Marketing Research

Within a Changing
Information Environment

McGraw-Hill/Irwin Series in Marketing

edition 3

Marketing Research

Within a Changing Information Environment

JOSEPH F. HAIR, JR.
Louisiana State University

ROBERT P. BUSH
University of Louisiana, Lafayette

DAVID J. ORTINAU
University of South Florida

McGraw-Hill
Irwin

Boston   Burr Ridge, IL   Dubuque, IA   Madison, WI   New York   San Francisco   St. Louis
Bangkok   Bogotá   Caracas   Kuala Lumpur   Lisbon   London   Madrid   Mexico City
Milan   Montreal   New Delhi   Santiago   Seoul   Singapore   Sydney   Taipei   Toronto

McGraw-Hill
Irwin

MARKETING RESEARCH: WITHIN A CHANGING INFORMATION ENVIRONMENT Published by McGraw-Hill/Irwin, a business unit of The McGraw-Hill Companies, Inc., 1221 Avenue of the Americas, New York, NY, 10020. Copyright © 2006, 2003, 2000 by The McGraw-Hill Companies, Inc. All rights reserved. No part of this publication may be reproduced or distributed in any form or by any means, or stored in a database or retrieval system, without the prior written consent of The McGraw-Hill Companies, Inc., including, but not limited to, in any network or other electronic storage or transmission, or broadcast for distance learning.

Some ancillaries, including electronic and print components, may not be available to customers outside the United States.

This book is printed on acid-free paper.

3 4 5 6 7 8 9 0 WCK/WCK 0 9 8 7 6 5

ISBN 0-07-283087-5

Editorial director: *John E. Biernat*
Publisher: *Andy Winston*
Developmental editor I: *Anna M. Chan*
Executive marketing manager: *Dan Silverburg*
Lead producer, Media technology: *Victoria Bryant*
Project manager: *Harvey Yep*
Senior production supervisor: *Rose Hepburn*
Designer: *Kami Carter*
Lead media project manager: *Becky Szura*
Supplement producer: *Gina F. DiMartino*
Developer, Media technology: *Brian Nacik*
Cover design: *Kami Carter*
Interior design: *Jenny El-Shamy*
Typeface: *10/12 Times Roman*
Compositor: *GTS–New Delhi, India Campus*
Printer: *Quebecor World Versailles Inc.*

Library of Congress Cataloging-in-Publication Data

Hair, Joseph F.
    Marketing research : within a changing information environment / Joseph F. Hair, Jr.,
  Robert P. Bush, David J. Ortinau.—3rd ed.
      p. cm.—(McGraw-Hill/Irwin series in marketing)
    Includes bibliographical references and index.
    ISBN 0-07-283087-5 (alk. paper)
    1. Marketing research. I. Bush, Robert P. II. Ortinau, David J. III. Title. IV. Series.
  HF5415.2.H258 2006
  658.8′3—dc22

                                                                        2004061113

dedication

To my loving and supportive wife, Dale, and to my son Joe III and his wife Kerrie.

—Joseph F. Hair, Jr., Baton Rouge, LA

This book is dedicated to my wife, Donny, and to my two boys, Robert Jr. and Michael.

—Robert P. Bush, Sr., Lafayette, LA

This book is dedicated to Carol Livingston, to my mom Lois, to my wonderful sister Nancy and her husband Jim Sasaki, and to brothers Dean and Denny along with their families for their unconditional love and support. And to all my past, present, and future students for enriching my life experiences as an educator on a daily basis.

—David J. Ortinau, Tampa, FL

about the authors

Joseph F. Hair, Jr., earned his Ph.D. in Marketing from the University of Florida, Gainesville. He currently holds the Alvin C. Copeland Endowed Chair of Franchising and is the Director, Entrepreneurship Institute, Ourso College of Business Administration, Louisiana State University. He has published over 25 books, including *Marketing,* 7th edition (SouthWestern, 2004); *Multivariate Data Analysis,* 6th edition (Prentice Hall, 2006); and *Essentials of Business Research Methods* (Wiley, 2003). He has also published numerous articles in academic journals, such as the *Journal of Marketing Research, Journal of Academy of Marketing Science, Journal of Business/Chicago, Journal of Advertising Research, Journal of Business Research,* and others. He has consulted with many companies, provided expert testimony in litigation matters, and developed numerous executive education programs. In May 2004, he was given the Academy of Marketing Science Outstanding Marketing Teaching Excellence Award. Under his leadership in 2003 the LSU Entrepreneurship Institute was recognized by *Entrepreneurship Magazine* as one of the top 12 programs nationally. Joseph F. Hair, Jr., is often invited to give lectures on research techniques to graduate programs at universities in Europe and in other countries abroad.

Robert P. Bush earned a B.A. in Psychology and Economic History from St. Mary's University and an M.A. and Ph.D. in Marketing at Louisiana State University. He began his teaching career at the University of South Florida before moving on to the University of Mississippi, the University of Memphis, and then the University of Louisiana, Lafayette. He was chairman of the committee on Grants and Research for the Fogelman College of Business from 1991 to 1997 and Director of the Ph.D. program at Memphis from 1995 to 1997. He has been a consultant for a wide range of corporations and institutes, as well as for the U.S. Department of Defense. Robert P. Bush is the coauthor of *Retailing for the 21st Century* (Houghton Mifflin, 1993) and a coeditor of *Advances in Marketing* (LSU Press, 1994). He is a regular contributor to such academic publications as *Journal of Advertising, Journal of Consumer Marketing, Journal of Marketing Education, Journal of Direct Marketing, Journal of Health Care Marketing,* and *Marketing Education Review.*

David J. Ortinau earned a B.S. in Management from Southern Illinois University, Carbondale, an M.A. in Business Administration, with a specialty in marketing research, from Illinois State University, and a Ph.D. in Marketing from Louisiana State University. He began his teaching career at Illinois State University and after completing his Ph.D. degree he moved to the University of South Florida, Tampa, where he continues to win awards for both outstanding research and for excellence in teaching. He has a wide range of research interests from research methodologies and scale measurement of attitude formation and perceptual differences in retailing and services marketing to interactive electronic marketing technologies and their impact on information research problems. He consults for a variety of corporations and small businesses, with specialties in customer satisfaction, customer service quality, customer service value, retail loyalty, and imagery. David J. Ortinau continues to serve as a member of the editorial review board for the *Journal of the Academy of Marketing Science (JAMS)* and the *Journal of Business Research (JBR).* He was co-editor of *Marketing: Moving Toward the 21st Century* (SMA Press, 1996). He remains an active leader in the Marketing discipline. He has held many leadership positions in the Society for Marketing Advances (a.k.a. Southern Marketing Association), served as co-chair of the 1998 Southern Marketing Association's Doctoral Consortium in New Orleans and the 1999 Society for Marketing Advances' Doctoral Consortium in Atlanta. He is a past President of SMA and was recognized as the 2001 SMA Fellow. He is currently serving as the (2004–2006) President of the SMA Foundation and recently served as the 2004 Academy of Marketing Science Conference Program co-chair. He has presented numerous papers at academic meetings and has been a regular contributor to and referee for such prestigious publications as the *Journal of the Academy of Marketing (JAMS), Journal of Retailing (JR), Journal of Business Research (JBR), Journal of Marketing Education (JME), Journal of Health Care Marketing (JHCM), Journal of Services Marketing,* and others.

preface

Building on the success of the first two editions of *Marketing Research: Within a Changing Information Environment,* the new third edition goes well beyond the basic idea of all marketing research books—to introduce students to the concepts and practices that make up the field—to show how marketing information research tools, skills, and understanding can be applied in solving marketing problems and creating business opportunities in our ever more rapidly changing information environment. With the growing availability, acceptance, and use of (1) the Internet and its related advanced technologies and communication systems and (2) gatekeeper technologies such as caller ID, electronic answering devices, and voice messengers to protect people's privacy; and in the context of (3) continuously changing internal organizational structures to improve the cross-functional sharing of information and (4) the movement of both large and small businesses toward globalization of marketing practices, tomorrow's information requirements will be more challenging than those of yesterday.

Objectives and Approach

Although the first two editions of *Marketing Research: Within a Changing Information Environment* were well received in the marketplace, it was most of all the positive comments made by adopters of the book and reviewers (both adopters and nonadopters) as well as students which encouraged us to write this third edition. Our objectives in the new edition of *Marketing Research* remain threefold. First, we present students a body of knowledge and a set of facts that are easy to study and understand and that will facilitate *practical self-learning* of the basics of information research. Second, we provide students solid tools and the chance to learn skills necessary to solve business problems and exploit business opportunities. And finally, we provide a solid educational learning resource for instructors who strive to bring understanding to frequently complex subject matter. As students develop information acquisition skills and an understanding of basic research tools, they will quickly see how these can be applied to a changing marketing environment, to other academic courses, and to their personal lives.

Rapid changes in the business world are creating new decision situations that demand creative solutions and better skills for the acquisition and use of information. As a result of many recent advances in communication technologies, high speed communication systems, and other electronic technological advances, business decision makers and the marketing research industry have been forced to rethink their notions of information and of the practices used to acquire and generate data and information. A unique feature of the third edition of *Marketing Research* is the detailed treatment of and significantly greater emphasis placed on identifying, searching, gathering, analyzing, and interpreting secondary data and information. Another unique feature is the book's detailed and expanded coverage of *customer relationship management* and the integrative role that marketing information research plays in making CRM one of the hottest topics in information research today. In addition, this text places a heavy emphasis on the use of technology for marketing research practices. Finally, students and instructors will have the opportunity to engage the book's new *interactive Web site* (www.mhhe.com/hair06) linking students to a wide variety of additional practical marketing research examples, exercises, applications, learning modules, cases, and points of interest relevant to better understanding marketing research information tools, skills, and practices.

The third edition of *Marketing Research: Within a Changing Information Environment* provides detailed insights into alternative ways of dealing with new information needs and demands brought about by environmental changes. These changes have had direct impact both on marketing research practices and on the operating environments of business practitioners. Additionally, there have been many changes in the educational environment that have implications for how people acquire knowledge and master the skills and tools customarily associated with the practice of marketing research. Given the strong acceptance of the information research process presented in the prior two editions of this text, we again use that process not only to cover the traditional marketing research concepts, but also to provide insights for meeting the information challenges of the 21st century. The third edition is written for people at a fairly basic level; it does not require a strong background in statistics or any prior knowledge of marketing research. It is not intended for people who wish to teach advanced multivariate statistics, yet it serves well as a supplement text for those procedures.

We believe that self-learning is a critical and necessary component of a student's overall educational experience. To that end we have incorporated the following characteristics into the third edition to enhance the self-learning process:

- Easy-to-understand writing style and organization.

- Clearly presented and informative exhibits, tables, and boxes that provide real business applications.

- Integrative examples that illustrate the links between various research concepts.

- End-of-chapter Marketing Research in Action Features that demonstrate how researchers integrate concepts discussed within the chapter.

- Detailed treatment of critical research skills and tools.

- In-depth treatment of secondary data/information as well as customer relationship management.

- New in-depth treatment of technology in a marketing research environment.

- A new interactive book Web site that links the students and instructors to additional examples and discussions on many different research topics.

Content and Organization

Positive comments and acceptance from reviewers, adopters, and students of the previous edition encouraged us to maintain the overall content for the third edition, which, however, provides significantly new and expanded coverage of a number of marketing research topics in the second edition. Part One of the book covers marketing research programs and processes. Chapter 1 presents an overview of the role of marketing research for the decision-making/planning process. It also provides a detailed discussion of ethics in the marketing research industry. Chapter 2 takes an information approach to explaining the marketing research process and sets the tone for the remaining chapters. Chapter 3 incorporates decision-making and customer relationship management issues pertaining to secondary data acquisition and retrieval.

Part Two is devoted primarily to technology and the marketing research process. Chapter 4 of the new edition provides a detailed discussion of customer relationship management (CRM) and explores various research decisions using CRM approaches for data acquisition and intra-organizational sharing of data and information. Chapter 5 focuses uniquely on how research-driven decision support systems are created and used to support a research environment. This chapter is also supplemented with a fundamental discussion on the role of geographic information systems (GIS) for marketing research purposes.

Part Three covers the various research designs used to collect accurate data and information. Chapter 6 provides a detailed discussion of exploratory designs of in-depth interviews and focus groups. There is new and expanded coverage of online focus group practices. Chapter 7 continues with descriptive research designs along with other quantitative data collection methods that are associated with descriptive research objectives. Part Three concludes with a discussion of the value of observation techniques for marketing research projects in Chapter 8. This chapter takes a unique approach in the discussion of observational research approaches, designing experiments in a research environment, test marketing, and causal research designs.

Part Four demonstrates the necessary approaches for gathering and collecting accurate data. In the new third edition, we provide two chapters on sampling. Chapter 9 explores sampling from a theory and design perspective with a detailed discussion on theoretical and statistical factors of sampling. Chapter 10 examines sampling approaches used in a variety of marketing research situations. Chapters 11 and 12 are devoted to the concept of measurement, first addressing the issues associated with construct development and scale measurement (Chapter 11) and following with attitude scale measurements as used in survey research. Finally, Chapter 13 illustrates an innovative and detailed approach to questionnaire design and development.

Part Five is devoted to data preparation and data analysis. These topics, often viewed as complex and technical, are developed in a reader-friendly format. Chapter 14 discusses a "hands-on," step-by-step approach for coding, editing, and the general preparation necessary for data analysis. Chapter 15 presents tests for significant differences and Chapter 16 presents tests for association. Both chapters are enlivened by a wide variety of examples, exercises, and SPSS highlights to enhance pedagogy and readability. Chapter 17 discusses multivariate statistics, again emphasizing readability, comprehension, and clarity. The new edition concludes with Chapter 18 which illustrates the design and execution of the marketing research report and visual presentation. To complement this chapter, a PowerPoint illustration is provided on the text's Web site (www.mhhe.com/hair06).

Pedagogy

Most marketing research textbooks are readable, but a more important question might be, "Can students comprehend what they are reading?" This book offers a wealth of pedagogical features, all aimed at answering the question in the affirmative. Here is a list of the major elements:

Learning Objectives. Each chapter begins with clear learning objectives that students can use to gauge their expectations for the chapter discussion in view of the nature and importance of the chapter's material.

Real-World Chapter Openers. Each chapter opens with an interesting and pertinent example of a real-world business situation that illustrates the focus and significance of the chapter's material.

Key Terms and Concepts.   These are bold-faced in the text and defined in the page margins. They are also listed at the end of the chapters along with page numbers to make reviewing easier and included in the Glossary at the end of the book.

A Closer Look at Research.   These illustrative boxes, found frequently throughout the chapters, come in three categories: Technology, Small Business, and In the Field. They are intended to expose the students to real-world marketing research issues.

Ethics.   Ethical issues are treated early in the book (Chapter 1), revisited throughout the text, and illustrated in Ethics boxes.

Global Insights.   These boxes encourage the student to see the international implications of, and opportunities for, marketing research.

Chapter Summaries.   The detailed chapter summations, organized by learning objectives, will help students remember key facts, concepts, and issues. They also serve as an excellent study guide for preparation for in-class exercises or exams.

Questions for Review and Discussion.   The Review Questions and Discussion Questions are carefully designed to enhance the self-learning process and to encourage the application of the concepts learned in the chapter to real business situations. There are two or three questions in each chapter directly related to the World Wide Web designed to provide students with opportunities for sharpening their electronic data gathering and interpretive skills.

Marketing Research in Action.   The cases found at the ends of the chapters provide students with additional insights into how key concepts in each chapter can be applied to real-world situations. These cases can serve as in-class discussion tools or applied case exercises. An ingoing case—the Santa Fe Grill—found in several chapters uses a single situation to illustrate various aspects of the marketing research process.

Santa Fe Grill.   The Santa Fe Grill continuing case is a specially designed business scenario embedded throughout the book for the purpose of questioning and illustrating chapter topics. First introduced in the Marketing Research in Action in Chapter 1, the Santa Fe Grill continuing case provides students with an ongoing example of applying marketing research concepts and the challenges associated with them as they appear in the text. A data set accompanies this useful learning example.

Supplements

This book offers a rich ancillary package. Here is a brief description of each element in the package.

Instructor's Resource CD-ROM.   This CD includes a thoroughly revised Instructor's Manual and PowerPoint slide presentation. A wealth of extra student projects and real-life examples provide additional classroom resources. The electronic test bank was also thoroughly revised and included on the CD.

Videos.   The video program contains two hours of material on marketing research from the McGraw-Hill/Irwin video library.

Web Site.   Students can use their Internet skills to log on to this book's dedicated Web site (www.mhhe.com/hair06) to access additional information about marketing research and evaluate their understanding of chapter material by taking the sample quizzes. Students can also prepare their marketing research projects with our online support system. Additional resources are offered for each chapter—look for prompts in the book that will guide you to the Web site for more useful information on various topics.

Data Sets.   Six data sets in SPSS format are available at the book's Web site (www.mhhe.com/hair06). The data sets can be used to assign research projects or with exercises throughout the book. These databases cover a wide variety of topics that all students can identify with, and offer an excellent approach to enhance teaching of concepts. The databases include the following: Santa Fe Grill continuing case, Deli Depot (restaurant example), Remington's Steak House (perceptual mapping example), Qualkote (B-to-B example), DVD sales (B-to-C example), and Back Yard Burgers (restaurant example).

SPSS Student Version.   Through an arrangement with SPSS, we offer the option of purchasing the textbook packaged with a CD-ROM containing an SPSS Student Version for Windows. This powerful software tool allows for the analysis of up to 50 variables and 1,500 cases. It contains all data sets and can be used in conjunction with data analysis procedures contained in the text.

Acknowledgments

While we took the lead in creating this book, many other people must be given credit for their significant contributions in bringing our vision to reality. We thank our colleagues in academia and industry for their helpful insights over many years on many different research topics.

In any textbook project, the peer reviewers play a very significant role in helping shape the content and pedagogy during the preparation of the various drafts. We wish to acknowledge them and to extend our thanks and appreciation to the following colleagues for their useful suggestions for improving the quality of this book.

David Andrus
Kansas State University
Jill Attaway
Illinois State University
Barry Babin
University of Southern Mississippi
Elisa Fredericks
Northern Illinois University
Susan Holak
CUNY/College of Staten Island
Harold Koch
Utah Valley State College
Karl Mann
Towson University
Joseph McAloon
Fitchburg State College

Tom O'Connor
University of New Orleans
Teresa Pavia
University of Utah
Peter Sanchez
Villanova University
Mary Schramm
College of Mount St. Joseph
Omar Shehryar
Louisiana State University
Ann Veeck
Western Michigan University
Ramanswamy Venkatesh
University of Pittsburgh
Mary Zimmer
Texas A&M University

We would also like to thank the many survey respondents, too numerous to mention here, whose comments contributed to this edition. And again we thank the following reviewers of the second edition:

Carol Anderson
Rollins College
Sandy Bravo
Boston College
P. K. Cannon
University of Maryland

Les Dlabay
Lake Forest College
Vicki Eveland
Mercer University
James Gould
Pace University

Janice Gygi
Utah Valley State College
Rich Hanna
Boston University
Arthur Money
Henley College
G. M. Naidu
University of Wisconsin, Whitewater
Rajan Natarajan
Auburn University
Lee Nordgren
Indiana University

Radesh Palakurthi
San Jose State University
Alan Sawyer
University of Florida
K. Sivakumar
University of Illinois, Chicago
Patrick Vargas
University of Illinois, Champaign-Urbana
Mark L. Wilson
University of Charleston

Finally, we'd like to thank our editors and advisors at McGraw-Hill/Irwin. Thanks go to Andy Winston, our publisher and executive editor; Anna Chan, our development editor; and Dan Silverburg, our marketing manager. We are also grateful to our very professional production team—Harvey Yep, project manager; Kami Carter, designer; Rose Hepburn, production supervisor; Gina DiMartino, supplement producer; and Becky Szura, media project manager.

Joseph F. Hair, Jr.
Robert P. Bush
David J. Ortinau

brief contents

part 4
Gathering and Collecting Accurate Data   305

part 5
Data Preparation, Analysis, and Reporting the Results   475

contents

part 1

The Role and Value of Marketing Research Information

chapter 1

Marketing Research for Managerial Decision Making

Learning Objectives

After reading this chapter, you will be able to

1. Describe and explain the impact marketing research has on marketing decision making.

2. Demonstrate how marketing research fits into the marketing planning process.

3. Provide examples of marketing research studies.

4. Understand the scope and focus of the marketing research industry.

5. Demonstrate ethical dimensions associated with marketing research.

6. Understand emerging trends and new skills associated with marketing research.

Marketing Research and Decision Making: It's a Jeep Thing, You Wouldn't Understand

Question the behavior of a loyal Jeep owner, and you're likely to hear these words: "It's a Jeep thing, you wouldn't understand." Because if there's one thing that dyed-in-the-wool Jeep drivers believe, it's that they are fundamentally different from the slew of SUV owners currently crowding the roads. Consider, for example, the outward appearance of a Jeep Cherokee. The prospect of being smacked by a roving shopping cart in a parking lot is the sort of thing that leads a Lexus SUV owner to park a half-mile from the closest car, but for the Jeep owner, scratches, dings, gashes, and chips are like medals of honor bestowed on the vehicle. The long history of the Jeep vehicle, the original 4 × 4, has brand recognition that has always been synonymous with a spirit of adventure, and Jeep owners are passionate about it.

One of the greatest challenges for the Jeep Division of DaimlerChrysler, AG, is keeping up with the changing needs, wants, desires, and diversity of its customer base. Forty years ago, Jeep made the only all-terrain vehicle, found mainly on army

bases, running remote trails, or venturing out on exotic safaris. Today, Jeeps are more likely to be spotted hauling kids to school or stockbrokers to the Hamptons. In fact, with so many other car companies attempting to market to the growing demand for SUVs, Jeep management realizes that learning about customers by convening focus groups and compiling surveys is no longer enough.

Rather, Jeep's marketing research efforts are focusing on individual consumers and creating a relationship between the Jeep brand and the buyer. Marketing research activities now focus on information technology and data gathering through event sponsorships. Over the years, Jeep has invited families to participate in such activities as off-road driving clinics, fly fishing contests, hiking and mountain-biking competitions solely for the purpose of collecting data. These activities are indeed expensive, but by generating face-to-face dialogue with thousands of customers they provide a great forum for learning more about customers and the relationship they have with their vehicles.

The greatest opportunity for Jeep comes when marketing researchers and engineers talk to consumers. Casual conversations among event attendees are carefully recorded by market research personnel, and almost 90 percent of all attendees complete and return customer feedback cards. Yet the most valuable information on customer expectations is generated by roundtable discussions between customers and Jeep engineers. The purpose of such discussions is to allow Jeep engineers to record tangible benefits from the customer encounter, namely, product ideas and improvements. By meeting directly with customers in a roundtable format, engineers and market researchers get feedback on model changes, lifestyles, and satisfaction. Such data collection methods appear to be working. According to Jeep sales research, owners who participate in sponsored activities are four times more likely to purchase another Jeep than are owners who do not participate. Jeep executives contend that not only do such events boost sales, but they also contribute to a vast database used to build long-term customer relationships and the loyalty car companies yearn for.

Value of Marketing Research Information

Jeep in the opening example illustrates how marketing research can operate to solve business issues. The example identifies new approaches and evolving processes in the marketing research industry. Implementing a sound marketing research process based on customer inquiry and feedback allows a business of any size to make confident, cost-effective decisions, whether in identifying new product opportunities or designing new approaches for communicating with customers.

Marketing research
The function that links an organization to its market through the gathering of information.

The American Marketing Association formally defines **marketing research** as follows:

> Marketing research is the function that links an organization to its market through the gathering of information. This information allows for the identification and definition of market-driven opportunities and problems. The information allows for the generation, refinement and evaluation of marketing actions. It allows for the monitoring of marketing performance and improved understanding of marketing as a business process.[2]

Applying this definition to the Jeep Division, we can see that Jeep used marketing research information to identify new product and model opportunities, as well as to implement new data-gathering processes to better understand customers, approaches known as *relationship marketing* and *customer relationship management,* discussed in detail in the section below.

Marketing research is a systematic process. The tasks in this process include designing methods for collecting information, managing the information collection process, analyzing and interpreting results, and communicating findings to decision makers. This chapter provides an overview of marketing research as well as a fundamental understanding of its relationship to marketing practices. We first explain why firms use marketing research and give some examples of how marketing research can help companies make sound marketing decisions. Next we discuss who should use marketing research, and when.

The chapter also provides a general description of the activities companies use to collect marketing research information. We present an overview of the marketing research industry in order to clarify the relationship between the providers and the users of marketing information. The chapter closes with a description of the role of ethics in marketing research. It also includes an appendix on careers in marketing research as well as one on how to use the statistical analysis software package SPSS.

Relationship Marketing and the Marketing Research Process

Marketing The process of planning and executing the pricing, promotion, and distribution of products, services, and ideas in order to create exchanges that satisfy both the firm and its customers.

The fundamental purpose of **marketing** is to enable firms to plan and execute the pricing, promotion, and distribution of products, services, and ideas in order to create exchanges that satisfy both the firm and its customers. The process of creating this exchange is the responsibility of the firm's marketing manager. Marketing managers attempt to stimulate the marketing process by following various decision criteria. More specifically, they focus on getting the right goods and services (1) to the right people, (2) at the right place and time, (3) with the right price, (4) through the use of the right blend of promotional techniques. Adhering to these criteria ultimately leads to the success of the marketing effort. However, the common denominator associated with each criterion is uncertainty. Uncertainty lies in the fact that consumer behavior is unpredictable. In order to reduce this uncertainty, marketing managers must have accurate, relevant, and timely information. Marketing research is the mechanism for generating that information.

Relationship marketing The name of a strategy that entails forging long-term relationships with customers.

Today, successful businesses, no matter how small or large, follow a business strategy known as **relationship marketing.** Companies that follow this strategy build long-term relationships with customers by offering value and providing customer satisfaction. The company is rewarded with repeat sales, increases in sales and market share, and profits. Dell Computers, for example, is highly focused on relationship marketing. Dell sees its customers as individuals with unique needs and desires. Its marketing research program is directed toward measuring these aspects of the customer, then developing its entire marketing program around such measures to build long-term relationships with customers.

The success of any relationship marketing program depends on knowledge of the market, effective training programs, and employee empowerment and teamwork:

- **Knowledge of the market.** For an organization to be focused on building relationships with customers, it must know all relevant information pertaining to those customers. This implies that the company must have an obsession with understanding customer needs and desires and using that information to deliver satisfaction to the customer. Nowhere is this more important than in the marketing research responsibilities of the company.

- **Effective training programs.** Building excellence in relationships begins with the employee. In the eyes of many consumers, the employee is the company. Therefore, it is critical, not only in a marketing research capacity, but throughout the entire company, that the actions and behaviors of employees be market oriented. Many organizations such as McDonald's, Walt Disney, and American Express have corporate universities designed to train employees in customer relations. Furthermore, many of these universities train employees in the proper techniques of gathering data from customers. Emphasizing informal customer comments, discussing issues on competing products, and encouraging customers to use comment cards are some ways in which American Express trains its employees in data gathering practices.

- **Employee empowerment and teamwork.** Many successful companies encourage their employees to be more proactive in solving customer problems. On-the-spot problem solving is known as empowerment. Additionally, organizations are now developing cross-functional teams dedicated to developing and delivering customer solutions. Teamwork designed to accomplish common goals is frequently used at the Jeep Division of Daimler-Chrysler. This is evident in the opening example, where marketing research and engineering personnel work together to better understand the requirements of their customers.

Empowerment and teamwork facilitate relationship building among customers. These two dimensions, along with training and knowledge of the market, form the catalyst for implementing the relationship marketing strategy commonly referred to as customer relationship management.

Relationship Marketing and Customer Relationship Management

Customer relationship management The process used for implementing a relationship marketing strategy.

Customer relationship management, or CRM, is the process used to implement a relationship marketing strategy. CRM gathers market-driven data to learn more about customers' needs and behaviors for the purpose of delivering added value and satisfaction to the customer. The data, in conjunction with information technology, is then used to develop stronger relationships with customers. Fundamentally, CRM is based on a number of concepts focusing on the marketplace and the consumer. Specifically, these concepts address:

Customer/market knowledge: This is the starting point of any CRM process. The role of marketing research is to collect and gather information from multiple sources as it pertains to the customer. Key data to be captured include demographics, psychographics, buying and service history, preferences, complaints, and all other communications the customer has with the company. Data can be internal, through customers' interaction with the company, or external, through surveys or other data collection methods.

Data integration: This process develops a data warehouse to integrate information from multiple sources into a single shared data source depository. The data, which are used to understand and predict customer behavior, are then made available to all functional areas of the company so that anyone who interacts with the customer will have a complete history of the customer.

Information technology: The role of marketing research is to facilitate data integration through technology-driven techniques. These techniques perform functions such as basic reporting on customers, data mining, statistical analysis procedures, and data visualization.

Creating customer profiles: Collected and integrated data are used to develop customer profiles. These profiles are then made available to all functional areas of the company utilizing the appropriate information technology.

These concepts are embodied in a variety of outcomes based on the decision-making and planning objectives of the company (e.g., introducing new products, growing new market segments, evaluating advertising campaigns). The overriding goal is to provide the necessary data and technology to monitor customer changes while building and maintaining long-term customer relationships. An overview of the impact of the CRM process on the marketing research process, including building, developing, and implementing the process, is provided in Chapter 4.

Marketing Planning and Decision Making

Within a market-planning framework, managers must make many critical marketing decisions. These decisions vary dramatically in both focus and complexity. For example, managers must decide which new markets to penetrate, which products to introduce, and which new business opportunities to pursue. Such broad decisions usually require decision makers to consider a variety of alternative approaches. Conversely, decisions regarding advertising effectiveness, product positioning, or sales tracking, while still very complex, are somewhat narrower in focus. Such decisions usually concentrate on a specific advertising campaign, a particular brand, or a specific market segment. Such decisions often center on monitoring performance or anticipating and initiating changes in a company's marketing practices.

Regardless of the complexity or focus of the decision-making process, managers must have accurate information to make the right decisions. The entire marketing planning process is a series of decisions that must be made with high levels of confidence about the outcome. It is therefore not surprising to realize that a sound marketing research process is the nucleus for market planning.

Exhibit 1.1 lists some of the research-related tasks necessary for confident marketing decision making. While this list is by no means exhaustive, it does provide a general illustration of the relationship between market planning and marketing research. The following sections describe this relationship in more detail.

ⓔXHIBIT 1.1 Marketing Decision Making and Related Marketing Research Tasks

Marketing Planning Process	Marketing Research Task
Marketing Situation Analysis	**Situation Research Efforts**
Market analysis	Opportunity assessment
Market segmentation	Benefit and lifestyle studies
	Descriptive studies
Competition analysis	Importance-performance analysis
Marketing Program Design	**Program-Driven Research Efforts**
Target marketing	Target market analysis
Positioning	Positioning (perceptual mapping)
New-product planning	Concept and product testing
	Test marketing
Marketing Program Development	**Program Development Research**
Product portfolio decisions	Customer satisfaction studies
	Service quality studies
Distribution decisions	Cycle time research
	Retailing research
	Logistic assessment
Pricing decisions	Demand analysis
	Sales forecasting
Integrated marketing communications	Advertising effectiveness studies
	Attitudinal research
	Sales tracking
Program Implementation and Control	**Performance Analysis**
Marketing control	Product analysis
	Environmental forecasting
Critical information analysis	Marketing decision support systems

Marketing Situation Analysis

Situation analysis To monitor the appropriateness of a firm's marketing strategy and to determine whether changes to the strategy are necessary.

The purpose of a **situation analysis** is to monitor the appropriateness of a firm's marketing program and to determine whether changes to the program are necessary. A situation analysis includes three decision areas: market analysis, market segmentation, and competition analysis. Within the context of a situation analysis, the purposes of marketing research are to

1. Locate and identify new market opportunities for a company (opportunity assessment).

2. Identify groups of customers in a product market who possess similar needs, characteristics, and preferences (benefit and lifestyle studies, descriptive studies).

3. Identify existing and potential competitors' strengths and weaknesses (importance-performance analysis).

Market Analysis

Opportunity assessment Involves collecting information on product markets for the purpose of forecasting how they will change.

The research task related to market analysis is **opportunity assessment.** It involves collecting information on product markets for the purpose of forecasting how they will change. Companies gather information relevant to macroenvironmental trends (political and regulatory, economic and social, and cultural and technological) and assess how those trends will affect the product market.

The role of marketing research is to gather and categorize information relating to macroenvironmental variables, and then interpret the information in the context of strategic consequences to the firm. Marketing researchers use three common approaches in the collection of macroenvironmental information:

1. Content analysis, in which researchers analyze various trade publications, newspaper articles, academic literature, or computer databases for information on trends in a given industry.

2. In-depth interviews, in which researchers conduct formal, structured interviews with experts in a given field.

3. Formal rating procedures, in which researchers use structured questionnaires to gather information on environmental occurrences.

These procedures will be discussed further in Chapters 11, 12, and 13.

Market Segmentation

Benefit and lifestyle studies Examine similarities and differences in consumers' needs. Researchers use these studies to identify two or more segments within the market for a particular company's products.

A research task related to market segmentation is **benefit and lifestyle studies,** which examine similarities and differences in consumers' needs. Researchers use these studies to identify segments within the market for a particular company's products. The research objective is to collect information about customer characteristics, product benefits, and brand preferences. This data, along with information on age, family size, income, and lifestyle, is then compared to purchase patterns of particular products (cars, food, electronics, financial services) to develop market segmentation profiles.

Creating customer profiles and understanding behavioral characteristics are major focuses of any marketing research project. Determining why consumers behave as they do becomes the critical interaction between marketing research and marketing program development. Chapter 9 will focus on this issue and examine, in detail, customer-driven marketing research approaches.

Competitive Analysis

A research task used in competitive analysis is **importance-performance analysis,** which is an approach for evaluating competitors' strategies, strengths, limitations, and future plans. Importance-performance analysis asks consumers to identify key attributes that drive their purchase behavior within a given industry. These attributes might include price, product performance, product quality, accuracy of shipping and delivery, or convenience of store location. Consumers are then asked to rank the importance of the attributes.

Following the importance rankings, researchers identify and evaluate competing firms. Highly ranked attributes are viewed as strengths, and lower ranked attributes are viewed as weaknesses. When the competing firms are analyzed in aggregate, a company can see where its competitors are concentrating their marketing efforts and where they are falling below customer expectations.

Marketing Strategy Design

Information collected during a situation analysis is subsequently used to design a marketing strategy. At this stage of the planning process, companies identify target markets, develop positioning strategies for products and brands, test new products, and assess market potential.

Target Marketing

Target market analysis provides useful information for identifying those people (or companies) that an organization wishes to serve. In addition, it helps management determine the most efficient way of serving the targeted group. Target market analysis attempts to provide information on the following issues:

- New-product opportunities.

- Demographics, including attitudinal or behavioral characteristics.

- User profiles, usage patterns, and attitudes.

- The effectiveness of a firm's current marketing program.

In order to provide such information, the marketing researcher must measure certain key variables as outlined in Exhibit 1.2.

Positioning

Positioning (or *perceptual mapping*) is a process in which a company seeks to establish a general meaning or definition of its product offering that is consistent with customers' needs and preferences. Companies accomplish this task by combining elements of the marketing mix in a manner that meets or exceeds the expectations of targeted customers.

The task of the marketing researcher is to provide an overview of the relationship between competitive product offerings based on judgments of a sample of respondents who are familiar with the product category being investigated. Consumers are asked to indicate how they view the similarities and dissimilarities among relevant product attributes for a set of competing brands. For example, positioning among beers may indicate that customers decide between "popular versus premium" and "regional versus national" brands.

ӨХHIBIT 1.2	**Target Market Characteristics and Associated Variables Measured in Target Market Analysis**

Target Market Characteristics	Key Variables to Measure
Demographics	Age, gender, race, income, religion, occupation, family size, geographic location, and zip code
Psychographics	Consumer activities, interests, and opinions
Product usage	Occasion (special use, gift); situation (climate, time of day, place); and usage context (heavy, medium, or light)
Brand preferences	Level of brand loyalty, salient product attributes, and product/brand awareness
Decision process	Size and frequency of purchase; propensity to purchase; risk of purchase (high, medium, low); and product involvement

This information is then used to construct perceptual maps, which transform the positioning data into "perceptual space." Perceptual mapping reflects the dimensions on which brands are evaluated, typically representing product features or attributes judged as important in a customer's selection process.

New-Product Planning

Concept and product testing and **test marketing** Information for decisions on product improvements and new-product introductions.

The research tasks related to new-product planning are **concept and product testing** and **test marketing,** which give management the necessary information for decisions on product improvements and new-product introductions. Product testing attempts to answer two fundamental questions: "How does a product perform for the customer?" and "How can a product be improved to exceed customer expectations?" In product tests, ideas are reshaped and redefined to identify those that not only meet but exceed market expectations. Specifically, product tests

1. Provide necessary information for designing and developing new products.

2. Determine whether new or improved products should replace current products.

3. Assess the appeal of alternative products for new target segments.

4. Identify products that are most preferred or actively sought compared to existing competitive offerings.

Marketing Program Development

The information requirements for marketing program development concentrate on all the components of the marketing mix: product, distribution, price, and promotion. Managers combine these components to form the total marketing effort for each market targeted. While at first this may appear to be an easy task, decision makers must remember that the success of the total marketing effort or program relies heavily on synergy. It is critical that the marketing mix not only contain the right elements but do so in the right amounts, at the right time, and in the proper sequence. Ensuring that this synergy occurs is the responsibility of market researchers.

Product Portfolio Analysis

Within product portfolio analysis, the total product line typically is the focal point of investigation. Market researchers design studies that help product managers make decisions about reducing costs, altering marketing mixes, and changing or deleting product lines. Two types of studies are customer satisfaction studies and service quality studies.

Customer satisfaction studies assess the strengths and weaknesses customers perceive in a firm's marketing mix. While these studies are usually designed to analyze the marketing mix collectively, many firms elect to focus on customer responses to one element at a time (e.g., satisfaction with pricing policy). Regardless of their scope, customer satisfaction studies concentrate on measuring customer attitudes. Research indicates that customers' attitudes are linked to purchase intentions, brand switching, perceptions of company image, and brand loyalty.[3] Attitude information allows management to make intelligent decisions regarding product or brand repositioning, new-product introductions, new market segments, and the deletion of ineffective products. Chapters 11 and 12 discuss the design and development of attitudinal research studies.

Service quality studies are designed to measure the degree to which an organization conforms to the quality level customers expect. Service quality studies concentrate on physical facilities and equipment, appearance and behavior of company personnel, and dependability of products and programs. Specifically, employees are rated on their general willingness to help customers and provide them with prompt, friendly, courteous treatment.

A popular service quality study is the mystery shopper study, in which trained professional shoppers visit, for example, retail stores and/or financial institutions, and "shop" for various goods and services. Atmosphere, friendliness, and customer appreciation are just a few of the dimensions evaluated by mystery shoppers. Some firms also patronize their competitors to see how their own performance compares. Data from service quality studies has been invaluable for decision making related to products or services. For example, firms can anticipate problems in product or service offerings before they get out of hand. Also, the data enable firms to assess themselves relative to competitors on key strengths and weaknesses.

Customer satisfaction studies These studies assess the strengths and weaknesses that customers perceive in a firm's marketing mix.

Service quality studies Are designed to measure the degree to which an organization conforms to the quality level customers expect.

Distribution Decisions

Distribution decisions take into account the distributors and retailers that link producers with end users. The distribution channel used by a producer can strongly influence a buyer's perception of the brand. For example, Rolex watches are distributed through a limited number of retailers that project a prestigious image consistent with the Rolex brand name. Three common types of distribution-related research methods are *cycle time research, retailing research,* and *logistic assessment.*

With many businesses moving to control inventory costs, automatic replenishment systems and electronic data interchange are becoming widely used. Closely associated with such inventory systems is **cycle time research,** which centers on reducing the time between the initial contact with a customer and the final delivery (or installation) of the product.[4] This research is most often concerned with large distribution networks (manufacturers, wholesalers, retailers). Cycle time research does not ignore shorter channels of distribution (direct to retailer or end user), for in many cases, such as direct marketing approaches, it becomes critical in exploring ways to increase customer satisfaction and fulfillment. Marketing research becomes responsible for collecting information that will help reduce costs in the total cycle time, as well as exploring alternative methods of distribution to reduce the time frame in the shipping and installation of goods.

Cycle time research A research method that centers on reducing the time between the initial contact and final delivery (or installation) of the product.

Two common research practices in this area are delivery expense studies and alternative delivery systems studies. Both seek to obtain information related to expense analysis for alternative forms of delivery (e.g., post office, FedEx, UPS), in connection with providing a high degree of customer satisfaction. Such studies are unique in that they rely heavily on internal company records or databases. Usually referred to as secondary research, these studies are becoming more common. Chapter 3 is devoted to information-gathering procedures at a secondary level.

Retailing research

Retailing research includes studies on a variety of topics. Because retailers are viewed as independent businesses, many of the studies we have discussed are applicable to the retail environment. Yet, at the same time, the information needs of retailers are unique. Market research studies peculiar to retailers include trade area analysis, store image/perception studies, in-store traffic pattern studies, and location analysis.

Studies on topics such as trade area analysis, store image/perception, in-store traffic patterns, and location analysis.

Because retailing is a high-customer-contact activity, much retailing research focuses on database development through optical scanning procedures. As illustrated in Exhibit 1.3, every time a salesperson records a transaction using an optical scanner, the scanner notes the type of product, its manufacturer and vendor, and its size and price. Marketing research then categorizes the data and combines it with other relevant information to form a database. As a result, retailers can find out what television programs their customers watch, the kinds of neighborhoods they live in, and the types of stores they prefer to patronize. Such information helps retailers determine what kind of merchandise to stock and what factors may influence purchase decisions.

Logistic assessment

Information in logistics allows market researchers to conduct total cost analysis and service sensitivity analysis.

Marketing research related to **logistic assessment** is an often overlooked area in distribution decisions. One reason for this is that it traditionally has been driven by secondary data, that is, information not gathered for the study at hand but for some other purpose. This

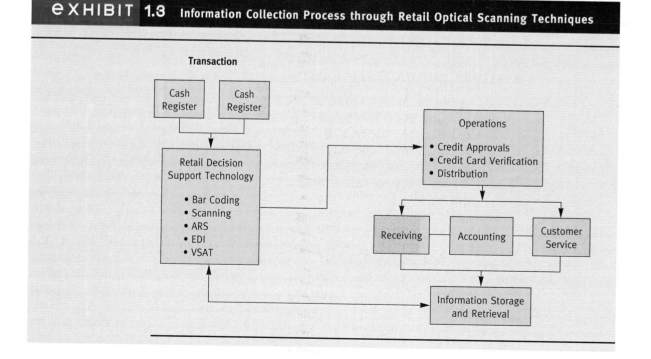

e X H I B I T 1.3 **Information Collection Process through Retail Optical Scanning Techniques**

type of information in logistics enables market researchers to conduct total cost analysis and service sensitivity analysis.

Total cost analysis explores the alternative logistic system designs a firm can use to achieve its performance objective at the lowest total cost. The role of marketing research is to develop an activity-based cost information system by identifying key factors that affect transportation, inventory, and warehousing costs.

Service sensitivity analysis helps organizations design basic customer service programs by evaluating cost-to-service trade-offs. In conducting this type of analysis, market researchers look for ways to increase various basic services by making adjustments in transportation activities, inventory levels, or location planning. Each adjustment is analyzed relative to its impact on corresponding total costs.

Pricing Decisions

Pricing decisions involve pricing new products, establishing price levels in test-market situations, and modifying prices for existing products. Marketing research must provide answers to such fundamental questions as the following:

1. How large is the demand potential within the target market?

2. How sensitive is demand to changes in price levels?

3. What nonprice factors are important to customers?

4. What are the sales forecasts at various price levels?

Pricing research can take a variety of forms. Two common approaches are *demand analysis* and *sales forecasting*.

When a company evaluates a new-product idea, develops a test market, or plans changes for existing products, a critical research challenge is estimating how customers will respond to different price levels. **Demand analysis** seeks to estimate the level of customer demand for a given product and the underlying reasons for that demand. For example, research indicates that customers often buy more of certain products at higher prices, which suggests that price may be an indication of quality.[5] The influence of price on perceptions of quality seems to occur most often when customers are unable to evaluate the product themselves. The chemical firm DuPont, using demand analysis, also obtains measures of nonprice factors for its products. Among those factors are delivery, service, innovation, brand name, and quality.

> **Demand analysis** A research method that seeks to estimate the level of customer demand for a given product and the underlying reasons for that demand.

Demand analysis often incorporates a test-marketing procedure. This involves the actual marketing of a product in one of several cities with the intent of measuring customer sensitivity to changes in a firm's marketing mix. Test marketing is discussed in detail in Chapter 8. Demand analysis can also incorporate end-user research studies and analysis of historical price and quality data for specific products.

> **Sales forecasting** Uses variables that affect customer demand to provide estimates of financial outcomes for different price strategies.

Closely associated with demand analysis is **sales forecasting.** After demand analysis identifies the variables that affect customer demand, sales forecasting uses those variables to provide estimates of financial outcomes for different price strategies.

Although a variety of sales forecasting techniques exist, most can be placed in one of two categories: qualitative or quantitative. Qualitative techniques include user expectation studies, sales-force composites, juries of executive opinion, and Delphi techniques. Quantitative forecasting techniques include market testing, time series analysis, and statistical demand analysis.

Integrated Marketing Communications

Promotional decisions, many times viewed as integrated marketing communications, are important influences on any company's sales. Companies spend billions of dollars yearly on various promotional activities. Given the heavy level of expenditures devoted to promotional activities, it is essential that companies design studies that will generate optimum returns from the promotional investment.

Marketing research methods used to acquire information about the performance of a promotional program must consider the entire program. Employing the appropriate methodology, estimating adequate sample sizes, and developing the proper scaling techniques are just three key areas of promotional research. Each of these areas is used when considering the three most common research tasks of integrated marketing communications: advertising effectiveness studies, attitudinal research, and sales tracking.

Because advertising serves so many purposes and covers so many objectives, advertising effectiveness studies often vary across situations. Advertising effectiveness studies may be qualitative, quantitative, or both. They may take place in laboratory-type settings or in real-life settings. Measures of an ad's effectiveness may be taken before or at various times after media placement. Regardless, the key elements of advertising effectiveness studies are what is being measured, when the measurement is made, and which medium is being used.

Most advertising effectiveness studies focus on measuring a particular ad's ability to generate awareness, communicate product benefits, or create a favorable predisposition about a product. In attempting to accomplish such measurement objectives, market researchers usually include attitudinal research within the advertising effectiveness study.

Attitudinal research can be categorized into three types. First is the *cognitive approach,* which attempts to measure consumers' knowledge and opinions about a given product or brand. Second, *affect approaches* measure consumers' overall impressions of a product or brand. These impressions are usually associated with dimensions like good/bad, pleasant/unpleasant, or positive/negative. Third, *behavioral approaches* seek to measure consumers' specific behaviors (brand loyalty, brand switching, etc.) with regard to a given product or brand. Because many promotional strategies are designed to affect consumers' attitudes, the results of attitudinal research play an important role in the design and implementation of promotional programs.

Personal selling also plays a major role in a firm's promotional mix. The objectives assigned to salespeople frequently involve expected sales results such as sales quotas. Non-sales objectives are also important and may include increasing new accounts, evaluating middlemen, or achieving set levels of customer service. Both forms of objectives are commonly tied to the evaluation of a salesperson's overall performance. Several variables must be considered in this evaluation process, which uses a technique commonly called *sales tracking.* From the standpoint of marketing research, key information must be gathered on salespeople and placed into the proper units of analysis in order to provide adjustments for factors beyond the control of individual salespeople. Sales-tracking procedures allow for this adjustment by assessing a combination of objective and subjective performance dimensions.

Exhibit 1.4 contains some actual data collected on a sales-tracking form. Some of the key variables are standard industrial classification (SIC) codes, annual sales, and number of employees. The form also illustrates the effectiveness of the selling function by documenting who sold the product, the number of sales calls required to close the sale, and the profit generated. A well-designed sales-tracking system such as this helps managers diagnose performance-related problems and determine corrective actions that may be necessary.

EXHIBIT 1.4   Computerized Sales Tracking Form Illustrating Key Sales Tracking Variables

Company Id:	5012
Job No:	7012
Name:	HERSHEY CHOCOLATE USA
Address:	27 WEST CHOCOLATE AVE
City ST Zip:	HERSHEY PA 17033-0819
Phone:	717-534-6488
DIV:	
SIC Code:	2066
Employees:	5
Annual Sales:	4
Region:	1
Primary Bus:	4
No. of Plants:	8
Projected Growth:	7
Primary Market:	2
No. of Product Line:	4
End Product:	4
Facility Address:	HERSHEY
Key Contact Person:	GARY HOMMEL
Division No.:	
Location:	1
System Price:	1
System Profit:	
Sales Call/Close Ratio:	
Sales Rep:	52

Marketing Program Implementation and Control

The key to marketing program implementation and control for any organization is the marketing plan. This plan indicates what the strategic goals are and how they will be accomplished. Marketing research provides managers information they need to analyze product markets, competition, and product performance with regard to the marketing plan. In addition, marketing research provides information for strategy implementation and long-term planning.

Marketing Program Control

Product analysis Identifies the relative importance of product selection criteria to buyers and rates brands against these criteria.

Two key areas of focus are product analysis and environmental forecasting. **Product analysis** attempts to identify the relative importance of product selection criteria to buyers and rate brands against these criteria. Such analysis is conducted throughout the life cycle of the product or brand. It is particularly useful when developing the strengths-and-weaknesses section of a marketing plan. Many of the standardized information services provided by marketing research firms, such as Information Resources and AC Nielsen, monitor the performance of competing brands across a wide variety of products.

Environmental forecasting A research method used to predict external occurrences that can affect the long-term strategy of a firm.

Environmental forecasting is used to predict external occurrences that can affect the long-term strategy of a firm. This technique usually involves a three-phase process that begins with a survey of customers and industry experts. This is followed with a market test to measure customer response to a particular marketing program and, finally, an analysis of internal company records to determine past buying behaviors. The net result is an accumulation of data pertaining to industry trends, customer profiles, and environmental changes that allows a company to adapt its strategy to anticipated future events.

Information Analysis

Information is vital to the market planning process. Just as market planning is the key to the long-term survival of the firm, information is the key to the accuracy of the marketing plan. Critical information allows firms to develop a competitive advantage. The role of marketing research is not only to collect and analyze data, but to categorize and process the data for maximum usage. This task is achieved through the development of a sophisticated **marketing decision support system (MDSS),** a company-developed database used to analyze company performance and control marketing activities.

Marketing decision support system (MDSS) A company-developed database used to analyze company performance and control marketing activities.

The MDSS includes standardized marketing research reports, sales and cost data, product-line sales, advertising data, and price information. This information is organized to correspond to specific units of analysis (market segments, geographic locations, particular vendors), and is used for various decisions from reordering inventory to launching new products. The value of the MDSS becomes most apparent when the system focuses on managerial decision making. An example of this relationship between market planning and marketing research is Northwest Airlines' ability to use an MDSS when focusing on the needs of specific market segments. The Northwest system, which determines mileage awards for frequent flyers and provides a reservation support database organized according to market segments, reveals that the top 3 percent of the company's customers account for almost 50 percent of its sales. These key customers are highlighted on all service screens and reports. Ticket agents are alerted when one of these customers phones in or arrives, so they can offer a variety of special services, such as first-class upgrades.[6]

New technologies for collecting, processing, and analyzing market research data are rapidly changing organizations in a variety of ways. Many experts predict that technologies associated with the MDSS will reduce the need for primary data collection methods in the future.[7] The impact of the MDSS on marketing research will be discussed in Chapter 5.

The Marketing Research Industry

The marketing research industry has experienced unparalleled growth in recent years. According to an *Advertising Age* study, revenues of U.S. research companies grew 15 percent in 2003, compared to 10 percent in 1997.[8] Even more dramatic were the revenues reported by international research firms, claiming a 20 percent increase in 2003. Marketing research firms have attributed these revenue increases to postsale customer satisfaction studies (one-third of research company revenues), retail-driven product scanning systems (also one-third of all revenues), database development for long-term brand management, and international research studies.

Types of Marketing Research Firms

Marketing research providers can be classified as either internal or external, custom or standardized, or brokers or facilitators. Internal research providers are normally organizational units that reside within a company. For example, General Motors, Procter & Gamble, and Kodak all have internal marketing research departments. Kraft Foods realizes many benefits by keeping the marketing research function internal; these benefits include research method consistency, shared information across the company, minimized spending on research, and ability to produce actionable research results.

Other firms choose to use external sources for marketing research. External sources, usually referred to as marketing research suppliers, perform all aspects of the research, including study design, questionnaire production, interviewing, data analysis, and report preparation. These firms operate on a fee basis and commonly submit a research proposal to be used by a client for evaluation and decision purposes. An actual example of a proposal is provided in the Marketing Research in Action at the end of Chapter 2.

Many companies use external research suppliers because, first, the suppliers can be more objective and less subject to company politics and regulations than internal suppliers. Second, many external suppliers provide specialized talents that, for the same cost, internal suppliers could not provide. And finally, companies can choose external suppliers on a study-by-study basis and thus gain greater flexibility in scheduling studies as well as match specific project requirements to the talents of specific research firms.

Marketing research firms also can be considered customized or standardized. Customized research firms provide specialized, highly tailored services to the client. Many firms in this line of business concentrate their research activities in one specific area such as brand-name testing, test marketing, or new-product development. For example, Namestormers assists companies in brand-name selection and recognition, Survey Sampling Inc. concentrates solely on sampling development for the restaurant industry, and Uniscore conducts studies designed around retail scanning data. In contrast, standardized research firms provide more general services. These firms also follow a more common approach in research design so that the results of a study conducted for one client can be compared to norms established by studies done for other clients. Examples of these firms are Burke Market Research, which conducts day-after advertising recall; AC Nielsen (separate from Nielsen Media Research), which conducts store audits for a variety of retail firms; and Arbitron Ratings, which provides primary data collection regarding commercial television.

Many standardized research firms also provide syndicated business services, which include purchase diary panels, audits, and advertising recall data made or developed from a common data pool or database. A prime example of a syndicated business service is a database established through retail optical scanner methods. This database, available from AC Nielsen, tracks the retail sales of thousands of brand-name products. This data can be customized for a variety of industries (snack foods, over-the-counter drugs, etc.) to indicate purchase profiles and volume sales in a given industry. The Closer Look at Research box illustrates how Yahoo and AC Nielsen, as a result of a blending of technology, provide customized data for the Internet.

A Closer Look at Research

Yahoo! and AC Nielsen: A Marketing Research Marriage through Technology

Yahoo! Inc., a leading global Internet company, and AC Nielsen, the world's leading market research firm, today released the results of the most recent Yahoo!/AC Nielsen Internet Confidence Index, a quarterly study designed to measure confidence levels in Internet products and services. The results of the Index show that consumer confidence and attitudes about the Internet and online shopping are up eight points higher than the same period last year. The survey also shows that consumers intend to spend a projected $19.6 billion online in the fourth quarter holiday season, a 23 percent increase from last year. The strong confidence level is driving an increased intent to spend more online during the fourth quarter, especially among broadband users, pointing to the growing mainstream acceptance of and reliance on the Internet as a medium for commerce. Year-over-year, there has been a statistically significant eight point increase in the Yahoo!/AC Nielsen Internet Confidence Index. The results of this current wave show that the steady rise in confidence among Internet users can be attributed in part to a greater confidence in the security of personal information online. "The increase in Internet confidence from last year's holiday season is good news for marketers who are utilizing the Internet for holiday shopping campaigns," said Travyn Rhall, managing director, AC Nielsen International. "Our data indicates that there is a strong correlation between higher confidence and higher consumer spending; marketers should therefore focus on bringing down the perceived barriers to e-commerce, including comfort regarding personal information online."

BROADBAND CONSUMERS HIGHLY CONFIDENT

This quarter's Internet Confidence Index examined broadband usage and those consumers' confidence in Internet products and services. Consumers with faster Internet access are the most confident in e-commerce transactions and have the highest intent to shop and spend during the next quarter. Three key motivators driving the increased confidence include convenience, high comfort levels with credit card usage, and a strong sense of security with personal information online.

Age also plays a factor in confidence level and spending habits. The confidence of the 25–34-year-old age group (currently the most confident demographic), and the 45+ year-old group have both increased significantly. The 25–34 age group shows an 11 point leap since last year and is up 16 points since the last quarter. Additionally, the 45+ age group has shown a 19 point increase in confidence levels in the last year and a 13 point increase since the last quarter.

ABOUT THE YAHOO!/AC NIELSEN INTERNET CONFIDENCE INDEX The Yahoo!/AC Nielsen Internet Confidence Index measures consumers' attitudes related to potential motivators and barriers to e-commerce, as well as various facets of purchasing behavior within the United States. The index score for the initial Yahoo!/AC Nielsen Internet Confidence Index was set at 100 for use as a baseline, allowing subsequent survey data to be converted into trended, indexed scores. Further information can be accessed at http://docs.yahoo.com/docs/info/yici/.

AC Nielsen, on behalf of Yahoo!, conducts research for the Index through computer-aided telephone interviewing with random digit dialing and utilizes a sample size audience of 1,000 adults, who may or may not be currently utilizing the Internet. Yahoo! publishes Index results on a quarterly basis, four times per calendar year and when special circumstances merit close examination of changes in consumer attitudes.

ABOUT AC NIELSEN AC Nielsen, a VNU business, is the world's leading marketing information company. Offering services in more than 100 countries, the company provides measurement and analysis of marketplace dynamics and consumer attitudes and behavior. Clients rely on AC Nielsen's market research, proprietary products, analytical tools, and professional service to understand competitive performance, to uncover new opportunities, and to raise the profitability of their marketing and sales campaigns.

Source: Reprinted by permission. Yahoo! Inc., Yahoo media relations press release.

Finally, marketing research firms can be distinguished as either brokers or facilitators. Broker services provide the ancillary tasks that complement many marketing research studies. For example, marketing research suppliers and clients who do not have the resources for data entry, tabulation, or analysis will typically use a broker service to facilitate the data management process. Brokers usually offer specialized programming, canned statistical packages, and other data management tools at low cost. P-Shat, Inc., for example, is a marketing research broker service that performs only three functions: data entry, data tabulation, and statistical analysis.

Facilitating agencies

Businesses that perform marketing research functions as a supplement to a broader marketing research project.

Facilitating agencies are companies or businesses that perform marketing research functions as a supplement to a broader marketing research project. Advertising agencies, field services, and independent consultants are usually classified as facilitators because they help companies complete broader marketing projects. Advertising agencies, for example, are in the business of designing, implementing, and evaluating advertising campaigns for individual clients. Many agencies use their own research services to guide the development of the campaign and test for effectiveness. In this instance, the ad agency provides marketing research to facilitate the ad campaign process.

Marketing research suppliers frequently employ field services, whose primary responsibilities are to schedule, supervise, and complete interviews. As a facilitating agency, a field service contributes data collection services toward the completion of the marketing research project. In addition, many independent consultants are hired ad hoc to complement strategic planning activities for clients. Many consultants, offering unique and specialized research skills, are hired by firms to facilitate a total quality management program, develop a marketing information system, or train employees in the procedures of marketing research.

As this discussion shows, marketing research is a diverse industry. Diversity, coupled with increased revenue growth in the industry, has created job opportunities for people with a variety of skills. Furthermore, as more and more marketing research projects take on international flavor, these opportunities will continue to expand. The following section addresses what skills will be needed in the industry.

Changing Skills for a Changing Industry

Marketing research employees represent a vast diversity of cultures, technology, and personalities. As marketing research firms expand their geographic scope to Europe, Asia, and the Pacific Rim, the requirements for successfully executing marketing research projects will change dramatically. Many fundamental skill requirements will remain in place, but new and innovative practices will require a totally unique skill base that is more comprehensive than ever before.

In a survey of 100 marketing research executives, basic fundamental business skills were rated high for potential employees. Communication skills (verbal and written), interpersonal skills (ability to work with others), and statistical skills were the leading attributes in basic job aptitude.[9] More specifically, the top five skills executives hope to find in candidates for marketing research positions are (1) the ability to understand and interpret secondary data, (2) presentation skills, (3) foreign-language competency, (4) negotiation skills, and (5) computer proficiency.[10] Results of this survey indicate there has been a shift from analytical to execution skill requirements in the marketing research industry. In the future, analyzing existing databases, multicultural interaction, and negotiation are likely to be important characteristics of marketing researchers. Marketing research jobs are discussed further in a careers appendix at the end of this chapter.

Ethics in Marketing Research Practices

There are many opportunities for both ethical and unethical behaviors to occur in the research process. The major sources of ethical dilemmas in marketing research are the interactions among the three key groups: (1) the research information user (e.g., decision maker, sponsoring client, management team, practitioner); (2) the research information provider (e.g., researcher, research organization or company, project supervisor, researcher's staff representative or employees); and (3) the selected respondents (e.g., subjects or objects of investigation).

Unethical Activities by the Client/Research User

Decisions and practices of the client or decision maker present opportunities for unethical behavior. One such behavior is when the decision maker requests a detailed research proposal from several competing research providers with no intention of selecting a firm to conduct the research. In this situation, companies solicit the proposals for the purpose of learning how to conduct the necessary marketing research themselves. Decision makers can obtain first drafts of questionnaires, sampling frames and sampling procedures, and knowledge on data collection procedures. Then, unethically, they can use the information to either perform the research project themselves or bargain for a better price among interested research companies.

Unfortunately, another common behavior of unethical decision makers is promising a prospective research provider a long-term relationship or additional projects in order to obtain a very low price on the initial research project. Then, after the researcher completes the initial project, the decision maker forgets about the long-term promises.

Unethical Activities by the Research Provider or Research Company

While there might be numerous opportunities for the researcher, the research company, or its representatives to act unethically in the process of conducting a study, there are four major sources of unethical activities that can originate with the research company. First, a policy of unethical pricing practices is a common source of conflict. For example, after quoting a set overall price for a proposed research project, the researcher may tell the decision maker that variable-cost items such as travel expenses, monetary response incentives, or fees charged for computer time are extra, over and above the quoted price. Such "soft" costs can be easily used to manipulate the total project cost.

Second, all too often research firms just simply do not provide the promised incentive (e.g., contest awards, gifts, even money) to respondents for completing the interviews or questionnaires. Also, many firms will delay indefinitely the fees owed to field workers (e.g., interviewers, data tabulators, data entry personnel). Usually, these parties are paid at the project's completion and thus lose any leverage they have with the research provider to collect on services rendered.

Third, it is not uncommon for the researcher or the organization to create respondent abuse. Research companies have a tendency to state that interviews are very short when in reality they may last up to one hour. Other situations of known respondent abuse include selling the respondents' names and demographic data to other companies without their approval, using infrared dye on questionnaires to trace selective respondents for the purpose of making a sales call, or using hidden tape recorders in a personal interviewing situation without the respondent's permission.

Finally, an unethical practice found all too often in marketing research is the selling of unnecessary or unwarranted research services. While it is perfectly acceptable to sell follow-up research that can aid the decision maker's company, selling bogus services is completely unethical. There are several other researcher-related unethical practices within the execution of the research design such as (1) falsifying data, (2) duplicating actual response data, and (3) consciously manipulating the data structures inappropriately.

A practice of data falsification known to many researchers and field interviewers is called curbstoning (or rocking-chair) interviewing. This occurs when the researcher's trained interviewers or observers, rather than conducting interviews or observing respondents' actions as directed in the study, will complete the interviews themselves or make up "observed" respondents' behaviors. Other falsification practices include having friends and relatives fill out surveys, not using the designated sample of sample respondents but rather anyone who is conveniently available to complete the survey, or not following up on the established callback procedures indicated in the research procedure.

Another variation of data falsification is duplication of responses or the creation of "phantom" respondents. This is a process whereby a researcher or field personnel (e.g., interviewer, field observer, or data entry personnel) will take an actual respondent's data and duplicate it to represent a second set of responses. This practice artificially creates data responses from people who were scheduled to be in the study but who for some reason were not actually interviewed. To minimize the likelihood of data falsification, research companies typically randomly verify 10 to 15 percent of the interviews. And finally, researchers act unethically when they either (1) consciously manipulate data structures from data analysis procedures for the purpose of reporting a biased picture to the decision maker or (2) do not report selected findings at all.

Unethical Activities by the Respondent

The primary unethical practice of respondents or subjects in any research endeavor is that of providing dishonest answers or of faking behavior. The general expectation is that when a subject has freely consented to participate, she or he will provide truthful responses, but truthfulness might be more difficult to achieve than one thinks. Some procedures are available to researchers to help evaluate the honesty of respondents' answers or actions. For example, bipolar questioning is used as a consistency check in surveys. Here the first question is framed in a positive way and the second question is framed in a negative way. The respondent's answers, if consistent, would be inversely related.

Other areas of possible ethical dilemmas within a researcher-respondent relationship are (1) the respondent's right to privacy; (2) the need to disguise the true purpose of the research; and (3) the respondent's right to be informed about certain aspects of the research process, including the sponsorship of the research.

Marketing Research Codes of Ethics

Of increasing importance to today's ethical decision-making processes is the establishment of company ethics programs. Special attention is provided here to these programs because they offer perhaps the best chance of minimizing unethical behavior. Today's marketing researchers must be proactive in their efforts to ensure an ethical environment, and the first step in being proactive is to develop a code of ethics. Many marketing research companies have established internal company codes of ethics derived from the ethical codes formulated by larger institutions that govern today's marketing research industry. Exhibit 1.5 displays the code developed by the American Marketing Association.[11] This code provides a framework for identifying ethical issues and arriving at ethical decisions in situations researchers sometimes face.

eXHIBIT	**1.5**	Code of Ethics of the American Marketing Association

The American Marketing Association, in furtherance of its central objective of the advancement of science in marketing and in recognition of its obligation to the public, has established these principles of ethical practice of marketing research for the guidance of its members. In an increasingly complex society, marketing research is more and more dependent upon marketing information intelligently and systematically obtained. The consumer is the source of much of this information. Seeking the cooperation of the consumer in the development of information, marketing management must acknowledge its obligation to protect the public from misrepresentation and exploitation under the guise of research.

Similarly the research practitioner has an obligation to the discipline he practices and to those who provide support of his practice—an obligation to adhere to basic and commonly accepted standards of scientific investigation as they apply to the domain of marketing research. It is the intent of this code to define ethical standards required of marketing research in satisfying these obligations.

Adherence to this code will assure the user of marketing research that the research was done in accordance with acceptable ethical practices. Those engaged in research will find in this code an affirmation of sound and honest basic principles which have developed over the years as the profession has grown. The field interviewers who are the point of contact between the profession and the consumer will also find guidance in fulfilling their vitally important roles.

AMA CODE OF ETHICS

Members of the American Marketing Association are committed to ethical professional conduct. They have joined together in subscribing to this Code of Ethics embracing the following topics:

Responsibilities of the Marketer

Marketers must accept responsibility for the consequences of their activities and make every effort to ensure that their decisions, recommendations and actions function to identify, serve and satisfy all relevant publics: customers, organizations and society.

Marketers' Professional Conduct must be guided by:

1. The basic rule of professional ethics: not knowingly to do harm;
2. The adherence to all applicable laws and regulations;
3. The accurate representation of their education, training and experience; and
4. The active support, practice and promotion of this Code of Ethics.

Honesty and Fairness

Marketers shall uphold and advance the integrity, honor and dignity of the marketing profession by:

1. Being honest in serving consumers, clients, employees, suppliers, distributors, and the public;
2. Not knowingly participating in conflict of interest without prior notice to all parties involved; and
3. Establishing equitable fee schedules including the payment or receipt of usual, customary and/or legal compensation for marketing exchanges.

Rights and Duties of Parties in the Marketing Exchange Process

Participants in the marketing exchange process should be able to expect that:

1. Products and services offered are safe and fit for their intended uses;
2. Communications about offered products and services are not deceptive;
3. All parties intend to discharge their obligations, financial and otherwise, in good faith; and
4. Appropriate internal methods exist for equitable adjustment and/or redress of grievances concerning purchases.

It is understood that the above would include, but is not limited to, the following responsibilities of the marketer:

In the area of product development and management:

- disclosure of all substantial risks associated with product or service usage;
- identification of any product component substitution that might materially change the product or impact on the buyer's purchase decision;
- identification of extra cost-added features.

In the area of promotions:

- avoidance of false and misleading advertising;
- rejection of high-pressure manipulations, or misleading sales tactics;
- avoidance of sales promotions that use deception or manipulation.

In the area of distribution:

- not manipulating the availability of a product for the purpose of exploitation;
- not using coercion in the marketing channel;
- not exerting undue influence over the reseller's choice to handle a product.

In the area of pricing:

- not engaging in price fixing;
- not practicing predatory pricing;
- disclosing the full price associated with any purchase.

In the area of marketing research:

- prohibiting selling or fundraising under the guise of conducting research;
- maintaining research integrity by avoiding misrepresentation and omission of pertinent research data;
- treating outside clients and suppliers fairly.

Organizational Relationships

Marketers should be aware of how their behavior may influence or impact the behavior of others in organizational relationships. They should not demand, encourage or apply coercion to obtain unethical behavior in their relationships with others, such as employees, suppliers, or customers.

1. Apply confidentiality and anonymity in professional relationships with regard to privileged information;
2. Meet their obligations and responsibilities in contracts and mutual agreements in a timely manner;
3. Avoid taking the work of others, in whole, or in part, and representing this work as their own or directly benefiting from it without compensation or consent of the originator or owner; and
4. Avoid manipulation to take advantage of situations to maximize personal welfare in a way that unfairly deprives or damages the organization of others.

Any AMA member found to be in violation of any provision of this Code of Ethics may have his or her Association membership suspended or revoked.

**AMERICAN MARKETING ASSOCIATION CODE OF ETHICS
FOR MARKETING ON THE INTERNET**

Preamble

The Internet, including online computer communications, has become increasingly important to marketers' activities, as they provide exchanges and access to markets worldwide. The ability to interact with stakeholders has created new marketing opportunities and risks that are not currently specifically addressed in the American Marketing Association Code of Ethics. The American Marketing Association

continued

Code of Ethics for Internet marketing provides additional guidance and direction for ethical responsibility in this dynamic area of marketing. The American Marketing Association is committed to ethical professional conduct and has adopted these principles for using the Internet, including online marketing activities utilizing network computers.

General Responsibilities

Internet marketers must assess the risks and take responsibility for the consequences of their activities. Internet marketers' professional conduct must be guided by:

1. Support of professional ethics to avoid harm by protecting the rights of privacy, ownership and access.
2. Adherence to all applicable laws and regulations with no use of Internet marketing that would be illegal, if conducted by mail, telephone, fax or other media.
3. Awareness of changes in regulations related to Internet marketing.
4. Effective communication to organizational members on risks and policies related to Internet marketing, when appropriate.
5. Organizational commitment to ethical Internet practices communicated to employees, customers and relevant stakeholders.

Privacy

Information collected from customers should be confidential and used only for expressed purposes. All data, especially confidential customer data, should be safeguarded against unauthorized access. The expressed wishes of others should be respected with regard to the receipt of unsolicited e-mail messages.

Ownership

Information obtained from the Internet sources should be properly authorized and documented. Information ownership should be safeguarded and respected. Marketers should respect the integrity and ownership of computer and network systems.

Access

Marketers should treat access to accounts, passwords, and other information as confidential, and only examine or disclose content when authorized by a responsible party. The integrity of others' information systems should be respected with regard to placement of information, advertising or messages.

While the codes of ethics advocated by marketing and survey research associations have given proactive guidance and the appearance of integrity to the marketing research industry, some researchers do not believe they are enough to guarantee continuous ethical behavior. As such, ethical dilemmas remain a never-ending concern for the parties involved with research practices.

Emerging Trends

The general consensus in the marketing research industry is that five major trends are becoming evident: (1) an increased emphasis on secondary data collection methods; (2) movement toward technology-related data management (optical scanning data, database technology); (3) an increased use of digital technology for information acquisition and retrieval; (4) a broader international client base; and (5) a movement away from pure data analysis and toward a data interpretation/information management environment.

Organization of this book is consistent with these trends. Part 1 (Chapters 1–3) explores marketing research information from the client's perspective, including how to evaluate marketing research projects. Part 2 (Chapters 4 and 5) provides an innovative outlook at customer relationship management and technology, with emphasis on technology-driven approaches for collecting data, and the design and development of databases. Part 3 (Chapters 6–8) discusses traditional marketing research project design issues (survey methods and research designs). While these methods are fundamental to the marketing research process, technological developments are changing the focus of these issues. Part 3 also includes collection and interpretation of qualitative data. Practical examples illustrating how they are used today in industry facilitate the discussion. Part 4 (Chapters 9–13) covers sampling, attitude measurement and scaling, and questionnaire design. Part 5 (Chapters 14–18) prepares the reader for management, categorization, and analysis of marketing research data. Computer applications of various statistical packages give readers a hands-on guide to a somewhat intimidating area. This part concludes with a presentation of marketing research findings. Key elements in preparing a written marketing research report and planning an oral presentation of results are treated succinctly. Data analysis packages and graphic and presentation aids highlight the discussion of these topics.

Each chapter in the book concludes with an illustrative example called *Marketing Research In Action,* whose goal is to facilitate the reader's understanding of chapter topics and to provide the reader with a "how-to" approach for marketing research methods.

mARKeTING ReSeARCH IN ACTION

Continuing Case Study

The Santa Fe Grill Mexican Restaurant

The Santa Fe Grill Mexican Restaurant was started 18 months ago by two former business students at the University of Nebraska, Lincoln. They had been roommates in college and both had an entrepreneurial desire. After graduating they wanted to start a business instead of working for someone else. The students worked in restaurants while attending college, both as waiters and one as an assistant manager, and felt they had the knowledge and experience necessary to start their own business.

During their senior year they prepared a business plan in their entrepreneurship class for a new Mexican restaurant concept. They initially intended to start the restaurant in Lincoln, Nebraska. After a demographic analysis of that market, however, they decided that Lincoln did not match their target demographics as well as did some other geographic areas.

After researching the demographic and competitive profile of several markets, they decided that Dallas, Texas, would be the best place to start their business. In examining the markets, they were looking for a town that would best fit their target market of baby boomers and young families. The population in Dallas consists of 4,299,258 people, of which 50.4 percent are between the ages of 35 and 64. This showed them there were a lot of baby boomers and others in their target market in the Dallas area. They also found that 51 percent of the population earn between $35,000 and $75,000 a year, which indicated the market would have enough income to eat out regularly. Finally, 56 percent of the population was married and many of them had children at home, which was consistent with their target of families.

The new restaurant concept was based upon the freshest ingredients, complemented by a festive atmosphere, friendly service, and cutting-edge advertising and marketing strategies. The key would be to prepare and serve the freshest "made-from-scratch" Mexican foods possible. Everything would be prepared fresh every single day. In addition to their freshness concept, they wanted to have a fun, festive atmosphere and fast, friendly service. The atmosphere would be open, brightly lit and bustling with activity. Their target market would be mostly baby boomers and families. Their marketing programs would be ahead of the pack, with the advertising designed to provide an appealing, slightly off-center, unrefined positioning in the market.

The Santa Fe Grill has been successful, but not as quickly as the owners anticipated. To improve restaurant operations, the owners need to better understand what aspects of the restaurant drive customer satisfaction and where they can improve. They have come up with a few questions to be researched. Are the customers satisfied and if not, why are they not satisfied? Are there problems with the food, the atmosphere, or some other aspect of restaurant operations (e.g., employees or service)? Is the target market correctly defined or do they need to focus on a different niche? What are the common characteristics of satisfied customers? Answering these and other similar questions will help the owners focus their marketing efforts, improve operations, and be in a position to expand their restaurant concept to other markets.

Hands-On Exercise

The owners need your help as follows:

1. Based on your understanding of Chapter 1, and specifically using Exhibit 1.1, what type(s) of research program(s) should the owners of the Santa Fe Grill consider?

2. Given the general questions that the owners have cited above, are there additional information/questions that you would suggest to the owners when designing their research program?

Summary of Learning Objectives

■ **Describe and explain the impact marketing research has on marketing decision making.**

Marketing research is the set of activities central to all marketing-related decisions regardless of the complexity or focus of the decision. Marketing research is responsible for providing managers with accurate, relevant, and timely information so that they can make marketing decisions with a high degree of confidence. Within the context of strategic planning, marketing research is responsible for the tasks, methods, and procedures a firm will use to implement and direct its strategic plan.

■ **Demonstrate how marketing research fits into the marketing planning process.**

Marketing research is the backbone of any relationship marketing process through the data collection operations of the research process. Specifically, marketing research facilitates the CRM process through the generation of customer/market knowledge, data integration, information technology, and the creation of customer profiles. The key to successful planning is accurate information. Information related to product performance, distribution efficiency, pricing policies, and promotional efforts is crucial for developing the strategic plan. The primary responsibility of any marketing research endeavor is to design a project that yields the most accurate information possible in aiding the development of a marketing plan.

■ **Provide examples of marketing research studies.**

The scope of marketing research activities extends far beyond examination of customer characteristics. The major categories of marketing research tasks include, but are not limited to, (1) situation research efforts (which include opportunity assessment, benefit and lifestyle studies, descriptive studies, and importance-performance analysis); (2) strategy-driven research efforts (which include target market analysis, positioning or perceptual mapping, concept and product testing, and test marketing); (3) program development research (which includes customer satisfaction studies, service quality studies, cycle time research, retailing research,

logistic assessment, demand analysis, sales forecasting, advertising effectiveness studies, attitudinal research, and sales tracking); and (4) performance analysis (which includes product analysis, environmental forecasting, and marketing decision support systems).

■ **Understand the scope and focus of the marketing research industry.**

Generally, marketing research projects can be conducted either internally by an in-house marketing research staff or externally by independent or facilitating marketing research firms. External research suppliers are normally classified as custom or standardized, or as brokers or facilitators.

■ **Demonstrate ethical dimensions associated with marketing research.**

Ethical decision making affects all industries, including marketing research. Ethical dilemmas in marketing research are likely to occur among the research information user, the research information provider, and the selected respondents. Specific unethical practices of research providers include unethical pricing practices, failure to meet obligations to respondents, respondent abuse, and selling unnecessary services. Unethical behavior by clients includes requesting research proposals with no intent to follow through and unethical practices to secure low-cost research services. The falsification of data and duplication of actual responses are unethical practices associated with the research firm.

■ **Understand emerging trends and new skills associated with marketing research.**

Just as the dynamic business environment causes firms to modify and change practices, so does this environment dictate change to the marketing research industry. Specifically, technological changes will affect how marketing research will be conducted in the future. Necessary skills required to adapt to these changes include (1) the ability to understand and interpret secondary data, (2) presentation skills, (3) foreign-language competency, (4) negotiation skills, and (5) computer proficiency.

Key Terms and Concepts

Review Questions

1. Provide three examples of how marketing research helps marketing personnel make sound managerial decisions.

2. What improvements in market planning can be attributed to the results obtained from customer satisfaction studies?

3. List the three basic approaches used in the collection of marketing research information. Briefly describe each method and comment on its application.

4. Discuss the importance of target market analysis. How does it affect the development of market planning for a particular company?

5. What are the advantages and disadvantages for companies maintaining an internal marketing research department? What advantages and disadvantages can be attributed to the hiring of an external marketing research supplier?

6. As the marketing research industry expands in the new century, what skills will future executives need to possess? How do these skills differ from those currently needed to function successfully in the marketing research field?

7. Identify and explain four potential unethical practices within the marketing research process and their contribution to "deceptive research results."

Discussion Questions

1. **EXPERIENCE THE INTERNET.** Go online to one of your favorite search engines (Yahoo!, Google, etc.) and enter the following search term: marketing research. From the results, access a directory of marketing research firms. Select a particular firm and comment on the types of marketing research studies it performs.

2. **EXPERIENCE THE INTERNET.** Using the Yahoo! search engine, specifically the Get Local section, select the closest major city in your area and search for the number of marketing research firms there. Select a company, e-mail that company, and ask to have any job descriptions for positions in that company e-mailed back to you. Once you obtain the descriptions, discuss the particular qualities needed to perform each job.

3. You have been hired by McDonald's to lead a mystery shopper team. The goal of your research is to improve the service quality at the McDonald's restaurant in your area. What attributes of service quality will you attempt to measure? What customer or employee behaviors will you closely monitor?

4. Contact a local business and interview the owner/manager about the types of marketing research performed for that business. Determine whether the business has its own marketing research department, or if it hires an outside agency. Also, determine whether the company takes a one-shot approach to particular problems or is systematic over a long period of time.

5. **EXPERIENCE THE INTERNET.** As the Internet continues to grow as a medium for conducting various types of marketing research studies, there is growing concern about ethical issues. Identify and discuss three ethical issues pertinent to research conducted using the Internet.

   Now go to the Internet and validate your ethical concerns. Using any browser and search engine, go to the Internet Fraud home page at www.fraud.org/ifw.htm. Click on the other links and browse the information. What unethical practices are plaguing the Net?

6. Identify and describe at least two situations in which marketing research should not be undertaken.

7. How is the Internet changing the field of marketing research?

8. Discuss how recent ethical developments are impacting the marketing research industry.

appendix 1.A

Careers in Marketing Research with a Look at Federal Express

Career opportunities in marketing research vary by industry, company, and size of company. Different positions exist in consumer products companies, industrial goods companies, internal marketing research departments, and professional marketing research firms. Marketing research tasks range from the very simple, such as tabulation of questionnaires, to the very complex, such as sophisticated data analysis. Exhibit A.1 lists some common job titles and the functions as well as compensation ranges for marketing research positions.

EXHIBIT A.1 Marketing Research Career Outline

Position*	Duties	Compensation Range (Annual, in Thousands)
Account executive research director	Responsible for entire research program of the company. Works as go-between for the company and client. Employs personnel and supervises research department. Presents research findings to company and/or clients.	$60 to $90+
Information technician statistician	Acts as expert consultant on application of statistical techniques for specific research problems. Many times responsible for research design and data analysis.	$40 to $70+
Research analyst	Plans research project and executes project assignments. Works with analyst in preparing questionnaire. Makes analysis, prepares report, schedules project events, and sets budget.	$35 to $65+
Assistant research analyst	Works under research analyst supervision. Assists in development of questionnaire, pretest, preliminary analysis.	$30 to $45+
Project coordinator Project director Field manager Fieldwork director	Hires, trains, and supervises field interviewers. Provides work schedules and is responsible for data accuracy.	$25 to $35+
Librarian	Builds and maintains a library of primary and secondary data sources to meet the requirements of the research department.	$35 to $45+
Clerical and tabulation assistant	Handles and processes statistical data. Supervises day-to-day office work.	$18 to $32+

*Positions are generalized, and not all companies have all of the positions.

Most successful marketing research people are intelligent and creative; they also possess problem-solving, critical-thinking, communication, and negotiation skills. Marketing researchers must be able to function under strict time constraints and feel comfortable with working with large volumes of data. Federal Express, for example, normally seeks individuals with strong analytical and computer skills to fill its research positions. Candidates should have an undergraduate degree in business, marketing, or information systems. Having an MBA will usually give an applicant a competitive advantage.

As is the case with many companies, the normal entry-level position in the marketing research area at Federal Express is the assistant research analyst. While learning details of the company and the industry, these individuals receive on-the-job training from a research analyst. The normal career path includes advancement to information technician and then research director and/or account executive.

Marketing research at Federal Express is somewhat unusual in that it is housed in the information technology division. This is evidence that, while the research function is integrated throughout the company, it has taken on a high-tech orientation. Marketing research at FedEx operates in three general areas:

1. **Database development and enhancement.** This function is to establish relationships with current FedEx customers and use this information for the planning of new products.

2. **Cycle time research.** Providing more information for the efficient shipping of packages, tracking of shipments, automatic replenishment of customers' inventories, and enhanced electronic data interchange.

3. **Market intelligence system.** Primarily a logistical database and research effort to provide increased customer service to catalog retailers, direct marketing firms, and electronic commerce organizations.

The entire research function is led by a vice president of research and information technology, to whom four functional units report directly. These four units are responsible for the marketing decision support system operation, sales tracking, new business development, and special project administration.

If you are interested in pursuing a career in marketing research, a good way to start is to obtain the following career guide published by the Marketing Research Association:

Career Guide: Your Future in Marketing Research
Marketing Research Association
2189 Silas Deane Highway, Suite 5
Rocky Hill, CT 06067
MRAH@aol.com

It is also a wise idea to obtain the *Marketing and Sales Career Directory*, available at your university library or by writing:

Marketing and Sales Career Directory
Gale Research Inc.
835 Penobscot Building
Detroit, MI 48226-4094

1. Go to the home Web page for Federal Express, and identify the requirements that FedEx is seeking in marketing research personnel. Write a brief description of these requirements, and report your findings to the class.

2. If you were seeking a marketing research position at FedEx, how would you prepare yourself through training and education for such a position? Put together a one-year plan for yourself identifying the college courses, special activities, interests, and related work experience you would engage in to obtain a marketing research position at FedEx.

appendix 1.B

Using SPSS with the Santa Fe Grill Database

The SPSS software package is very user-friendly and enables you to easily learn the various statistical techniques without having to use formulas and calculate the results. The approach is a simple Windows-based "point-and-click" process. In this appendix, we provide a brief overview of how to use the package and click-through sequences for the techniques you will be using. This will be a quick reference point for you to refresh your memory on how to run the various techniques.

When you run the SPSS software, you will see a screen like that in Exhibit B.1. The case study database is available from our Web site at www.mhhe.com/hair/06 or from your instructor. You will note the columns are blank because the data has not been entered into the SPSS software.

When you load SPSS a screen in the top left-hand corner labeled Untitled—SPSS Data Editor should be visible in the background. In the foreground is a dialog box called SPSS for Windows Student Version. If you have never run SPSS you will have to tell the program where to find the data. If you have previously run the SPSS program you can simply highlight the location of the database and click on OK at the bottom of the screen. The SPSS Data Editor screen without the dialog box in the foreground is shown in Exhibit B.1.

Across the top of the screen is a toolbar with a series of pull-down menus. Each of these menus leads you to several functions. An overview of these menu functions is shown below.

Menus

There are 10 "pull-down" menus across the top of the screen. You can access most SPSS functions and commands by making selections from the menus on the main menu bar. Below are the major features accessed from each of the menus on the Student Version 12 of the SPSS software.

File = create new SPSS files; open existing files; save a file; print; and exit.

Edit = cut and/or copy text or graphics; find specific data; change default options such as size or type of font, fill patterns for charts, types of tables, display format for numerical variables, and so forth.

View = modify what and how information is displayed in the window.

Data = make changes to SPSS data files; add variables and/or cases; change the order of the respondents; split your data file for analysis; and select specific respondents for analysis by themselves.

Transform = compute changes or combinations of data variables; create new variables from combinations of other variables; create random seed numbers; count eXHIBIT **B.1** SPSS Data Editor Window with No Data

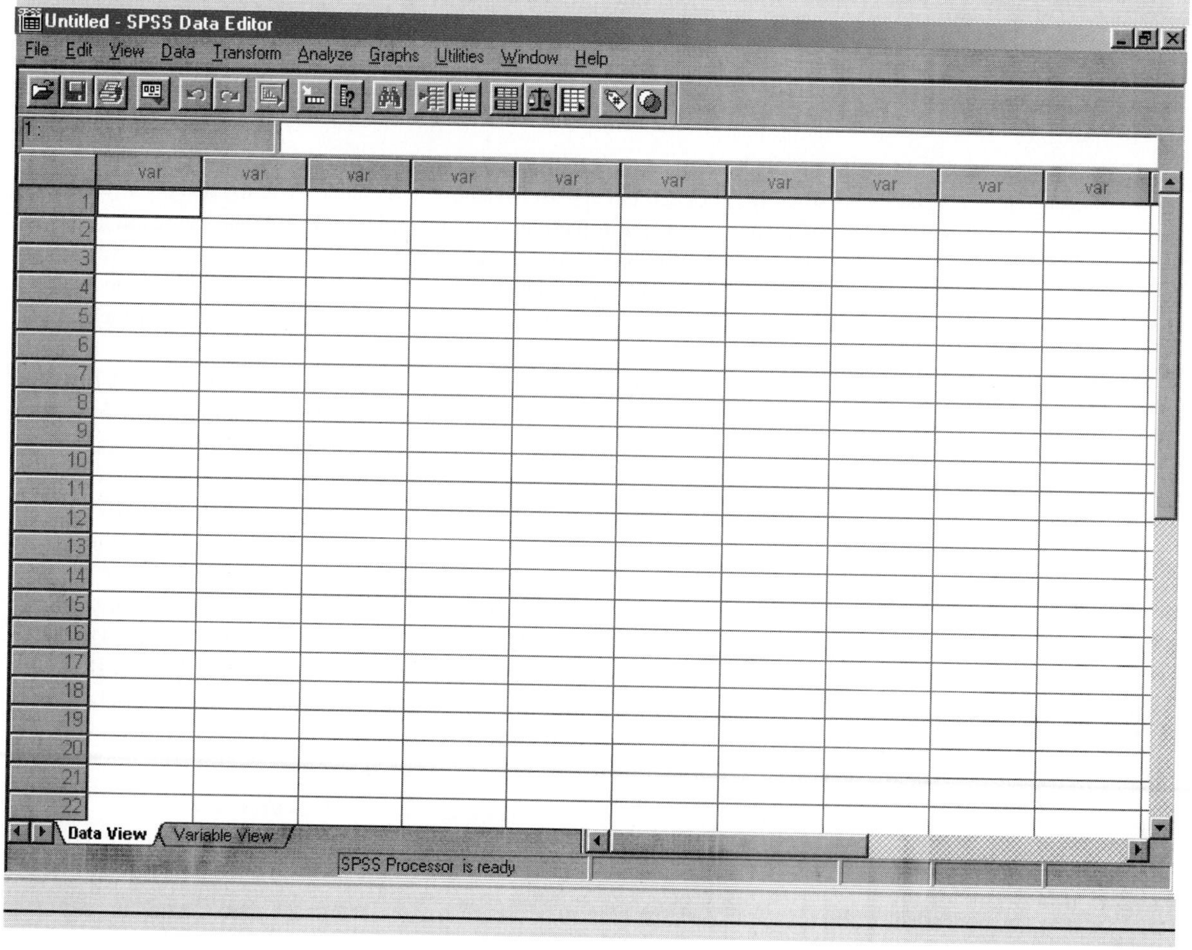

occurrences of values within cases; recode existing variables; create categories for existing variables; replace missing variables; and so on.

Analyze = prepare reports; execute selected statistical techniques such as frequencies, correlation and regression, factor, cluster, and so on.

Graphs = prepare graphs and charts of data, such as bar, line, and pie charts; also boxplots, scatter diagrams, and histograms.

Utilities = information about variables such as missing values, column width, measurement level, and so on.

Window = minimize windows or move between windows.

Help = a brief tutorial of how to use SPSS; includes a link to the SPSS home page at www.spss.com.

Entering Data

There are two ways you can enter data into SPSS files. One is to enter data directly into the Data Editor window. This can be done by creating an entirely new file or by bringing data in from another software package such as Excel. The other is to load data from a file that has been created in another SPSS application.

Let's begin with explaining how to enter data directly into the Data Editor window. The process is similar to entering data into a spreadsheet. The first column typically is used to enter a respondent ID. Use this to enter a respondent number for each response. The remaining columns are used to enter data. You can also "cut and paste" data from another application. Simply open the Data Editor window and minimize it. Then go to your other application and copy the file, return to the Data Editor window and paste the data in it, making sure you correctly align the columns for each of the variables.

Now let's talk about how to load a previously created SPSS file, such as the one that comes with your text. Load the SPSS software and you should see an Untitled SPSS Data Editor screen. Click on the Open File icon and you will get an Open File dialog box. Click on "Look in" to indicate where to look for your file. For example, look on your CD or other storage device. This will locate your SPSS files and you should click on the Santa Fe Grill survey. This will load up your file and you will be ready to run your SPSS analysis.

Data View

When you load up your SPSS file it will show the Data View screen. Exhibit B.2 shows the Data View screen for the Santa Fe Grill survey. This screen is used to run data analysis and to build data files. The other view of the Data Editor is Variable View. The Variable View shows you information about the variables. To move between the two views go to the bottom left-hand corner of the screen and click on the view you want. We discuss the Variable View screen in the next section.

The survey database is set up in columns. The first column on the far left labeled "id" is a unique number for each of the 400 respondents in your database. The remaining columns are the data from the interviews conducted at the restaurant. In the first 3 columns to the right of the id you have the values for the three screening questions. Then, you have the first six variables of the survey–the lifestyle variables (X_1–X_6). For example, respondent 1 gave the Santa Fe Grill a "6" on the 7-point scale for the first variable (X_1). Similarly, that same respondent rated the restaurant a "4" on the second variable (X_2) and a "5" on the third one (X_3). Exhibit B.2 shows only the id, the three screening variables, and the first six variables of the survey. But on your SPSS screen if you scroll to the right you will see the data for all of the survey variables.

Variable View

Exhibit B.3 shows the Variable View screen for the Santa Fe Grill survey. In this view the variable names appear in the far left-hand column. Then each of the columns defines various attributes of the variables as described below:

Name = This is an abbreviated name for each variable.

Type = The default for this is numeric with 2 decimal places. This can be changed to express values as whole numbers or it can do other things such as specify the values as

EXHIBIT   B.2   Data View of the Santa Fe Grill Database

	id	x_s1	x_s2	x_s3	x1	x2	x3	x4	x5	x6
1	1	1	1	1	6	4	5	3	4	5
2	2	1	1	1	4	3	4	2	4	4
3	3	1	1	1	3	4	7	3	4	7
4	4	1	1	1	6	5	7	4	4	7
5	5	1	1	1	4	4	5	2	4	5
6	6	1	1	1	4	6	7	2	4	7
7	7	1	1	1	5	4	5	3	2	5
8	8	1	1	1	6	4	6	4	4	6
9	9	1	1	1	6	5	6	2	5	5
10	10	1	1	1	5	5	6	3	4	6
11	11	1	1	1	4	4	5	3	5	5
12	12	1	1	1	6	3	4	4	5	4
13	13	1	1	1	5	2	3	4	4	3
14	14	1	1	1	6	5	7	3	5	7
15	15	1	1	1	6	3	4	4	2	4
16	16	1	1	1	6	5	7	4	4	6
17	17	1	1	1	5	5	7	4	4	7
18	18	1	1	1	6	5	6	4	4	5
19	19	1	1	1	4	2	3	3	3	3
20	20	1	1	1	6	4	5	3	5	5
21	21	1	1	1	5	4	6	4	3	6
22	22	1	1	1	5	2	3	4	3	3
23	23	1	1	1	6	6	7	4	5	7
24	24	1	1	1	4	5	7	4	4	6
25	25	1	1	1	5	3	3	3	4	3
26	26	1	1	1	6	5	6	2	2	6
27	27	1	1	1	6	3	4	4	5	4
28	28	1	1	1	6	5	4	2	4	4
29	29	1	1	1	6	5	7	4	3	7
30	30	1	1	1	4	2	3	3	4	3
31	31	1	1	1	6	5	7	3	2	6

Data_Santa Fe Grill_N = 400.sav - SPSS Data Editor
File   Edit   View   Data   Transform   Analyze   Graphs   Utilities   Window   Help

id : 1

Data View / Variable View

SPSS Processor is ready

Start | Eudora | Eudora | Data_San... | Ch_17_3e... | Appendix ...

dates, dollar, custom currency, and so forth. To view the options click first on the Numeric cell and then on the three shaded dots to the right of the cell.

Label = In this column you give a more descriptive title to your variable. For example, with the Santa Fe Grill survey variable X_1 is labeled as X_1—Try New and Different Things and variable X_2 is labeled as X_2—Party Person. When you have longer labels and want to be able to see all of them you can go to the top of the file and click between the Label and Values cells and make the column wider.

Values = In the values column you can assign a label for each of the values of a variable. For example, with the Santa Fe Grill survey data variable X_1—Try New and Different Things we have indicated that a 1 = Strongly Disagree and a 7 = Strongly Agree. To view the options click first on the Values cell and then on the three shaded dots to the right of the cell. You can add new labels or change existing ones.

EXHIBIT B.3 **Variable View of the Santa Fe Grill Survey Data**

	Name	Type	Width	Decimals	Label	Values	Missing
1	id	Numeric	4	0	ID	None	None
2	x_s1	Numeric	4	0	Regularly Dine at Casual Dining Restaurants	None	None
3	x_s2	Numeric	4	0	Have Dined at Other Mexican Restaurants In last 6	None	None
4	x_s3	Numeric	4	0	Gross Annual Income $15,000 or More	None	None
5	x1	Numeric	4	0	X1 -- Try New And Different Things	{1, Strongly Disagree}...	None
6	x2	Numeric	4	0	X2 -- Party Person	{1, Strongly Disagree}...	None
7	x3	Numeric	4	0	X3 -- People Come to Me	{1, Strongly Disagree}...	None
8	x4	Numeric	4	0	X4 -- Avoid Fried Foods	{1, Strongly Disagree}...	None
9	x5	Numeric	4	0	X5 -- Likes to Go Out Socially	{1, Strongly Disagree}...	None
10	x6	Numeric	4	0	X6 -- Friends Come to Me	{1, Strongly Disagree}...	None
11	x7	Numeric	4	0	X7 -- Self-Confident	{1, Strongly Disagree}...	None
12	x8	Numeric	4	0	X8 -- Eat Balanced, Nutritious Meals	{1, Strongly Disagree}...	None
13	x9	Numeric	4	0	X9 -- Buy New Products	{1, Strongly Disagree}...	None
14	x10	Numeric	4	0	X10 -- Careful About What I Eat	{1, Strongly Disagree}...	None
15	x11	Numeric	4	0	X11 -- Try New Brands	{1, Strongly Disagree}...	None
16	x12	Numeric	4	0	X12 -- Friendly Employees	{1, Strongly Disagree}...	None
17	x13	Numeric	4	0	X13 -- Fun Place to Eat	{1, Strongly Disagree}...	None
18	x14	Numeric	4	0	X14 -- Large Size Portions	{1, Strongly Disagree}...	None
19	x15	Numeric	4	0	X15 -- Fresh Food	{1, Strongly Disagree}...	None
20	x16	Numeric	4	0	X16 -- Reasonable Prices	{1, Strongly Disagree}...	None
21	x17	Numeric	4	0	X17 -- Attractive Interior	{1, Strongly Disagree}...	None
22	x18	Numeric	4	0	X18 -- Excellent Food Taste	{1, Strongly Disagree}...	None
23	x19	Numeric	4	0	X19 -- Knowledgeable Employees	{1, Strongly Disagree}...	None
24	x20	Numeric	4	0	X20 -- Proper Food Temperature	{1, Strongly Disagree}...	None
25	x21	Numeric	4	0	X21 -- Speed of Service	{1, Strongly Disagree}...	None
26	x22	Numeric	4	0	X22 -- Satisfaction	{1, 1 = Not Satisfied At All}...	None
27	x23	Numeric	4	0	X23 -- Likely to Return	{1, Not Likely At All}...	None
28	x24	Numeric	4	0	X24 -- Likely to Recommend	{1, Definitely Will Not Recommend}...	None
29	x25	Numeric	4	0	X25 -- Frequency of Patronizing Santa Fee Grill	{1, Occasionally (less than once a month)}...	None
30	x26	Numeric	4	0	X26 -- Price	{1, Most Important}...	None
31	x27	Numeric	4	0	X27 -- Food Quality	{1, Most Important}...	None
32	x28	Numeric	4	0	X28 -- Atmosphere	{1, Most Important}...	None

Missing = Missing values are important in SPSS. If you do not handle them properly in your database it will cause you to get incorrect results. Use this column to indicate values that are assigned to missing data. A blank Numeric cell is designated as system-missing and a period (.) is placed in the cell. The default is no missing data but if you have missing data then you should use this column to tell the SPSS software what is missing. To do so, you can record one or more values that will be considered as missing data and will not be included in the data analysis. To use this option, click on the Missing cell and then on the three shaded dots to the right. You will get a dialog box that shows the default of no missing data. To indicate one or more values as missing click on Discrete missing values and place a value in one of the cells. You can record up to three separate values. The value most often used for missing data is a 9. If you want to specify a range of values click on this option and indicate the range to be considered as missing.

Column = Click on the Column cell to indicate the width of the column. The default is 8 spaces but it can be increased or decreased.

Align = The default for alignment is initially left, but you can change to either center or right alignment.

Let's look at the Variable View screen for the Santa Fe Grill database. It is shown in Exhibit B.3. To see the Variable View screen go to the bottom left-hand corner of the screen and click on "Variable View." The name of the variable will be in the first column, but if you look at the fifth column it will tell you more about the variable. For example, variable X_1 is "Try New and Different Things" while X_2 is "Party Person." All of the remaining variables have a similar description. Also, if you look under the Values column it will tell you how the variable is coded; for example, 1 = Strongly Disagree and 7 = Strongly Agree.

Running a Program

The two menus you will use most often are "Analyze" and "Graphs." Let's do a simple chart to show you how easy it is to use SPSS. Click on the "Graphs" pull-down menu first. When you do, select Bar and you will get a dialog box called Bar Charts. There are three options on the top left but for now use "Simple," which is the default (already checked). We also use the default in the "Data in Chart are:" box. This default tells the program to create a bar chart showing the count of the number of responses in each of the categories of the 7-point scale for this question. Now click Define and use the default = N of cases. Your database variables are shown in a window to the left of the screen. Highlight variable X_{22}—Satisfaction and then click on the "arrow button" to the left of the Category Axis box to move this variable into the box. Now click OK and you will get the bar chart shown in Exhibit B.4.

There are several things we can learn about this variable from the bar chart. First, the highest rating on the 7-point scale is a 6 and the lowest rating is a 3 (7 = Very Satisfied and 1 = Not Satisfied At All). Second, the rating given most often is a 5 and the one given least often is a 2. Recall the question for this variable read: "Please indicate your view on each of the following questions: How satisfied are you with the Santa Fe Grill?" Based on how the respondents answered this question, the bar chart tells us that overall the respondents are somewhat satisfied. We recommend you explore some of the other pull-down menus at this point and take the tutorial to begin familiarizing yourself with the SPSS software. As you go through the chapters we will give you the "Click-through" sequence for each of the problems we ask you to examine. But for a quick reference to the major procedures, we provide an alphabetic listing of these sequences in the following section. This will help you to easily apply and learn the statistical techniques that are most often used in analyzing data for business research reports and managerial decision making.

Click-Through Sequences for Selected Procedures

ANOVA
The click-through sequence is ANALYZE → GENERAL LINEAR MODEL → UNIVARIATE. Highlight the dependent variable X_{24}—Likely to Recommend by clicking on it and move it to the Dependent Variable box. Next, highlight X_{30}—Distance Driven and X_{32}—Gender, and move them to the Fixed Factors box. Click OK, since we don't need to specify any other options for this test.

eXHIBIT B.4 **SPSS Bar Chart of Variable X$_{22}$—Satisfaction**

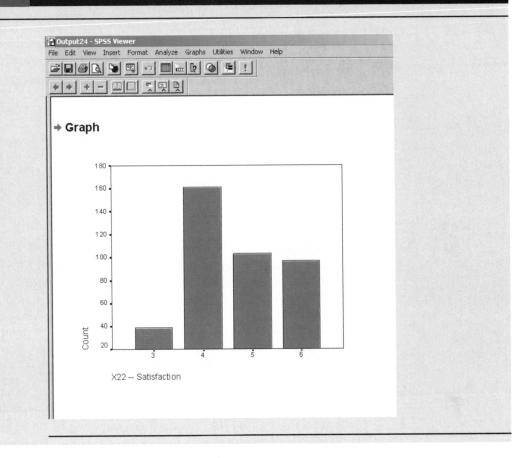

Bar Charts

The click-through sequence to prepare a bar chart for variable X$_{22}$—Satisfaction is: ANALYZE → DESCRIPTIVE STATISTICS → FREQUENCIES. Highlight X$_{22}$ and click on the arrow box to move it into the Variables box. Click on Charts and Bar Charts, and then Continue. Next click OK to execute the program.

Bivariate Regression

The click-through sequence for bivariate regression is ANALYZE → REGRESSION → LINEAR. Click on X$_{22}$—Satisfaction and move it to the Dependent Variable box. Click on X$_{16}$—Reasonable Prices and move it to the Independent Variables box. We will use the defaults for the other options, so click OK to run the bivariate regression.

Compare Means

The click-through sequence is ANALYZE → COMPARE MEANS → MEANS. Highlight the dependent variable X$_{24}$—Likely to Recommend by clicking on it, and move it to the Dependent List box. Next, highlight X$_{30}$—Distance Driven and X$_{32}$—Gender, and move them to the Independent List. Then click OK.

Chi-Square

The click-through sequence for Chi-Square is ANALYZE → DESCRIPTIVE STATISTICS → CROSSTABS. Click on X_{30}—Distance Traveled for the Row variable and on X_{32}—Gender for the Column variable. Click on the Statistics button and the Chi-Square box, and then Continue. Next click on the Cells button and on Expected frequencies (Observed frequencies is usually already checked). Then click Continue and OK to execute the program.

Cluster Analysis

The SPSS click-through sequence is ANALYZE → CLASSIFY → HIERARCHICAL CLUSTER, which leads to a dialog box where you select variables X_{22}, X_{23} and X_{24}. After you have put these variables into the Variables box, look at the other options below. Keep all the defaults that are shown on the dialog box. You should also use the defaults for the Statistics and Plots options below. Click on the Method box and select Ward's under the Cluster Method (you have to scroll to the bottom of the list), but use the default of squared euclidean distances under Measure. We do nothing with the Save option at this point, so you can click OK at the top of the dialog box to execute the cluster analysis.

Discriminant Analysis

The SPSS click-through sequence is ANALYZE → CLASSIFY → DISCRIMINANT, which leads to a dialog box where you select the variables (see Exhibit 17.19). The dependent, nonmetric variable is X_{31} and the independent, metric variables are X_{15}, X_{18} and X_{20}. The first thing you do is transfer variable X_{31} to the Grouping Variable box at the top, and then click on the Define Range box just below it. You must tell the program what the minimum and maximum numbers are for the grouping variable. In this case the minimum is 0 = Do Not Recall Ads and the maximum is 1 = Recall Ads, so just put these numbers in and click on Continue. Next you must transfer the food perceptions variables into the Independents box (X_{15}, X_{18}, and X_{20}). Then click on the Statistics box at the bottom and check Means, Univariate ANOVAS, and Continue. The Method default is Enter, and we will use this. Now click on Classify and Compute from group sizes. We do not know if the sample sizes are equal, so we must check this option. You should also click Summary Table and then Continue. We do not use any options under Save, so click OK to run the program.

Discriminant Analysis with Cluster Analysis

The SPSS click-through sequence is ANALYZE → CLASSIFY → DISCRIMINANT, which leads to a dialog box where you select the variables. The dependent, nonmetric variable is clu2_1, and the independent, metric variables are X_4, X_8, and X_{10}. First transfer variable clu2_1 to the Grouping Variable box at the top, and then click on the Define Range box just below it. Insert the minimum and maximum numbers for the grouping variable. In this case the minimum is 1 = cluster one and the maximum is 2 = cluster two, so just put these numbers in and click on Continue. Next you must transfer the food perceptions variables into the Independents box (X_4, X_8, and X_{10}). Then click on the Statistics box at the bottom and check Means, Univariate ANOVAS, and Continue. The Method default is Enter, and we will use this. Now click on Classify and Compute from group sizes. We do not know if the sample sizes are equal, so we must check this option. You should also click Summary Table and then Continue. We do not use any options under Save, so click OK to run the program.

Factor Analysis

The SPSS click-through sequence is ANALYZE → DATA REDUCTION → FACTOR, which leads to a dialog box where you select variables X_{12}–X_{21}. After you have put these variables into the Variables box, look at the data analysis options below. First click on the

Descriptives box and unclick the Initial Solution box because we do not need it at this point. Now click Continue to return to the previous dialog box. Next go to the Extraction box. In this one you leave the default of principal components and unclick the unrotated factor solution under Display. We will keep the other defaults, so now click the Continue box. Next go to the Rotation box. The default is None. We want to rotate, so click on Varimax as your rotational choice and then Continue. Finally, go to the Options box and click Sorted by Size, and then change the Suppress Absolute Values from .10 to .30. These last choices eliminate unneeded information, thus making the solutions printout much easier to read. We do not need Scores at this point, so we can click on OK at the top of the dialog box to execute the factor analysis. Exhibit 17.6 shows examples of some of the dialog boxes for running this factor analysis.

Independent Samples t-test

The SPSS click-through sequence is ANALYZE → COMPARE MEANS → INDEPENDENT SAMPLES T-TEST. When you get to this dialog box click variable X_{22}—Satisfaction into the Test Variables box and variable X_{32}—Gender into the Grouping Variable box. For variable X_{32} you must define the range in the Define Groups box. Enter a 0 for Group 1 and a 1 for Group 2 (males were coded 0 in the database and females were coded 1) and then click Continue. For the Options we will use the defaults, so just click OK to execute the program.

Mean, Median, and Mode

The SPSS click-through sequence is ANALYZE → DESCRIPTIVE STATISTICS → FREQUENCIES. Let's use X_{25}—Frequency of Patronage of Santa Fe Grill as a variable to examine. Click on X_{25} to highlight it, and then on the arrow box for the Variables box to use in your analysis. Next open the Statistics box and click on Mean, Median, and Mode, and then Continue and OK. Recall that if you want to create charts, open the Charts box. Your choices are Bar, Pie, and Histograms. For the Format box we will use the defaults, so click on OK to execute the program.

Multiple Regression

The SPSS click-through sequence to examine this relationship is ANALYZE → REGRESSION → LINEAR. Highlight X_{22} and move it to the Dependent Variables box. Highlight X_{15}, X_{18} and X_{20} and move them to the Independent Variables box. We will use the defaults for the other options so click OK to run the multiple regression.

Multiple Regression with Factor Analysis

The SPSS click-through sequence is ANALYZE → REGRESSION → LINEAR, which leads you to a dialog box where you select the variables. You should select X_{22} as the dependent and fac1_1, fac2_1, fac3_1, and fac4_1 as the independents. Now click on the Statistics button and check Descriptives. There are several additional types of analysis that can be selected, but at this point we will use the program defaults. Click OK at the top right of the dialog box to execute the regression.

Paired Samples t-test

The click-through sequence is ANALYZE → COMPARE MEANS → PAIRED SAMPLES T-TEST. When you get to this dialog box, highlight both X_{18}—Food Taste and X_{20}—Food Temperature, and then click on the arrow button to move them into the Paired Variables box. For the Options we will use the defaults, so just click OK to execute the program.

Pearson Correlation

The SPSS click-through sequence is ANALYZE → CORRELATE → BIVARIATE, which leads to a dialog box where you select the variables. Transfer variables X_{22} and X_{24} into the Variables box. Note that we will use all three default options shown below: Pearson correlation, two-tailed test of significance, and flag significant correlations. Next go to the Options box, and after it opens click on Means and Standard Deviations and then continue. Finally, when you click on OK at the top right of the dialog box it will execute the Pearson correlation.

Range, Standard Deviation, and Variance

The Santa Fe Grill database can be used with the SPSS software to calculate measures of dispersion, just as we did with the measures of central tendency. The SPSS click-through sequence is ANALYZE → DESCRIPTIVE STATISTICS → FREQUENCIES. Let's use X_{22}—Satisfaction as a variable to examine. Click on X_{22} to highlight it and then on the arrow box to move X_{22} to the Variables box. Next open the Statistics box, go to the Dispersion box in the lower-left-hand corner, and click on Standard deviation, Variance, Range, Minimum and Maximum, and then Continue. If you would like to create charts, then open the Charts box—your choices are Bar, Pie, and Histograms. For the Format box we will use the defaults, so click on OK to execute the program.

Sample Subgroups

To split the sample into groups, the click-through sequence is: DATA → SPLIT FILE. First click on the Data pull-down menu and scroll down and highlight and click on Split File. You will now see in the Split File dialog box where the default is Analyze all cases. Click on the Compare groups option, highlight the variable you want to split the groups with (e.g., X_{32}—Gender), and click on the arrow box to move it into the Groups Based on: box. Next click on OK and you will be analyzing the males versus females groups separately. That is, your output will have the results for males and females separately.

Spearman Rank Correlation

The SPSS click-through sequence is ANALYZE → CORRELATE → BIVARIATE, which leads to a dialog box where you select the variables. Transfer variables X_{27} and X_{29} into the Variables box. You will note that the Pearson correlation is the default along with the two-tailed test of significance, and flag significant correlations. "Unclick" the Pearson correlation and then click on Spearman. Then click on OK at the top right of the dialog box to execute the program.

Summated Scores

The restaurant perceptions variables include three measures related to satisfaction. They are variables X_{22}, X_{23}, and X_{24}. To calculate the summated score, the click-through sequence is TRANSFORM → COMPUTE. First type a variable name in the Target Variable box. In this case we are calculating a summated score for the satisfaction variables so let's use the abbreviation Sum_Sat for Summated Satisfaction. Next click on the Numeric Expression box to move the cursor there. Look below at the buttons and click on the parenthesis to place it in the Numeric Expression box (make sure cursor is between parentheses). Now highlight variable X_{22} and click on the arrow box to move it into the parenthesis. Go to the buttons below and click on the plus (+) sign. Go back and highlight variable X_{23} and click on the arrow box to move it into the parenthesis. Again click on the plus (+) sign. Finally, go back and highlight variable X_{24} and click on the arrow box to move it into the parenthesis. Now put the cursor at the right end of the parentheses and click on the divide sign (/)

and then 3 to get the average. Next click on OK and you will get the average summated score for the three variables. You can find the new variable at the far right-hand side of your data editor screen.

Univariate Hypothesis Test

The click through sequence is ANALYZE → COMPARE MEANS → ONE SAMPLE T-TEST. When you get to the dialog box, click on X_{16}—Reasonable Prices to highlight it. Then click on the arrow to move X_{16} into the Test Variables box. In the box labeled Test Value, enter the number 4. This is the number you want to compare the respondents' answers against. Click on the Options box and enter 95 in the confidence interval box. This is the same as setting the significance level at .05. Then, click on the Continue button and OK to execute the program.

chapter 2

The Marketing Research Process

Learning Objectives

After reading this chapter, you will be able to

1. Describe the major environmental factors influencing marketing research and explain their impact on the research process.

2. Discuss the phases and steps of the research process and explain some of the key activities within each step.

3. Explain the differences between raw data, data structures, and information, and describe the process by which raw data are transformed into information that managers can use.

4. Illustrate and explain the critical elements of problem definition in marketing research.

5. Distinguish between exploratory, descriptive, and causal research designs.

6. List the critical issues in the development of a sampling plan, and explain the basic differences between a probability and nonprobability sampling plan.

7. Identify and explain the major components of a research proposal.

Using the Research Process to Address Marketing Problems, Questions, and Opportunities

Bill Shulby is president of Carolina Consulting Company, a marketing strategy consulting firm based in Raleigh-Durham, North Carolina. He was recently working with the owners of a regional telecommunications firm located in Texas on improving service quality processes. Toward the end of their meeting, one of the owners, Dan Carter, asked him about customer satisfaction and perceptions of the company's image as they related to service quality and customer retention. During the discussion, Carter stated that he was not sure how the company's telecommunications services were viewed by current or potential customers. He said, "Just last week, the customer service department received eleven calls from different customers complaining about everything from incorrect bills to taking too long to get DSL (high speed internet service) installed. Clearly, none of these customers were happy about our service." Then he asked Shulby, "What can I do to find out how satisfied our customers are overall and what can be done to improve our image?"

Shulby indicated that answers could be obtained to his questions by conducting a marketing research study. Dan Carter responded that the company had not done research in the past so he did not know what to expect from such a study. Shulby then gave several examples of studies the Carolina Consulting Company had conducted for other clients and explained how the information had been used, making sure not to disclose any confidential information. Carter then asked, "How much would it cost me to do this study and how long would it take to complete?" Shulby then explained he would like to ask a few more questions so he could better understand the issues, and he then would prepare a research proposal summarizing the approach to be used, the deliverables from the study, the cost, and the time frame for completion. The proposal would be ready in about a week and they would meet to go over it in detail.

Value of the Research Process

As the chapter opening example illustrates, owners and managers frequently identify potential problems they need help to resolve. In such situations, additional information often is needed to make a decision or solve a problem. One solution is a marketing research study conducted following a standardized research process. This chapter uses an information perspective to explain the marketing research process. It begins with a discussion of the critical environmental factors that directly influence the scope of the research process. Much of the chapter provides an overview of the four basic phases that make up the research process and the specific steps involved in each phase, as well as activities and questions a researcher must address within each step. The final section of the chapter explains how to develop an information research proposal.

This chapter, the textbook's designated overview chapter, serves as a preview of some of the central topics in the text. Much of the discussion is descriptive in nature. Overall, this chapter provides the general blueprint for understanding the information research process. The topics introduced are discussed in much more detail in subsequent chapters.

Changing View of the Marketing Research Process

Internet A network of computers and technology linking computers into an information superhighway.

Secondary data Historical data structures of variables previously collected and assembled for some research problem or opportunity situation other than the current situation.

Primary data Firsthand raw data and structures which have yet to receive any type of meaningful interpretation.

Gatekeeper technology Advanced telecommunication technologies that allow a person to screen incoming contact messages from other people or organizations.

Organizations, both for-profit and not-for-profit, increasingly are confronted with new and more complex challenges and opportunities that are the result of changing legal, political, cultural, technological, and competitive issues. Exhibit 2.1 summarizes several key environmental factors that are significantly impacting business decision making and the marketing research process.

Perhaps the most influential factor is the **Internet.** The rapid technological advances and growing use of the Internet by people worldwide are making the Internet a driving force in many current and future developments in marketing research. Traditional research philosophies are being challenged as never before. For example, there is a growing emphasis on secondary data collection, analysis, and interpretation as a basis of making business decisions. **Secondary data** is information previously collected for some other problem or issue. In contrast, **primary data** is information collected for a current research problem or opportunity.

A by-product of the Internet is the ongoing collection of data that is placed in a data warehouse and is available as secondary data to help understand business problems and to make better decisions. Many of today's larger businesses (e.g., Dell Computers, Bank of America, Marriott Hotels, Coca-Cola, IBM, McDonald's, Wal-Mart) are using interlinkages between online scanning of customers' real-time purchase behavior with offline customer profiles in the data warehouse to enhance their ability to understand shopping behavior and better meet customer needs. But even medium- and small-sized companies are building databases of customer information to serve current customers more effectively and to attract new customers.

Second, there is increased use of **gatekeeper technologies** (e.g., caller ID and automated screening and answering devices) as a means of protecting one's privacy against intrusive marketing practices such as telemarketers and illegal scam artists. Marketing researchers' ability to collect consumer data using traditional methods like mail and telephone surveys has been severely limited by the combination of gatekeeper devices and

eXHIBIT 2.1   Environmental Factors That Affect Marketing Research Practices in the New Millennium

Environmental Factors	Impact on Marketing Research and Examples
Internet and e-commerce	Revolutionizing the methods of collecting data and information. *Examples:* increased emphasis on secondary data structures; increases in the need for and integration of technology-driven online and offline databases; shorter acquisition and retrieval time requirements; greater proficiency in interactive multimedia systems.
Gatekeeper technologies and data privacy legislation	Raising concerns about consumers' right to privacy, to what extent consumer information can be shared, and increased difficulties of reaching people for their input on attitudes and behaviors. *Examples:* increased employment of caller ID, electronic answering, and voice messenger devices; increases in intrusive telemarketing practices and scam artists; stronger, more restrictive data privacy laws; mandated opt-out opportunities.
Global market expansion	Creating multicultural interaction problems, opportunities, and questions for marketing decision makers as well as new language and measurement challenges for researchers. *Examples:* different cultural-based market needs and wants; different global data requirements for segmentation; use of different, yet compatible measurement schemes for market performance, attitude, and behavior data.
Marketing research as a strategy	Leading businesses to reposition marketing research activities with more emphasis on strategic implications. *Examples:* use of marketing research for developing CRM and customer and competitor intelligence strategies; marketing researchers' deeper involvement in developing online/offline databases.

recent federal and state data privacy legislation. For example, marketing researchers must contact almost four times more people today to complete a single interview than was true five years ago. Similarly, online marketers and researchers must provide opt-in/opt-out opportunities when soliciting business or collecting information. Advances in gatekeeper technologies will continue to challenge marketers to be more creative in developing new ways to reach respondents.

A third challenge facing marketing decision makers is the widespread expansion into global markets. Global expansion introduces marketing decision makers to new sets of cultural issues that force researchers to not only focus on data collection tasks, but also on data interpretation and information management activities. For example, one of the largest full-service global marketing information firms, NFO (National Family Opinion) Worldwide, Inc., located in Greenwich, Connecticut, with subsidiaries in North America, Europe, Australia, Asia, and the Middle East, has adapted many of its measurement and brand tracking services to accommodate specific cultural and language differences encountered in global markets.

Fourth, marketing research is being repositioned in businesses to play a more important role in strategy development. Marketing research increasingly is being used to identify new business opportunities and to develop new product, service, and delivery ideas. It also is being viewed not only as a mechanism to more efficiently execute CRM (customer relationship management) strategies, but also as a critical component in developing competitive intelligence. For example, Sony uses its Playstation Web site (www.playstation.com) to collect information on PlayStation gaming users and to build closer relationships. The PlayStation Web site is designed to create a community of users who can join PlayStation Underground where they will "feel like they belong to a subculture of intense gamers." To achieve this objective the Web site offers online shopping, opportunities to try new games, customer support, and information on news, events, and promotions. Interactive features include online gaming and message boards, as well as other relationship-building aspects. Marketing researchers at Sony and other companies are becoming more like cross-functional information experts, assisting in collecting not only marketing information, but information on all types of business functions.

While many other factors are influencing the marketing research process, these are the key ones now forcing managers and researchers to view marketing research as an information management function. The term information research reflects the evolving changes occurring in the market research industry impacting organizational decision makers. Indeed, a more appropriate name for the traditional marketing research process is the information research process. The **information research process** is a systematic approach to collecting, analyzing, interpreting, and transforming raw data into decision-making information. While many of the specific tasks involved in marketing research remain the same, understanding the process of transforming raw data into usable information from a broader information processing framework expands the applicability of the research process in solving organizational problems and creating opportunities.

Information research process The systematic task steps in the gathering, analyzing, interpreting, and transforming of data structures and results into decision-making information.

Determining the Need for Information Research

Before we introduce and discuss the phases and specific steps of the information research process, it is important that you understand when the research process is needed and when it is not. Moreover, increasingly researchers must interact closely with managers in recognizing business problems, questions, and opportunities.

While many marketing research texts suggest the first step in the marketing research process is for the researcher to establish the need for marketing research, this places a lot of responsibility and control in the hands of a person who might not be trained in understanding the management decision-making process. Decision makers and researchers frequently are trained differently in their approach to identifying and solving business problems, questions, and opportunities, as illustrated in the Closer Look at Research box. Until decision makers and information researchers become closer in their thinking, the initial recognition of the existence of a problem or opportunity should be the primary responsibility of the decision maker, not the researcher.

To help prevent the differences between decision makers and researchers from complicating the initial business problem definition process, the decision makers should be given the responsibility of initiating the activities in recognizing and defining the problem or opportunity situation. For now, a good rule of thumb is to ask, "Can the stated decision-making problem (or question) be resolved by using subjective information (e.g., past experience, assumptions, emotional feelings)?" If "No" is the logical response, the information research process needs to be considered and perhaps implemented.

In most cases when some type of additional information is needed to address a problem, decision makers will need assistance in determining the problem, collecting and analyzing the data, and interpreting that information. The need to activate the research process basically comes from decision makers' ability to recognize problem and opportunity situations as well as monitor market performance conditions.

A key to understanding when the information research process should be undertaken is the notion that marketing research no longer focuses on just the activities of collecting,

A Closer Look at Research

Management Decision Makers and Marketing Researchers

MANAGEMENT DECISION MAKERS ... Tend to be decision-oriented, intuitive thinkers who want information to confirm their decisions. They want additional information now or "yesterday," as well as results about future market component behavior ("What will sales be next year?"), while maintaining a frugal stance with regard to the cost of additional information. Decision makers tend to be results oriented, do not like surprises, and tend to reject the information when they are surprised. Their dominant concern is market performance ("Aren't we number one yet?"); they want information that allows certainty ("Is it or isn't it?"); and they advocate being proactive but often allow problems to force them into reactive decision-making modes.

In the Field

MARKETING RESEARCHERS ... Tend to be scientific, technical, analytical thinkers who love to explore new phenomena; accept prolonged investigations to ensure completeness; focus on information about past behaviors ("Our trend has been ..."); and are not cost conscious about additional information ("You get what you pay for"). Researchers are results oriented but love surprises; they tend to enjoy abstractions ("Our exponential gain ...") and the probability of occurrences ("May be," "Tends to suggest that ..."); and they advocate the proactive need for continuous inquiries of market component changes, but feel most of the time that they are restricted to doing reactive ("quick and dirty") investigations due to management's lack of vision and planning.

analyzing, and interpreting primary data for solving management's problems. Increasingly, secondary research and data warehouse information are being used to address decision-making situations. Technological advances in the Internet, high-speed communication systems, and faster secondary and primary data acquisition and retrieval systems are dramatically changing marketing research practices. As a result, the constraints used in determining whether to conduct research are less restrictive than in the past.

There are four situations in which the decision to commission a marketing research project may be ill advised.[1] These are listed and discussed in Exhibit 2.2. One of the shortcomings of this approach to deciding when to conduct research is that in each situation the decision maker is assumed to have prior knowledge about the "true" availability of existing information, the necessary time and staff, adequate resources, or clear insight into the expected value of the resulting information. As technology advances, these assumptions become more suspect.

The main responsibility of today's decision makers is to initially determine if the research process should be used to collect the needed information. The initial question the decision maker must ask is: *Can the problem and/or opportunity be resolved using only subjective information?* Here the focus is on deciding what type of information (subjective, secondary, or primary) is required to answer the research question(s). In most cases, decision makers should undertake the information research process any time they have a question or problem or believe there is an opportunity, but either do not have the right subjective information or are unwilling to rely on subjective information to resolve the problem. In reality, conducting secondary and primary research studies costs time, effort, and

---

EXHIBIT 2.2 Situations When Marketing Research Might Not Be Needed

---

When information already available When the decision maker has substantial knowledge about markets, products and services, and the competition, enough information may exist to make an informed decision without doing marketing research. Some experts believe advancements in computer and information processing technology ensure the right information gets to the right decision makers in a timely fashion.

When insufficient time frames When the discovery of a problem situation leaves inadequate time to execute the necessary research activities, decision makers may have to use informed judgment. Competitive actions/reactions sometimes emerge so fast that formalized marketing research studies are not a feasible option.

When inadequate resources When there are significant limitations in money, manpower, and/or facilities, then marketing research typically is not feasible.

When costs outweigh the value When the benefits to be gained by conducting the research are not significantly greater than the costs, then marketing research is not feasible.

---

money. Exhibit 2.3 displays a framework that illustrates the factors and examples of the questions that must be asked and answered to determine whether the research process is necessary.

After deciding that subjective information alone will not resolve the identified problem, the next question to be answered by the decision makers focuses on the nature of the decision: *Does the problem/opportunity situation have strategic or tactical importance?* Strategic decisions tend to have broader time horizons but are much more complex than tactical decisions. Most strategic decisions are critical to the company's operations and bottom-line profitability objectives. In turn, on the basis of the investment associated with a tactical decision, undertaking the research process might be the appropriate alternative for collecting data and information. For example, Outback Steakhouse recently made a tactical decision to update its menu both in appearance and in food offerings. Researching the opinions of known customers proved helpful in determining new food items to be included and those items that should not be on the menu but rather offered as occasional "chef's specials." Bottom line—if the problem situation has strategic or significant tactical importance, then a research expert should be consulted at this point.

Another key managerial question deals with the availability of existing information. With the assistance of the research expert, decision makers face the next question: *Does adequate information for addressing the defined problem already exist within the company's internal record systems?*

In the past, if the necessary marketing information was not available in the firm's internal record system, then a customized marketing research project would be undertaken to produce and report the information. Today, advances in computer technology and changing management philosophy toward the cross-functional sharing of information enable management to record, store, and retrieve huge amounts of operating data (e.g., sales, costs, and profitability by products, brands, sales region, customer groups) with greater ease and speed. CRM has reduced some of management's past concerns about availability of information.

With input from the research expert, decision makers must assess the "time constraints" associated with the problem/opportunity: *Is there enough time to conduct the necessary*

ҽXHIBIT 2.3 Determining When to Undertake the Information Research Process

Type of Information

Can the decision problem and/or opportunity be resolved using only subjective information?

(Decision maker's responsibility)

→ **YES**

Do Not Undertake the Information Research Process

Nature of Decision ↓ **NO**

Is the problem/opportunity situation of strategic or tactical importance?

(Decision maker's responsibility)

→ **NO**

↓ **YES**

Decision maker should bring in the marketing researcher for advice

Availability of Data ↓

Is existing secondary information inadequate for solving the decision problem situation or exploiting the opportunity?

(Decision maker's responsibility with researcher's advice)

→ **NO**

Time Constraints ↓ **YES**

Is there a sufficient time frame available for gathering the information before the final managerial decision must be made?

(Decision maker's responsibility with researcher's advice)

→ **NO**

Resource Requirements ↓ **YES**

Are there sufficient levels of money, staff, and skills to meet the costs and marketing research requirements?

(Decision maker's responsibility with researcher's advice)

→ **NO**

Benefits versus Costs ↓ **YES**

Does the expected value of the information exceed the costs of conducting the research?

(Decision maker's responsibility with researcher's advice)

→ **NO**

↓ **YES**

Move on to Phase I of the Information Research Process

research before the final managerial decision must be made? Today's decision makers often need information in real time. But in many cases, systematic research that delivers high-quality information may take several months. If the decision maker needs the information immediately, then there is insufficient time to complete the research process. Another fundamental question focuses on the availability of marketing resources (e.g., money, staff, skills, facilities): *Is money budgeted for doing formalized research?* For example, many small businesses simply lack the necessary funds to consider doing any type of formal research.

Some type of cost-benefit assessment should be made regarding the overall value of the research compared to the cost: *Do the benefits of having the additional information outweigh the costs of gathering the information?* This type of question remains a challenge for today's decision makers. While the cost of doing marketing research varies from project to project, generally it can be estimated accurately. Yet, predetermining the true value of the expected information remains somewhat subjective. In addition to the foregoing considerations that help to determine whether to use the research process, decision makers should give thought to the following set of evaluative questions:

- What is the perceived importance and complexity of the problem?

- Is the problem realistically researchable? Can the critical variables in the proposed research be adequately designed and measured?

- Will conducting the needed research give valuable information to the firm's competitors?

- Will the research findings be implemented?

- Will the research design and data represent reality?

- Will the research results and findings be used as legal evidence?

- Is the proposed research politically motivated?

In deciding whether to employ the research process, another useful approach involves an always elusive question: *Why should the decision maker conduct information research?* Although there is no agreed-upon set of rules for determining when to conduct research other than the general notion initially described, there are some conditional reasons to consider when deciding whether to conduct research:

1. If the information will clarify the problem or identify marketplace changes that directly influence the company's product/service responsibilities.

2. If the information helps the company to acquire meaningful competitive advantages within its market environment.

3. If the information leads to marketing actions that will achieve marketing objectives.

4. If the information provides proactive understanding of future market conditions.

Overview of the Information Research Process

The marketing research process typically is described as a set of standardized phases. In this text, we will define it as an information research process that consists of four distinct yet interrelated phases: (1) determine the research problem, (2) select the appropriate research design, (3) execute the research design, and (4) communicate the research results (see Exhibit 2.4). Researchers must ensure that all phases of the process are completed properly if the best possible information is to be available for organizational decision makers. Each phase, however, should be viewed as a separate process that consists of a combination of integrated research steps.

Scientific method Formalized research procedures that can be characterized as logical, objective, systematic, reliable, valid, impersonal, and ongoing.

The four phases are guided by the principles of the **scientific method,** which involves formalized research procedures that can be characterized as logical, objective, systematic, reliable, valid, impersonal, and ongoing. Traditional marketing research emphasizes the collection and analysis of primary data. But the information research process places equal emphasis on the use of secondary data.

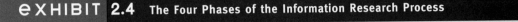

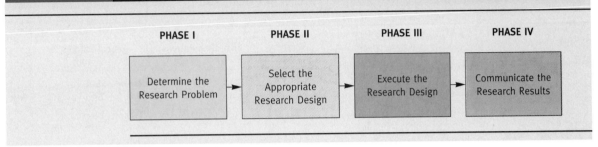

EXHIBIT 2.4 The Four Phases of the Information Research Process

PHASE I	PHASE II	PHASE III	PHASE IV
Determine the Research Problem	Select the Appropriate Research Design	Execute the Research Design	Communicate the Research Results

Transforming Raw Data into Information

The primary goal of the information research process is to provide organizational decision makers with secondary or primary information that will enable them to resolve a problem, answer an existing question, or pursue an opportunity. Information is created only after the data have been collected, analyzed, interpreted, and transformed into narrative expressions decision makers can understand and use. To understand this process, one must know the difference between raw data, data structures, and information.

First, **raw data** represent the actual firsthand responses that are obtained about an object or subject of investigation by asking questions or observing actions. These initial responses have not been analyzed or given an interpretive meaning. Some examples of raw data are (1) the actual individual responses on a questionnaire; (2) the words recorded during a focus group interview; (3) the tally of vehicles that pass through a specified intersection; (4) the list of purchases, by product type, recorded by an electronic cash register at a local supermarket.

All secondary and primary marketing information is derived from the following process: *gather raw responses; apply some form of data analysis to create usable data structures;* and then *have someone (a researcher or decision maker) interpret those data structures.*

Gather raw data → Create data structures → Provide interpretation

Data structures are the result of combining individual raw responses into groups of data using some type of quantitative or qualitative analysis procedure (e.g., content analysis, calculation of sample statistics). The results can reveal data patterns or trends, which in turn can be simple or complex. Some examples are (1) the average number of times 500 moviegoers patronize their favorite movie house; (2) the frequency distribution of 1,000 college students eating at several predetermined restaurants in a 30-day time frame; (3) the sampling error associated with the overall expressed satisfaction of 250 new Acura 3.2TL automobile owners; and (4) the z-testing results of comparing hotel selection criteria means for first-time and repeat patrons of a particular hotel.

Information is derived from data only when someone—either the researcher or the decision maker—takes the time and effort to interpret the data and attach a meaning. To illustrate this process, consider the following hotel example. Recently, the corporate executives of JP Hotel, Inc., in Atlanta, Georgia, were assessing ways to improve the firm's bottom-line profit figures. Specifically, they were seeking ways to cut operating costs. The vice president of finance suggested cutting back on the "quality of the towels and bedding" in the rooms. Before making a final decision, the president asked the marketing research department to interview the hotel's business customers using a scientifically sound research process.

Raw data Actual firsthand responses obtained about the subject of Investigation.

Data structures Results of combining raw data into groups using some type of quantitative or qualitative analysis.

Information The set of facts derived from data structures when someone—either the researcher or decision maker—interprets and attaches narrative meaning to the data structures.

eXHIBIT 2.5 Summary of Overall Importance Differences of Selected Hotel-Choice Criteria Used by First-Time and Repeat Business Patrons

Hotel Selection Criteria	Total (n = 880) Mean[a] Value	(SG)[b]	First-Time Patrons (n = 440) Mean Value	Std. Error	(SG)	Repeat Patrons (n = 400) Mean Value	Std. Error	(SG)	z Test
Cleanliness of the room	5.65	(A)	5.75	.06	(A)	5.50	.05	(A)	*
Good-quality bedding and towels	5.60	(A)	5.55	.06	(A)	5.62	.07	(A)	
Preferred guest card options	5.57	(A)	5.42	.07	(A)	5.71	.06	(A)	*
Friendly/courteous staff and employees	5.10	(B)	4.85	.09	(B)	5.45	.07	(B)	*
Free VIP services	5.06	(B)	4.35	.10	(C)	5.38	.11	(B)	*
Conveniently located for business	5.04	(B)	5.25	.09	(B)	4.92	.10	(B)	*
In-room movie Entertainment	3.63	(D)	3.30	.13	(D)	4.56	.11	(C)	*

[a]Importance scale: a six-point scale ranging from 6 (extremely important) to 1 (not at all important).

[b]Significant groupings (SG): (A) = definitely strong factor; (B) = strong factor; (C) = moderately strong factor; (D) = weak factor.

*Mean importance difference between the two patron groups is significant at $p < .05$.

Exhibit 2.5 summarizes the study's key results. In the study, 880 people were asked to indicate the degree of importance they placed on seven criteria when selecting a hotel. Respondents used a six-point importance scale ranging from (6) "Extremely important" to (1) "Not at all important." The individual responses represent the raw data. The researcher used the raw data to calculate the overall average importance for each of the criteria using a simple "mean analysis" procedure, where the resulting means represent the data structures associated with each selection criterion across all respondents and for both first-time and repeat patrons. In fact, all the numbers are data structures. In addition, there is evidence the data structures were statistically analyzed (e.g., see significant groupings [SG] results), but these results, by themselves, do not provide the management team with any meaningful information to assist in determining whether or not "quality towels and bedding" should be cut back to reduce operating costs.

When he was shown the results, the president asked this question: "I see a lot of impressive numbers, but what are they really telling me?" The director of marketing research quickly responded by explaining what the numbers concerning the "quality towels and bedding" criterion were suggesting: "Among our first-time and repeat business customers, they consider the quality of the hotel's towels and bedding one of the three most important selection criteria that impact their choice of a hotel to stay at when an overnight stay is required for business." In addition, business travelers feel "the cleanliness of the room and offering preferred guest card options are equally important to the quality of towels and bedding criterion, yet first-time business patrons place significantly stronger importance on cleanliness of the room ($x = 5.75$) than do our repeat business patrons ($x = 5.50$)." In turn, repeat business customers "place significantly more importance on the availability of our preferred guest card options ($x = 5.71$) in their hotel selection process than do first-time business patrons ($x = 5.42$)." Upon understanding the information being provided by the data, the executives decided it would not be wise to cut back on the quality of towels or bedding as a way to reduce operating expenses and improve profitability.

Interrelatedness of the Steps and the Research Process

As soon as decision makers recognize they need assistance, they should meet with the marketing researcher and begin executing a formalized, scientific research process. Exhibit 2.6 shows the interrelated steps included in the four phases of the research process.

Although in most instances researchers would follow the four phases in order, the individual steps may be shifted or omitted. Often the complexity of the problem, the urgency for solving the problem, the cost of alternative approaches, and the clarification of information needs will directly impact how many of the steps are taken and in what order. For example, secondary data or "off-the-shelf" research studies may be found that could eliminate the need to collect primary data, thus eliminating the need for a sampling plan. Similarly, pretesting the questionnaire (step 7) might reveal weaknesses in some of the scales being considered (step 6), resulting in further refinement of the scales or even selection of a new research design (back to step 4).

What might happen if the research process is not appropriately followed? Substantial time, energy, and money can be spent with the result being incomplete, biased, or wrong information for proper decision making. For example, the Food and Beverage Committee at the Alto Lakes Golf and Country Club in Alto, New Mexico, wanted to determine its members' overall satisfaction with the "beverage cart" services being provided on the golf course and gain insight to how to improve those services. Not knowing the research process, the committee instinctively designed a simple rating card asking members to rate the beverage cart service using a six-point scale ranging from (6) "Outstanding" to (1) "Terrible" and supplying a space for written comments. After reviewing only 50 cards returned, the committee found that members' comments suggested that there were several activities associated with the beverage

---

e X H I B I T 2.6   Phases and Steps in the Information Research Process

Phase I: Determine the Research Problem

Step 1: Identify and clarify management's information needs

Step 2: Specify the research questions and define the research problem

Step 3: Confirm research objectives and assess the value of the information

Phase II: Select the Appropriate Research Design

Step 4: Determine the research design and data sources

Step 5: Develop the sampling design and sample size

Step 6: Assess measurement issues and scales

Step 7: Pretest the questionnaire

Phase III: Execute the Research Design

Step 8: Collect and prepare data

Step 9: Analyze data

Step 10: Transform data structures into information

Phase IV: Communicate the Research Results

Step 11: Prepare and present final report to management

cart operations that were associated with overall satisfaction. But the rating scheme was measuring overall performance rather than satisfaction. The committee did receive data and information about the beverage cart service, but it was not what they were looking for. Although the committee had blindly incorporated some of the key activities found within the information research process, the data did not help them address their initial problem.

Phase I: Determine the Information Research Problem

The process of determining the information research problem involves three interrelated activities: (1) identify and clarify information needs; (2) specify the research questions and define the research problem; and (3) confirm research objectives and assess the value of the information. These activities bring researchers and decision makers together under the notion that management has recognized the need for some type of information to deal with an issue concerning firm performance.

Step 1: Identify and Clarify Information Needs

Usually, before the researcher becomes involved, decision makers have prepared a formal statement of what they believe is the problem. At this point, researchers then assist decision makers in making sure the problem or opportunity has been correctly defined and that the decision maker is aware of the information requirements. Remember that a **decision problem** exists when management has established a specific objective that may be achieved through any of several courses of action. The question becomes: Which is the best option?

For researchers to gain a clear understanding of the decision problem, they must use an integrated problem definition process, as shown in Exhibit 2.7. There is no one best process. But any process undertaken should include the following activities: (1) determine the decision maker's purpose for the research, (2) understand the complete problem situation,

Decision problem A situation in which a manager is not certain which course of action will help him or her accomplish a specific objective.

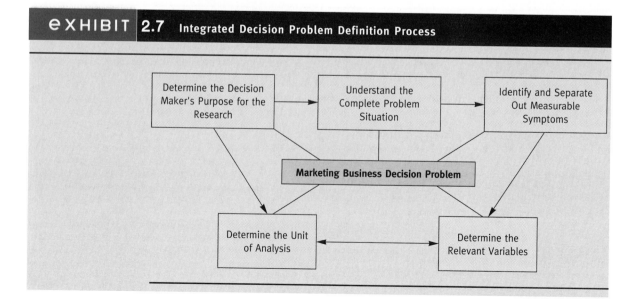

EXHIBIT 2.7 Integrated Decision Problem Definition Process

Determine the Decision Maker's Purpose for the Research → Understand the Complete Problem Situation → Identify and Separate Out Measurable Symptoms

Marketing Business Decision Problem

Determine the Unit of Analysis ↔ Determine the Relevant Variables

A Closer Look at Research

"Can I Get a New Coke, Please!"

In an effort to gain market share, the Pepsi Cola Company conducted a series of blind taste tests and determined that soft-drink consumers preferred the sweetness of Pepsi to the crisper taste of Coke. On the basis of what was called the Pepsi Challenge, Pepsi developed a marketing program concentrating on younger soft-drink customers and labeling them the Pepsi Generation.

The Coca-Cola company's initial response was to increase its advertising budget and develop a claim of product superiority. Nonetheless, Coke's own taste tests validated Pepsi's claims that customers preferred a sweeter product. Using information obtained in the development of Diet Coke, Coca-Cola created a new, sweeter Coke product and embarked on one of the most extensive marketing research programs in the history of the soft-drink industry.

Coke's market research lasted three years and asked over 200,000 customers to participate in blind taste tests conducted in shopping malls across the country. The information research question that guided Coca-Cola's research program was: "What will be the ultimate consumer reactions to the taste of the new Coke product?" Results of the marketing research indicated that when asked to compare unmarked beverages, consumers favored the new Coke formula over the original Coke

In the Field

product by a margin of 55 percent to 45 percent. When both soft drinks were identified, 53 percent of those taking the test still preferred the new Coke formula over the original Coke.

Based on these research results, Coca-Cola decided to introduce a new sweeter-formula Coke. The product was introduced with the name New Coke and the original Coke was discontinued. Within three months, however, old Coke was put back on the market. By the end of the year, the new Coke formula, the one marketing research showed to be preferred by drinkers, was discontinued. What happened? Where did Coca-Cola go wrong? What should have been measured? What if Coca-Cola had put the new product under the old label? These remain good topics of discussion within marketing research. From one perspective, Coca-Cola can be accused of being too narrow in the scope of its research question and defining the problem so that researchers investigated and tested only one aspect—consumers' preferences of taste associated with cola soft drinks. In this situation, researchers can be criticized for not also investigating the extent to which consumers have emotional attachment and loyalty to existing brand names and the impact of such loyalty on purchase and consumption behavior. Among other things, Coca-Cola's research failed to ask the respondents if the new Coke product should replace the original Coca-Cola.[2]

(3) identify and separate out measurable symptoms, (4) determine the appropriate unit of analysis, and (5) determine the relevant variables. Being able to correctly define and understand the actual decision problem is an important first step in determining if it is really necessary to conduct research. A poorly defined decision problem can easily produce research results that are unlikely to have any value, as in the New Coke example, illustrated in the Closer Look at Research box.

Purpose of the Research Request

Determining the research purpose is the beginning of any good problem definition process. The decision maker has the initial responsibility of deciding there might be a need for the services of a researcher in addressing a recognized decision problem or opportunity. Once brought into the situation, the researcher begins the problem definition process by asking the decision maker to express his or her reasons for thinking there is a need to undertake research. Using this type of initial questioning procedure, researchers begin to develop insights as to what the decision maker believes to be the problem. Having some basic idea of why research is needed focuses attention on the circumstances surrounding the problem. The researcher then asks questions that distinguish between the symptoms and actual causal factors. One method that might be employed here is for researchers to familiarize the decision maker with the iceberg principle, displayed in Exhibit 2.8.

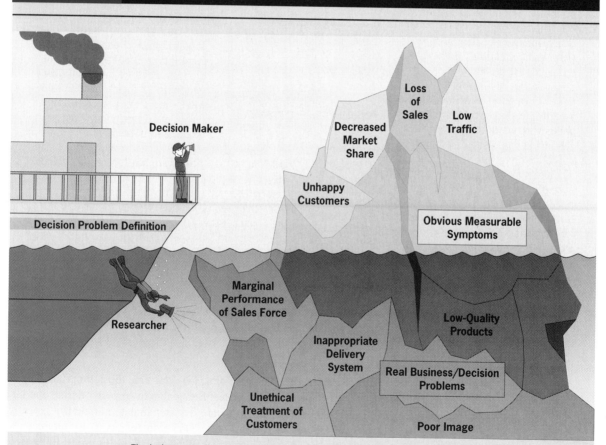

EXHIBIT 2.8   The Iceberg Principle

Decision Maker

Loss of Sales

Decreased Market Share

Low Traffic

Unhappy Customers

Obvious Measurable Symptoms

Decision Problem Definition

Marginal Performance of Sales Force

Researcher

Low-Quality Products

Inappropriate Delivery System

Real Business/Decision Problems

Unethical Treatment of Customers

Poor Image

The iceberg principle states that in many business problem situations the decision maker is aware of only 10 percent of the true problem. Often what is thought to be the problem is nothing more than an observable outcome or symptom (i.e., some type of measurable market performance factor), while 90 percent of the problem is neither visible to nor clearly understood by decision makers. For example, the problem may be defined as "loss of market share" when in fact the problem is ineffective advertising or a poorly trained sales force. The real problems are submerged below the waterline of observation. If the submerged portions of the problem are omitted from the problem definition and later from the research design, then decisions based on the research may be less than optimal.

Understand the Complete Problem Situation

Both the decision maker and the researcher must understand the complete problem. This is easy to state but quite often difficult to execute. To gain such understanding, researchers and decision makers should perform a situation analysis of the circumstances surrounding the problem area. A **situation analysis** is a popular tool that focuses on the gathering of background information to familiarize the researcher with the overall complexity of the decision area. A situation analysis attempts to identify the events and factors that have led to the current decision problem situation, as well as any expected future consequences. Complete awareness of the problem situation provides better perspectives on (1) the decision maker's needs; (2) the complexity of the problem situation; and (3) the types of factors involved.

Situation analysis A tool that focuses on the informal gathering of background information to familiarize the researcher with the overall complexity of the decision area.

Conducting a situation analysis can enhance communication between the researcher and the decision maker. The researcher must develop complete knowledge of the client's overall business. To objectively understand the client's situation (i.e., industry, competition, product lines, markets, and in some cases, production facilities), the researcher cannot rely solely on information provided by the client because many decision makers do not know or will not disclose all needed information. Only when the researcher sees the client's business practices objectively can the true problem be clarified. In short, researchers must develop expertise in the client's business.

Identify and Separate Out Measurable Symptoms

Once the researcher understands the overall problem situation, he or she must work with the decision maker to separate the root problems from the observable and measurable symptoms that may have been initially perceived as being the decision problem. For example, many times managers view declining sales or loss of market share as problems. After examining these issues, the researcher may see that they are the result of more concise issues such as poor advertising execution, lack of sales force motivation, or inadequate distribution. The challenge facing the researcher is one of clarifying the real decision problem by separating out possible causes from symptoms. Is a decline in sales truly the problem or merely a symptom of lack of planning, poor location, or ineffective sales management?

Determine the Unit of Analysis

As a fundamental part of problem definition, the researcher must determine the appropriate unit of analysis for the study. The researcher must be able to specify whether data should be collected about individuals, households, organizations, departments, geographical areas, or some combination of these. The unit of analysis will provide direction in later activities such as scale development and sampling. For example, in an automobile satisfaction study the researcher must decide whether to collect data from the purchaser (i.e., individual) of a specific vehicle or from a husband-wife dyad representing the household in which the vehicle is driven.

Determine the Relevant Variables to the Situation

The researcher and decision maker jointly determine the specific variables for the research questions that need to be answered. The primary focus is on identifying independent and dependent variables. Determination must be made as to the types of information (i.e., facts, predictions, relationships) and specific constructs that are relevant to the decision problem.

EXHIBIT **2.9** **Examples of Constructs Investigated in Marketing**

Constructs	Operational Description
Brand awareness	Percentage of respondents having heard of a designated brand; awareness could be either unaided or aided.
Attitudes toward a brand	The number of respondents and their intensity of feeling positive or negative toward a specific brand.
Purchase intentions	The number of people planning to buy the specified object (e.g., product or service) within a designated time period.
Importance of factors	To what extent do specific factors influence a person's purchase choice?
Demographics	The age, gender, occupation, income level, and other characteristics of individuals providing the information.
Psychographics	The attitudes, opinions, interests, and lifestyle characteristics of individuals providing the information.
Satisfaction	How people evaluate their postpurchase consumption experience with a particular product, service, or company.

A construct is a hypothetical variable consisting of several component responses or behaviors thought to be related. Exhibit 2.9 provides several examples of constructs that are often investigated with marketing research.

Step 2: Specify the Research Questions and Define the Research Problem

Next, the researcher must reformulate the problem in scientific terms. That is, the researcher must redefine the problem as a research question. This is necessary because scientific approaches are superior in executing a systematic approach to problem solving. This is the responsibility of the researcher. In fact, from here on the researcher assumes most of the responsibility for the satisfactory outcome of the research process.

Redefining the problem into a research question is the most critical step in the marketing research process, because how the research problem is defined greatly influences all of the remaining research steps. The researcher's task is to restate the initial variables associated with the problem in the form of one or more key question formats (how, what, where, when, or why). For example, management of Lowe's Home Improvement Warehouse, Inc., was concerned about the overall image of Lowe's retail operations as well as its image among customers within the Atlanta metropolitan market. The initial research question was, "Do our marketing strategies need to be modified to increase satisfaction among our current and future customers?" After Lowe's management met with consultants at Corporate Communications and Marketing, Inc., to clarify the firm's information needs, the consultants translated the initial problem into the specific questions displayed in Exhibit 2.10. With assistance of management, the consultants then identified the attributes in each research question. For example, specific "store/operation aspects" included convenient operating hours, friendly/courteous staff, and a wide assortment of products and services.

When research questions are written, two approaches can be taken to determine the level of detail to use. One approach is to phrase the question using a general focus that includes only the category of possible factors to develop the data requirements without specifying

eXHIBIT **2.10** Initial and Redefined Research Questions for Lowe's Home Improvement Warehouse, Inc.

Initial research question:

Do our marketing strategies need to be modified to increase satisfaction among our current and future customer segments?

Redefined research questions:

What store/operation aspects do people believe are important in selecting a retail hardware/lumber outlet?

How do customers evaluate Lowe's retail outlets on store/operation aspects?

What are the perceived strengths and weaknesses of Lowe's retail operations?

How do customers and noncustomers compare Lowe's to other retail hardware/lumber outlets within the Atlanta metropolitan area?

What is the demographic/psychographic profile of the people who patronize Lowe's retail outlets in the Atlanta market?

the actual individual factors. For example, with the demographic question in the Lowe's example (Exhibit 2.10), the phrasing is somewhat ambiguous because it expresses only the need for a "demographic/psychographic profile" of customers without specifying which particular demographic characteristics (e.g., age, income, education level, marital status) or psychographic factors (e.g., price conscious, do-it-yourself, brand loyalist, information seeker) should be investigated. The other approach is to be much more specific in phrasing the research questions. For example, if Lowe's management team is interested in determining the price range for a particular Black & Decker power drill, the research questions would be phrased as follows: (1) "What are the price ranges customers expect to pay for the Black & Decker RX power drill?" and (2) "What are the price ranges customers are willing to pay for the Black & Decker RX power drill?" Here each research question focuses on a specific data requirement—expected price ranges and then actual price ranges.

After redefining the problem into research questions and identifying the information requirements, the researcher must make initial assessments about the types of data (e.g., secondary or primary) that will best answer each research problem. Although final decisions on types of data are part of Step 4 (Determine the Research Design and Data Sources), the researcher begins the process in Step 2. The researcher asks the question, "Can the specific research question be addressed with data that already exist or does the question require new data?" To answer this fundamental question, researchers ask a series of additional questions concerning data availability, data quality, costs, and time constraints.

Finally, Step 2 enables the researcher to determine whether the information being requested by management is necessary. This step must be completed before going on to Step 3.

Step 3: Confirm Research Objectives and Assess the Value of Information

The research objectives should be confirmed based on the definition of the research problem in Step 2. Formally stated research objectives provide guidelines for determining which other steps must be undertaken. The assumption is that if the objectives are achieved, the decision maker will have the information needed to solve the problem.

A Closer Look at Research

Ford Foundation

Several years ago, the Ford Foundation of the Performing Arts, located in Vail, Colorado, successfully completed a $5 million fund-raising drive to build an amphitheater to house performing arts events. The Foundation's Amphitheater Design Team faced some difficult decisions. They were not sure which design features should be included in the structure to handle different types of events (theatrical productions, music concerts, dance productions, etc.). Further, they could not decide if the structure should accommodate indoor events, outdoor events, or a combination. They questioned the seating capacity and worried about ticket prices, parking requirements, availability of refreshments, and types of events most desired by local residents and visitors. The foundation hired a marketing research consultant to assist in gathering both primary and secondary data needed to address the team's questions and concerns. After several meetings with the design team, the researcher presented his research proposal, which stated that the "primary research objective focused on the collection of attitudinal and behavioral information to be used in addressing several questions posed by the Ford Amphitheater Design Team. The questions focused on performing arts events and possible design features for the proposed amphitheater structure." Three of the key research questions were:

Small Business Implications

1. What type of performing arts programs would residents and guests most prefer to see offered in the Vail Valley area?
2. What prices should be charged for the various types of events?
3. What type of summer-evening performing arts programs would people prefer attending at an indoor versus outdoor facility? If outdoors, what type of protection should be provided to the audience and the performers?

These questions were then transformed into the following research objectives:

1. To determine how often people attended performing arts events in the past 12 months and what three types of events (dance productions, theatrical productions, music concerts, etc.) they would be most interested in attending while staying in Vail Valley.
2. To determine, by event type, the average price range a person would expect and be willing to pay for an adult-reserved-seat ticket to the events presented in Vail Valley.
3. To determine the extent to which people would prefer to attend a specific type of event at an indoor or outdoor facility and the specific type of protection that should be offered the audience if the event was held at an outdoor facility.[3]

In some ways, research objectives serve as the justification for management and researchers to undertake an information research project. Consider the Ford Foundation example in the Closer Look at Research box. Notice that the three information objectives listed at the end are different from the foundation's statement of the research problem and the researcher's information problem. Before researchers move beyond Phase I of the research process, they must make sure a complete definition is given to each factor in the study. There also must be clear justification for the relevancy of each factor. For example, what does the Ford Foundation really mean by "protection"? Protection from what—rain or cold or snow, or perhaps something else?

Before moving to Phase II of the information research process, the decision maker and the researcher must evaluate the expected value of the information. This is not an easy task because a number of factors come into play. "Best guess" answers have to be made to the following types of questions: (1) "Can the information be collected at all?" (2) "Can the information tell the decision maker something not already known?" (3) "Will the information provide significant insights?" (4) "What benefits will be delivered by this information?" In most cases, information research should be conducted only when the expected value of the information to be obtained exceeds the cost of doing the research.

Phase II: Select the Appropriate Research Design

The main focus of Phase II is to select the most appropriate research design for a given set of research objectives. The steps in this phase are briefly outlined below.

Step 4: Determine the Research Design and Data Sources

The research design serves as a master plan of the methods used to collect and analyze the data. Determining the most appropriate research design is a function of the information research objectives and the specific information requirements. In this plan, the researcher must consider the type of data, the data collection approach (survey, observation, etc.), the sampling method, the schedule, and the budget. Although every research problem is unique, most research objectives can be met by using one of three types of research designs: exploratory, descriptive, and causal.

Exploratory Research Designs

Exploratory research

Research that focuses on collecting either secondary or primary data and using an unstructured format or informal procedures to interpret them.

Exploratory research focuses on collecting either secondary or primary data and using an unstructured format to interpret them. Of the three types of research designs, exploratory research includes the fewest characteristics of the scientific method. It often is used simply to classify the problems or opportunities and is not intended to provide conclusive information to determine a course of action. Some examples of exploratory research techniques are focus-group interviews, in-depth interviews, and pilot studies. Exploratory research also may use some forms of secondary data (e.g., online databases). Exploratory research can be somewhat intuitive and is used by many decision makers who monitor market performance measures for their company or industry. Exploratory designs will be treated in more detail in Chapter 6.

Descriptive Research Designs

Descriptive research

Research that uses a set of scientific methods and procedures to collect raw data and create data structures that describe the existing characteristics of a defined target population or market structure.

Descriptive research uses a set of scientific methods and procedures to collect raw data and create data structures that describe the existing characteristics (e.g., attitudes, intentions, preferences, purchase behaviors, evaluations of current marketing mix strategies) of a defined target group. Descriptive research designs are appropriate when the research objectives include determining the degree to which marketing variables are related to actual market phenomena. Here, the researcher looks for answers to the who, what, when, where, and how questions.

Descriptive studies provide information about customers, competitors, target markets, environmental factors, or other phenomena of concern. For example, there is a growing trend among chain restaurants to conduct annual studies that describe customers' attitudes, feelings, and patronage behavior toward their restaurants as well as toward the main competitors. These studies, referred to as either image assessment surveys or customer satisfaction surveys, describe how customers rate different restaurants' customer service, convenience of location, food quality, overall quality, and so on. Information generated from descriptive designs provides decision makers with information to select a course of action. Descriptive designs will be discussed further in Chapter 7.

Causal Research Designs

Causal research Research designed to collect raw data and create data structures and information that will allow the researcher to model cause-and-effect relationships between two or more market (or decision) variables.

Causal research is designed to collect raw data and create data structures that will enable the decision maker to determine cause-and-effect relationships between two or more decision variables. Causal research is most appropriate when the research objectives include the need to understand which decision variables (e.g., advertising) are the cause of the dependent phenomenon (e.g., sales) defined in the research problem.

Causal research can be used to understand the relationships between the causal factors and the outcome predicted. This type of research design enables decision makers to gain the highest level of understanding in the research process. In addition, understanding the cause-effect relationships among market performance factors enables the decision maker to make "If—then" statements about the variables. For example, the owner of a men's casual clothing store in Chicago might be able to say, "If I expand the assortment of brand-name shirts, increase my advertising budget by 15 percent, have an introductory 30 percent-off sale on the new shirts, and keep the rest of my marketing mix strategies unchanged, then overall sales volume should increase by 40 percent."

While causal research designs provide an opportunity to assess and explain causality among critical market factors, they tend to be complex, expensive, and time-consuming. Experimental designs have the greatest potential for establishing cause-effect relationships because they enable researchers to examine changes in one variable while manipulating one or more other variables under controlled conditions. Causal research designs are treated in more depth in Chapter 8.

Secondary and Primary Data Sources

The sources of data structures and information needed to solve information research problems can be classified as either secondary or primary, determination of which is based on three fundamental dimensions: (1) whether the data already exist in some type of recognizable format, (2) the degree to which the data have been interpreted by someone, and (3) the extent to which the researcher or decision maker understands the reason(s) why the data were collected and assembled. Sources of secondary data include inside a company, at public libraries and universities, on Internet Web sites, purchased from firms specializing in providing secondary information, and so on. Chapters 3 through 5 cover secondary data and sources.

Primary data represent "firsthand" raw data and data structures that have not had any type of meaningful interpretation. Primary data are the result of conducting some type of exploratory, descriptive, or causal research project that employs either surveys or observation to collect the data. Primary data are collected and assembled specifically for a current information research problem. The nature and collection of primary data are covered in Chapters 6 through 13.

Step 5: Determine the Sample Plan and Sample Size

If the decision is made to conduct some type of secondary research, then Step 5 (sampling) is not directly undertaken by the researcher. The researcher must still determine what population is being represented by the secondary data and decide if that population is relevant to the current research problem. Relevancy of secondary data is covered

---

EXHIBIT **2.11** Critical Questions and Issues in the Development of a Sampling Plan

- Given the problem, research objectives, and information requirements, who would be the best person (or object) to question or observe?
- What demographic (e.g., gender, occupation, age, marital status, income levels, education) and/or behavioral traits (e.g., regular/occasional/nonshopper; heavy user/light user/nonuser; customer/noncustomer) should be used to identify population membership?
- How many population elements must be in the sample to ensure it is representative of the population?
- How reliable does the information have to be for the decision maker?
- What are the data quality factors and acceptable levels of sampling error?
- What technique should be used in the actual selection of sampling units?
- What are the time and cost constraints associated with executing the appropriate sampling plan?

Target population A specified group of people or objects for which questions can be asked or observations made to develop required data structures and information.

Census A procedure in which the researcher attempts to question or observe all the members of a defined target population.

Sample A randomly selected subgroup of people or objects from the overall membership pool of a defined target population.

in Chapter 3. When conducting primary research, consideration must be given to sampling issues.

If predictions are to be made about market phenomena, the sample and its representativeness must be clearly understood. Typically, marketing decision makers are most interested in identifying and resolving problems associated with their target markets. Therefore, researchers need to identify the relevant **target population.** In collecting data, researchers can choose between two basic approaches. The first is referred to as a census of the target population. This may be the preferred approach for a small population. In a **census,** the researcher attempts to question or observe all the members of a defined target population.

The second approach, used when the defined target population is large, involves the selection of a **sample** from the overall membership pool of a defined target population. Researchers must use a representative sample of the population so the resulting information is generalizable. To achieve this objective, researchers develop a sampling plan as part of the overall research design. A sampling plan serves as the blueprint for defining the appropriate target population, identifying the possible respondents, establishing the procedures for selecting the sample, and determining the appropriate size of the sample. Exhibit 2.11 lists the critical questions and issues researchers typically faced when developing a sampling plan.

Sampling plans can be classified into two general types: probability and nonprobability. In probability sampling, each member of the defined target population has a known chance of being selected. Also, probability sampling gives the researcher the opportunity to assess the sampling error. In contrast, nonprobability sampling plans cannot measure sampling error and limit the generalizability of any information to the population.

Sample size affects data quality and generalizability. Researchers must therefore determine how many people to include or how many objects to investigate. Chapters 9 and 10 discuss sampling in more detail.

Step 6: Assess Measurement Issues and Scales

Step 6 is the second most important step in the research process. This step focuses on identifying the dimensions to investigate and measuring the variables that underlie the problem. The measurement process determines how much raw data can be collected and also the amount of information that can be inferred from the data.

Given the importance of measurement to the process of creating information, researchers must be able to answer questions such as: (1) What level of information is needed from a variable? (2) How reliable does the information need to be? (3) How valid does the information need to be? (4) How does one ensure that the scale measurements are reliable and valid? (5) What dimensions underlie the critical factors being investigated? and (6) Should single measures or multi-item measures be used to collect the data? For example, researchers must know what scaling assumptions or properties must be built into a scale design to ensure management's information needs are met. Chapters 11 and 12 discuss measurement and scale design procedures as well as other important measurement issues.

Although most of the specific activities involved in Step 6 are related to primary research, understanding these activities is important in secondary research studies as well. For example, in executing data mining with database variables, researchers must consider the basic measurement issues involved with the database. They must have an understanding of the measurement principles that were used in creating the database as well as the potential biases associated with the data. Lack of understanding can easily lead to misinterpretation of the secondary data and reporting of inappropriate or inaccurate information.

Step 7: Pretest the Questionnaire

Researchers must always pretest the questionnaire. Pretesting is done with individuals representative of those who will be asked to actually complete the survey. In a pretest respondents are asked to complete the questionnaire and comment on issues like clarity of instructions and questions, sequence of the topics and questions, and anything that is potentially difficult or confusing.

Phase III: Execute the Research Design

The execution phase is the heart of the research process. The main objectives of this phase are to finalize all necessary data collection forms, gather and prepare the data, analyze the data and create appropriate data structures, and interpret those structures to understand the initial problem. To achieve this overall objective, researchers must execute the next three interactive steps of the research process: (8) data collection and preparation, (9) data analysis, and (10) transforming data structures into information. As in the first two phases, researchers here must be cautious to ensure potential biases or errors are either eliminated or at least minimized.

Step 8: Collect and Prepare Data
Data Collection Methods

There are two fundamental approaches to gathering raw data. One is to have interviewers ask questions about variables and market phenomena or to use self-completion questionnaires. The other is to observe individuals or market phenomena. Self-administered surveys, personal interviews, computer simulations, telephone interviews, and focus groups are just some of the tools researchers use to collect data (see Exhibit 2.12).

еХHIBIT	2.12	Data Collection Tools Used in Marketing Research

Observation Tool	**Description**
Trained observers	Highly skilled people who use their senses (sight, hearing, smell, touch, taste) to observe and record physical phenomena. *Examples:* mystery shoppers; traffic counters; focus-group moderators.
Mechanical/electronic devices	High-technology instruments that can artificially observe and record physical phenomena. *Examples:* security cameras; videotaping equipment; scanning devices; Internet technology; tape recorders; air-hose traffic counters.
Questioning Tool	
Trained interviewers	Highly trained people who ask respondents specific questions and accurately record their responses. *Examples:* face-to-face interviewers; telephone interviewers; group survey leaders.
Interviewer/electronic devices	Highly skilled people who use high-technology devices during encounters with respondents. *Examples:* computer-assisted personal interviews; computer-assisted telephone interviews.
Fully automatic devices	High-tech devices that interact with respondents without the presence of a trained interviewer. *Examples:* on-site fully automatic interviews; fully automatic telephone interviews; computer-disk mail surveys; electronic-mail surveys; computer-generated fax surveys; Internet surveys.
Direct self-administered questionnaires	Survey instruments that are designed to have the respondent serve the roles of both interviewer and respondent. *Examples:* direct mail surveys; most group self-administered surveys.

A major advantage of questioning approaches over observation is they enable the researcher to collect a wider array of data. Survey data can pertain not only to current behavior but also to state of mind or intentions. In short, it can be used to answer why people are behaving as they are, not just how.

Observation methods can be characterized as natural or contrived; disguised or undisguised; structured or unstructured; direct or indirect; and human, electronic, or mechanical. For example, researchers might use trained human observers or a variety of mechanical devices such as a video camera, tape recorder, audiometer, eye camera, or pupilometer to record behavior or events.

As technology advances continue, researchers are moving toward integrating the benefits of technology with existing questioning tools that enable faster data acquisition. Online primary data studies (e.g., e-mail surveys, online focus-group interviews, Internet surveys) are increasing as well as secondary database research studies. Data collection instruments and methods are covered in Chapters 6, 7, 8, 12, and 13.

Preparation of Data

Once the primary data are collected, the researcher must perform several activities before doing data analysis. A coding scheme is needed so the raw data can be entered into computer files. Typically, researchers assign a logical numerical descriptor (code value) to all response categories. After the responses are entered, the researcher inspects the computer files to verify they are accurate. The researcher then must clean the data for coding or data-entry errors. As part of the data-cleaning process, each variable's data structure is tabulated. Chapter 14 discusses data preparation.

Data preparation in secondary research studies is somewhat different from that used with primary research. Researchers focus on evaluating the use of a single or multiple databases to obtain the needed information. When the data exist in multiple databases, different databases must be merged into one comprehensive database, or accessible via Internet connections. At times, overlaying one database on another can be very challenging and may require restructuring of one or more databases to achieve compatibility. Another activity is determining which data should be included in the analysis. Chapter 5 covers secondary data preparation and other key issues.

Step 9: Analyze Data

In Step 9, the researcher begins the process of turning raw data into data structures that can be used to generate useful information for the decision maker. The researcher analyzes the data and creates data structures that combine two or more variables into indexes, ratios, constructs, and so on. Analysis procedures vary widely in sophistication and complexity, from simple frequency distributions (percentages) to sample statistics (e.g., mean, median, mode) and perhaps even multivariate data analysis for data mining. Different procedures enable the researcher to (1) statistically test hypotheses for significant differences or correlations among several variables, (2) evaluate data quality, and (3) test models of cause-effect relationships. Chapters 15 through 17 provide an overview of data analysis techniques.

Step 10: Transform Data Structures into Information

Information is created for decision makers in Step 10. Researchers, or in some cases, the decision maker interpret the results of the statistical analysis. This does not mean a simple narrative description of the results. Interpretation means integrating several aspects of the findings into statements that can be used to answer the initial question. The data are similar to colors that can be used to paint a comprehensive picture.

Phase IV: Communicate the Research Results

The last phase of the information research process focuses on reporting the research findings and newly created information to management. The overall objective is to develop a report that is useful to a non-research-oriented person.

Step 11: Prepare and Present the Final Report to Management

Step 11 is preparing and presenting the final research report to management. The importance of this step cannot be overstated. There are some sections that should be included in any research report (e.g., executive summary, introduction, problem definition and objectives, methodology, results and findings, and limitations of study). The researcher asks the decision maker whether specific sections need to be included or expanded, such as recommendations for future actions or further information needs. In some cases, the researcher not only submits a written report but also makes an oral presentation of the major findings. Chapter 18 describes how to write and present research reports.

Develop an Information Research Proposal

Research proposal A specific document that serves as a written contract between the decision maker and the researcher.

By understanding the four phases of the research process, a researcher can develop a research proposal that communicates the research framework to the decision maker. A **research proposal** is a specific document that serves as a written contract between the decision maker and the researcher. It lists the activities that will be undertaken to develop the needed information, the research deliverables, how long it will take, and what it will cost.

The research proposal is not the same as a final research report. But some of the sections appear similar. There is no best way to write a research proposal. Exhibit 2.13 shows the sections that should be included in most research proposals. The exhibit presents only a general outline, but an actual proposal can be found in the Marketing Research in Action at the end of this chapter. Additional examples of research proposals are available at www.mhhe.com/hair06.

---

e X H I B I T 2.13   General Outline of a Research Proposal

TITLE OF THE RESEARCH PROPOSAL

I. Purpose of the Proposed Research Project
Includes a description of the decision problem and specific research objectives.

II. Type of Study
Includes discussions of the type of research design (i.e., exploratory, descriptive, causal), and secondary versus primary data requirements, with some justification of choice.

III. Definition of the Target Population and Sample Size
Describes the overall target population to be studied and determination of the appropriate sample size, including a justification of the size.

IV. Sample Design and Data Collection Method
Includes a substantial discussion regarding the sampling technique used, the actual method for collecting the data (e.g., observation or survey), incentive plans, and justifications.

V. Specific Research Instruments
Discusses the method used to collect the needed data, including the various types of scales.

VI. Potential Managerial Benefits of the Proposed Study
Discusses the expected values of the information to management and how the initial problem might be resolved, including the study's limitations.

VII. Proposed Cost for the Total Project
Itemizes the expected costs associated with conducting the research project, including a total cost figure and anticipated completion time frames.

VIII. Profile of the Research Company Capabilities
Briefly describes the main researchers and their qualifications as well as a general overview of the company.

IX. Optional Dummy Tables of the Projected Results
Offers examples of how the data might be presented in the final report.

MARKETING RESEARCH IN ACTION

What Does an Information Research Proposal Look Like?

The JP Hotel Preferred Guest Card Information Research Proposal

Purpose of the Proposed Research Project

The purpose of this proposed research project is to collect attitudinal, behavioral, motivational, and general demographic information to address several key questions posed by management of Louis Benito Advertising and W. B. Johnson Properties, Inc., concerning the JP Hotel Preferred Guest Card, a recently implemented marketing strategy. The key questions are as follows:

1. Is the Preferred Guest Card being used by cardholders?

2. How do cardholders evaluate the privileges associated with the card?

3. What are the perceived benefits and weaknesses of the card, and why?

4. To what extent does the Preferred Guest Card serve as an important factor in selecting a hotel?

5. How often do the cardholders use their Preferred Guest Card?

6. When do the cardholders use the card?

7. Of those who have used the card, what privileges have been used and how often?

8. What general or specific improvements should be made regarding the card or the extended privileges?

9. How did the cardholders obtain the card?

10. Should the Preferred Guest Card membership be complimentary or should cardholders pay an annual fee?

11. If there should be an annual fee, how much should it be? What would a cardholder be willing to pay?

12. What is the demographic profile of the people who have the JP Hotel Preferred Guest Card?

Type of Study

To collect the data needed to address the above-mentioned managerial questions, the research should be of a structured, nondisguised design characterized as exploratory and descriptive. The study will be descriptive to the extent that most of the questions focus on identifying the perceived awareness, attitudes, and usage patterns of the JP Hotel Preferred Guest Card as well as the demographic profiles of the current cardholders. It will be exploratory with regard to the investigation of possible improvements to the card and its privileges, the pricing structure, and the perceived benefits and weaknesses of the current card's features.

Definition of the Target Population and Sample Size

The target population to be studied consists of adults who are known to be current cardholders of the JP Hotel Preferred Guest Card. At present, this population frame is approximately 17,000 individuals across the United States. Statistically, a conservative sample size would be 384. But realistically, a sample of approximately 1,500 should be used to enable examination of sample subgroups. The bases for this approximation are (1) the likely response rate based on the sampling method and questionnaire design, (2) a predetermined level of precision of $\pm 5\%$ sampling error and a desired confidence level of 95%, (3) general administrative costs and trade-offs, and (4) the desirability of having a prespecified minimum number of randomly selected cardholders for the data analyses.

Sample Design, Technique, and Data Collection Method

A probabilistic random sampling technique will be used to draw the needed sample for the project from W. B. Johnson Properties, Inc.'s central cardholder bank. Using a mail survey, cardholders randomly selected as prospective respondents will be mailed a personalized self-administered questionnaire. Attached to the questionnaire will be a carefully designed cover letter that explains the generalities of the study as well as inducements for respondent participation. Given the nature of the study, the perceived type of cardholder, the general trade-offs regarding costs and time considerations, and the utilization of updated incentives to induce respondent participation, a mail survey would be more appropriate than other methods.

The Questionnaire

The questionnaire will be self-administered. That is, respondents will fill out the survey in the privacy of their home and without the presence of an interviewer. All the questions in the survey will be pretested by a convenience sample to assess clarity of instructions, questions, and administrative time dimensions. Response scales used in the actual questions will conform to standard questionnaire design guidelines and industry wisdom.

Potential Managerial Benefits of the Proposed Study

Given the scope and nature of this proposed research project, the study's findings will enable JP Hotel's management to answer questions regarding the Preferred Guest Card as well as other marketing strategy issues. Specifically, the proposed study will help JP management to

- Better understand the types of people that hold and use the Preferred Guest Card and the extent of that usage.

- Identify specific feature problems that could serve as indicators for evaluating (and possibly modifying) current marketing strategies or tactics as they relate to the card and its privileges.

- Develop specific insights concerning the promotion and distribution of the card to additional segments.

Additionally, the proposed research project will initiate a customer-oriented database and collection system to assist JP's management in better understanding its customers' hotel service needs and wants in the future. Customer-oriented databases will be useful in developing promotional strategies as well as pricing and service approaches.

Proposed Project Costs

Questionnaire/cover letter design and reproduction costs	$ 2,800
Development	
Typing	
Pretest	
Reproduction (1,500)	
Envelopes (3,000)	
Sample design and plan costs	1,620
Administration/data collection costs	3,840
Questionnaire packet assembly	
Postage and P.O. box	
Address labels	
Coding and predata analysis costs	4,000
Coding and setting of final codes	
Data entry	
Tab development	
Computer programming requirements	
Computer time	
Data analysis and interpretation costs	6,500
Written report and presentation costs	2,850
Total maximum proposed project cost*	$21,610

*Costing policy: Some costs may be less than what is stated on the proposal. Cost reductions, if any, will be passed on to the client. Additionally, there is a ± 10% cost margin associated with the pre- and actual data analysis activities depending on client changes of the original tab and analyses requirements.

Principal Researcher's Profile

The research for this proposed project will be conducted by the Marketing Resource Group (MRG), a research firm that specializes in a wide array of research approaches. MRG is located in Tampa, Florida, and has conducted numerous marketing research studies for many Fortune 1000 companies. The principal researcher and project coordinator will be Mr. Alex Smith, Senior Project Director at MRG. Mr. Smith holds a PhD in Marketing from Louisiana State University, an MBA from Illinois State University, and a BS from Southern Illinois University. With 25 years of marketing research experience, he has conducted numerous projects within the consumer packaged-goods products, hotel/resort, retail banking, automobile, and insurance industries, to name a few. He specializes in projects that focus on customer satisfaction, service/product quality, market segmentation, and general consumer attitudes and behavior patterns as well as interactive electronic marketing technologies. In addition, he has published numerous articles on theoretical and pragmatic researching topics.

A Dummy Table Example of Findings

In an effort to illustrate the potential types of findings that can be expected from the proposed research, the following dummy data table is provided in this proposal (see Exhibit 2.14). It is used to illustrate the type of data table that would be useful in addressing the research question: "To what extent does the Preferred Guest Card serve as an important factor in selecting a hotel?"

EXHIBIT 2.14 Summary of Overall Importance Differences of Selected Hotel-Choice Criteria Used by First-Time and Repeat Business Patrons

Hotel Selection Criteria	Total (n = 880)		First-Time Patrons (n = 440)			Repeat Patrons (n = 440)			
	Mean[a] Value	(SG)[b]	Mean Value	Standard Error	(SG)	Mean Value	Standard Error	(SG)	Z-Tests
Cleanliness of the room	5.65	(A)	5.75	.06	(A)	5.50	.05	(A)	*
Good-quality bedding and towels	5.60	(A)	5.55	.06	(A)	5.62	.07	(A)	
Has preferred guest card options	5.57	(A)	5.42	.07	(A)	5.71	.06	(A)	*
Friendly/courteous staff and employees	5.10	(B)	4.85	.09	(B)	5.45	.07	(B)	*
Offers free VIP services	5.06	(B)	4.35	.10	(B)	5.38	.11	(B)	*
Conveniently located for business	5.04	(B)	5.25	.09	(B)	4.92	.10	(B)	*
In-room movie entertainment	3.63	(D)	3.30	.13	(D)	4.56	.11	(C)	*

[a]Importance scale: a six-point scale ranging from 6 ("extremely important") to 1 ("not at all important").

[b]Significant groupings (SG): (A) = "definitely strong factor"; (B) = "strong factor"; (C) = "moderately strong factor"; (D) = "weak factor."

*Mean importance difference between the two patron groups is significant at $p < .05$.

Hands-On Exercise

1. If this research proposal is implemented, will it achieve the purposes of the management of J P Hotels?

2. Is the target population being interviewed the appropriate one? Why or why not?

3. Are there any other questions you believe should be included in the project?

Summary of Learning Objectives

■ **Describe the major environmental factors influencing marketing research and explain their impact on the research process.**

Several key environmental factors have significant impact on changing the tasks, responsibilities, and efforts associated with marketing research practices. The Internet and e-commerce, gatekeeper technologies and data privacy legislation, new global market structure expansions, and repositioning marketing research as a strategy are forcing researchers to balance their use of secondary and primary data to assist decision makers in solving decision problems and taking advantage of opportunities. Researchers are being asked to improve their ability to use technology-driven tools and databases. There are also greater needs for faster data acquisition and retrieval, analysis, and interpretation of cross-functional data and information among decision-making teams within global market environments.

■ **Discuss the phases and steps of the research process and explain some of the key activities within each step.**

The information research process was discussed in terms of four major phases, identified as (1) determination of the research problem, (2) development of the appropriate research design, (3) execution of the research design, and (4) communication of the results. To achieve the overall objectives of each phase, researchers must be able to successfully execute 10 interrelated task steps: (1) determine and clarify management's information needs, (2) redefine the decision problem as a research problem, (3) establish research objectives and determine the value of the information, (4) determine and evaluate the research design and data sources, (5) determine the sample plan and sample size, (6) determine the measurement issues and scales, (7) collect and process data, (8) analyze data, (9) transform data structures into information, and (10) prepare and present the final report to management. The overview of the steps highlighted the importance of each step and showed how it was related to the other steps in the research process.

■ **Explain the differences between raw data, data structures, and information and describe the process by which raw data are transformed into information that managers can use.**

Researchers and decision makers must understand that raw data, data structures, and information are different constructs. Raw data consist of the responses obtained by either questioning or observing people or physical phenomena. Data structures are created by submitting the raw data to some type of analysis procedure. In turn, information is created only when either the researcher or decision maker interprets the data structures.

■ **Illustrate and explain the critical elements of problem definition in marketing research.**

Phase I of the research process consists of three important task steps: (1) determine and clarify management's information needs; (2) redefine the decision problem as a research problem; and (3) establish research objectives and evaluate the value of information. The most critical step to the success of any research endeavor is the second one. Before redefining the initial decision problem as a set of more specific research questions, the decision maker needs to work with the researcher to determine or clarify the true information needs of the situation. Defining the decision problem correctly requires the use of a five-step model that includes uncovering the decision maker's purpose, understanding the complete problem situation, separating out the measurable symptoms, determining the appropriate unit of analysis, and determining the most relevant factors of the situation. Defining decision problems as research questions allows the researcher to focus on the how, what, which, who, when, where, and why questions needed to guide the formulation of the research objectives and clarify the pertinent information requirements. All the effort, time, and money spent to execute marketing research will be wasted if the true information research problems are misunderstood.

■ **Distinguish between exploratory, descriptive, and causal research designs.**

The main objective of exploratory research designs is to create information that the researcher or decision maker can use to (1) gain a clearer understanding of the decision problem; (2) define or redefine the initial problem, separating the symptom variables from the independent and dependent factors; (3) crystallize the problem and the objective; or (4) identify the specific information requirements (e.g., facts, estimates, predictions, variable relationships). Exploratory research designs are not intended to provide conclusive information from which a particular course of action can be determined.

Descriptive research designs focus on using a set of scientific methods to collect raw data and create data structures that are used to describe the existing characteristics (e.g., attitudes, intentions, preferences, purchase behaviors, evaluations of current marketing mix strategies) of a defined target population. The researcher looks for answers to how, who, what, when, and where questions. Information from this type of research design allows decision makers to draw inferences about their customers, competitors, target markets, environmental factors, or other phenomena of concern.

Finally, causal research designs are most useful when the research objectives include the need to understand why market phenomena happen. The focus of this type of research design is to collect raw data and create data structures and information that will allow the decision maker or researcher to model cause-and-effect relationships between two or more variables.

■ **List the critical issues in the development of a sampling plan, and explain the basic differences between a probability and nonprobability sampling plan.**

A sampling plan is a blueprint for correctly defining the appropriate target population, establishing the procedural steps needed to draw the required sample, and determining the appropriate size of the sample. Some of the critical questions that researchers must address when developing a sampling plan are the following:

Who would be the best type of person to question or observe? What explicit demographic or behavioral traits should be used to identify population membership? How many population elements must be drawn into the sample to ensure the representativeness of the population membership? How reliable does the resulting information have to be for the decision maker? What technique should be used in the actual selection of sampling units? What are the time and cost constraints associated with developing and executing the appropriate sampling plan?

■ **Identify and explain the major components of a research proposal.**

Once the researcher understands the different phases and task steps of the information research process, he or she can develop a research proposal. The proposal serves as a contract between the researcher and decision maker. There are nine specific content sections suggested for inclusion: (1) purpose of the proposed research project; (2) type of study; (3) definition of the target population and sample size; (4) sample design, technique, and data collection method; (5) specific research instruments; (6) potential managerial benefits of the proposed study; (7) proposed cost structure for the total project; (8) profile of the researcher and company; and (9) optional dummy tables of the projected results.

Key Terms and Concepts

Causal research 64

Census 65

Data structures 53

Decision problem 56

Descriptive research 63

Exploratory research 63

Gatekeeper technologies 46

Information 53

Information research process 48

Internet 46

Primary data 46

Raw data 53

Research proposal 69

Sample 65

Scientific method 52

Secondary data 46

Situation analysis 59

Target population 65

Review Questions

1. Identify the significant changes taking place in today's business environment that are forcing management decision makers to rethink their views of marketing research. Also discuss the potential impact that these changes might have on marketing research activities.

2. In the business world of the 21st century, will it be possible to make critical marketing decisions without marketing research? Why or why not?

3. How are management decision makers and information researchers alike? How are they different? How might the differences be reduced between these two types of professionals?

4. Explain the specific differences that exist between raw data, data structures, and information. Discuss how marketing research practices are used to transform raw data into meaningful bits of information.

5. Comment on the following statements:
   a. The primary responsibility for determining whether marketing research activities are necessary is that of the marketing research specialist.
   b. The information research process serves as a blueprint for reducing risks in making marketing decisions.
   c. Selecting the most appropriate research design is the most critical task in the research process.

6. How can you determine when marketing research might be needed to solve a problem or pursue an opportunity?

7. Why is determining the decision problem as a research problem the most critical step in any research endeavor?

8. Discuss the activities involved in the problem definition process. What should be the researcher's responsibilities in that process?

9. How can the iceberg principle be used to help decision makers gain a clearer understanding of their decision problem? What are the major differences between problem symptoms and decision problems?

10. Explain the value of preparing a research proposal.

Discussion Questions

1. For each of the four phases of the information research process, identify the corresponding steps and develop a set of questions that a researcher should attempt to answer.

2. What are the differences in the main research objectives of exploratory, descriptive, and causal research designs? Which design type would be most appropriate to address the following question: "How satisfied or dissatisfied are customers with the automobile repair service offerings of the dealership from which they purchased their new 2004 Acura 3.2 TL?"

3. When should a researcher use a probability sampling method rather than a nonprobability method?

4. **EXPERIENCE THE INTERNET.** Using your Internet browser and a search engine, go to the Gallup Poll Organization's home page at www.gallup.com. Select the "Take poll" option and review the results by selecting the "Findings" option. After reviewing the information, outline the different phases and task steps of the information research process that might have been used in the Gallup Internet Poll.

5. Using McDonald's as a case company, discuss how doing a situation analysis can help the researcher in determining an information research problem.

6. The program manager at Time Warner would like to know how many viewers are likely to tune in to a proposed new weekly TV show called *Leave it on the Table*. Identify three situations in which doing a marketing research study to address the program manager's question might prove to be inappropriate, and explain why.

7. What kind of research design would be best for a Santa Fe Grill project whose purpose is to learn more about what current customers like or dislike about the restaurant?

8. How would you define the problem facing the owners of the Santa Fe Grill?

chapter 3

Information Management for Marketing Decisions: Secondary Data Sources

Learning Objectives

After reading this chapter, you will be able to

1. Understand how secondary data fit into the marketing research process.
2. Explain how secondary data fit into the customer relationship management process.
3. Demonstrate how secondary data can be used in problem solving.
4. List sources of traditional internal secondary data.
5. Know how to use and extract external secondary data.
6. Identify sources of external secondary data.
7. Understand the availability and use of syndicated sources of secondary data.
8. Understand the changing focus of secondary data usage.

Know Your Customer: Making the Most of an Information-Rich Environment

Dell, Inc., recently responded to a disgruntled customer by building a better box—shipping box, that is. The customer was one of many that had been invited to the company's usability lab to test the length of time needed to get a new PC up and running. While unpacking a Dell Dimension tower, the customer struggled and struggled with the shipping box. He finally became so frustrated that he picked it up and turned it upside down. The tower fell to the floor and crashed. Although the purpose of the test was to learn how long it took a customer to install a computer, seeing someone destroy a tower was so startling executives quickly decided to redesign the box and its packing material.

Cisco Systems, Inc., a global leader in the networking market, recognized the potential of information and its impact on building customer relationships long before its competitors. After realizing it could not hire enough engineers to support its growing customer base, Cisco began looking at information solutions. "Our strategy is to empower customers and let them provide us with information they believe is important in maintaining a relationship," says Peter Solvik, senior VP of information systems. Known as Cisco Connect On-line, the Web-driven information connection allows customers to provide information to and access information from Cisco for the purposes of helping in the buying process, getting facts about the company's products, learning about customer training programs, and so on. Customers also use site features to configure and price their purchases, track order status, manage service contracts, and submit returns. Uniquely, this customer connect system also incorporates an electronic customer council that allows Cisco to conduct online focus groups, collect customer comments via e-mail, and hold chat sessions between customers and corporate officials.[1]

Value of Secondary Data

The examples of Dell and Cisco may not at first appear to fully illustrate the traditional notion of using secondary data. Yet these examples illustrate use of an emerging form of secondary data, referred to as *customer-volunteered information* or *customer knowledge information.* Given new information technology available, many companies are now using a variety of techniques to collect, store, and categorize customer data for future marketing decisions. Information gathered from electronic customer councils, customer usability labs, e-mail comments, and chat sessions is increasingly used to exploit a data-rich environment based on customer interaction. As more and more such data become available, many companies are realizing the data can be used to make sound marketing decisions. Data of this nature are more readily available, often more valid, and usually less expensive to secure than company-gathered primary data.

This chapter focuses on the types of secondary data available, how they can be used, the benefits they offer, and the impact of the Internet on the use of secondary data.

The Nature and Scope of Secondary Data

One of the basic tasks of marketing research is to obtain information that helps a company's management make the best possible decisions. Focusing on the particular marketing problem to be analyzed, the researcher needs to determine whether useful information already exists, how relevant the information is, and how it should be obtained. Existing sources of information are more widespread than one might expect, as illustrated in the chapter opening example, and should always be considered first in any data collection procedure.

Secondary data Data not gathered for the immediate study at hand but for some other purpose.

The term **secondary data** refers to data not gathered for the immediate study at hand but for some other purpose. There are two types of secondary data—internal and external. **Internal secondary data** are data collected by a company for accounting purposes, marketing activity reports, and customer knowledge. **Customer knowledge information** is provided by customers for purposes that may be outside the marketing function of an organization. For example, information may be provided to engineers, logistical support personnel, or information technology departments for issues relating to product improvement, packaging, or Web registration. Nonetheless, data of this type, if properly warehoused and categorized, can be an invaluable form of secondary data for marketing decisions as they relate to customer relationship management (CRM). CRM focuses on customer involvement and interactions throughout many of the processes of an organization.

Internal secondary data Data collected by the individual company for accounting purposes, marketing activity reports, and customer knowledge.

Customer knowledge information Information provided by customers that is unsolicited and can be used for marketing planning purposes.

External secondary data consist of data collected by outside agencies such as the federal government, trade associations, or periodicals. External data may also be available through standardized marketing research services such as NPD Marketing Research's food consumption reports, store audits, or consumer purchase panels. Finally, secondary data may be obtained from computerized data sources. Computerized secondary data sources are usually designed by specific companies and include internal and external data combined with online information sources. These computerized information sources may include information vendors, private Web sites, mailing lists, or direct marketing clearing and fulfillment services.

External secondary data Data collected by outside agencies such as the federal government, trade associations, or periodicals.

The Role of Secondary Data in Marketing Research

The role of secondary data in the marketing research process has changed in recent years. Traditionally, research based on secondary data was viewed as nonoriginal. It often was outsourced to a corporate librarian, syndicated data collection firm, or junior research analyst. The main functions of secondary data research were to provide historical background for a current primary research endeavor and to allow longitudinal trend analysis within an industry. In other words, secondary data research was viewed as the filler, attachment, or appendix to the formal primary research report. With the increased emphasis on business and competitive intelligence and the ever-increasing availability of information from proprietary online databases, secondary data research is gaining importance in the marketing research process.

Secondary research approaches are applied more often to specific marketing problems than are primary techniques due to the relative speed and cost-effectiveness of gathering secondary data. Many large corporations are redefining the role of the secondary research analyst to that of a business unit information professional or specialist linked to the information technology area. This individual creates contact and sales databases, prepares competitive trend reports, develops customer retention strategies, and so forth.

Secondary Data and Customer Relationship Management

Recall that customer relationship management (CRM) is a process used to learn more about customers' needs and behaviors in order to develop stronger relationships with customers. Customer relationship management uses a combination of technology and human resources to gain insights into the behaviors of customers and the value those customers hold for the organization. For any CRM initiative to be effective, an organization must first decide what kind of customer information it is looking for and what it intends to do with that information. For example, many financial institutions keep track of customer life cycle stages in order to determine the right time to market appropriate banking products like mortgages or IRAs.

The organization must then look into all of the different ways customer information comes into the business, where and how the data are stored, and how data are currently being used. For example, one company may interact with customers in a variety of ways including mail campaigns, Web sites, brick and mortar stores, call centers, salespersons, and advertising efforts. CRM links these sources of secondary data. The data then flow between operational systems (e.g., sales and inventory systems) and analytical systems that help sort through the data for customer patterns. Marketing research analysts then comb through the data to obtain an overall view of each customer and pinpoint areas where service enhancements are needed. For example, if someone has a mortgage, a business loan, an investment account, and a large commercial checking account with one bank, the person needs to have a positive experience each time he or she has contact with the financial institution.

Secondary data provide the nucleus for the CRM process. While many CRM activities are indeed supported by primary data, the emphasis on primary data is limited by the vast network of data collection and storage points in the CRM system.

Secondary Data Research Tasks and the Marketing Research Process

In many areas of marketing research, secondary research plays a subordinate role to primary research. In product and concept testing, focus groups, and customer satisfaction surveys, only primary research can provide answers to marketing problems. Yet when the data are appropriately selected for specific situations, secondary data research can not only save time and money, but also provide the researcher with a broad avenue of answers. In many instances, secondary data can be used to directly assess the research problem at hand. For example, in many research situations secondary data collection is the starting point in defining the actual research that needs to be conducted. If the problem can be solved based on available secondary data alone, then the company can save time, money, and effort. If the level of secondary data is not sufficient to solve the specific research problems, then primary data collection needs to be considered.

Exhibit 3.1 illustrates the functional roles of secondary data research. These roles typically are viewed in terms of their focus and value. If the focus of the research project is on external market dynamics, it will likely be a secondary research responsibility. One task of secondary research is trend analysis, which uses past market data to project future changes in a dynamic marketplace. Additionally, secondary data collection is a vital support task in providing business and competitive intelligence. Both tasks involve the acquisition of secondary data and information about all aspects of a competitor's marketing and business activities. In short, external market dynamics is an area that requires proactive secondary research.

If the research focus is on the external customer, secondary research adds value to the research process. Researchers may, for example, use internal company documents to profile the current customer base. This existing customer base can then be used to identify significant characteristics of potential new customers. Finally, needs analysis, which identifies critical problems or requirements of specific customer groups, is an additional secondary research task. The third type of secondary research involves providing internal support data for the company. Here the focus switches to providing support for primary research activities, sales presentations, and decision-making functions. It's important to realize that a marketing organization cannot survive without sales generated by professional presentations or decisions on product, price, place, and promotion. Also, the organization needs to know

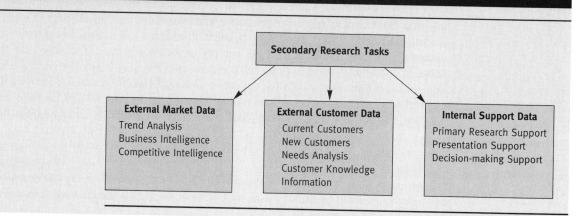

EXHIBIT 3.1   Functional Roles of Secondary Data Research

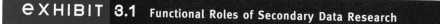

Secondary Research Tasks

External Market Data
Trend Analysis
Business Intelligence
Competitive Intelligence

External Customer Data
Current Customers
New Customers
Needs Analysis
Customer Knowledge
Information

Internal Support Data
Primary Research Support
Presentation Support
Decision-making Support

how markets are changing under its strategic planning process. Providing need-to-have planning tools is a primary task of secondary research.

To clarify the role of secondary research in the marketing research process, the Society of Competitive Intelligence Professionals conducted a survey among marketing research firms. Sixty percent of the sample reported using secondary research on a regular basis. The survey also revealed the following uses of secondary data:[2]

- Monitoring competitive and business intelligence—82 percent.
- Providing functional support for primary research projects—75 percent.
- Managerial presentations—59 percent.
- Specific business decisions—57 percent.
- Validating internal data and primary data collection—48 percent.

As the required skills and technology for acquiring new forms of data continue to evolve, the importance and value of secondary data research within the research process will increase.

Use and Evaluation of Secondary Data Sources

The primary reason for using secondary data is to save the researcher time and money. Usually, secondary data collection involves locating the appropriate source or sources, extracting the necessary data, and recording the data for the research purpose in question. This usually takes only several days, and in some cases only a few hours. Primary data, in contrast, can take months to accurately collect. When you consider the process of designing and testing questionnaires, developing a sampling plan, actually collecting the data, and then analyzing and tabulating them, you can see that primary data collection can be a long and involved procedure.

In addition to taking a long time, primary data collection can cost thousands of dollars. Fees for services rendered by market research firms typically range from $10,000 to $500,000. Clearly, the scope and magnitude of the research project play a significant role in the fee charged for a particular project. Yet with any primary data collection project it is difficult to avoid wages and expenses, transportation and data collection costs, and clerical and field services charges. In contrast, with many secondary data sources such costs are nonexistent or minimal. Expenses associated with secondary data are usually either incurred by the original data source, as with published secondary data sources (the U.S. census, corporate surveys of buying power, state and county demographic data), or shared between the user and the commercial provider of the data. Regardless, obtaining secondary data usually costs significantly less than securing primary data.

Because of time and cost savings, the first general rule of thumb associated with any research endeavor is to exhaust all potential sources of secondary data. If for some reason the particular research problem cannot be solved with secondary data, then consideration should be given to collecting primary data. In today's environment of information abundance, many firms, both consumer and industrial, are finding secondary data sources adequate for solving many of their marketing research problems. Indeed, by 2010 almost half of all marketing research objectives are expected to be accomplished using secondary data.[3]

As information becomes more abundant, and technology allows for greater refinement and categorization of the information, the emphasis on secondary data is likely to increase. In addition, secondary data are likely to become more accurate. Bar coding, optical scanning, and database point-of-purchase data often provide companies with all the information they need for much of their marketing research.

With the increasing emphasis on secondary data, researchers will develop better procedures to evaluate the quality of information obtained via secondary data sources. The new procedures should be based on six fundamental principles:

1. **Purpose.** Since most secondary data are collected for purposes other than the one at hand, the data must be carefully evaluated on how they relate to the current research objective. Many times the original collection of the data is not consistent with a particular market research study. These inconsistencies often stem from the units of measure employed. For example, much of the data regarding product consumption patterns in the *Survey of Buying Power* published by *Sales and Marketing Management* is based on average expenditure patterns. Each figure is assigned an arbitrary weight to account for environmental or situational differences. While the results represent a good average, they may not provide the necessary precision for profiling a highly defined target market relative to actual dollars spent on some particular product category.

2. **Accuracy.** When assessing secondary data, researchers need to keep in mind what was actually measured. For example, if actual purchases in a test market were measured, were they first-time trial purchases or repeat purchases? Researchers must also assess the generalizability of the data. Were the data collected only from certain groups (e.g., men, women, children) or randomly? Were the measures for the study developed properly? For example, a specific question might be, "Were dichotomous forced-choice questions used instead of interval scales when attempting to measure attitudes toward foreign automobile imports?" Researchers must further evaluate the data based on classification information. Were the data presented as a total of responses from all respondents, or were they categorized by age, sex, or socioeconomic status?

    Researchers must assess when the secondary data was collected. For example, a researcher tracking the sales of imported Japanese autos in the U.S. market needs to consider changing attitudes, newly imposed tariffs that may restrict imports, and even fluctuations in the exchange rate. Factors such as these not only can distort the accuracy of the data but also make it useless. With regard to the accuracy of secondary data, researchers must keep in mind the data were collected to answer a different set of research questions than the ones at hand. Thus, they may not accurately address all aspects of a research issue, or flaws may exist in the research design and method that are not apparent in the secondary data results.

3. **Consistency.** When evaluating any source of secondary data, a good strategy is to seek out multiple sources of the same data to assure consistency. For example, when evaluating the economic characteristics of a foreign market, a researcher may try to gather the same information from government sources, private business publications (*Fortune, BusinessWeek*), and specialty import/export trade publications.

4. **Credibility.** Researchers should always question the credibility of the secondary data source. Technical competence, service quality, reputation, and training and expertise of personnel representing the organization are some of the measures of credibility.

5. **Methodology.** The quality of secondary data is only as good as the methodology employed to gather it. Flaws in methodological procedures can produce results that are invalid, unreliable, or not generalizable beyond the study itself. Therefore, the researcher must evaluate the size and description of the sample, the response rate, the questionnaire, and the overall procedure for collecting the data (telephone, Internet, or personal interview).

6. **Bias.** Researchers must try to determine the underlying motivation or hidden agenda, if any, behind secondary data. It is not uncommon to find secondary data sources published to advance the interests of commercial, political, or other special interest groups. Sometimes secondary data are published to incite controversy or refute other

data sources. Researchers must try to determine if the organization reporting the data is motivated by a certain purpose. For example, statistics on animal extinction reported by the National Hardwood Lumber Association or deaths attributed to handguns as reported by the National Rifle Association should be validated before they can be relied on as unbiased sources of information.

Traditional Internal Sources of Secondary Data

The logical starting point in searching for secondary data is the company's own internal information. Many organizations fail to realize the wealth of information their own records contain. Additionally, internal data are the most readily available and can be accessed at little or no cost at all. Yet, while this appears to be an overwhelming rationale for using internal data, researchers must realize that a majority of this information comes from past business activities. This is not to say that internal data is not usable for future business decisions. As will be evident in the following discussion, internal data sources can be highly effective in helping decision makers plan new-product introductions or new distribution outlets.

Types of Internal Secondary Data

Generally, internal data will consist of sales or cost information. Data of this type are commonly found in internal accounting or financial records. The two most useful sources of information are sales invoices and accounts receivable reports. But quarterly sales reports and sales activity reports are also useful. Exhibit 3.2 lists key variables found in each of these internal sources of secondary data.

---

e XHIBIT 3.2 Common Sources of Internal Secondary Data plus Key Variables

1. **Sales invoices**
   a. Customer name
   b. Address
   c. Class of product/service sold
   d. Price by unit
   e. Salesperson
   f. Term of sales
   g. Shipment point

2. **Accounts receivable reports**
   a. Customer name
   b. Product purchased
   c. Total unit and dollar sales
   d. Customer as percentage of sales
   e. Customer as percentage of regional sales
   f. Profit margin
   g. Credit rating
   h. Items returned
   i. Reason for return

3. **Quarterly sales reports**
   a. Total dollar and unit sales by:
      Customer   Geographic segment
      Customer segment Sales territory

   Product   Sales rep
   Product segment
   b. Total sales against planned objective
   c. Total sales against budget
   d. Total sales against prior periods
   e. Actual sales percentage increase/decrease
   f. Contribution trends

4. **Sales activity reports**
   a. Classification of customer account
      Mega
      Large
      Medium
      Small
   b. Available dollar sales potential
   c. Current sales penetration
   d. Existing bids/contracts by
      Customer location
      Product

Sales Invoices

Sales invoices contain a wealth of data pertaining to both current and past customers. As a secondary data research tool, such invoices can provide customer profiles, sales trends, unit sales history, and other key items of information.

Accounts Receivable Reports

Accounts receivable reports contain information relative to both past and current customers. They also provide information on relative profit margins; reasons behind customer returns and chargebacks; and revenues by industry, segment, or geographic location. With such information, accounts receivable reports can provide indirect measures of customer satisfaction/dissatisfaction, price tactics, and sales history.

Quarterly Sales Reports

Quarterly sales reports normally illustrate planned sales activities relative to actual sales results. These reports are invaluable sources of information on sales territories, effective sales techniques, and competitive intelligence. The information is often useful in sales training and presentation planning.

Sales Activity Reports

Sales activity reports typically are prepared each month by individual sales representatives and usually contain data on sales, competition, territory activities, and changes in the marketplace. In general, most selling organizations require their sales personnel to include

---

e X H I B I T | 3.3 | Additional Sources of Secondary Data

Source	Information
Customer letters	General satisfaction/dissatisfaction data
Customer comment cards	Overall performance data
Mail-order forms	Customer name, address, items purchased, quality, cycle time of order
Credit applications	Full and detailed biography (demographic, socioeconomic, credit usage, credit ratings) of customer segments
Cash register receipts	Dollar volume, merchandise type, salesperson, vendor, manufacturer
Salesperson expense reports	Sales activities, competitor activities in market
Employee exit interviews	General internal satisfaction/dissatisfaction data, internal company performance data
Warranty cards	Sales volume; names, addresses, zip codes, items purchased, reasons for product return
Past marketing research studies	A variety of data pertaining to the situation in which the marketing research was conducted
Internet-provided information	Customer registration information, tracking, Web site visits, e-mail correspondence

competitive activities on these reports, making them an excellent source of data for competitive intelligence.

Other Types

Other types of internal data that exist among company records can be used to complement the information thus far discussed. Exhibit 3.3 outlines other potential sources of internal secondary data.

A lot of internal company information is available for marketing research activities. If maintained and categorized properly, internal data can be used to analyze product performance, customer satisfaction, distribution effectiveness, and target market strategies. These forms of internal data are also useful for planning new-product introductions, product deletions, promotional strategies, competitive intelligence, and customer service tactics.

Using and Extracting External Sources of Secondary Data

After searching for internal secondary data, the next logical step for the researcher to focus on is external secondary data. There are three sources of external secondary data: (1) published data in periodicals, directories, or indexes; (2) data compiled by an outside agency (syndicated or commercial) that can be acquired on an as-needed basis for a nominal fee; or (3) data contained in online databases or available through computer-facilitating agencies or vendors. This section will focus on the first two sources of external secondary data: published sources and syndicated/commercial sources. We then discuss the Internet as a source of secondary data.

Planning for the External Secondary Data Search

The major challenge associated with external secondary data is finding and securing the appropriate sources from which to extract the data. U.S. Department of Defense researchers say there is enough information available today to solve a majority of managers' questions and problems. But 90 percent of that information is not categorized in any particular form.[4] Thus, the problem often is not finding out whether information exists. It is finding out where the information resides.

When seeking secondary data sources, it is best to follow some sort of plan or strategy. A simple procedure when searching for secondary data is the "GO-CART approach" (for **g**oals, **o**bjectives, **c**haracteristics, **a**ctivities, **r**eliability, and **t**abulation).

1. **Goals.** Focus your information search on topics and concepts relevant to the specific research question at hand. If the research question is how to develop market or target market profiles, seek out information relevant to this topic (demographics, socioeconomic data, SIC codes, etc.). If the research question is how to understand customer satisfaction as it relates to product usage, seek out information on the product, for example, how it is manufactured, distributed, and transported. Let this information point to potential reasons for satisfaction or dissatisfaction.

2. **Objectives.** Many experts believe the best way to manage primary data is to initially gather a lot of it and then categorize it into specific topics. Managing a secondary data source is similar. Seek out as much information as you can on the topic. Then check

all references and citations that may enable you to address more specific topics. Keep in mind that many sources of secondary data are compiled from specific categories of information and reported in a general format. Backtracking through references and citations will allow you to narrow down the information. For example, much of the data reported in the *Survey of Buying Power* is general in reference to a standard metropolitan area. Yet analyzing how the data were compiled could lead to information by city limits, areas of a city, or even specific zip codes.

3. **Characteristics.** Always define the specific characteristics of information you are seeking. Write out a list of topics that need to be explored in your search. If you are seeking psychographic data, identify the specific characteristics of the data you wish to uncover. Are you looking for activities, interests, opinions (i.e., lifestyles)? If so, relative to what topics? Television viewing patterns, product usage, political affiliations, and so on? Focus your data search on a list of characteristics you're seeking as an aid in answering the research question.

4. **Activities.** Outline the places, people, events, and tasks that will be part of your secondary data search. You will probably need to visit libraries and speak with reference librarians. You may need to go to trade associations, state or county planning commission offices, newspaper file rooms, or even seminars. Document what needs to be done, where you need to do it, and who can help you along the way.

5. **Reliability.** Try to find several data sources on the same topic. This will enable you to assess consistency and will lead to greater levels of reliable data.

6. **Tabulation.** Document all sources of your data search. If possible, cross-reference the various sources. Finally, verify that what you have collected is indeed what needs to be collected to answer the research question at hand. If not, an additional data search may be necessary.

The GO-CART approach for planning a secondary data search is by no means the only way to collect secondary data. It does, however, provide an agenda to follow in order to prioritize elements of the search process. Because the search for secondary data can range from very simple to highly complicated, a specific plan for a data search is necessary for each situation the researcher faces. Without any type of plan, the time and cost benefits typically associated with secondary data may not be realized.

Key Sources of External Secondary Data

The amount of secondary information is indeed vast. But the information needs of many researchers are connected by a common theme. Data most often sought by researchers includes demographic characteristics, employment, economic statistics, competitive and supply assessments, regulations, and international market characteristics. Exhibit 3.4 provides examples of specific variables within these categories.

Several key sources of secondary data enable the researcher to create a hierarchy of information sources to guide a secondary data search, regardless of the variables sought. Developing a hierarchy of secondary data sources is consistent with the second task of the GO-CART approach—initially look for as much information as can be obtained easily and quickly. Then work to tailor your data search to specific needs. Several broad to narrow data sources are described below to help guide the researcher through the jungle of secondary information.

eXHIBIT 3.4 Key Variables Sought in Secondary Data Search

Demographics
Population growth: actual and projected
Population density
In-migration and out-migration patterns
Population trends by age, race, and ethnic
background

Employment Characteristics
Labor force growth
Unemployment levels
Percentage of employment by occupation categories
Employment by industry

Economic Data
Personal income levels (per capita and median)
Type of manufacturing/service firms
Total housing starts
Building permits issued
Sales tax rates

Competitive Characteristics
Levels of retail and wholesale sales
Number and types of competing retailers
Availability of financial institutions

Supply Characteristics
Number of distribution facilities
Cost of deliveries
Level of rail, water, air, and road transportation

Regulations
Taxes
Licensing
Wages
Zoning

International Market Characteristics
Transportation and exporting requirements
Trade barriers
Business philosophies
Legal system
Social customs
Political climate
Cultural patterns
Religious and moral backgrounds

North American Industry Classification System (NAICS)

North American Industry Classification System (NAICS) codes Numerical industrial listings designed to promote uniformity in data reporting procedures for the U.S. government.

An initial step in any secondary data search is to use the numeric listings of the **North American Industry Classification System (NAICS) codes.** NAICS codes were designed to promote uniformity in data reporting by federal and state government sources and private business. The federal government assigns every industry an NAICS code. Businesses within each industry report all activities (sales, payrolls, taxation) according to their code. Currently, there are 99 two-digit industry codes representing everything from agricultural production of crops to environmental quality and housing. Within each two-digit industry classification code is a four-digit industry group code representing specific industry groups. All businesses in the industry represented by a given four-digit code report detailed information about the business to various sources for publication. For example, as shown in Exhibit 3.5, NAICS code 12 is assigned to coal mining and NAICS code 1221 specifies bituminous coal and lignite, surface extraction. It is at the four-digit level where the researcher will concentrate most data searches.

Government Documents

Detail, completeness, and consistency are major reasons for using U.S. government documents. More specifically, U.S. Bureau of the Census reports are the statistical foundation for most of the information available on U.S. population and economic activities. Exhibit 3.6 lists some of the common sources of secondary data available from

---

exHIBIT 3.5 Sample List of North American Industry Classification System Codes Numeric Listing

10—Metal Mining
1011   Iron Ores
1021   Copper Ores
1031   Lead & Zinc Ores
1041   Gold Ores
1044   Silver Ores
1061   Ferroalloy Ores Except Vanadium
1081   Metal Mining Services
1094   Uranium, Radium & Vanadium Ores
1099   Metal Ores Nec*

12—Coal Mining
1221   Bituminous Coal & Lignite—Surface
1222   Bituminous Coal—Underground
1231   Anthracite Mining
1241   Coal Mining Services

13—Oil & Gas Extraction
1311   Crude Petroleum & Natural Gas
1321   Natural Gas Liquids
1381   Drilling Oil & Gas Wells
1382   Oil & Gas Exploration Services
1389   Oil & Gas Field Services Nec*

14—Nonmetallic Minerals Except Fuels
1411   Dimension Stone
1422   Crushed & Broken Limestone
1423   Crushed & Broken Granite
1429   Crushed & Broken Stone Nec*
1442   Construction Sand & Gravel
1446   Industrial Sand

*Not elsewhere classified.

Source: Ward Business Directory of U.S. Private and Public Companies, 2003.

---

exHIBIT 3.6 Common Government Documents Used as Secondary Data Sources

U.S. Census Data
Census of Agriculture
Census of Construction
Census of Government
Census of Manufacturing
Census of Mineral Industries
Census of Retail Trade
Census of Service Industries
Census of Transportation
Census of Wholesale Trade
Census of Housing
Census of Population

U.S. Census Reports
Guide to Industrial Statistics
County and City Data Book
Statistical Abstract of the U.S.
Fact Finders for the Nation
Guide to Foreign Trade Statistics

U.S. Department of Commerce Data
U.S. Industrial Outlook
County Business Patterns
State and Metro Area Data Book
Business Statistics
Handbook of Cyclable Indicators
Monthly Labor Review
Measuring Markets: Federal and State Statistical Data

Additional Government Reports
Aging America: Trends and Population
Economic Indicators
Economic Report of the President
Federal Reserve Bulletin
Statistics of Income
Survey of Current Business

the U.S. government. These include specific census data (e.g., censuses of agriculture or construction), census reports (e.g., the *County and City Data Book*), U.S. Department of Commerce data, and a variety of additional government reports.

There are two notes of caution about census or other secondary data. First, census data is collected only every 10 years with slight periodic updates, so researchers always need to be aware of the timeliness issue of census data. Second, census data can be misleading. Not every person or household is reflected in census data. Those who have recently changed residences or were simply not available for contact at census time are not included in census data.

A final source of information available through the U.S. government is the *Catalog of Government Publications* compiled by Marcive, Inc. (www.marcive.com). This catalog indexes major market research reports for a variety of domestic and international industries, markets, and institutions. It also provides an index of publications available to researchers from July 1976 to the current month and year.

Secondary Sources of Business Information

It is virtually impossible to document all of the sources of secondary data available from businesses. Most sources are, however, classified by some index, directory, or standardized guidebook, so researchers should consult a directory of business information. Such directories identify statistical information, trade associations, trade journals, market characteristics, environmental trends, and so on.

The following are some commonly used sources of business information:

Business Organizations, Agencies, and Publications Directory

Directory of Corporate Affiliation

Fortune Magazine Directory

International Directory of Corporate Affiliations

Million Dollar Directory

F & S Index: Domestic, International, Europe

Standard and Poor's Registry of Corporations

Thomas' Register of American Manufacturers

Marketing Economics Guide

Business Index

Business Periodical Index

A key source of business information is the ABI Inform Database (www.cas.org). This database is available both online and on CD-ROM. It provides indexes and abstracts of business periodicals relating to a broad range of business topics. Electronic access to most business articles is also available. Gathering market information through business sources, in most cases, will lead the researcher to three widely used sources of data: *Sales and Marketing Management's Survey of Buying Power, Editors and Publishers Market Guide,* and *Source Book of Demographics and Buying Power for Every Zip Code in the U.S.A.* As illustrated in the Closer Look at Research box, a variety of secondary data is based on selected business sources.

A Closer Look at Research

Secondary Data and the CRM Process: Placing a Value on Customer Information

Organizations are now treating secondary data as a valuable balance sheet asset. Industry leaders in the CRM process are placing a clear value on customer information in order to size, rank, and cost overall CRM investment. Companies that do not articulate a clear business rationale—based on customer information, revenue sources, and exit barrier considerations—for CRM applications and integration priorities are wasting their significant investment.

In the Field

In directing their CRM investment, catalog retailers such as Lands' End, Fingerhut, and JC Penney use vast amounts of secondary data to calculate the lifetime value of customers. Knowing, for example, that a specific type of customer will likely buy $900 in merchandise over 10 transactions allows these companies to place a clear value on that relationship and budget for CRM programs that will retain or enhance customer relationship value by building exit barriers and cross-selling campaigns. Analytical applications that improve data quality, such as data warehousing and data mining, are of course critical components of the process.

Sales and Marketing Management's Survey of Buying Power

A popular source of information on area buying power is *Sales and Marketing Management's Survey of Buying Power* (www.salesandmarketing.com). Published annually, the survey covers all metropolitan statistical areas (MSA), counties, cities, and states in the United States. It provides data on retail sales by merchandise categories, total retail sales by area, population projections, and effective buying income. Exhibit 3.7 shows typical data from the survey for aspects relating to the Leavenworth County, Kansas, market.[5]

Among the most useful data the survey provides are estimates of an area's effective buying income. **Effective buying income (EBI)** is a measure of personal income (wages, salaries, interest, dividends, and profits) less federal, state, and local taxes.[6] It is expressed as a total dollar amount.

When combined with retail sales and population size, the EBI is an overall indicator of an area's buying power, known as the **buying power index (BPI).** The BPI is expressed as a percentage of total U.S. sales. The higher the BPI, the greater the ability of the market area to generate spendable income. For example, in Exhibit 3.7 the BPI for the Kansas City Metro Area (.6977) is greater than those of the city of Leavenworth (.0130) and Leavenworth County (.0194), which indicates that Kansas City has a greater market potential for a variety of new product purchases.

The BPI actually is a weighted average of the population, retail sales, and effective buying income of an area. Each of these criteria is assigned a weight based on its importance to the study at hand. For example, if population is the most important variable, it should receive the highest weight. Using weights of 5, 3, and 2, the buying power index can be calculated as follows:

$$\text{BPI} = \frac{(\text{Population} \times 5) + (\text{Retail sales} \times 3) + (\text{Effective buying income} \times 2)}{10 \ (\text{Sum of the weights})}$$

Effective buying income (EBI) A measure of personal income less federal, state, and local taxes.

Buying power index (BPI) A weighted average of population, retail sales, and effective buying income of an area.

EXHIBIT 3.7   Example of Effective Buying Income for Leavenworth County, Kansas

Retail Sales by Store Group ($000)

	Total Retail Sales	Food & Beverage Stores	Food Serv. & Drinking Estab.	General Merch.	Furnit. & Home Furnish. and Electron. & Appliances	Motor Veh. & Parts Dealers
Leavenworth County						
2003	433,208	92,015	38,085	69,750	5,255	80,223
2002	445,399	94,876	35,879	59,742	4,675	91,140
1994	222,635	69,517	*	52,377	*	52,377
1990	148,535	48.482	*	31,004	*	31,004
City of Leavenworth						
2003	287,915	62,712	24,883	62,579	4,369	60,465
2002	307,970	65,396	25,071	53,573	3,838	65,069
Kansas City Metro Area						
2003	28,026,033	2,885,541	2,465,865	4,718,260	1,708,655	6,808,595
2002	27,294,827	3,192,895	2,329,156	3,897,668	1,589,420	7,171,291

Effective Buying Income

	Total EBI*	Median Hsld EBI	% of Households by EBI Group			Buying Power Index**
			$20,000–$34,999	$35,000–$49,999	$50,000 & Over	
Leavenworth County						
2003	1,176.798	44,493	22.1	21.5	41.7	0.0194
2002	1,110,616	43,220	23.0	22.2	39.4	0.0190
City of Leavenworth						
2003	524,533	37,474	26.8	20.9	33.0	0.0130
2002	515,754	38,199	26.6	22.5	32.5	0.0099
Kansas City Metro Area						
2003	37,032,035	42,308	22.7	20.4	39.4	0.6977
2002	36,642,397	42,221	22.8	20.5	39.2	0.6965

Population

	Total Population (000s)	% of Population by Age Group				Households (000s)
		18–24	25–34	35–49	50+	
Leavenworth County						
2003	70.5	9.1	12.5	26.3	26.5	24.0
2002	69.0	8.5	13.4	26.3	24.8	23.3
City of Leavenworth						
2003	35.3	8.9	14.3	25.9	23.7	12.1
2002	35.3	9.2	15.3	25.2	22.4	12.0
Kansas City Metro Area						
2003	1,821.2	8.8	13.5	23.9	27.7	715.5
2002	1,798.5	8.7	14.1	24.1	26.7	704.9

continued

| ⊖XHIBIT | **3.7** | **Example of Effective Buying Income for Leavenworth County, Kansas**, *continued* |

5-Year Projections		
Population		
	Leavenworth County	**Kansas City**
1/1/03 Total Population (000s)	70.5	1,821.2
1/1/08 Total Population (000s)	73.3	1,895.5
% Change 2003–2008	4.0	4.1
1/1/08 Total Households (000s)	25.5	751.1
% Change 2003–2008	6.3	5.0
Effective Buying Income		
	Leavenworth County	**Kansas City**
2008 Total EBI ($000)	1,452,645	44,804,006
% Change 2003–2008	23.4	21.0
Average Household EBI ($)		
2003	49,033	51,757
2008	56,966	59,651
Retail Sales		
	Leavenworth County	**Kansas City**
2008 Total Retail Sales ($000)	469,772	34,050,163
% Change 2003–2008	8.4	21.5
Retail Sales per Household ($)		
2003	18,050	39,170
2008	18,422	45,334
Buying Power Index		
	Leavenworth County	**Kansas City**
2003	0.0194	0.2342
2008	0.0193	0.2541

*Not available

Effective buying income (EBI)* is a measurement of disposable income, and the buying power index (BPI)**, for which the *Survey* is best known, is a unique measure of spending power that takes population, EBI, and retail sales into account to determine a market's ability to buy. The higher the index, the better.

A major drawback of the BPI is that it is useful only for estimating the potential for general merchandise categories sold at median prices. For specialized merchandise, such as men's shoes, a customized BPI must be constructed.

Editors and Publishers Market Guide

An additional source of secondary information on buying potential is the *Editors and Publishers Market Guide.* This guide provides much the same information as the *Survey of Buying Power,* plus some unique city-by-city variables useful in making comparisons. The guide includes information on infrastructure, transportation, principal industries, banks, and retail outlets. The data provides a detailed profile of economic activity within a given geographic area and is used for comparison purposes when selecting markets for new stores or product introductions. For more information on this guide go to their Web site: http://www.editorandpublisher.com/eandp/resources/market_guide.jsp.

Source Book of Demographics and Buying Power for Every Zip Code in the U.S.A.

This source book provides information on population, socioeconomic characteristics, buying power, and other demographic characteristics for zip code areas across the United States. Each zip code area is analyzed relative to its consumption potential across a variety of product categories, and a purchasing potential index is calculated. The index is based on a national average score of 100.[7] For example, if zip code 55959 generates a score of 110 for furniture consumption, then that zip code area has a 10 percent greater potential to purchase furniture than the U.S. average.

Statistical Sources of Information

Statistical sources of secondary data can lead the researcher to specific statistical publications or can provide actual reprints of data extracted from numerous other secondary data sources. If actual data are located in the sourcebook, rather than in indexed references, these sources can save considerable research time. The following are examples of statistical data sources:

Merchandising: "Statistical and Marketing Report"

Standard and Poor's Industrial Surveys

Data Sources for Business and Market Analysis

American Statistics Index

Statistical Reference Index

Federal Statistical Directory

Commercial Publications and Newspapers

Newspapers and commercial publications (*Time, Newsweek, BusinessWeek, Forbes, Fortune*) are important sources of secondary information. Because these publications are circulated on a daily, weekly, or monthly basis, the information they contain is very recent. In addition, many publications are archived in some manner, allowing the researcher access to historical information. The problem with commercial publications and newspapers is volume. There are probably more than 1,000 business-related commercial publications available. Many of these publications, especially newspapers, are not indexed in traditional reference books. Those that do provide indexing are usually associated with major metropolitan markets. For example, the following newspapers are indexed from 1979 to the present:

The New York Times

The Wall Street Journal

Christian Science Monitor

Los Angeles Times

Chicago Tribune

Boston Globe

Atlanta Constitution

The *Business Periodical Index* is the primary index for commercial publications.

Syndicated Sources of Secondary Data

A major trend in marketing research is toward a greater dependency on syndicated (or commercial) data sources. The rationale for this is quite simple. Companies can obtain substantial information from a variety of industries at a relatively low cost. Also, because most of the data contained in these sources was collected at the point of purchase, the information represents actual purchase behavior rather than purchase intentions.

The Society of Competitive Intelligence Professionals reports that over 80 percent of marketing research firms purchase and use secondary research reports from commercial vendors. In addition, firms spend more than $15,000 annually for syndicated reports and devote at least 10 hours per week to analyzing the data.[8] Indeed, syndicated reports available online are rapidly replacing traditional paper-based sources.

Characteristics of Syndicated Data Sources

Syndicated (or commercial) data Data that have been compiled according to some standardized procedure; provides customized data for companies, such as market share, ad effectiveness, and sales tracking.

Syndicated (or commercial) data normally consist of data that have been collected and compiled according to some standardized procedure. In most cases these data are collected for a particular business or company, with a specific reason or purpose motivating the data collection procedure. This information is then sold to different client companies in the form of tabulated results or reports prepared specifically for a client's research needs. Commonly, these reports are personalized and tailored to the client by reporting units. For example, reports can be organized by geographic region, sales territory, market segment, product class, or brand. In order for these data sources to be effective, suppliers of commercial/syndicated data must have in-depth knowledge of the industry and generate timely data. Suppliers have traditionally employed one of two methods of data collection: consumer panels and store audits. A third method that is gaining ground—optical-scanner technology—will be discussed in a later chapter.

Consumer Panels

Consumer panels Large samples of households that provide specific, detailed data for an extended period of time.

Consumer panels consist of large samples of households that have agreed to provide specific, detailed data for an extended period of time. Data provided by these panels usually consist of product purchase information or media habits. Information typically is reported on the consumer package goods industry. But gradually this information is being replaced by optical-scanner generated information.

Panels typically are designed and developed by marketing research firms. Panels use a rigorous data collection approach. Panel respondents are required to record detailed behaviors at the time of occurrence on a highly structured questionnaire. The questionnaire contains a large number of questions related directly to actual product purchases or media exposure. This is usually an ongoing procedure whereby respondents report data back to the company on a weekly or monthly basis.

Panel data are then sold to a variety of clients after being personalized and tailored to the client's research needs. A variety of benefits are associated with panel data. These include (1) lower cost than primary data collection methods; (2) rapid availability and timeliness; (3) accurate reporting of socially sensitive expenditures (i.e., products may include beer, liquor, cigarettes, generic brands); and (4) high level of specificity (i.e., data pertain to actual products purchased or media habits, not merely intentions or propensities to purchase). When selecting a consumer panel data source, researchers should consider a number of issues. Inherent problems with these sources include reporting errors by respondents, inability to answer ambiguous questions, and forgetting brand names or product characteristics. More specifically, consumer panels tend to suffer from three primary weaknesses:

1. **Sampling error.** Most consumer panels underrepresent minorities. In fact, many panels report a sampling distribution that is highly skewed to white, middle-class respondents.

2. **Turnover.** No one panel member is obligated to stay on the panel for the entire duration. Many members leave the panel, have other family members perform the response activities, or simply don't respond at all. This feature seriously jeopardizes the representativeness and internal validity of the data.

3. **Response bias.** Many panel respondents have a tendency to answer questions in a socially desirable manner, knowing their purchases are being scrutinized. Leaving certain questions blank and recording wrong answers can lead to high levels of response bias among the panel data.

There are two types of panel-based data sources: those reflecting actual purchases of products and services and those reflecting media habits. The discussion below provides some examples of both types.

Examples of Consumer Panel Data Sources.
A variety of companies offer panel-based purchasing data. Two of the largest companies are National Family Opinion (NFO) and the NPD Group (www.npd.com). NPD collects continuous data from a national sample consisting of approximately 15,000 members. Data collection centers on consumer attitudes and awareness of such products as toys, apparel, textiles, sporting goods, athletic footwear, automotive products, home electronics, and cameras.[9]

Three of NPD's most commonly used data sources are the Consumer Report on Eating Share Trends (CREST), National Eating Trends (NET), and a service that provides data on the food service industry in general. CREST is based on over 14,000 households that report data on restaurant habits. NET provides continuous tracking of in-home food and beverage consumption patterns. ISL, a Canadian subsidiary of the NPD Group, provides similar purchase data through the Consumer Panel of Canada.

National Family Opinion (NFO) maintains a consumer panel of over 450,000 households to conduct product tests; concept tests; and attitude, awareness, and brand-usage studies. In connection with the panel, NFO offers a proprietary software program called Smart-System. This system enables clients to access and analyze complex information quickly, with easy cross-referencing on major data variables. In addition, NFO maintains highly targeted panels referred to as the Hispanic Panel, the Baby Panel, the Mover Panel, and SIP (Share of Intake Panel on Beverage Consumption).

The following list describes additional companies and the consumer panels they maintain:

- Market Facts, Inc., provides panel data for forecasting models, brand equity/loyalty models, and brand tracking information.

- The Bases Group specializes in new-product planning, evaluation, and forecasting using consumer panels and simulated test markets.

- J. D. Power and Associates maintains a consumer panel of car and light-truck owners to provide data on product quality, satisfaction, and vehicle dependability.

- Roper Starch Worldwide provides data on consumption patterns for the 6- to 18-year-old age market.

- Creative and Response Research Services has a consumer panel called Kidspeak that provides advertising and brand tracking among children.

- Chilton Research Services conducts highly specialized research for the automotive, financial, and health care industries.

- Yankelovich Partners, Inc., has the Yankelovich monitor system that tracks values in the United States.

Examples of Media Panel Data Sources. Media panels and consumer panels are similar in procedure, panel composition, and design. They differ only in that media panels primarily measure media consumption habits as opposed to product or brand consumption. As with consumer panels, a multitude of media panels exist. This section provides examples of the more commonly used syndicated media panel data sources.

Nielsen Media Research is by far the most widely known and accepted source of media panel data. The flagship service of Nielsen is the National Television Index (NIT). Based on a 5,000-household sample, the NIT provides an estimation of national television audiences measuring "ratings" and "share." Ratings refer to the percentage of households that have at least one television set tuned to a program for at least 6 of every 15 minutes a program is aired. Share constitutes the percentage of households that have a television tuned to one specific program at one specific time.[10] Data are collected on television, cable, and home video viewing habits through an electronic device, called a people meter, connected to a television set. The people meter continuously monitors and records when a television set is turned on, what channels are being viewed, how much time is spent on each channel, and who is watching. The data are communicated back to the central computer by telephone.

The primary purpose of the NIT data is to assist media planners in determining audience volume, demographics, and viewing habits. This information is then used to calculate media efficiency measured as cost per thousand (CPM); that is, how much it costs to reach 1,000 viewers. CPM measures a program's ability to deliver the largest target audience at the lowest cost.

While most data are collected by the people meter, Nielsen still maintains diary panels in 211 local markets measuring the same media habits. In addition, Nielsen also operates an 800-household sample of Hispanic TV viewers designed to measure Spanish-language media usage in the United States.

Arbitron Inc. is primarily a media research firm that conducts ongoing data collection for electronic media. Arbitron is organized into five media research business units.[11] Arbitron Radio provides radio audience data for more than 250 local market areas. Utilizing a 2 million-plus customer panel, Arbitron Radio collects over 1 million weekly listening diaries that are the basis of Arbitron Radio's station rating reports. The data are used primarily by media planners, advertising agencies, and advertisers. Arbitron also sells syndicated data on local media, consumer listening habits, and retail advertising impact data across 58 of the major U.S. markets. Currently, 600 newspapers, radio stations, television stations, and cable systems are predominant users of this syndicated data source.

The following list describes media panels maintained by other companies:

- Local Motion Retail Ratings provides syndicated data on TV, radio, and cable systems. Data collection is a combination of media diary panels and telephone panels collected in 11 market areas across the United States.

- Arbitron Newmedia provides syndicated data on emerging market segments regarding electronic media usage, including interactive TV, online services, interactive cable systems, and direct broadcast satellites.

- Media Marketing Technologies, owned by Arbitron, has a database known as Mediamaps. Based on a media diary panel of 100,000 listeners, Mediamaps profiles prospective radio station listeners using geodemographic mapping.

- Macro International, Inc., has four syndicated data sources developed on a consumer media/purchase panel of more than 100,000 respondents. Europinion is a database that provides quarterly reports on consumption attitudes and behaviors in Eastern European countries.

- Simmons Marketing Research Bureau (SMRB) Group, Ltd., publishes an Annual Report on Media and Markets. Simmons also sells syndicated reports tailored to teenage, child, and Hispanic markets.

- ASI Marketing Research, Inc., maintains two advertising copy syndicated data sources. Targeted Copy Testing (TCT) measures advertising recall and copy effectiveness. Kid Copy Testing (KCT) uses touch-screen, multimedia, digital voice technology to capture moment-by-moment response measures on the creative content of advertising directed to children 6 to 11 years of age.

Store Audits

Store audits Formal examination and verification of how much of a particular product or brand has been sold at the retail level.

Store audits consist of formal examination and verification of how much of a particular product or brand has been sold at the retail level. Based on a collection of participating retailers (typically discount, supermarket, and drugstore retailers), audits are performed on product or brand movement in return for detailed activity reports and cash compensation to the retailer. The audits then operate as a secondary data source. Clients can acquire the data relative to industry, competition, product, or specific brand. Store audits provide two unique benefits: precision and timeliness. Many of the biases of consumer panels are not found in store audits. By design, store audits measure product and brand movement directly at the point of sale (usually at the retail level). Also, sales and competitive activities are reported when the audit is completed, making the data timely and readily available to potential users.

An inherent problem of the traditional store audit is representativeness. In most audit situations only 75 to 85 percent of retail stores are included.[12] Rarely can an audit be performed at all stores in any given area. Therefore, what is reported can be somewhat misleading. Areas in which product sales are extremely high or low may be ignored for the audit process. While this may not affect inferences regarding national sales averages, it can distort sales figures at the regional or local level. Despite this inherent problem, store audits provide much valuable data.

Data Gathering in the Store Audit. Key variables being measured in the store audit typically include beginning and ending inventory levels, sales receipts, price levels, price inducements, local advertising, and point-of-purchase (POP) displays. Collectively, these data allow users of store audit services to generate information on the following factors:

1. Product/brand sales in relation to competition.

2. Direct sales and inventory levels at retail.

3. Effectiveness of shelf space and POP displays.

4. Sales at various price points and levels.

5. Effectiveness of in-store promotions and point-of-sale coupons.

6. Competitive marketing practices.

7. Direct sales by store type, product location, territory, and region.

Two of the major providers of in-store audit services are AC Nielsen (Nielsen Retail Index) and Information Resources (Infoscan). Collectively, these two organizations conduct over 150,000 store audits in more than 40,000 separate retail locations. The Nielsen Retail Index provides information on a wide range of causal marketing factors that affect consumer responses to grocery, health and beauty, drug, and beverage products. Nielsen audits are developed on a stratified sampling procedure of store size, type, population, and geographic location. Actual stores used in the audit are randomly selected from designated strata. Audits typically are performed on a monthly basis at the point-of-sale level.

Infoscan provides census-based information rather than information based on a sample of representative stores. Through the Infoscan census, all stores within a particular retail chain (e.g., Wal-Mart, Kroger, Target) are audited. Information from the audit is then compiled and disseminated to each store within the chain for store-level marketing applications. The data are also used within specific industries to develop customer response programs at the manufacturer or wholesale level.

A variety of smaller audit services exist, such as Audits and Surveys, Inc., which provides syndicated product movement data in the automotive, sporting goods, home improvement, and entertainment industries. Through the audit service called National Total Market, Audits and Surveys provides a retail census of distribution for any specific company (AutoZone, Hand City, etc.) and in-store data on shelf-space availability, brand-name sales, mystery-shopper programs, and in-store promotional impacts.

The Internet as a Growing Source of Secondary Data

The Internet has dramatically accelerated the speed at which anyone can obtain useful secondary information. Web sites describe products and services and provide information that can be used to evaluate corporate structure and marketing positioning strategies. Finding a company's Web page can be fairly easy when companies use their name as the URL. Many times, however, multiple companies have the same or a similar name, although operating in different industries. A solution to this problem is to search for competitive companies using "KnowThis" (www.knowthis.com). This is a specialty search engine for a virtual marketing library that contains Internet addresses for more than a million sites. An actual listing of these records in the library is displayed in Exhibit 3.8. Currently,

eXHIBIT 3.8 Example of Marketing Virtual Library

Knowledge source for market research, marketing plans, internet marketing, marketing careers & much more!

MarketingVirtualLibrary

Search

[ ] GO

Advanced Search

FEATURED SITE

MONTHLY   RETAIL TRADE SURVEY

Facts and figures from U.S. Census Bureau on retail sales including a report that examines online (e-commerce) retail sales.
SEE MORE LIKE THIS

Marketing News
Dead But Not Gone

About KnowThis
Media Requests

Member of the
World Wide Web
Virtual Library

Main Areas
Advertising
Careers & Jobs
Customer-Focused
Education
General Resources
Groups & Meetings
International
Internet Marketing
Legal
Market Research
Planning & Mgmt.
Publications
Retail & Consumer
Selling

ADVERTISING & PROMOTION

Advertising
Basics, Advertising Agencies, Ad Examples
Direct Mail & Direct Marketing
Basic Information, Mailing Lists, Contact Lists
Internet Advertising
Basics, Banner Ads, Rich Media, Ad Rates
Media Issues & Find Media Outlets
Find Media, Media Ratings, Research, Newspapers
Other Promotional Strategies
Sales Promotion & Others, Sponsorships, Events
Public Relations
Basics, How-to, Release Services & Wire Services

CAREERS & JOBS

Career Help
Marketing Careers, Job Hunting Advice
Marketing Jobs
Job Listings, Listing Services, Freelance Jobs

CUSTOMER-FOCUSED MARKETING

Customer-Facing Technologies
Call Centers, Kiosks, Sales Force Automation
Customer Relationship Management
Basics of CRM
Database & Target Marketing
Basics, Data Mining, Bus. Intelligence, Targeting
Personalization
Web Site Personalization & 1-to-1 Marketing
Referral & Word-of-Mouth Marketing
Grassroots Marketing, Viral Marketing

EDUCATION

Academic Research
Basics, Funding/Grants, Journals, Locations
Higher Education
Departments, Schools, Distance Education
Professionals
Professional Education & Training
Students
Competitions, Groups, Help, Internships
Teachers
Case Studies, Teaching Ideas

GENERAL RESOURCES

Basics, Principles & How-To's
Articles & Tutorials, History, Exhibits
Definitions & Terms
Web Dictionaries & Glossaries
Marketing, Business, Technology News
Current Marketing News, News Portals, Updates
Other Marketing Areas
Distribution & Purchasing, Pricing, Other Areas, Social Marketing & Ethics, Specific Industries

GROUPS & MEETINGS

Associations and Organizations
Academic, Professional, Others
Conferences, Meetings, Trade Shows
Academic, Meeting Locators
Online Discussion Groups, Forums
Marketing Groups, Group Locators

INTERNATIONAL MARKETING & TRADE

Doing Business & Managing
Culture, Trade/Import/Export, Portals
International Marketing
General, International Market Research

INTERNET MARKETING & E-BUSINESS

Definitions & Terms
Web Dictionaries & Glossaries
Electronic Commerce
General, Research, Smart Cards, Transactions
Internet Basics
Basics, Internet History
Internet Marketing & Strategies
Affiliate Programs, Email, Site Design, Strategies
Search Engine Marketing
Search Engine Rankings, Optimization

LEGAL ISSUES IN MARKETING

Basic Coverage
Marketing & Advertising, Internet & E-Commerce
Intellectual Property
Patents, Trademarks & Copyrights
Legal Assistance
Forms and Contracts

MARKET RESEARCH

Basics of Marketing Research
General Info, Research Design, Other MR
Company, Industry & Competitive Info.
Annual Reports, Competitive Intelligence, Corporate History, Company Rankings, Lists
Finding Companies & Information
Business Directories, Help Finding Information
US Government & Social Science Data
Gov't Reports, Demographic Data, Population Stats
Expert Sources
Find Experts, Ask Experts, Event Speakers
Internet Marketing Research
Domain Name Search/Info, Reports & Summaries,
Web Metrics & Stats, Other Reports & Stats
Market Research Firms
Find MR Firms, Leading MR Firm Sites
Market Research Reports
Sources for Research Reports
Online Searching
Databases, Search Help, Top Search Tools

MARKETING STRATEGY & MANAGEMENT

Marketing Strategy & Planning
Marketing Strategy, Writing a Marketing Plan
Product Management & Branding
Basic Information
Starting & Running a Business
Starting a Business, Running a Business

PUBLICATIONS, BOOKS & JOURNALS

Books & Textbooks
Online Texts, Textbook Publishers, Search Retailers
Directories
Academic, E-zines, Publishers, Trade
Leading Publication Sites
Academic, Print, Web-Only Publications & Journals

RETAILING, SHOPPING & CONSUMERS

Consumers
Consumer Behavior, Education, Protection
Online Shopping & Offline Shopping
Basics, Coupons, Help Shopping
Retailing
Brick-and-Mortar, Internet Retailing

SELLING & SALES MANAGEMENT

Personal Selling
General, Generate Sales Leads, Sales Presentations
Sales Management
Manufacturers' Reps, Sales Training
Sales Meetings

.com (commercial), .net (network providers), .edu (education), .gov (government), .org (noncommercial organizations), .mil (military), .us (United States), .nom (individual), .info (information provider), .arts (art related organizations) and .store (online store) URLs are provided. The Internet has many electronic discussion groups that include controversy, conflict, or rumors about competitors' products or services. "Hate Walmart" is one such group that allows customers to express their dissatisfaction with Wal-Mart operations. Two references for finding such discussion groups are www.reference.com and www. dejanews.com.

Company management, financial, and marketing information are necessary components for any business intelligence program (BIP) and most of the information can be found easily on the Internet. An excellent starting point is a specialty Web site known as "Corporate

---

ΘXHIBIT 3.9   **Selected Internet Information Sources**

Source	Description of Data	Web Address
International Business Research	Provides international business information and links to useful data sources	www.infotoday.com
BUSLIB-L	Collection of business research articles and e-mail discussion groups	www.montague.com
@BRINT	Guide to business research sites with editorial comments	www.brint.com
CI Resource Index	Listing of sites by category for finding competitive intelligence sources	www.ciseek.com
European Research Gateways	Stores 60,000 records of R&D projects currently in operation in Europe	www.cordis.lu/ergo/home
Intellifacts.com	230,000 company profiles and business locators	www.intellifact.com
International Business Resource	Vast directory of regional trade and trade-related statistics	www.globaledge.msu.edu
The Internet for Competitive Intelligence	Web resources for finding corporate and industry intelligence	www.freeprint.com
Internet Intelligence Index	600 intelligence-related sites	www.fuld.com
Powerize.com	Version of Hoover.com, contains over 32 million business filings	www.powerize.com
PR Webpress Database	Press releases of business and industry over the preceding 90 days	www.prweb.com
American Demographics/Marketing Tools	Searches the full text of *American Demographics* and *Marketing Tools*	www.marketingtools.com
EconData	An excellent site for researchers interested in economics and demographics	www.econdata.net
Harris Info Service	Provides business-to-business data on American manufacturers	www.harrisinfo.com
Nielsen Media Research	Data on media usage in United States	www.nielsenmedia.com
U.S. Census Bureau	Useful source for all census data	www.census.gov
World Opinion	Excellent site for the marketing research industry. Many research studies referenced here.	www.worldopinion.com
USA Data	Consumer lifestyle data on a local, regional and national basis	www.usadata.com

A Closer Look at Research

Computer Technology and Real-Time Data

As computer technology continues to change and more people become versed in Boolean search strategies for databases, the role of secondary research will continue to change. Secondary data researchers will become more involved with a company's internal technology department as

In the Field

they begin to tap into real-time inventory and client or production systems to add more customization of information to the secondary data that they find online. Try it for yourself. Go to the Internet and contact www.freeedgar.com. You will find hundreds of documents on U.S. companies that are not only updated daily but also highly customized from a secondary data perspective.

Information" (www.corporateinformation.com). This site contains links to public and private companies in more than 100 countries and recently added a search engine for accessing a database of 100,000 companies.

An additional use of the Internet is to track and monitor current alerts about competitors. Press releases and news stories contain a wealth of information about a competitor's services, products, and markets. Two valuable sources for this type of information are Excite's News-tracker Clipping Service (www.news.excite.com) and Company Sleuth (www.companysleuth.com).

Perhaps one of the greatest assets of the Internet is the various search engines. Sites such as AltaVista, Excite, Yahoo!, and Google are very popular with researchers looking for secondary information on the Internet. These organizations offer search engines that scan the Internet looking for information on a designated topic. Each search engine uses its own indexing system to locate relevant information. Google is by far the most popular search engine, but Microsoft is developing its own search engine and will launch it in the near future. Remember, the Internet has no restrictions on what is published there. Search engines yield files with a wide range of quality from a variety of searches. Try multiple sites when researching a particular topic.

There is no question the Internet has become a significant tool and in the future may be the only source needed to supply information for a BIP (Business Intelligence Program). Exhibit 3.9 provides additional sources of BIP information on the Internet. It's essential to proceed with caution, though, since the quality and reliability of Internet information—for that matter, any information—must be questioned and its quality and reliability confirmed.

The Future of Secondary Data Sources

This chapter has focused on traditional secondary data sources. But 90 percent of the information referenced here currently exists online. As the technology of information management becomes more acceptable and accessible, more and more secondary data will be available at the push of a computer key. This is already happening, and is more fully described in Chapter 5. More important, as communication technology begins to merge with computer technology (interactive television and shopping, two-way satellite communications, at-home on-demand shopping), the amount of secondary data is expected to mushroom. Although this increase may not be the purpose of the technology, it will be the result of the interaction process. More actual purchase information than ever before will become available in a timely and cost-efficient manner.

As more and more organizations begin to realize the full value of database development and information systems management, they will be able to customize secondary data sources (see the Closer Look at Research box).

marketing research in action

Continuing Case Study

Santa Fe Grill Anticipating Expansion

As you recall from Chapter 1, the Santa Fe Grill is a new restaurant concept that currently operates in Dallas, Texas. The owners of the restaurant, when developing their five-year plan, anticipated the opening of two additional locations within Texas, after five years of successful operation at the Dallas location. The owners were planning to expand to Houston and possibly San Antonio, Texas.

After revisiting the five-year plan, the owners have realized they lack data and information relevant to these two cities. In fact, the only information they have are the population size and growth of these two cities. Realizing this, they have decided to develop an area profile of Houston and San Antonio relative to the restaurant market.

Key secondary data must be collected. Population characteristics, economic conditions, competitive trends in the restaurant industry, and market factors appear to be the starting point of the secondary data search. The owners, realizing these factors may be too broad for facilitating an expansion decision, have requested the help of a local university marketing research class to conduct a secondary data search for specific information on Houston and San Antonio. At this point, the owners need your help in the secondary data search—designing the approach, deciding on types of data needed, collecting the data, and presenting conclusive evidence.

Hands-On Exercise

1. Develop a list of the specific variables that need to be examined regarding demographic characteristics, economic characteristics, competitive dimensions of the restaurant market, and other relevant customer data pertaining to Houston and San Antonio, Texas.

2. Based on the information in this chapter and what you've learned in the chapter, perform a secondary data search on all key variables you identified in your answer to question 1.

3. Develop a comparative profile of the two cities (Houston, San Antonio) based on your secondary data and provide the owners with a report showing evidence that one, both, or neither of the cities would be desirable for possible restaurant expansion.

Summary of Learning Objectives

■ **Understand how secondary data fit into the marketing research process.**

The task of a marketing researcher is to solve the problem in the shortest time, at the least cost, with the highest level of accuracy. Therefore, before any marketing research project is conducted, the researcher must seek out existing information that may facilitate a decision or outcome for a company. Existing data are commonly called secondary data.

■ **Explain how secondary data fit into the customer relationship management process.**

Secondary data frequently are considered the nucleus of the customer relationship management (CRM) process because of the vast amount of customer data that must be collected and stored on a historical basis. Customer knowledge information, or information volunteered by consumers, is often collected on an ongoing basis and consistently stored and monitored as part of CRM initiatives.

■ **Demonstrate how secondary data can be used in problem solving.**

If secondary data are to be used to assist the decision-making process or problem-solving ability of the manager, they need to be evaluated on six fundamental principles: (1) purpose (how relevant are the data to achieving the specific research objectives at hand?); (2) accuracy (are the data collected, measured, and reported in a manner consistent with quality research practices?); (3) consistency (do multiple sources of the data exist?); (4) credibility (how were the data obtained? what is the source of the data?); (5) methodology (will the methods used to collect the data produce high-quality data?); and (6) biases (was the data-reporting procedure tainted by some hidden agenda or underlying motivation to advance some public or private concern?).

■ **List sources of traditional internal secondary data.**

Internal secondary data are usually sorted into three categories. First are the internal accounting or financial records of the company. These typically consist of sales invoices, accounts receivable reports, and quarterly sales reports. Other forms of internal data include past marketing research studies, customer credit applications, warranty cards, and employee exit interviews.

■ **Know how to use and extract external secondary data.**

Because of the volume of external data available, researchers need to ensure that the right data are located and extracted. A simple guideline to follow is called the GO-CART approach: define *goals* the secondary data need to achieve; specify *objectives* behind the secondary search process; define specific *characteristics* of data that are to be extracted; document all *activities* necessary to find, locate, and extract the data sources; focus on *reliable* sources of data; and *tabulate* all the data extracted.

■ **Identify sources of external secondary data.**

External secondary data can be obtained from a wide variety of sources. The most common forms of external data are North American Industry Classification System (NAICS) codes, government documents (which include census reports), business directories, trade journals, statistical sources, commercial publications, and newspapers.

■ **Understand the availability and use of syndicated sources of secondary data.**

Syndicated (or commercial) data sources consist of data that have been systematically collected and compiled according to some standardized procedure. Suppliers of syndicated data have traditionally used one of two approaches in collecting data: consumer panels and store audits. (A third approach, optical-scanner technology, will be discussed in a later chapter.) With most syndicated data sources, the objective is quite clear: to measure point-of-sale purchase behaviors or to measure media habits.

■ **Understand the changing focus of secondary data usage.**

The computerization of secondary data is revolutionizing the marketing research industry as is the Internet. Online services are making more data available that are more applicable to business needs than ever before. In addition, databases and information systems are bringing the use of secondary data to monumental proportions. Technology will make secondary data more customized and applicable for many businesses.

Key Terms and Concepts

Buying power index (BPI) 92

Consumer panels 96

Customer knowledge information 80

Effective buying income (EBI) 92

External secondary data 80

Internal secondary data 80

North American Industry Classification System (NAICS) codes 89

Secondary data 80

Store audits 99

Syndicated (or commercial) data 96

Review Questions

1. What characteristic separates secondary data from primary data? What are three sources of secondary data?

2. Explain why a company should use all potential sources of secondary data before initiating primary data collection procedures.

3. List the six fundamental principles used to assess the validity of secondary data.

4. List the three methods of data collection typically used by the suppliers of commercial data sources, and discuss the advantages and disadvantages associated with each.

5. How can information from a sales activity report be used to improve a company's marketing research efforts?

6. Briefly discuss the GO-CART approach of secondary data search management.

7. How is the Internet changing the nature and use of secondary data?

8. Describe the value of *Sales and Marketing Management*'s *Survey of Buying Power* as a source of secondary data.

Discussion Questions

1. **EXPERIENCE THE INTERNET.** Go online to your favorite browser (e.g., Netscape) and find the home page for your particular state. For example, www.mississippi.com would get you to the home page for the state of Mississippi. Once there, seek out the category that gives you information on county and local statistics. Select the county where you reside and obtain the vital demographic and socioeconomic data available. Provide a demographic profile of the residents in your community.

2. **EXPERIENCE THE INTERNET.** Go to the home page of the U.S. census, www.census.gov. Select the category Current Economic Indicators and browse the data provided.

3. What specific industry information could executives at Procter & Gamble obtain from the *Source Book of Demographics and Buying Power for Every Zip Code in the U.S.A.?* How would this information improve Procter & Gamble's marketing strategies?

4. You are planning to open a coffee shop in one of two areas in your local community. Conduct a secondary data search on key variables that would allow you to make a logical decision on which area is best suited for your proposed coffee shop.

5. Using the data you collected in the MRIA exercise in this chapter, should the Santa Fe Grill open restaurants in other markets?

6. What is the value of panel data in making marketing research decisions?

part 2

Technology in the Research Process

chapter 4

Customer Relationship Management and the Marketing Research Process

Learning Objectives

After reading this chapter, you will be able to

1. Understand the essential elements that make up a customer relationship management program.

2. Describe the relationship that exists between marketing research and customer relationship management.

3. Understand the meaning of market intelligence.

4. Illustrate the process of data collection for a customer relationship management program.

5. Illustrate and define a marketing research database.

6. Illustrate the development and purpose of the data warehouse.

7. Explain the process of data mining as it relates to the data warehouse.

8. Understand the role of modeling in database analysis.

Customer Relationship Management Allows Continental Airlines to Survive

Wouldn't it be nice if just once, one of those surly airline employees offered a sincere and unequivocal apology for losing your luggage or for a delayed flight? If you fly first class with Continental Airlines, you may finally get that apology.

The Houston-based carrier has been enhancing in-flight reports it provides to flight attendants just before takeoff with more detailed information on passengers. For example, in addition to indicating passengers that have ordered special meals, the expanded reports flag the airline's high-value customers and detail such things as whether they've had their luggage lost in the recent past or experienced a delayed flight. Armed with this information, flight attendants can now approach these customers during the flight to apologize for the inconveniences. Such high-touch, personalized service increases customer loyalty, particularly among Continental's most valuable patrons, and that loyalty in turn drives revenue. Continental breaks customers into different levels of profitability: Since building its new system, the

airline reports earning an average of $200 in revenue on each of its 400,000 valuable customers, and an additional $800 in revenue from each of the 35,000 customers it places in its most profitable tier—all because it accords them better service.

Continental's desire to improve its ranking in a competitive industry drove it to build a real-time data warehouse. When the data warehouse was first being developed its initial purpose was to bring data from some 27 systems together so that the company could more accurately forecast revenue. Since then, the company has used it to determine if customer loyalty initiatives really affect revenue. By testing a sample of 30,000 customers who experienced delays, Continental found that those individuals to whom the airline sent a letter of apology and some sort of compensation (either in the form of a free cocktail on their next flight or extra frequent flier miles) forgot the event and didn't hold a grudge. In fact, Continental says that revenue from those passengers who received letters jumped 8 percent.

Using operational and customer data in the data warehouse, the data warehousing team developed a solution to one of the biggest headaches gate agents face: accommodating passengers inconvenienced by a cancellation or delay. The team created a program that automates the rebooking process. Before the program was developed, gate agents had to figure out on their own how to reroute passengers. Now, when a cancellation or delay occurs, the system does the work for them. For example, when the system identifies a high-value customer whose flight has been cancelled, the gate agent may decide to put that traveler on a competitor's flight just to make the individual happy and to get him on his way as fast as possible.

Currently, Continental is trying to use customer and operational data in the data warehouse to come up with a way for flight attendants to get information about baggage that's been mislaid and to inform passengers while they're still on the plane that their luggage has gone astray. The airline thinks being proactive will mitigate passengers' annoyance over their bags being lost. If flight attendants have a way to tell individuals not to bother going to baggage claim and to take the address so they can send the suitcase when it arrives, the airline will save that person the time and frustration associated with filing a claim for lost luggage.

"Before the data warehouse, the person who yelled the loudest got the best service. Now our most valuable customers get the best service," says Alicia Acebo, Continental's data warehousing director. That strategy is helping the company narrow its losses during a period of great instability in the airline industry.[2]

Value of Customer Relationship Management

Customer relationship management (CRM)
Management of customer relationships based on the integration of customer information throughout the business enterprise in order to achieve maximum customer satisfaction and retention.

Customer relationship management (CRM) is neither a concept nor a project. Instead, it's a business strategy that aims to understand, anticipate, and manage the needs of an organization's current and potential customers. As illustrated in the opening example of Continental Airlines, CRM is a combination of strategic, process, organizational, and technological change, whereby a company seeks to better manage its own enterprise around customer information. Acquiring and deploying knowledge about customers and using this information across all areas of the business is the focus of CRM. The outcomes are high customer knowledge, increased revenues and profits, increased service quality, and maximum customer satisfaction.

Recently, Allied Medical Corporation, a medical service provider, faced some interesting challenges similar to those many other businesses face. The company lacked a customer-driven information focus. It failed to respond to the rapidly changing and evolving customer. Its technology infrastructure was insufficient to support information for customer decisions. As a result, customers and the agents who sold the company's services were defecting, customer retention rates were falling, and operating costs were escalating. There was an immediate need to establish a customer relationship management strategy, to ensure the culture would take hold, and to translate it into changed behaviors. What Allied Medical Corp. had previously failed to recognize was the following:

1. There is a strong correlation between customer satisfaction and customer retention. Recent studies indicate that 95 percent of customers who rate service as "excellent" will repurchase from an organization and are "highly unlikely" to switch to another product or service provider.

2. For every 100 dissatisfied customers more than half will defect from the company if not given the proper opportunity to complain about the product or their service encounter. Moreover, information generated from complaint behavior is a key data ingredient for a CRM strategy.

3. The focus on "making and selling" will not work in today's competitive environment. Knowing your customer and increasing value-added components to the customer is a key dimension to profitability. Business and market intelligence tools are key to obtaining information from customers and understanding customer behaviors.

Learning these truths, Allied Medical Corp. adopted a CRM strategy to improve revenues through increased customer satisfaction and retention by better collection and dissemination of customer information throughout the organization. This new focus led the organization to implement a total CRM approach, including all facets of the business as well as suppliers and retailers.[3]

Essentials of Customer Relationship Management

Enterprise The total business unit, including all facets of the business as well as suppliers and retailers.

Customer relationship management has many names. Some call it customer management; others refer to it as customer value management, customer-centricity, or customer-centric management. Regardless of the term used, customer relationship management (CRM) is the management of customer relationships based on the integration of customer information throughout the business **enterprise** (all facets of the business, including suppliers and retailers) to achieve maximum customer satisfaction and retention.

Businesses often must respond to rapidly changing environments. Environmental change has been a business focus for decades. Now, a well-established newcomer is changing the traditional business environment even more: the Internet and electronic commerce are the new players disrupting the business environment. Travelocity in the travel industry, Autobytel in auto retailing, and eBay in auctions are new entrants that are invading old industries. Even more critical is the development of entirely new businesses, for instance, Mannesmann (www.mannesmann.com) and Lending Tree (www.lendingtree.com). Given these changes, businesses have rediscovered that, more than ever, in the face of increased competition, mature markets, and ever-demanding customers, treating existing customers well is the best source of profitability and sustained growth. In short, the focus is on retaining and growing the best customers. Keeping customers is a lot cheaper than trying to attract new ones—by a ratio of one to five in sales and marketing expenditures.

CRM is the implementation process for relationship marketing. In the past few years businesses have been transformed: where they once sold products or services on a transaction basis and behaved as if they were constantly in a customer acquisition mode, they now strive to retain customers. Today, businesses are "enterprises" and are driving toward establishing a dialogue with customers, understanding and anticipating customer change, and attempting to maximize the lifetime value of the customer. Exhibit 4.1 provides an overview of the CRM process.

Customer interaction The relationship between the enterprise and the customer.

CRM is the way the small corner grocer used to treat customers—on a one-to-one basis. CRM now attempts to do this on an "institutionalized" basis for millions of customers. CRM focuses on one customer at a time, but for millions of customers. To accomplish such a task, CRM operates on a simple yet often misunderstood concept—customer interaction. In a CRM context, **customer interaction** is the relationship between two parties—the enterprise and the customer. However, being a virtual entity, the enterprise does not have relationships per se because there is no one person in the enterprise that a customer can develop a relationship with. Therefore, the relationship is based on the perception the customer has of the enterprise. This perception is the end result of

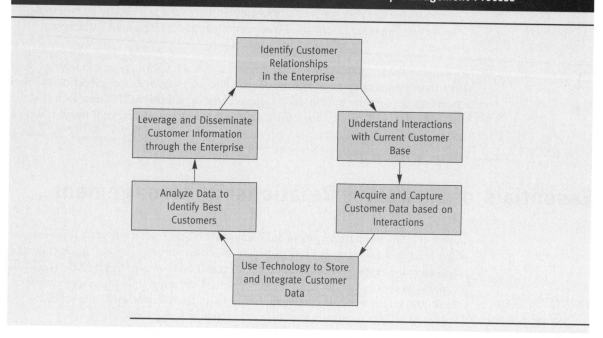

EXHIBIT 4.1   A Flow Model of the Customer Relationship Management Process

the interactions the customer has with the enterprise, directly or indirectly. These can be either internal, through customers' interactions with different parts of the enterprise (distributors, sales, customer service), using different communication channels (face-to-face, telephone, e-mail, Web sites), or external (via advertising campaigns, direct mail, surveys). CRM becomes the management of the capability to interact with the customer such that every interaction is positive and reinforces the relationship; and, more important, every interaction becomes a stored and usable information source for the CRM program. In short, the interaction becomes the major data collection method for customer relationship management.

Storage and use of customer interaction information are critical components of the CRM program. This information becomes what is known in CRM as customer knowledge. **Customer knowledge** is the customer interaction information used to create customer profiles to tailor interactions, segment customers for appropriate products and services, and build stronger relationships. Marketing research becomes the tool for collecting, storing, and analyzing customer interaction information. Coca-Cola, Wal-Mart, Nike, Dell and most all other companies collect and maintain knowledge about their customers' needs and buying patterns.

CRM begins with the enterprise determining the types of relationships it has with its customers. Next, the enterprise interacts with the customer base to acquire and capture customer information. Technology is used to support the CRM process by storing and integrating the customer data. Information on customers is then analyzed to determine the best customer segments based on profitability. Once analyzed, information is disseminated throughout the enterprise for all business units to use when contacting

Customer knowledge
The collection of customer interaction information used to create customer profiles that can be used to tailor interactions, segment customers, and build strong customer relationships.

customers. The objective is to build stronger relationships with profitable customers for maximum customer retention and growth. This chapter is organized around these critical CRM topics.

Marketing Research and Customer Relationship Management

Market intelligence
The use of real-time customer information (customer knowledge) to achieve a competitive advantage.

A primary function of marketing research in the CRM process is to collect, store, and analyze customer interaction information (customer knowledge). In doing so, marketing research takes on a new role that is unique to the CRM environment. This role is to transform the practice of marketing research into one of **market intelligence.** The approach goes beyond the traditional market research practice of data gathering to one where data acquisition is strategic and transactional in focus. In short, market intelligence is based on real-time customer information.

Market intelligence begins with the notion of customer knowledge, which is the necessary starting point for any CRM process. An enterprise cannot meet its customers' needs and wants, and thereby offer value, unless it understands clearly the evolution and change of the customer. In a CRM environment a major use of customer knowledge is to assess profitability and provide increased value to targeted customer segments. Therefore, from a marketing research perspective, the major questions to answer in the CRM process are:

1. What kind of relationship will add value to the enterprise's customers (loyalty programs, preferred customer status, etc.)?

2. What is the value perception of the customer segment, and how can the value be enhanced (direct communication to customers, new services, etc.)?

3. What products and services, and what mode of delivery, have value to the customer segment (e.g., stock market alerts via Web-enabled cell phones)?

4. What are customers' responses to marketing and sales campaigns?

To answer these questions, marketing researchers capture and integrate information about consumers from multiple sources. This includes demographic and psychographic data, behavioral and preference data, complaint behavior, and all other direct and indirect communications with the enterprise. Data of this nature are used for two purposes: to create customer profiles that can be used to tailor interactions with customers; and to segment customers in order to develop appropriate product and service offerings, marketing campaigns, and growth and retention programs.

Silo Data in one functional area of a business not shared with other areas exist in silos.

Collecting and capturing the information involves the development of a market intelligence culture. This culture ensures that collected data are integrated into all facets of the enterprise. Most customer data in an enterprise exist in **silos.** That is, data that are exclusive to one functional area of the enterprise are not shared with other areas of the enterprise. For example, late payment notices from accounting are often not shared with customer service departments attempting to introduce customers to a new product or program. Data such as these must be shared with all departments of the business so that informed understanding of the customer is gained by all who interact with the customer. This level of knowledge and integration comes about only through market intelligence.

Transforming Marketing Research into Market Intelligence

South Central Bell (SCB) recently lost almost 27 percent of its intrastate long-distance telephone customers to other long-distance providers. Using highly refined information on the profitability of those customers, SCB segmented its defectors and tailored a strategy to win them back. The company was able to re-sign 7 percent of those who left for another service provider. This resulted in the retention of almost 50 percent of SCB's most profitable customers, leaving the unprofitable customers with the competition. Through additional research, SCB gained important information from those customers, including how competitors lured them away and how those customers rated the service quality of SCB. The company learned that its service was weak and needed to be enhanced quickly.

This example illustrates a well-known premise that approximately 20 percent of a company's customer base provides a significantly high percentage of revenues and profit. For example, Coca-Cola found that one-third of its Diet Coke drinkers consumed 84 percent of total Diet Coke sales.[4] On the basis of this type of data, companies are fighting to increase profits from high-consumption customers. Like Coca-Cola and South Central Bell, many companies are following an enterprisewide focus, examining all organizational departments for the purpose of sharing and leveraging information. The goal of this process is to transform the company from a marketing research, information-acquisition company, to a market intelligence enterprise that shares information for the purpose of being connected, responsive, and proactive to customers.

Granular data Highly detailed, highly personalized data specifically structured around an individual customer.

The market intelligence enterprise follows a different business model from traditional companies. The model provides a competitive advantage by using customer information at the **granular data** level. That is, data are detailed, highly personalized, and specifically structured around the individual customer. The enterprise embraces the vision that targeting customers is not sufficient—capturing and retaining customers is the overall goal. On the basis of granular customer information, market intelligence enterprises anticipate the desires of the customer and refine their offerings according to this anticipation. This is commonly referred to as a customer-centric approach in a CRM environment. A **customer-centric approach** facilitates convenience and efficiency for customers in their interactions with the enterprise. Interactions are used to obtain information from the customer in order to build and solidify a relationship. The Closer Look at Research box illustrates how the process works in the financial services industry.

Customer-centric approach Use of granular data to anticipate and fulfill customers' desires.

The market intelligence enterprise has four unique characteristics that shape and define its character. These characteristics are also the basis of a sound CRM program: (1) the strategic use of customer information; (2) information based on transactions; (3) enterprisewide approach to the use of information; and (4) technology support of the CRM structure.

Strategic Use of Customer Information

Two key questions driving CRM programs are "What does my customer value?" and "What is the value of my customer?" An enterprise driven by market intelligence addresses these questions through its unending effort to strategically use customer information to sort customers into profitable and unprofitable segments. Information from various sources both within and outside the enterprise must be organized and categorized into the firm's data warehouse. The primary information collected includes customer information from transactions (purchase frequency, credit information), salespeople (competitive information), call centers (customer service lines), sales promotions (purchase habits), survey data

A Closer Look at Research

CRM in the Financial Services Industry

MIECO, a financial services company, tailors its products to each customer's needs. One particular customer's package includes a money market fund; a mutual fund; a credit card; a home mortgage; and home, life, and auto insurance. MIECO knows the customer travels frequently for work and relays this information to its credit card partner to prevent unnecessary calls to the customer for authorization when there are periods of heavy use.

Having accumulated customer preferences by learning habits and trends through each transaction, MIECO sends offers that have a high degree

of acceptance (e.g., information on vacation home real estate opportunities and car lease changes). The company also provides information on the tax implications of owning a second home and reviews the customer's financial holdings, offering suggestions on how to finance a second mortgage. And when interest rates drop, MIECO e-mails the customer about speaking with a MIECO representative concerning refinancing the first mortgage. Using family information from the insurance policy, the company sends timely information on college loan programs, something the customer has agreed to receive. This customer asked to be contacted by e-mail, never by phone, and MIECO makes sure that this happens.

(customer satisfaction), in-store interactions, the Internet, kiosks, demographic information, service bureaus, database marketing companies, and even motor vehicle registration. The enterprise then performs statistical analysis of a customer's value, likes and dislikes, lifetime value, and profitability. Using this information, the enterprise refines its product and service offering to meet the needs of the most profitable customer segments, build loyalty among these customers, and manage positive relationships with them.

In the consumer electronics industry, for example, young single adults purchase DVD players for home and auto; childless newlyweds buy small appliances for the home; new parents often want camcorders; and established families look for multiple televisions, digital cameras, and home computers. Retired adults buy electronics for second homes; divorced couples spend to set up new households. This is the type of information that can be profitable to a market intelligence enterprise.

Information Based on a Transactional Focus

In every contact with customers an opportunity exists to capture customer information, invest in the customer relationship, and build loyalty. Real-time communication between the buyer and the enterprise enables the firm to enhance its positive interaction with the customer. During real-time communication, the enterprise has the opportunity to capture information beyond the transaction, for example, not just what the customer purchases when a desired item is not available (e.g., having to buy a Pepsi when a Coke is not available), but what each customer actually desires and why. The enterprise then shares that information throughout product planning and production to respond to the reason for needing the product or service.

Beyond the transaction, enterprises can collect information relating to the context of the interaction. Through contextual marketing, a bank, for example, might learn that a particular customer generally phones the bank's call center on Sunday evenings. When the bank wants to communicate with that customer, that would be a good time and the telephone would be an excellent way of conducting the interaction.

Enterprisewide Approach to the Use of Information

The process of gathering information during each transaction or at each contact with the customer and using that information is critical to the success of a CRM program. It is also critical that the information not remain in the hands of marketing or advertising but be disseminated throughout the enterprise. Successful CRM enterprises use information across all business units to manage the supply chain, create customized products and pricing structures, acquire new customers, and improve service and quality. In a CRM context, this is referred to as "information at every **touchpoint.**" That is, all individuals in the enterprise having direct or indirect contact with the customer must be exposed to the identical level of information pertaining to that customer.[5] All business units—accounting, engineering, production, marketing, distribution, and so on—not only share information about customers, but share the same information about customers. This level of shared information must even extend beyond the firm to include all facets of the enterprise—suppliers, independent contractors, facilitating agencies, and retailers.

Touchpoint Specific customer information gathered and shared by all individuals in an enterprise.

Technology Support of the CRM Structure

Technology support makes it possible to develop a strategic, information-rich CRM infrastructure. Technology provides the platform for turning customer data into customer knowledge. In short, information technology enables companies to maximize profitability through precise targeting of market segments. We are in a new era of marketing research that leverages relationships through the use of technology. For example, an enterprise collects customer data relating to demographics, billings, transactions, satisfaction levels, and service quality. These data, with additional primary and secondary data, are integrated and stored in a centralized database called a data warehouse. The data are then analyzed through such techniques as data mining. With powerful new technological approaches, companies are now leveraging technology so that information itself becomes a primary product. Wal-Mart and Target, for example, require all vendors not only to access and use information in their data warehouse, but to cooperate in capturing information by using RFID (Radio Frequency Identification tags) tracking technology to manage the supply chain.

Data Collection in a CRM Environment

Growth in the electronic marketplace and the resultant increase in the availability of customer data have been major drivers of the accelerated pace at which enterprises are adopting technology-based solutions for CRM. Technology is the driving force behind not only the integration and sharing of data, but also collecting customer data. In most CRM programs data are tracked at the point of customer interaction. This may occur at point-of-sale terminals or on the Web. Regardless of the source, the goal is to collect all relevant customer interaction data, store the data in the data warehouse, and subsequently analyze the data to develop profitable customer profiles.

Accessing Customer Data over the Internet

Many customers surf the Internet under the illusion that their activities are private and anonymous. Signing onto the Internet, visiting virtual storefronts, sending and receiving e-mail, or chatting in newsgroups—all these activities are increasingly being tracked by various businesses. Many businesses use CRM to gather information about current or prospective customers. Such searches are classified as passive, active, or directed.

Passive Data

Passive data Data supplied to a business when a consumer visits the company's Web site.

Passive data, frequently referred to as automatic data, are automatically given to a business once a consumer visits a particular Web site. The data obtained by the business is the Internet address, and it can appear in two forms. The internet protocol (IP) address is the numeric location of a computer physically attached to the Internet. Each computer has its own unique and individualized IP address. The domain name (DN) is the second form of data obtained over the Internet. This type of data combines geographical and specific user information. For example, look at Harold@memphis.edu. Harold is the user name, Memphis is the server name, and edu is the location, in this case an educational institution.

Passively gathered data can be used by businesses in several ways. The information a surfer leaves by just visiting a site can easily be used to categorize individuals into larger groups or segments. The business can narrow its customer demographic base by determining if there are any commonalities in the domain location of the customers and can target advertising or promotional material to this common domain.

Active Data

Active data Data acquired by a business when customers interact with the business's Web site.

Active data are acquired by a business when customers interact with the business's Web site. Through the use of "cookies" or online application forms filled out by the customer, a tremendous amount of information about the customer can be obtained. A cookie is a small piece of information a Web server can store with a Web browser and later read back from that browser. The user cookie is a unique identifier, assigned by the Web server and saved on a customer's computer that is provided back to the Web server upon request. Using this technology, a business can track a customer's progress through a Web site page by page. Once a customer visits a Web site, the customer will have the business added to his or her cookie file, indicating that this was a visited site. Consequently, every time the customer accesses the business's Web site, the business will have the customer's information and will then be able to track the number of times that customer searched that Web site.

Added to passive data, active data increase the level of customer knowledge for the enterprise. E-mail addresses, other volunteered information, and surfing patterns tracked through cookies can be used to enhance knowledge of the customer. The information can also be used to predict the tastes, desires, preferences, and buying patterns of the customer. For example, a customer can visit www.target.com and select items such as clothing, DVDs, toys, or sporting goods. As the customer adds these items to the shopping cart on the Web site, the list of these items is kept in the customer's browser's cookie file so that all the items can be paid for at once at the end of the shopping experience. Of course, if the customer makes a purchase, e-mail addresses, credit card information, and geographic location of the customer are also retained in the file. On the basis of a simple shopping trip, Target now knows who the customer is, where the customer lives, various forms of financial information, what was bought and in what quantity, and how to contact this customer for future communications. The interactive nature of this data collection method enables companies to use the information obtained to target market efforts so narrowly that marketing efforts can be personalized for each individual customer.

Directed Data

Directed data Comprehensive data about customers collected through the use of computers.

Directed data are the most comprehensive data available on customers. Directed data are not necessarily new information on customers but can be considered newly accessed information on customers. For example, starting with only a customer's last name, the Internet can be used to find a person's full address, get a map of the exact street location, a zip code, motor vehicle registration, even the amount of political contributions made by the individual. From a source called the "Stalker Home Page," a wealth of information on a person can be obtained in a matter of minutes. This information is based on an individual's credit report, and, although it contains no financial information, it does contain an individual's name, address, phone number, and social security number.

This type of data can yield all possible information about a customer. It can be used to track a person's visits on the Web and buying habits, and even generate a complete profile of the individual. In fact, an organization known as "Personal Agents, Inc." has developed the technology to log and analyze a person's browser patterns and, additionally, searches outside of its home site and collects data from potential customers.

Marketing Research and Customer Management: The Database Process

As illustrated in the chapter opening example, the foundation of any CRM process is its ability to provide shared information across the organization to develop better programs for individual customers. For this to occur there must be a blending of marketing research and information technology. The process includes collecting and storing customer data in a data warehouse, partitioning and categorizing the data in a customer database, and utilizing data analysis techniques to profile individual customers and react to their desires.

What Is a Database?

Database Collection of information indicating what customers are purchasing, how often they purchase, and the amount they purchase.

A marketing database is a central repository of all relevant information concerning a company's customers. Specifically, a **database** is a collection of information indicating what customers are purchasing, how often they purchase, and the amount they purchase. A well-designed database incorporates information from a multitude of diverse sources, including actual transactions, history of promotional effectiveness, consumer surveys, secondary data, and other past marketing research project data. Unlike operational databases that reflect accounting and financial data, a true research database enables users to analyze purchase behavior, not intentions, over some predetermined time frame, event, or business situation.

A typical database is structured around transactional information that is chronologically arranged to reflect each purchase occasion. Additional information (demographics, lifestyles, media habits) is entered into the transactional data so a company can develop a complete picture of its customers. The outcome is a complete customer profile based on actual purchase frequency and amount at any given point in time. When categorized effectively, the information provides a company with a total customer portfolio to be used in making product or brand decisions, resource allocations, and decisions on communication tools and distribution channels.

The information in a marketing database is generated by the customer via sales invoices, warranty cards, telephone calls, market research projects, and so forth. The information is then logically arranged to allow for instant access whenever the customer contacts a company or vice versa.

Such databases typically are linked to an interactive computer system that can automatically display a customer profile on demand. This enables the user of the database to recognize customers by name, purchase history, general interests, and product uses, as well as future product needs. In addition, most marketing databases are complemented with information pertaining to a company's total product mix. This tells the database user exactly what a company makes or sells, which items are the most popular, and which are most suitable for certain customers.

At the core of the database is a network that provides specific information on each and every product or service provided by the company. With such information companies can tell customers which replacement parts to order for their dishwasher, how to change a filter on their air conditioner, what games are available for their Nintendo system, and what each would cost. Even technical questions, such as those regarding installation of a home television satellite system, can be routed to a company expert.

Airlines and travel agencies provide excellent examples of marketing database development and usage. These service providers can book customers on complicated tours around the world; have hotel rooms and rental cars waiting at each destination; and deliver tickets, boarding passes, and itineraries overnight. This happens because of a networked database that links airlines, hotels, car rental services, and express delivery systems. The enhanced marketing database takes this concept one step further. With database information, the service provider knows a particular customer prefers a window seat, usually travels with Delta Airlines, always flies first class, is a Crown Room member, and uses Hertz Number One Gold Club Auto Rentals. The service provider knows the address to which the tickets are to be delivered, the spouse's name, and the home and office phone numbers. All of the customer's information is stored in the database and can be accessed instantly anytime the service provider needs it.

Purposes of a Customer Database

In the broadest sense, the purpose of any customer database is to help a firm develop meaningful, personal communication with its customers. This level of communication deals with the proper products or brands, the various prices of the product offering, the level of customer service to be built into the total offering, and how much access customers have to the product. In short, a customer database allows a company to communicate at the right place, at the right time, with the right product, to the right customer. Lands' End, Dell, Nike, Coca-Cola, Target, Procter and Gamble, and most other consumer goods companies have extensive databases to better serve their customers.

More specific purposes of the customer database are (1) to improve the efficiency of market segmentation, (2) to increase the probability of repeat purchase behavior, and (3) to enhance sales and media effectiveness. To fulfill these purposes, the successful customer database must enable users to measure, track, and analyze customer buying behaviors. The role of marketing research, then, becomes one of generating, developing, and sustaining the database.

Marketing databases are constructed to achieve or enhance customer relationships. The databases bring back the level of individual service lost due to mass merchandising. In the past, local retailers knew each customer and his or her family members. They established a bond with customers that included two-way communication, instilled customer loyalty, increased customer satisfaction, and fostered the growth of the business. Mass merchandising and discount retailing ended this relationship. Price, not loyalty, began to drive customers' purchase decisions. While quality of merchandise went up, personal service went down. Today the situation is reversing itself. By giving a firm access to information on each customer's family demographics, leisure activities, purchase history, media interests, and personal socioeconomic factors, the modern database can help that firm re-create personal service.

Four fundamental areas in which the database benefits the firm are (1) exchanging information with customers, (2) determining heavy users, (3) determining lifetime customer value, and (4) building segment profiles.

One of the most valuable benefits of a database involves the exchange of information between a firm and its customers. Information on product availability, special features, competitive product comparisons, repairs, and warranties is critical for customer service.

Most businesses, through internal secondary data, have this information available. The task becomes providing it to customers to allow them better decision-making capabilities.

At the same time, customers possess a wealth of information absolutely essential for any business. Why do customers buy a certain product? What features and benefits do they seek? What other products are they likely to purchase? Successful databases constantly provide such exchange of information. Every contact with a customer becomes an occasion to provide more information to a database. Also, as a business learns more about its customers, it understands what information customers want from it.

Information exchange tells a business that all customers are not alike. With a database, businesses can distinguish heavy, medium, and light users of their product or service and adjust their strategy accordingly. The database's ranking system for all customers can help the business tailor products, benefits, and services to each class to keep heavy users loyal and stimulate medium and light users to buy more.

Within each user class, the business can also determine the expected lifetime value per customer. When a customer is acquired, the database enables the business to determine what it can expect from that customer. Calculating contribution to profit and overhead for a customer's lifetime with the company is a major task. Using this lifetime value, the company can determine how much to spend on marketing activities to keep the customer satisfied and loyal.

Finally, a marketing database enables the business to answer the crucial question: "Why do some consumers buy our products or services regularly, while others do not?" The simple premise behind a database is that consumers themselves can provide the information necessary to answer this question. Other questions that can be answered using the database include:

- How do our products compare with the competition?

- What is the relationship between perceived value and price of the product?

- How satisfied are customers with the service level and support for the product?

- What are the comparisons among lifestyles, demographics, attitudes, and media habits between heavy, medium, and light users of the product?

Through various modeling techniques, individuals can be profiled on the basis of selected characteristics that will likely distinguish buyers from nonbuyers.

Marketing Research and Data Enhancement

Data enhancement The overlay or partitioning of information about new or existing customers for the purpose of better determining their responsiveness to marketing programs.

The primary role of a database is to serve as an information and intelligence resource for a company. Central to this objective is the process of **data enhancement,** which is defined as the overlay (adding) of information about customers to better determine their responsiveness to marketing programs. Data enhancement gives organizations three distinct advantages:

1. **More knowledge of customers.** Knowing exactly who buys products or services is extremely valuable in adjusting a company's marketing plan. Most databases are built with this purpose and concentrate on internal company data for current users of a product or service. Data enhancement enables external primary data to be woven into current internal data to gain a more accurate categorization of customers based on their true value to the company. The external data normally contain, but are not limited to, demographic, psychographic, behavioral, and motivational data about various consumers.

2. **Increased effectiveness of marketing programs.** Through data enhancement, the marketing function of an organization can gain greater insights into communications, distribution, and new-product development. When internal data about customers are

enhanced with external data, usage profiles by consumer can be tailored to reflect the unique desires of various customer groups.

3. **Better Prediction of response to new marketing programs.** Having concise information on various customer groups allows for increased targeting efficiency. Efficiency is increased when current customer profiles are used to predict the probability of targeting new yet similar customers with a new marketing plan. In short, the probability of success regarding new programs and procedures can be calculated according to the enhanced data.

Effective Development of Enhanced Databases

A typical database contains three critical data units that can be interactively categorized for unique customer profile reports: geodemographic factors, attribute data, and target market dimensions. Exhibit 4.2 shows the interactive properties of these data units.

Two levels of geodemographic factors are generally used: geographic market and residential area. At the residential level, information requirements center on the individual, the household, and the zip code where current customers reside. The geographic market level requires data at a more aggregate level representing metropolitan or regional market areas.

Typically, attitudinal data reflect an individual's preferences, views, and feelings toward a particular product or service offering. Attitudinal data reflect a person's overall attitude toward the product, specific brands, and product features and are an important component of database development because they are related to purchase behavior. When individuals prefer a product or brand, they are more inclined to buy it than when they have no preference.

Motivational data refer to the drive, desire, or impulse that channels an individual's behavior toward a goal. Motivational data typically involve those factors behind why people behave as they do. Seeking particular product benefits, shopping at stores that are convenient and comfortable, or simply enjoying the interaction with certain salespeople may all constitute motivational characteristics that drive a purchase decision. In short, motivational data reflect the activities behind the purchase. Whether the issue is brand loyalty, store loyalty, or media influence, motivational data describe those circumstances that direct a customer's behavior toward a goal.

Target market characteristics describe heavy product users versus light users on such dimensions as demographics, purchase volume, and purchase frequency. Other data reveal household consumption patterns, shopping patterns, advertising effectiveness, and price sensitivity information.

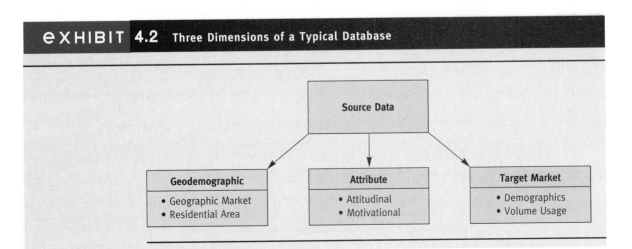

EXHIBIT 4.2 Three Dimensions of a Typical Database

The key to database enhancement, of course, is the availability of data to increase the interactive efficiency of the data units. In most database development, the geodemographic unit is called the driver dimension because it determines (or drives) the type and amount of additional data that can be generated for cross-reference purposes. For example, a company may have a limited database of its current customers. But it wants to use a promotional campaign to increase awareness of its product offering among potential new users. Analysis of its database based on geodemographic factors reveals useful information on where current customers reside. However, it provides little value regarding the targeting of new customers except for similar residential locations. Therefore, the data requirement shifts to obtaining external data on attributes and target market characteristics of current users in order to enhance the transferability of current customer profiles to potential new customers.

In this simple example, geodemographic data served as the driver for determining additional data requirements. Depending on the level and amount of information available on a geodemographic level, additional data requirements are then determined. Electronic databases are also effective tools for data enhancement.

The Dynamics of Database Development

A database is "a comprehensive collection of interrelated data." The data comes from many sources both internal and external to the company. Regardless of where the information comes from, a database is only as good as the information it contains. If the information required to make marketing decisions is not in the database, the database is useless. From a marketing perspective, information generated for a database must possess the following:

1. **Affinity.** Data must reflect prior usage of the product or service in question. Data reflecting past usage by current customers is one of the best predictors of future purchases.

2. **Frequency.** Information reflected in a database must give users the ability to categorize customers by frequency of purchase. Available information should reflect the amount of business each individual has conducted with the company.

3. **Recency.** Length of time between purchases is a very powerful predictor of future purchases. Because of this, recency of purchase is a critical factor in database dynamics. Recency assumes that a customer who purchased from a particular business last month has a greater probability of repurchase than a customer whose last purchase occurred six months ago.

   Using recency, customers are profiled on the basis of their most recent purchase, the most recent having the highest probability and the least recent having the lowest probability of repurchase. Each customer is assigned a recency code (1 = most recent, 5 = least recent, for example) and sorted into groups based on the assigned codes.

   Once these profiles are established, decision makers view these customers in a totally different light. Certain customer groups can receive new-product promotions, while others may be targeted with specially designed marketing efforts to increase repeat purchases. Recency allows the business to build better relationships with different customer classes. It enables the researcher to determine which ones are most important and which groups need additional cultivation.

4. **Amount.** How much a customer purchases from any one company is a good predictor of future usage status. Therefore, the data must facilitate categorization of customers into specific usage groups (light, medium, heavy users).[6]

Many companies go beyond the above guidelines and consider profitability as well. Customers may purchase frequently and in large amounts, but if they purchase only items that are on sale or deeply discounted they are less profitable to the firm. Wachovia National Bank groups its customers into 10 segments based on profitability. Customers in the more profitable segments are called by relationship managers to make them aware of new products and services, or just to tell them they appreciate their business. Less profitable customers are encouraged to use less costly approaches like the Internet.[7] Some banks even charge customers to talk with a bank representative.

While it is important to realize that the information for a database must contain certain characteristics, researchers must never lose sight of the fact that database development is unique to each company. The amount and type of information relevant to one business may not be relevant to another. Database development is highly specific, yet within this specificity lies the art of maximizing the relevancy of the information.

Rules of Thumb in Database Development

Given the value a well-developed database can add to a company, management should view the total process of database development as a commitment to a long-term data acquisition plan. Thus, the development of a database should be budgeted as a multiyear process. Researchers should begin with collecting the data that will have the greatest amount of predictive power.

Depth The overall number of key data fields or key variables that will make up the data record.

Second, management should view the data acquisition process in terms of the width and depth of the database. **Depth** refers to the overall number of key data fields or variables that make up the data record (all data pertaining to the individual or company). **Width,** in contrast, refers to the total number of records contained in the database (total number of individuals or companies in the database).

Width The total number of records contained in the database (also referred to as sample size).

Finally, companies should avoid jumping onto the database bandwagon (i.e., developing a database just because everyone else is) and then failing to commit the necessary resources. A marketing research database is a constant and ongoing process. A database will not succeed unless the company makes a commitment to long-term data acquisition and enhancement.

Database Technology

Most companies have data on almost every aspect of their operations. Many companies even have data on how much data they have. What are data? Data are verbal or numerical facts that can be used for reasoning or calculating. In database terminology, a data item or **data field** is a basic characteristic about a customer or client (e.g., sex, age, name, address). Data fields have little value when treated individually. But when they are combined in a manner that makes them useful for making decisions, they acquire value and can be regarded as information.

Data field A basic characteristic about a customer.

Database technology The tools that are used to transform data into information.

Database technology refers to the tools used to transform data into information. Database technology processes data and stores it in a single databank. It consists of two unique features: a database management system and a data dictionary. A database management system is a computer program that creates, modifies, and controls access to the data in the database. Users of these programs follow basic instructions to combine data and produce a desired output. The output of a typical database management system is shown in Exhibit 4.3. A data dictionary provides descriptions of the data in the database.

eXHIBIT 4.3 Typical Output of a Database Management System

PRIMARY BUSINE	KEY CONTACT PE	DELIVERY STREET	STATE	ZIP CODE	PHONE	FAX	CUSTOMER PO	ORDER NO.
	Douglas				2882231	0	100541	52117
banks	Ernest Stevens		AL	35203-	2052521161	2053266220	020890-2	299568
snack food	DENNY TAVERES				7176324477	7176327207	VERBAL PER DEN	572117
	Richard Trotter						2179	342422
food	John Lock		W	54467	7153415960	7153415966	21259	59571
food			W	54467	715341596	7153415566	29060	127397
	DALE COWART				5014245403	5014245228	MH51114	376271
			OR	97220-	5036664545	5036692223	DM90099	222620
pers care			PR	00709	3154322287	0	BM00030	54200
pers care			PR	00709	0	0	BM	109800
pers care	FRANCK		PR	00709	3154322287	315432411	VERBAL	96175
pers care	Ben Sepulveda		PR	00709	8098340185	8098331095	20464	48541
pers care	Ben Sepulveda		PR	00709	8098340185	8098001095	20464	48541
pers care	JERRY WOOSTER		VA	22021	2019266786	2019266782	M-01202	60067
	MILLOS CIKASA				8185494	8185496638	101071	53582
	OLIVIER DULAUN				6096632260	6096650474	5586	407602
					6096632260	0	1187	780000
building products					2154858959		72748	74000
					2068728400	2063957701	F-35580	145560
	MARK MIKA		WA	98032	2063957596	2063957591	D67428	3977000
							84007	194076
	CAROL COLLINS		MI	48043	6144386312	0	LMT104737	48897
			PA	19363	7088332900	7088331025	K-53167	43188
	PAUL MORGAN				6155976700	6155975243	13362	42009
	ALLEN RANSOM		IN	46041	8032815292	0	B883D150061	312743
snack foods			IN	46041	2143534893	0		375954
snack foods					0	0	U9914	383478
snack foods			NC		0	0		360140
snack foods			MD		0	0	EU10443	403937
snack foods	Royce Shafer							957600
snack foods					0	0	U9914	383478
snack foods								42960
snack foods	Engineering Accou		IN	46041-	2143534893	0	EU-7308	375954
snack foods	BRUCE FISHER/II		MD		2143344940	2143345175	EU-14060	997554
snack foods	DAN PREMUS		OR	97005	2143344940	2145345175	EV14247	596553
snack foods	Bruce Fisher	Aberdeen	MD	21001			EV15168	325766
food	ED CASSATERI		IL	60185	7082311140	7082316968	WC-072810	189319
	D. WHEL		KS	66031	9137648100	9137646520	VERBAL	550691
	NANCY HOLLAND				8002556837	0	H2924	56861
		Burlingame	CA	94010			1717	222430
	Roland Gage						1717	787745
snack food					2159329330	2159325698	SM12067	98481
food	CHRISTINE ALLEN	HERSHEY	PA	17033			2R5076221	49428

It formats the data and assigns meaning to the data fields or variables. Together, the database management system and data dictionary constitute what is called the database processing system.

Two types of database processing systems exist: sequential and relational. A **sequential database system** organizes data in a very simple pattern; that is, a simple path, linkage, or network. In a sequential database only two single data fields can be paired. Once paired, they can be linked to a third data field. Once this group is connected, it can be linked to a fourth, and then to a fifth, and so on, as illustrated in Exhibit 4.4.

Many companies choose to develop sequential databases because they allow users to easily access detailed data linked to a specific data field or variable (e.g., region of country). Also, database systems are commonly used in companies that require reports based on consistent data in a given format.

A **relational database system** operates somewhat differently from a sequential database system. The major difference is that relational databases require no direct relationship between data fields or variables. Data are structured in tables with rows and columns, with the tables (not the data fields) being linked together depending on the output desired. With a relational database system, the table becomes an individual file, rows correspond to records (width), and columns represent data fields or variables (depth) within each record.

In Exhibit 4.5, for example, each row represents the number of customers for that particular field. The primary market attribute, for example, is divided into regional, national, and international fields. Each column contains the breakdown of each customer by primary

Sequential database system Data in a very simple pattern; that is, a simple path, linkage, or network.

Relational database system A system that structures a database in tables with rows and columns, with the tables (not data fields) being linked together depending on the output desired.

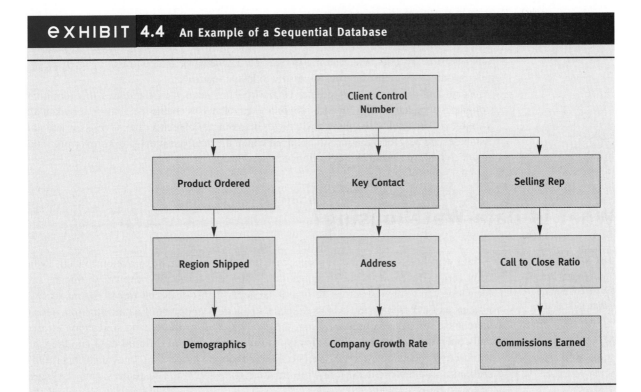

eXHIBIT 4.4 **An Example of a Sequential Database**

eXHIBIT 4.5 A Relational Database That Shows a Customer Profile by Industry Segment

	Bakery (15)	Chemical (7)	Pharmaceutical (35)	Snack food (42)	Other (11)
Primary Market Served					
Regional	1(6.7)	1(14.3)		3(7.1)	1(9.1)
National		2(28.6)	7(20)	37(88.1)	3(27.3)
International	3(20)	2(28.6)	8(22.9)		5(45.5)
No. of Product Lines					
One	(6.7)	1(14.3)	1(2.9)		3(27.3)
Two	6(40)		2(5.7)	2(4.8)	2(18.2)
Three		1(14.3)	5(14.3)	1(2.4)	1(9.1)
Four	1(6.7)	3(42.9)	4(11.4)	4(9.5)	—
Five		1(2.9)			—
Six	1(6.7)				1(9.1)
Seven					
Region					
N.E.	5(33.3)		13(37.1)	9(21.4)	2(18.2)
S.E.	1(1.7)	6(85.7)	4(11.4)	1(2.4)	5(45.5)
M.W.	4(26.7)	1(14.3)	3(8.6)	23(54.8)	2(18.2)
West	5(33.3)		1(2.9)	2(4.8)	2(18.2)
CAN/Other			13(37.1)	7(16.7)	

business (bakery, chemical, pharmaceutical, etc.). The rows and columns together constitute the table, which profiles customers by industry segment.

Relational databases offer greater flexibility than sequential databases in examining complex data relationships. In addition, relational databases enable the analyst to look at all variables or data fields simultaneously rather than one variable at a time. Overall, relational databases are best for dynamic situations in which the database must expand over time and in which multiple variable applications are needed.

What Is Data Warehousing?

Data warehouse Central repository for all significant parts of information that an organization collects.

A **data warehouse** is a central repository for the information an organization collects. Data from various functions of the organization are stored in a central computer so that the information can be shared across all functional departments of the business. The major significance of a data warehouse is its purpose. From the standpoint of data collection, a data warehouse serves two purposes. First, the data warehouse collects and stores data for the daily operations of the business. This type of data is called **operational data** and the system used to collect operational data is online transaction processing, known as OLTP. Operational data represent not only information collected from customers, but also data collected from suppliers and vendors.[8]

Operational data Data for the daily operations of the business.

Informational data
Data available for
analysis purposes.

The second purpose of the data warehouse is to collect, organize, and make data available for analysis. This enables the business to use the data warehouse as a decision-making tool for marketing programs. This type of data is commonly referred to as **informational data** and the system used to collect and organize informational data is online analytical processing, known as OLAP. This process involves the development of customer categories based on relationships among the data.[9] For example, purchase history, frequency, store visits, and brand preference may all share a common relationship among a group of customers and are therefore grouped and categorized to form a profile of a particular customer group, similar to that of a market segment profile. The data warehouse provides the company with a system that is driven toward shared information; that is, information that can be used by any and all functional departments of the business.

A data warehouse is comparable to a campus library, both as a resource for and as a service to the entire university. The value of your campus library resource is determined by the variety and assortment of books, periodicals, and professional information it contains. The value of your campus library service is based on how quickly and easily the staff can assist you in finding and using what you need. In a data warehouse, the value of the resource is determined by the amount and variety of data collected and stored in the warehouse. The value of the service is determined by the ease of use and the extent to which the information can be shared throughout the entire business.

Marketing-Related Data and Data Warehousing

The type of data collected and stored is a key determinant in the success of any data warehouse. Data collected for a warehouse is highly specific to the business, yet the common feature of all data, regardless of the business, is that it is centered on the customer. Hospitals collect data on patient procedures, financial institutions collect data on financial services used, and insurance companies collect data on types of policies and risk associated with types of events that might occur. Although all three differ in their product/service offerings, they are similar in collecting data related to the customer. Aside from secondary and primary data stored in the warehouse, two unique forms of customer data most commonly collected for a data warehouse are (1) real-time transactional data and (2) customer-volunteered data.

Real-time transactional data Data that are collected at the point of sale.

Real-time transactional data are collected at the point of sale. This type of data is usually collected through a customer loyalty program or preferred buying program. Customer loyalty cards identify who the customer is, what the customer is buying and in what quantity and frequency, and at what retail outlet (either brick and mortar or online). The key dimension is that data are collected at the time of purchase, so manufacturers can identify how customers respond to a specific marketing program being used at that point in time. For example, sales of Miller beer may be tracked via point-of-sale data where price may vary over certain days along with point-of-sale promotional activities. In this case, the retailer can identify the impact of price and promotional variations on the sale of Miller beer.

Customer-volunteered information Data that are provided by the customer without any solicitation.

Customer-volunteered information is provided by the customer without any solicitation. This type of data includes customer comment cards or complaints, customer registration information from Web sites, customer communications via chat rooms, and data obtained through customer advisory groups.

Wal-Mart has both real-time data and customer-volunteer information in its data warehouse. Its data warehouse, second in size only to the Pentagon, contains over 200 terabytes (trillions of characters) of transactional data. Among other things, Wal-Mart uses it warehouse database to help stores select and adapt merchandising mixes to match local neighborhood preferences.

Data Mining: Transforming Data into Information

Many businesses have implemented systematic processes for collecting data from a variety of sources. Justification for these efforts focuses on specific marketing questions facing the business. Data warehouses are designed to answer marketing-related questions. Many businesses are drowning in data while starving for useful information about customers. This data overload has led to widespread interest in data mining.

Data mining Process of finding hidden patterns and relationships among variables/characteristics contained in data stored in the data warehouse.

Data mining is the process of finding hidden relationships among variables contained in data stored in the data warehouse. Data mining is an analysis procedure known primarily for the recognition of significant patterns of data for particular customers or customer groups. Marketing researchers have used data mining for many years, but the procedures usually were performed on small data sets containing 1,000 or fewer respondent records. Today, with the development of sophisticated data warehouses, the size of data sets being analyzed has increased to thousands, even millions of respondent records. For example, Ford's database has over 50 million names, Kraft Foods has more than 25 million names, Citibank has over 30 million names, American Express has 20 million names, and so on. Special data-mining tools have been developed for the specific purpose of analyzing customer patterns found in very large databases.

Data mining finds not easily identifiable relationships among several customer dimensions within large data warehouses. The procedure is conducted when the market researcher has limited knowledge of a particular subject. For example, management in a casino business may ask the question, "What are the characteristics of the gaming customers who spent the most in our casino last year?" Data-mining techniques are used to search the data warehouse, capture the relevant data, categorize the significant characteristics, and develop a profile of the high-budget gambler.

The Data-Mining Process

Exhibit 4.6 illustrates a framework of what is involved in the data-mining process. This framework focuses on four elements: the marketing research question, data-mining approaches, the mining implementation process, and the visual data-mining product.

Marketing Research Question

Description The process of discovering patterns, associations, and relationships among key customer characteristics.

Prediction Uses patterns and relationships to predict future trends and behaviors.

This is the starting point in any data-mining analysis. For example, management may want answers to questions such as "Which customers are most likely to visit our casino in the month of July and why?" To provide an answer, data-mining tools analyze two key requirements: description and prediction.

Description is the process of discovering patterns, associations, and relationships among key customer characteristics such as demographic variables, gambling expenditures, frequency of casino visits, amount of wagers won/lost, day of the week, month, time of day, number of hours engaged in gambling. **Prediction** uses these patterns and relationships to predict future trends and behaviors, such as why customers visit during a given month, what activities they engage in during that month, how much they gamble during the month, what special event they attend, if any, during that particular time.

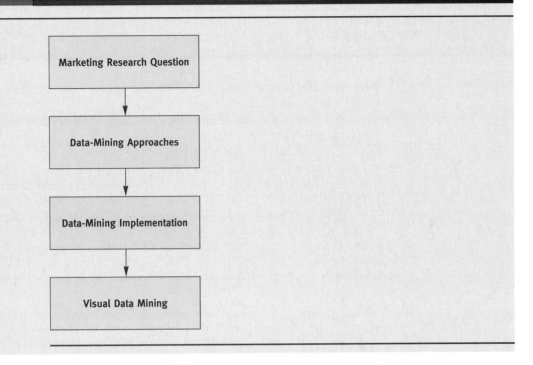

EXHIBIT 4.6 A Data-Mining Framework for Marketing Decisions

Marketing Research Question

Data-Mining Approaches

Data-Mining Implementation

Visual Data Mining

Data-Mining Approaches

Data mining uses several approaches for description and prediction. One or more of these approaches can be used, for example, to profile groups based on age, sex, income, race, and lifestyle using consistent or sequential behavior patterns, or to predict customer satisfaction levels based on friendliness of employees, cleanliness of surroundings, quality of services, and reputation of the business. Exhibit 4.7 lists the most commonly used data-mining approaches and some business applications in which they are applied.

Data-Mining Implementation

During this process the researcher first identifies how the data contained in the warehouse are stored and categorized. Categorization and storage determines which data-mining approach is most appropriate to find answers to the marketing question.

Visual Data Mining

No matter which data-mining approach is used, deciding how the results will be presented is a critical part of any data-mining activity. Remember, data mining is the combination of two concepts, automatic pattern discovery among customer characteristics and visual presentation of those patterns. A data-mining approach may be very good at discovering patterns, but if those patterns are not effectively visualized, the power to make strategic decisions using the information is lost. Thus, the success of any data-mining procedure relies heavily on the ability of the researcher to access and comprehend the results of the analysis relative to the marketing question being answered.

EXHIBIT 4.7   **Most Commonly Used Approaches in Data Mining**

Decision Trees

This is a set of rules that uses a tree-like structure to classify customers into segments or other relevant groups. Examples of this approach include:

Retail: What are the differences between frequent and infrequent shoppers at Wal-Mart?

Medical: Which factors affect kidney transplant survival rates?

Telemarketing: Which prospects are good risks and therefore an attempt should be made to sell them a mortgage?

Rule Induction

This process develops "If . . . then . . . " rules to classify individuals in a database. While decision trees use a set of rules, rule induction methods generate a set of independent rules that are unlikely to form a tree and may form better classification patterns. Examples include:

Retail: Will the likelihood of purchase of a one-year extended warranty on a new digital camera from Best Buy be greater than, equal to, or less than 10 percent?

Medical: What are the "good risk" criteria that must be met before trying a particular treatment on a cancer patient?

Direct mail: Will the response to a mail campaign for Office Depot be greater than 5 percent?

Neural Networking

This is a nonlinear predictive model that learns how to detect patterns that match a particular profile. The name comes from the fact that the process resembles that of the human brain. The results typically are based on clustering or sequencing of patterns. Examples include:

Retail: Which brand of DVD player is a prospect most likely to purchase?

Medical: What disease is a person likely to contract?

Direct Mail: Who will respond to a particular mailing?

Fuzzy Logic

This approach handles imprecise concepts like "small, large, big, young, old, high, and low" and is more flexible. It examines fuzzy types of data classifications rather than those with more precise boundaries.

Retail: Who is a likely customer for our new line of HDTV products?

Medical: Which smokers are likely to develop lung cancer?

Direct Mail: Who might be a likely person to respond to our new promotional campaign?

Genetic Algorithms

These are not used to find patterns, but rather to guide the learning process of neural networking. The approach loosely follows the pattern of biological evolution in which members of one generation compete to pass on their characteristics to the next generation until the best model is found. Examples include:

Retail: What is the optimal store layout for a particular location?

Medical: What is the optimal treatment for a particular disease?

Direct Mail: What is the optimal demographic profile of an individual who is likely to invest $20,000 or more in a mutual fund this year?

Database Modeling

Before conducting any modeling, the researcher needs to review, refine, and format the raw data in the database so it can be easily processed using statistical packages. This data interface process is necessary for successful query and modeling activities.

A Closer Look at Research

Database America Introduces SalesLeads™—First Web-Based Lead-Generating Service for Consumers and Small Businesses

Database America markets SalesLeads™, a Web-based direct marketing database designed to generate sales leads for small to medium-sized businesses. SalesLeads provides anyone with access to the Internet a cost-effective means of building targeted prospect lists from Database America's file of in-depth information on more than 14 million U.S. and Canadian businesses and over 200 million people in 104 million households. While on the Web site users can develop highly customized mailing lists by paying a minimal charge for the names they download.

Anyone with a computer and an Internet connection can access SalesLeads via the Database America Web site (www.database-america.com). The system provides an easy interface for selecting marketing criteria such as geographic and demographic attributes and honing the list to specify details such as sales volume or employee size. Uses for SalesLeads range from students researching employment prospects, to hobbyists building a list of regional churches or associations sponsoring craft fairs, to commercial real estate agents generating leads to sell properties. There is no charge for looking and no minimum requirements. Customers pay only a few cents for each prospect they download and can pay via a secure credit card transaction on the system.

"Database America is drawing on more than 40 years of expertise in business-to-business direct mail marketing. We pride ourselves on leading the market with the latest technology," says Al Ambrosino, president of Database America. "As an online service, SalesLeads provides the small business and home office audience access to the identical database information previously geared toward much larger organizations."

SalesLeads is the first lead-generating product of its kind on the Web offering real-time delivery of information that can be easily updated. Users can conduct their searches by filling in criteria in an easy-to-use graphical form on the Database America Web page. Criteria include business name, business type via NAICS (North American Industry Classification System) codes, geography, zip code, number of employees, and sales volume.

Once users have determined their search criteria and built a mailing or telemarketing list, they can download the file to their computers. The list is created in a standard character file format that is compatible with virtually all desktop word processing and spreadsheet programs. The list includes business names, addresses, and phone numbers for printing out as address labels. Database America also offers users the option of purchasing the data for shipment in hardcopy labels.

Source: www.databaseamerica.com

Database analysis and modeling are designed to summarize what companies already know about their best customers and at the same time indicate what else they need to learn about these individuals. When a database model fails to predict a customer's future behavior, the database analyst needs to ask whether the company truly knows enough about its customers. The Closer Look at Research box highlights one of the largest database firms in the world.

Many companies find themselves data rich and information poor. The process of customer modeling often points to a company's information shortages and triggers new ideas for future marketing research endeavors. An effective approach to handling database modeling is to start where the process will end and then work backward. The question then becomes: "How will the information be used?" or "What will the information enable us to do?" With this approach the researcher knows how the modeling output will be usable for the decision maker. Among the many modeling procedures that exist in database analysis, two of the more traditional are scoring models and lifetime value models.

EXHIBIT 4.8 An Example of a Gains Table

Group Number	Number of Customers	Percentage of Customers	Cumulative Number of Customers	Cumulative Percentage	Average Profile per Customer	Predicted Total Profit	Cumulative Total	Cumulative Average per Customer
1	100,000	20%	100,000	20%	$20	$2,000,000	$2,000,000	$20.00
2	100,000	20	200,000	40	15	1,500,000	3,500,000	17.50
3	100,000	20	300,000	60	10	1,000,000	4,500,000	3.50
4	100,000	20	400,000	80	5	500,000	5,000,000	1.25
5	100,000	20	500,000	100	1	100,000	5,100,000	.20

Scoring Models

Scoring models Database models used to predict consumption behavior; each individual in the database is assigned a score based on his or her propensity to respond to a marketing variable or make an actual purchase.

Scoring models are used to predict consumption behavior. Each individual in the database is assigned a score based on his or her propensity to respond to a marketing variable or make an actual purchase. High scores are indications of very desirable customers; low scores represent less desirable segments. The initial objective is to rank customer segments based on their potential profitability to the company. The primary feature of scoring models is called the gains table. An example of a gains table is presented in Exhibit 4.8.

Using a gains table, a database analyst can project and manage the profitability of various customer segments. For example, according to the data in Exhibit 4.8, the customer base is composed of 500,000 persons divided into five equal segments of 100,000, or five segments of 20 percent of the market. The gains table ranks each of these segments based on its profit potential. Group 1 customers have the highest profit potential, and group 5 the lowest. Group 1 is estimated to draw approximately $2 million in future profit, or an estimated $20 per customer, and so on. Combined, groups 1, 2, and 3 are expected to generate $4.5 million in total future profits, or an estimated $20, $17.50, and $3.50, respectively, per customer. As you move through the gains table, the percentage of profitability per segment begins to decrease. This approach reinforces the basic marketing principle that customers are not homogeneous and, more specifically, the conventional wisdom that 20 percent of customers represent 80 percent of a company's profits.

Key Variables in Scoring Models

Key variables in the scoring model enable researchers to determine which factors can be used to separate customers into purchase groups. Scoring models use weights to multiply assigned values in each customer's record. For example, suppose five factors are useful in separating heavy users from light users of hair spray—age, income, occupation, number of children under 18, and home value. On the basis of customer characteristics in the database, the scoring model determines that for heavy users of hair spray, the variables are arranged in the following order and assigned a corresponding weight: home value, .130; age, .050; occupation, .042; number of children under 18, .022; and income, .012. Obviously, the real weights produced by the model would be quite different, since they are to be multiplied by numbers (e.g., age in years, occupation in assigned coded value, income in thousands). For our discussion, however, let's assume these are real values.

In this example, home value is an important factor, with income being a less important factor for classifying customers into a heavy user group. The model permits a researcher to run a program that takes each of the relevant factors in the customer record and multiplies it by the appropriate weight. The weights are then added together to get an overall score. The score represents the likelihood of a customer's being a heavy user (or a medium user, etc.) of the product.

Variables used to generate scoring model gains tables should be from actual purchase behavior data. Key variables include demographics, psychographics, lifestyle data, and purchase habits including frequency, volume, and amount spent at a given time. These variables would then be assigned weights or scores depending on their ability to predict purchase behavior. For example, men may purchase more power tools than women. Therefore, on the basis of the single demographic variable of gender, men would be assigned a 10, women a 4. Each variable classification is assigned a weight or score. The scoring weight structure for two customer groups based on gender might look like the following:

Customer Group A		Customer Group B	
Female	2 pts	Male	10 pts
Volume: $100	5 pts	Volume: $50	10 pts
Frequency: 2 weeks	4 pts	Frequency: 1 month	8 pts
Product purchased: dry cleaning	6 pts	Product Purchased: dry cleaning	6 pts
Total:	17 pts	Total:	34 pts

As can be seen, Group B (with 34 points) has better matching variables than Group A (with only 17 points). The total scores for each group are then converted to dollars. So 34 points would become $34, and 17 points would become $17. This conversion becomes the foundation for predicting future profitability in gains table analysis.

Scoring models have a limited period of effectiveness. The life of the model is directly related to changes in customer demand. Therefore, scoring models need to be revised and changed as the market changes.

Lifetime Value Models

Lifetime value models
Database models developed on historical data, using actual purchase behavior, not probability estimates, to predict future actions.

The fundamental premise behind **lifetime value models** is that customers, just like physical and tangible machinery, represent company assets. Moreover, customers represent a continuous stream of cash flow based on transactions they conduct with the business. All too often, the outcome of many marketing research projects is to obtain information that can be used to generate new customers only. Lifetime value models demonstrate that it is more valuable for businesses to concentrate on qualified customers first. Then focus on growing them rather than constantly seeking new customers. Database information in most lifetime value models includes the following:

1. **Price variables:** The initial product or service cost and any price changes that occur.

2. **Sales promotional variables:** Type used, cost of the incentive, value to the customer.

3. **Advertising expenditures:** Direct costs of advertising expenses.

4. **Product costs:** Direct costs, plus quality of goods/services.

5. **Relationship-building efforts:** Type and costs of relationship-building devices; value of building long-term relationships.

eXHIBIT 4.9   A Hypothetical Lifetime Value Model for a Fast-Food Restaurant

PERIOD	1	2	3	4
CUSTOMERS	10,000			
REPEAT		3,500	1,225	428
REPEAT %		35%	35%	35%
REVENUE				
AVE, TICKET	$4.30	$4.50	$4.75	$4.75
PRICE INC.	.90			
TOTAL	34,000	15,750	5,818	2,033
EXPENSES				
DIRECT COSTS	60%	60%	60%	60%
TOTAL	20,400	9,450	3,491	1,219
REPEAT EFFORT				
TARGET	10,000	3,500	1,225	428
REPEAT %	35%	35%	35%	35%
RATE	3,500	1,225	428	150
TOTAL MAIL	10,000	3,500	1,225	428
COST	$3,800	$1,330	$465	$162
TOTAL EXP.	$24,200	$10,780	$3,956	$1,381
CONTRIB.	9,800	4,970	1,862	652
INVEST.	3,800	1,330	465	162
TOTAL LIFETIME VALUE	$6,000	$9,460	$11,037	$11,527
CUSTOMER VALUE	$.60	$.96	$1.10	$1.15

Database information is used to identify the most profitable customers. Exhibit 4.9 represents the output from a hypothetical lifetime value model for a fast-food restaurant. In this example 10,000 new customers are targeted for the marketing effort. The average amount spent by customers is about $4.30, and a free sandwich (with a cost of 90 cents) is the incentive to attract the customers. Therefore, the estimated revenue is about $34,000. Expenses amount to approximately 60 percent of total revenues, for a total expense of $20,400.

The business averages a 35 percent return rate of its customers. Therefore, mailing out 10,000 free sandwich coupons should yield 3,500 responses at a cost of $3,800. Total expenses for this planned effort are now estimated at $24,200. With an initial investment of $3,800, the total contribution should result in a $9,800 return to the business. This, in turn, equates to a total lifetime customer value of $6,000, or 60 cents per customer during the first period of the promotion. Given expected rates of return for customers over the next three promotional periods, total contribution would fall to $652, with investment costs down to $162. Total lifetime value over four periods would increase to $11,527, or $1.15 per customer. The four-period lifetime value for an individual customer is $1.15.

To summarize, as a database tool lifetime value models examine the asset value of customers. In contrast to purchase intention data, lifetime value models are based on actual purchase data, which is often a better predictor of customer behavior.

marketing research in action

The Function of Databases within the Financial Services Industry

Leading with Data[10]

Credit card issuers and bankers have big appetites for customer data and are using it to drive their businesses. As a representative of Jackson, MS–based Trustmark National Bank recently said, "If we don't know our customers and their behavior patterns, we can't make decisions that harness those behavior patterns into desired actions."

Never has such knowledge been more crucial. The banking industry is in transition, with new electronic delivery channels changing traditional banker–client relationships, replacing them with a fluid market system in which consumers can shop for products and services on price. Loyalty is difficult to come by, as products become increasingly commoditized, and channels of delivery more abundant. In this environment, banks are grooming a new breed of data-savvy executives who can lead by following the data trail.

Courting Profitable Customers

According to Acxiom Corporation (www.acxiom.com), bankers are at different levels in their mastery of the data basics of segmentation and data enhancement. But competition is forcing quick transformations of those who are not on board. The collection, integration, enhancement, and analysis of customer data have become must-do disciplines for improving marketing efficiency. Major credit card issuers have been using advanced database techniques for years. But other financial services businesses are just beginning to use such information technology. Mutual fund issuers are beginning to take advantage of consumer data sources. Retail bankers also are very involved in customer databases (called master customer information files or MCIFs), while commercial banking is only beginning to use these approaches.

Many banks are concerned with the warehousing of multiple streams of customer and prospect data and with providing analytical tools to their executives to support customer acquisition and retention efforts. Some of this work is being outsourced to service bureaus and consultants to help bring projects to rapid completion. And new data service providers are cropping up in unexpected places. MasterCard International, for example, has thousands of member banks that access consumer transaction data by account number.

While data is driving more acquisition and retention programs, New York City–based research firm First Manhattan Consulting Group (www.fmcg.com) reports that only 10 percent of America's top 50 banks use data for the more sophisticated profitability analysis at the account or household level. Profitability analysis involves obtaining operating costs, by product, identifying profit components from each transaction file, creating a formula for each product, and validating the accuracy of the calculated data. For example, CoreStates Bank (www.corestatesbank.com) uses profitability analysis to measure a customer's return. CoreStates' initial profitability analysis showed that 20 percent of customers were very profitable, 20 percent were very unprofitable, and 60 percent were marginal. Going further, CoreStates analyzed two of its branches. Branch "A" was in an affluent neighborhood and very profitable, while Branch "B" was in a blue-collar area and losing money.

To management's surprise, the two branches were comparable in loan ratios and all other areas except one: no-fee checking. That product alone pushed Branch "B" into the red. This knowledge allowed the product manager to change the minimum balance, raise fees, and use other alternatives to improve the profitability of both the accounts and the branch. Conventional wisdom holds that blue-collar customers are a bank's bread and butter because affluent customers often establish more than one banking relationship, but analysis showed that wasn't true in this case. Because the affluent customers' balances were so much higher—double that of other households, even without the total banking relationship—they produced a much better return.

At the other end of the spectrum is a small, 15-branch community bank that was very proficient at identifying the most profitable branch portfolios. They used an MCIF system to determine who the most profitable customers were in each branch and to evaluate product profitability by customer. The analysis has enabled the bank to generate multimillion-dollar returns in customer acquisition and retention campaigns.

Mastering the Basics

Acxiom recommends that all banks use the following:

- **RFM segmentation.** Segmenting customers by the three key variables of behavior: recency, frequency, and monetary value (RFM). Transaction data remains the most powerful predictor of future behavior and can help banks identify the best prospects and possible defectors.

- **Data enhancement.** Appending demographic and geographic data to customer records permits various modeling and mining efforts to be undertaken, including:
  1. **Profiling.** Create a profile of individual customers and households in each of your key segments, comparing the incidence of a particular type of buyer in your customer universe to the larger marketplace.
  2. **Cross-selling the existing customer base.** Identify best customers and target those who are prime candidates for additional products and services. Analytical models pinpoint variables that will lift response—which means you can mail to fewer people and get a greater response on what you do mail.
  3. **Upselling or reactivating customers.** Low-balance depositors and noncredit customers can be upgraded to more profitable status with appropriate product targeting. Inactive customers may likewise be viable prospects for other offerings.
  4. **Retention.** Reduce churn in your customer base by identifying factors predictive of defection and testing programs to turn likely defectors into your most loyal customers.
  5. **Acquisition.** Data can be used in various ways to improve acquisition. Your profile of your best customers points the way to the prospect most likely to respond and be profitable over time. This data can drive your offer, your creative, your media selection, and your fulfillment approach. Large mailers or telemarketers can also screen prospect lists by running them through a regression model, since they have considerable bargaining power in the list rental marketplace.

The Loyalty Connection

Developing deeper customer loyalty is an ongoing challenge for every financial institution. It is compounded by the industry's increasing reliance on technology, both for developing products and executing transactions. As reliance on brick-and-mortar branch infrastructures and personal relationships lessens, low-cost, high-tech options such as automated teller machines (ATMs) and online banking are increasingly homogenizing product offerings, and banks may lose the opportunity to cross-sell and up-sell to their own customers because newcomers, not tied to banking's traditional branch infrastructure, can deliver services more cheaply. While it may be hard to think of bank products and services as commodities that we can shop around for like bread or milk, that mindset is changing.

Newcomers to banking such as Net Bank (www.netbank.com) are making some inroads with Internet-happy customers. But there is an upside for established players who are expanding their own online offerings. Electronic transactions generate transactional data that, when handled proactively, can help banks stand out from the crowd. For example, data captured on which ATM locations a customer uses, where the ATM is located in relation to the consumer's home and work, and what type of transactions each consumer conducts by time of day, week, or month, can be very illuminating. Banks can use such data resources to increase overall ATM usage, to redirect traffic to underutilized sites, or to increase usage during low-peak evening and weekend hours.

Designing Win-Win Situations

Leading with data in financial services is not without its challenges. One of the key problems is that a model profitable customer—one who runs high balances on credit cards or other revolving loan programs—is also a model candidate for bankruptcy. That problem has been worsened by industry practices in issuing preapproved credit cards, which has contributed to rising bad debt for both consumers and issuers.

The delinquency crunch has attracted some nonbank innovators to the marketplace. Merchandise cataloger Fingerhut of Minnetonka, MN (www.fingerhut.com), decided to pursue high-risk customers as a lucrative credit card market. Using the company's catalog database containing 500 pieces of information on the cataloger's 50-million-name file, Fingerhut opened 670,000 credit card accounts with $500 million in receivables in less than a year, making it one of the largest card issuers in the United States. Factoring in the inherent risk of extending credit to low- to middle-income families, Fingerhut allowed a 6 percent write-off for bad debt and a competitive interest rate on its co-branded Visa and MasterCards. Fingerhut attributed the company's success to data—"It all goes back to the database," said their CEO.

Sensitivity Prevails

Another sophisticated use of data is segmented pricing based on customers' and prospective customers' risk and return profiles. Such customization, however, while used successfully in the insurance industry, faces consumer resistance when it comes to accessing credit. In fact, some issuers have raised consumer ire by offering preapproved cards without revealing all of the facts about the offered rate. Variable rates and "as low as" offers are clearly on shaky ethical and legal ground (federal law requires issuers to disclose in writing the interest rate in preapproved offers). And recent amendments to the Fair Credit Reporting Act require all companies using credit bureau lists to inform consumers of their opt-out rights. Issuers must factor in these business realities as they experiment with data-driven programs.

Data can also help bankers to think about customers in fresh ways. Data helps banks to develop traditional or emerging channels and to glean all the information they possibly can. Trustmark National Bank (www.trustmark.com), for example, offers senior citizens, who generally appreciate high-touch over high-tech service, the opportunity to have someone reconcile their check registers with their bank statements. Does that sound time consuming and unprofitable? It could be, but Trustmark added a relational database field to track which seniors opened savings accounts for their grandchildren, and markets to them accordingly.

Banks are entering a new era of relationship-oriented strategies. Intensely transaction-driven, they have realized that product-oriented strategies will give way to more targeted and focused marketing efforts. Gemini Consulting (www.gemini.com) outlines the benefits banks derive as they adopt relationship-building strategies that lead with data:

- They efficiently sell the maximum amount of the banking products targeted to the right segments of their databases.

- Basic segmentation and cross-selling become easier, as preferred pricing and service strategies emerge for customers who buy multiple products and keep their business close to home.

- They build multiple product relationships with targeted customer segments, as sophisticated modeling techniques and profitability analysis at the account level allow customized value offerings and pricing.

To overcome the increasing homogenization of banking products via Internet banking and other online services, banks must position and distribute distinct initiatives associated with a bank's brand identity.

Hands-On Exercise

1. Using the CRM process model in Exhibit 4.1, explain where in the process the financial services firms are in your community. Give examples of some banks that are appealing to students using CRM and how.

2. Using the knowledge you acquired in this chapter about CRM, suggest ways banks and other companies can use CRM to better serve their customers.

Summary of Learning Objectives

■ **Understand the essential elements that make up a customer relationship management program.**
Customer relationship management (CRM) is the management of customer relationships based on the integration of customer information throughout the business enterprise in order to achieve maximum customer satisfaction and retention. To accomplish such a task, CRM operates on a simple yet often misunderstood concept—customer interaction. Customer interaction (in a CRM context) is based on the relationship between the enterprise and the customer.

■ **Describe the relationship that exists between marketing research and customer relationship management.**
One of the primary roles of marketing research in the CRM process is to collect, store, and analyze customer interaction information (customer knowledge). In doing so, marketing research takes on a new role that is unique to the CRM environment. This role is to transform the practice of marketing research into one of market intelligence.

■ **Understand the meaning of market intelligence.**
The market intelligence enterprise follows a business model different from that of the more traditional companies. This model promotes a competitive advantage by using customer information at the "granular" level; that is, data that are highly detailed, highly personalized, and specifically structured around the individual customer. This enterprise embraces the vision that targeting customers is not sufficient; capturing customers is the goal.

■ **Illustrate the process of data collection for a customer relationship management program.**
In most CRM programs data are tracked at the point of customer interaction. This may occur at point-of-sale terminals (registers) or on the Web. Regardless of the source, the goal is to collect all relevant customer interaction data, store the data in the data warehouse, and subsequently analyze the data to render profitable customer profiles.

■ **Illustrate and define a marketing research database.**
A marketing research database is a central repository of information on what customers are purchasing, how

often, and in what amount. The fundamental purpose of any customer database is to help a firm develop meaningful, personal communication with its customers. Other, more specific purposes of this database are to improve efficiency of market segment construction, increase the probability of repeat purchase behavior, and enhance sales and media effectiveness.

■ **Illustrate the development and purpose of the data warehouse.**
A data warehouse is a central repository for all significant parts of information that an organization collects. Data from various functions of the organization are stored and inventoried on a central mainframe computer so that information may be shared across all functional departments of the business. The major significance of a data warehouse is its purpose. From the standpoint of data collection, a data warehouse serves two purposes: (1) to collect and store data for the daily operations of the business, and (2) to collect, organize, and make data available for analysis purposes.

■ **Explain the process of data mining as it relates to the data warehouse.**
Data mining is the process of finding hidden relationships among variables contained in data stored in the data warehouse. Data mining is a data analysis procedure known primarily for the recognition of significant patterns of data as they pertain to particular customers or customer groups.

■ **Understand the role of modeling in database analysis.**
The purpose of database modeling is twofold: (1) to summarize what companies already know about their customers, and (2) to show companies what they need to learn about their customers. Two common modeling techniques exist in database analysis. Scoring models, using a gains table, are designed to predict consumption behavior. Lifetime value models measure the value customers represent to the firm. Both models rely on actual purchase behavior, not probability estimates based on purchase intentions.

Key Terms and Concepts

Review Questions

1. What are the three major benefits that a company can realize from a CRM program?

2. Briefly describe the basic essentials of a CRM program.

3. Briefly explain the following concepts as they apply to a CRM environment: the strategic use of customer information, information based on a transactional focus, enterprisewide approach to the use of information, and technology support of the CRM structure.

4. What role does technology play in a CRM program?

5. Describe the significant implications that exist when companies collect the following data: active data, passive data, and directed data.

6. List the three advantages that data enhancement provides and explain how Nike (www.nike.com) could use each one.

7. Explain the differences between a sequential database and a relational database. What advantages are associated with each?

8. Describe how data mining works and how it is helping companies to improve their decision making.

9. What is the value of database modeling in understanding customer behavior?

Discussion Questions

1. Describe the CRM process and discuss the potential contributions this process has for a business enterprise.

2. **EXPERIENCE THE INTERNET.** Conduct an Internet search on customer relationship management. In your search, try to identify 10 companies that are currently practicing CRM.

3. **EXPERIENCE THE INTERNET.** Conduct an Internet search for consulting firms that provide CRM assistance for businesses. Select a firm and provide a brief write-up on what that firm provides regarding CRM.

4. Why are transactional data collection techniques important to Anheuser-Busch and other companies?

5. Briefly describe the differences between lifetime value models and scoring models. In what situations would each modeling procedure be most appropriate?

6. Could the Santa Fe Grill benefit from using database modeling in its operations? If so, how?

7. Would the application of CRM principles improve the Santa Fe Grill operations? If so, how?

8. What are the major types of information the Santa Fe Grill should include in building a data warehouse?

chapter 5

Marketing Decision Support Systems

Learning Objectives

After reading this chapter, you will be able to

1. Understand the purpose of a marketing decision support system (MDSS).

2. Describe the various information requirements used to design an MDSS.

3. Understand the role of transactional data in the MDSS.

4. Explain the relationship between information processing and the MDSS.

5. Understand the various models used in an MDSS.

6. Provide examples of output from an MDSS.

7. Discuss the relationship that exists between the decision support system and business intelligence.

Sears: Consolidating Data for Real-Time Decisions

Sears knows a lot about its more than 48 million active Sears customer households. But before installing a decision support system, it did not know which of its customers were the same people. Under the Sears umbrella (www.sears.com), which includes almost 900 full-line stores and over 1,000 specialty stores, customers could get a credit card, then use it to buy clothes from a catalog, Craftsman tools, or Kenmore appliances. They could have their hair dyed red, then have their picture taken while waiting to have their auto repaired or to buy a Diehard battery. Sears goes to millions of customers' houses each year to kill termites, install fences, and deliver air-conditioning units. But each purchase record appeared in a different Sears database. In its previous system, eight separate transactions would appear to be from eight different people, although that might not have been the case. Sears management needed to tie together the records that made up individual customer profiles, but first they had to figure out which records belonged to the same person. Consolidation of Sears customer purchase records was particularly important because with the acquisition of Lands' End (www.landsend.com) the company would need to make a seamless connection between its existing

customer base and millions of new Lands' End customers.

To further complicate the problem, system consistency had to be superimposed because the data sources had different underlying structures: the hair salon indexed records by customer name, the credit card database identified customers by social security numbers, and the appliance repair center tracked customers by home phone number. Sears had to standardize and make sense of all the data. The decision support system known as "unified data view" seemed to be the answer. The system allowed Sears to build a single picture of each customer, creating a powerful decision tool to improve service and increase customer retention.

Customer retention is a goal of both retailers and manufacturers. The advent of more powerful decision support tools, advanced analytical processes such as data mining, and rich customer data sources is powering this business trend. The benefit of these technologies is realized when data associated with the customer is merged with data generated by ongoing business operations. This infrastructure is known as a decision support system, and it is increasingly being used by successful companies in the United States and abroad.[1]

Value of the Marketing Decision Support System

When businesses find themselves in uncertain competitive situations, they must make strategic decisions. Such decisions may involve changing personnel, implementing new pricing policies, introducing new products, or exploring new promotional methods. The task then evolves to selecting the best action to solve the problem and generate the desired outcome. For example, if a change in price policy is recommended, a manager must know what prices to set, how the new pricing will affect customer perceptions, and how the competition will react. Similarly, if a new promotional method is recommended, what method should be used? How much will it cost? How effective will the new method be? Questions such as these can be answered only by properly interpreting the most appropriate information available.

Rapid advancement of technology over the past decade has made it possible for businesses to collect, condense, and categorize information in a highly efficient manner. But while this has produced an unprecedented level of information availability, it has not generated much improvement in managers' ability to correctly interpret information. Interpretation requires more than the ability to correctly read rows and columns of numbers, percentages, and absolute values. It begins with an understanding of where the information comes from, how the information is obtained, and what relevance the information has to the business situation being examined. Decision makers must anticipate the kinds of information that will be required to reduce uncertainty in the decision-making process. This involves selecting the proper information sources and knowing how to obtain information from those sources.

Correct interpretation of information is also affected by time. Information that was collected yesterday may be outdated today. For information to be correctly interpreted it must be collected in a timely, ongoing manner. A systematic gathering of longitudinal information reinforces a manager's ability to correctly interpret that information for decision making.

Finally, the ability to correctly interpret information centers on its accuracy. Even if researchers establish careful criteria for information collection, it is inevitable that biases will arise out of personal or environmental factors. In order to reduce such biases, researchers should collect information from several sources or use several different approaches. Different information sources relevant to the decision problem can enhance accuracy in the interpretation process.

CRM and the Marketing Decision Support System

Growth in the electronic marketplace and the resultant increase in the availability of and access to customer data have been major drivers of the accelerated pace at which businesses are adopting technology-based systems for customer relationship management (CRM). Businesses are using technology to better align their operations, resources, and strategies to maximize the value customers derive from their products and services. Applications have focused on automating customer operational procedures for the purpose of interaction and data collection. However, "customer-centric" businesses are increasingly embracing a view that goes beyond the functionality of such applications to include a full range of support system components. These approaches foster a more sophisticated view of CRM based on the creation of a closed-loop decision support system.

While the CRM process has a variety of strategic outcomes, two of the most common are the decision support system and the business intelligence program. As we will see in the first part of this chapter, the decision support system is a CRM tool designed to assist a business in making marketing decisions. Early decision support systems were designed as business intelligence tools. In today's technological arena, with vast amounts of consumer and competitive information available, decision support systems and business intelligence programs each serve unique purposes for business. Business intelligence programs will be discussed later in the chapter.

The Marketing Decision Support System

Marketing decision support system (MDSS) A computer-based system intended for use by particular marketing personnel at any functional level for the purpose of solving semistructured problems.

A **marketing decision support system (MDSS)** is a computer-based system used by marketing personnel at any functional level (e.g., sales, product or brand management, advertising). The output is special reports, mathematical simulations, or tracking devices.

The MDSS and the marketing information system (MIS) have been viewed as almost identical. Based on the emergence of new technology, however, the two systems have evolved into unique research tools. The MDSS, in contrast to the MIS, possesses several unique characteristics:

1. It focuses on specific research problems to support individual marketing personnel.

2. It provides information to facilitate a specific decision (new-product planning, advertising effectiveness, distribution alternatives).

3. Its primary purpose is to evaluate alternative solutions to marketing-related problems and to identify the best course of action.

4. It solves more limited problems such as facilitating the design of sales territories, evaluating outcomes of new-product or brand launches, or even profiling specific target markets for marketing actions.

5. Its emphasis is twofold: information storage and categorization, and resultant solutions.

Marketing Decision Support Systems, Inc. (www.mdssworld.com), is a major supplier of MDSS solutions. Examples of how it has helped clients solve MDSS problems include: developed a marketing database for a consumer electronics company to track sales patterns and sales force productivity, set up a system for a durable goods manufacturer that uses monthly industry forecasts to set factory production schedules, and helped a household goods manufacturer analyze data from more than 350,000 product registration forms so it could distribute marketing information to the dealers that sell its products. FACTIVITY is a specialized MDSS solution (www.mdss.net) that is an example of an off-the-shelf product. It is designed to control shop floor labor and work-in-process production as well as provide real-time data collection for an MDSS database that can be used to manage supply chain issues.[2]

A Marketing Decision Support System Diagram

Exhibit 5.1 illustrates how an MDSS supports marketing personnel in various capacities. The MDSS stores and categorizes three groups of marketing information: environmental, transactional, and competitive. This information is contained within an information-processing system consisting of a computer, a marketing research database, and specialized software. This information-processing system enables the user to examine information and obtain output in the form of specialized reports, responses to database queries, and model simulations. Reports and database queries are used most often to identify market-related problems. Simulations are helpful in planning alternative solutions to problems.

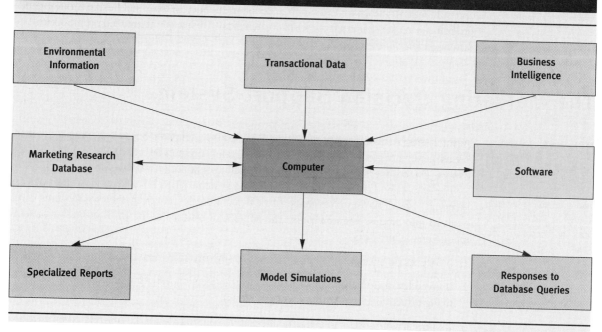

EXHIBIT 5.1 A Marketing Decision Support System

The purpose of this chapter is to acquaint the reader with how an MDSS is used. Chapters 3 and 4 provided discussions of secondary data, information technology, and database development, which together form the foundation for understanding the MDSS.

Information Requirements

Much of the information in the MDSS is secondary. Because the MDSS is designed to provide solutions to current problems in the marketplace, it contains actual market data, not intentions or attitudes. Information used in the MDSS provides marketing personnel with a picture of what happened in the past, so the present and the future can be put in perspective. Market activities are reported quickly, as they actually happen, so marketing personnel can act accordingly. For example, when Miller Brewing Company (www.millerbrewing.com) introduced its Miller Red Beer, managers needed to know how the beer was selling at different stores, at different price points, under different promotional campaigns. Corrective actions to change or enhance the marketing effort had to take place immediately. Thus, the most valuable data were the direct, point-of-sale, transactional data linked into the MDSS from various store locations. Transactional data revealed that sales were less than estimated at convenience stores in the southwestern United States. It happened that Budweiser was doing a massive point-of-sale campaign for its Michelob brand, undermining all marketing efforts by Miller. Within 24 hours, Miller distributors were instructed to contact convenience store managers in the Southwest and offer them a $1 buydown per case if they would remove all Michelob promotions and exclusively promote Miller.

On the basis of a simulation of transactional data, Miller estimated a sales increase of 40 percent, which would more than offset the lost revenue resulting from the $1 buydown. In addition, the model estimated that individual store units would average 700 cases sold per week, resulting in $700 extra revenue for the store. Armed with this data, distributors were able to persuade convenience store managers to change their emphasis to Miller. This rapid reaction would not have been possible without point-of-sale data and MDSS simulations. The key to the success of this decision was showing managers at Miller what happened in the past, what was happening today, and what would happen tomorrow.

Environmental Information

Environmental information Information pertaining to suppliers and distributors.

Within the context of the MDSS, **environmental information** is that pertaining to suppliers and distributors. Information on suppliers is particularly important, because cooperation and coordination of activities with these firms ensure that a company has the necessary raw materials and services to react to changes in the market. Specifically, companies must have reliable information on supply considerations such as cost, quality, and product reliability.

In an MDSS, suppliers are ranked by the dollar volume of business they do with a company. A series of related criteria is established and stored within the information processing unit of the MDSS. This information can then be analyzed using software that evaluates all suppliers on the following dimensions:

1. Dollar volume by season and year.

2. Growth or shrinkage of annual dollar volume.

3. Accuracy of shipping and billing.

4. Timeliness of deliveries.

5. Price terms and allowance.

6. Returns and procedures.

A sample output of supplier processing software is shown in Exhibit 5.2. Perhaps the greatest advantage of such a system is that a supplier can be selected or replaced immediately so that the company can avoid shortages or excessive inventory and, ultimately, customer dissatisfaction.

Distribution Partners

Distributors are typically referred to as service wholesalers. They are businesses that secure products from the manufacturer and sell them to retailers. Service wholesalers are widely used because they offer many advantages over selling direct to retail. For example, they offer packaging and shipping services, reduce inventory carrying needs, reduce credit risks, and simplify bookkeeping. Many businesses, such as grocery stores and convenience stores, have no choice but to use wholesalers due to the wide merchandise variety they must maintain. Thus, the profitability of service wholesalers is continually evaluated. Hard data related to wholesalers should include:

1. Levels of inventory carried by various wholesalers.

2. On-time delivery performance.

3. Minimum ordering requirements.

4. Transportation costs.

5. Repairs, allowances, and adjustments.

6. Level of service (e.g., automatic merchandise replacement, markups, inventory management).

| **e X H I B I T** | **5.2** | **Example of Output from Supplier Processing Software** |

Dept. No.

Date

Resource

Merchandise   Top Grade _____   Medium _____   Low-End _____

Activity (Mfr., Jobber, Importer, etc.)

Sales Office Address   Telephone _____

Factory or Warehouse Address

Company Officers and Titles

Buyer Contacts—State peculiarities or special handling required by
  a. Sales Office   b. Factory

Rating—Dun & Bradstreet

Ethics of Firm

Ranking in Industry

Vendor Importance to Store

Store Importance to Vendor

Record of All Arrangements (Terms, Trade Discounts, Cash Discounts, Cooperative Advertising, etc.)

Remarks (State clearly any additional information not covered above that will guide any member of our organization who may have to deal with this vendor.)

Semiannual

Date   By Whom

Exhibit 5.3 shows a document from a wholesaler evaluation system, included in many marketing decision support systems. As you can see, the system allows for quick, efficient comparative evaluation among wholesalers. Here again, the accuracy and timeliness of data are necessary in order for the system to be effective in the decision-making process.

Business Intelligence

Business intelligence
A procedure for collecting daily operational information pertinent to the company and the markets it serves.

An additional informational requirement of a marketing decision support system is **business intelligence.** Business intelligence activities lack the structure and rigor of more formal information-gathering practices associated with suppliers or distributors, but they represent an important informational input into the MDSS. Business intelligence collects daily operational information pertinent to the company and markets it serves. Business intelligence information is usually collected by reading trade publications, books, and newspapers, as well as by talking to customers, suppliers, wholesalers, and other personnel within the company.

Transactional Data

Transactional data Information resulting from a transaction usually between a consumer and a retailer.

Transactional data is information resulting from a transaction usually between a consumer and a retailer. New methods of collecting transactional data are emerging and will significantly change the practice of marketing research. Today, five technologies interact to help researchers collect and maintain transactional data: *bar coding, optical scanning, automatic replenishment, electronic data interchange,* and *reader sorters.*

еXHIBIT 5.3 Example of Wholesaler Evaluation System

```
VENDOR INQUIRY                              PROGRAM-NAME: 201U5031
                                            PFKEY  1 - RESTART
   DEPT    20    LADIES SPORTSWEAR          PFKEY 16 - EXIT
   VENDOR  437801  LONGSTREET INDUSTRIES, LTD.
   DATE    06/8-

   RECEIPTS:                MARKDOWNS:
      UNITS    420             UNITS     56      ADV CONTRIBUTIONS:   .00
      @ RTL   6715.80          @ RTL   280.23
      @ COST  3156.45                           # P.O.'S PLACED:   6

                              PURCHASES:
   SALES:                                       # SHIPMENTS:       5
                                @ RTL   7438.20
      UNITS    324              @ COST  4462.92  OVER SHIPMENTS:    0
      @ RTL   5389.77
      @ COST  3108.45        INVOICED AMTS:      UNDER SHIPMENTS:   1

   RETURNS:                    INVOICE  3782.40
                               DISC      231.18
      UNITS     23             FREIGHT    45.20
      @ RTL    367.77          RETAIL   6715.80
                                        Press "ENTER" to continue *
```

Bar coding A pattern of varied-width bars and spaces that represents a code of numbers and letters.

Optical scanner A light-sensitive device that "reads" bar codes; that is, captures and translates unique bar code numbers into product information.

Bar coding is a pattern of varied-width bars and spaces that represents a code of numbers and letters. When decoded through an optical scanning device, the code points to important product information. Brand name, style, size, color, and price are some of the data represented by bar codes. Bar codes also provide data on inventory levels, percentage of markup on the item, stock turn rate on merchandise, and quantity levels necessary for reordering.

Bar coding operates in conjunction with optical scanners. An **optical scanner** is a light-sensitive device that "reads" bar codes; that is, it captures and translates unique bar code numbers into product information and thus facilitates data entry into the MDSS. Two scanning techniques are commonly employed. First, the universal product code (UPC) is a generally accepted bar code for the retail industry. A UPC is a 12-digit number used for merchandise identification. Second is the shipper container marking (SCM). An SCM is a bar code that facilitates the identification and shipping of containers between manufacturers, distributors, and retailers. UPCs and SCMs can be read by a variety of optical scanners. Stores like Target, Home Depot, and Wal-Mart use handheld scanners for speed and convenience. Optical scanning wands are used predominantly by department stores like Dillard's and Macy's because of loosely attached price tags. Flatbed scanners or in-line conveyers are used mainly by supermarkets due to the volume of items and coupons that need scanning.

Every time an optical scanner reads a bar code, it electronically records what was bought, the manufacturer and vendor, the size, and price. This information is then archived in a database and enhanced with market intelligence and other research-related information.

eXHIBIT 5.4   HomeScan: Scanner Data for Decision Making

Men are more active buyers of products in many categories than had been thought, according to new data from NPD/Nielsen's Advertising Services division.

The first data released from Nielsen's HomeScan database cover a year of magazine reading and product purchases in 18,000-plus households nationally, part of Nielsen's household panel.

While HomeScan's single-source information service is similar to annual surveys from Mediamark Research Inc. (MRI) and Simmons Market Research Bureau, HomeScan gathers purchasing information electronically, via a scanning wand, MRI and Simmons respondents record purchase information in response to a written questionnaire or interview.

HomeScan tracks magazine readers' use of 1,500 brands in 1,000 product categories, Among initial findings is the high number of package-goods purchases made by men.

"We are finding that men are a lot more important [as consumers]. Overall, about 30 percent of the dollars recorded by package goods were purchased by men," said Steve Coffey, vice president of NDP/Nielsen.

For example, among mouthwash brands, men bought 52 percent of all Viadent purchased and 22 percent of Colgate Tartar in the year ended June 1.

Nielsen isn't sure why HomeScan shows more purchases by men than previous estimates. But Coffey said it may be because other surveys typically designate a single member of each household as a homemaker who provides information about product purchases, while HomeScan distinguishes between household members and records their age and sex.

Another finding is that magazine audience levels are higher than those recorded by MRI and Simmons, Overall, HomeScan shows 44 percent higher audience levels than MRI and 86 percent higher than Simmons in the 140 magazines HomeScan tracks.

This disparity may be caused by interviewer bias in other surveys, Coffey said. Unlike MRI and Simmons, HomeScan collects readership information electronically, not through an interviewer.

As a result, some magazines—particularly those responders might feel awkward reporting they read, such as *The National Enquirer* and *Playboy*—post higher audience levels than in other surveys. Other categories, including newsweeklies, post audience levels similar to those reported by MRI and Simmons.

HomeScan subscribers can access the database, updated in October and April, via an online service or compact disc. Subscribers include *Parade; Reader's Digest; USA Today;* Kraft; General Foods; Leo Burnett Co.; Foote, Cone Belding Communications; and Walter Thompson USA.

Automatic replenishment system (ARS) A continuous automated system designed to analyze inventory levels, merchandise order lead times, and forecasted sales.

Electronic data interchange (EDI) A computerized system designed to speed the flow of information and products from producer to distributor to retailer.

The resulting database has the potential to reveal what consumers watch on television, what type of neighborhood they live in, and what kinds of stores they shop at.

Exhibit 5.4 describes how scanner data can be cross-referenced as well as the value it holds for marketing researchers. Information in the exhibit is based on AC Nielsen Homescan (www.acnielsen.com/products/reports/homescan/), a consumer packaged goods purchase information service with key insights on consumers in 18 countries.

An **automatic replenishment system (ARS)** is a continuous, automated system designed to analyze inventory levels, merchandise order lead times, and forecasted sales. It also generates purchase orders for merchandise that needs quick replenishment. ARS helps firms carry the lowest possible levels of inventory while still maintaining a sufficient quantity to avoid stock-outs. Inventory levels are optimized because order quantities are smaller and ordering is more frequent. In addition, inventory movement is improved because reordering is automatic, stock turn rates are higher, and the cost of spoilage and shrinkage is decreased dramatically.

Electronic data interchange (EDI) is a computerized system that speeds the flow of information and products from producer to distributor to retailer, contributing to increased sales, reduced markdowns, and lowered inventory carrying costs. EDI differs from an automatic replenishment system (ARS) in that additional benefits are derived from reductions in costs of clerical and administrative activities associated with merchandise ordering. EDI centers mainly on electronic exchange of information such as purchase orders, invoices, advanced shipping notices, and product return notices. In essence, EDI is the information arm of an automatic replenishment system.

EDI is available in two formats: direct data interchange (from retailer to vendors or distributors) and third-party networks, which operate as clearinghouses or electronic mailboxes for retailers. While slight differences exist between these two formats, their benefits are much the same. EDI reduces the costs of clerical work and data entry, postage, handling, and form printing. The speed of communication reduces inventory carrying costs, improving the efficiency of vendor and retailer.

Automatic replenishment systems and electronic data interchange are keys to the MDSS. Toys "R" Us (www.toysrus.com), for example, is a $13 billion dollar business with approximately 1,500 stores worldwide that is networked to over 500 vendors. Being a highly seasonal company (60 percent of sales occur between Thanksgiving and Christmas), Toys "R" Us depends on inventory control for its survival. It attributes its growth and profitability to the inventory and information components of the MDSS. Transmitted data include orders and shipment confirmations. Sales and inventory records are also transmitted, providing information to buyers and vendors on which toys are sold at which stores worldwide, and when the items need to be replenished. More specifically, through EDI Toys "R" Us can monitor sales trends and communicate with vendors automatically. Toys "R" Us stores in California, for example, sell more trend and fad merchandise than other stores. EDI enables buyers to create a balanced product mix of these goods with other, less seasonal goods.

Reader-sorter A computerized device located at the point of sale that resembles a miniature automated teller machine (ATM); it enables consumers to pay for transactions with credit cards, ATM cards, or debit cards.

The final element used in generating transactional data is the **reader-sorter.** The reader-sorter is a computerized device located at the point of sale that resembles a miniature automated teller machine (ATM). It enables consumers to pay for transactions with credit or debit cards. The magnetic strip on the back of each card contains a wealth of consumer data. On this tiny strip an individual's personal, historical data are stored, along with other relevant data such as at which store the card was used, what was actually purchased and when, along with significant demographic and lifestyle data.

At the point of sale, when a consumer uses the reader-sorter as a payment method, data from both the magnetic strip and the current purchase are automatically collected. The optical scanner (via a bar code) is collecting and recording product purchases while the reader-sorter (via the credit or debit card) is collecting and recording information on who is making the purchase. Both groups of information are then stored in the central database of the MDSS. When compiled with other consumer purchases, a specific product-related profile can be generated based on weekly, even daily, store activities.

Exhibit 5.5 contains a sample MDSS report on individuals who purchased Pepsi products at a particular supermarket. On the basis of the database information, we learn these individuals also listen to contemporary rock music, visit theme parks, drink vodka, rent videocassettes, give cookouts and barbeques, are pro football watchers, and use a personal computer at home. While this is only a small amount of the data it would be possible to gather on Pepsi drinkers, it represents actual data collected at the point of sale and stored in the database.

With this information Pepsi can anticipate daily sales, plan in-store promotional activities, anticipate reactions to price and packaging changes, and maintain an accurate description of its target market. Since the data were generated on actual product purchases, not propensity to purchase Pepsi, the information has high predictive accuracy. Thus, the benefits of an MDSS are not only its ability to collect and categorize relevant customer information, but also to predict based on the information-processing element of the MDSS. Virtually all

EXHIBIT 5.5 Sample MDSS Report on Pepsi Buyers

TARGET LIFESTYLES/MEDIASTYLES/DEMOGRAPHICS FOR PEPSI

TARGET: SOUTH AO DDT HEAVY USER

Demographics	Penetration			Demographics	Penetration		
	Total	Target	Index		Total	Target	Index
Bought Heavy Rock Music	7.76	13.11	109	Go Power Boating	4.83	5.82	120
Bought Cntmpry Rock Music	15.90	24.85	156	Professional Wrestling Fans	10.95	13.17	120
Attended Pop/Rock Concerts	8.91	13.53	152	Drink Vodka	18.74	22.24	115
Ride Motorcycles	3.71	5.46	147	Go Bicycling	16.77	19.63	117
Bought Soul/R&B/Black Music	8.13	11.65	143	First Time Truck Buyers	7.12	8.31	117
Play Racquetball	4.53	6.45	143	Bought Pre-Rec Audio Csstte	23.44	27.26	116
Downhill Skiers	3.98	5.65	143	Tapes			
Bought Cntmpry Pop Vcl Music	17.10	24.18	141	Rented Video Cassettes 1st yr	48.06	35.70	115
Do Weight Training	9.84	13.87	141	Bought Traditional/Cntmpry Jazz	5.97	6.81	114
Water Skiers	3.94	5.53	140	Bought 3-Door/Hatchback New	2.70	3.05	113
Joggers/Runners	9.16	12.61	138	Bought Foreign Car New	12.28	13.85	113
Go Horseback Riding	4.26	5.35	137	Smoke Menthol Cigarettes	9.15	10.26	112

consumer packaged good companies like Procter and Gamble, Heinz, Campbell's Soup, ConAgra, General Mills, Nabisco, and Tyson's, to name a few, use this kind of information in their MDSS systems.

Information Processing and the MDSS

The three key elements of the information-processing component of the MDSS are the database, the computer facilities, and the software system. We have already discussed database development, so our focus here is on the computer and the software system.

The computer and the software system serve one primary function in the MDSS: to produce reports valuable to the decision maker. The computer and software system of the MDSS should:

- Reflect the needs for the user, not the analyst.

- Provide reports for the user within minutes.

- Sort and print highly specific report data.

- Be easy to read, use, and manipulate.

- Be custom-made versus prewritten. While prewritten systems are less expensive, if the system does not meet the user's needs, it is useless.

Two general types of software systems exist for MDSS: statistical software systems and managerial function software systems.

Statistical Software Systems

Statistical software systems MDSS systems that analyze large volumes of data and compute basic statistics such as means and standard deviations.

Statistical software systems analyze large volumes of data and compute basic statistics such as means and standard deviations. They also compare sets of numbers and use such tests as t-tests and chi-square tests to determine how similar or different the numbers are. More sophisticated routines like multiple regression and analysis of variance are also available.

While a variety of statistical software systems exist, SAS (www.sas.com) and SPSS (www.spss.com) are the most robust packages for the MDSS. Statistical knowledge is needed to use these packages. But they are usually the favorite choice of the research analyst. Therefore, managerial function software systems are also included in the MDSS.

Managerial Function Software Systems

Managerial function software systems MDSS systems used by managers; these include forecasting systems, product/brand management systems, and promotional budget systems.

In the MDSS environment, three **managerial function software systems** are commonly employed: forecasting systems, product/brand management systems, and promotional budget systems.

Many forecasting systems enable sales or marketing managers to project future occurrences. They all use the types of data described earlier as a basis for predicting sales. For example, if transactional data indicate that purchases increase with increased presence of the product at retail, the relationship could be stated in mathematical (i.e., modeled) terms. Forecasting systems usually produce sales or profitability projections in a report form such as the one in Exhibit 5.6.

Product/brand management software systems enable managers to plan for new-product introduction. One such package, called brand planning, is based on a critical path analysis and displays the output in the form of a Gantt chart. The brand-planning package plans the sequencing of activities (production, sales, packaging, etc.) that must be performed simultaneously in order to have a successful product launch.

Promotional budget systems enable managers to predict and control promotional expenditures. Limits are set for each element of the promotional budget—sales, advertising, sales promotion, and media spending. Reports are issued on a monthly basis indicating how actual expenses relate to budget projections. An example of a promotional budget system is the ADBUG.[3] This model evaluates sales response to advertising. Conceptually, the system is quite simple in that it examines what is happening to an entire industry, product class, or even brand within the class, with respect to the brand's market share. The system uses what-if assumptions and performs a series of sensitivity analyses to measure sales response based on the effects of share advertising, media effectiveness, product seasonality, trends, competition, and price.

In order to develop the sales response function, the ADBUG user makes a number of assumptions. These include:

1. A certain level of advertising expenditures will maintain brand share at some given level.

2. A floor exists where brand share will fall by a fixed amount with zero advertising.

3. A ceiling exists where brand share will increase given large advertising expenditures.

The ADBUG system has two main objectives: (1) to determine the optimum level of advertising expenditures to achieve a desired level of sales and (2) to determine how to change advertising expenditures over time to maximize profits.

Regardless of which MDSS software system is used, the goal is to produce information from data in order to facilitate decisions. The common denominator of all MDSS software systems is that modeling capabilities are used to provide direct support to the manager for solving problems. Therefore, before we cover MDSS output we provide a brief discussion of models.

EXHIBIT 5.6 Illustration of Output from Sales Forecasting System

PROJECTS QUOTED RECAP: September
RECAP BY INDUSTRY:

Industry	Type	Total w/Revisions by Indus. & Type	Total w/Revisions by Indus.	Total Complete by Indus. & Type	Total Complete by Indus.	No. Quotes
BAKING:	Systems (S)	$550,004.00		$2,398,425.00		3
	Screeners (CS)	$38,761.91		$38,761.91		1
	Rotary Valves (CV)	$0.00		$0.00		0
	Miscellaneous (M)	$0.00	$588,765.91	$0.00	$2,437,186.91	0
PLASTIC:	Systems (S)	$0.00		$0.00		0
	Screeners (CS)	$0.00		$0.00		0
	Rotary Valves (CV)	$0.00		$0.00		0
	Miscellaneous (M)	$0.00	$0.00	$0.00	$0.00	0
CHEMICAL:	Systems (S)	$314,980.00		$559,519.00		4
	Screeners (CS)	$19,140.00		$19,140.00		3
	Rotary Valves (CV)	$10,860.00		$10,860.00		2
	Miscellaneous (M)	$0.00	$344,980.00	$0.00	$589,519.00	0
PHARMACEUTICAL:	Systems (S)	$69,918.00		$129,918.00		4
	Screeners (CS)	$0.00		$0.00		0
	Rotary Valves (CV)	$0.00		$0.00		0
	Miscellaneous (M)	$200,000.00	$269,918.00	$252,000.00	$381,918.00	2
FOOD:	Systems (S)	$13,670,547.00		$22,409,527.00		12
	Screeners (CS)	$155,667.00		$155,667.00		6
	Rotary Valves (CV)	$28,120.00		$28,120.00		3
	Miscellaneous (M)	($67,100.00)	$13,787,234.00	$317,200.00	$22,910,514.00	1
DAIRY:	Systems (S)	$0.00		$0.00		0
	Screeners (CS)	$13,374.00		$13,374.00		1
	Rotary Valves (CV)	$0.00		$0.00		0
	Miscellaneous (M)	$0.00	$13,374.00	$0.00	$13,374.00	0
PARTS:	General (Parts)	$0.00	$0.00	$0.00	$0.00	0
Powder Paint: (PP)	Systems (S)	$0.00		$0.00		0
	Screeners (CS)	$46,065.00		$97,584.00		3
	Rotary Valves (CV)	$0.00		$0.00		0
	Miscellaneous (M)	$0.00	$46,065.00	$0.00	$97,584.00	0
		$15,050,336.91	$15,050,336.91	$26,430,095.91	$26,430,095.91	45

Total w/Revisions	Total Complete	No. Quotes
$311,987.91	$363,506.91	19
$0.00	$0.00	0
$138,918.00	$138,918.00	3
$13,485,890.00	$21,758,234.00	7
$655,000.00	$655,000.00	2
$458,541.00	$3,514,437.00	14
$0.00	$0.00	0
$0.00	$0.00	0
$0.00	$0.00	0
$15,050,336.91	$26,430,095.91	45

MDSS Models and Output

When the information contained in the MDSS is categorized and classified by the software system, the result is some form of output for the decision maker. When the output provides a solution to the problem, it is most likely generated by a modeling technique. A model is an abstraction that explains some phenomenon or activity. For example, a model is a way to explain how a company's sales fluctuate in response to advertising expenditures. Modeling capabilities enable the MDSS to produce output. The most common types of MDSS outputs are reports, simulations, and queries.

An MDSS Sales Analysis Output Example

An example of MDSS output is a series of sales analysis reports produced from accounting and sales transaction data. The data used in preparing the records are sorted into various sequences to provide a sales manager with information describing the firm's sales by customer, region, and salesperson. A sales-by-customer report is shown in Exhibit 5.7. Customers are listed in descending order based on year-to-date sales and percentage contribution to total sales. This enables the sales manager to analyze customers on a percentage-of-sales basis. The same technique is used in the sales-by-region report in Exhibit 5.8. The sales manager can then analyze sales made by salespeople within their region.

e X H I B I T 5.7 Output of Sales-by-Customer Report for System Products

Customer	Region	Sales $	% of Sales	% of System Sales
Emerald Industries	mw	$3,272,428	21.6%	31.2%
Keebler	mw	1,067,051	7.0%	10.2%
Merck Sharp & Dohme	ot	1,038,019	6.8%	9.9%
Pretzels Inc	mw	776,218	5.1%	7.4%
Snyders of Hanover	ne	632,505	4.2%	6.0%
Syntex	ot	590,717	3.9%	5.6%
Floor Daniel (Frito)	w	330,270	2.2%	3.1%
Ore-Ida Foods	w	300,830	2.0%	2.9%
Schultz Foods	ne	252,122	1.7%	2.4%
Sterling Drug	ne	233,028	1.5%	2.2%
Golden Flake	ne	178,000	1.2%	1.7%
M&M Mars	ne	172,725	1.1%	1.6%
Glaxo	ne	147,868	1.0%	1.4%
Continental Mills	w	145,560	1.0%	1.4%
Marion Merrell Dow	mw	125,688	0.8%	1.2%
Reading (troyer)	ne	117,644	0.8%	1.1%
Warner Lambert	ot	106,678	0.7%	1.0%

еXHIBIT 5.8 Output of Sales-by-Region Report for Northeast Region

Customer Name	Product	Sales $	% of Sales	% of System Sales
Snyders of Hanover	sys	$632,505	4.2%	26.6%
Schultz Foods	sys	252,122	1.7%	10.6%
Sterling Drug	sys	233,028	1.5%	9.8%
Golden Flake	sys	178,000	1.2%	7.5%
M&M Mars	sys	172,725	1.1%	7.3%
Glaxo	sys	147,868	1.0%	6.2%
Reading (troyer)	sys	117,644	0.8%	4.9%
Reading (keystone)	sys	98,806	0.7%	4.2%
Congoleum Corp	engr	74,000	0.5%	3.1%
Hershey Chocolate	sys	66,939	0.4%	2.8%
IFF	sys	63,801	0.4%	2.7%
Schultz Foods	inst	60,850	0.4%	2.6%
Brystol Meyers	sys	59,667	0.4%	2.5%
Kline Process	sys	31,050	0.2%	1.3%
Union Carbide	vlv	30,050	0.2%	1.3%
Wasca Foods	vlv	18,982	0.1%	0.8%
Glatt Air Technology	vlv	18,523	0.1%	0.8%
A & G Machine	scr	15,073	0.1%	0.6%
M&M Mars	vlv	15,062	0.1%	0.6%
Union Carbide	vlv	15,025	0.1%	0.6%

Geographic Information Systems

Most MDSS models have simulation capability and the process of using the tool is *simulation.* A commonly used MDSS simulation is a geographic information system (GIS). GIS uses spatial modeling in conjunction with data drawn from the MDSS. It enables users to display spatial data organized as map layers.

GIS market areas are analyzed to learn where defined demographic characteristics overlap. In fact, neighborhoods can be clustered into categories and defined by both demographic and lifestyle data. The data is then linked to household information to produce neighborhood profiles that are useful for sales planning. An example of GIS is described in the Marketing Research in Action at the end of this chapter.

Using GIS, geographic parameters are examined to identify regions or locations based on spatial coincidence of relevant factors. For example, GIS can be used to examine environmental, economic, and political factors to identify potential store location sites as well as the environmental impact of a proposed development. The main advantage of GIS is its ability to pose what-if scenarios.

Hilton Corporation (www.hilton.com), for example, uses GIS to help reduce the risk of locating new hotels and casinos. GIS what-if scenarios were used to determine whether to enter the casino market on the Mississippi Gulf Coast. Demographic, socioeconomic, and psychographic features were considered, along with the location of competing sources of entertainment in the area. After GIS indicated saturation on the Mississippi Gulf Coast, Hilton decided not to open a casino there. Exhibit 5.9 indicates how GIS operates to provide companies with crucial location information and, hence, actual location decisions.

exHIBIT 5.9   How a GIS Works

GIS at Work

A vinyl siding company wants to identify for its local distributor the areas in Shelby County that hold the greatest potential for sales. Its target is based on (a) the location of homes 15 years old and older that are (b) owned by people with annual median household incomes of at least $35,000. Using the query capability of GIS software, along with census data coded in the GIS database, the user can categorize census tracts based on age of homes (A) and annual median income (B). With overlaying of the two map layers, a final layer that identifies various categories of needs and affordability can be quickly isolated (C).

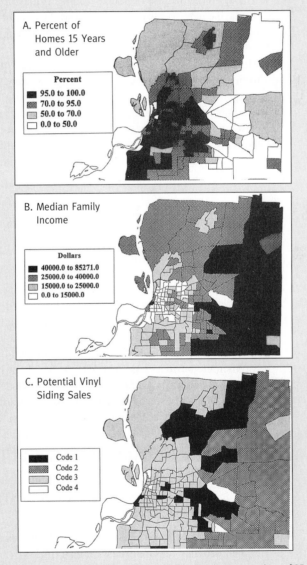

A. Percent of Homes 15 Years and Older

Percent
- 95.0 to 100.0
- 70.0 to 95.0
- 50.0 to 70.0
- 0.0 to 50.0

B. Median Family Income

Dollars
- 40000.0 to 85271.0
- 25000.0 to 40000.0
- 15000.0 to 25000.0
- 0.0 to 15000.0

C. Potential Vinyl Siding Sales

- Code 1
- Code 2
- Code 3
- Code 4

Code 1 = Over 60% of homes 15 years old or older; median family income above $35,000

Code 2 = High median income, less than 60% of homes 15 years old or older

Code 3 = Low median income, over 60% of homes 15 years old or older

Code 4 = Low median income, less than 60% of homes 15 years old or older

The use of GIS will expand with satellite imagery. Availability of satellite images as a data source will lead to more sophisticated use of global positioning systems (GPS) to find the best locations.

MDSS and Queries as an Output Resource

Query A segment of the MDSS that enables the user to retrieve information from the system without having to have special software.

A **query** is another component of the MDSS that facilitates data retrieval. It enables the user to retrieve information from the system without having to use special software. The response, either on screen or in hard-copy form, has the same general appearance as a regular MDSS report.

The unique feature of MDSS queries is they arise after data are provided to the analyst, that is, the need to use query operations arises after the analyst reviews the results of an earlier report. For example, a loan manager interested in cross-selling bank services can request a display of customer use of banking products (e.g., loans, credit cards, savings accounts), which would then be used to formulate detailed queries about the customer's financial information. This would enable the manager to view various services the customer may not be using, hence providing a cross-selling opportunity for the bank. A query enables the analyst to combine input and output forms, so that inputs (new bank services to cross-sell) are always given in the context of the previous MDSS output (current product use). Additionally, the analyst can fill in or select inputs that can modify the current output or result in different output altogether, such as selection/evaluation criteria for new-product offerings.

Business Intelligence Programs

A business intelligence program (BIP) is a formal, continuously evolving process by which a business assesses the evolution of its industry and the capabilities of current and potential competitors to develop and maintain a competitive advantage. Thus, it is an ongoing and integral component of a business's CRM process. The purpose of BIPs is to gather accurate and reliable information. The groundwork for this is accomplished through a business intelligence audit. A business intelligence audit reviews the business's operations to determine what is actually known about competitors and their operations.

When the business has some knowledge about its competitors and its own BIP needs, it gathers BIP data. Based on BIP needs, relevant data is gathered from the business's sales force and marketing research staff, customers, industry periodicals, competitors' promotional material, analysis of competitors' products and annual reports, trade shows, and distributors.

Tools and Techniques for Gathering BIP Data

Although a variety of approaches can be used to gather BIP data, the most appropriate technique depends on the objective of the intelligence program. The following eight sources are used for gathering BIP data:

1. **Governmental agencies.** Government sources can yield valuable data for the BIP, but their use may require excessive lead time.

2. **Online databases.** With increasing sophistication and affordability of information technology, this technique will proliferate as a data gathering method. Database search rarely provides information that has not been released to the public or that has not yet been collected.

3. **Company and investment community resources.** Some types of data that are not widely available from databases can be obtained by contacting a particular corporation or investment community sources.

4. **Surveys and interviews.** Surveys can yield data about competitors and products, while interviews can provide more in-depth perspectives from a limited sample.

5. **Drive-by and on-site observations.** Observing competitors' parking spaces, new construction in progress, customer service at retail stores, volume and patterns of trucking activities, and so on, can provide useful BIP data about the state of a competitor's business.

6. **Benchmarking.** A leading competitor is identified and its operations are analyzed and compared with the business's own operations.

7. **Defensive competitive intelligence.** A company monitors and analyzes its own business activities as competitors and outsiders see them.

8. **Reverse engineering.** Unraveling of competitors' products and services may provide important information about their quality and costs.

Each of these techniques provides unique information concerning competitors and market activity. As previously mentioned, databases are becoming a primary source of business intelligence. Accordingly, the Internet is providing easy access to such databases, and it has had a major impact on BIP activities in recent years.

marketing research in action

Geographic Information System[4]

Using a GIS

Geographic Information System (GIS) is one of the most important tools for CRM applications of "niche" marketing strategies, and it has applications in a wide variety of other industries industries as well. In fact, GIS can facilitate problem solving and decision making in many areas of marketing, resource management, planning, and environmental monitoring. GIS combines layers of information about a place to give you a better understanding of that place. The layers of information you combine depends on your purpose—finding the best location for a new store, analyzing environmental damage, viewing similar crimes in a city to detect a pattern, and so on.

Like most tools, however, GIS is only as good as the person using it. Using word processing software, for example, does not make one an accomplished writer. Effective use of GIS requires an understanding of the fundamental concepts of geographic data and systems (GPS), map coordinate systems and registration, data integrity and accuracy, overlay analysis, and database manipulation. GIS technology integrates spatial modeling, database management, and computer graphics in a system for managing and manipulating geographic data. Exhibit 5.10 shows the four major components of a GIS: data input, data analysis, data management, and data output.

The key to proper application of GIS technology is the database. A GIS application typically uses a relational database management system to manipulate attribute information.

---

exHIBIT 5.10 Components of a GIS—Data Input, Data Analysis, Data Management, and Data Output

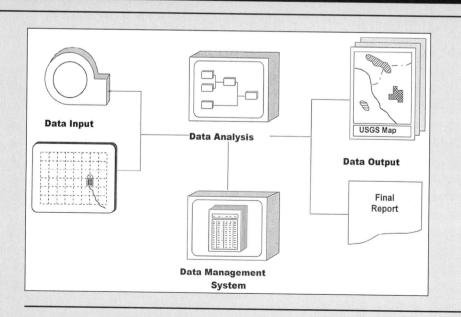

exHIBIT 5.11

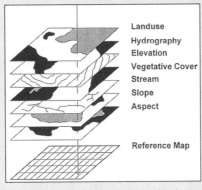

Landuse
Hydrography
Elevation
Vegetative Cover
Stream
Slope
Aspect

Reference Map

A GIS database may be conceptualized as a stack of floating map layers registered to a common map base.

The GIS database contains map layers representing geographic themes organized in a digital format. The map layers, which are geocoded to a standard coordinate system, can be conceptualized as a stack of floating maps tied to a common map base, as shown in Exhibit 5.11. Each map layer can be independently accessed. When combined, information and related attributes from individual layers can be referenced to one another from a spatial standpoint.

In addition to the map layers, a GIS database also includes a data file containing attribute information about features indicated on each map layer. For example, the data for a map layer of the road network of Shelby County, Tennessee, may include information such as road name, road type, physical distance, class type, and address range. GIS spatial analysis involves manipulation of map layers, individually or in combination, to derive solutions to spatial problems that assist the user in decision making.

Applications

GIS enables marketers to "layer" information within a neighborhood or larger geographic areas. Market areas can be examined to learn where defined demographic characteristics—age, sex, income, and race, for example—overlap. Neighborhoods are then "clustered" into categories and defined by demographic data and lifestyle information. Moreover, geodemographic information is linked with other types of household information to produce sophisticated profiles of neighborhoods that are a valuable tool for all types of target marketing. Some marketing research firms offer databases that allow businesses to look at their market area in levels as fine as several blocks.

Sylvania (www.sylvania.com) used GIS to help Stuart C. Irby Company (www.irby.com), an electrical goods supplier based in Jackson, Mississippi, increase sales of Sylvania products. The Irby Company provided Sylvania with information about the types of products it sells to customers and their geographic locations: Sylvania developed a plan of action to help Irby increase its Sylvania sales.

Lichliter, Jameson & Associates (www.ljaengineering.com), a Houston–based consulting engineering firm, uses GIS for transportation planning and engineering projects. In one project, GIS was used to assess environment impacts, manage asset data, and analyze effects of project alternatives for constructing a 200 m.p.h. passenger rail system serving Houston, Dallas, Austin, and San Antonio, Texas.

These are but a few of the applications of GIS as a planning tool by marketers, resource scientists, and land use planners. The availability and expanded use of satellite imagery for GIS applications will have a marked effect on GIS technology. There will be increased use of satellite images as GIS data sources, which in turn will lead to greater integration of GIS applications with remote sensing technology. There also will be expanded and more sophisticated use of the Global Positioning System (GPS) in data location and registration.

Hands-On Exercise

1. How could GIS be used to identify a location for a new Wal-Mart supercenter?

2. Could GIS be used by a sales manager to design sales territories for sales people? How?

3. What are some other examples of how GIS could be used in marketing research?

Summary of Learning Objectives

■ **Understand the purpose of a marketing decision support system (MDSS).**

The MDSS is designed to help marketing personnel with decision-making activities. These activities are highly focused on a specific problem and information required to solve that problem. With proper information, the MDSS allows the manager to identify and evaluate the best course of action in solving market-related problems. Therefore, the primary purpose of the MDSS is to manipulate information to provide problem solutions.

■ **Describe the various information requirements used to design an MDSS.**

The bulk of the information contained in the MDSS comes from secondary data. The common forms of information used in the MDSS are environmental information, transactional data, and business intelligence. The primary purpose of the data is to provide managers with the information they need for making immediate market-reaction decisions.

■ **Understand the role of transactional data in the MDSS.**

Considered the most important information requirement, transactional data provide information resulting from point-of-sale transactions. This information allows managers to track and react to daily sales fluctuations, evaluate the effectiveness of point-of-sale marketing activities, and develop predictive models based on actual product sales data.

■ **Explain the relationship between information processing and the MDSS.**

The key elements of the information-processing components of the MDSS are the database, the computer facilities, and the software system. Collectively, these elements must provide the manager or user with the capability to produce timely and accurate reports. The driving force behind report generation is the specific software system employed by the MDSS. The two most common forms of software systems are statistical software systems and managerial function software systems.

■ **Understand the various models used in an MDSS.**

There are several different ways to classify MDSS models. Regardless of the model employed, the objective is to provide the manager with a set of usable outputs. These outputs most commonly include reports, simulations, and queries.

■ **Provide examples of output from an MDSS.**

The most common forms of MDSS output are reports, simulations, and queries. The reports are normally generated around the marketing elements and attempt to determine profitability or performance measures on the mix. Simulations are used to produce what-if scenarios. A valuable simulation for many MDSS users is the geographic information system (GIS). Finally, queries enable users to retrieve information from the system without having to have a unique software program.

■ **Discuss the relationship that exists between the decision support system and business intelligence.**

Decision support systems and business intelligence programs serve unique purposes for business. The purpose of a BIP is to gather accurate and reliable information. The groundwork for this is accomplished through a business intelligence audit, which is primarily a review of a business's operations to determine what is actually known about competitors and their operations.

Key Terms and Concepts

Automatic replenishment system (ARS) 152

Bar coding 151

Business intelligence 150

Electronic data interchange (EDI) 152

Environmental information 149

Managerial function software systems 155

Marketing decision support system (MDSS) 147

Optical scanner 151

Query 160

Reader-sorter 153

Statistical software systems 155

Transactional data 150

Review Questions

1. What advantages of a marketing decision support system are not present in a management information system?

2. Why is it important to use secondary marketing information in a marketing decision support system?

3. List the five methods of collecting and maintaining transactional data, and provide an explanation of how each method can affect a company's marketing strategy.

4. What ethical implications are associated with the use of electronic scanning devices and electronic information storage procedures?

5. What are three key elements that make up the information processing component of the MDSS?

6. What is the purpose of a business intelligence system?

7. What is the value of a business intelligence audit?

Discussion Questions

1. **EXPERIENCE THE INTERNET.** Go to www.yahoo.com and search for companies that use and develop MDSSs. Provide a brief report on the number of companies that develop the systems and the applications for which they are used. Now try www.google.com and see if your results differ.

2. **EXPERIENCE THE INTERNET.** Go to www.gis.com. What is the purpose of this Web site? How would it help someone interested in GIS?

3. Discuss the differences associated with statistical software systems and managerial function software systems. Why are managerial function software systems used more frequently in actual business situations?

4. What is the most important advantage of a geographic information system (GIS)? What information would a GIS provide for a professional sports franchise seeking to relocate? Explain.

5. Could the Santa Fe Grill benefit from using an MDSS in it operations? If so, how?

6. Would the application of geographic information system (GIS) principles improve the Santa Fe Grill operations? If so, how?

7. What are the major types of business intelligence the Santa Fe Grill should be collecting for its MDSS?

part 3

Designing the Marketing Research Project

chapter 6

Exploratory Designs:
In-Depth Interviews
and Focus Groups

Learning Objectives

After reading this chapter, you will be able to

1. Identify the fundamental differences between qualitative and quantitative research methods and explain their appropriateness in creating useful managerial information.

2. Describe and explain two popular qualitative techniques used in gathering primary data.

3. Explain the basic pros and cons of using qualitative methods of data collection.

4. Explain focus groups, the importance of a moderator, and how the findings are used to improve decision making.

"What new banking services or changes in existing service offerings does Barnett Bank need to consider to assure customer service quality and satisfaction?"

—LAURA W. GAUTHIER
Vice President and Sales Manager
Barnett Bank of Pasco County

Using Focus Group Interviews to Gain Insights into Bank Customer Satisfaction

The Barnett Bank of Pasco County (BBPC) found itself in a position of declining market share among the senior citizen market structure for the fourth consecutive quarter. Although the bank conducted quarterly satisfaction surveys and the results indicated strong satisfaction among its senior customers, bank records indicated that an increasing number of senior customers were switching their accounts to BBPC's competitor banks. Not understanding this trend, BBPC's management called on the marketing research department to gather information among BBPC's senior customers regarding their attitudes, perceptions, and behaviors toward the bank's service offerings and current service delivery methods as well as how the bank might improve its service quality and ensure customer satisfaction.

A series of moderated small-group discussions was conducted among both current and past BBPC senior banking customers to determine their expectations and attitudes about BBPC's service. To assist the researcher in later in-depth analysis, each of the focus group sessions was videotaped.

The findings revealed that these particular current and past customers wanted (1) very friendly and courteous treatment by BBPC's staff and management; (2) a personalized relationship with someone who demonstrated trust, diagnostic competence, reliability, credibility, and understanding of their banking needs; and (3) clear and correct answers to their questions. In turn, the discussions indicated that those senior customers who switched banks had experienced (1) their "favorite" teller losing his or her job or being transferred to another location; (2) a lack of empathy and concern on the part of the bank's employees; and (3) difficulty with the loan department.

The research afforded BBPC's management insights into potential problems in the delivery system used to service the senior customer market. BBPC learned that its methods of dealing with customers were too inflexible to handle attitudinal differences among demographic market segments. Front-line service personnel were being trained to treat all customers the same way. As a result of the additional insights gained through the focus group interviews, BBPC modified its training programs to teach its employees that demographically different customers hold different perceptions about banking services and delivery methods. New training programs stressed the need for more flexibility among its customer service and teller staff. Staff members were retrained to exhibit patience and extra politeness toward senior customers. Be sure to read the Marketing Research in Action at the end of this chapter for a detailed illustration of how the BBPC focus groups were planned and executed.

Value of Qualitative Research Information

The BBPC opening example illustrates several important issues business decision makers must be aware of to resolve marketing problems and questions. First, management quite often is faced with problem situations where important questions cannot be adequately addressed or resolved merely with secondary information. Meaningful insights can be gained only through the collection of primary data. Recall that primary data typically are collected using a set of formal procedures in which researchers question or observe individuals and record their findings. Second, collecting only qualitative data does not ensure management will fully understand the problem. Collecting quantitative data might be necessary as well.

As we continue our examination the research process, attention turns away from research activities that emphasize secondary data. This chapter begins a series of three chapters that discuss the three basic types of research design (exploratory, descriptive, and causal) used to collect primary data and create information. As discussed in earlier chapters, the research objectives and information requirements are the keys to determining the type of research design that is most appropriate in collecting data. For example, exploratory research is used when the research objectives focus on gaining background information and clarifying the research problems to create hypotheses and establish research priorities. Descriptive designs are used when the research objectives emphasize describing and measuring marketing issues at a particular point in time. Data from a descriptive design provide answers to information research questions framed in who, what, where, when, how many, how much, and how often formats as they relate to management's initial decision problem situation. But descriptive designs often are not as useful in collecting primary data to explain why the marketing phenomena are happening. As discussed in Chapter 2, information for addressing many why questions is obtained with causal research designs. Causal research designs are used to determine causality in relationships between marketing factors and research problems as well as testing "if-then" statements about the various issues being investigated.

At this point, recall two important points. First, although exploratory, descriptive, and causal research designs might appear to be mutually exclusive, in many cases it is the complete set of information questions that will determine whether one particular research design or a combination of designs will be used to collect the appropriate data. A second point to remember is that although the information research process might implicitly suggest that exploratory research should always be undertaken before descriptive or causal research, there are cases in which exploratory research is used after some other design. To illustrate this point, look at the BBPC chapter opening example again. After collecting the satisfaction data through a descriptive research design on the bank's senior market segment, management turned to data collected through an exploratory design (i.e., focus group research) to gain a clearer understanding of the conflicting information that indicated senior customers rated the bank high on satisfaction yet switched their accounts to competitor banks.

At the heart of any research design are the methods actually used to collect the required data. Advances in technology and the Internet are rapidly changing the techniques researchers use in creating research designs and the speed of conducting data acquisition activities. With these changes also come changes in the terminology describing the methods used in planning the three traditional types of research designs, especially exploratory research. In recent years, methods for collecting data have been classified into two very broad categories: qualitative and quantitative. As you read on, you will see how we have integrated the qualitative and quantitative research methods in discussing exploratory, descriptive, and causal research designs. Keep in mind that to achieve a study's overall research objectives, in some cases researchers will use a multiple design approach, where data are collected using both qualitative and quantitative methods. This chapter introduces several popular research methods used mainly in exploratory research designs to collect qualitative, or "soft," data structures. As such, the term "qualitative" is interchangeable with "exploratory." In contrast, Chapter 7 focuses on the different quantitative methods (e.g., surveys) used by researchers in developing and executing descriptive research designs. Chapter 8 includes detailed discussions of the different quantitative methods (e.g., observation, experiments, test markets) used in causal research designs.

Observation and Questioning as Methods of Collecting Primary Data

Prior to discussing the different classifications of methods used by researchers to collect primary data, it is important to remember that there are actually two basic ways to collect primary data. Researchers can either use some form of *observation* to record human behavior or market phenomena or they can use some form of *questioning and recording* to capture a person's attitudes, feelings, and/or behaviors. Overall, observation techniques require the use of either a human observer or some type of mechanical or electronic device to capture and record specific human behaviors or phenomena of interest that take place during the observing time frame. In contrast, the questioning/recording method focuses on asking specific questions and recording the responses. This method of capturing data may or may not require an interviewer. In some situations, researchers may use both forms in order to obtain the required primary data to answer the research questions. Although some marketing researchers consider observation methods to be an exploratory research design, this method of obtaining primary data also is used in both descriptive and causal research designs. As you learn about exploratory, descriptive, and causal research designs, you will see how researchers can use both observation and questioning in any research design.

An Overview of Qualitative and Quantitative Research Methods

Quantitative research
Research that places heavy emphasis on using formalized standard questions and predetermined response options in questionnaires or surveys administered to large numbers of respondents.

Prior to discussing the qualitative techniques used in exploratory research designs, we will identify some of the fundamental differences between qualitative and quantitative research methods. Although there are vast differences between the two approaches, there is no single agreed-on set of factors that distinguishes them as being mutually exclusive. The factors listed in Exhibit 6.1 offer some insights on the general differences.

Quantitative Research Methods

Quantitative research is commonly associated with surveys or experiments and is considered the mainstay of the research industry for collecting marketing data. **Quantitative research** places heavy emphasis on using formalized questions and predetermined response options in questionnaires administered to large numbers of respondents. For example, when you think of

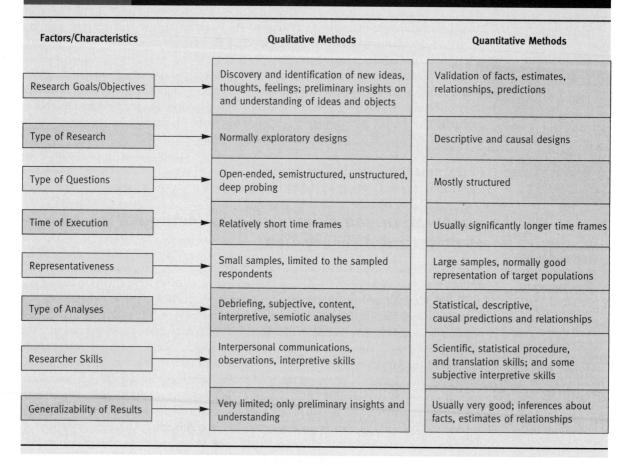

EXHIBIT 6.1 Differences between Qualitative and Quantitative Research Methods

Factors/Characteristics	Qualitative Methods	Quantitative Methods
Research Goals/Objectives	Discovery and identification of new ideas, thoughts, feelings; preliminary insights on and understanding of ideas and objects	Validation of facts, estimates, relationships, predictions
Type of Research	Normally exploratory designs	Descriptive and causal designs
Type of Questions	Open-ended, semistructured, unstructured, deep probing	Mostly structured
Time of Execution	Relatively short time frames	Usually significantly longer time frames
Representativeness	Small samples, limited to the sampled respondents	Large samples, normally good representation of target populations
Type of Analyses	Debriefing, subjective, content, interpretive, semiotic analyses	Statistical, descriptive, causal predictions and relationships
Researcher Skills	Interpersonal communications, observations, interpretive skills	Scientific, statistical procedure, and translation skills; and some subjective interpretive skills
Generalizability of Results	Very limited; only preliminary insights and understanding	Usually very good; inferences about facts, estimates of relationships

quantitative research, think of J. D. Power and Associates conducting a nationwide mail survey on customer satisfaction among new car purchasers or American Express doing a nationwide survey on travel behaviors with telephone interviews. In certain situations, however, observation techniques also are used to collect nonverbal and/or behavioral data from respondents during the questioning process. With quantitative research, the research problems typically are specific and well defined, and the decision maker and researcher have agreed on the precise information needs. Quantitative research methods are more directly related to descriptive and causal research designs but can be associated with exploratory designs as well. Success in collecting primary data is more a function of correctly designing and administering the survey instrument than of the communication and interpretive skills of an interviewer or observer.

The main goals of quantitative research are to provide specific facts decision makers can use to (1) make accurate predictions about relationships between market factors and behaviors, (2) gain meaningful insights into those relationships, (3) validate the existing relationships, and (4) test various types of hypotheses. In quantitative research practices, researchers are well trained in construct development, scale measurement, questionnaire design, sampling, and statistical data analysis skills. In addition, researchers must have a solid ability to translate numerical data into meaningful narrative information. Data reliability and validity issues are serious concerns with quantitative research.

eXHIBIT	6.2	Guidelines for Using Quantitative Research Methodologies

Quantitative research methods are appropriate when decision makers or researchers are:

- Validating or answering a business problem or opportunity situation or information requirements.
- Obtaining detailed descriptions or conclusive insights into the motivation, emotional, attitudinal, and personality factors that influence marketplace behaviors.
- Testing theories and models to explain marketplace behaviors or relationships between two or more marketing constructs.
- Testing and assessing the reliability and validity of scale measurements for investigating specific market factors, consumer qualities (e.g., attitudes, emotional feelings, preferences, beliefs, perceptions), and behavioral outcomes.
- Assessing the effectiveness of their marketing strategies on actual marketplace behaviors.
- Interested in new-product/service development or repositioning current products or service images.
- Segmenting and/or comparing large or small differences in markets, new products, services, or evaluation and repositioning of current products or service images.

When to Use Quantitative Research Methods

In most descriptive and many causal research endeavors, the data will be gathered using quantitative data collection approaches. Exhibit 6.2 lists some guidelines for determining when it is appropriate to use quantitative research methods. These guidelines are by no means exhaustive and will be discussed in detail in Chapters 7 and 8.

Qualitative Research Methods

Qualitative research
Research used in exploratory designs to gain preliminary insights into decision problems and opportunities.

Over the past decade, **qualitative research** has come to refer to selected research methods used in exploratory research designs. One of the main objectives of qualitative research is to gain *preliminary insights* into research problems. On the surface, qualitative research methods incorporate some scientific elements but normally lack the critical elements of true reliability. Qualitative research tends to focus on the collection of detailed amounts of primary data from relatively small samples of subjects by asking questions or observing behavior. Researchers well trained in interpersonal communication and interpretive skills use either open-ended questions that allow for in-depth probing of the subjects' initial responses or specific observational techniques that allow for analysis of behavior. In most cases, qualitative data can be collected within relatively short periods of time, but it is difficult to quickly summarize the data into meaningful findings. Data analysis typically involves subjective content, interpretation, or semiotic analysis procedures.

The nonstructured format of the questions and the small sample size tend to limit the researcher's ability to generalize (or infer) qualitative data to the population. Nevertheless, qualitative data have important uses in understanding and resolving business problems, especially in the areas of initial discovery and preliminary explanation of marketplace or customer behavior and decision processes. For example, qualitative data can be invaluable in providing researchers with initial ideas about specific problems or opportunities; theories, models, or constructs; or the designing of new, specific scale measurements. Yet qualitative data generally is not relied on in recommending a final course of action.

---

e X H I B I T 6.3   Guidelines for Using Qualitative Research Methodologies

Qualitative research methods are appropriate when decision makers or researchers are:

- Identifying a business problem, opportunity situation, or establishing information requirements.
- Obtaining preliminary insights into the motivation, emotional, attitudinal, and personality factors that influence marketplace behaviors.
- Building theories and models to explain marketplace behaviors or relationships between two or more marketing constructs.
- Developing reliable and valid scale measurements for investigating specific market factors, consumer qualities (e.g., attitudes, emotional feelings, preferences, beliefs, perceptions), and behavioral outcomes.
- Trying to determine the preliminary effectiveness of their marketing strategies on actual marketplace behaviors.
- Interested in new-product or service development, repositioning current product, or service images.

When to Use Qualitative Research Methods in Exploratory Designs

In most exploratory research projects, the raw data is gathered through qualitative data collection practices. Exhibit 6.3 lists some guidelines for determining when it is appropriate to use qualitative research methods for collecting information with exploratory designs.

Advantages and Disadvantages of Qualitative Research Methods

Like other primary data collection techniques, qualitative research methods offer several advantages to today's researchers. Exhibit 6.4 summarizes the main advantages and disadvantages.

Major Advantages

One general advantage of qualitative research methods is that they are both *economical and timely* compared to most quantitative methods. Due in part to the use of small samples, researchers can complete their investigations quicker and at a significantly lower cost than is true with other types of methods. Another advantage is the *richness of the data.* The unstructured

---

e X H I B I T 6.4   Advantages and Disadvantages of Using Qualitative Research Methods

Advantages of Qualitative Methods	Disadvantages of Qualitative Methods
Economical and timely data collection	Lack of generalizability
Richness of the data	Inability to distinguish small differences
Accuracy of recording marketplace behaviors	Lack of reliability and validity
Preliminary insights into building models and scale measurements	Difficulty finding well-trained investigators, interviewers, and observers

nature of qualitative techniques enables the researcher to collect in-depth data about the subjects' attitudes, beliefs, emotions, and perceptions, all of which may strongly influence their observable market behaviors. Such in-depth data can be invaluable in gaining a preliminary understanding of those behaviors. Some qualitative techniques allow decision makers to gain *firsthand experiences* with customers and can provide very revealing information about their thinking patterns. The richness of the qualitative data can often supplement the facts gathered through other primary data collection techniques. Some qualitative methods enable the investigator to accurately record *actual behaviors,* not just reported behaviors.

Some qualitative research methods provide researchers with excellent preliminary insights into building marketing models and scale measurements. In addition, qualitative data play a critical role in *identifying marketing problems.* The in-depth information enhances the researcher's ability to predict consumer behavior in the marketplace, as well as to develop better marketing constructs and more reliable and valid scale measurements of those constructs.

Major Disadvantages

Although qualitative research produces useful information, it has two main potential disadvantages: sample size limitations and the need for well-trained interviewers or observers. First, qualitative data normally *lack generalizability* (or representativeness). That is to say, due to the use of small, nonrandom samples, the information generated by qualitative research techniques cannot be generalized to larger groups of individuals. This *lack of representativeness* of the defined target population severely limits the use of qualitative information in helping decision makers select and implement final action strategies. For example, the attitudes and behaviors of a group of 8 to 12 college students are unlikely to be representative of all college students in the United States, of college students at a particular university, of business majors at that university, or even of marketing majors. Small sample sizes make it virtually impossible for researchers to extend findings beyond the group used to collect the data.

Another disadvantage is the raw data generated through qualitative methods are limited by their *inability to distinguish small differences.* Many times marketing successes and failures are based on small differences in marketing mix strategies. Using small samples of subjects to provide critical information does not allow researchers to evaluate the impact of small differences. Moreover, researchers are forced to analyze qualitative data at aggregate, not disaggregate, levels. Aggregation of the findings eliminates the opportunity to study individual differences. In most cases, the reliability of data collected using qualitative research methods cannot be assessed. Decision makers often are reluctant to use information that cannot be assessed for reliability.

Finally, the *difficulty of finding well-trained interviewers and observers* to conduct qualitative research can be a potential disadvantage. Due to the informal, unstructured nature of obtaining qualitative data, few researchers have the extensive formal training needed to be an expert in the qualitative field. Moreover, it is difficult for the unsuspecting practitioner to discern the researcher's qualifications or the quality of the research. In spite of these disadvantages, researchers still should integrate both qualitative and quantitative techniques in order to make the research program complete.

Questioning Techniques in Qualitative Research

In today's technology-driven business environment many marketing problems can be solved only by looking beyond secondary data. Frequently decision makers need current information that can be obtained only through real-time observations of individual behaviors or by directly asking people questions. Observation and interviewing techniques play important roles in exploratory research designs. Since observation methods employ approaches that can capture both qualitative and quantitative data, we will discuss observation methods separately in Chapter 8. The focus here is on introducing and detailing the interviewing techniques and activities associated with collecting primary data using qualitative methods. There is a distinct "family" of interviewing approaches that can be used to collect primary qualitative data, including in-depth interviews, focus groups, case studies, experience interviews and projective interviewing techniques. All these approaches are useful in providing information to decision makers, but we will focus primarily on in-depth interviews and focus group interviews, techniques that are the most popular methods of choice among many decision makers and researchers, while highlighting the others.

In-Depth Interviews

In-Depth Interviewing Techniques

In-depth interview A formalized process in which a well-trained interviewer asks a subject a set of semistructured questions in a face-to-face setting.

As a qualitative technique, an **in-depth interview,** also referred to as a "depth" or "one-on-one" interview, represents a formal process in which a trained interviewer asks a subject a set of semistructured, probing questions usually in a face-to-face setting. Depending on the research objectives, the typical setting for this type of interview would be either the subject's home or office, or some type of centralized interviewing center that is convenient for the subject. In special situations, in-depth interviews can be conducted by telephone or through a high-tech telecommunication system that allows face-to-face interchanges through a television or computer. Exhibit 6.5 lists several of the main objectives of in-depth interviewing methods.

In-depth interviewing allows the researcher to collect both attitudinal and behavioral data from the subject that spans all time frames (past, present, and future). Let's say, for example, that corporate management of Marriott Hotels wants to understand how to deliver better on-site services to business customers. Marriott's researchers can conduct on-site, in-depth interviews with selected business travelers that include the following semistructured questions:

1. What were the specific factors you used in selecting Marriott for overnight accommodations during your business trip to San Diego, California? (Motives)

2. What hotel services did you use during your stay? (Behavior)

3. How satisfied or dissatisfied are you with those services? (Current feelings)

4. How likely are you to stay at a Marriott Hotel next time you are in San Diego for business, and why? (Future intended behavior)

EXHIBIT 6.5   Main Research Objectives of In-Depth Interviewing

To gain preliminary insights into **what** the subject thinks or believes about the topic of concern or **why** the subject exhibits certain behaviors.

To obtain unrestricted and detailed comments revealing feelings, beliefs, or opinions that can help the interviewer better understand the different elements of the subject's thoughts and the reasons they exist.

To have the respondent communicate as much detail as possible about his or her knowledge and behavior toward a given topic or object.

A unique characteristic of this data collection method is that the interviewer uses *probing questions* as the mechanism to get more data on the topic from the subject. By taking the subject's initial response and turning it into a question, the interviewer encourages the subject to further explain the first response and creates natural opportunities for a more detailed discussion of the topic. The general rule of thumb is that the more a subject talks about a topic, the more likely he or she is to reveal underlying attitudes, motives, emotions, and behaviors. To illustrate the technique of using probing questions, let's use the second question from the above Marriott example. The dialogue might go as follows:

Interviewer: "What hotel services did you use during your stay?"

Subject: "I used the front desk, restaurant, and the hotel's fitness center."

Interviewer: "With regard to the front desk, what were some of the actual services you requested?"

Subject: "Well, besides checking in, I inquired about the availability of a fitness room and car rental."

Interviewer: "Why were you interested in information about the hotel's fitness center and car rental service?"

Subject: "When I am away on business, I enjoy a good workout to help relieve stress buildup and I find my energy level improves."

Interviewer: "While at the hotel, how did renting a car fit into your plans?"

Subject: "I had a business meeting the next day at 9:30 A.M. across town; afterward I planned to play a round of golf."

Interviewer: "Which rental car company do you usually prefer to use?"

Subject: "Hertz—they are the best! I have Gold VIP status with them and I receive frequent flier miles."

Interviewer: "Besides using the fitness center and renting a car, what other hotel services might you request during your stay?"

Subject: "I might rent a movie at night."

Interviewer: "Rent a movie? What kinds of movies do you prefer."

Subject: "When away from home, I enjoy watching action-oriented movies as a means to relax after a long day on the road. I do not get much of a chance when I am at home with the wife and the kids."

Interviewer: "Are there any other services you would consider using?"

Subject: "No." (With this response, the interviewer would move on to the next topic.)

By interpreting this dialogue and those involving other participants, the researcher can create theme categories that reveal not only what hotel services the guests used, but why those particular services were used during their stay at the Marriott. Here, management learns the property's fitness center, availability of in-room movie entertainment, and on-property car rental service are some of the hotel features that must be in place to attract business travelers to the hotel. In addition, the movie entertainment and fitness center features could be promoted with a theme toward "stress reduction" activities during the customer's stay at the hotel.

A word of caution about probing questions: it is critically important that the interviewer avoid framing questions that allow the subject to reply with a simple but logical "no." Unless the interviewer intends to bring closure to the discussion, probing questions should not be framed in formats like "Can you tell me more about that point?" "Could you elaborate on that?" "Do you have some specific reasons?" or "Is there anything else?" All these formats allow the subject to logically say no. Once a no response is given, it becomes very difficult to continue probing the topic for more detailed data.

Skills Required for Conducting In-Depth Interviews

Interpersonal communication skills The interviewer's ability to articulate questions in a direct and clear manner.

Listening skills The interviewer's ability to accurately interpret and record the subject's responses.

Probing questions Questions that result when an interviewer takes the subject's initial response to a question and uses that response as the framework for the next question (the probing question) in order to gain more detailed responses.

For in-depth interviewing to be an effective data collection tool, interviewers must have excellent interpersonal communication and listening skills. **Interpersonal communication skills** relate to the interviewer's ability to ask the questions in a direct and clear manner so the subject understands to what she or he is responding. **Listening skills** include the ability to accurately hear, record, and interpret the subject's responses. Depending on the complexity of the topic and the desired data requirements, most interviewers ask permission from the subject to record the interview using either a tape recorder or possibly a video recorder rather than relying solely on handwritten notes.

As mentioned above, without excellent probing skills, the interviewer may inadvertently allow the discussion of a specific topic to end before all the potential data are revealed. **Probing questions** need to be precise and include the subject's previous reply. Interpretive skills relate to the interviewer's ability to accurately understand and record the subject's responses. These skills play a critical role in the process of transforming the actual raw data into usable information. An interviewer's weak interpretive skills will have a negative impact on the quality of the data collected. For example, if the interviewer does not understand the subject's response, he or she is not likely to follow up with a probing question that will move the dialogue where it was intended to move. The resulting data may not be meaningful to the initial area of inquiry. Finally, the personality of the interviewer plays a significant role in establishing a "comfort zone" for the subject during the question/answer process. Interviewers should be easygoing, flexible, trustworthy, and professional. Respondents who feel at ease with a person are more likely to reveal their hidden attitudes, feelings, motivations and behaviors.

Advantages of In-Depth Interviews

As a qualitative data collection method, in-depth interviewing offers researchers several benefits. First is flexibility. One-on-one personal interviews enable the researcher to ask questions on a wide variety of topics. The question-and-answer process gives the researcher the flexibility to collect data not only on the subject's activities and behavior patterns, but also on the attitudes, motivations, and opinions that underlie those reported behaviors. Probing questions allow researchers to collect highly detailed data from the subject regarding the topic at hand. Once a certain comfort zone is reached in the interviewer–subject relationship, subjects willingly reveal their inner thinking.

Disadvantages of In-Depth Interviews

Data collected by in-depth interviews is subject to the same general limitations as all qualitative methods. Although in-depth interviews can generate a lot of detailed data, the findings lack generalizability, reliability, and the ability to distinguish small differences. Inaccurate findings may be caused by the introduction of interviewer–respondent artifacts (e.g., interviewer illustrates empathy toward the respondent's answers); respondent bias (e.g., faulty recall, concern with social acceptability, fatigue); or interviewer errors (e.g., inadequate listening, faulty recording procedures, fatigue). Other factors that limit the use of this questioning approach are the costs for both setup and completion and the extensive length of time required.

Steps in Conducting an In-Depth Interview

In planning and conducting an in-depth interview, there are a number of logical and formalized steps. Exhibit 6.6 highlights those necessary steps.

EXHIBIT 6.6 Key Steps in Conducting an In-Depth Interview

Steps

Description and Comments

Step 1 **Understand Management's Initial Decision Question(s)/Problems**

- Researcher must gain a complete understanding of management's critical initial problem situation and decision question(s).
- Researcher must engage in dialogue with the decision maker that focuses on bringing clarity and understanding of the current problem situation (factors, thoughts, concerns) that have lead the decision maker to state his/her questions.

Step 2 **Create a Set of Appropriate Research Questions**

- A set of appropriate research questions must be developed that will serve as the "backbone" of the in-depth interview.
- Using new-found understanding of the problem situation, the "how, what, when, where, who, etc." framing technique, the research questions should directly focus on the major elements of the initial decision questions or problem(s)
- The research questions should be arranged using a logical flow from "general" to "specific."

Step 3 **Decide on the Best Environment for Conducting the Interview**

- Researcher must decide on the best location for the interview, understand the characteristics of the prospective subject, and use a relaxed, comfortable interviewing setting.
- The setting should allow for a private conversation without outside distractions.

Step 4 **Select, Screen, and Secure the Prospective Subjects**

- There is no one "best" method for selecting potential subjects, but each must be screened to assure they meet some set of specified criteria for being the "right person" to interview.
- Decision maker and researcher make a joint decision on the critical qualifying criteria.
- Sometimes particular demographic, attitudinal, emotional, and/or behavioral factors are used.

Step 5 **Contact Prospective Subjects, Provide Guidelines, Create Comfort Zone, Begin Interview**

- Researcher (interviewer) meets the subject and provides the appropriate introductory guidelines for the interviewing process.
- Obtains permission to tape-record the interview.
- Spends the first few minutes prior to the start of the questioning process creating a "comfort zone" for the subject, using warm-up questions.
- Begins the interview by asking the first listed research questions.

Step 6 **Conduct the In-Depth Interview**

- Using the subject's response to the initial research questions, researcher uses "probing" questions to obtain as many details from the subject as possible on the topic before moving to the next question.
- For each listed question, the researcher repeats the probing questioning technique, until the last question is discussed.
- On completing the interview, thank the subject for participating and provide the predetermined incentives, if any.

Step 7 **Analyze the Subject's Narrative Responses**

- Researcher begins interpreting the responses of each subject interviewed by either using predetermined classification systems or by using the raw responses to first create a classification system and then go back and code the raw responses.
- This analysis is very similar to that of a focus group. For more guidelines, go to Exhibit 6.13.

Step 8 **Write a Summary Report of the Results**

- Whether one or several interviews are conducted, writing up a summary report is very similar to writing a report for a "focus group." Refer to Exhibit 6.14 for the guidelines.

Focus Group Interviews

Nature of Focus Group Interviews

Focus group research
A formalized process of bringing a small group of people together for an interactive, spontaneous discussion on one particular topic or concept.

The second and most popular qualitative method we discuss is focus group research. **Focus group research** involves bringing a small group of people together for an interactive and spontaneous discussion of a particular topic or concept. Focus groups normally consist of 8 to 12 participants who are guided by a professional moderator through an unstructured discussion that typically lasts about 1½ hours. By getting the group members to talk in detail about a topic, the moderator draws out as many ideas, attitudes, and experiences as possible about the specified issue.

The overall goal of focus group research is to give researchers, and ultimately decision makers, as much information as possible about how people regard the topic of interest. That topic is typically a product, service, concept, or organization. Unlike many other types of questioning techniques, focus group research is not restricted to just asking and answering questions posed by an interviewer. Its success relies heavily on the group dynamics, the willingness of members to engage in an interactive dialogue, and the professional moderator's ability to keep the discussion on track. The fundamental idea behind the focus group approach is that one person's response will spark comments from other members, thus generating a spontaneous interplay among all of the participants. The overall cost of conducting a focus group can vary from $2,000 to $5,000 per session.[1]

Focus Group Research Objectives

There are many reasons focus group research is the most popular qualitative research method. As noted earlier, data collected in focus groups can offer preliminary insights into hidden marketing phenomena. Exhibit 6.7 lists some other pertinent objectives of focus group research. Each of these is described in more detail below.

To Provide Data for Defining and Redefining Marketing Problems

In those situations where managers or researchers experience difficulties in identifying and understanding a specific marketing problem, focus groups can help distinguish the differences between symptoms and problems. For example, the marketing department chairperson at a major southwestern university was not sure why undergraduate enrollment levels were continually declining. The chairperson called for a departmental faculty meeting using

---

EXHIBIT 6.7 **Main Focus Group Research Objectives**

1. To provide data for defining and redefining marketing problems.
2. To identify specific hidden information requirements.
3. To provide data for better understanding results from other quantitative studies.
4. To reveal consumers' hidden needs, wants, attitudes, feelings, behaviors, perceptions, and motives regarding services, products, or practices.
5. To generate new ideas about products, services, or delivery methods.
6. To discover new constructs and measurement methods.
7. To help explain changing consumer preferences.

a focus group format. The discussion revealed several unexpected factors that provided the marketing department preliminary insights into why enrollment levels were declining. One of these had to do with whether the current marketing curriculum was offering marketing majors the kinds of skills currently demanded by businesses. The marketing department investigated this issue and found significant gaps between the two perspectives as to which skills undergraduate marketing majors needed. The department began a reassessment of its own curriculum in an attempt to realign the skills being taught to those being mandated by the business world.

To Identify Specific Hidden Information Requirements

In some situations decision makers and researchers are not totally sure what specific types of data or information should be investigated. In these situations, focus groups can reveal unexpected aspects of the problem and thus can directly help researchers determine what specific data should be collected. For example, the directors of the Ford Foundation of Performing Arts in Vail, Colorado, were faced with the difficulty of deciding what design features should be included in the construction of a new $5 million Performing Arts Center. The foundation's research team conducted several focus groups consisting of local residents and seasonal visitors. From the groups' spontaneous, unstructured discussions, specific features and concerns such as different types of indoor and outdoor events, parking requirements, availability of refreshments, seating design and capacity, pricing of tickets, and protection from bad weather were revealed as being important factors that needed further understanding.

To Provide Data for Better Understanding Results from Other Quantitative Studies

There are situations where quantitative research investigations leave the decision maker or researcher asking why the results came out the way they did. Focus groups can be conducted to help explain the findings of other surveys. For example, corporate management of JP Hotels, Inc., conducted a survey among business guests at its hotels concerning free in-room entertainment services. The results indicated that 85 percent of the business guests were aware of the availability of the entertainment services but only 15 percent actually used them. Not understanding this gap between awareness and actual use, JP Hotels conducted several focus groups among its business guests regarding these services. The focus group discussions revealed that business travelers were either too busy doing necessary paperwork or too exhausted to watch any type of TV at night. They preferred to read or listen to music as a means of relaxing after a long workday.

To Reveal Consumers' Hidden Needs, Wants, Attitudes, Feelings, Behaviors, Perceptions, and Motives Regarding Services, Products, or Practices

Focus group interviews provide researchers with excellent opportunities to gain preliminary insights into what consumers think or feel about a wide array of products and services. For example, a manufacturer like Procter & Gamble uses focus groups to obtain data that reveal consumers' attitudes for and against using Crest toothpaste. These data help the company understand how consumer brand loyalty is developed and what marketing factors are necessary to reinforce it.

A Closer Look at Research[2]

Dimensions of Service Quality

Researchers at the University of South Florida conducted exploratory research in an effort to bring clarity to the dimensionality controversy that continues to plague the "service quality" construct. Using available secondary information from earlier research on service quality reported in the literature, several focus group interviews were conducted among known patrons of retail commercial banking services. A trained professional moderator led the participants through unstructured and spontaneous discussions using a predetermined series of topical questions relating to the generic aspects of service quality. The qualitative data resulting from the discussions revealed seven possible sets of interpersonal behavior activities that consumers relied on when

In the Field

assessing the existence of service quality. These activities were subjectively described as service provider's communication/listening capabilities; diagnostic competence—understanding customers' needs/wants; empathy with customers' needs/wants; tactful responsiveness to customers' questions; reliability/credibility of the service provider; technical knowledge; and interpersonal social skills. In addition, the data supplied the researchers with preliminary insights into specific behavioral interchanges between service providers and customers. In turn, the interchanges were useful in building a 75-item inventory of interpersonal behavior activities and were used in a quantitative survey designed to test which behavioral interchanges were associated with these behaviors.

To Generate New Ideas about Products, Services, or Delivery Methods

This particular objective of focus group interviews has long been a mainstay among decision makers and researchers. Here, focus groups generate interactive discussions about new or existing products and services. Data collected through these discussions provides valuable preliminary insights into new-product development, new usages of existing products and services, possible changes for improving products or services, or identifying better delivery systems. A classic example is how Arm & Hammer discovered new in-home uses for baking soda. Periodically, the company conducts focus group interviews among known users of Arm & Hammer baking soda. Data generated from these discussions has revealed that baking soda is used for such things as cleaning kitchens and bathrooms, cleaning around babies, deodorizing everything from carpets to cat litter boxes, freshening laundry, soothing and conditioning skin, and cleaning teeth. Today, Arm & Hammer baking soda is marketed as a natural product with "a houseful of uses."

To Discover New Constructs and Measurement Methods

For academicians and practitioners alike, focus group interviews play a critical role in the process of developing new marketing constructs and creating reliable and valid construct measurement scales. In the exploratory stage of construct development, researchers may conduct focus groups concerning a particular marketing idea to reveal additional insights into the underlying dimensions that may or may not make up the construct. These insights can help researchers develop scales that can be tested and refined through larger survey research designs. Take the important construct of service quality, for example. Researchers have been trying to refine the measurement of this construct for the past 15 years. They continue to ask such questions as "What does service quality mean to consumers, practitioners, and academicians?" "What is the underlying dimensionality of the construct—is it unidimensional or multidimensional?" and "What is the most appropriate way of measuring service quality?" Read the nearby Closer Look at Research box to see how these questions have been investigated.

To Help Explain Changing Consumer Preferences

This objective refers to the use of focus group interviews to collect data that can be useful in understanding how customers describe their experiences with different products and services. This type of qualitative data can be valuable in improving marketing communications as well as in creating more effective marketing segmentation strategies. For example, a manufacturer of a brand-name line of lawn care products may be interested in such questions as "What do consumers like about lawn care and gardening?" "What words or terms do they use in describing lawn care/gardening products and their use?" "Why do they do their own lawn work?" and "How do they take care of their lawns and gardens?"

Conducting Focus Group Interviews

While there is no one particular approach acceptable to all researchers, focus group interviews can be viewed as a process divided into three logical phases: planning the study, conducting the focus group discussions, and analyzing and reporting the results (see Exhibit 6.8).

еXHIBIT 6.8 The Three-Phase Process for Developing a Focus Group Interview

Phase 1: Planning the Focus Group Study

- This is the most critical phase.
- Researchers must have an understanding of the purpose of the study, a precise definition of the problem, and specific data requirements.
- Key decisions focus on who the appropriate participants would be; how to select and recruit respondents; what size the focus group should be; and where to have the sessions.

Phase 2: Conducting the Focus Group Discussions

- One of the key players in this phase is the focus group moderator.
- To ensure a successful interactive session, the moderator's role and pertinent characteristics must be clearly understood by everyone involved.
- A necessary activity in this phase is the development of a moderator's guide that outlines the topics, questions, and subquestions that will be used in the session.
- The actual focus group session should be structured with beginning, main, and closing sections.

Phase 3: Analyzing and Reporting the Results

- After the actual session is completed and if the sponsoring client's representatives are present, the researcher should conduct a debriefing analysis with all the key players involved to compare notes.
- The researcher should conduct a content analysis on the raw data obtained from the participants during the interviewing session and write a formal report that communicates the findings.
- Key to the researcher here is to remember who will be the reading audience, the purpose of the report, and the nature of reporting the results as well as an appropriate report style format.

Phase 1: Planning the Focus Group Study

As with most other types of marketing research, the planning phase is most critical for successful focus group interviews. In this phase, researchers and decision makers must have a clear understanding of the purpose of the study, a precise definition of the problem, and specific data requirements. There must be agreement to such questions as: "Why should such a study be conducted?" "What kinds of information will be produced?" "What types of information are of particular importance?" "How will the information be used?" and "Who wants the information?" Answers to these types of questions can help eliminate the obstacles (organizational politics, incomplete disclosure, and hidden personal agendas) that can delay agreement and create problems between decision makers and researchers. Other important decisions in the planning phase relate to who the participants should be, how to select and recruit respondents, size of the group, and where to have the focus group sessions.

Focus Group Participants

In deciding who should be included as participants in a focus group, researchers must give strong consideration to the purpose of the study and think about who can best provide the necessary information. While there is no one set of human characteristics that can guarantee the right group dynamics, the focus group must be as homogeneous as possible but with enough variation to allow for contrasting opinions. Central factors in the selection process are the potential group dynamics and the willingness of members to engage in dialogue. Desirable commonalities among participants may include occupation; past use of a product, service, or program; educational level; age; gender; or family structure. The underlying concern is the degree to which these factors influence members' willingness to share ideas within group discussions. Having a homogeneous focus group in which participants recognize their common factors and feel comfortable with one another is likely to create a more natural and relaxed group environment than having a heterogeneous group. Furthermore, participants in homogeneous focus groups are less likely to be eager to present contrived or socially acceptable responses just to impress other group members or the moderator. Researchers need to remember that in most cases, focus group participants are neither friends nor even acquaintances but typically strangers. Many people can feel intimidated or hesitant to voice their opinions, feelings, or suggestions to strangers.

A factor often overlooked in the selection of focus group participants is that of individuals' existing knowledge level of the topic. Researchers must determine whether prospective participants have some prior knowledge about the topics to be discussed in the interview. Lack of knowledge on the part of participants severely limits the opportunities for creating spontaneous, interactive discussions that will provide detailed data about a specific topic. For example, bringing together a group of people who sell women's shoes for a discussion about the operations of a nuclear power plant is likely to produce few meaningful insights pertinent to that topic.

Selection and Recruitment of Participants

Selecting and recruiting appropriate participants are keys to the success of any focus group. We have already noted the necessity for homogeneous groups. Now it becomes critical to understand the general makeup of the target audience that needs to be represented by the focus group. Exhibit 6.9 lists some general rules for the selection process.

EXHIBIT 6.9 General Rules for the Selection of Focus Group Participants[3]

General Rule Factors	Description of Rule Guidelines
Specify exact selection criteria	Interacting with the decision maker, the researcher needs to identify, as precisely as possible, all the desired characteristics of the group members.
Maintain control of the selection process	The researcher must maintain control of the selection process. A screening mechanism that contains the key demographic or socioeconomic characteristics must be developed and used to ensure consistency in the selection process. In those situations where the researcher allows someone else to do the selection, precise instructions and training must be given to that individual.
Beware of potential selection bias	Selection bias tends to be overlooked by researchers and decision makers alike. Biases can develop in subtle ways and seriously erode the quality of the data collected. Beware of participants picked from memory, or because they expressed an interest or concerns about the topic, or because they are clones of the person doing the selection.
Incorporate randomization	Whenever possible, randomize the process. It will help ensure a nonbiased cross section of prospective participants. This will work only if the pool of respondents meets the established selection criteria.
Check respondents' knowledge	For any given topic, prospective participants may differ in knowledge and experience. Lack of experience and knowledge may directly affect respondents' abilities to engage in spontaneous topical discussions.
Keep in mind that no process is perfect	Researchers have to make the best choices they can with the knowledge they have at the time of selection. The process may overlook certain aspects of the problem and inadvertently neglect individuals with unique points of view.

Selection of Participants. To select participants for a focus group, the researcher must first develop a screening form that specifies the characteristics respondents must have to qualify for group membership. Researchers also must choose a method for contacting prospective participants. They can use lists of potential participants supplied by either the company sponsoring the research project, a screening company that specializes in focus group interviewing, or a direct mail list company. Other methods are piggyback focus groups, on-location interviews, snowball sampling, random telephone screening, and placing ads in newspapers and on bulletin boards. Regardless of the method used to obtain the names of prospective participants, the key to qualifying a person is the screening form. A sample telephone screening form is shown in Exhibit 6.10. This form illustrates the format, key information questions, and screening instructions.

Sampling Procedures for Focus Groups. The issue of sampling requires some special thought when planning focus group interviews. Traditionally, researchers try to randomize the process of identifying prospective subjects. While randomization is critical in quantitative surveys, it is not as necessary in qualitative studies. Focus groups tend to require a more flexible research design. While a degree of randomization is desirable, it is not the primary factor in selection. Participant credibility during the focus group discussions is one of the

---

EXHIBIT 6.10 Telephone Screening Questionnaire to Recruit Focus Group Participants: Performing Arts Programs among Adults in Vail, Colorado*

Respondent's Name: _____   Date: _____

Mailing Address: _____   Phone #: _____

_____   Fax #: _____

(City)   (State)   (Zip Code)

Hello, my name is _____, and I'm calling for the Marketing Resources Group in Tampa, Florida. We are conducting a short interesting survey in your area and would like to include your opinions. The Marketing Resources Group is conducting a study on performing arts programs offered in your metropolitan area and I would like to ask you a few questions. The questions will take less than two minutes. Let me begin by asking . . .

1. Do you or any member of your immediate household work for a research firm, advertising agency, or a firm that produces or markets performing arts programs or events?
   (__) Yes **[THANK THE PERSON AND TERMINATE AND TALLY]**
   (__) No **[CONTINUE]**

2. Have you attended a performing arts event in the past month?
   (__) Yes **[CONTINUE]**
   (__) No **[THANK THE PERSON AND TERMINATE AND TALLY]**

3. Are you a permanent resident of Summit County?
   (__) Yes **[CONTINUE]**
   (__) No **[THANK THE PERSON AND TERMINATE AND TALLY]**

4. Are you currently employed full-time or part-time outside the home?
   (__) Full-time **[CONTINUE]**
   (__) Part-time **[THANK THE PERSON AND TERMINATE AND TALLY]**
   (__) Not currently employed **[THANK THE PERSON AND TERMINATE AND TALLY]**

5. Please stop me when I come to the age category to which you belong.
   (__) Under 20 **[THANK THE PERSON AND TERMINATE AND TALLY]**
   (__) 21 to 35 **[RECRUIT AT LEAST 12]**
   (__) 36 to 50 **[RECRUIT AT LEAST 12]**
   (__) 51 to 65 **[RECRUIT AT LEAST 12]**
   (__) Over 65 **[THANK THE PERSON AND TERMINATE AND TALLY]**

[PARTICIPANT RECRUITMENT PART—READ BY INTERVIEWER]

(Mr., Mrs., Ms.) **(Person's Last Name Here)**, the **Marketing Resources Group (MRG)** is sponsoring a meeting with people, like yourself, to discuss performing arts programs and events. We understand that **many people are busy yet enjoy attending performing arts events and have opinions about different topics concerning the arts.** We would like you to join a group of people, like yourself, to **discuss** and **get your opinions** about some performing arts topics. This **is not** a sales meeting, **but strictly a research project.** The group will meet on **Wednesday evening, August 15th, at the Vail Chamber of Commerce Office,** in downtown Vail. We would like you to be our guest. The **session will start promptly at 7:00 P.M.,** there will be refreshments and the **session will be over by 9:30 P.M.** Those people **who participate will receive $100** as our token of appreciation for participating in this important discussion session. Will you be able to attend?

(__) Yes **[CONFIRM NAME, ADDRESS, PHONE, AND FAX NUMBERS]**
(__) No **[THANK THE PERSON AND TERMINATE AND TALLY]**

[If YES], I will be sending you a **letter and information packet in a few days confirming the meeting and your participation.**

If you have **any questions or need to cancel,** please telephone our office at **[GIVE OFFICE PHONE NUMBER].** On behalf of MRG, **thank you and have a pleasant (day or evening).**

Author's note: The items that absolutely must be included in a screening/recruitment form are in boldface type for identification purposes.

key factors researchers want to achieve. Randomization can help reduce the selection bias inherent in some forms of personal recruitment, but there is never total assurance.

Recruitment of Participants. Once a prospective participant is identified, contacted, and qualified for group membership, the task becomes one of obtaining that person's willingness to actually join the group. Securing the respondent's willingness to participate is not an easy process. The researcher must invite the respondent to participate in the discussion of an interesting and important topic. There is no one best method of achieving this task, but there are some key factors that must be incorporated in the process. The researcher should use only professionally trained people as recruiters. They must have good interpersonal communication skills, as well as such characteristics as a positive, pleasant voice, a professional appearance, polite and friendly manners, and a "people-to-people" personality. The recruiter must establish a comfort zone with the respondent as quickly as possible.

To bring legitimacy to the research project, the recruiter must be able to clearly articulate the general interest and importance of the topic. It must be made clear to the respondent that because of the small group size, his or her opinions and feelings on the topic are very important to the success of the project. The recruiter must make it clear that the group meeting is not a sales meeting, but strictly a research project. Other information factors that must be included are the date, starting/ending times, location of the focus group, the incentives for participating, and a method of contacting the recruiter if the prospective participant has any questions or problems concerning the meeting. Exhibit 6.10 shows an example of the recruitment part of a screening form for a focus group session.

After the respondent commits to participating in the focus group, the researcher must send out a formal confirmation/invitation letter that includes all the critical information about the focus group meeting. The main purpose of this type of letter is to reinforce the person's commitment to participate in the focus group. Exhibit 6.11 displays a hypothetical confirmation letter. The last activity in the recruiting process is that of calling the respondent the day before (or the morning of) the actual focus group session to further reinforce his or her commitment to participate in the session.

Size of the Focus Group

Most experts agree that the optimal number of participants in any type of focus group interview is from 8 to 12. Any size smaller than eight participants is not likely to generate the right type of group dynamics or energy necessary for a beneficial group session. Too few participants create a situation where one or two people can dominate the discussion regardless of the efforts of the moderator. Also there is the increased probability of the moderator's having to become too active and talkative to keep the discussions flowing. In contrast, having too many participants can easily limit each person's opportunity to contribute insights and observations.

One of the reasons for the wide range of members (8 to 12) directly relates to the fact that it is difficult to predict just how many respondents will actually show up at the focus group session. It is not uncommon for 12 people to agree to participate but for only 8 to show up. Some researchers may try to hedge on actual response rates by inviting more people than necessary, in hopes that only the right number will show up. In cases where too many respondents show up, the researcher is forced to decide whether or not to send some home. The greatest fear of a focus group researcher is that no one will show up for the session, despite promises to the contrary.

Focus Group Incentives. While using screening forms, professionally trained recruiters, personalized invitations, and follow-up phone calls can help secure a person's willingness to participate, incentives are also needed because participation requires both time and effort. Participants usually must reserve time out of a busy schedule and are likely to incur

EXHIBIT | 6.11 Sample of Confirmation/Invitation Letter to Focus Group Members*

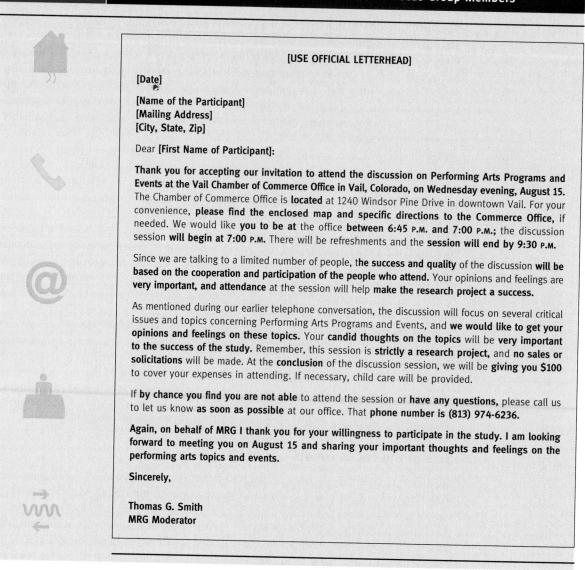

[USE OFFICIAL LETTERHEAD]

[Date]

[Name of the Participant]
[Mailing Address]
[City, State, Zip]

Dear [First Name of Participant]:

Thank you for accepting our invitation to attend the discussion on Performing Arts Programs and Events at the Vail Chamber of Commerce Office in Vail, Colorado, on Wednesday evening, August 15. The Chamber of Commerce Office is **located** at 1240 Windsor Pine Drive in downtown Vail. For your convenience, **please find the enclosed map and specific directions to the Commerce Office,** if needed. We would like **you to be at** the office **between 6:45 P.M. and 7:00 P.M.;** the discussion session **will begin at 7:00 P.M.** There will be refreshments and the **session will end by 9:30 P.M.**

Since we are talking to a limited number of people, t**he success and quality** of the discussion **will be based on the cooperation and participation of the people who attend.** Your opinions and feelings are **very important, and attendance** at the session will help **make the research project a success.**

As mentioned during our earlier telephone conversation, the discussion will focus on several critical issues and topics concerning Performing Arts Programs and Events, and **we would like to get your opinions and feelings on these topics.** Your **candid thoughts on the topics** will be **very important to the success of the study.** Remember, this session is **strictly a research project,** and **no sales or solicitations** will be made. At the **conclusion** of the discussion session, we will be **giving you $100** to cover your expenses in attending. If necessary, child care will be provided.

If **by chance you find you are not able** to attend the session or **have any questions,** please call us to let us know **as soon as possible** at our office. That **phone number is (813) 974-6236.**

Again, on behalf of MRG I thank you for your willingness to participate in the study. I am looking forward to meeting you on August 15 and sharing your important thoughts and feelings on the performing arts topics and events.

Sincerely,

Thomas G. Smith
MRG Moderator

*Author's note: All parts that are in boldface type are information that must be included in the letter.

expenses such as for child care, travel, and meals. Finally, participants will typically spend time (between 90 minutes and two hours) in the actual session. In some cases the total time is three hours—two hours for the session and an additional hour for pre- and post-interviewing activities.[4] Consequently, group members need to be compensated for their "investments" associated with their willingness to participate.

The incentive should not be viewed as a reward or salary, but rather as a stimulus to get prospective participants to attend the scheduled session on time. Focus group incentives can remind people that their commitment to participate is worth the effort, incline them to keep the promised time slot from being preempted by other factors, and communicate to the participants that the discussion session is important. While different types of incentives have different effects on participation, money is by far the best incentive choice. The advantages of using money as an incentive are that (1) it is immediately recognized and understood by the participants, (2) it is portable and fits into small spaces, (3) most people like to receive immediate cash, and (4) it has a proven track record of working. The dollar amount per participant will vary from project to project, with most ranging between $75 and $200.[5]

Number of Focus Group Sessions. Depending on the complexity of the issues to be discussed, one or more focus group sessions must be held. "Just how many sessions should be conducted?" is an elusive question. There is no set standard. The rule of thumb is there should be a minimum of two sessions but that sessions should continue until no more new ideas, thoughts, or feelings are offered by different groups of respondents.

Focus Group Locations

The last element in the planning phase is where to hold the focus group sessions. This component is important because of the length of the discussions. Since a focus group session can last between 90 minutes and two hours, it is necessary to ensure that the setting is comfortable, uncrowded, and conducive to spontaneous, unrestricted dialogue among all group members—such as a large room that allows for a roundtable format and is quiet enough so that at least audiotaping can take place with minimum disturbances. Depending on the researcher's budget constraints, focus groups can be held in such locations as the client's conference room, the moderator's home, a meeting room at a church or civic organization, and an office or hotel meeting room, to name a few.

While all of the sites listed above are adequate, in most instances the best location is a professional focus group facility. Such facilities offer a set of specially designed rooms for conducting focus group interviews. Normally, each room has a large table and comfortable chairs for up to 13 people (12 participants and a moderator), a relaxing atmosphere, built-in recording equipment, and usually a one-way mirror so that researchers or decision makers can view and hear the discussions without being seen. Also available is videotaping equipment used to capture the participants' nonverbal communication behaviors. Using a professional focus group facility usually adds to the overall data collection costs. Depending on which services are used, extra costs can range between $800 and $2,500 per focus group session.[6]

Phase 2: Conducting the Focus Group Discussions

The success of the actual focus group session depends heavily on the moderator and his or her communication, interpersonal, probing, observation, and interpretive skills. The moderator must be able not only to ask the right questions but also to stimulate and control the direction of the participants' discussions over a variety of predetermined topics.

The Focus Group Moderator

Focus group moderator
A special person who is well trained in interpersonal communication skills and professional manners.

The **focus group moderator** is well trained in interpersonal communication skills and professional manners. Moderators draw from the participants the best and most innovative ideas about the assigned topic or question. The moderator's objectives are to seek the best ideas from each group member and to stimulate spontaneous interactive and detailed discussions. The moderator is responsible for creating positive group dynamics and a comfort zone between himself or herself and each group member as well as among the members themselves. Although there is no one set of traits or characteristics that describe the type of

eXHIBIT	6.12	Important Traits of a Focus Group Moderator

The following descriptions represent some of the important traits that a researcher must consider in the selection of an excellent moderator for the focus group session:

1. The person must be well trained in interpersonal communications and have excellent listening, observation, and interpretive skills.
2. The moderator must display professional mannerisms and personality, have a good memory for names, create positive group dynamics and a comfort zone for spontaneous and interactive dialogue.
3. The moderator must be comfortable and familiar with group dynamics and processes, and must be able to exercise mild, unobtrusive control over participants.
4. The moderator must have good understanding and background knowledge of the specified topics and questions and the ability to guide the participants from one topic to the next.
5. The person must be well trained in asking follow-up probing questions, and must demonstrate respect and sensitivity for the participants and their expressed opinions and feelings.
6. The moderator must be able to communicate clearly and precisely both in writing and verbally, and must be objective, self-disciplined, and focused.
7. The person should exhibit a friendly, courteous, enthusiastic, and adaptive personality, along with a sense of humor.
8. The person should be experienced in focus group research.
9. The moderator must have a quick mind capable of noting new ideas that come from the group.
10. The moderator must know how and when to bring closure to one topic and move the discussion to the next.

person who would make the best focus group moderator, Exhibit 6.12 lists some of the traits researchers have used in selecting focus group moderators.

Moderator's Characteristics and Role. Moderators must be comfortable and familiar with group dynamics and processes. The moderator must manage the participants and be able to guide them from one topic to the next while maintaining group enthusiasm and interest for the topic. Successful moderating requires knowing when to bring closure to one topic and move on to the next. The moderator should not only have a good understanding of the specified topics and questions but also demonstrate a curiosity toward each topic and each participant's response. This curiosity may result in follow-up probing questions that uncover ideas, avenues, or connections that shed new light on the topic. Another important trait is that of demonstrating respect and sensitivity for participants and their expressed opinions and feelings on the topic. Showing respect for the group members can directly affect the value and quality of the data collected.

The moderator must have sufficient background knowledge on the topic to place all comments in perspective and follow up with appropriate questions.[7] Moreover, the moderator must be able to communicate clearly and precisely both verbally and in writing. Moderating the session requires objectivity, self-discipline, concentration, and careful listening on the part of the moderator. He or she must guard against interjecting personal opinions about the topic or a participant's response, and must instead focus on eliciting the perceptions of the group members. In addition, the moderator must be mentally prepared and completely familiar with the questioning route, yet flexible enough to allow follow-up probing questions.

A Closer Look at Research

Moderator's Guide for Vail Performing Arts Program Focus Group Interview Sessions

I. INTRODUCTION

   a. Welcome the participants.

   b. Briefly highlight the focus group format . . . get consent forms signed and turned in (if necessary).

   c. Explain ground rules for session:

      No correct answers—only your opinions and feelings . . . you are speaking for other people like yourself . . . want to hear from everyone.

      Briefly explain the audiotaping of the session and why . . . so I don't have to take many notes. If necessary, mention the one-way mirror and that some of my associates are observing the session . . . because they are extremely interested in your opinions.

      Only one speaks at a time . . . please no side discussions . . . I do not want to miss anyone's comments.

      Do not worry if you do not know much about a particular topic we talk about . . . it is OK and important for me to know . . . if your views are different from someone else's that's all right . . . it is important for me to know that too . . . please do not be afraid of having different opinions, just express them . . . remember there is no one right answer.

      This is an informal discussion . . . a research project, not a sales meeting . . . I will not be contacting you later on to try to sell you anything . . . I want you to be comfortable and relax . . . just express your opinions and feelings.

   d. Any questions? [Answer all questions of participants.] Let's begin.

II. WARMUP [Use opening question format.]

   Tell us your name and one or two things about yourself. [Ask this of each participant.] (Build group dynamics and comfort zone among group members.)

III. INTRODUCE FIRST TOPIC

[Use an introductory question format.]

"FROM YOUR VIEWPOINT, TO WHAT EXTENT DO YOU ENJOY ATTENDING PERFORMING ARTS PROGRAMS AND/OR ENTERTAINMENT EVENTS?"

Probe for:

   a. Types of programs and events that have been attended in the past and would attend in the future.

   b. Types of programs and events most preferred to see offered in the Vail Valley area.

   [Use transition question format to move to next topic.]

IV. SECOND MAJOR TOPIC

[Use a critical question format.]

Now I want you to think about how people make their decisions to attend performing arts events.

"WHAT PERFORMING ARTS/ENTERTAINMENT FEATURES DO PEOPLE DEEM IMPORTANT IN DECIDING TO ATTEND A PROGRAM OR EVENT?"

Probe for:

   a. Detail and clarification of features.

   b. Understanding of importance of identified features. [Use transition question format to move to the next topic.]

V. SPECIFIC DESIGN FEATURES

[Use a critical question format.]

Now think about the facilities used to present performing arts programs and events.

"WHAT FACTORS SHOULD BE INCLUDED IN FACILITY STRUCTURE DESIGN?"

Probe for:

   a. Specific design features and why.

   b. Thoughts and feelings about indoor versus outdoor event capabilities.

   c. Types of protection features for outdoor events for the audience, the performers. [Use transition question format to move to closure of session.]

Continued

A Closer Look at Research

Continued

VI. CLOSE SESSION WITH SUGGESTIONS AND FINAL THOUGHTS [Use ending question format.]

"TAKING INTO CONSIDERATION OUR DISCUSSIONS, WHAT SPECIFIC ACTIONS WOULD YOU SUGGEST OR RECOMMEND TO THE DESIGN TEAM TO HELP MAKE VAIL'S NEW PERFORMING ARTS FACILITY THE BEST POSSIBLE?"

Probe for clarity of specific ideas and details as to why.

Features: ___ structure designs
___ seating requirements
___ theater style vs. auditorium style
___ quality of sound system/ acoustics
___ outdoor event protection features

"ANY LAST THOUGHTS, FEELINGS, OR COMMENTS?"
[Ask and probe for each participant.]

VII. END THE FOCUS SESSION

a. Thank the participants for their cooperation and input.

b. Give each participant his or her gift of appreciation.

c. Extend a warm wish to drive home carefully.

Moderator's guide A detailed outline of the topics, questions, and subquestions used by the moderator to lead the focus group session.

Preparing a Moderator's Guide. To ensure that the actual focus group session is productive, it is necessary to prepare a detailed moderator's guide. A **moderator's guide** represents a detailed outline of the topics and questions that will serve as the basis for generating the spontaneous interactive dialogue among the group participants. The nearby Closer Look at Research box shows a moderator's guide that was incorporated in the Vail Performing Arts example mentioned earlier. Using a structured outline format, a sequence is established for asking a series of opening, introductory, transition, and ending questions. Opening questions are asked at the beginning of the focus group and can be answered quickly to identify characteristics participants have in common. These questions are normally factual and are important in establishing the group's comfort zone and internal dynamics. Introductory questions also are used to introduce the general topic of discussion as well as provide group members with the opportunity to reflect on past experiences and their connection with the overall topic. Typically, these questions are not critical to the final analysis but are important in creating spontaneous, interactive discussions. The objective of transition questions is to direct the conversation toward the main topics of interest. Transition questions help group members view the topic in a broader scope and let the participants know how others feel about the topic. In general, these questions serve as the logical link between introductory and substantive questions. From a content perspective, substantive questions drive the overall study. The moderator uses these questions to get to the heart of discussing the critical issues underlying the topics of interest. Finally, ending questions are asked to bring closure to the discussion. They allow participants to reflect on previous comments and feelings, and they encourage members to summarize any final thoughts.

The Actual Focus Group Session

Beginning the Session. As the participants arrive for the session, they should be warmly greeted by the moderator and made to feel comfortable. If name cards have not been prepared in advance, participants should be instructed to write their first names, in large letters, on the cards. Before the participants sit down, there should be an opportunity (about 10 minutes) for sociable small talk, coupled with refreshments. The purpose of these pre-session activities is to create a friendly, warm, comfortable environment in which participants feel at ease. During the socializing period, the moderator should use his or her observation skills to notice how well group members interact and talk with one another. If the moderator can identify dominant talkers and shy listeners, this can be used to place members strategically around the table.

If consent forms are required, participants should sign them and give them to the moderator before the session begins. The moderator should briefly discuss the ground rules for the session: only one person should speak at a time, everyone should understand the purpose of the session and act accordingly, and so on. In some cases, a brief mention of the sponsoring client is in order (e.g., the sponsoring client looks forward to the group's discussion on the topic as a way to decide on an important issue). In most cases, the sponsoring client is not identified to avoid introducing bias into the discussion. If the situation requires the use of a one-way mirror or audio/video equipment for taping purposes, the moderator should tell participants and briefly explain their logical use in the session. Sometimes group members are asked to introduce themselves with a few short remarks. This approach breaks the ice, gets each participant to talk, and continues the process of building positive group dynamics and comfort zones. After completing the ground rules and introductions, the moderator asks the first question using an opening question format. This question is designed to engage all participants in the discussion.

Main Session. Using the moderator's guide, the first topic area is introduced to the participants. As the discussion unfolds, the moderator must be able to use probing techniques to gain as many details as possible. If there is a good rapport between group members and the moderator, it should not be necessary for the moderator to spend a lot of time merely asking selected questions and receiving answers. Because there are no hard-and-fast rules on how long the discussion should last on any one particular topic, the moderator must use his or her judgment in deciding when to bring closure to one topic and move on to the next. In general, the session should move toward the study's critical questions at a pace that ensures enough time for depth probing of as many ideas and opinions as possible.

Closing the Session. After all of the prespecified topics have been covered, participants should be asked an ending question that encourages them to express final ideas or opinions. To enhance this closure process, the moderator can briefly summarize the group's main points and ask if these are accurate. During the summary activities, the moderator should observe the body language of the participants for signs of agreement, disagreement, hesitation, or confusion. For example, it would be appropriate for the moderator to present a final overview of the discussion and then ask the participants, "Have we missed anything?" or "Do you think we've missed anything in the discussion?" Responses to these types of closing questions may reveal some thoughts that were not anticipated. Upon final closure, participants should be given a short debriefing of the session, thanked for participating, given the promised incentive gift or cash, and wished a safe journey home.

Phase 3: Analyzing and Reporting the Results
Analysis Techniques

Debriefing Analysis. If the researcher or the sponsoring client's representatives are present, they and the moderator should conduct a **debriefing analysis** and wrap-up activities immediately after the focus group members leave the session. These activities give the researcher, client, and moderator a chance to compare notes. The key players who have heard the discussion need to know how their impressions compare to those of the moderator. Insights and perceptions can be expressed concerning the major ideas, suggestions, thoughts, and feelings from the session.

> **Debriefing analysis** An interactive procedure in which the researcher and moderator discuss the subjects' responses to the topics of the focus group session.

Ideas for improving the session can be uncovered and applied to further focus group sessions. For example, strong points can be identified and emphasized, and errors noted, while they are fresh in everyone's mind. Some researchers like to use debriefing analysis because it (1) provides an opportunity to include the opinions of marketing experts with those of the moderator; (2) allows the sponsoring client's representatives or researcher to learn, understand, and react to the moderator's top-of-mind perceptions about what was said in the group discussion; and (3) can offer opportunities for brainstorming new ideas and implications of the main points expressed in the discussion. In contrast, potential shortcomings of debriefing include (1) a clear possibility of creating interpretive bias; (2) faulty recall on the part of the moderator due to recency or limited memory capabilities; and (3) misconceptions due to lack of time for reflecting on what was actually said by the participants.[8]

> **Content analysis** The systematic procedure of taking individual responses and grouping them into larger theme categories or patterns.

Content Analysis. Although **content analysis** is an appropriate analysis tool to use in any type of qualitative research, it is probably the most widely used formalized procedure by qualitative researchers in their efforts to create meaningful findings from focus group discussions. This procedure requires the researcher to implement a systematic procedure of taking individual responses and categorizing them into larger theme categories or patterns.

Depending on how the group discussion was recorded and translated (e.g., transcript, audiotape, videotape, session notes), the researcher reviews the participants' raw comments and creates a report according to common themes or patterns. This process requires the researcher to consider several analysis and interpretive factors (see Exhibit 6.13).

Reporting Focus Group Results

To properly report the findings, the researcher must understand the audience, the purpose of the report, and the expected format. The researcher must have a strong understanding of the people who will be using the results—their preferences in receiving information and their demographic profile, including educational level, occupation, and age, to name only a few factors. Overall, the report should stress clarity and understanding and should support the findings. In many cases, the writing style can be informal and the vocabulary familiar. The researcher should use active rather than passive voice and incorporate quotations, illustrations, and examples where appropriate.

In writing the report, the researcher must be aware of its basic purpose. First, the report should communicate useful insights and information to the audience. It should be a clear and precise presentation tailored to the individual information needs of the specific users. It must offer a logical sequence of findings, insights, and recommendations. The researcher should also keep in mind the report will serve as a historical record that likely will be reviewed at some point in the future.

e X H I B I T 6.13	**Important Analysis and Interpretive Factors When Analyzing Focus Group Data**[9]

Analysis/Interpretive Factors	Description and Comments
Consider the words	Thought must be given to both the words used by the participants and the meanings of those words. Because there will be a variety of words and phrases used by the group members, the researcher will have to determine the degree of similarity and classify them accordingly. It should be remembered that editing messy quotations is a difficult but necessary task.
Consider the context	The researcher will have to gain an understanding of the context in which participants expressed key words and phrases. The context includes the actual words as well as their tone and intensity (voice inflection). It must be remembered that nonverbal communication (body language) can also provide meaningful bits of data worth analyzing.
Consider the frequency of participants' comments	In most situations, some of the topics presented in the session will be discussed by more (extensiveness) and some comments made more often (frequency) than others. The researcher should not assume that extensiveness and frequency of comments are directly related to their importance.
Consider the intensity of comments	Sometimes group members will talk about specific aspects of a topic with passion or deep feelings. While left undetected in transcripts alone, the intensity factor can be uncovered in audio- or videotapes by changes in voice tone, talking speed, and emphasis placed on certain words or phrases.
Consider the specificity of responses	Those responses that are associated with some emotional firsthand experience probably are more intense than responses that are vague and impersonal. For example, "I feel that the new McDonald's McArch burger is a ripoff because I ate one and it tasted just terrible, especially at the price they are charging" should be given more weight than "The new McArch burger does not taste very good, considering what it costs."
Consider the big picture	Because data from focus groups come in many different forms (words, body language, intensity, etc.), the researcher needs to construct an aggregate theme or message of what is being portrayed. Painting a bigger picture of what group members are actually saying can provide preliminary insights into how consumers view the specified product, service, or program. Caution should be used when trying to quantify the data. Use of numbers can inappropriately convey the impression that the results can be projected to a target population, which is not within the capabilities of qualitative data.

Format of the Report

Traditionally, focus group reports have been presented in a narrative style that uses complete sentences supported by direct quotes from the group discussion. An alternative is to use an outline format supported with bulleted statements that use key words or phrases to highlight the critical points from the group discussion. Regardless of the style, the report must be written in a clear, logical fashion and must look professional. Although there is no one best format, Exhibit 6.14 describes the essential components of a typical report.

EXHIBIT 6.14   Components of a Written Focus Group Research Report[10]

Components of the Report	Description and Comments
Cover page	The front cover should include the title, the names of people receiving or commissioning the report, the names of the researchers, and the date the report is submitted.
Executive summary	A brief, well-written executive summary should describe why the focus group session was conducted and list the major insights and recommendations. It should be limited to two pages and be able to stand alone.
Table of contents	This section provides the reader with information on how the report is organized and where various parts can be located. (It is optional for short reports.)
Statement of the problem, question, methods	This section describes the purpose of the study and includes a brief description of the focus interviews, critical questions, the number of focus group sessions, the methods of selecting participants, and the number of people included in each session.
Results and findings	The results are most often organized by critical questions or overall ideas. The results can be presented in a number of ways using bulleted lists or narrative formats, listing raw data, summarizing the discussion, or using an interpretative approach.
Summary of themes	Statements in this section are not limited to specific questions but rather connect several questions into a larger picture.
Limitations and alternative explanations	This section can be placed within the results section, if it is brief. Limitations reflect those aspects of the study that reduce the application of the findings or affect different interpretations of the findings.
Recommendations	This optional section is not automatically included in all focus group reports. The recommendations suggest what might be done with the results.
Appendix	The appendix should include any additional materials that might be helpful to the reader. Most often a copy of the moderator's guide, screening form, or other relevant material would go into the appendix.

Advantages of Focus Group Interviews

With an understanding of the process and activities of conducting focus group interviews, we can see the advantages and disadvantages associated with this popular qualitative research method. There are basically five major advantages to using focus group interviews: they stimulate new ideas, thoughts, and feelings about a topic; foster understanding of why people act or behave in certain market situations; allow client participation; elicit wide-ranging participant responses; and can bring together hard-to-reach subject groups.

New Ideas

The spontaneous, unrestricted interaction among focus group participants during discussions can stimulate new ideas, thoughts, and feelings that may not be raised in one-on-one interviews. There is a high likelihood that respondents will offer creative opinions about a subject topic. With an effective moderator, participants are more at ease in expressing their candid opinions than in a one-on-one situation with an interviewer. In a spontaneous, interactive environment, participants are encouraged to freely engage in group creativity that induces a "snowballing" process where additional responses are triggered by someone else's comments.

Underlying Reasons of Behavior

Focus groups allow researchers to collect detailed data about the underlying reasons people act as they do in different market situations. A trained moderator can help in directing the focus group discussion so that participants feel comfortable in expressing why they hold certain beliefs or feel the way they do about particular discussion topics such as the product's attributes, service components, brand images, or particular marketing practices, to name a few.

Client Participation

Focus group interviews offer another advantage by allowing the decision makers the opportunity to be involved in the overall process from start to finish. Clients can have an interactive role in creating the research objectives and setting the focus groups' overall agenda and initial research questions. The energetic atmosphere during the actual sessions enables the client's representatives and researchers to observe firsthand (from behind a one-way mirror) the group dynamics and how participants respond to information on the topics and questions of interest. This participation can lead to impressions and results that suggest specific actions. In some cases, clients formulate and begin action plans based on their observations even before the data are analyzed and submitted as a final report.

Breadth of Topics Covered

Focus group interviews can range over an unlimited number of topics and management issues as well as very diverse groups of subjects like children, teenagers, senior citizens, and so on. Sessions can incorporate prototypes of new products to be demonstrated or advertising copy being evaluated. In addition, other types of projective data collection methods could be included (e.g., balloon tests, role-playing activities, word association tests, picture tests) to stimulate spontaneous discussions of a topic. Recent technology has added new flexibility to the process by allowing clients located in different geographic regions to participate in and observe the live sessions without having to be at the specific facility location.

Special Market Segments

Another advantage is the technique's unique ability to bring together groups of individuals, such as doctors, lawyers, and engineers, to name a few, who might not otherwise be willing to participate in a study. The focus group format allows these hard-to-interview individuals an opportunity to interact with their peers and compare thoughts and feelings on common topics and issues of interest.

Disadvantages of Focus Group Interviews

As with any exploratory research design, focus group interviews are not a perfect research method. The major weaknesses of focus groups are inherently similar to all qualitative methods: the findings lack generalizability to the target population, the reliability of the data is questionable, the interpretation is subjective, and the cost per participant is high.

Low Generalizability of Results

As with any qualitative method, the findings developed from focus group interviews tend to lack representativeness with regard to the target population. This makes it very difficult, if not impossible, for the researcher to generalize the results to larger market segments. For example, Procter & Gamble's brand manager of Crest toothpaste as well as the researcher might run substantial risks in believing that the attitudes and feelings toward a new formula change in the product obtained from 12 Crest users in a focus group are truly representative of the typical attitudes and feelings of the millions of Crest users in the market.

Questions of Data Reliability

Given the type of data collected in focus group interviews, the researcher has no way to evaluate reliability. In addition to having to deal with extremely small sample sizes, the unstructured nature of the data (nominal nature of the verbalized comments and nonverbal body language) precludes analyzing the results in standard statistical formats (e.g., percentage and mean values). Adding to this weakness is the possibility that some degree of the known "Hawthorne effect" has impacted the data collected from the participants: the focus group process can easily create an environment that makes some of the participants think they are "special" and act accordingly when offering their comments.

Another potential problem relates to effects of moderator interaction bias. Because of the social interaction in focus groups, the moderator must guard against behaving in ways that might prejudice participants' responses. For example, a moderator that is aggressive or confronting in nature could systematically lead participants to say whatever they think the moderator wants to hear. In contrast, a moderator's attempts to play dumb or too supportive to participants' comments may create a sense of phoniness on the moderator's part, thus causing some respondents to stop making comments. While difficult to measure, these conditions may reduce the reliability of the data.

Subjectivity of Interpretations

Given the nature of the data collected, selective use of the data by either the researcher or the client's representatives can create problems. For example, if the client enters the focus group process with preconceived ideas of what will emerge from a focus group, that client often can find something in the data (e.g., participants' comments) that can be subjectively interpreted as being supportive of these views while ignoring any opposing data. In addition, there is always the possibility of moderator interpretation bias, which can quickly reduce the credibility and trustworthiness of the information being provided to marketing decision makers.

High Cost per Participant

The costs of identifying, recruiting, and compensating focus group participants along with the costs of the moderator(s) and facilities are overall quite high (e.g., ranging from $5,000 to $8,000 per session), resulting in a cost-per-participant average of between $500 and $800, assuming the data came from 10 participants. This average per participant is significantly greater than the cost of other qualitative methods.

Focus groups are popular not only in the United States, but globally. The Global Insights box describes focus group research practices in other countries and compares them with those used in the United States.

Understanding Focus Group Research Abroad[11]

As more companies enter the global market, there is an increasing need for qualitative research information, both to help assess the demand for items and to identify the optimal way of marketing in foreign countries. Many U.S. companies are expanding their use of focus group research to their overseas markets. There are some major differences in doing focus groups outside the United States and Canada, according to Thomas L. Greenbaum, president of Groups Plus, Inc., in Wilton, Connecticut. One cannot simply take the same materials used to conduct focus groups in the United States and send them to a research organization in a foreign country and expect to get comparable, or even reliable, results. The following insights are offered within seven key components of focus group research:

1. **Time frame.** Whereas many companies are accustomed to developing a project on Monday and having it completed by the end of the following week, this is almost impossible to do in foreign countries. Lead times tend to be much longer, with the Far East being particularly troublesome. If it takes two weeks to set up groups in the United States, figure almost double that in most of Europe and even more than that in Asia.

2. **Structure.** Eight to 10 people in a group is a large number for most foreign groups, which often consist of 4 to 6 people, our minigroup. Further, the length of sessions outside the United States can be up to four hours. Be very specific when arranging for international focus groups. Most foreign research organizations seem to adapt well to our format if properly informed and supervised.

3. **Recruiting and rescreening.** In general, the United States is much more rigid in adhering to specifications both in recruiting and screening. These processes must be monitored very carefully.

4. **Approach.** Foreign moderators tend to be much less structured and authoritative, which can result in a great deal of downtime during the sessions. Also they tend to use fewer writing exercises and external stimuli such as concept boards and photos. This must be considered when planning foreign sessions.

5. **Project length.** Projects can take much longer to execute. In the United States, we are accustomed to doing two, sometimes three or four, groups a day, but in many overseas markets, one group is the limit because of the time they are scheduled, the length of the sessions, or demands of the moderators. Also, some moderators have a break in the middle of the group, which would be very unusual in U.S. sessions.

6. **Facilities.** The facility environment outside the United States and Canada is much like the setup here 20 years ago. For example, it is more common than not to watch a group in a residential setting on a television which is connected to the group room by cable. Many of the facilities with one-way mirror capabilities simply do not have the amenities we are accustomed to in the United States.

7. **Costs.** Finally, the cost of conducting focus group research varies considerably by region and country. It would not be unusual to pay almost twice as much per group for sessions conducted in Europe and almost three times as much for many areas in Asia.

In light of these differences, it is important that companies take action to ensure that they get the results needed from foreign research. Greenbaum suggests having the international research managed by the same people who run the U.S. studies or use a U.S.-based foreign research company that can be a central point of contact and will handle the details abroad. So if you are going to conduct qualitative research outside the United States, spend the extra time and money, and do it right. It will be a small investment over the long term.

Advancing Technology Moves Focus Groups into the 21st Century

Online focus group
Subjects are gathered in a centralized location and the session is carried in real time across the Internet to clients and researchers at other locations.

Few would argue that the future of focus group interviewing is very bright. Improved sophistication in Internet, telecommunications, and computer technology is leading the way toward new trends in conducting focus groups that will keep this qualitative data collection method popular well into the 21st century.

A high-tech version of focus group interviewing, promoted as **online focus groups,** is becoming more widely used. With this approach, a special group of service application providers (SAPs), not marketing researchers, have successfully integrated many of the benefits of the high-speed computer and telecommunication technologies into focus group research. For example, interactive marketing technologies (IMTs) facilitate conducting telephone, video, and Internet focus group interviews through such formats as teleconference networks. TeleSessions, FocusVision Networks, and itracks Internet software use videoconferencing and online Internet systems to complete focus groups.[12] In addition, Market Opinion Research (MOR), FocusVision Worldwide, Inc., Interactive Tracking Systems, Inc. (hppt://www.itracks.com), and others offer interactive group research systems that allow customization of any business's needs, whether they involve testing new TV ads, product or advertising concepts, or observing consumers' reactions to words, phrases, or visuals.[13]

The rapid introduction and continuous improvements of Internet technologies are driving how, what, when, where, and how fast qualitative data are collected, analyzed and disseminated to researchers and decision makers. High-speed Internet-assisted approaches are making it easier to reach today's hard-to-reach subjects and are shortening the time cycle in completing focus group research projects, while allowing decision makers to interact with the process in real time.[14] In turn, the advances in technology-driven approaches for conducting online focus groups and videoconferencing have increased the costs of collecting qualitative data, at least in the short run.

Online versus Offline Focus Group Research

Opinions differ on whether the future of focus group research will be online methods or offline (e.g., traditional focus group practices as discussed in this chapter) practices, based on acknowledged new speed and flexibility requirements. For now, it is important to understand the driving forces behind online practices. The push is coming not from marketing researchers, but rather from the new breed of specialized focus group data collection facilities. Once limited to providing researchers with a "professional" taping facility for conducting the actual focus group sessions, with the integration of high technology these service providers shorten the data acquisition, analysis, and reporting activities of focus groups. Decision makers have embraced the real-time dimension and flexibility these service providers offer. But at present few focus group facilities have the expensive computer and software technologies necessary to offer online focus groups.

Overall, the processes, guidelines, and decisions that are required in the "planning" and "execution" stages of an online focus group session are, for the most part, the same for conducting a traditional offline focus group session. For example, both methods require that the decision maker and researcher fully understand the nature of focus group interviews and together develop the focus group objectives. Similar activities for identifying the appropriate type of people for inclusion in the focus group, the sampling, selection, and recruitment of the prospective participants, as well as the critical decisions concerning size and number of focus groups, incentives, and location must be jointly undertaken by the researcher and decision maker regardless of the approach. In conducting the actual focus group session, both methods require participants and a trained moderator to be located in a specific central location for taping the interview.

It is here that differences begin to appear. For example, the technology driving the data-capturing activities during the focus group session is much more sophisticated for online than for offline methods, requiring online moderators to have a greater technological aptitude and understanding of the devices used to gather the data in real time. Online focus groups provide significantly greater flexibility to client participation before, during, and after the session. Offline methods require that the client's representatives be at the focus group, located behind a one-way mirror, and communication capabilities with the moderator are limited and antiquated (e.g., a moderator headset, handwritten notes, or specified breaks in the session). In contrast, online methods use advanced communication technologies that enable clients to directly participate from anywhere in the world—all they need is a computer and Internet access.

Offline focus groups have the advantage of gaining additional information from each of the participants through the moderators' and clients' ability to directly observe the participants' nonverbal communication habits and body language during the actual group interview. In certain forms of online group interviews (e.g., chat room discussions, bulletin boards, newsgroups, discussion lists, etc.) the lack of face-to-face interaction makes obtaining this type of additional information impossible. In turn, the lack of face-to-face exposure might well make online participants feel more comfortable in giving more candid responses than those in an offline group interview. In any of the online methods (excluding those that use some form of face-to-face interactions), incentives needed to recruit participants are normally cheaper or less extensive than the incentives needed to secure participants in offline group interviews.

The greatest differences between the two methods are in the last phase of the process (analyzing and reporting of the results). Online focus group interviewing allows for data manipulation, retrieval, and reporting of the qualitative data results in real time, whereas offline methods typically take researchers days, if not weeks, to manipulate and report the findings to decision makers. For more insights into online focus group research practices, visit the book's Web site at www.mhhe.com/hair06.

Other Qualitative Research Methods

Case Studies

Case study An exploratory research technique that intensively investigates one or several existing situations which are similar to the current problem/opportunity situation.

Case studies are exploratory research that involves intense investigation of one or a few past problem situations that are viewed as similar to the researcher's current problem situation. The premise underlying the case study approach is that for any current research issue there are probably several past situations that have some very similar elements. The case study approach requires the researcher or decision maker to conduct an in-depth examination of the element of interest. The specific element can be a customer, salesperson, store, firm, market area, and so forth. This approach of gathering data is best when researchers need to obtain substantial detail about the issue or when they do not know exactly what they are looking for or are trying to find important clues and ideas concerning a current research problem.

Very often success in using the case study method is a function of the investigator's ability to use common sense and imagination during the data gathering process. Typical objectives of the case study method are to (1) identify relevant variables, (2) indicate the nature and order of the existing relationships between the variables, and (3) identify the nature of the problem and/or opportunity present in the original decision. The overall goal is to develop a comprehensive description of the issues leading to a better understanding of the current problem situation and the potential impact of the interacting elements. Take for example Custom Doors, Inc., a manufacturer of doors used in commercial buildings. Management wanted to expand its market to include commercial businesses in Japan but was unaware of the key factors necessary to be successful. The executives at Custom Doors researched several of the leading Japanese construction companies using their annual financial reports and available information on their distribution systems. They also had detailed discussions with several of their own current material suppliers that had experience in Japanese commercial markets and held personal interviews with two architects at one of the largest Japanese architectural firms in Tokyo. As a result of their in-depth analysis of the information obtained, management gained a better understanding of the key elements for landing Japanese ventures. The key elements focused on the company's ability to (1) secure high-quality raw materials, (2) produce commercial doors that met very strict product specifications, (3) be adaptable with design changes, and (4) make assurances on the delivery of the final product on time. As a consequence, Custom Doors, Inc. (1) developed strong relationships with four U.S.-based suppliers that guaranteed the needed high-quality raw material, (2) spent about 2 million U.S. dollars to purchase laser guided manufacturing equipment for improving its ability to meet product specifications, (3) developed a system for handling short notice architectural specification changes, and (4) contracted with a Japanese-based delivery company. Today, Custom Doors, Inc., has expanded its annual commercial door business to about 12 million dollars just within the Japanese market.

Experience Interviews

Experience interviews
Informal gathering of information from individuals thought to be knowledgeable on the issues relevant to the information research problem.

Experience interviews gather opinions and insights informally from people considered to be knowledgeable on the issues associated with the research problem. For example, if the research problem involves difficulties in purchasing books online from Amazon.com, then interviews among dissatisfied online Amazon purchasers might be conducted. If a company like Procter & Gamble has a research problem that deals with estimating future demands for its newly created Web site "Consumer Corner" (http://www.consumercorner.com), the company could begin by contacting several Web site "experts" and asking their opinions on the issues.

For the most part, experience interviews differ from other types of interviewing approaches in that there is no attempt to ensure that the findings are representative of any overall defined group of subjects. To illustrate this point, let's take an instructor at your institution who is asked to teach a marketing research course for the first time. The fundamental research problem here simply deals with which topics should be covered in what detail within a specified time frame. The instructor could contact several other people who have experience in teaching a marketing research course and ask their opinions about topics and depth of coverage. Although these "experts" may provide useful information, there is a high likelihood their opinions and suggestions would differ from the collective opinions of all people who have experience teaching marketing research.

Protocol Interviews

Protocol interviewing
The subject is placed in a specified decision-making situation and asked to verbally express the process and activities that he or she would undertake to make a decision.

Protocol interviewing places a person in a specified decision-making situation and asks the person to verbally express the process and activities that are considered in making a decision. This technique is useful when the research problem focuses on selected aspects (e.g., motivational or procedural) of making a purchase decision. For example, Dell Computer

Company wants to understand the difficulties associated with the various decision criteria customers use when making online purchases of Dell PCs. By asking several Dell PC purchasers to verbalize the steps and activities they went through, the researcher is able to work backward and identify the different processes used in making online purchase decisions. This can provide the researcher with insights and understanding of those motivational and/or procedural activities that might be potential obstacles keeping other potential customers from making an online purchase from Dell.

Articulative Interviews

Articulative interviews
A qualitative-oriented interviewing technique that focuses on the listening for and identifying of key conflicts in a person's orientation values toward products, services, or concepts.

Articulative interviews are qualitative group interviews that focus on listening for and identifying key conflicts in a person's orientation values toward products and services. This method gets subjects to articulate their orienting values as well as their inherent conflicts with those values that otherwise might seem inexpressible. An articulative interview is structured to elicit narratives as opposed to gaining factual truths. The interview focuses on uncovering what subjects find worthy and unworthy in their lives; how they live in particular roles and in certain domains of activity. The line of questioning used by an articulative interviewer requires the subjects to express a narrative that incorporates a past-present-future structure of the topic of concern. During the story-telling process, the interviewer raises questions about the parts of the story that were left out that tend to bring out expressions of conflict. By questioning the narrative context, subjects are encouraged to describe how the roles they hold are in conflict resulting in seemingly insoluble dilemmas.

In conducting articulative interviews, the researcher must be able to achieve two goals: identify the subjects' orienting values toward the product or service being investigated and clarify existing value conflicts. To identify subjects' orienting values, the researcher must be able to (1) question the obvious and listen for differences, (2) study the present, (3) know the past, and (4) learn the descriptive vocabulary used by the participants. For example, researchers studying parents from different cultures and economic classes about their values taught to their children initially found that most parents universally expressed: "I want what is best for my children. And that is that they 'do well' in life." By questioning the obvious, it was learned that among parents in middle-class Mexican culture, "doing well" means visibly achieving the next economic class status, but in low-income Mexican culture, "doing well" means the children will have their own home without regard to whether it came by good fortune or hard work.

As a result of articulative interviewing, the researchers were able to identify significantly different shadings of "doing well."[15] In order to expose a participant's value conflicts, the researcher must be able to (1) listen for confusion, awkwardness, resignations, and contradictions among the subjects; (2) listen for invidious distinctions and self-righteous expressions; (3) identify the roles the subject plays in relation to the product or service category; and (4) elicit defining narratives of life changes. To illustrate the latter technique, researchers studied female college graduates regarding their orienting value of "being taken seriously." When asked to reflect back as undergraduate students, many of the subjects thought their future careers would mean everything to them. Being taken seriously meant doing anything to get ahead in a career. But after entering the workforce, a new value arose—being able to live a balanced, "quality" life. For most this meant having a family, engaging in healthy physical activities, taking vacations, and being a serious person. To better understand the changing meaning of "being taken seriously" and the conflicts of living a "quality life," researchers used follow-up questions such as "Where do you see your professional lives moving in the future?" "What do you wish you could keep from the old way of being serious?" "How does having a family fit in?" and/or "How do you view yourself in comparison to your mother?"

Projective Interviewing Techniques

Projective technique
An indirect method of questioning that enables a subject to project beliefs and feelings onto a third party, into a task situation, or onto an inanimate object.

Projective techniques constitute a "family" of qualitative data collection methods where participants are asked to project themselves into specified buying situations, then asked questions about the situations. The underlying objective is to learn more about the participants in situations where they might not reveal their true thoughts under a direct questioning process. These techniques were initially developed in the motivational area of social and clinical psychology and include word association tests, sentence completion tests, picture tests, thematic apperception tests (TAT), cartoon or balloon tests, and role-playing activities.

Word Association Tests

Word association test
A projective technique in which the subject is presented with a list of words or short phrases, one at a time, and asked to respond with the first thing that comes to mind.

In interviews using **word association tests,** a participant is read a preselected set of words, one at a time, and asked to respond with the first thing that comes to her or his mind regarding that word. For example, what comes to your mind when you hear the word "red"? Some people might respond with hot; others might say danger, apple, stop, fire truck, or Santa Claus. After completing the list of words, researchers then look for hidden meanings and associations between the responses and the words being tested on the original list. Advertising researchers employ word association tests in efforts to develop meaningful ad copy a target market can quickly identify with the message. Research companies like the Discovery Group, a New England–based youth firm, use word association techniques to find out the latest slang words or phrases peculiar to East Coast kids 11 to 17 years of age. Exhibit 6.15 illustrates some of the new words and phrases most popular in teen-speaking today. Marketers and advertisers can gain better insight into how to communicate more effectively to teens by understanding the latest teen lexicons.

Sentence Completion Tests

Sentence completion test A projective technique where subjects are given a set of incomplete sentences and asked to complete them in their own words.

In **sentence completion interviews,** respondents are given incomplete sentences and asked to complete them in their own words in hopes that the respondents will reveal some hidden aspects about their thoughts and feelings toward the investigated object. From the data collected, researchers interpret the completed sentences to identify meaningful themes or concepts. For example, let's say the local Chili's restaurant in your area wants to find out what modifications to its current image are needed to attract a larger portion of the college student market segment. Researchers could interview college students in the area and ask

EXHIBIT 6.15 From the Mouths of Teens

Word/Phrase	Definition	Used in a Sentence
"Be easy"	Relax, calm down	"Yo, son, be easy. Sit down."
"Jump off"	Hot: really happening	"That party is the jump off."
"Mad" or "Madd"	A lot: very	"This shirt is mad cool."
"Shorty"	A girl	"She's my shorty."
"Cheesin'"	Smiling broadly	"Yo. That chick is cheesin'."

Source: The Discovery Group and *American Demographics* (May 2003).

them to complete the following sentences:

People who eat at Chili's are _____.

Chili's reminds me of _____.

Chili's is the place to be when _____.

College students go to Chili's to _____.

My friends think Chili's is _____.

While the researcher could (and should) separately identify different themes from the data provided from each question, integrating the data could reveal overall themes that might prove more useful in creating a dining experience likely to attract significantly more college students. For example, an interpretation of the data from the first sentence might reveal the theme of "older, more mature restaurant patrons," suggesting that serious changes would be needed to attract those college students not interested in spending their dining experience in a restaurant setting where mature people eat. The theme for the second sentence might be "family-oriented," suggesting that Chili's is perceived as an eating establishment where there are a lot of small children, not appealing to many college students. The next sentence might support a theme of "great place to take a date," indicating college students think of Chili's as a place to eat dinner when out on a date. Data from the next sentence might suggest the theme of "a place to hang out with friends and watch sporting events." Here it would be important for the restaurant to make sure its advertisements convey this theme to college students. The final sentence might generate data that supports the theme "fun atmosphere," indicating that students like going to Chili's when they want to have fun. Now combining the information, Chili's management will know the college market perceives the restaurant as being an enjoyable place to meet friends, watch sporting events, and have dinner with a date, but a place that is too family oriented and caters to noncollege patrons.

Picture Tests

Picture test A qualitative interviewing method where subjects are given a picture and instructed to describe their reactions by writing a short narrative story about the picture.

In **picture tests,** respondents are given a picture and instructed to describe their reactions by writing a short narrative story about the picture. Researchers interpret the content of the written stories to identify the respondent's positive, neutral, or negative feelings or concerns generated by the picture. Traditionally, this method has proven very useful to ad agencies testing the impact of pictures for use on product packaging, print advertisements, and brochures. For example, a test print advertisement for a Virgin Mobile cell phone designed to possibly attract more college student consumers depicted a fogged-up back window of a car with the ad headline written on the window that said "Hello Lovers: get a Hot Virgin Mobile cell phone for as low as $59." A picture test may divulge some aspects about the ad that are negative or not believable. Perhaps some college students might not make the connection because they do not have a significant other or they just went through a tough relationship breakup. In turn, the picture may be perceived as not having much relevancy to college students or the $59 rate as not being a bargain or not generating the types of feelings toward staying connected as intended by Virgin Mobile's ad agency. Regardless of the stories communicated by the respondents, without the picture test it would be difficult for management at Virgin Mobile to determine the audience's reactions to the ad.

Thematic Apperception Test (TAT)

Thematic apperception test (TAT) A specific projective technique that presents the subjects with a series of pictures and asks them to provide a description of or a story about the pictures.

Similar to yet different from the picture test is the **thematic apperception test (TAT).** Instead of asking the participant to write a short story about what a single picture is communicating, the TAT method presents participants with a series of pictures where the consumer and/or products/services are the main focus in each picture. Typically there is some level of continuity among the pictures. Participants are asked to provide their descriptive interpretation of what is happening in the pictures or a story about the pictures and what the people might do next. The researcher then conducts a content analysis of the descriptions and stories. The goal is to create interpretable themes based on the descriptions or stories attached to the pictures.

One of the keys in using TAT is that pictures or cartoon stimuli must be sufficiently interesting to the participants to induce discussions, yet ambiguous enough not to give away the nature of the research project. It is important that hints not be given to the picture characters' positive or negative predispositions. For example, a designer clothing manufacturer wanting to test the potential of a new pair of jeans having a positive appeal to female college students might use TAT by showing selected females a set of pictures with the first one portraying three college age females at the local department store discussing the jeans. The second picture might show one of the females getting dressed in the jeans and the final picture might have a female dancing in the jeans at a party. After viewing the pictures, participants are asked to provide their interpretation of what is going on in each picture. The researcher then does a content analysis of the descriptions or stories to uncover latent themes that might represent either positive or negative elements of the jeans. While TATs are fun to do, the complexity factor of the picture or stimuli used can cause difficulties in analysis. Insights gained from TAT research can prove useful in better understanding elements use in product design, packaging, print advertisements, and brochures.

Cartoon or Balloon Tests

Cartoon (balloon) test
A qualitative data collection method in which the subject is given a cartoon drawing and suggests the dialogue in which the character(s) might engage.

Cartoon (balloon) tests involve the use of cartoons similar to those in your local newspaper. Typically, one or two characters are arranged in a setting, sometimes predescribed and other times ambiguous. Normally the characters themselves are presented in a vague manner, without expression, to ensure the respondent is not given any clues regarding a suggested type of response. The researcher places an empty balloon above one or both of the characters and instructs respondents to write in the balloon(s) what they believe the character(s) are saying. The researcher then interprets these written thoughts to identify the respondent's latent feelings about the situation being portrayed in the cartoon. For example, when shown a cartoon situation of a male and female character in a pet store in which the female is making the statement, "Here is a multilevel cat condo on sale for $165," the respondent is asked how the male character in the drawing would respond and asked to write it in the balloon above the male character. After the response is provided, the researcher then uses his or her interpretive skills to evaluate the respondent's reactions.

Role-Playing Interviews

Role-playing interview
Subject is asked to act out someone else's behavior in a specified setting.

In **role-playing interviews,** participants are asked to take on the identity of a third person, such as a neighbor or friend, placed in a specific, predetermined situation, and then asked to verbalize how they would act in the situation. In other cases where the research interest lies in how the participant would respond to a specific statement, rather than what respondents think, the statement is phrased in terms of "your neighbors" or "most people" or another third-party format. For example, rather than asking a person why she does not use the Internet more frequently to purchase online consumer products for her home, the researcher would ask, "Why don't many people use the Internet more often to purchase online consumer products for their home?"

marketing research in action

Designing and Implementing a Focus Group Interview

Barnett Bank Customer Satisfaction

This discussion will illustrate the research activities used by the Barnett Bank of Pasco County (BBPC) to resolve the decision problem situation described at the beginning of this chapter. Integrating the information presented in this and earlier chapters on research problems and objectives, the following discussion will show how focus group interviews were planned and executed to collect the information needed by BBPC's management team.

The Decision Problem Situation

BBPC's management found that its seniors market segment indicated overall high satisfaction regarding the bank's products and service offerings, but the bank had lost market share in this segment to competing banks in the region. More specifically, management could not understand the existing relationship between the bank's senior customers' expressed satisfaction and the fact that a significant number of them had been closing their BBPC accounts and switching to competing financial institutions. (Bank management defined "senior customer" as anyone over 54 years old.) Therefore, BBPC's management asked the bank's marketing department to find the answers. The vice president of marketing was given the task of gathering information about BBPC's senior customers' banking attitudes, perceptions, and behaviors toward the product and service offerings and current service delivery methods as well as how the bank might improve its service quality and assure customers of satisfying experiences.

Realizing that she was not an expert in marketing research, the vice president of marketing solicited the help of a research expert. After a telephone conversation, the researcher scheduled an initial meeting with the vice president of marketing and the bank's president to discuss the bank's situation.

Identifying the Research Problems and Objectives

At that first meeting, the researcher listened to management's view of the problem. Using a situation analysis framework, the researcher asked many background questions and employed the iceberg principle to help management obtain a clearer picture of the present problem. The main concern was to understand why senior bank customers were leaving BBPC for other financial institutions even though records indicated they were satisfied overall with BBPC's banking services. In turn, the researcher asked management such research questions as the following:

- What bank selection criteria did senior customers use to select BBPC initially?

- Which bank products and services are most important to this particular market segment?

- How do the bank's senior customers rate the quality of service they receive from BBPC?

- What banking practices and procedures does BBPC conduct in an effort to keep customers satisfied?

- Who is empowered to ensure bank customer satisfaction?

Using management's responses to the questions, the background information provided by management, and the researcher's knowledge of research design, the following research objectives were proposed for BBPC's approval:

1. To gain preliminary understanding of those banking factors that are important in selecting a retail banking institution, with emphasis on products, service offerings, facilities, and parking features.

2. To identify and understand senior customers' attitudes toward the various methods of
conducting banking transactions, particularly inside, drive-up, 24-hour ATM, phone,
mail, and online methods.

3. To gain an understanding of the senior customers' perceptions of bank service quality
related to BBPC's current delivery mechanisms.

4. To discover how the satisfaction of BBPC's senior customers affects their bank loyalty.

After establishing the basic research objectives, the researcher discussed with the vice president of marketing different possible qualitative and quantitative research designs that
could be used to collect the necessary information as well as the time and cost constraints
associated with each design alternative.

Given that management needed to understand why happy senior customers were switching banks and what banking practices might need changing to ensure service quality and satisfying banking experiences, the researcher suggested holding a series of six focus groups
among both current BBPC senior customers and those who had switched banks. The researcher prepared a complete research proposal that suggested two focus group sessions,
each with 10 participants, be conducted among current senior customers and four 10-person
sessions be conducted with senior customers who had left BBPC. The proposal indicated
that each focus group session would cost BBPC about $2,500. The research proposal was
approved by management, and the researcher began planning the focus group interviews.

Planning the Focus Group Interviews

In designing the focus group sessions, the researcher's focus was on defining, selecting, and
recruiting prospective participants for the six sessions. BBPC's records showed there were approximately 26,000 current senior bank customers living within BBPC's service market area.
Records also indicated that about 4,000 senior customers had closed their accounts with BBPC
within the past 12 months. A random probability sampling procedure was used to select the 20
current senior customers along with 40 alternates and 40 ex-customers with 100 alternates. A
multiphase process was used to contact and recruit the focus group participants. Selected
prospective participants were first contacted and screened for eligibility by telephone using the
"screening" instrument displayed in Exhibit 6.16. Next, each selected individual who agreed
to participate in the focus group study was mailed a thank-you/confirmation letter, displayed
in Exhibit 6.17, that provided the specific date, time, location, and other information pertinent
to his or her scheduled focus group session. Since the sessions were going to be videotaped,
each participant was also mailed a consent form (Exhibit 6.18) to sign and bring to the session.

As prospective participants were being recruited, the researcher also developed the
scripted moderator's guide that would be used to conduct the focus group sessions. The main
function of a moderator's guide is to provide the framework and necessary guidance of what
and how topics are to be covered in the session. The guide is really nothing more than an outline that helps ensure the required topics are covered. Exhibit 6.19 shows the moderator's
guide used in the BBPC study.

Conducting the Focus Group Discussions

Since senior consumers do not like to drive at night, the two focus group sessions that had
participants age 65 or older were held from 5:00 to 7:00 P.M. All other sessions were scheduled for 6:30 to 8:30 P.M. The times were appropriate since the two sessions were conducted

---

eXHIBIT 6.16 Telephone Screening Questionnaire Used to Recruit Focus Group Participants for Barnett Bank of Pasco County Study

---

Respondent's Name: _____   Date: _____

Mailing Address: _____   Phone #: _____

_____   Fax #: _____
(City)   (State)   (Zip Code)

Hello, my name is _____, and I'm calling for the Marketing Resources Group in Tampa, Florida. We are conducting a short interesting survey in your area and would like to include your opinions. The Marketing Resources Group is conducting a study on retail banking practices in your metropolitan area and I would like to ask you a few questions. The questions will take less than two minutes. Let me begin by asking . . .

1. Do you or any member of your immediate household work for a retail bank, for a research firm, or for an advertising agency that produces or markets banking products or services?
    (__) Yes **[THANK THE PERSON AND TERMINATE AND TALLY.]**
    (__) No **[CONTINUE.]**

2. Do you conduct some of your banking transactions at a retail commercial bank?
    (__) Yes **[CONTINUE.]**
    (__) No **[THANK THE PERSON AND TERMINATE AND TALLY.]**

3. Please stop me when I come to the age category to which you belong.
    (__) Under 20 **[THANK THE PERSON AND TERMINATE AND TALLY.]**
    (__) 21 to 35 **[THANK THE PERSON AND TERMINATE AND TALLY.]**
    (__) 36 to 54 **[THANK THE PERSON AND TERMINATE AND TALLY.]**
    (__) 54 to 65 **[RECRUIT AT LEAST 40.]**
    (__) Over 65 **[RECRUIT AT LEAST 20.]**

[PARTICIPANT RECRUITMENT PART—READ BY INTERVIEWER]

(Mr., Mrs., Ms.) **(Person's Last Name Here),** the Marketing Resources Group (MRG) is sponsoring a meeting with people, like yourself, to discuss retail banking practices. We understand that many people are busy yet have opinions about different topics concerning retail banking practices. We would like you to join a group of people, like yourself, to discuss and get your opinions about some banking topics. This is not a sales meeting, but strictly a research project. The group will meet on Tuesday, June 15, at the Youth and Family Service Center, in New Port Richey. We would like you to be our guest. The session will start promptly at 5:00 P.M., there will be refreshments and the session will be over by 7:00 P.M. Those people who participate will receive $100 as our token of appreciation for participating in this important discussion session. Will you be able to attend?

    (__) Yes **[CONFIRM NAME, ADDRESS, PHONE, AND FAX NUMBERS.]**
    (__) No **[THANK THE PERSON AND TERMINATE AND TALLY.]**

[If YES], I will be sending you a letter and information packet in a few days confirming the meeting and your participation. If you have any questions or need to cancel, please telephone our office at **[GIVE OFFICE PHONE NUMBER].** On behalf of MRG, thank you and have a pleasant (day or evening).

---

during June and July, when there was sufficient daylight to allow the participants to drive back home before dark. For each session, participants were contacted by telephone the night before their scheduled session to reconfirm their attendance and were asked to arrive about 15 minutes prior to the start of their session. This time was used to check in participants and allow some informal socializing to get to know the moderator and other participants. Another critical objective of this pre-session time frame was to give the participants, initially strangers, an opportunity to relax and become familiar with the setting.

EXHIBIT 6.17 Thank You/Confirmation Letter

June 8, 2004

Mr. Henry C. Aniello
2305 Windsor Oaks Avenue
New Port Richey, FL 34655

Dear Mr. Aniello:

Thank you for agreeing to participate in the retail banking focus group study being held on Tuesday, June 15, at 5:00 P.M. I look forward to meeting you and hearing your comments and suggestions about the retail banking industry.

This letter is to confirm the date, time, and location that the focus group will meet. There is a map enclosed for your convenience. I have arranged to have sandwiches and beverages provided for you. As discussed via telephone, I will be videotaping our session to assist me with the study.

Please bring the enclosed videotaping consent form to the focus group meeting on Tuesday.

There is no particular "dress code" for the meeting. I would suggest you wear something comfortable and casual. Please try to be at the meeting location (The Youth and Family Service Center) at about 4:45 P.M. so that I can begin the focus group as close to 5:00 P.M. as possible.

DATE: TUESDAY, JUNE 15, 2004

TIME: 5:00 P.M. TO 7:00 P.M.

PLACE: THE YOUTH AND FAMILY SERVICE CENTER

Thank you in advance for your willingness and cooperation in participating in this focus group. The success of this stage of the research project depends heavily on the opinions of all the participants of the focus group.

If you have any questions, please call me at our MRG offices (813) 974-2313.

Sincerely,

Thomas G. Smith
MRG Moderator

EXHIBIT 6.18 Videotaping Consent Form

VIDEOTAPE CONSENT FORM

Retail Banking Study Focus Group 06/15/04

I have given my consent to Thomas G. Smith and Market Resources Group, Inc., to videotape my comments during the retail banking customer focus group to be held on Tuesday, June 15, 2004. I fully understand this tape will not be used for commercial purposes or monetary gains.

_____

(Participant's Signature and Date)

EXHIBIT 6.19   Moderator's Guide Used in the BBPC Study

I. INTRODUCTION AND WARMUP

A. Welcome the participants! As a warmup, have each participant introduce and say one or two things about himself or herself; create the comfort zone.

B. Explain the rules of the session.

C. Ask if anyone has any questions; clearly address each question.

II. INTRODUCE FIRST TOPIC—GENERAL DISCUSSION ABOUT CHANGING TRENDS IN BANKING

A. Consumers' viewpoints of changing trends
"FROM YOUR VIEWPOINT, HOW HAS RETAIL BANKING CHANGED OVER THE PAST FIVE YEARS?"
(Probe for clear, meaningful, and specific changes.)

B. Banks' ability to handle or manage those changes
"HOW (OR WHAT) HAVE RETAIL BANKS DONE TO MANAGE THOSE CHANGES, MAKING THEM UNDERSTANDABLE TO US CONSUMERS?"
(Probe for detail and clarification; if necessary, use ATM technology example.)

C. Today's retail banks' operating motives and/or missions
(Set up following scenario: Some people believe that today's retail banks are "BIG BUSINESSES" like the General Motors Corp. with their primary goal being one of "making large profits at all cost," but other consumers view retail banks more like an extension of the government—federal, state, local—with the goal of "serving people at the lowest possible cost.")
"WHAT ARE YOUR FEELINGS ABOUT RETAIL BANKS OPERATING SOLELY FOR THE PURPOSE OF MAKING A PROFIT? HOW MUCH IS TOO MUCH PROFIT?"
(Where appropriate, probe for specifics.)

III. RETAIL BANK SELECTION CRITERIA

A. Consumers' perceptions of important banking factors used to select a bank to do business with
"IN DECIDING WHERE TO BANK, WHAT BANKING CHARACTERISTICS OR FACTORS DO PEOPLE USE IN THEIR SELECTION PROCESS?"
(Use the factors below to help guide the discussion.)

B. "WHAT ARE SOME IMPORTANT AND NOT SO IMPORTANT BANKING FEATURES TO YOU?"
(Probe for features and reasons of importance.)

Bank's Product and Service Offerings

__ Checking	__ Regular savings	__ CDs
__ Money markets	__ Credit lines	__ IRAs
__ Visa/MC cards	__ Installment loans	__ Trusts
__ Senior partner	__ Brokerage services	__ Safety deposit
__ Ease of statement	__ Accuracy of statements	__ Mortgages
__ Community support	__ Interest rates on deposits	__ Online loans

Bank's Facilities and Parking Availability

__ Inside the bank comfortability	__ Has 24-hour ATMs	__ Banking hours
__ Easy-to-get-to location	__ Clean facilities	__ Easy to reach by phone
__ Parking availability	__ Has many service outlets	__ Has online banking services
__ Lobby hours	(branches)	

Banking Methods

__ Inside the bank	__ 24-hour ATMs	__ Drive-up windows
__ Bank by phone	__ Bank by mail	__ Online banking

Bank's Personnel and Staff

__ Courteous/friendly people	__ Using your name
__ Availability to answer questions	__ Speed of handling transaction
__ Explains things clearly and correctly	__ Ability to resolve problems
__ Responsive to customer's needs/wants	__ Knowledgeable staff personnel
__ Accuracy in completing transaction	__ Professional in appearance

continued

EXHIBIT 6.19 **Moderator's Guide Used in the BBPC Study,** *continued*

IV. RETAIL BANK SERVICE QUALITY

A. Consumers' view of what retail bank service quality means
"WHAT DOES RETAIL BANK SERVICE QUALITY MEAN?"
(Probe for clarity and details.)

B. "WHAT CAN (SHOULD) RETAIL BANKS DO TO ENSURE OR IMPROVE SERVICE QUALITY TO THEIR CUSTOMERS?"
(Probe for details and clarity.)

C. "WHAT DO YOU FEEL RETAIL BANKS DO WRONG RESULTING IN A LOWER SERVICE QUALITY TO CUSTOMERS?"
(Probe for clarity and specifics.)

V. RETAIL BANK CUSTOMER SERVICE SATISFACTION

A. Consumers' view of what customer service satisfaction means
"WHAT DOES BANK CUSTOMER SERVICE SATISFACTION MEAN?"
(Probe for clarification of thoughts.)

B. "WHAT DO YOU FEEL RETAIL BANKS CAN (OR SHOULD) DO TO ENSURE OR IMPROVE THEIR CUSTOMERS' SERVICE SATISFACTION?"
(Probe for specific ways and clarity.)

C. "WHERE DO RETAIL BANKS GO WRONG IN THEIR EFFORT TO CREATE CUSTOMER SATISFACTION?"
(Probe for specifics and clarity.)

VI. CLOSING SESSION WITH SUGGESTIONS AND FINAL THOUGHTS

A. Overall, what specific action(s) would you suggest or recommend to improve customer service quality and satisfaction in today's retail banking industry?
(Make sure every participant has an opportunity to answer.)

B. Introduce the fact that everyone is (or used to be) a customer of BBPC.
If session is with current customers, ask:
"WHAT COULD BARNETT BANK DO (IF ANYTHING) TO IMPROVE YOUR BANKING RELATIONSHIP WITH THEM?"
If session is with ex-customers, ask:
"PLEASE SUMMARIZE YOUR SPECIFIC REASON(S) FOR ENDING YOUR BANKING RELATIONSHIP WITH BBPC."
(Probe for specific answers.)
"WHAT COULD BARNETT BANK HAVE DONE (IF ANYTHING) TO HAVE KEPT YOU FROM ENDING YOUR RELATIONSHIP WITH THEM?"
(Probe for specific ideas.)

C. End the focus group session.
Debrief the participants.
Thank them for their cooperation and input.
Give each participant his or her gift of appreciation.
Extend a warm wish to drive home carefully.

Each two-hour focus session was segmented into three parts: beginning, main, and closing. The beginning part of the session included introductions and warmup activities. Here, participants were formally welcomed and thanked again for their willingness to participate; the moderator highlighted and explained the guidelines for the session and made every effort to quickly establish a comfort zone for the participants. In addition, it was important for the subjects to get comfortable about being videotaped and forget about the individual who was operating the camera. As part of this process, the moderator began the actual discussion by focusing on general changing trends in banking. For example, the first question for participants' discussion was, "From your viewpoint, how has retail banking changed over the past five years?" The main function of this first question was to relax the participants rather than to obtain their opinions about a critical item to bank management's situation. The questions presented to the participants moved from general to specific.

The main section of the session focused on topics relevant to retail bank selection criteria, bank service quality, and bank customer service satisfaction (see Exhibit 6.19 for the actual questions used for each topic area). The moderator kept control over the flow, direction, and depth of the discussions. Using listening and interpersonal communication skills, the moderator led the discussions by asking probing questions. While presentation of the complete transcripts of the actual dialogues between the focus group participants is beyond the scope of this example, the following illustrates the questioning approach used by the moderator.

Focus Group 4 held Tuesday, June 15, 2004: Ex-Customer Group (Subjects 65 and Older)

Moderator: "To bring closure to our session today, I would like for you to discuss and respond to this question: 'What were some of the specific reasons for ending your banking relationship with Barnett Bank of Pasco County?'"

Sally P: "For me it was that I got tired of being treated like a 'stupid' person when asking the loan officer questions about my house mortgage. That loan officer made me feel like I was not important and wasting his time."

Henry A: "Yep, I had the same problem with several of the tellers when asking questions about my saving account balance."

Moderator: "Sally, what did that loan officer say or do to make you feel stupid and not very important?"

Sally P: "I remember two specific things. First, his facial expressions when I asked a question. And second, his phone rang three times and each time he would answer it and carry on a conversation with that person and just left me sitting there."

Moderator: "What kinds of facial expressions did that loan officer exhibit when you were asking your questions?"

Sally P: "He would wrinkle up his forehead and nose as though he was saying 'So what do you want me to do about that?' or that he could not understand why I was asking."

Moderator: "Henry, was your experience with the tellers similar?"

Henry A: "Yes and no! My problem was somewhat different. One time, the teller came across as though I was asking the wrong person my questions about my saving account, but could not direct me to the right individual. I guess it was similar in that the teller just had a bad attitude toward helping me. She made it appear that saving accounts were not her area of interest or responsibility."

Mary F: "I just got tired of all the errors on my monthly statements. With one error, the bank said I had $300 less in my checking account than what my records showed. It took the bank three months to correct their mistake and then they wanted to charge me a $21 service charge! That's when I decided to close out all my accounts with Barnett and go to Bank of America."

A full report of the focus group research is beyond the scope of this illustration, but a couple of points are worth mentioning. After completing the focus group interviews, the researcher used the responses from the six separate sessions and performed a content analysis to identify the overall themes of what the subjects were expressing. Working with BBPC's management team, the researcher could present the results a number of ways. One approach might be a comparison of identified themes between current and ex-customer groups. Another possibility would be between BBPC's 55-to-64 and over-65 senior market segments.

Hands-On Exercise

Using the information presented in Exhibit 6.8, critique the approach that was used to conduct the above BBPC focus group interviews and answer the following questions:

1. What are the strengths and weaknesses of the approach taken?

2. Analyze the data provided from Focus Group 4 and write a brief summary report.

Summary of Learning Objectives

■ **Identify the fundamental differences between qualitative and quantitative research methods and explain their appropriateness in creating useful managerial information.**

In business problem situations where secondary information alone cannot answer management's questions, primary data must be collected and transformed into usable information. Researchers can choose between two types of data collection methods: qualitative or quantitative. There are many differences between these two approaches with respect to their research objectives and goals, type of research, type of questions, time of execution, generalizability to target populations, type of analysis, and researcher skill requirements.

Moreover, qualitative methods focus on generating exploratory, preliminary insights into decision problems. Qualitative methods focus on collecting detailed amounts of data from relatively small samples by questioning or observing what people do and say. These methods require the use of researchers well trained in interpersonal communication, observation, and interpretation. Data are normally collected using open-ended or nonstructured questioning formats that allow for either probing of hidden attitudes or behavior patterns or human/mechanical/electrical observation techniques for current behaviors or events. While the data can be collected quickly, it is difficult to analyze and transform into generalized inferences about the defined target group.

In contrast, quantitative or survey research methods place heavy emphasis on using formalized, structured questioning practices where the response options have been predetermined by the researcher. These questions tend to be administered to significantly large numbers of respondents. Quantitative methods are directly related to descriptive and causal types of research projects where the objectives are either to make more accurate predictions about relationships between market factors and behaviors or to validate the existence of relationships. Quantitative researchers are well trained in construct development, scale measurements, questionnaire designs, sampling, and statistical data analyses.

■ **Describe and explain two popular qualitative techniques used in gathering primary data.**

While there are many qualitative methods available for collecting data, this chapter focuses on in-depth interviews and focus groups. An in-depth interview is a formalized process of asking a subject a set of semistructured, probing questions in a face-to-face setting. Focus groups involve bringing a small group of people together for an interactive and spontaneous discussion of a particular topic or concept. While the success of in-depth interviewing depends heavily on the interpersonal communication and probing skills of the interviewer, success in focus group interviewing relies more on the group dynamics of the members, the willingness of members to engage in an interactive dialogue, and the moderator's abilities to keep the discussion on track.

Both types of questioning approaches are guided by similar research objectives: (1) to provide data for defining and redefining marketing problem situations; (2) to provide data for better understanding the results from other quantitative survey studies; (3) to reveal and understand consumers' hidden needs, wants, attitudes, feelings, behaviors, perceptions, and motives regarding services, products, or practices; (4) to generate new ideas about products, services, or delivery methods; (5) to discover new constructs and measurement methods; and (6) to better understand changing consumer preferences.

■ **Explain the basic pros and cons of using qualitative methods of data collection.**

The general advantages of qualitative research methods include the economy and timeliness of data collection; richness of the data; accuracy of recording marketplace behaviors; and preliminary insights into building models and scale measurements. The potential disadvantages include the lack of generalizability of the data to larger target groups; inability of the data to distinguish small differences; lack of data reliability; and difficulty of finding well-trained investigators, interviewers, and observers.

■ **Explain focus groups, the importance of a moderator, and how the findings are used to improve decision making.**

A focus group is a small group of people (8 to 12) brought together for an interactive, spontaneous discussion. The three phases of a focus group study are planning the study, conducting the actual focus group discussions, and analyzing and reporting the results. In the planning of a focus group, critical decisions have to be made regarding who should participate, how to select and recruit the appropriate participants, what size the group should be, what incentives to offer to encourage and reinforce participants' willingness and commitment to participate, and where the group sessions should be held. Exhibit 6.12 lists important traits of the focus group moderator, and Exhibit 6.13 illustrates a modera-tor's guide. Different analysis techniques are appropriate for analyzing and interpreting the results, and the findings can be written up in a professional report format.

Key Terms and Concepts

Articulative interviews 203

Cartoon (balloon) test 206

Case study 201

Content analysis 194

Debriefing analysis 194

Experience interviews 202

Focus group moderator 189

Focus group research 180

In-depth interview 176

Interpersonal communication skills 178

Listening skills 178

Moderator's guide 192

Online focus groups 200

Picture test 205

Probing questions 178

Projective technique 204

Protocol interviewing 202

Qualitative research 173

Quantitative research 171

Role-playing interviews 206

Sentence completion test 204

Thematic apperception test (TAT) 205

Word association test 204

Review Questions

1. What are the major differences between quantitative and qualitative research methods? What skills must a researcher have to develop and implement each type of design?

2. Compare and contrast the unique characteristics, main research objectives, and advantages/disadvantages of the in-depth and focus group interviewing techniques.

3. Explain the pros and cons of using qualitative research methods as the means of developing raw data structures for each of the following situations:
   a. Adding carbonation to Gatorade and selling it as a true soft drink.
   b. Finding new consumption usages for Arm & Hammer baking soda.
   c. Inducing customers who have stopped shopping at Sears to return to Sears.
   d. Advising a travel agency that wants to enter the cruise ship vacation market.

4. What are the characteristics of a good focus group moderator? What is the purpose of a moderator's guide?

5. Why is it important to have 6 to 12 participants in a focus group? What difficulties might exist in meeting that objective?

6. Why are the screening activities so important in the selection of focus group participants? Develop a screening form that would allow you to select participants for a focus group on the benefits and costs of leasing new automobiles.

7. What are the advantages and disadvantages of "online" focus group interviews compared to "offline" group interviews?

8. How are focus group participants recruited, and what are the common difficulties (problems) associated with the recruitment of these people?

9. What are the main differences between articulative interviews and in-depth interviews?

10. Develop a word association test that will provide some insight into the following information research question: "What are college students' perceptions of their university's student union?

Discussion Questions

1. What type of exploratory research design (observation, projective interview, in-depth interview, focus group) would you suggest for each of the following situations and why?
   a. The research and development director at Calvin Klein suggests a new type of cologne for men that could be promoted by a sports celebrity like Michael Jordan.
   b. The director of on-campus housing at your university proposes some significant changes to the physical configuration of the current on-campus dorm rooms for freshmen and new transfer students.
   c. The vice president of marketing in charge of new-store locations for Home Depot must decide on the best location for a new store in your hometown.
   d. The senior design engineer for the Ford Motor Company wishes to identify meaningful design changes to be integrated into the 2007 Ford Taurus.
   e. The general manager at Clyde's Restaurant in Washington, D.C., wishes to offer customers two "new and exciting" dinner items that would be a blend of spicy herbs, chicken, and lemon.
   f. A retail supermarket manager would like to know the popularity of a new brand of cereal produced by General Mills.

2. Develop a moderator's guide that could be used in a focus group interview to investigate the following question: Why do 30 percent of Time Warner cable subscribers disconnect their cable services after the initial three-month special package offer?

3. Thinking about how most participants are recruited for focus groups, identify and discuss three ethical issues that the researcher and decision maker must consider when using a focus group research design to collect primary data and information.

4. **EXPERIENCE THE INTERNET.** Go to the Internet and find a college student–oriented bulletin board and conduct a focus group interview among some college students at universities in Illinois, Michigan, and Nebraska regarding decision factors they use when choosing a destination in Colorado for a spring break skiing trip.

5. Conduct an "in-depth" interview and write a brief summary report on the following decision question: "Do cell phone owners use the same criteria for selecting their cell phone service provider as for selecting their Internet provider?"

6. Outback Steakhouse, Inc., is concerned about the shifting attitudes and feelings of the public toward the consumption of red meat. Chris Sullivan, CEO and co-founder of Outback Steakhouse, Inc., thinks that the "red meat" issues are not that important because his restaurant also serves fish and chicken entrees. Select any two "projective interviewing" techniques that you feel would be appropriate in collecting data for the above situation. First, defend your choice of each of your selected projective

interviewing techniques. Second, describe in detail how each of your two chosen techniques would be applied to Sullivan's research problem at hand.

7. Refer to the Santa Fe Grill Mexican Restaurant case first presented at the end of Chapter 1. In their quest for better understanding the consumers' attitudes and feelings toward casual dining-out experiences, the two young owners of the Santa Fe Grill Mexican Restaurant asked two important questions: (1) Do specific restaurant features differ in importance to consumers when deciding where to go for their casual dining experience? (2) Do consumers prefer dining out in a festive atmosphere or a quiet romantic restaurant atmosphere? Using your understanding of the "in-depth interviewing" data collection method, develop and execute a 45-minute in-depth interview that will allow you to capture the necessary data/information for answering the owners' two questions. After completing the interview, analyze your data and write a one- or two-page summary report that answers the owners' two questions.

chapter 7

Descriptive Research Designs: Survey Methods and Errors

Learning Objectives

After reading this chapter, you will be able to

1. Explain the advantages and disadvantages of using quantitative, descriptive survey research designs to collect primary data.

2. Discuss the many types of survey methods available to researchers. Identify and discuss the factors that drive the choice of survey methods.

3. Explain how the electronic revolution is affecting the administration of survey research designs.

4. Identify and describe the strengths and weaknesses of each type of survey method.

5. Identify and explain the types of errors that occur in survey research.

> "The basic techniques of market research—interview, focus groups, surveys, observation—are used in all corners of the globe."
>
> —MICHAEL R. CZINKOTA AND ILKKA A. RONKAINEN[1]

The JP Hotel Preferred Guest Card Study

Several years ago, JP Hotel's corporate management team implemented a new marketing strategy designed to attract and retain customers in their business traveler market. The overall strategy consisted of marketing a VIP hotel card system to business travel customers that provided privileges to the cardholder not offered to other hotel patrons. In some ways the initial system was similar to the airline industry's "frequent flier" programs. At the time, management thought the hotel card program, named "JP Hotel Preferred Guest Card," would help increase the hotel chain's market share of business travelers and create a sense of loyalty among those who were in the program. To become a member of the preferred guest program, a business traveler had to fill out an application at any of the hotel's properties across the country. There were no costs to join and no annual card fee to members. JP Hotel's corporate accounting records indicated the initial implementation costs associated with the program were approximately $55,000 with annual operating costs of about $85,000. At the end of the program's third year, the membership was 17,000.

Last year at a corporate management team meeting, the CEO asked the following questions concerning the Preferred Guest Card Program: "Is the guest card strategy working? Does it serve as a competitive advantage? Has the program increased the hotel's market share of business travelers? Is the company making money (profit) from the program? Is the program helping to create loyalty among our business customers?" Taken by surprise by this line of questions, the corporate VP of marketing replied by saying those were great questions but he had no answers at that time. After having his assistants investigate corporate records to obtain the needed information, the VP of marketing realized that all he had was a current membership listing and a total of the program costs to date (about $310,000). He did not have any good information on the attitudes and behaviors of cardholders and his best guess at revenue benefits was about $85,000 a year. At best, the current productivity of the program was basically close to a break-even point.

Realizing he needed help, the vice president contacted his friend, Alex Smith, the senior project director at Marketing Resource Group (MRG). MRG located in Tampa, Florida, is a marketing research firm that specializes in a wide array of exploratory, descriptive, and causal research designs and practices. An informal meeting was scheduled to discuss the situation and begin the necessary research process. At this first meeting, the vice president of marketing restated the questions asked by the CEO concerning the JP Hotel Preferred Guest Card program and added that the company did not have any information that could address the attitudinal, behavioral, or motivational questions about current cardholders. In the vice president's words, "JP does not know whether the preferred guest card program is a money maker or an unnecessary expense being accrued for the benefit of a few business patrons." Alex suggested a second meeting was needed that included a representative from the advertising agency being used to promote the card program. At this second meeting, Alex listened to the concerns of both JP Hotel and the ad agency's representative regarding the card program. Using situational analysis and the iceberg principle, Alex asked the following questions: What was the purpose of the Preferred Guest Card Program? What were the factors that led to creating such a program? What were the short-term and long-term gains hoped for by offering such a program? What types of benefits were included in the program? How was the program being promoted to business travelers? Through which media was the program being advertised? What message about card membership was being communicated? To what extent were cardholders using the card? How important was being a cardholder in selecting hotel accommodations? This questioning approach brought clarity to the following two problems:

1. JP Hotel needed information that would aid in determining whether or not the company should continue the Preferred Guest Card program.

2. The ad agency needed attitudinal, behavioral, motivational, and demographic information that would help fine-tune promotional strategies to attract new members, retain current cardholders, and increase card usage.

To transform these key problems into research questions, Alex collected some additional qualitative information by conducting several in-depth interviews with the general manager (GM) of three JP Hotel properties and a focus group session with 10 known JP Hotel Preferred Guest Cardholders. All this additional background information led Alex to form the following five research objectives:

1. To determine the card usage patterns among known JP Hotel Preferred Guest Cardholders.

2. To identify and evaluate the privileges associated with the card program and how important the card is as a factor in selecting a hotel for business purposes.

3. To determine business travelers' awareness of the card program.

4. To determine whether or not JP Hotel should charge an annual fee for card membership.

5. To identify profile differences between heavy users, moderate users, light users, and nonusers of the card.

After establishing the research objectives, Alex's next concern was determining what type of research design would be most appropriate for achieving the research objectives. Make sure you read the Marketing Research in Action at the end of this chapter to learn how Alex went about determining the right research design to use in collecting the necessary data.

Value of Descriptive Survey Research Designs

The chapter opening example shows that sometimes the research problem requires primary data that can only be gathered by questioning a large number of respondents who are representative of the defined target population. Survey research can play an important role in providing the necessary information to guide a firm's development of new marketing strategies.

This chapter is the second of three chapters devoted to methods for collecting primary data. Whereas discussions in Chapter 6 were limited to qualitative methods used in exploratory research, this chapter will focus on survey designs used in descriptive research. Observation practices and experimental research designs will be covered in Chapter 8.

We begin this chapter by discussing the interrelatedness of descriptive research designs and survey research methods. Then we provide an overview of survey research methods and their main objectives. The next section examines the various types of survey methods in more detail. This is followed by a discussion of factors in survey method selection. The remainder of the chapter deals with types of errors common in survey research.

Interrelatedness of Descriptive Research Designs and Survey Research Methods

Before we discuss the methods employed in conducting descriptive research, it is necessary to understand the interrelationships among descriptive research designs, quantitative methods, and survey methods as well as how researchers interchange these concepts in their efforts to collect primary data. First, determination of whether the research design should be descriptive is based on three factors: (1) the nature of the initial decision problem/opportunity, (2) the set of research questions, and (3) the research objectives. When the nature of the initial research problem/opportunity is either to describe specific characteristics of existing market situations or to evaluate current marketing mix strategies, then descriptive research design is an appropriate choice. Second, if the management's research questions focus on issues such as the who, what, where, when, and how elements of target populations or market structures, then a descriptive research design may be appropriate. Finally, if the task is to identify meaningful relationships, determine whether true differences exist, or verify the validity of relationships between the marketing phenomena, then descriptive research designs should be considered. Keep in mind that these factors do not by themselves automatically determine the need to use descriptive research designs.

Researchers also must give consideration to the quantitative aspects associated with descriptive research designs. Quantitative research practices are driven by the need to collect substantial information from enough members of the target population so that accurate inferences can be made about the market factors and phenomena under investigation. Most researchers believe that descriptive research designs are for the most part quantitative in nature.

The final element in determining the use of descriptive research designs focuses on how to collect the primary data. There are two basic approaches to collecting primary data—observation and asking questions. Although these approaches are used in any type of research design (exploratory, descriptive, causal), descriptive designs more frequently use data collection procedures that heavily emphasize asking respondents structured questions about what they think, feel, and do rather than observing what they do. Thus, descriptive research designs are viewed as survey research methods for collecting quantitative data from large groups of people through the question/answer process.

Overview of Survey Research Methods

Survey research methods
Research procedures for collecting large amounts of raw data using question-and-answer formats.

Marketing researchers can observe behaviors, survey respondents, or conduct experiments. **Survey research methods** are the mainstay of marketing research in general and are typically associated with descriptive and causal research situations. One of the distinguishing factors of survey research methods is the need to collect data from large groups of people

EXHIBIT	7.1	Advantages and Disadvantages of Quantitative Survey Research Designs

Advantages of Survey Methods

- Can accommodate large sample sizes and generalize the results
- Can distinguish small differences
- Ease of administering and recording questions and answers
- Ability to use advanced statistical analysis
- Factors and relationships not directly measurable can be studied

Disadvantages of Survey Methods

- Difficulty of developing accurate survey questionnaires
- Limits to the in-depth detail of data
- Limited control over timeliness, and potentially low response rates
- Evaluating whether respondents are responding truthfully
- Misinterpretation of data and inappropriate use of analysis procedures

(e.g., 200 or more). This size factor necessitates the use of "bi-directional communication practices," which means that individuals are asked questions and their responses are recorded in a structured, precise manner. Most marketing research is conducted through one or more of the various survey methods.

Success in collecting primary data is more a function of correctly designing and administering a survey questionnaire than of relying on the communication and interpretive skills of an interviewer or observer. The main goal of quantitative survey research methods is to provide specific facts and estimates—from a large, representative sample of respondents—that decision makers can use to (1) make accurate predictions about relationships between market factors and customer behaviors; (2) understand the relationships and differences; and (3) validate the existing relationships.

Survey research focuses on collecting data that enable the researcher to understand and resolve marketing problems. The advantages and disadvantages of survey research designs are summarized in Exhibit 7.1 and discussed more fully in the following sections.

Advantages of Survey Methods

One major advantage of surveys is their ability to accommodate large sample sizes at relatively low costs. Using a large sample increases the geographic flexibility of the research. When implemented correctly, the data obtained from survey methods can increase the researcher's ability to make inferences about the target population as a whole. Moreover, the data can be analyzed in many different ways based on the diversity of the variables. For example, data can be analyzed according to gender, income, occupation, or any other variable included in the survey. The analysis also can be based on multiple variables. For example, an analysis of product purchasing behaviors among households headed by female single parents in the Northeast can be compared to purchasing behaviors among households headed by female single parents in the Southeast to reveal small differences in regional preferences that may not be apparent in simpler data analysis approaches. Thus, another factor in favor of surveys is they collect quantitative data that can be used with advanced statistical analysis to identify hidden patterns and trends in the data.

Another major advantage of surveys is their ease of administration. Most surveys are fairly easy to implement because there is no need for sophisticated devices to record actions and reactions, as with observations or experiments. Even personal interviews can be relatively simple. Surveys facilitate the collection of standardized common data since all respondents give answers to the same questions and have the same set of responses available to them. This allows direct comparisons between respondents.

A final advantage of surveys is their ability to tap into factors that are not directly observable (e.g., attitudes, feelings, preferences). Through both direct and indirect questioning techniques, people can be asked why they prefer, say, one package design over another. Predetermined questions determine what thought process a customer used to select a particular brand or how many brands were considered. Observation, for example, would show only that an individual selected a particular brand. Most survey research methods enable the researcher to collect all types of data and all potential time frames (i.e., the past, the present, and the future).

Disadvantages of Survey Methods

While quantitative research holds distinct advantages over qualitative exploratory research, survey methods are not without problems. Implementation is fairly easy, but developing the appropriate survey method can be very difficult. To ensure precision, the researcher must resolve a variety of issues associated with construct development, scale measurements, and questionnaire designs. Inappropriate treatment of these issues can produce many kinds of errors in survey findings. As the possibility of systematic error increases, so does the likelihood of collecting irrelevant or poor-quality data. The development, measurement, and design issues associated with surveys are discussed in Chapters 11, 12 and 13.

A second potential disadvantage of survey designs relates to their limited use of probing questions. In general, survey designs limit the use of extensive probing by the interviewer and rarely use unstructured or open-ended questions. Consequently, the data may lack the detail the researcher needs to address the initial research problems. A third disadvantage of surveys is the lack of control researchers have over their timeliness. Depending on the administration techniques, surveys can take significantly longer to complete than other methods. In direct mail surveys, for example, the researcher must carefully develop a questionnaire packet, disseminate the packets, and wait for them to be returned via the postal service. The researcher can only estimate how long it will take the postal service to actually get the questionnaire packet to each selected respondent, how long the respondents will take to complete the survey, and how long it will take the postal service to return the packets. In reality, the researcher loses control of the process as soon as the questionnaire packets are given to the postal service. While the researcher might estimate that the process will take 14 days to complete, direct mail designs can take 45 days or longer. Getting the surveys out and back within a reasonable amount of time remains a great challenge for researchers using direct mail surveys. Associated with the problem of response time is the problem of guaranteeing a high response rate (or return rate of completed surveys). As new data collection technologies emerge, the timeliness disadvantage will be reduced.

A fourth disadvantage of some survey designs is that it can be difficult to know whether the selected respondents are being truthful. This difficulty varies depending on the actual method employed by the researcher. For example, in designs that incorporate a trained interviewer in a face-to-face communication process (e.g., personal in-home or mall-intercept interviews) this problem is minimal since the interviewer can either observe facial expressions and other body language of the respondent or use probing techniques for more clarity. In contrast, in self-administered surveys (e.g., mail, fully automatic computer-assisted surveys, Internet surveys) truthfulness becomes a greater concern. Finally, although surveys are designed to collect quantitative data, the statistical techniques selected may introduce subtle levels of subjectivity to interpretation of data. Such subjectivity may not be as apparent in survey research as it is in qualitative research.

Types of Errors in Survey Methodology

Before discussing the appropriate quantitative research methods and the types of descriptive designs, it is important to discuss the types of errors that can occur in any survey. Errors (also referred to as bias) and their sources can quickly reduce the accuracy and quality of the data the researcher collects. To select the best strategy, decision makers must assess the overall accuracy of the research results being provided by the researcher. In any research design, whether qualitative or quantitative, numerous opportunities exist for careless researchers to let in errors. This is particularly true with survey research designs.

Potential survey research errors can be classified as being either *sampling errors* or *nonsampling errors*. Exhibit 7.2 provides an overview of the various forms of survey errors researchers must be aware of and attempt to either reduce or at least control.

Sampling Error

Any survey research design that involves collecting primary data from a sample will have a certain amount of error due to fluctuations in the data. In simple terms, sample error is the statistically measured difference between the actual sample results and the true population results. With appropriate sampling approaches, this type of error is reduced by increasing the sample size. Sampling error is discussed in Chapters 9 and 10.

Systematic Errors (Nonsampling Errors)

Systematic error All errors that can enter the survey research design that are not related to the sample method or sample size.

In survey research, the counterpart to sampling error is systematic error (nonsampling error). **Systematic error** represents all errors that can enter the survey research design that are not related to the sampling method or sample size. Most types of nonsampling errors can be traced back to four major sources: respondent errors, measurement/design errors, faulty problem definition, and project administration errors.

Regardless of the survey research method used to collect primary data, there are several common characteristics among all systematic errors. First, they tend to create some form of "systematic variation" in the data that is not considered a natural occurrence or fluctuation on the part of the surveyed respondents. Systematic variations usually result from imperfections in the survey design or from mistakes in the execution of the research process. Second, nonsampling errors are controllable. They are the result of some type of human mishap in either the design or execution of a survey. Consequently, the responsibility for reducing or eliminating systematic errors falls on the researcher and requires that a set of controls be imposed during the design and execution processes of any type of survey research project.[2]

Third, unlike sampling error that can be statistically measured, nonsampling error cannot be directly measured. Finally, nonsampling errors are interactive in nature. One type of error can potentially allow other types of errors to enter the data collection process. For example, if the researcher designs a bad questionnaire, the errors can potentially cause respondent errors. Overall, nonsampling errors can only lower the quality level of the data being collected and the information being provided to the decision maker.

EXHIBIT 7.2   Types of Error Sources with Survey Research Designs

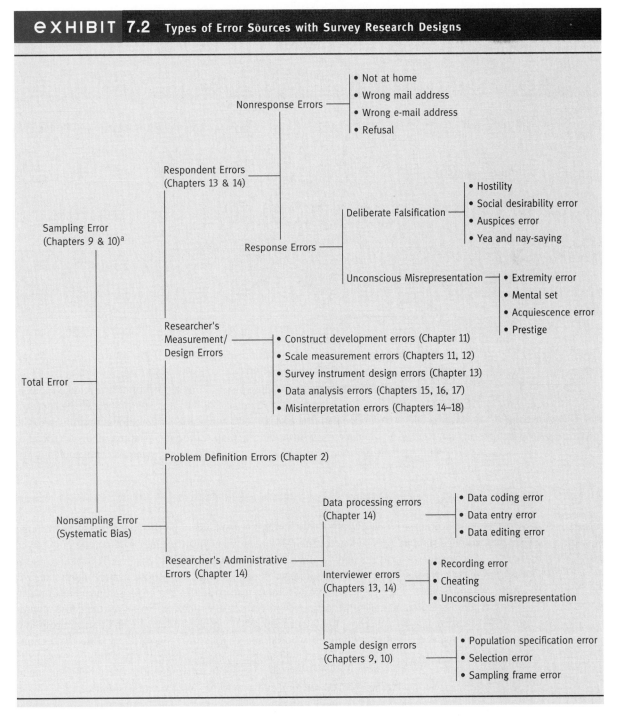

[a]Other chapters that discuss error.

EXHIBIT 7.3 Types of Respondent Errors in Survey Research Methods

Type of Errors	Error Sources
Nonresponse error	Not at home
	Wrong mailing address
	Wrong e-mail address
	Refusal
Response error	Deliberate falsification:
	Feeling of hostility
	Social desirability
	Prestige imaging
	Auspices errors
	Yea and nay-saying
	Unconscious misrepresentation:
	Mental set errors
	Extremity errors
	Acquiescence errors
	Prestige

Respondent Errors

This type of nonsampling error occurs when respondents either cannot be reached to participate in the survey process, do not cooperate, are unwilling to participate in the survey's question/answer exchange activities, or respond incorrectly or in an unnatural way to the questions asked in the survey. Exhibit 7.3 summarizes the major components that lead to respondent errors in survey research practices. The two major sources for respondent error are termed *nonresponse error* and *response error.*

Nonresponse Error

Nonresponse error A systematic bias that occurs when the final sample differs from the planned sample.

Nonresponse error is a systematic bias that occurs when the final sample differs from the planned sample. This situation is likely to occur when a sufficient number of the preselected prospective respondents in the sample cannot be reached for participation. The major reasons for this type of error are not at home, wrong mailing address, wrong e-mail address, and/or wrong/changed telephone numbers. Nonresponse error also can be caused when a sufficient number of the initial sampled respondents refuse to participate. No matter the cause, nonresponse errors can severely limit the generalizability of the findings. In addition, nonresponse error can occur when individuals who do not respond have significantly different feelings from those who do respond. When the nonresponse rate is high, the risk of biased results is increased. People choose to participate in a survey for a variety of reasons including social rewards, monetary incentives, boredom, and sometimes just for the experience.

Nonresponse is caused by many factors. Some people do not trust the research sponsor and/or have little commitment toward responding,[3] some prospective respondents resent what is perceived as an invasion of privacy, or the subject matter may be too sensitive. The differences between people who do and who do not respond can be striking. For example, some research has shown that for mail surveys, where the response rate tends to be lower than most other primary data collection methods, respondents tend to be more educated than nonrespondents and have higher scores on other related variables such as income.

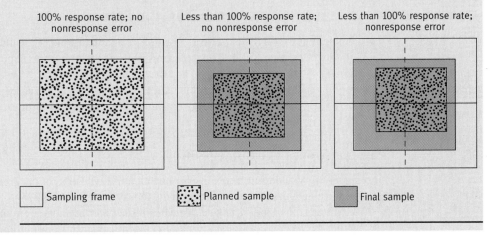

EXHIBIT 7.4 Impact of Nonresponse Error

Two important points can be drawn from the discussion of nonresponse error:

1. Nonresponse error can occur even if there is no sampling frame error. Even selecting a probability sample from a representative sampling frame cannot guarantee there will be no nonresponse error.

2. Nonresponse error depends on the composition of the final sample compared to the planned sample. Remember, a response rate of less than 100% does not automatically imply there is nonresponse error.

100% response rate; no nonresponse error | Less than 100% response rate; no nonresponse error | Less than 100% response rate; nonresponse error

Sampling frame   Planned sample   Final sample

In addition, respondents are more likely to be female.[4] The effect of other sociodemographic variables is not well understood. But no matter the research method, community size, gender, age, education, and income of those who respond to second- and third-wave solicitations are different from nonrespondents.[5]

To reduce the nonresponse rate, researchers attempt to be less intrusive on the respondent's life.[6] Other practices for improving response rates include multiple callbacks, mailing waves, building credibility of the research sponsor, and shorter questionnaires.[7] Exhibit 7.4 further illustrates the impact of nonresponses and some methods to improve survey response rates.

Response Bias

When the researcher asks questions, one of two basic mechanisms begin operating. One mechanism is for the respondents to search their memory, retrieve their attitudinal recollections, and provide them as their response. If this doesn't happen automatically, however, or if respondents aren't motivated to search their memory, the responses may be biased in some manner. For example, the respondents may give a socially desirable response, a response that enhances their ego, or simply guess.

The human memory is also a source of response bias. People can have impaired memory and be unable to respond accurately. This is termed *faulty recall*. If the questions relate to a new attitude, the respondent may answer on the basis of some combination of short-term memory and the context of the question.[8] Human memory is an inexact thing. It is subject to telescoping, selective perception, and the compression of time, such that respondents may think they recall things that happened when they actually do not. Another memory problem is termed *averaging*. Averaging refers to assuming the norm behavior or belief to be the actuality. For example, a person who commonly has fried chicken for Sunday dinner may be unable to recall that last week's Sunday dinner was pot roast. In addition, respondents sometimes leave out information the researcher would like to know about. Although in most cases respondents try to give more information rather than less, the respondent may be tired or there may not be a good rapport with the interviewer.

Researchers have found that measurement of the time between when a question is asked and the response is given is one technique that is useful to evaluate response bias. Responses that are expressed very fast and those that are given slowly may be biased. Fast response is indicative of a hurried response or a simple information request, while slow responses are indicative of a difficult question that requires a more extended thought process.[9]

Measurement and Design Error

In addition to respondent errors, researchers and decision makers must recognize that the quality of data can suffer from problems of bias resulting from inappropriate design of the constructs, scale measurements, and the survey questionnaire.[10] Bias makes getting meaningful results from the data problematic. Exhibit 7.5 summarizes the five major sources of bias researchers must understand and attempt to reduce or control to enhance the collection of high-quality data.

Construct Development Error

In any survey design, researchers must identify the different data requirements (i.e., concepts, objects, topics, etc.) that form the focus of the investigation. Nonsampling errors can be introduced to the survey design when researchers are not careful in identifying the constructs to be used in the study. When critical constructs are not completely defined, for example, there is a strong likelihood that problems of inappropriate dimensionality will occur resulting in underidentifying the subcomponents that make up the construct. When data requirements are not fully developed, data quality, reliability, validity, and ability to make generalizations about the defined target population become problematic.

---

exHIBIT 7.5   Types of Measurement and Design Errors in Survey Research Methods

Type of Errors	Error Sources
Construct development error	Incomplete constructs
	Low reliability of construct
	Low construct validity
Scale measurement error	Lack of precision
	Lack of discriminatory power
	Ambiguity of question/setup
	Inappropriate use of scale descriptors
Survey instrument design error	Improper sequence of questions
	Lack of instructions
	Length of questionnaire
Data analysis error	Inappropriate analysis technique
	Predictive bias
Misinterpretation error	Interpretive bias
	Selective perception

Scale Measurement Error

Another area where nonsampling errors can be introduced is in the process of creating the scale measurements used to collect data from groups of respondents. Once the constructs are identified, the researcher must create the appropriate scale measurements attached to those constructs. Measurement errors could be created through either the design of inappropriate questions, scale attributes, or scale point descriptors used to collect respondents' answers. In the design process, researchers must control for errors that might result from (1) a lack of precision in the measurement, (2) a lack of discriminatory power among the scale descriptors, (3) ambiguity of the scale's questions, or (4) use of inappropriate scale descriptors. These types of bias sources will negatively impact the reliability and validity of the data.

Survey Instrument Error

The survey instrument may induce some tainting of the data in several ways. Instrument bias can result from many things related to questionnaire design and the context in which the questions themselves are interpreted.[11] In many cases, instrument bias is a result of leading questions—ones that suggest an appropriate answer. Leading questions put words in a respondent's mouth rather than drawing out what the respondent actually thinks. For example, asking a respondent "Why do you think this is a high-quality product?" encourages only positive responses. Leading questions do not encourage respondents to give their true feelings about the topic being investigated. More often, leading questions elicit the responses we want to hear. While careful design of the individual measurements can reduce bias, it does not guarantee it. For example, improper sequencing of scale measurements used to make up a questionnaire can create systematic errors that are not directly related to scale measurement problems. Moreover, questionnaire design errors can result in both nonresponse and response type errors.

Data Analysis Error

Measurement and instrument design errors can directly influence researchers to create analysis errors. One of the greatest nonsampling errors is selecting an inappropriate analysis procedure. Incorrect statistical estimates invalidate the researcher's ability to predict and test relationships between important factors.

Misinterpretation Error

The two main bias sources are *interpretive error* and *selective perception error*. First, interpretive bias is created when the wrong inference is made by the researcher about the real world or target population due to some type of extraneous factor. For example, the researcher might present the results in such a way that the findings appear to support the initial thoughts of the researcher. Selective perception bias occurs in situations where the researcher uses only a selected portion of the survey results to give support to a tainted picture of reality. For example, leaders in the tobacco industry for years manipulated test results of nicotine as an addictive substance to hide the truth about the effects of nicotine as an ingredient in cigarettes.

Faulty Problem Definition Errors

Survey research designs, like any other type of research methodology, can easily suffer when the initial problem situation is not clearly or correctly identified by management. In these situations, *faulty problem definition error* occurs when the decision maker and/or researcher misinterprets the true nature of the problem situation. The main causes that create

EXHIBIT 7.6 Types of Administrative Errors in Survey Research Methods

Type of Errors	Error Sources
Data processing error	Data coding errors
	Data entry errors
	Data editing errors
Interviewer/observer error	Unconscious mispresentation
	Recording errors
	Cheating
Sample design error	Population specification error
	Sample selection errors
	Sampling frame error

faulty problem definition error are (1) management's lack of understanding of the real problem, (2) misinterpreting market performance factors (e.g., decrease in sales revenues) as being the problem rather than the symptom, or (3) the researcher inaccurately transforming the problem into research questions. Regardless of the cause, incorrectly defining the decision problems will make survey research results useless. For example, let's say the product manager for Nike requests a study to test the best media mix for athletic shoes. If the true problem is the company's pricing strategies, then any research conducted, no matter how technically correct, will not be helpful to the manager.

Researcher's Administrative Error

In survey research, administrative errors occur from improper execution of the steps involved in gathering and processing data. In Exhibit 7.6, administrative errors are grouped into three basic sources: data processing error, interviewer error, and sample design error.

Data Processing Error

Nonsampling errors that occur in data processing are characterized as being either data *coding, entry,* and/or *editing* in nature. In any type of survey research method, the accuracy of data processed by computers can be compromised by mistreatment of any of these human activities. For example, coding error occurs when a person incorrectly assigns a computer code to a response. In turn, data entry errors occur when those codes are incorrectly entered into their designated column in the computer's data file. Editing errors result from careless verifying procedures. These types or errors can be minimized by establishing and implementing careful control procedures for verifying each step in data processing.

Interviewer Error

Interviewer bias distorts information from respondents in a manner similar to instrument bias. While instrument bias is a result of an interaction between the measurement instrument and the respondent, interviewer bias is a result of an interaction between the interviewer and the respondent. The three primary sources of interviewer error are *recording error, unconscious misrepresentation,* and *cheating.* Unconscious misrepresentation can occur when the interviewer somehow induces a pattern of responses that is not indicative of the target population. For example, the respondent may interpret the interviewer's body language, facial expression, or tone of voice as a cue to how to respond to a question. It is important that interviewers remain as neutral as possible during interviews to reduce interviewer-induced bias. Proper training, supervision, and practice all help to reduce interviewer bias.

In other situations, interviewer cheating involves *deliberate falsification* of responses by incorrectly recording responses, by making up entire questionnaires, or by filling in answers to questions that have been intentionally skipped by respondents. For example, some interviewers cheat to finish an interview as quickly as possible in order to complete their assignment or to avoid asking sensitive topic questions. On the other hand, recording errors occur when interviewers inadvertently check the wrong prelisted response or may be unable to write fast enough to capture the response verbatim. These are all examples of interviewer error. Quality control techniques that detect interviewer error whether deliberate or inadvertent should be used.

Sample Design Error

Sample design error A family of nonsampling errors that occur when sampling plans are not appropriately developed and/or the sampling process is improperly executed by the researcher.

Critical to any survey design is asking questions and recording responses from the "right" respondents. The "right" respondents are those that are representative of the defined target population. To achieve this goal, most survey research projects incorporate a sampling design process to determine the "right" respondents to represent the larger target population. A number of systematic errors can occur during the sampling process. The three primary types of errors associated with developing and executing sample designs are population specification error, sample selection error, and sampling frame error.

Population specification error An incorrect definition of the true target population to the research question.

Population specification error (also known as population frame error) is the term used to describe an incorrect definition of the target population of interest to the research question. Correctly defining the target population to be studied is a critical step in research. Imagine if we design and conduct a study thinking that only individuals who earn more than $50,000 are of interest and then discover that individuals earning $30,000 to $50,000 also use the product. The entire class of people earning $30,000 to $50,000 and their responses would not be represented. Population specification error is discussed in Chapters 9 and 10.

Sample selection error A specific type of sample design bias that occurs when an inappropriate sample is drawn from the defined target population because of incomplete or faulty sampling procedures or because the correct procedures have not been carried out.

In addition to population specification, errors can occur due to drawing an inappropriate sample from the defined target population. **Sample selection errors** occur when incomplete or incorrect sampling procedures are used. Sample selection error can occur even if the target population is correctly specified. For example, interviewers may avoid some members of the target population in a mall-intercept survey because the individuals appear scruffy or unattractive in some way. Quality controls should include checks on the sample selected to ensure the data is collected from randomly selected members of the target population.

Sampling frame error An error that occurs when a sample is drawn from an incomplete list of potential or prospective respondents.

In sample designs, the sampling frame is the list of population elements or members from which the prospective respondents (or sampling units) are selected. **Sampling frame error** occurs when an incomplete or inaccurate sampling frame is used. The main problem with frame error is that the sample is likely to not be representative of the defined target population. An example of a sample design that is likely to include sampling frame error is one that uses a published telephone directory as the sample frame for a telephone survey. Many individuals or households are not listed or not listed accurately in the current telephone directory because they either (1) do not want to be listed, (2) have recently moved and missed the publication deadline date, or (3) have recently changed their telephone number. Research has shown that people who are listed in telephone directories are systematically different from those who are not listed.[12]

Types of Survey Methods

There are probably as many ways of gathering primary data as there are types of communication and researchers. Recent improvements in computer hardware and software and telecommunications have created many new survey approaches. Nevertheless, almost all survey methods can be classified as *person-administered, self-administered,* or *telephone-administered.* Exhibit 7.7 provides an overview of survey methods being used to collect data.

EXHIBIT 7.7 Types of Survey Research Methods

Type of Survey Research	Description
Person-Administered	
In-home interview	An interview takes place in the respondent's home or, in special situations, within the respondent's work environment (in-office).
Executive interview	A business executive is interviewed in person.
Mall-intercept interview	Shopping patrons are stopped and asked for feedback during their visit to a shopping mall.
Purchase-intercept interview	The respondent is stopped and asked for feedback at the point of purchase.
Telephone-Administered	
Telephone interview	An interview takes place over the telephone. Interviews may be conducted from a central telephone location or the interviewer's home.
Computer-assisted telephone interview (CATI)	A computer is used to conduct a telephone interview; respondents give answers by pushing buttons on their phone.
Completely automated telephone surveys (CATS)	The survey is completely administered by a computer without the use of any human interviewer.
Wireless phone survey	The survey is conducted over the respondent's wireless phone in either text-based or voice-based formats.
Self-Administered	
Mail panel survey	Surveys are mailed to a representative sample of individuals who have agreed in advance to participate.
Drop-off survey	Questionnaires are left with the respondent to be completed at a later time. The surveys may be picked up by the researcher or returned via mail.
Mail survey	Questionnaires are distributed to and returned from respondents via the postal service.
Computer-Assisted (Online)	
Fax survey	Surveys are distributed to and returned from respondents via fax machines.
E-mail survey	Surveys are distributed to and returned from respondents via electronic mail.
Internet survey	The Internet is used to ask questions of and record responses from respondents.

Person-Administered Surveys

Person-administered surveys Data collection techniques that require the presence of a trained human interviewer who asks questions and records the subject's answers.

Person-administered survey methods are distinguished by the presence of a trained interviewer (or observer) who asks questions and records the subject's answers. Once the primary method used by researchers to collect data, traditional person-administered survey methods are being seriously challenged today by the growing acceptance and use of sophisticated Internet and telecommunications technologies as well as decision makers' demands for faster data acquisition. Nevertheless, person-administered survey techniques will continue to be used by researchers in the future, just at a lower frequency than in past years. Depending on the research problem and data requirements, different types of methodologies offer unique strengths and weaknesses to researchers. Exhibit 7.8 highlights some of the advantages and disadvantages associated with person-administered surveys.

In-Home Interviews

In-home interview A structured question-and-answer exchange conducted in the respondent's home.

An **in-home interview** is a face-to-face structured question-and-answer exchange conducted in the respondent's home. Sometimes the interviewer/respondent exchange occurs in the respondent's work environment rather than in the home, in which case the term becomes *in-office interview*. This method has several advantages. The interviewer can explain confusing or complex questions, use visual aids or other stimuli to elicit responses, and assess contextual

---

eXHIBIT 7.8 General Advantages and Disadvantages of Person-Administered Surveys

Advantages	Comments
Adaptability	Trained interviewers can quickly adapt to respondents' differences.
Rapport	Not all people are willing to talk with strangers when asked to answer a few questions. Interviewers can help establish a "comfort zone" during the questioning process.
Feedback	During the questioning process, interviewers can answer respondents' questions and increase the respondents' understanding of instructions and questions, and capture additional verbal and nonverbal information.
Quality of responses	Sometimes the interviewer must screen to qualify prospective respondents based on a set of characteristics like gender, age, etc. Interviewers can help ensure respondents are correctly chosen. Respondents tend to be more truthful in their responses when answering questions in a face-to-face situation.

Disadvantages	
Speed of data acquisition	Interviewers are sometimes slow in recording responses.
Possible recording error	Humans often use selective perception in listening to and recording responses to questions, which can cause inaccuracies in the respondent's answers.
Interviewer-respondent interaction error	Respondents may interpret the interviewer's body language, facial expression, or tone of voice as a clue to how to respond to a question.
High expense	Overall cost of data collection using an interviewer in a face-to-face environment often is higher than other data collection methods.

conditions. This helps generate large amounts of feedback from the respondent. In addition, respondents are in a comfortable, familiar environment where they feel safe and secure, thus increasing the likelihood of respondents' willingness to answer the survey's questions.

Frequently, in-home interviewing is accomplished through door-to-door canvassing of geographic areas. This canvassing process is one of the disadvantages of in-home interviewing. Interviewers who are not constantly supervised may skip homes they find threatening or may simply fabricate interviews. To ensure the safety of the interviewer, researchers may have to provide training on how to avoid potentially threatening situations. In addition, in-home or in-office interviews are expensive and time consuming.

Executive Interviews

Executive interview A personal exchange with a business executive conducted in his or her office.

An **executive interview** is a personal exchange with a business executive that frequently takes place in the executive's office. In general, executive interviews focus on collecting primary data concerning industrial products or service offerings because few executives are willing to share business hours to discuss nonbusiness or personal preferences.

Conducting executive interviews is very expensive, not only in terms of interviewer compensation but also travel expenses. In addition, securing an appointment with an executive can be a time-consuming process, and even then his or her agreement or commitment to be interviewed can be problematic. Finally, executive interviews require the use of well-trained and experienced interviewers because the topics often are highly technical.

Mall-Intercept Interviews

Mall-intercept interview A face-to-face personal interview that takes place in a shopping mall.

The expense of in-home and executive interviews has forced many researchers to conduct their surveys in a central location, frequently within regional shopping centers.[13] A **mall-intercept interview** is a face-to-face personal interview that takes place in a shopping mall. Mall shoppers are stopped and asked to complete a survey. The survey may take place in a common area of the mall or in the researcher's on-site offices.

Mall-intercept interviews share the advantages of in-home and in-office interviews except for the familiarity of the environment for the respondent. However, the mall-intercept is less expensive and more convenient for the researcher. A researcher spends little time or effort in securing a person's agreement to participate in the interview because both are already at a common location. In addition, the researcher benefits from reduced screening costs and time because interviewers can easily identify potential members of the target population by using their observation skills on location.

The disadvantages of mall-intercept interviews are similar to those of in-home or in-office interviews in terms of time, but as respondents are easy to recruit and travel time is nil, the total time investment is lower. However, mall patrons may not be representative of the general population. In addition, individuals representative of the general population may shop at different stores or at different times during the day. Typically, mall-intercept interviews are considered a nonprobability sampling approach for selecting prospective respondents. As you will learn later, nonprobability sampling approaches can have adverse effects on the ability to generalize survey results. Marketing researchers using mail-intercept interviews need to be sensitive to these issues.

Purchase-Intercept Interviews

Purchase-intercept interview A face-to-face interview that takes place immediately after the purchase of a product or service.

As in a mall-intercept, in a **purchase-intercept interview,** potential respondents are stopped and asked for feedback while on a shopping trip. However, purchase-intercepts are different in that the intercept takes place after the interviewer has observed a prespecified behavior, usually the selection or purchase of a particular product. An advantage of this type of interview is that the recency of the behavior aids the respondent's recall capabilities.

There are two major disadvantages to purchase-intercept interviews in addition to those of mall-intercepts. First, many stores are reluctant to allow their customers to be intercepted and their shopping interrupted in the store. Second, purchase-intercepts involve only those individuals who demonstrate some observable behavior. Thus, consumers who are considering a purchase but do not buy are excluded from this type of data collection technique.

Telephone-Administered Surveys

Traditional Telephone Interviews

Telephone interviews
Question-and-answer exchanges that are conducted via telephone technology.

Telephone interviews are a major source of market information. Compared to face-to-face interviews, telephone interviews are less expensive, faster, and more suitable for gathering data from large numbers of respondents. On a basic level, **telephone interviews** are simply personal interviews conducted via telephone technology. Individuals working from their homes or from central locations use telephones to ask questions and record responses.

Advantages of Telephone Interviews. Telephone survey methods have a number of advantages over face-to-face survey methods. One advantage is that interviewers can be closely supervised if they work out of a central location. Supervisors can record calls and review them later, and they can listen in on calls. Reviewing or listening to interviewers ensures quality control and can identify training needs. When interviewers work out of their own home, they can set hours that are convenient for them, within limits prescribed by the employer and the law.

Telephone interviews are less expensive than face-to-face interviews in a number of ways. They allow individual interviewers to do more surveys in a given time period, and they reduce travel time and time spent on searching for respondents. Although there is the added cost of the telephone call and related equipment, wide area telephone service (WATS) has made telephone calling a cost-efficient survey medium. Telephone interviews also facilitate interviews with respondents across a wide geographic area.

Another advantage of telephone surveys is that they enable interviewers to call back respondents who did not answer the telephone or respondents who found it inconvenient to grant interviews when first called. Callbacks are very inexpensive compared to follow-up personal surveys. A fourth advantage is that respondents perceive telephone surveys to be more anonymous and may feel less threatened and therefore be more candid.[14] Anonymity also reduces the opportunity for interviewer bias. Finally, telephone survey designs may well be the best hope for conducting executive interviews. While executives may not make time for a personal interview, they often take time for a telephone call. The same is true for many busy, hard-to-reach people. Using the telephone at a time convenient to the respondent facilitates collection of information from many individuals who would be almost impossible to interview personally.[15]

Disadvantages of Telephone Interviews. While some researchers believe the above advantages have made telephone survey designs the dominant form of collecting primary data, the telephone method, like any other data survey method, has several drawbacks. One disadvantage is that pictures or other nonaudio stimuli cannot be presented over the telephone. A second disadvantage is that it is difficult for telephone respondents to perform complex tasks. For example, imagine the confusion in the mind of a respondent asked to remember seven brands of a product, each with multiple variations, throughout an entire interview. Third is that

 **eTHICS**

Using Technology

Sugging Is a Federal Offense[18]

Sugging is the term used for the illegal telemarketing practice of selling under the guise of research. Sugging has been described as the bane of telephone research and especially the researcher. Researchers are frequently forced to deal with respondents who challenge them to prove the call is a legitimate research effort and not a disguised sales solicitation.

Consumer outrage at the practice of sugging prompted the U.S. Congress to pass the Telemarketing Sales Act (TSA), which went into effect under Federal Trade Commission implementation rules. The final rules state:

> The legislative history of the Telemarketing Act noted the problem of deceptive telemarketers contacting potential victims under the guise of conducting a poll, survey, or other such type of market research. To address these problems, the Commission believes that in any multiple purpose call where the seller or telemarketer plans, at least in some of the calls, to sell goods or services, the disclosures required by this Section of Rule should be made "promptly," in the first part of the call, before the non-sales portion of the call takes place.

The TSA follows the Telephone Consumer Protection Act (TCPA), which prescribed the hours of 8:00 A.M. to 9:00 P.M. local time as the only hours during which telephone solicitations can be made. Under the provisions of both the TCPA and the TSA, the telephone research industry is clearly exempted. The new laws apply to telemarketers, those persons making calls to or receiving calls from a customer in connection with a sales transaction. A "telephone solicitation" is defined as "the initiation of a telephone call or message for the purpose of encouraging the purchase or rental of, or the investment in, property, goods, or services, which is transmitted to any person." Telemarketing and marketing research using the telephone are different.

The Direct Marketing Association, the National Association of Attorneys General, and the Council for Marketing and Opinion Research combined to support the outlawing of sugging. The intent of the law is to ensure that the recipient is informed about a call from someone he or she doesn't know. The call recipient can choose whether or not to participate in legitimate telephone survey research or make a purchase from a telemarketer.

telephone surveys tend to be shorter than personal interviews because people hang up on long telephone calls. Telephone surveys also are limited, at least in practice, by national borders—the telephone is seldom used in international research. Probably the greatest disadvantage, though, lies in the restrictions on the types of data that can be collected over the phone.[16] For example, it is difficult to use multiple levels of agreement/disagreement, likes/dislikes, and so on, and all but impossible to accurately ask a brand-image question that would require the respondent to answer using a semantic differential scale (see Chapter 13).

Another disadvantage is the poor perception of telephone research in some people's minds, due in part to the increased use of telemarketing practices and the misperception that this type of research is the same as telemarketing.[17] The Ethics box describes the illegal and unethical act of "sugging," or selling under the guise of research, which no doubt contributes to this poor perception. The public has been vocal enough regarding sugging that it is against federal law. Even so, some people are annoyed by telephone research because it interrupts their privacy, their dinner, or their relaxation time. The federal government has responded with legislation limiting the hours of telephone interviews and telemarketing. Generally, the most productive hours from the researcher's standpoint are during the day to reach homemakers. Evening hours during the week and mid-morning to early evening on weekends are good times to reach people who work during the week.

A difficult but critical task in being able to conduct telephone interviewing is selecting the telephone number to be called. Using a telephone directory does not produce a random sample because many people choose to have unlisted numbers. In some cases, the client will supply the researcher with a customer list or another prescribed list, but most marketing research studies need a random sample. Three techniques—plus-one dialing, systematic random digit dialing, and random digit dialing—have been developed to overcome the telephone-number selection problem.

Plus-one dialing. In plus-one dialing, the researcher generates telephone numbers to be called by choosing numbers randomly from a telephone directory and adding 1. For example, suppose the telephone number 727-7119 is selected from the directory. Adding 1, we would dial 727-7120. This method is easy and allows for the possibility of unlisted telephone numbers to be included in the sample. But researchers should remember any telephone directory provides an initial weak sampling frame in most situations.

Systematic random digit dialing. Systematic random digit dialing is a technique in which researchers randomly dial telephone numbers, but only numbers that meet specific criteria. For example, numbers that are not within a specified area code would be ignored. Assuming the researcher is interested in consumer responses, exchanges that are devoted to government or business organizations would also be ignored. With this method, the marketing researcher randomly selects a telephone number as a starting point and uses a constant, or "skip," pattern in the selection process. The starting point, or seed number, is based on the sample interval. Specifically, the skip interval is added to the seed on the basis of the number of telephone numbers available divided by the number to be interviewed. For example, say that there are 10,000 telephone numbers in the 727 exchange. Assuming the researcher wants to interview 500 households within that exchange, the skip interval would be 10,000/500 = 20. The researcher would randomly choose a telephone number between 727-0000 and 727-0020, say 727-0009. Then, to generate additional numbers, the researcher would add the interval. Thus, the second number dialed in this example would be 727-0029, the third 727-0049, and so on.

The advantages of this method are that each number within an exchange has a known but not equal chance of being called. Thus, within an area, the selection of respondents is random. If the same number of calls is made in several exchanges, the sample will tend to share the attributes of the area and have the same geographic dispersion. Finally, the method is fairly simple to set up and administer.

Random digit dialing. Random digit dialing refers to a random selection of area code, exchange, and suffix numbers. The advantage is that all numbers have an equal chance of being called—the unlisted numbers are just as likely to be called as listed numbers. However, the random digit dialing is costly because many numbers either are not in service or are in use by people or organizations not included in the scope of the researcher's survey design.

Computer-Assisted Telephone Interviews

Computer-assisted telephone interviewing (CATI) Integrated telephone and computer system in which the interviewer reads the questions off a computer screen and enters respondents' answers directly into the computer program.

Advances in telecommunication, computer, and software technologies have totally revolutionized telephone survey methods. Most research firms have computerized the central location telephone interviewing process. With faster, more powerful computers and affordable software, even small research firms (e.g., fewer than five employees) can use **computer-assisted telephone interviewing (CATI)** systems. Although different systems are available, CATI systems basically integrate advanced telecommunication technologies with the traditional telephone survey methods. Interviewers are equipped with a "hands-free" headset and is seated in front of a keyboard, "touch-screen" computer terminal, or personal computer. Upon activating the system, the computer dials the prospective respondent's phone number automatically and provides the interviewer with the appropriate introduction screen. When the qualified respondent is on the line, the interviewer activates the interviewing process by pressing a key or series of keys on the computer's keyboard or pressure-sensitive screen. Following the introductory comments, another simple keystroke brings up to the screen the first question and a prelisted set of choice responses.

Many CATI systems are designed to have one question per screen. The interviewer then reads the question and records the respondent's answer. Note that depending on the question/scale design, the interviewer might read not only the question but also a list of possible answer choices. By recording the respondent's answer, the computer automatically skips ahead to the appropriate next question. For example, when Procter & Gamble conducts a clothes detergent purchasing behavior study using a CATI system, one question asked by the interviewer might be "In the past 30 days have you purchased any clothes cleaning products?" If the answer is yes, a series of specific questions focusing on the types of clothes cleaning products the person buys might follow. If the answer is no, those questions might be inappropriate to ask the respondent. The computer is programmed to skip to the next appropriate question on the basis of the respondent's answer. Here, the next question might be something like "How often do you purchase clothes cleaning products?" When programmed to react in a predetermined way based on the respondent's initial response to the question, the computer can eliminate human error which exists in surveys conducted using the traditional paper-and-pencil telephone interview mode.

CATI systems can be used to customize questions. Consider a J. D. Power and Associates study on new-car purchasers' satisfaction. In the early part of the survey, the respondent is asked to provide the years, makes, and models of the cars owned in the past 10 years. Later in the interview, the interviewer might be prompted to ask the respondent to rate the safety features for a particular car owned. The question might appear as "You said you owned a 2004 Acura 3.2 TL. How would you rate each of the following safety features of that car?" The interviewer would first describe the scale and its use, then ask about the first safety feature on the screen. The process would continue until all the prelisted safety features were rated. Although these types of questions can be handled in a traditional telephone interview mode, the computerized version handles them much more efficiently because the interviewer does not have to physically flip questionnaire pages back and forth or remember a respondent's previous responses. Today's CATI systems have alleviated most of the problems associated with manual systems of callbacks, complex quotas, skip logic, rotations, and randomization.

Advantages of Computer-Assisted Telephone Interviews.

Although many of the advantages of computer-assisted telephone interviews are based on lower costs per call, there are other advantages as well. In sophisticated systems, it is possible to switch from one questionnaire to another during the interview. Switching capabilities allow for interviewing family members other than the head of household, for example. The advantage is that common information is shared between all the questionnaires, saving the need for multiple calls. Another advantage is ownership of the call. Sometimes people need to stop in the middle of an interview but are willing to finish at another time. Computer technology has the capability of routing inbound calls to a particular interviewer who "owns" the interview. Not only is there greater efficiency in terms of labor per call, but there can be cost savings as well. A cost advantage, perhaps not so obvious, is the ability of computer systems to select the least expensive routing for a particular call.

CATI systems also eliminate the need for separate editing and data entry tasks associated with manual systems. The researcher does not edit or clean complete questionnaires for errors or manually create data computer files, because there is no physical questionnaire and the responses are automatically entered directly to a computer file at the end of the interview. The possibility for coding or data entry errors is eliminated with CATI systems because it is impossible to accidentally record an improper response from outside the set of prelisted responses established for a given question. Here is an easy example to remember that illustrates this point. The respondent is asked the question "How important is it for your new car to have an automatic seatbelt safety system?" The response choices are prelisted as (a) "Extremely important," (b) "Important," (c) "Somewhat important," and (d) "Not at all important." If the interviewer, by mistake, enters any code other than one of the four established codes, the computer will ask for the answer to be reentered until an acceptable code is entered.

Given the sophistication of the CATI systems' software, tabulation of results can be run in real time at any point of the study. Real-time reporting of the results is not possible using traditional paper-and-pencil methods. Quick preliminary results can be beneficial in determining when certain questions can be eliminated because enough information has been obtained or when some additional questions are needed because of unexpected patterns uncovered in the earlier part of the interviewing process. Overall, use of CATI systems continues to grow at a rapid rate because decision makers have embraced the cost savings, quality control, and time-saving aspects of these systems.

Disadvantages of Computer-Assisted Telephone Interviews.

CATI systems have two problem areas. Setting up and activating CATI systems require substantial initial investment and operating costs. The investment in computers, especially for large and sophisticated systems, is still high, considering how quickly a computer system becomes obsolete. Software to control the hardware, monitor calls, and record responses in real-time fashion is also expensive and rapidly changing, especially if customized, and can be very time-consuming to develop and debug. Second, in addition to having traditional skills, interviewers must have specific computer skills to effectively administer this type of survey. As the costs of both computer hardware and software go down and more people develop better computer literacy, these problems will diminish.

Completely Automated Telephone Interviews

Completely automated telephone surveys (CATS) A telephone interviewing system in which a computer dials a phone number and a recording is used to introduce and administer the survey, leaving the subject to interact with the computer directly.

Using more sophisticated software than CATI systems, some research companies have fully automated their telephone interviewing data collection process. This type of system is referred to as a **completely automated telephone surveys (CATS)** system and uses no human interviewer. The survey is completely administered by a computer. After the system is activated, the computer dials a phone number and a recording is used to introduce the survey to the prospective respondent and give directions. The actual survey is conducted by the respondent by listening to the electronic voice and responding by pushing keys on the Touch-Tone telephone keypad. Although still relatively new, CATS has been successfully employed in service quality monitoring, product/warranty registrations, customer satisfaction studies, in-home product tests, and in election day polls.[19] One of the difficulties experienced in using this fully automated system is there is a high "disconnect" rate among prospective respondents. While research is under way to investigate this disconnect behavior, some informal evidence suggests invasion of home privacy and the impersonal, one-way communication involved in responding to an unsolicited electronic voice are problematic.

Wireless Phone Surveys

Wireless data networking and advanced database technologies offer researchers a promising new innovative data collection technique for doing marketing research studies—the wireless phone survey.[20] With a **wireless phone survey** data are collected from wireless phone users. Researchers can survey in either text-based or voice-based formats or a combination of both. In a text-based format, the respondent can access the survey and display it as text messages on a wireless phone screen. The respondent uses the phone's dial pad to answer the questions. All responses are sent, in real time, back to a backend database through the wireless network and the Internet. In contrast, a voice-based survey allows the respondent to listen to the questions on the wireless phone and answer them by speaking. All survey questions and answers are automatically processed and analyzed by voice synthesis and recognition software on voice extensible markup language (VoiceXML) equipment. One of the unique characteristics of wireless phone surveys is their ability to deliver instant answers—anytime, anywhere. They also enable researchers to capture data from respondents in their natural shopping and consumption environments.

Advantages of Wireless Phone Surveys. Although this data collection method is in infancy stage, there are a number of potential advantages over online, other telephone, and paper-and-pencil–based methods. First, wireless phone surveys are contemporaneous—they capture consumers' real experiences at the moment of purchase or consumption. Another advantage is the mobility associated with wireless phones. Almost like a watch, a wireless phone is with the consumer wherever she goes. This mobility factor brings a tremendous degree of convenience for respondents. Third, wireless surveys are less intrusive to the respondent because they can be sent without interrupting respondents' lives. In turn, respondents have full control of the time and place to fill out the survey. In cases where a respondent must complete the survey at a particular moment, such requirements are agreed upon by the respondent prior to sending the survey and are not viewed as obtrusive.[21]

Capturing data via wireless phones increases the potential of implementing longitudinal types of studies. Normally, a wireless phone is a personal belonging and can be associated with each individual, thus making it easier for researchers to keep track of each respondent over time. Another advantage relates to the flexibility of retrieving data from respondents. Wireless networks enable respondents to send their answers to a database in real time during the survey. In addition, the survey can be programmed similar to CATI and CATS surveys to branch questions automatically based on previous answers. Finally, wireless phone surveys provide geographic flexibility and facilitate completing surveys on location-sensitive topics such as during a shopping trip at a particular mall or theme park.

Disadvantages of Wireless Phone Surveys. There are several challenges facing the use of wireless phone surveys. First, there are limited display spaces on wireless phone screens. Therefore, the questions must be kept short and simple in both text-based and voice-based formats. Consequently, wireless phone surveys are not suitable for research that involves long and/or complex questions and responses. Second, wireless phones have limited capacity to handle graphics. Therefore, wireless surveys may not be appropriate for studies that require visual stimuli for answering certain types of research questions. Third, the initial technology costs (both hardware and software) required for implementing and maintaining wireless phone surveys are very high. Finally, researchers conducting wireless phone surveys must be well trained in information technology skills in addition to other research skills.

Self-Administered Surveys

Self-administered survey
A data collection technique in which the respondent reads the survey questions and records his or her own answers without the presence of a trained interviewer.

The third type of interviewing exchange is the **self-administered survey.** A self-administered survey is a data collection technique in which the respondent reads the survey questions and records his or her own responses without the presence of a trained interviewer. The advantages are low cost per survey and interviewer bias—but the latter comes at a price since there is no interviewer to probe for a deeper response. For example, on a self-administered survey a respondent may indicate that he or she did not purchase a certain product, but that respondent can also fail to answer "Why not?"

While the emergence of telecommunications technology has allowed delivery systems for self-administered surveys to expand, the most common type of self-administered survey is still a mail survey. Exhibit 7.9 highlights some of the advantages and disadvantages associated with self-administered data collection methods. We discuss three types of self-administered surveys: direct mail, mail panel, and drop-off.

---

eXHIBIT 7.9 General Advantages and Disadvantages of Self-Administered Surveys

	Comments
Advantages	
Low cost per survey	With no need for an interviewer or computerized assistance device, self-administered surveys are by far the least costly method of data acquisition.
Respondent control	Respondents are in total control of how fast, when, and where the survey is completed; thus the respondent creates his/her own comfort zone.
No interviewer-respondent bias	There is no chance of introducing interviewer bias or respondent interpretive error based on the interviewer's body language, facial expression, or tone of voice.
Anonymity in responses	Respondents are more comfortable in providing honest and insightful responses because their true identity is not revealed.
Disadvantages	
Minimize flexibility	The type of data collected is limited to the specific questions placed initially on the survey. It is impossible to obtain additional in-depth data, because of the lack of probing and observation capabilities.
High nonresponse rates	In some cases, it is impossible to guarantee that the respondent will complete and return the survey at all. The respondent may get frustrated with questions that need clarification.
Potential response errors	The respondent may not fully understand a survey question and provide an erroneous response or mistakenly skip sections of the survey, resulting in inaccurate answers. Without an interviewer, respondents may unconsciously commit numerous errors while believing they are properly responding.
Slow data acquisition	In many cases, the time required to acquire the data and enter it into a computer file for analysis is significantly longer than in many other data collection methods.
Lack of monitoring capability	Not having an interviewer present could lead to increases in misunderstanding of questions and instructions on how to respond to certain questions.

Mail Surveys

Mail survey A self-administered question-naire that is delivered to selected respondents and returned to the researcher by mail.

In situations where the researcher decides that a **mail survey** is the best method, a questionnaire is developed and mailed to a list of people who return the completed surveys by mail. The researcher must be careful to select a list that accurately reflects the target population of interest. Sometimes obtaining the required mailing addresses is an easy task. But in other cases it can be time-consuming and difficult. In addition, there are production considerations. For example, the envelope needs to be designed to stimulate the potential respondent's interest enough that the questionnaire is not simply thrown out. The questionnaire itself needs to be carefully designed to gather as much information as possible and still be short enough for people to complete in a reasonable length of time.

Advantages of Mail Surveys. This type of survey is inexpensive to implement. There are no interviewer-related costs such as compensation, training, travel, or search costs. Plus, most of the production expenses are one-time costs that can be amortized over many surveys. The variable costs are primarily postage, printing, and the cost of the incentive. Another advantage is that mail surveys can reach even hard-to-interview people.

Disadvantages of Mail Surveys. Mail surveys have several drawbacks. One major drawback is that response rates tend to be much lower than with face-to-face or telephone interviews. The risk of nonresponse bias is very real with mail surveys since the researcher gives up control over who responds. The researcher is never exactly sure who filled out the questionnaire, leaving the question of whether someone else provided the answers instead of the intended person. For example, in sending a mail survey to Mr. Jones in Dallas, Texas, on Network Television Programming, the researcher cannot determine precisely whether Mr. Jones or some other member of his household answered the survey.

Another problem is that of misunderstood or skipped questions. Mail surveys make it difficult to handle problems of both vagueness and potential misinterpretation in question-and-answer setups. People who simply do not understand a question may record a response the researcher did not intend or expect. Or the respondent may skip one or more questions entirely. These are all problems associated with not having a trained interviewer available to assist the respondent. Finally, mail surveys are also slow as there can be a significant time lag between when the survey is mailed and when the survey is returned.

Mail Panel Surveys

Mail panel survey A questionnaire sent to a group of individuals who have agreed in advance to participate.

To avoid some of the drawbacks of mail surveys, a researcher may choose a mail panel survey method. A **mail panel survey** is a questionnaire sent to a group of individuals who have agreed in advance to participate. The panel can be tested prior to the survey so the researcher knows that the panel is representative; the prior agreement usually produces high response rates. In addition, mail panel surveys allow for longitudinal research. That is, the same people can be tested multiple times over an extended period. This enables the researcher to observe changes in the panel members' responses over time.

The major drawback to mail panels is that members are very likely not to be representative of the target population at large. For example, individuals who agree to be on a panel may have a special interest in the topic or may simply have a lot of time available. There is little information on how much, if any, these aspects of mail panels bias the results of the research. Researchers should be cautious, therefore, regarding the degree of generalizability of the findings.

It is important to remember that the different survey methods are not necessarily mutually exclusive. It is quite common for several methods to be employed on the same project.

For example, the researcher may contact potential in-home respondents via the mail to help improve the response rate or as a part of the screening process. Telephone calls may be used to inform people of impending mail surveys. Sending multiple copies of a mail survey to nonrespondents is frequently a useful way to increase response rates.

Drop-Off Surveys

Drop-off survey A self-administered question-naire that a represen-tative of the researcher hand-delivers to selected respondents; the com-pleted surveys are re-turned by mail or picked up by the representative.

One common combination technique is termed the **drop-off survey.** In this method, a representative of the researcher hand-delivers survey forms to respondents. Completed surveys are returned by mail or picked up by the representative. The advantages of drop-off surveys include the availability of a person who can answer general questions, screen potential respondents, and spur interest in completing the questionnaire. The disadvantage to drop-offs is they are fairly expensive in comparison to mail surveys.

Online Survey Methods

Marketing research practices and the delivery systems being used in collecting primary data have changed dramatically as people have increasingly accepted Internet technologies, telecommunications, and researchers' demand for faster data acquisition and real-time reporting of results. Many traditional survey methods have been revised by technology-savvy researchers to use new "online" platforms. Although many of the fundamental principles that underlie traditional survey methods remain the same, the speed of data acquisition and reporting systems has created new benchmarks for improving how primary data will be collected in years to come. Online advances that were just visions a few years ago are now part of reality.[22] Exhibit 7.10 summarizes online data collection techniques that are in the process of replacing or augmenting traditional survey research methods. The following discussion focuses on three online survey designs—fax, e-mail, and Internet surveys—researchers increasingly are using to collect primary data.

Fax Surveys

Fax survey A self-administered question-naire that is sent to the selected subject via fax.

A **fax survey** is essentially a mail survey sent by fax. The fax survey allows researchers to collect responses to visual cues, as in a mail survey, as well as semantic differential or constant sum scales (see Chapter 12), which are difficult to use in telephone interviews.[23] The potential benefit of fax surveys is that the flexibility of mail can be combined, to an extent, with the speed of the telephone.[24]

In comparison to mail surveys, the fax delivery facilitates faster delivery and response speed and may even be less expensive. Administrative and clerical functions also can be reduced because there is no need to fold surveys and stuff envelopes. Finally, a fax survey implies urgency and is not perceived as being junk mail by many recipients. Even in a regular mail survey, merely offering the option to respond by fax can increase the response rate.[25]

One disadvantage of fax surveys is that many consumers and small businesses do not have fax machines and therefore cannot be contacted. In addition, respondents may have to pay to fax back their responses, which can reduce response rates. Sending a prepaid mailing label increases response time, and using a toll-free fax response line increases costs. In addition fax surveys can be delayed or not delivered because of operator error, equipment malfunctions, or busy signals. These problems may be particularly acute in high-volume operations. The relative lack of privacy may cause response problems as well. Finally, fax surveys may lack the clarity of image of a printed mail survey, and a color fax may be too expensive.

Nevertheless, fax surveys offer an attractive alternative to direct mail surveys under proper conditions. Fax surveys can provide relatively faster responses, higher response

EXHIBIT 7.10   Online Computer Technology Integrates with Offline Survey Data Collection Methods

Offline Method	Online Method	Comments
Personal interview	Computer-assisted personal interview	The respondent sits with the interviewer, and interviewer reads the respondent the questions from a laptop computer screen and directly keys in the responses.
Handout self-administered interview	Computer-assisted self-interview	The researcher directs a respondent to a specified computer terminal where the respondent reads questions from the screen and directly enters responses.
Self-administered interview	Fully automated self-interview	The respondent independently approaches a central computer station (kiosk) and reads and responds to the questions, all without researcher intervention.
Telephone interview	CATI	The interviewer calls respondent at home or office, reads questions from a computer screen, and directly enters the responses into the computer system.
Telephone interview	CATS	The computer calls respondents and an electronic voice gives directions and asks questions. The respondent uses the keypad of a Touch-Tone telephone to enter responses.
Direct mail self-administered survey	Computer disks by mail (CDM)	A computer disk is mailed to the respondent, who completes the survey on his or her computer and returns the disk to the researcher by mail.
Mail panel survey	Online panel survey	Through various methods, groups of people agree to become members of a selected panel of consumers. Initially these consumers fill out a form on background data on specific demographic and purchase factors. Later these respondents are sent surveys from time to time via e-mail. They complete the survey and return it via e-mail or direct mail.
Self-administered survey	E-mail survey	The batch feature available on most e-mail systems is used to send a "mass mailing" to potential respondents, the respondent completes an opt-in/opt-out option, and those respondents who opt in continue and complete the survey. Surveys are returned via e-mail.
Self-administered survey	Computer-generated fax survey	A computer is used to dial and send a survey to potential respondents via fax. The respondent completes the survey and returns it via fax.
Self-administered survey	Internet survey	The survey is placed on a specific Web site, a respondent has to click on the specified Web site, complete the survey, then click the Send button. Or the survey is placed on a specified Web site, the respondent is contacted separately by letter or e-mail about the survey and its Web site location and given a unique password in order to access the survey, and the respondent completes the survey and returns it by clicking the Send button.

rates, and similar data quality. In addition, fax surveys can be cheaper due to low transmission and paper-handling costs. Still, the image-quality and limited-reach problems are not likely to be resolved in the foreseeable future.

E-mail Surveys

E-mail survey A self-administered data collection technique in which the survey is delivered to and returned from the respondent by e-mail.

An **e-mail survey** is a self-administered data collection technique in which the survey is electronically delivered to and returned by e-mail. E-mail surveys have become one of the popular methods within the "family" of online surveys used by marketing researchers. Using the improvements of the batch feature associated with today's e-mail systems, the researcher creates a standardized e-mail message, sometimes in the format of a cover letter, and appends the online survey as an attachment. The e-mail message and survey are then electronically transmitted as a "mass mailing" to a large number of prospective respondents. Once the respondent opens the e-mail, she or he is given an opt-in or opt-out approval option that serves to gain the respondent's permission to participate in the study. The opt-in/opt-out option is required by federal consumer and data privacy laws to protect people from receiving "spam" or "sugging" mailings.[26] *Spam* and *sugg* are terms for the illegal marketing practice of selling unsolicited products or services under the guise of conducting research. By law, respondents who select the opt-out option do not participate in the attached survey, and their e-mail addresses are supposed to be automatically removed from the researcher's mailing list, so they receive no future e-mail from that originating source. In turn, respondents who select the opt-in option, granting permission, continue the survey following on-screen directions. After completing the survey, the respondent returns it via e-mail. Today, returning an e-mail survey is as easy as clicking a single Submit or Return button located normally at the end of the survey.

Proponents of e-mail surveys favor this method for its capabilities of collecting a variety of data at lightning speed at a very low cost-per-participant figure. In addition, as with other computer-assisted or online research methods, errors like data nonresponse caused by interviewer error, interviewer interaction bias, and data entry errors are eliminated by technology-based controls. E-mail surveys have grown in popularity as a method of conducting fast and inexpensive research for international consumer products and services studies.

Like any online survey method, there are still some difficulties that must be overcome. First, not everyone has access to the Internet. Experts estimate that 60 to 65 percent of individuals in the United States have access to the Internet.[27] But in other global markets the percentage is much smaller. These percentages are expected to grow slowly in the United States, but increase significantly in most global markets, like Latin America, Europe, and the Pacific Rim.[28] Online researchers will have to continue their efforts to establish legitimacy in generalizing their results to large target populations. The second significant problem revolves around data privacy. All research firms have been forced to integrate opt-in strategies in building the numbers for their online panel groups. Yet differences in strictness and enforcement of data privacy laws remain a sticking point, especially between global market governments.[29]

Internet Surveys

Internet survey A self-administered questionnaire that is placed on a World Wide Web site for prospective subjects to read and complete.

Internet surveys are another method gaining strong interest among many marketing research firms. This type of online survey method is tightly integrated into Web site technology. Some characteristics of Internet surveys are similar to e-mail surveys, but there are some distinct differences. An **Internet survey** is a self-administered questionnaire that is placed on a Web site for prospective subjects to read and complete. This type of survey method requires prospective respondents to first commit to becoming a member of a special club or advisory panel that is directly controlled by the particular organization conducting the survey. After

A Closer Look at Research

Virtual Reality in Marketing Research[30]

Tom Allison, president of Allison Hollander in Atlanta, Georgia, thinks that a computer program can do a better job of tabulating what customers will actually do rather than what the customers think they will do. The problem, according to Allison, is that people communicate in words but do not think or feel in words. People think and feel in pictures. Computer technology has the added bonus of reducing interviewer and consumer bias as well.

To illustrate the problem of consumer bias as a result of thinking in pictures and communicating in words, Allison asks audiences to think of the following sentence: "You are standing by the water's edge." Then, he produces four images: an ocean scene, a lake scene, a river scene, and a stream. Each image elicits different feelings, according to Allison. In practice, this consumer bias is the reason that people react differently to a can of Coca-Cola than they do to an old-style bottle of Coca-Cola.

The prescription, according to Allison, is to take the consumer to the McDonald's restaurant instead of simply talking about a McDonald's. In this way, the researcher can get a truer picture of the consumer's reactions than time-lagged thoughts and feelings allow. The way to take the consumer to McDonald's is by computer simulation.

By using full-scale electronic simulations, the consumer can be exposed to menus, store shelves, coolers, and vending machines. The realism of the simulations allows for accurate communications with respondents and also for meaningful data collection. Allison suggests that the simulation should be engaging and short enough to hold the respondent's attention. Letting the respondent do, observe, and question elicits the entire selection process. And the computer can track and record the mental process step by step.

Allison says that consumer companies can use simulations in many different ways. For example, a consumer might be asked to build a stereo system, spending only a given amount of money. The researcher using the computer simulation could see what the respondent would buy. Another example could be a sunglasses boutique. The consumer could have his or her face scanned into a computer and then electronically "try on" sunglasses by clicking a mouse.

Other researchers think that virtual reality may offer an exciting way of testing. The consumer could "shop" the store, picking up items from shelves as he or she would in an ordinary store. The computer could track the respondent's actions and reactions. This virtual reality testing would allow companies to very accurately pretest pricing changes, packaging, promotions, shelf layout, new-product interest, and substitution behaviors.

Proponents of the computer simulation research say the tests are becoming faster and the cost is decreasing as technology advances. Other benefits include a realistic context for the respondent; a controlled, low-risk environment; and no need for back data or norms.

---

agreeing to the company's opt-in membership requirements, prospective respondents then select unique "login" and "password" codes, which serve as entrance keys for participation. Following Web site instructions, respondents complete and submit their survey.

Another distinct difference is that respondents have the option of accessing the results of the survey in real time. Some companies, like Procter & Gamble through its "Consumercorner.com" panel system, even encourage respondents to scroll through the results and have additional options that allow respondents to make and share testimonial comments about the products being surveyed with other group members. Read the nearby Closer Look at Research box, which illustrates the use of computer simulations as a creative method of integrating computer technologies with survey research.

EXHIBIT 7.11 Computer-Assisted Data Collection Methods[31]

Benefits	Personal — Computer-Assisted Personal Interview	On-Site — Computer-Assisted Self-Interview	On-Site — Fully Automated Self-Interview	Telephone — Computer-Assisted Telephone Interview	Telephone — Fully Automated Telephone Interview	Mail — Computer Disks by Mail	Online Panel — Online Panel Survey	E-mail — Electronic-Mail Survey	Fax — Computer-Generated Fax Survey	Internet — Self-Administered Survey
No need for respondents to have computer-related skills	X			X	X		X		X	X
Allows respondents to choose own schedule for completing survey		X	X			X	X	X	X	X
Can incorporate complex branching questions into survey	X	X	X	X	X	X	X*	X*		X*
Can incorporate respondent-generated words in questions	X	X	X	X	X	X	X*	X*		X*
Can accurately measure response times to questions	X	X	X	X	X	X	X*	X*		X*
Can display graphics and directly relate them to questions	X	X	X			X	X*	X*		X*
Eliminates the need to encode data from paper survey forms	X	X	X	X	X	X	X*	X		X
Errors in data less likely compared to manual methods	X	X	X	X	X	X	X	X		X
Speedier data collection and encoding compared to manual methods	X	X	X	X	X	X	X	X	X	X

*Assumes interactive e-mail population specification.

While the benefits are many, there are still difficulties that results in nonresponse bias. In addition, response bias remains a problem because Internet surveys are available to everyone without being targeted to anyone. Internet surveys are initially passive in nature: a prospective respondent must seek out the Web site, and thus only those who have a prior interest are likely to even find the survey, let alone complete it. Exhibit 7.11 summarizes the benefits of using computer-assisted and online survey methods for collecting primary data. Refer to this book's Web site at www.mhhe.com/hair06 for more discussion and examples of online survey methods.

Factors for Selecting the Appropriate Survey Method

Researchers must consider several factors when choosing a survey method. Yet merely selecting any method the researcher finds interesting or convenient may not produce usable, cost-efficient data. For example, in determining the appropriate method, the researcher must consider a number of important factors such as those listed in Exhibit 7.12. The following sections describe these situational, task, and respondent characteristics in more detail.

EXHIBIT 7.12   Important Factors to Consider in Selecting a Survey Method

Factors and Characteristics	Important Issues and Questions
Situational Characteristics	
Budget of available resources	What degree of appropriate resources can be committed to the project? What are the total dollars and worker-hours available for committing to the research project's activities of gathering raw data, developing data structures, and creating/presenting information? What is the cost of collecting the required data?
Completion time frame	How much time is needed for completing the research project? How quickly do data-gathering, analysis, and information-generation activities have to be completed?
Quality requirements	How accurate and representative is the derived information to the research problem?
Completeness of the data	How much information and what degree of detail are needed for the defined research problem?
Generalizability	At what level of confidence does the researcher want to make inferences about the defined target population from the data results?
Precision	What is the acceptable level of error that the data results may have in representing true population parameters?
Task Characteristics	
Difficulty of the task	How much effort is required by the respondent to answer the questions? How hard does the subject have to work to answer the questions? How much preparation is required to create a desired environment for the respondents?
Stimuli needed to elicit a response	How much physical stimulus does a respondent need? Do specific stimuli have to be used to elicit a response? How complex do the stimuli have to be?
Amount of information needed	How detailed do the respondent's answers have to be? Will probing activities be needed? How many questions should there be? How long should the respondent expect to take?
Research topic sensitivity	To what degree are the survey's questions socially, politically, and/or personally sensitive?
Respondent Characteristics	
Diversity	What commonalities exist among the prospective respondents? How many and which common characteristics have to exist?
Incidence rate	What percentage of the defined target population has the key characteristics to qualify for being included in the survey?
Degree of survey participation	Are the selected respondents able to completely interact in the question-and-answer process? What is the person's ability to participate? What is the person's degree of willingness to participate? What is the knowledge-level requirement for a person to participate in the survey process?

Situational Characteristics

In an ideal situation, the researcher's sole focus would be on the collection of accurate data. However, we live in an imperfect world and researchers must reckon with the competing objectives of budget, time, and data quality. In most survey research methods, the goal is to produce usable data in as short a time as possible at the lowest cost. Finding the optimal balance between these three factors is frequently a ticklish task. It is easy to generate large amounts of data in a short time if quality is ignored. But excellent data quality can be achieved only through expensive and time-consuming methods. In selecting the survey method, the researcher commonly considers all the situational characteristics in combination.

Budget

The budget is the amount of resources available to the researcher. While budgets are commonly thought of in terms of dollar spending, other resources such as staff size can have similar constraining effects. All researchers face budget constraints. The resources available for a study can greatly affect choice of the method. For example, if only 500 hours are available in the research department, it would be impossible to conduct more than 1,000 personal interviews of 30 minutes each. The researcher might select a mail survey method because developing the survey form, mailing it, and collecting the responses would take much less time than personal interviews. In a similar manner, a $20,000 budget for a 1,000-person study limits the researcher to spending $20 per person. Given this constraint, the researcher might elect to use a telephone survey because the cost per response can be lower than in a personal interview. It should be noted that the researcher is not required to spend all the budgeted money or personnel resources in conducting any type of quantitative survey, but most researchers will try to keep the research design and activities cost-effective if at all possible.

In truth budget determinations are frequently much more arbitrary than researchers would prefer. However, it is rare that the budget is the sole determinant of the survey method. Much more commonly, the budget is considered along with the data quality and time factors.

Completion Time Frame

For decisions to be effective, they often must be made within a specified time period. The time frame commonly has a direct bearing on the data-gathering method. Long time frames allow the researcher the luxury of selecting the method that will produce the best data. In many situations, however, the affordable time frame is much shorter than desired, forcing the researcher to choose a method that may not be the researcher's ideal one. Some primary data surveys, such as direct mail or personal interviews, require relatively long time frames. Other methods, such as telephone surveys or mall-intercepts, can be done more quickly.

Quality Requirements

Data quality is a complex issue that encompasses issues of scale measurement, questionnaire design, sample design, and data analysis. Data quality is too complex to discuss in this section, but a brief overview of three key issues will help explain the impact of data quality on the selection of survey methods.

Completeness of Data. The first key data quality issue is the completeness of the data. Completeness refers to the depth and breadth of the data. Having complete data allows the researcher to paint a total picture, fully describing the information from each respondent.

Incomplete data will lack some detail, resulting in a picture that is somewhat vague or unclear. Personal interviews can be very complete, while mail surveys may not be. In some cases, the depth of information needed to make an informed decision will dictate that an in-depth personal survey be the appropriate method. In other cases, a telephone interview that allows for short calls and brief response times may be the appropriate choice.

Data Generalizability. The second data quality issue is generalizability. Generalizability refers to the data being an accurate portrait of the defined target population. Data that are generalizable accurately describe the population being studied. In contrast, data that are not generalizable cannot accurately reflect the population. In this situation, the data can lead only to estimates about the population and may truly reflect only the respondents who supplied it. For example, primary data from mail surveys are frequently thought of as being relatively less generalizable due to low response rates or small samples.

Data Precision. The third data quality issue is precision. Precision is related to, but still distinct from, completeness. Precision refers to the degree of exactness of the data in relation to some other possible response. For example, a car company may want to know what colors will be "hot" for their new models. Respondents may indicate their preference for a bright color for automobiles. The completeness issue refers to the respondents' preference for red, for example. Precision refers to the preference of red over blue by a two-to-one margin. If all we need to know is that bright colors are preferred, then fairly incomplete and imprecise data will suffice. If we need to know that red is preferred by a two-to-one margin, then both complete and precise data are needed. Mail surveys can frequently deliver precise results, but may not always produce the most generalizable results. Telephone surveys may be generalizable but may lack precision due to short questions and short interview times.

Task Characteristics

The characteristics of the task placed on respondents also influences the method used to collect data. The respondent's task characteristics can be categorized into four major areas: (1) the difficulty of the task; (2) the stimuli needed to elicit a response from the respondent; (3) the amount of information the respondent is asked to give; and (4) the sensitivity of the research topic.

Difficulty of the Task

Task difficulty How hard a survey respondent needs to work and how much preparation the researcher needs to do.

Task difficulty refers to how hard a respondent needs to work. Some marketing research questions involve very difficult tasks. For example, taste tests require respondents to sample foods prepared under very controlled conditions. In this example, the task difficulty is primarily in creating exactly the same stimulus for each respondent. In other cases, the respondent may have to work very hard to answer the questions. Sometimes product or brand preference testing involves many similar products and therefore can be laborious for the respondents. In general, the more complex the survey environment the greater the need for trained individuals to complete the interviews. Regardless of the difficulty of the survey task, the researcher should try to make it easy for the respondent to fully answer the questions.

Stimuli Needed to Elicit the Response

Frequently, researchers need to expose respondents to some type of stimulus in order to elicit a response. The stimuli may consist of products (as in taste tests), promotional visuals (as in advertising research), or some physical entity used to elicit the respondent's opinion. Some sort of personal involvement is needed in situations where respondents have to touch, see, or taste something. It is very difficult for the researcher to maintain control over such situations without a trained interviewer. In product concept research, for example, respondents frequently need to see and touch the product in order to form an opinion.

The actual form of the personal interview may vary. It is not always necessary to design a one-on-one interview. For example, people may come in groups to a central location for taste testing, or people in mall-intercepts can be shown videotapes to elicit their opinions on advertising.

Amount of Information Needed from the Respondent

Researchers are always looking for ways to get more data from respondents. But respondents have limits in time, knowledge, and patience, among other things. Generally speaking, if a large amount of detailed information is required from respondents, the need for personal interaction with a trained interviewer increases. Conversely, if very simple information is needed in small amounts, very little interviewer interaction is needed.

While some people tend to be resistant to long mail surveys, this might not cause a dramatic drop in response rates. Although some people will terminate long interviews at shopping malls, some may not even stand for short interviews. People hang up on long telephone calls, too. The survey researcher's task is to achieve the best match between the survey method and the amount of information needed. Consequently, a researcher has to assess the trade-off between getting more information and risking respondent fatigue.

Research Topic Sensitivity

Topic sensitivity The degree to which a survey question leads the respondent to give a socially acceptable response.

In some cases, the problem may require researchers to ask some socially or personally sensitive questions. **Topic sensitivity** is the degree to which a specific survey question leads the respondent to give a socially acceptable response. In general, topic sensitivity relates to questions about income, but from time to time sensitive questions may be asked about racial issues, environmental issues, politics, religion, and personal hygiene. In these areas, and perhaps a few others, the researcher should be careful. When asked about a sensitive issue, some respondents will feel they should give a socially acceptable response even if they actually feel or behave otherwise. In addition, some respondents simply refuse to answer questions they consider too personal or sensitive. Others may even terminate the interview. Typically, the less sensitive research topics are those that relate to brand preference, shopping behaviors, and satisfaction levels. Such questions are usually viewed as being nonintrusive or otherwise not problematic. Another sensitivity issue is competitor confidentiality—sometimes the sponsoring client of the survey just does not want written surveys to get into the wrong hands (i.e., the competition).

Respondent Characteristics

Since most marketing research projects target prespecified types of people, the third major factor in selecting the appropriate survey method is the respondents' characteristics. The extent to which members of the target group of respondents share common characteristics will have some influence on the survey method selected. The following discussion will center on three facets of respondent characteristics: diversity, incidence, and participation.

Diversity

Diversity of respondents refers to the degree to which respondents share characteristics. The more diverse the respondents, the fewer similarities they share. The less diverse the respondents, the more similarities. For example, if the defined target population is specified as people who own or have access to a fax machine, then diversity is low and a fax survey can be an effective and cost-efficient method. However, if the defined target population does not have convenient access to a fax machine, fax surveys will fail.

There are cases where the researcher may assume a particular personal characteristic or behavior is shared by many people in the defined target population, when in fact very few share that characteristic. For example, the rates of unlisted telephone numbers vary significantly by geographic area. In some areas (e.g., small rural towns in Illinois), the rate of unlisted numbers is very low (less than 10%), while in others (e.g., large cities like New York or Los Angeles), the rate is very high (more than 50%).[32]

If researchers select prospective respondents for telephone surveys from published numbers, there often are significant problems with the accuracy of the data. People who do not have listed numbers may be different from people with listed telephone numbers. In general, the more diverse the defined target population, the greater the need for trained interviewer intervention. For example, public opinion polls on welfare reform, government spending, and education are commonly conducted via telephone surveys because most people have opinions on these issues. Compare that to a situation in which the Acura division of Honda America Motor Corporation wants to ask Acura TL 3.2 automobile owners about their satisfaction with the service provided with that car. With this less diverse target population a mail survey would most likely be the method chosen.

Incidence Rate

The term **incidence rate** refers to the percentage of the general population that is the subject of the market research. Sometimes the researcher is interested in a large portion of the general population. In those cases, the incidence rate is high. For example, the incidence rate of auto drivers is very high in the general population. In contrast, if the defined target group is small in relation to the total general population, then the incidence rate is low. The incidence rate of airplane pilots in the general population is much lower than that of car drivers. Normally, the incidence rate is expressed as a percentage. Thus, an incidence rate of 5 percent means that 5 out of 100 members of the general population have the qualifying characteristics sought in a given study.

Complicating the incidence factor is the persistent problem of contacting prospective respondents. For example, a researcher may have taken great care in generating a list of prospective respondents for a telephone survey, but may then discover that a significant number of them have moved, changed their telephone number, or simply been disconnected (with no further information). In this case, the incidence rate will be lower than initially anticipated.

As you may imagine, the incidence rate can have an impact on the cost of conducting survey research. When the incidence rate is very low, the researcher will spend considerably more time and money in locating and gaining the cooperation of enough respondents. In low-incidence situations, personal interview surveys would be used very sparingly—it costs too much to find that rare individual who qualifies. In cases where the defined target group is geographically scattered, a direct mail survey may be the best choice. In other cases, telephone surveys can be very effective as a method of screening. Individuals who pass the telephone screen, for example, could receive a mail survey. In doing survey research, the researcher has the goal to reduce the search time and cost of qualifying prospective respondents while increasing the amount of actual, usable raw data.

Respondent Participation

Respondent participation involves three basic forms: the respondent's ability to participate, the respondent's willingness to participate, and the respondent's knowledge level of the topic or object. **Ability to participate** refers to the ability of both the interviewer and the respondent to get together in a question-and-answer interchange. The ability of a respondent to share his or her thoughts with the researcher or interviewer is an important method-selection consideration. It is very frustrating to the researcher to find a qualified respondent who is willing to respond but for some reason is unable to participate in the study. For example, personal interviews require uninterrupted time. Finding an hour to personally interview a busy executive can present real problems for both the researcher and the executive. Similarly, while they might like to participate in a mall-intercept survey, some shoppers may be in a hurry to pick up children from day care or school. An optometrist may have only five minutes until the next patient. The list of distractions is endless. A method such as a mail survey, in which the time needed to complete the questions does not need to be continuous, may be an attractive alternative in such cases. As the above examples illustrate, the inability-to-participate problem is very common. To get around it, most telephone surveys, for example, allow for the respondent to be called back at a more convenient time. This illustrates the general rule that marketing researchers make every possible effort to respect the respondent's time constraints.

A second component of survey participation is the prospective respondent's **willingness to participate,** that is, the respondent's inclination to share his or her thoughts. Some people will respond simply because they have some interest in the subject. Others will not respond because they are not interested, wish to preserve their privacy, or find the topic objectionable for some reason. In any case, a self-selection process is in effect. The type of survey selected affects the self-selection process. People find it much easier to ignore a mail survey or hang up on a telephone call than to refuse a person in a mall-intercept or personal in-home interview.

Knowledge level is the degree to which the selected respondents feel they have the knowledge or experience to answer questions about the survey topic. The respondents' knowledge level plays a critical role in whether or not they agree to participate. The knowledge-level component also has a direct impact on the quality of the data collected. For example, a large manufacturer of computer software wanted to identify the key factors that small wholesalers use to decide what electronic inventory tracking system (EITS) they would need for improving their just-in-time delivery services to retailers. The manufacturer decided to conduct a telephone survey among a selected group of 100 small wholesalers that did not currently use any type of EITS. In the process of trying to set up the initial interviews, the interviewers noticed that about 80 percent of the responses were "not interested." In probing that response, they discovered that most of the respondents felt they were not familiar enough with the details of EITS to be able to discuss the survey issues. As a general rule, the more detailed the information needed the higher the respondent knowledge level must be to get them to participate in the survey.

Over the years, researchers have developed various strategies to increase participation levels. One frequently used strategy is that of offering some type of incentive. Incentives can include both monetary "gifts" such as a dollar bill and nonmonetary items such as a pen, a coupon to be redeemed for a food product, or entry into a drawing. For example, let's assume the researcher decides to collect data by executing a personal interview design.

Ability to participate The ability of both the interviewer and the respondent to get together in a question-and-answer interchange.

Willingness to participate The respondent's inclination or disposition to share his or her thoughts.

Knowledge level The degree to which the selected respondents feel they have knowledge of or experience with the survey's topics.

A Closer Look at Research

Farmers Speak Their Mind[33]

"Farmers as a group, when compared to the general population, show relatively high levels of cooperation in telephone surveys," says Tony Blum, vice president of Kansas City–based Market Directions, Inc. However, that high response rate may not last. In a recent study of Midwest farmers who had more than 250 acres and had participated in prior research studies, Blum found that farmers have a generally negative and skeptical attitude toward marketing research.

In the study, Blum found that 78 percent of farmers had some level of disagreement with the statement that marketing research serves a useful purpose, and that 44 percent thought answering public opinion polls was a waste of time. A whopping 92 percent said they do not entirely believe that surveys give people the opportunity to provide feedback to manufacturers.

Still, the response rate from farmers is quite high. In the study by Blum, 70 percent of those called participated in the study, which did not include an incentive. The response from farmers is approximately double the nonfarm response rate experienced by Market Directions. Incentives can help the response rate even for farmers. Cenex/ Land O' Lakes Ag Services, of St. Paul, Minnesota,

finds that farmers consider $15 to $20 for a 30 minute interview to be fair compensation. Growthmark, of Bloomington, Illinois, finds that for its usual four-page survey, $5 seems to work well. Blum says that the $20 incentive is the best amount to offer farmers. According to him, 86 percent of farmers participate in his studies with a $20 incentive. The response rate is virtually identical for a $5 and $15 incentive, at 80 percent and 81 percent, respectively. No incentive reduces the response rate to 70 percent.

Maintaining the high response rate from farmers is important to agricultural researchers. Researchers suggest that changing farmers' attitudes regarding the value of marketing research over the long term is the key to maintaining high participation levels. The researchers think that sharing results with farmers, even in a summarized form, may help show the value of research. Companies are urged to follow up with farmers and tell them that the company is making changes based on what they learned in the research. The problem with providing research results to farmers, at least according to one marketing researcher, is that farmers want some meaty results. The research sponsor may not be willing to share the meat.

A strategy to increase the overall response rate might be to offer respondents money, product samples, or T-shirts. Another strategy might be to personally deliver the questionnaire to potential respondents. In survey designs that involve group situations, researchers can use social influences to increase participation. It is important to note that incentive strategies should not be promoted as a "reward" for respondent participation. Rewards can serve as the wrong motivator for people deciding to participate in a survey. In general, the researcher tries to get as much participation as possible to avoid the problems associated with nonresponse bias. Read the nearby Closer Look at Research box for a specific case involving farmers' participation in surveys.

marketing research in action

Determining and Planning the Appropriate Survey Method

The JP Hotel Preferred Guest Card Study

This illustration is designed to integrate the chapter's information on survey research methods with the ongoing example of JP Hotels. The objective is to illustrate the activities a researcher undertakes in deciding which communication mode is appropriate when using survey research methods to collect primary data. These activities normally begin Phase II of the research process (Select the Appropriate Research Design). To enhance understanding of this illustration, it will be helpful to review the information on the JP Hotel Preferred Guest Card study presented in earlier chapters.

Selecting and Planning the Appropriate Survey Method

Initially, the research objectives and data requirements identified in Phase I of the research process play a key role in determining whether an observation, a survey, or an experiment should be used to collect the needed primary data. Previously the researcher, Alex Smith, described the five research objectives of the JP Hotel study as follows:

1. To determine card usage patterns among known JP Hotel Preferred Guest Card holders.

2. To identify and evaluate the privileges associated with the card program and how important the card is as a factor in selecting a hotel for business purposes.

3. To determine business travelers' awareness of the card program.

4. To determine whether or not JP Hotel should charge an annual fee for card membership.

5. To identify profile differences between heavy users, moderate users, light users, and nonusers of the card.

An assessment of these objectives shows that some type of descriptive research study should be conducted. The corresponding data requirements suggest the need for attitudinal, behavioral, and demographic data from the respondents. These research objectives and data requirements led Smith to decide that a survey design would be the most effective approach to collect the data. Now a decision had to be made regarding the most feasible mode for asking the questions and recording responses. In other words, should the survey approach use a person-administered, telephone-administered, or self-administered approach.

While there are many factors to consider, Smith conducted a comparison analysis of the three basic approaches using some of the situational, task, and respondent characteristics displayed in Exhibit 7.12. Smith created an evaluation matrix (see Exhibit 7.13). Using his knowledge of the three alternative approaches and their strengths and weaknesses, he cross-evaluated the survey methods by ranking how well each method would achieve each of the listed factors. His ranking scheme consisted of using 1 to represent "excellent," 2 for "good," 3 for "weak," and N/A for "not applicable." As he did the actual evaluations, his rankings were influenced by such factors as cost and time considerations, the need to use multiattribute scales (see Chapter 12), the difficulty of the question/response process, and the geographic diversity of the defined target population.

EXHIBIT 7.13 Survey Design Selection Factors

Factors	Personal Interviews	Telephone Interviews	Self-Reporting Surveys
Resource budgets			
Need for available dollars	3	2	1
Need for available staff	3	2	1
Total completion time	3	1	2
Data quality			
Completeness	1	3	2
Generalizability	1	2	2
Precision	1	2	2
Difficulty of task			
Amount of thought	3	2	1
Preparation time	3	2	1
Information requirements			
Amount of information	1	3	2
Depth of information	1	3	2
Type of data	1	3	1
Length of survey/interview	1	3	1
Topic sensitivity	3	2	1
Diversity of respondents	1	1	2
Geographic dispersion	3	1	1
Incidence rate	1	1	1
Search/contacting time	3	2	1
Survey participation			
Ability to participate	3	2	2
Willingness to participate	3	2	2
Knowledge level of topics	1	1	1
Overall cost per respondent	3	2	1
Likely response rate	1	2	2
Control of potential errors			
Interviewer errors	3	2	[N/A]
Response errors	2	2	2
Nonresponse errors	1	2	2

The Survey Design Decision

After reviewing the results, Smith determined the appropriate mode for conducting the survey would be a self-reporting one where the selected respondents would read and respond to the survey's questions without the aid of any trained interviewer. How did he arrive at that decision? Initial interpretation of the cross-evaluation suggested that any of the three alternative modes for administering a descriptive survey could be appropriate. There is no one method that stands out as being the best. They all have their own benefits and weaknesses.

In this situation, the final decision was influenced by the fact that the defined target population was 17,000 business travelers spread across the country. The cost and time requirements in using a person-administered design outweighed the potential increased quality.

Given the attitudinal, behavioral, and demographic requirements to fulfill the research objectives, the survey would have to include a significant number of question scales. In addition, some of the question scales would have to use multisensitive scale descriptors to meet the study's information requirements. Consequently, employment of a telephone-administered survey would not be desirable for two reasons. First, questions that use multisensitive scale descriptors are difficult for respondents to complete over the phone because they cannot easily visualize the different scale point alternatives. Second, the respondents are businesspeople who generally will not answer a survey that takes more than 7 to 10 minutes to complete. Given the research objectives and information requirements, any survey would be too long for this group.

In this situation, a self-administered survey would not encounter the same problems associated with either person- or telephone-administered methods. Overall, self-administered surveys are less expensive than the alternatives. Major concerns are low response rates, control over possible nonresponse errors, overall time frame for completing data collection activities, and data quality. Alex Smith was concerned about these weaknesses, but felt that good planning and execution of the processes underlying the self-administered survey method would minimize the weaknesses while still meeting the study's information requirements.

Hands-On Exercise

Assume the role of Alex Smith, research consultant in the JP Hotel Guest Card Study situation. Using your newfound knowledge about various online survey methods, create a new Exhibit 7.13 by adding any two of the computer-assisted or online survey methods discussed in the chapter, then go through and rank the five methods using the same three-point scheme described above. After creating the new ranking, analyze them and answer the following questions:

1. Given the new data structures on your "Survey Design Selection Factors" table, what type of survey design would you now recommend to JP Hotel's management team? Why?

2. Should additional factors be included on your table of factors? If not, why not? If yes, what factors and why?

3. In this new situation, should the management team give final approval for this research project? Why or why not?

Summary of Learning Objectives

■ **Explain the advantages and disadvantages of using quantitative, descriptive survey research designs to collect primary data.**

Some of the main advantages of using survey designs to collect primary data from respondents are the ability to accommodate large sample sizes; generalizability of results; ability to distinguish small differences between diverse sampled groups; ease of administering and recording questions and answers; increased capabilities of using advanced statistical analysis; and identifying latent factors and relationships. In contrast, the main disadvantages of survey research designs tend to focus on potential difficulties of developing accurate survey instruments; inaccuracies in construct and scale measurements; and limits to the depth of the data structures. In addition, researchers can lack control over long time frames and potentially low response rates, among other problems.

■ **Discuss the many types of survey methods available to researchers. Identify and discuss the factors that drive the choice of survey methods.**

Survey methods are generally divided into three generic types. One is the person-administered survey, in which there is significant face-to-face interaction between the interviewer and the respondent. Second is the telephone-administered survey. In these surveys the telephone is used to conduct the question-and-answer exchanges. Computers are now used in many ways in telephone interviews, especially in data recording and telephone-number selection. Third is the self-administered survey. In these surveys, there is little, if any, actual face-to-face contact between the researcher and prospective respondent. The respondent reads the questions and records his or her answers. Most of the emerging technology's survey methods are self-administered, although some, such as virtual reality, will require human intervention.

There are three major factors affecting the choice of survey method: situational characteristics, task characteristics, and respondent characteristics. With situational factors, consideration must be given to such elements as available resources, completion time frame, and data quality requirements. Also, the researcher must consider the overall task requirements and ask questions like "How difficult are the tasks?" "What stimuli will be needed to evoke responses?" "How much information is needed from the respondent?" and "To what extent do the questions deal with sensitive topics?" Finally, researchers must be concerned about the diversity of the prospective respondents, the likely incidence rate, and the degree of survey participation. Maximizing the quantity and quality of data collected while minimizing the cost and time of the survey generally requires the researcher to make trade-offs.

■ **Explain how the electronic revolution is affecting the administration of survey research designs.**

With the increasing advances in telecommunication and computer technologies, numerous new, fast techniques are available to researchers for collecting primary raw data from people. The range of new techniques continues to grow and includes such methods as computer-assisted telephone interviewing methods; fully automated self-administered techniques; and e-mail, fax, and Internet surveys. There is little doubt that the time requirements of collecting data will significantly decrease with these new methods.

■ **Identify and describe the strengths and weaknesses of each type of survey method.**

It is important to remember that all methods have strengths as well as weaknesses. No single method is the best choice under all circumstances. Nor is the information researcher limited to a single method. Innovative combinations of survey methods can produce excellent results, as the strengths of one method can be used to overcome the weaknesses of another.

■ **Identify and explain the types of errors that occur in survey research.**

The researcher needs to evaluate the errors in the research results. All errors are either sampling errors or nonsampling errors. By far the greatest amount of error that can reduce data quality comes from nonsampling error sources. Three major sources of error are respondent error (i.e., nonresponse errors and response biases); measurement and design error (i.e., construct development, scale measurement, and survey instrument design errors); and administrative errors (i.e., data processing, interviewer, and sample design errors). In survey research, systematic errors decrease the quality of the data being collected.

Key Terms and Concepts

Review Questions

1. Identify and discuss the advantages and disadvantages of using quantitative survey research methods to collect primary raw data in marketing research.

2. What are the three critical components for determining data quality? How does achieving data quality differ in person-administered surveys and self-administered surveys?

3. Explain why survey designs that include a trained interviewer are more appropriate than computer-assisted survey designs in situations where the task difficulty and stimuli requirements are extensive.

4. Explain the major differences between in-home interviews and mall-intercept interviews. Make sure you include their advantages and disadvantages.

5. How might measurement and design errors affect respondent errors? Develop three recommendations to help researchers increase the response rates in direct mail and telephone-administered surveys.

6. What possible issues associated with customer behavior and consumption patterns might be extremely sensitive ones to directly question respondents about? How might researchers overcome the difficulties of collecting sensitive data?

7. What is "nonresponse"? Identify four types of nonresponse found in surveys.

8. How does a wireless phone survey differ from CATI and CATS surveys?

9. What are the advantages and disadvantages associated with "online" surveys?

10. How might a faulty problem definition error on the part of the researcher impact the implementation of a mail survey?

Discussion Questions

1. Develop a cross-table of the factors used to select from person-administered, telephone-administered, self-administered, and computer-assisted survey designs. Then discuss the appropriateness of those selection factors across each type of survey design.

2. What impact, if any, will advances in telecommunication and computer technologies have on survey research practices? Support your thoughts.

3. Situation: The regional sales manager for Procter & Gamble interviews its sales representatives in the Midwest and asks them questions about the percentage of their time spent making presentations to new potential customers, talking on the telephone with current customers, working on the computer, and engaging in on-the-job activities. What potential sources of error might be associated with the manager's line of questioning?

4. Revisiting Exhibit 7.2, which describes the different types of sampling and nonsampling errors found in survey research designs, identify five potential sources of error that have direct ethical implications. Write a short report that discusses the ethical issues associated with each type of error source and the strategies that a researcher should implement to resolve each issue.

5. **EXPERIENCE THE INTERNET.** Go to the latest Gallup Poll survey (www.gallup.com) and evaluate the survey design being used. Write a two-page report that points out the design's strengths and weaknesses.

6. What types of research studies lend themselves to using e-mail as the communication method in surveying respondents? What are the advantages and disadvantages of using e-mail surveys?

7. Comment on the ethics of the following situations:
   - A researcher plans to use invisible ink to code his direct mail questionnaires to identify those respondents who return the questionnaire.
   - A telephone interviewer calls at 10:00 P.M. on a Sunday and asks to conduct an interview.
   - A manufacturer purchases 100,000 e-mail addresses from a national e-mail distribution house and plans to e-mail out a short sales promotion under the heading "We Want to Know Your Opinions."

8. Recall from previous chapters the continuing example of the Santa Fe Grill Mexican Restaurant. The owners gained some preliminary insights into customers' attitudes and restaurant patronage behaviors from conducting 50 qualitative in-depth interviews. Now, they believe it is critical to obtain more descriptive detailed attitudinal and behavioral information representative of their larger potential target market of customers within the Dallas/Fort Worth metropolitan area. They decide they need to conduct some type of quantitative-based survey research, but are not sure which research method would be more effective in gathering the necessary data. Their budget is limited to about $5,000 and they need the information within the next 45 days. Using your understanding of the material in this chapter, respond to the following and provide support for your recommendations.
   a. Develop a list of possible information research questions (IRQs) that might be useful in helping the restaurant owners better understand the restaurant aspects that

potential customers like and dislike about Mexican-theme dining experiences, what creates a satisfying dining experience, the media/communication sources people use to gain knowledge of the different types of restaurants available to dine out at, as well as a demographic profile of who these potential customers are.

b. Select one "offline" and one "online" survey research method which you would recommend as feasible methods to conduct a proposed survey that would gather the needed data/information for answering your listed information research questions. Compare and contrast your selected methods based on the strengths and weaknesses of the methods.

c. What general or specific potential systematic errors should the owners be aware of with respect to the two methods that you have recommended above?

d. What particular concerns do these potential errors raise about the accuracy and quality of the data that could be collected using your recommended survey research designs?

e. Based on your responses to the above items, which of the two specific survey research designs would you recommend to the owners and why?

chapter 8

Observation Techniques, Experiments, and Test Markets

Learning Objectives

After reading this chapter, you will be able to

1. Discuss the characteristics, benefits, and weaknesses of observational techniques, and explain how these techniques are used to collect primary data.

2. Describe and explain the importance of and differences between the variables used in experimental research designs.

3. Explain the theoretical importance and impact of internal, external, and construct validity measures in experiments and interpreting functional relationships.

4. Discuss the three major types of experimental designs used in marketing research. Explain the pros and cons of using causal designs as a means of assessing relationship outcomes.

5. Explain what test markets are, the importance and difficulties of executing this type of research design, and how the resulting data structures are used by researchers and marketing practitioners.

Lee Apparel Company: Using Test Marketing to Gauge New-Product Acceptance

The new-product development team at Lee Apparel Company was excited about their recent efforts in coming up with a new apparel line of jeans for females. The design team suggested the company go with the brand name *Riders* because it was a hip, stylish name for the new jeans. Based on past knowledge of launching other apparel lines, the company's marketing team decided to conduct a series of extensive market tests on Riders. After much discussion, a decision was made to test the product design and brand name in five major market areas in the United States. The overall objective of these tests would be to gain greater insights into female purchase decisions, attitudes, motivations, and potential repeat purchase behavior for the new line of jeans. In addition the company was determined to create a complete customer database that would be shared by the manufacturer and all channel members (wholesalers and retailers, alike). Company officials were determined to test and evaluate the entire marketing program for Riders before any decision was made regarding a national launch of the product.

In several test cities, design styles and colors are now being manipulated. The brand name and different advertising strategies are being monitored and evaluated based on customer sales. Even the colors of the product—brown, blue, red, and tan—are being tested for customer reaction. Several different promotional themes and vehicles are being used to evaluate brand name awareness and test product positioning strategies. Point-of-sale coupons and price discounts are being varied across different retail stores as a way to monitor price sensitivity. Operating in conjunction with a battalion of data-collection personnel, Lee Apparel is attempting to determine customer intentions to purchase using different marketing programs for the new jeans apparel line. Based on initial results, company officials are hopeful the test marketing for Riders jeans will be highly successful. In addition to positive customer reaction indicated by early test results, Lee Apparel hopes to create a stronger information sharing process that will enable the company to enjoy a successful product introduction.[2] Make sure you read the Marketing Research in Action at the end of the chapter to discover how the Lee Apparel Company successfully launched its Riders brand of female jeans and created partnerships with retailers.

Value of Experimentation and Test Marketing

As the chapter opening example suggests, a growing area in marketing research is that of test marketing using causal research designs. *Test marketing* consists of controlled field experiments usually conducted in limited market areas on specified market performance indicators. Its main objective is to predict sales, uncover valuable market information, or anticipate adverse consequences of a marketing program for a particular product. With growing popularity, experimental procedures and observational techniques are employed to investigate and collect important cause-effect relationship data regarding new products or improvements of existing products. Many practitioners use test marketing to determine customer attitudes toward new-product ideas, service delivery alternatives, or marketing communication strategies. While qualitative exploratory and descriptive survey studies are extremely effective for collecting primary data in certain situations, they do not necessarily establish causal links between various events. Causal research designs are powerful methods that can provide researchers with the appropriate data to understand why certain events occur. The primary focus of this chapter will be introducing and discussing experimental and test marketing designs. But we begin by discussing observational techniques that can be used with all research designs to collect behavioral data about people and/or marketplace phenomena. We also discuss reliability and validity issues that are important to all research designs.

Overview of Observational Techniques

Observational techniques are *tools* researchers can use to collect primary data about human behavior and marketing phenomena regardless of the nature of research designs (e.g., exploratory, descriptive, causal). The main characteristic of observational techniques is that researchers must rely heavily on their powers of observing rather than actually communicating with people. Basically, the researcher depends on watching and recording what people or objects do in different research situations. Much information about the behavior of people and objects can be observed: *physical actions* (e.g., consumers' shopping patterns or automobile driving habits), *expressive behaviors* (e.g., the tone of voice and facial expressions of respondents during a personal interview), *verbal behavior* (e.g., telemarketing phone conversations), *temporal behavior patterns* (e.g., the amount of time spent online shopping or at a particular Web site), *spatial relationships and locations* (e.g., the number of vehicles that move through a traffic light or movements of people at a theme park), *physical objects* (e.g., which brand-name items are purchased at supermarkets or which make/model SUVs are driven), and so on. These types of data can be used to augment data patterns collected through other research designs by providing complementary evidence concerning individuals' true feelings.

Observation of nonverbal symbols exhibited by people can add much to the researcher's understanding of a given situation. For example, consider the focus groups used by Barnett Bank of Pasco County to examine customers' satisfaction and their behavior toward switching accounts to competitors' banks. The videotapes of the interviews revealed distinct nonverbal communication symbols from the participants' facial expressions and hand gestures that supported the existence of negative feelings and unhappiness when discussing bank switching behavior.

Observation The systematic activities of witnessing and recording the behavioral patterns of objects, people, and events without directly communicating with them.

In marketing research, **observation** refers to the systematic activities of observing and recording the behavioral patterns of objects, people, events, and other phenomena without directly communicating with them. The main reason for using observational techniques is

e X H I B I T 8.1 Conditions for Using Observational Techniques

Condition	Brief Description
Information	Current behavior patterns must be part of the data requirements.
Type of data	Necessary data must be observable.
Time frame	Data patterns must meet repetitiveness, frequency, and predictability factors in a prespecified time frame.
Setting	Behavior must be observable in some public or laboratory setting.

to collect data structures about behavioral patterns. Observational techniques require two elements: a behavior or event that is observable and a system of recording it. Researchers record the behavior patterns by using trained human observers or devices such as videotapes, movie cameras, audiotapes, computers, handwritten notes, or some other tangible recording mechanism. The main weakness of observation techniques is they cannot be used to capture cognitive elements such as attitudes, preferences, beliefs, or emotions.

Appropriate Conditions for Using Observational Techniques

Several conditions are required for the successful use of observation. The research objectives must clearly indicate that some type of event or behavior is to be observed. For the most part, the event or behavior must be repetitive, frequent, and relatively predictable. Finally, the behavior normally should take place in some public setting that enables the researcher to observe the behavior directly. Exhibit 8.1 summarizes these important conditions.

Information Condition

Trying to collect current-behavior data using any other method might lessen the data's accuracy and meaningfulness due to faulty recall by subjects. For example, people might not accurately recall the number of times they zap commercials while watching their favorite one-hour TV program on Monday nights. New technology developed and used by companies like AC Nielsen Media Research can capture commercial zapping behavior among those members of its Nielsen Television Index (NTI) consumer panel groups.

Type-of-Data Condition

If the researcher wants to know why an individual purchased one brand of cereal over the other brands available, observational techniques will not provide the answers. Thus, observation is used only when a respondent's feelings are relatively unimportant to the research objective or believed to be readily inferrable from the behavior. For example, in studying children playing with toys, it is possible to use facial expressions as an indicator of a child's attitudes or preferences toward the toys because children often react with conspicuous physical expressions. However, this type of observation method means the observer must have excellent interpretive skills.

Time-Frame Condition

For observational techniques to be feasible, the behaviors or events being examined need to happen within a relatively short time span. That means they also must be repetitive and frequent. For example, attempting to observe all the activities involved in the process of buying a new home or automobile would not be feasible in terms of data collection costs and time. In turn, behaviors associated with someone purchasing food items in a super-market, people waiting in line inside a bank, or children watching a TV program could lend themselves to observation techniques.

Setting Condition

Activities are limited to those the investigator can readily observe firsthand or through a device such as a video camera. Normally, activities such as private worshiping or using in-home products (e.g., products used when cooking, turning up and down air-conditioning controls, or washing clothes) are not readily observable.

It is important to recognize that all four conditions for using observational techniques apply to those situations involving *current* events. They do not hold for situations in which researchers are interested in collecting data on past events, since it is impossible to observe those events firsthand. Some experts suggest that indirect observational techniques can be used to accurately infer past behaviors or events. What researchers normally observe in those situations is some type of artifact (e.g., a video- or audiotape, a written transcript).[3] These artifacts are often like secondary data. The main emphasis would be on interpreting the reported outcomes and making preliminary inductive statements about the actual behavior.

Unique Characteristics of Observational Techniques

There are four general characteristics of observational techniques. Depending on the re-searcher's need for (1) directness, (2) subjects' awareness, (3) structure, and (4) a specific type of observing/recording mechanism, he or she can choose from a number of ways to observe events and record primary data. These characteristics directly influence the frame-work for conducting the observations. With good designs, researchers can eliminate, or at least control for, methodological problems that could prevent the gathering of consistent and generalizable data. See Exhibit 8.2.

ǝXHIBIT **8.2** **Unique Characteristics of Observation Research Methods**	
Characteristic	**Description**
Directness of observation	The degree to which the researcher or trained observer actually observes the behavior/event as it occurs. Researchers can use either direct or indirect observation techniques.
Subjects' awareness of being observed	The degree to which subjects consciously know their behavior is being observed and recorded. Researchers can use either disguised or undisguised observation techniques.
Structuredness of observation	The degree to which the behavior, activities, or events to be observed are specifically known to the researcher prior to doing the observations. Structured and unstructured techniques can be used to collect primary behavioral data.
Type of observing mechanism	How the behavior activities or events will be observed and recorded. Researchers have the option either of using a trained human observer or some type of mechanical or electronic device.

Directness of Observation

Direct observation   The process of observing actual behaviors or events and recording them as they occur.

Direct observation is the process of observing actual behavioral activities or events and recording them as they occur.[4] Direct observation uses a human being, rather than a mechanical device, for observing and recording actual behaviors. For example, if researchers were interested in conducting a field experiment to find out how often people read tabloid magazines while waiting to check out at a supermarket, they could use any of several different direct observation techniques. In contrast, some experts believe that indirect observation techniques can be used to capture subjects' past behaviors in special situations.[5] **Indirect observation** focuses on directly observing the artifacts that represent specific behaviors from some earlier time. It can be easily argued that this direct observing of artifacts of past human behavior is really nothing more than a trained investigator interpreting a form of secondary data. While indirect observation might allow a researcher some insights into past behaviors, those insights should be viewed as tenuous, at best. For example, management of Tech Data, a company that sells computer systems nationwide, can review and interpret the company's telephone logs to find out how many long-distance telephone calls its sales department made during the previous month. After interpreting the logs, management might make general inferences concerning the impact of cold-calling behaviors of highly productive salespeople compared to less productive salespeople. Secondary sources that record past behavior are referred to as archives, physical audits, or traces.[6] These types of artifacts represent tangible evidence of some past event. For example, a retail chain looking to expand its operations to new locations might directly observe the amount of graffiti on existing buildings around proposed locations to estimate the potential crime factor in those areas.

Indirect observation   The process of directly observing the recorded artifacts of past behaviors.

Subjects' Awareness of Being Observed

This characteristic refers to the degree to which subjects consciously know their behavior is being observed and recorded. When the subjects are completely unaware they are being observed, the observation method is termed **disguised observation.** A popular and easy-to-understand example of disguised observation is the "mystery shopper" technique used by many retailers.[7] A retailer such as Wal-Mart might hire a research firm to send in observers disguised as ordinary shoppers to observe how well the stores' employees and staff interact with customers. The observers might look for interpersonal behavior that would demonstrate attributes like friendliness, courtesy, helpfulness, and store/product knowledge. The resulting data can aid Wal-Mart's management in determining how its employees' interpersonal skills can enhance the customers' overall shopping experience. Wal-Mart's management can use other methods (e.g., one-way mirrors and hidden cameras) to prevent its employees from finding out they are being observed. Disguised observations are used because when people know they are being watched, they naturally tend to modify their normal behavior. The resulting behavior would therefore be atypical. For example, how would a sales representative for Wal-Mart act if told she or he was going to be watched for the next several hours? Most likely the representative would be on best behavior for that time period.

Disguised observation   A data collection technique where the subjects of interest are completely unaware that they are being observed.

New consumer right-to-privacy legislation may limit the use of disguised observing techniques. These laws restrict the conditions for which disguised techniques are appropriate by requiring the approval of the subject. For example, 22 states currently have "stalking" laws while another 16 states have pending laws that make it a crime to track people unknowingly.

Researchers may, however, face situations in which it is impossible to keep the subjects from knowing they are being observed, for example, observing activities such as the interpersonal behavior of a new waiter or waitress with customers at a restaurant like T.G.I.F. in Washington, D.C., or textbook sales representatives' behavior with faculty members on sales calls. Similarly, AC Nielsen Media Research would find it difficult to use its

Undisguised observation
The data recording method where the subjects are aware that they are being watched.

audiometers on in-home TV sets without the subjects' knowledge. Whenever subjects are aware they are being watched, the process is termed **undisguised observation.** As a general practice, the researcher should minimize the presence of the observer to avoid the possibility of atypical behavior by subjects.

Structure of Observation

Structured observation
A method of recording specifically known behaviors and events.

This characteristic refers to the degree to which the behaviors or events are specifically known to the researcher prior to the observation. When a researcher knows specifically which behaviors or events are to be recorded, a **structured observation** technique is most appropriate. In these situations, the trained observer ignores all other behaviors. Researchers use some type of checklist or standardized recording form to help the observer restrict his or her attention to just those prespecified behaviors or events. For example, the produce manager at a local Safeway supermarket is deciding whether to prepackage the tomatoes or display them individually, because he is concerned about the extent to which customers handle and squeeze the tomatoes in selecting which ones to buy. Using a structured observation approach, he assigns a store employee to hang out in the produce department and observe 100 customers as they select tomatoes. The employee simply focuses on the following behaviors: number of times individual tomatoes are picked up and handled; number of times prepackaged tomatoes are picked up and handled; and any noticeable squeezing of individual and prepackaged tomatoes. The tallied results show that 75 percent of the customers observed picked up and handled the individual tomatoes, while only 35 percent picked up and handled the prepackaged ones. Also, 55 percent of those observed actually squeezed the individual tomatoes, while only 40 percent did the same to the prepackaged ones. Do these numbers justify prepackaging? Even though individual tomatoes got handled and squeezed more frequently, the produce manager feels uncomfortable going to the store manager to suggest that all tomatoes be prepackaged to reduce spoilage. Now think about what other behaviors should have been recorded.

Unstructured observation
The data recording format that does not place any restrictions on the observer regarding what behaviors or events should be recorded.

In contrast, **unstructured observation** formats place no restrictions on the observer regarding what should be recorded. Ideally, all events would be observed and recorded. When an unstructured technique is used, what usually happens is researchers brief the trained observers on the research objectives and information requirements and then allow them to use their own discretion in determining what behaviors are actually recorded. For example, the director of parks and recreation in a town or city wants to develop a proposal for renovating several of the city's aging parks. Not sure what type of equipment should be included in the renovations, he sends out two park supervisors to observe people using the facilities at several of the city's most popular parks. The data collected could be useful not only in redesigning the aging parks but also in providing ideas about how to make the parks safer for people.

Type of Observing Mechanism

Human observation
Data collection by a researcher or trained observer who records text, subjects' actions, and behaviors.

This characteristic relates to how the behaviors or events will be observed. The researcher can choose between human observers and mechanical or electronic devices. With **human observation,** the observer is either a person hired and trained by the researcher or is a member of the research team. To be effective, the observer must have a good understanding of the research objectives and strong observation and subjective interpretive skills. For example, the professor of a marketing research course can use observation skills to capture not only students' classroom behavior but also nonverbal communication symbols exhibited by students during class (e.g., facial expressions, body postures, movement in chairs, hand gestures), which allows him or her to determine, in real time, if students are paying attention to what is being discussed, when students become confused about a concept, or if boredom begins to set in.

Mechanical/electronic observation Data collection using some type of mechanical or electronic device to capture human behavior, events, or marketing phenomena.

In many situations the use of a mechanical or electronic device is more suitable than employing a person in collecting the primary data. **Mechanical/electronic observation** is the use of some type of mechanical or electronic device (videotape camera, traffic counter, optical scanner, eye tracking monitor, pupilometer, audio voice pitch analyzer, psychogalvanometer, to name a few) to capture human behavior, events, or marketing phenomena. Such devices may reduce the cost and improve the flexibility, accuracy, or other functions in the data collection process. For example, when the Department of Transportation (DOT) conducts a traffic-flow study, air pressure lines are laid across the road and connected to a counter box that is activated every time a vehicle's tires roll over the lines. Although the data will be limited to the number of vehicles passing by within a specified time span, this method is less costly and more accurate than using human observers to record traffic flows. Other examples of situations where mechanical/electronic observation would be appropriate include using security cameras at ATM locations to detect problems that customers might have in operating the ATM, using optical scanners and bar-code technology (e.g., universal product code [UPC]) to count, in real time, the number and types of products purchased at a retail establishment, and using turnstile tick-o-meters to count the number of fans at major sporting or entertainment events.

With advances in technology, telecommunications, and computer hardware and software, mechanical/electronic observation techniques are rapidly becoming very useful and cost-effective for monitoring human behaviors and marketing phenomena.[8] For example, AC Nielsen recently upgraded its Television Index (NTI) system in the United States by integrating its People Meter technology into the NTI system. The People Meter is a microwave-based, computerized television rating system that replaces the old passive meters and handwritten diary system with state-of-the-art electronic measuring. Using AC Nielsen's TV household panel members, when the TV is turned on, a simple question mark symbol appears on the screen to remind the viewers to indicate who is watching the program. Using a handheld electronic device similar to the TV's remote control, the viewer(s) record who is watching. Another device attached to the TV automatically sends prespecified information (e.g., viewer's age, sex, program tuned in to, time of program) to AC Nielsen's computers. These data are used by AC Nielsen to generate overnight ratings for shows as well as demographic profiles.

Another technology-driven device is the new software used to monitor people's interactive behavior with Internet Web sites. Companies like Itracks, FocusVision Worldwide, Inc., HarrisInteractive, and Burke have pioneered developments in new tracking software used to monitor people's interactive Web site behavior and track popularity of participating Web sites and online Internet providers (e.g., America Online, Yahoo, MSN). This type of tracking software is installed on participating consumers' personal computers and allows for tracking Web sites consisting of multiple pages, page by page, as well as the paths or sequence of pages visitors follow.

Scanner-based panel A group of participating households which have a unique bar-coded card as an identification characteristic for inclusion in the research study.

Advances in scanner-based technology are quickly replacing traditional consumer purchasing diary methods. In brief, a **scanner-based panel** is made up of a group of participating households that are assigned a unique bar-coded card that is presented to the checkout clerk at the register. The household's code number is matched with information obtained from previous scanner transactions. The system enables the researcher to observe and build a purchase behavior database on each household. More recent technology advances enable researchers to combine these offline tracking systems with online-generated demographic and psychographic information databases of the households, which provide more complete customer profiles. Scanner-based observation data provide marketers with week-by-week information on how products are doing in individual stores and track sales against price changes and local ads or promotion activities.

Techniques Used in Measuring Physiological Actions and Reactions

For years, researchers have used mechanical observations to evaluate consumers' physical and physiological reactions to various stimuli such as ad copy, packaging, and new products. These techniques are used when the researcher is interested in recording actions and reactions the subjects are unaware of or when subjects are unwilling to provide honest responses to the effects of the stimulus being studied. Traditionally, there are four categories of mechanical observation devices used to measure physiological reactions: voice pitch analyzers, pupilometers, eye tracking monitors, and psychogalvanometers.

Voice pitch analyzer A computer system that measures emotional responses by changes in the subject's voice.

The **voice pitch analyzer** is a computer system that measures emotional responses by changes in the subject's voice. This technique uses sophisticated audio-adapted computers to detect abnormal frequencies in the subject's voice caused by changes in the person's autonomic nervous system. It is similar to a lie detector test, but the subject is not hooked up to a lot of wires. Computerized analysis compares the subject's voice pitch patterns during a warm-up session (benchmarked as the normal range) to those patterns obtained from the recorded verbal responses to a given stimulus (e.g., a TV commercial).

Pupilometer A mechanical instrument that observes and records changes in the diameter of a subject's pupils.

The **pupilometer** mechanically observes and records changes in the diameter of a subject's pupils. The subject is instructed to view a screen on which the stimulus is projected. As the distance and brightness of the stimulus to the subject's eyes are held constant, changes in pupil sizes are recorded and are interpreted as some type of unobservable cognitive activity. The assumption underlying the use of a pupilometer is the belief that increases in pupil size within a controlled environment reflect a positive attitude or interest in the stimulus.

Eye tracking monitor A mechanical device that observes and records a person's unconscious eye movements.

The **eye tracking monitor** is a device that observes and records a person's unconscious eye movements. Invisible infrared light beams record the subject's eye movements while reading or viewing the stimulus (e.g., a magazine ad, TV commercial, package design) and another video camera records what part of the given stimulus is being viewed at the movement. The two databases are overlaid and the system can determine what parts of the stimulus were seen and which components were overlooked. In advertising, this type of data can provide insights to possible points of interest and impacts to selling points.

Psychogalvanometer An electronic instrument that measures involuntary changes in the electronic resistance of a subject's skin; also referred to as the galvanic skin response (GSR).

Finally, the **psychogalvanometer** measures involuntary changes in the electronic resistance of a subject's skin, referred to as the galvanic skin response (GSR). This mechanical observation technique indicates when the person's emotional arousal or tension level changes toward the stimulus, and these changes are assumed to be created by the presence of the stimulus.

While all these mechanical observation techniques are interesting, they are based on the unproven assumption that physiological actions and reactions are predictors of people's thoughts or emotions. There is no theoretical consensus this assumption is valid. Moreover, the accuracy of the measurements obtained from these techniques is questionable, and the technology needed is expensive. In addition, external validity remains an issue because use of these types of physiological observation requires that subjects be brought into controlled artificial laboratory environments, which do not represent reality.

Selecting the Appropriate Observation Method

To determine the most appropriate type of observation method for collecting primary data, researchers must integrate their knowledge and understanding of the research objectives, information requirements, conditions for using observations, and characteristics of observation methods.

The first step in determining the right observation method is for the researcher to understand the information requirements and consider how that information will be used later on. Without this understanding, the task of deciding a technique's appropriateness becomes significantly more difficult. The researcher must answer the following questions prior to method selection:

1. What types of behavior are pertinent to the research problem?

2. How simple or complex are the behaviors?

3. How much detail of the behavior needs to be recorded?

4. What is the most appropriate setting (natural or contrived) for the behavior?

The second step involves integrating the researcher's knowledge of the conditions for observing behavior and the characteristics of observation methods in order to develop an objective method of observing and recording the specified behavior. The issues that must be addressed include the following:

1. How complex is the required public setting?

2. Is it available for observing the specified behaviors or events?

3. To what extent are the desired behaviors or events repetitious and frequently exhibited?

4. What degrees of directness and structure should be associated with observing the behaviors or events?

5. How aware should the subjects be that they and their behaviors are being observed?

6. Are the observable behaviors or events complex enough to require the use of a mechanical/electronic device for observing the behavior? If so, which specific method would be most appropriate?

The last step focuses on the cost, flexibility, accuracy, efficiency, and objectivity factors associated with observational techniques, as well as the ethical issues. Prior to implementing any observation method, the researcher must evaluate the proposed method's ability to accurately observe and record the specified behavior. The costs—time, money, manpower—involved must be determined and compared to the expected efficiency of collecting the data based in part on the number of subjects needed in the investigation. In addition, the researcher must consider the possible ethical issues that might exist with the proposed observation method. The Ethics box discusses ethical issues associated with observation methods.

The Benefits and Limitations of Observational Techniques

Observational data collection techniques have several specific strengths and weaknesses (see Exhibit 8.3). Probably the most obvious benefit is that observational techniques allow for very accurate gathering of consumers' actual behavior patterns or events rather than reported activities. This is especially true in situations where the subjects are observed in a natural public setting using a disguised technique. In situations where the behaviors or events are complex and unstructured, mechanical/electronic observation techniques are particularly useful. In addition, observation techniques can help in reducing potential subject recall error, response bias, and refusal to participate, as well as in reducing potential observer errors. In many situations, observation techniques enable the researcher to gather and record in-depth details about current behavior or events. Usually, the data can be collected in less time and at a lower cost than through other types of collection procedures.

Observation techniques have several limitations. One of the ongoing shortcomings of observation techniques is they produce data that are difficult to generalize beyond those test

eTHICS

Subjects' Unawareness Can Raise Many Questions

Subjects' awareness of observation methods raises some ethical questions worth noting. When using observations to collect primary behavior data, should the subjects be informed that they are being observed? If so, what changes in their natural behavior might occur? Remember, the researcher wants to capture the subjects' natural behavior as it actually occurs and relates to the specified situation. Subjects being observed might feel uncomfortable about their true behavior or actions and try to behave in a more socially acceptable manner. For example, a marketing professor at a university is told by his department chair that as part of his annual performance review, an outside observer will be in class Monday to observe the professor's teaching style. How likely will the professor be to modify his "normal" classroom

behavior for that Monday's class session to make doubly sure his effectiveness meets or exceeds the standards? Would you behave in a more socially acceptable manner if you knew someone was going to be observing you? In disguised observations, the researcher uses some degree of deceit in order to observe behavior without the subjects' knowledge. In this situation, the ethical questions focus on the subjects' right to privacy. Are there certain public or private behaviors that are protected by U.S. law? Is spying on people an acceptable norm of our society? These are tough but pertinent questions that a researcher must address prior to conducting research with observational techniques, and there are no easy, clear-cut answers. In part, ethical issues concerning the use of disguised techniques might be related to whether or not the investigated behaviors are legal versus illegal.

subjects who were actually observed. Typically, observation methods are used in research projects that focus on a small number of subjects (between 5 and 60) under unique or special circumstances, thus reducing the representativeness of larger groups of people.[9] Given the nature of observation methods, it is extremely difficult for the researcher to logically explain why the observed behaviors or events took place. This inability to interrogate the subjects on their attitudes, motives, feelings, and other nonobservable factors means that any resulting insights into the behavior should be considered subjective. Understanding of the observed behavior is therefore limited to "educated guesses."

In those situations where the natural public setting includes a large number of subjects, it is difficult even for trained observers to note all the activities occurring at the same time. While an observer is focused on the behavior of one particular subject, she or he is likely to completely miss that of the other subjects in the setting during that same time frame. Disguised observation situations pose an additional limitation in that human observers cannot instantaneously or automatically record the behavior activities as they occur. There is

eXHIBIT 8.3 Benefits and Limitations of Observation Techniques

Major Benefits of Observation	Limitations of Observation
Accuracy of actual behavior	Lack of generalizability of data
Reduction of confounding factors	Inability of explaining behaviors or events
Detail of the behavioral data	Complexity of setting and recording of behavior(s) or events

some lag time between observing the behavior or event and recording what was observed. With this natural lag time, there is the possibility of faulty recall on the part of the observer. One way to overcome these potential limitations is that the observations should be made with the appropriate mechanical/electronic device whenever possible.

The Nature of Experimentation

Variable Any observable and measurable element (or attribute) of an item or event.

Marketing research requires the measurement of variables. **Variables** are the observable and measurable elements (or attributes) of an item or an event. They are the qualities the researcher specifies, studies, and draws conclusions about. They can vary in different situations and at different times. To illustrate this concept, let's take the vehicle you are currently driving. Your automobile or truck is really a composite of many different attributes. The color, the make and model, the number of cylinders, the miles per gallon, and the price are all variables. Furthermore, different automobiles and trucks possess different variables, and any one vehicle has one given set of variables at any given time. Whenever an object, idea, or event is described, every element by which it could be observed and measured can be considered a variable, including where it is, how it is used, and what surrounds it.

When conducting an experiment, the researcher attempts to identify the relationships among different variables. Let's consider, for example, the following research question: "How long does it take a customer to place and receive an order from the drive-through at a Wendy's fast-food restaurant?" The time it takes to receive a food order is a variable that can be measured quantitatively. That is to say, the different values of the time variable are determined by some method of measurement. But how long it takes a particular customer to receive a food order is complicated by a number of other variables. For instance, what if there were 10 cars waiting in line, or it was 12:00 noon, or it was raining? Additionally, such factors as the number of drive-up windows, the training level of order takers, and the number of patrons waiting are all variables. Consequently, all of these variables can have some effect on the time variable.

Functional relationship An observable and measurable systematic change in one variable as another variable changes.

In turn, the make of the car the person is driving, the number of brothers or sisters he has, and the quantity of food he orders are also variables. But the first two variables are unlikely to have much effect on order time. However, there is a relationship between the quantity of the order and the waiting time, because the more items in the order, the longer it takes to prepare. If it is true that the quantity of food ordered increases one's wait at a drive-through, the researcher can say that there is a **functional relationship** between food quantity ordered and waiting time. As such, it can be concluded that waiting time at a fast-food drive-through is a function of the amount of food being ordered. In causal research designs that use experimental procedures, the researcher investigates the functional relationships between variables. The focus is on investigating the systematic change in one variable as another variable changes. The Closer Look at Research box illustrates a version of this called BehaviorScan.

Types of Variables Used in Experimental Designs

In using experimental designs, researchers must be especially careful to confirm that the relationships they find between the variables being investigated actually do exist. Attempts must be made to hold constant the influence of extraneous variables so that accurate measures can be made of the variables under investigation. When designing causal research experiments, researchers must understand the four types of variables that are critical in the design process: independent, dependent, control, and extraneous. See Exhibit 8.4.

A Closer Look at Research

BehaviorScan: A Device Used for Testing New Products and Marketing Programs

BehaviorScan is a one-of-a-kind, in-market laboratory for testing new products and marketing programs under tightly controlled yet real-world conditions. The impact of the test program can be measured in terms of both total store sales and household-level purchasing behavior. BehaviorScan offers the only targetable TV service in the nation, capable of delivering different ad copy and/or media weight to two or three selected groups of households within a given market. In seven markets around the United States, Information Resources Inc. (IRI), the company providing BehaviorScan, has facilities optimally designed for test marketing. IRI handles everything from retail sell-in to product stocking and promotion execution to data collection and analysis. IRI can control the

distribution, price, shelf placement, trade, consumer promotion, and TV advertising for each product in a test. This ability to control all the variables enables highly accurate evaluation of the test variable.

In each BehaviorScan market, a large, ongoing household panel is maintained, making it possible to track household purchasing behaviors on an item-by-item level over time. Panel data collection is passive: members need only present their "Shopper's Hotline ID" card at checkout in participating retailers. Scanner sales data are collected on an ongoing basis from groceries, drugstores, and mass merchandisers. In-store promotion activity in most categories is monitored as well as documented pricing, displays, and features by item. Data from other outlets, such as convenience stores or hardware stores, can be collected on a custom basis. More details on BehaviorScan can be obtained at www.infores.com.

Independent variables
Variables whose values are directly manipulated by the researcher.

Independent variables are those whose values are directly manipulated by the researcher in an experiment. The researcher is interested in identifying functional relationships between independent and dependent variables. In many market research experiments, marketing mix variables such as price levels, product/package designs, distribution channel systems, and advertising themes are treated as independent variables. Let's say, for example, that

еXHIBIT 8.4 Types of Variables Used in Experimental Research Designs

Type of Variable	Comments
Independent variable	Also called predictor or treatment variable (X). An attribute or element of an object, idea, or event whose values are directly manipulated by the researcher. The independent variable is assumed to be the causal factor of a functional relationship with a dependent variable.
Dependent variable	Also called criterion variable (Y). An observable attribute or element that is the outcome on specified test subjects that is derived from manipulating the independent variable(s).
Control variables	Variables the researcher controls so they do not affect the functional relationship between the independent and dependent variables included in the experiment.
Extraneous variables	Uncontrollable variables that should average out over a series of experiments. If not accounted for, they can have a confounding impact on the dependent variable measures that could weaken or invalidate the results of an experiment.

Procter & Gamble (P&G) is interested in determining the relationship between several new package designs for its Tide brand of laundry detergent and Tide's unit sales. Using experimental design procedures, the researchers could observe customers' purchasing of the product on four different occasions. On each occasion, the researchers can change the package design from, say, round to square, to rectangular, to oval. Every time the package design is changed, sales can be measured. Since the researchers directly manipulated it, package design serves as the independent variable.

Dependent variables are measures of outcome that occur during the experiment. They also are referred to as measures of change in the conditions that exist after the experiment is completed. These variables may include such market performance factors as unit sales, profit levels, and market shares. While values of independent variables are assigned before the experiment begins, this is not possible with dependent variables. Dependent variables are attributes or elements that are affected by the process of the experiment. Their specific outcome values cannot be measured before the experiment begins. In the P&G package design example, the dependent variable is Tide's unit sales. This variable is measured under each manipulation of the package design. If the researchers want to state the results in terms of a functional relationship, they would say that Tide's unit sales (the dependent variable) is a function of package design (the independent variable).

Control variables are the conditions or elements that make the research design a true experiment. These are variables that the researcher controls, or does not allow to vary freely or systematically with independent variables. Thus, the average value of a control variable or its impact should not change as the independent variable is manipulated. Researchers must design the experiment so that control variables cannot systematically affect the relationship between the independent and dependent variables. Control variables can present a major problem in using experimental designs to investigate hypothesized functional relationships. For example, if P&G wants to investigate the true relationship between Tide's unit sales and package design alternatives, the researchers do not want any other variables to influence the measure of unit sales. They would want to make sure the conditions surrounding Tide's unit sales (the dependent variable) are as similar as possible for each of the package design manipulations (the independent variable). For example, the customers should (1) shop at the same store during each package design manipulation; (2) shop at the same time of day with the same amount of store crowding; and (3) shop on successive days without being exposed to any advertised message for Tide. In addition, the price and shelf location of Tide should remain the same on all successive package design manipulations. This points to the problem that there are so many possible influences on Tide's unit sales that the researchers cannot possibly control all of them. The researchers must, however, control as many as they can.

Extraneous variables, such as changes in temperature, mood, health, or even physical conditions of the store, to name a few, cannot be controlled by the researchers. These types of variables may average out over the different manipulations of the independent variables, and thus not have systematic influences on the dependent variable. But they also may weaken the results of the experiment. One method P&G researchers could use to reduce the effects of extraneous variables is to randomize the same manipulation condition of the package design across a number of customers and then measure unit sales. This procedure would have to be accomplished across all of the package design manipulations until a significant number of customers were measured for Tide unit sales under each manipulation. This procedure is referred to as **complete randomization** of subjects. The desired outcome is that the influence of the extraneous variables will average out over all manipulations of the independent variable. While the measured results under these conditions might not be very precise for any individual test subject, they should be precise enough to show a fairly accurate relationship between the independent and dependent variables.

Dependent variables
Measures of effect or outcome that occur during the experiment, or measures of change in the conditions that exist after the experiment is completed.

Control variables Variables that the researcher does not allow to vary freely or systematically with independent variables; control variables should not change as the independent variable is manipulated.

Extraneous variables
Variables that cannot be controlled by researchers but that should average out over different trials and thus not systematically affect the results of the experiment.

Complete randomization
The procedure whereby many subjects are assigned to different experimental treatment conditions, resulting in each group averaging out any systematic effect on the investigated functional relationship between the independent and dependent variables.

The Role of Theory in Experimental Designs

Theory A large body of interconnected propositions about how some portion of a certain phenomenon operates.

From an experimental design perspective, **theory** is a large body of interconnected propositions about how some portion of a phenomenon operates. Theory underpins the development of hypotheses about relationships. As such, hypotheses are smaller versions of theories. **Experimental research** is primarily a hypothesis-testing method and can therefore be referred to as **deductive research.** Researchers derive a hypothesis from a theory, design an experiment, and gather data to test the hypothesis. There are situations when researchers use causal designs to generate hypotheses in order to create new theories or extend existing theories about a phenomenon. These are referred to as **inductive research.** In practice, researchers often use both deductive and inductive design methods. A researcher may begin an investigation using causal research procedures to test some hypotheses that focus on the cause-effect relationships between variables, but then develop new hypotheses when he sees the data results. Existing theoretical insights can help a researcher in identifying the critical independent variables that might bring about changes in dependent variables. It is important to understand that experimental and other causal research designs are most appropriate when the researcher wants to find out why certain events occur and why they happen under certain conditions and not others. Identifying and being able to explain cause-effect relationships enables marketing researchers to be in a position to make reasonable predictions about marketing phenomena.

Experimental research An empirical investigation that tests for hypothesized relationships between dependent variables and manipulated independent variables.

Deductive research Experimental investigations that are undertaken to test hypothesized relationships.

Inductive research An investigation that uses causal design procedures to generate and test hypotheses that creates new theories or extends existing theories.

Validity Concerns with Experimental Research Designs

To better understand causal research designs, we first must examine validity issues that directly affect these designs. Extraneous variables are numerous and difficult to control when using causal designs for testing hypothesized relationships. Their presence may result in contamination of the functional relationship. This contamination clouds the researcher's ability to conclusively determine whether the results of the experiment are valid. **Validity** refers to the extent to which the conclusions drawn from the experiment are true. In other words, do the differences in the dependent variable found through experimental manipulations of the independent variables really reflect a cause-effect relationship? While there are many ways to classify the validity of causal research designs, we will discuss three: *internal* validity, *external* validity, and *construct* validity.

Validity The extent to which the conclusions drawn from the experiment are true.

Internal Validity

Internal validity The extent to which the research design accurately identifies causal relationships.

Internal validity refers to the extent to which the research design accurately identifies causal relationships. In other words, internal validity exists when the researcher can rule out other explanations for the observed conclusions about the functional relationship. For example, in an experiment on the effects of electricity, if you shock someone (experimental treatment) and he jumps (observed effect), and he jumps only because of the shock and for no other reason, then internal validity exists.

Why is establishing internal validity of causal research designs important to researchers? The following example illustrates the answer. Let's say a small bakery in White Water, Wisconsin, wanted to know whether or not putting additional frosting on its new cakes would cause customers to like the cakes better. Using an experimental design, it tested the hypothesis that its customers liked additional frosting on their cakes. As the amount of frosting was being manipulated, the bakery discovered the additional frosting allowed the cakes to stay more moist. Consequently, it might have been the moistness and not the frosting that caused the customers' positive reaction to the new cakes. In an attempt to assess internal validity,

EXHIBIT 8.5   Validity Types and Threats to Validity[11]

THREATS TO INTERNAL VALIDITY

History	When extraneous factors that enter the experiment process between the first and later manipulations affect measures of the dependent variable.
Maturation	Changes in the dependent variable based on the natural function of time and not attributed to any specific event.
Testing	When learned understanding gained from the first treatment and measures of the dependent variable distort future treatments and measurement activities.
Instrumentation	Contamination from changes in measurement processes, observation techniques, and/or measuring instruments.
Selection bias	Contamination created by inappropriate selection and/or assignment processes of test subjects to experimental treatment groups.
Statistical regression	Contamination created when experimental groups are selected on the basis of their extreme responses or scores.
Mortality	Contamination due to changing the composition of the test subjects in the experiment.
Ambiguity	Contamination from unclear determination of cause-effect relationship.

THREATS TO EXTERNAL VALIDITY

Treatment vs. treatment	When test subjects in different treatment groups are exposed to different amounts of manipulations.
Treatment vs. testing	When the premeasurement process sensitizes test subjects to respond in an abnormal manner to treatment manipulations.
Treatment vs. selection	Generalizing the results to other categories of people beyond those types used in the experiment.
Treatment vs. setting	Generalizing the results to other environments beyond the one used in the experiment.
Treatment vs. history	Using the existing functional relationship to predict future phenomenon outcomes.

THREATS TO CONSTRUCT VALIDITY

Inadequate preoperationalization of variables	Contamination due to inadequate understanding of the complete makeup of the independent and preoperationalization dependent variables included in the experimental design.
Mono-operation bias	Contamination created by using only one method to measure the outcomes of the dependent variable.
Mono-method bias	Contamination due to assessing multiattribute treatment manipulations (independent variables) using single-item measuring instruments.
Hypothesis-guessing	Contamination by test subjects believing they know the desired functional relationship prior to the manipulation treatment.
Evaluation apprehension	Contamination caused by test subjects being fearful that their actions or responses will become known to others.
Demand characteristics	Contamination created by test subjects trying to guess the true purpose behind the experiment, thus giving abnormal socially acceptable responses or behaviors.
Diffusion of treatment	Contamination due to test subjects discussing the treatment and measurement activities with individuals that have not received the treatment.

control groups were established consisting of customers who were not exposed to the treatment (extra frosting, original moistness), but all other conditions (original moistness) were kept the same.[10] Adding the control group to the experimental design reduced the possibility that the observed effect of the new cakes was caused by something other than the treatment. In this case, if it was the frosting, then the treated group should like the new cake more than the control group. But if it was the moistness, then both groups would like the new cake equally.

Exhibit 8.5 displays the types of threats that can negatively affect internal, external, and construct validities associated with causal research designs. The latter two will be discussed in the next sections. Here we will discuss the threats to internal validity. History threats would involve events that occur between the first measurement of the dependent variable and the second measurement. If the objective of the manipulation was to measure changes in a person's attitude about political integrity (dependent variable) resulting from a political history course, the results could be strongly affected if a major political scandal occurred between the first and second manipulation treatments (i.e, while the person was taking the political history course).

Without a doubt, our attitudes and behaviors change as we grow older, and these changes can also represent a maturation threat to internal validity. The threat of testing refers to the second administration of the treatment where the experience with the first administration may well affect scores on the second administration. Changes in observers' attitudes, reduced accuracy of scorers, or changed administration techniques are all examples of the instrumentation threat to internal validity.

When strict random assignment to treatment and control groups is not followed, then selection bias resulting in noncomparable groups could occur, threatening internal validity. Mortality involves the loss of subjects from groups due to natural causes, thereby creating groups of subjects that are no longer comparable. Ambiguity of causal direction may also be a problem. For instance, do higher family incomes result from higher education levels, or do higher income levels allow higher education levels? Such ambiguities reduce the researcher's ability to differentiate between cause and effect.

Statistical regression is where human beings score differently on each trial in an experiment, with the recorded scores regressing toward the true population mean. In other words, the errors balance out. In those cases where subjects are selected for particular groups based on extreme pretreatment responses, the observed posttreatment measures will be even more biased. The primary weapon against threats to internal validity is random selection of subjects from a heterogeneous target population and then random assignment to treatment groups. This is considered standard practice in experimental research studies.

External Validity

External validity The extent to which a causal relationship found in a study can be expected to be true for the entire target population.

External validity refers to the extent to which a causal relationship found in a study can be expected to be true for the target population.[12] For example, let's say a food company wanted to find out if its new dessert would appeal to a commercially viable percentage of U.S. citizens between the ages of 18 and 35. It would be too costly to ask each 18- to 35-year-old in the United States to taste the product. Therefore, using experimental design procedures, the company could randomly select test subjects of the defined target population (18–35) and assign them to different treatment groups, varying one component of the dessert for each group. The subjects then taste the new dessert. If 60 percent indicated they would purchase the product, and if in fact 60 percent of the entire population did purchase the new product when it was marketed, then the results of the study would be considered externally valid.

Threats to external validity include interactions of treatment with history, setting, selection, testing, and treatment exposures. Interactions with history that might lessen external validity could include testing on a special day such as Christmas or Halloween. If the researcher were interested in charitable behavior, then a treatment manipulation and effect measures administered on Christmas Day might give quite different results than one given at some other less notable time. After watching several movies emphasizing charity and love for our fellow man, the average subject might react significantly differently on this day than on some other. By the same token, polls on gun control might very likely be affected if taken immediately after the assassination of a major public figure. Generalizability to other time frames would therefore be considerably reduced.

Similar reductions in external validity might occur if the location or setting of the experiment influenced the observed results. Surely, a fear-of-heights scale administered on top of a mountain would have different results than one administered in a classroom. The final threat of selection bias occurs when the sample is not truly representative of the target population. Asking subjects to participate in a survey or experiment requiring several hours will limit the actual sample to only those who have the spare time and may not generate a truly representative sample.

Another possible threat to external validity can occur when some of the test subjects experience more than one treatment in the experimental setting. The conclusions drawn could not be generalized to situations where individuals received fewer or more treatments. For example, if an experiment was designed to study the effects of a price reduction on product sales in which the product was displayed in two separate locations, the results could not be generalized to situations where only one display was used. Here, the extra display competes with price reduction as an explanation for sales.

Construct Validity

Construct validity The extent to which the variables under investigation are completely and accurately identified prior to hypothesizing any functional relationships.

Critical to all causal research designs is the ability to accurately identify and understand the independent and dependent variables included in the study. In addition, researchers must be able to accurately measure those variables in order to assess their true functional or cause-effect relationships. Consequently, researchers must attempt to assess the construct validity of both independent and dependent variables prior to executing their experimental or causal research design. **Construct validity** can simply be viewed as the extent to which the variables under investigation are completely and accurately identified prior to hypothesizing any functional relationships. Establishing construct validity for the variables can be an elusive goal. Of the many approaches to establishing construct validity, one that is used widely consists of three steps.[13]

First, the relationship between the constructs (or variables) of interest must be accurately identified. To illustrate, let's assume a researcher wanted to use a construct called motivation to succeed (MTS) as an independent variable in predicting the likelihood of individuals' life success. Those who measure the highest on the MTS construct would be those most likely to have succeeded in life. The fundamental question that must be addressed is "What are the observable, real-life indicators of such success?" Using a process referred to as specifying the domain of observable subcomponents related to the construct,[14] let's assume that peer respect, academic achievement, and personal financial security represent success in the society being investigated. The precise nature of this specification is necessary so that the hypothesized relationship can be empirically tested with real data. Otherwise, the details collected will be insufficient to either support or refute the hypothesis.

Second, the researcher executes an experimental design that manipulates MTS and measures the outcome "life success." If it is determined the data are both positive and substantial in support of the hypothesized functional relationship, then evidence of construct validity exists. Researchers would also attempt to determine what other constructs these observable subcomponents might be related to, such as social position, inherited wealth, or athletic prowess. To the extent the observable subcomponents are not related to MTS, but rather to other alternative constructs, then the evidence in support of construct validity would be weakened. For example, peer respect and personal financial security might be the result of inherited wealth and have little to do with motivation to succeed. As a result, it would be necessary to find other observable subcomponents that are more closely related to MTS and that could not generally be caused by other variables.

Third, prior to executing the experiment, researchers compare the proposed measures of the independent and dependent variables with other similar measures. When existing measures of the same construct are highly correlated with the researcher's measures, then there

Convergent validity
When the researcher's measures of a construct are highly correlated with known existing measures of the same construct.

Discriminant validity
The existence of a negative correlation between the experiment's measuring methods and those measurements of completely different constructs.

Inadequate preoperationalization Contamination to construct validity measures due to inadequate understanding of the complete makeup of the independent and dependent variables included in the experimental design.

Monomethod bias A particular type of error source that is created when only a single method is used to collect data about the research question.

Demand characteristics Contamination to construct validity measures created by test subjects trying to guess the true purpose behind the experiment and therefore give socially acceptable responses or behaviors.

Evaluation apprehension Contamination to construct validity measures caused by test subjects being fearful that their actions or responses will become known to others.

is evidence of **convergent validity** in support of the construct validity we seek. Additional evidence, called **discriminant validity,** may come from a negative correlation between the experiment's measures and those designed to measure completely different constructs.[15]

Key Threats to Construct Validity

Construct validity can be threatened in many ways, including (1) inadequate preoperationalization of constructs; (2) mono-operation bias; (3) monomethod bias; (4) hypothesis-guessing; (5) demand characteristics; (6) evaluation apprehension; and (7) diffusion of treatment.

To avoid **inadequate preoperationalization,** the researcher should carefully and completely define the construct as precisely as possible. Fear of heights cannot simply be defined as a fear of high places, since some people are afraid of being on high mountain roads but not in an office in a high building or on an airplane. As a researcher, it is essential that you know exactly what form of fear you are trying to measure. Then, once the definition has been refined in light of the purpose of the study, you can more precisely select measurable, observable constructs.

Mono-operation and **monomethod bias** can threaten construct validity through contamination created by using only one method or single-item measurements. Where possible, researchers should use more than one measuring method (pen and pencil, interview, or physical reactions) and more than a single measure in each method to collect data.[16] Researchers have found that many subjects try to guess the purpose of the research and respond as they feel the researcher wants them to respond. Called the **demand characteristic,** this threat can be reduced by making the hypothesis difficult to guess. For example, one clever psychologist invited people to participate in an experiment, had them wait in an outer office, and then took them into a room where they were asked several questions. In actuality, the experiment involved interpersonal conversational patterns and took place in the waiting room with the help of confederates posing as subjects (without the knowledge of the real subjects).[17]

Most of us have exhibited **evaluation apprehension** before a college entrance exam, sports physical, or even our first job interview. Because such apprehension can seriously bias the results of many studies, researchers will attempt to reduce it as much as possible. One approach frequently used in marketing research involves ensuring the anonymity of respondents. Careful briefing of respondents by the research team also can help reduce this threat.

The final threat to construct validity involves the **diffusion of treatment.** Since it is rarely possible to completely isolate subjects, the control group may exchange information with the treatment group, or those who previously completed a questionnaire may discuss it with those who have yet to participate. Although the researcher cautions subjects not to discuss the research, such efforts are usually unsuccessful. Taking several samples from the target population at various locations and under different conditions usually reduces this threat. In fact, using different samples from the population of interest is a good way to reduce threats to construct and other types of validity.

Reliability of Experimental Research Designs

We also must understand reliability in causal research designs. For **experimental design reliability** to exist, researchers must be able to demonstrate that their experiment can be repeated and similar conclusions will be reached. While there tends to be little reward in repeating the experiments of other researchers, there can be significant benefits in repeating the procedures used in causal research designs. For example, a company such as AT&T, which has many different types of telecommunication products, might standardize its design and testing procedures for investigating new-product acceptance. Such standardization of procedures could lead to significant cost reductions within AT&T's research and development activities.

Diffusion of treatment
Contamination to construct validity measures due to test subjects discussing the treatment and measurement activities with individuals yet to receive the treatment.

Experimental design reliability The degree to which the design and its procedures can be replicated and achieve similar conclusions about hypothesized relationships.

Improving the Internal and External Validity of Experimental Designs

The ultimate goal of experimental research is determining the true causal or functional relationship between the independent and dependent variables. Researchers must minimize the extent to which extraneous variables confound experimental results. As a way to counter threats to internal and external validity, researchers can implement several techniques unique to experimental designs.

Inclusion of Control Groups

When designing an experiment, the researcher must determine who will be assigned to the groups that will be exposed to the manipulation and who will be assigned to the control group that does not receive the manipulation. Control groups represent the greatest strength of the experiment and the best way to ensure internal validity.

Time Order of the Manipulation Exposure

The researcher also must determine which variables, independent or dependent, will occur first. This can be accomplished by using pre-experimental measures of the variables prior to manipulation or by establishing experimental treatment and control groups that do not differ in terms of influencing the dependent variable before the manipulation takes place.

Exclusion of Nonsimilar Test Subjects

To increase internal validity, the researcher can select only those test subjects who have similar and controllable characteristics. Let's say, for example, that the researcher is interested in certain product-purchasing behaviors among a targeted group of consumers. This study's results might be confounded by differences in age and occupational status of the test subjects. To counter this possibility, the researcher would select only those test subjects with age and occupational status characteristics similar to the target market. By doing so, the researcher is eliminating extraneous variation due to age and occupation.

Matching Extraneous Variables

Through the process of matching, the researcher measures certain extraneous variables on an individual basis. Those who respond similarly to the variables are then allocated to the experimental and control groups. This process can control for selection bias and enhance internal validity.

Randomization of Test Subjects to Treatment Groups

Randomization of the assignment of test subjects to the experimental and control groups can help make the groups equivalent. The key to true randomization of test subjects is that the randomness must be secured in a carefully controlled manner. To enhance external validity, the researcher should also randomly select settings and times for the experiment based on the population or events under investigation. By ensuring the above procedures are followed in the experimental design, the researcher increases the experiment's ability to accurately identify true causal or functional relationships. Moreover, these procedures help the researcher control contamination of the relationships between the independent and dependent variables.

Types of Experimental Research Designs

Experimental designs can be classified into three groups: (1) pre-experiments, (2) true experiments, and (3) quasi-experiments. (See Exhibit 8.6.) The main difference among these groups is the degree of control the researcher exercises in the design and execution. To facilitate understanding of the different types of experimental designs, we use the following set of symbols:[18]

X = The exposure of an independent variable (treatment manipulation) to a group of test subjects for which the effects are to be determined.

O = The process of observation or measurement of the dependent variable (outcome) on the test subjects.

EXHIBIT 8.6   Types of Experimental Research Designs in Marketing Research

Pre-experimental Designs

One-shot study	A single group of test subjects is exposed to the independent variable treatment X, and then a single measurement on the dependent variable is taken (O_1).
One-group pretest-posttest	First a pretreatment measure of the dependent variable is taken (O_1), then the test subjects are exposed to the independent treatment X, and then a posttreatment measure of the dependent variable is taken (O_2).
Static group comparison	There are two groups of test subjects: one group is the experimental group (EG) and is exposed to the independent treatment, and the second group is the control group (CG) and is not given the treatment. The dependent variable is measured in both groups after the treatment.

True Experimental Designs

Pretest-posttest control group	Test subjects are randomly assigned to either the experimental or control group, and each group receives a pretreatment measure of the dependent variable. Then the independent treatment is exposed to the experimental group, after which both groups receive a posttreatment measure of the dependent variable.
Posttest-only control group	Test subjects are randomly assigned to either the experimental or the control group. The experimental group is then exposed to the independent treatment, after which both groups receive a posttreatment measure of the dependent variable.
Solomon Four Group	This design combines the "pretest-posttest control group" and "posttest-only control group" designs and provides both direct and reactive effects of testing. Not used in marketing research practices because of complexity and lengthy time requirements.

Quasi-experimental Designs

Nonequivalent control group	This design is a combination of the "static group comparison" and the "one-group pretest-posttest" pre-experimental designs.
Separate-sample pretest-posttest	Two different groups of test subjects are drawn; neither group is directly exposed to the independent treatment variable. One group receives a pretest measure of the dependent variable. Then after the insignificant independent treatment occurs, the second group of test subjects receives a posttest measure of the dependent variable.
Field experiment	This is a causal design that manipulates the independent variables in order to measure the dependent variable in the natural setting of the event or test.
Factorial Designs	Experimental designs used to investigate the simultaneous effects of two or more treatment (independent) variables on single or multiple dependent (outcome) variables.
Latin square	This design manipulates one independent variable and controls for two additional sources of extraneous variations by restricting randomization to row and column.

[R] = The random assignment of test subjects to separate treatment groups.

EG = The experimental group of test subjects.

CG = The control group of test subjects.

$\rightarrow$ = A movement through time, normally displayed as left-to-right movement.

Note also that vertical alignment of symbols implies those symbols refer to activities that occur simultaneously at a prescribed point in time, and that horizontal alignment of symbols implies all those symbols refer to a specific treatment group of test subjects.

Pre-experimental Designs

Three specific pre-experimental designs are available to marketing researchers: the one-shot study; the one-group pretest-posttest; and the static group comparison. These designs are commonly referred to as crude experiments and should be undertaken only when a stronger experimental design is not possible. These designs are characterized by an absence of randomization of test subjects. Their major weakness is the inability to meet internal validity criteria due to a lack of equivalent group comparisons.[19]

One-Shot Study

The one-shot case study can be illustrated as follows:

$$(\text{EG}): \quad X \rightarrow O_1$$

An example of this design would be when a researcher wishes to measure customer reactions to a product display in a single store. A design of this nature does not control extraneous variables. It ignores the process of group comparisons that is fundamental in the experimental process. The only comparisons made are those based on common knowledge, past experiences, or general impressions of what the condition would have been had the manipulation not occurred. In this instance, even careful development of accurate measures will not compensate for the inadequate design.

One-Group Pretest-Posttest

The value of the "one-group pretest-posttest" design is its ability to provide the researcher with a comparison measure. It is diagrammed as follows:

$$(\text{EG}): \quad O_1 \rightarrow X_1 \rightarrow O_2$$

The design is subject to the same extraneous confounding factors as with the one-shot study. In addition, history contamination is a major weakness, given events may occur between O_1 and O_2. Even environmental noise (sirens, thunder, phones) can affect results. The only way to control for the occurrence is to isolate the experiment in a controlled environment. Unfortunately, this is a widely used design in marketing research, often to measure advertising effects among consumers. Many advertisers take a pretest criterion measure of ad recall, product involvement, media habits, or purchase history. Then an experimental independent treatment manipulation is delivered (e.g., exposure to an ad during a TV program), followed by a posttest measure of the dependent variable, usually ad recall. Experimental designs such as these are further affected by maturation and instrumentation problems. The effect of the pretest measure also introduces problems with the testing factor. One advantage of the "one-group pretest-posttest" design is its lack of selection bias. Since only one group exists, it automatically eliminates the problem of differential selection. Overall, this design has imperfect safeguards to internal validity and should be used only when nothing better is available.

Static Group Comparison

Static group comparison is a two-group experimental design consisting of an experimental group (EG) and a control group (CG) of test subjects, but it lacks any randomization. The experimental group receives the independent treatment manipulation, with the second operating as the control. It can be illustrated as follows:

$$(EG): \quad X \rightarrow O_1$$
$$(CG): \quad\quad\quad O_2$$

Selection bias is the major defect of this design mainly because the groups are formed on a nonrandom basis. For example, many studies look at two store settings or heavy users versus light users when comparing new-product trials or sales. While the groups are randomly selected, in theory there is no assurance the two groups are equivalent. Yet in comparison to the other pre-experimental designs, the static group comparison is substantially less susceptible to history, maturation, instrumentation, and testing contaminations.

True Experimental Designs

There are three forms of true experimental designs: (1) pretest-posttest control group; (2) posttest-only control group; and (3) Solomon Four Group. The common denominator is that all three designs ensure equivalence between experimental and control groups by random assignment to the groups.[20]

Pretest-Posttest Control Group—Completely Randomized Design

The "pretest-posttest control group" design consists of one experimental group and one control group of test subjects, who are assigned to either group by the process of complete randomization. This process randomly assigns each experimental unit (subject) to the treatments. Randomization of experimental units is the researcher's attempt to control all extraneous variables while manipulating a single treatment variable. It can be illustrated as follows:

$$(EG): \quad [R] \, O_1 \rightarrow X \rightarrow O_2$$
$$(CG): \quad [R] \, O_3 \longrightarrow O_4$$

With the treatment effect (TE) of the experimental manipulation being:

$$TE = (O_2 - O_1) - (O_4 - O_3)$$

This experimental design controls for extraneous factors contributing to the contamination of internal validity, but does not necessarily ensure true internal validity. For example, if extraneous history events produce a difference between O_2 and O_1, and a difference between O_4 and O_3, it can be assumed the researcher has controlled for history contamination. Yet the researcher cannot directly determine whether exactly the same history events occurred in both groups. Certain events may have taken place in the experimental group and not the other, even if the results suggest there is internal validity. This can occur due to some disturbance, diversion, or environmental factor influencing the test subjects in the control group. To prevent this problem, the researcher would first randomly assign individuals into experimental and control groups, then have each individual tested for any such disturbance.

Regression, testing, and maturation threats are controlled since differences should be measured equally in experimental and control groups. An instrumentation problem might arise from the researcher knowingly modifying the measuring instrument between the pretest and posttest measures of the dependent variable. Differences in dropout rates among group members can also develop into a mortality issue. Selection is adequately handled through the process of randomization, with match techniques being employed to improve equivalency. Matching should be used only as a supplement to randomization.

Procedural operations of this design are quite simple. To illustrate this point, let's consider testing the impact of a direct mail promotional message regarding customers' knowledge of automobiles. To begin, a sample of individuals is selected at random. Half are randomly assigned to the control group, the other half to the experimental group (e.g., the group that receives direct mail on automobiles). Everyone selected is measured on automobile knowledge. The experimental group then receives the promotional message, and after an acceptable period of time, the "automobile knowledge" measure is again administered to all subjects.

Sources of extraneous variation are realized if differences occur between the measures of O_4 less O_3 (e.g., an actual product recall occurred during the experiment). However, if this type of extraneous effect did occur, it would be measured equally on those individuals in the experimental group. While the design produces adequate control for internal validity, it does not necessarily do so for external validity. Two factors serve as threats to the external validity of this design: testing and selection. Pretests run the risk of introducing bias into the design based on the mere topic area being pretested. This can cause unusual attitudes to develop among experimental group subjects that can ultimately bias the posttest measures. In addition, a high mortality rate of subjects can destroy the intentions of sound randomization procedures. If this is a factor, replication of the experiment over time among different groups is necessary to ensure external validity.

Posttest-Only Control Group

This experimental design is identical to the previous completely randomized design except the pretest measures of the dependent variable are absent. This type of causal design works well if the process of randomization is totally assured. The design is illustrated as follows:

$$(EG): \quad [R] \; X \rightarrow O_1$$

$$(CG): \quad [R] \qquad O_2$$

Take for example a completely randomized posttest only control group design that might be used by a research company like J. D. Powers and Associates in its efforts to examine the effects of various incentive alternatives used to increase the response rate of its direct mail new automobile owner satisfaction survey. The two experimental treatment incentive alternatives of interest are personal monetary payments of 10 dollars to prospective respondents versus a 10-dollar contribution to a charitable organization selected by the respondent. When a control group of respondents is used in the design, there are actually three treatment groups: (1) no incentive offered to the control group of respondents, (2) $10 charity incentive, and (3) $10 personal incentive. Let's assume the researchers determine the overall sampling frame would need to be 1,500 new automobile owners resulting in 500 prospective respondents (n) being randomly assigned to each of the three treatment groups. Below are the hypothetical results of the experiment:

	Response Rate Experimental Treatment Groups		
Groups	$10 Personal Incentive	$10 Charity Incentive	Control: No Incentive
Response Rates	39.4%	24.3%	25.7%
# of respondents (n)	500	500	500

In comparing the above response rate (dependent variable) of each of the three treatment groups, the results suggest that personal payment incentives have the strongest influence on response rate. From a managerial perspective, J. D. Powers and Associates could expect a significantly higher survey response rate by including a $10 personal payment with each of the new automobile owner satisfaction surveys mailed.

Solomon Four Group

Although a highly complex design, the Solomon Four Group enables the researcher to learn more about internal and external validity than any other experimental design does. But because of its complexity, marketing researchers do not use it as widely as the other design alternatives. It is illustrated as follows:

Design 1

$$(EG): \quad [R] \, O_1 \rightarrow X \rightarrow O_2$$

$$(CG): \quad [R] \, O_3 \longrightarrow O_4$$

Design 2

$$(EG): \quad [R] \qquad X \rightarrow O_5$$

$$(CG): \quad [R] \qquad O_6$$

The design is a combination of the "pretest-posttest control group" and the "posttest only control group" experimental designs. It provides both direct and reactive effects of testing, based on $O_1 \rightarrow X \rightarrow O_2$ and $X \rightarrow O_5$, respectively. External validity is enhanced, along with true experimental effect assurance by comparing $[O_2$ less $O_1]$, $[O_2$ less $O_4]$, $[O_5$ less $O_6]$, and $[O_5$ less $O_3]$. When these four comparisons agree, the researcher's ability to infer that the resulting functional relationship between the dependent and independent variables is being caused by the experimental independent variable treatment dramatically increases.

Quasi-experimental Designs

Between the extremes of pre-experimental designs (which have little or no control) and true experimental designs (based on randomization), we have the quasi-experimental designs. (See Exhibit 8.7.) These designs are appropriate when the researcher can control some variables (e.g., price level, media vehicle, package design) but cannot establish equal experimental and control groups based on randomization (e.g., store types or customer groups). While there are many different types of quasi-experimental designs available to marketing researchers, we will focus only on the two more widely used ones: (1) nonequivalent control group and (2) separate-sample pretest-posttest.[21]

Nonequivalent Control Group

Commonly used in marketing research, the "nonequivalent control group" design differs from true experimental designs in that the experimental and control groups are not equivalent. It can be illustrated as follows:

$$\text{Group 1} \quad (EG): \quad O_1 \rightarrow X \rightarrow O_2$$

$$\text{Group 2} \quad (CG): \quad O_3 \qquad O_4$$

This quasi-experimental design operates at two levels. The intact equivalent design allows experimental and control groups to be formed in natural settings. For example, many marketing research quasi-experiments recruit test subjects from established organizations such

exHIBIT 8.7	Summary of Other Quasi-experimental Designs Used in Marketing Research Practices
Nonequivalent dependent variable design	Single group of test subjects and pretest measures on two scales, one that is expected to change due to treatment manipulation and one that is not. This design is restricted to theoretical contexts where differential change is predicted. The design must be powerful enough to determine that the nontreated variable is reliably measured. These results are interpretable only when the two outcome measures are conceptually similar and both would be affected by the same nontreatment effect.
Removed treatment design with pretest and posttest	There could be an ethical problem in the removing of the treatment manipulation in the second scenario. There needs to be a noticeable discontinuity after the removal of the second treatment; otherwise, it could be that the initial treatment had no long-term effects.
Repeated treatment design	This design is most interpretable when the results of the first experiment occur in the same direction as the second experiment and the initial pretest measure differs from any of the following test measures. This design is best when there are unobservable treatments and long periods between a treatment and its reintroduction.
Reversed-treatment, nonequivalent control group design	This design requires both pretest and posttest measures and directional hypotheses. There is potential for high construct validity, but it depends on the research revealing the existence of an inverse relationship.
Cohort designs with cyclical turnover	*Cohorts* are test subjects who follow each other through a formal institutional environment such as school or work. In this type of design, the researcher pretests a group of test subjects, then gives the treatment manipulation to the next group and collects posttest measures from the second group. The major underlying premise to this type of quasi-experimental design is that the samples are drawn from the same population. This design can eliminate the threats of history and testing by stratifying the treatment groups.
Regression discontinuity design	This causal design is used when the experimental groups are given rewards or those in special need are given extra assistance. The regressed lines for the treatment and nontreatment groups should be different due to the effect of the treatment. Interpretation of the results becomes difficult with the possibility of curvilinear relationships. Knowledge of the reward could lead to extra actions in order to receive it.

as church clubs or civic groups. They also use customers from similar stores. Ideally, the groups should be as similar as possible. In this self-selected experimental group design, group membership is based on the subject's interest or desire to participate. Many times, this is accomplished by selecting test subjects from a shopping mall, whereas control subjects are selected on the basis of availability. The difference between O_1 and O_3 becomes an indication of equivalency between the experimental and control groups. If pretest measures are significantly different, group compatibility must be seriously questioned. However, if the measures appear similar, then there is an increased certainty of internal validity. While this design may conform to sound validity practices, it is highly dependent on the circumstances that lead to the selection of test subjects.

Separate-Sample Pretest-Posttest

When it is virtually impossible to determine who is to receive the independent treatment manipulation, but when measures of the dependent variable can be determined, a "separate-sample pretest-posttest" design is an appropriate choice. This design can be illustrated as follows:

$$\text{Sample 1} \quad O_1 \rightarrow (X)$$
$$\text{Sample 2} \qquad (X) \rightarrow O_2$$

When the experimental treatment manipulation (X) is insignificant to the research, it simply indicates the experimental group of test subjects cannot be controlled for treatment. Although this is a weak design, it is not an uncommon situation in marketing research practices. This type of quasi-design is most often used when the population is large, a pretest measure will not produce any meaningful information, and there is no way to control for application of the experimental manipulation. This quasi-experimental framework is commonly used in advertising research. Let's say, for example, that the advertising agency for Home Depot, the "do-it-yourself" building supply chain, may be launching a major image campaign. First, it draws two samples of test subjects. One sample is interviewed about their perception of Home Depot's image (dependent variable) prior to the image campaign. After the campaign ends, test subjects in the second group are interviewed about their perception of Home Depot.

Obviously, this design must deal with a number of threats to internal validity. History and mortality are the greatest concerns. Repetition of the experiment over several settings can reduce these effects somewhat. Yet this quasi-experimental design is considered superior to true experiments with regard to external validity. This occurs from its natural setting and the use of large samples of test subjects who are representative of the target group. Overall, the reason why quasi-experimental designs are practiced in marketing research is they are in a natural setting. Thus, they are a type of field experiment. Field experiments, to which we devote the next section of this chapter, provide valuable information to researchers because they allow both functional and causal relationships to be generalized to the target population.

Field Experiments

Field experiments
Causal research designs that manipulate the independent variables in order to measure the dependent variable in a natural setting of the test.

Field experiments are experimental research designs that manipulate the independent variables in order to measure the dependent variable in the natural setting of the test. Field experiments are often conducted in retail environments such as malls, supermarkets, or other retail stores. These settings tend to create a high level of realism. However, high levels of realism contribute to a lack of control of the independent variables and increase problems with extraneous variables. Problems with control can occur in several ways. For example, conducting a field experiment of a new product in a supermarket requires the retailer's commitment to authorize the product in the store. Today, retailers are becoming more hesitant about adding new products, given the large number of new-product introductions each year. Even if the product is authorized, proper display and retailer support are needed to appropriately conduct the experiment. Competition can also negatively influence a field experiment. In some field experiments of new products, competitors have negatively affected sales of the experimental product by using heavy price discounts and promotions to increase sales of their own products at the time of the test. When field experiments are used, there are two types of designs: *factorial* and *latin square* designs.

Factorial Designs

In marketing, researchers are often interested in investigating the simultaneous effects of two or more independent (treatment) variables on single or multiple dependent (outcome) variables. When the effects of two or more independent variables are investigated in a field experiment situation, researchers should use some type of factorial design. For example, Dell Computer's corporate vice president of marketing is interested in measuring the effects of the company's sales training procedure and the compensation plan (independent variables) on sales performance (dependent variable) for its online sales representatives. There are two different types of sales training procedures (STP): (1) sales manager's on-the-job training and (2) video-based off-the-job self-training. The compensation plan (CP) also has two different types of schemes: (1) straight commission of 9 percent and (2) salary plus a 4 percent commission. So in this example there are two independent variables each consisting of two alternatives resulting in what is called a 2×2 factorial design. This design has four cells ($2 \times 2 = 4$) in the design matrix. Each cell can be considered a "treatment" group. The overall experimental design matrix would look as follows.

	Compensation Plan (CP)	
Training Procedure (STP)	**(CP_1)** **Combination** **Salary + 4%**	**(CP_2)** **Straight** **Commission**
(STP_1) On-the-job training	STP_1, CP_1	STP_1, CP_2
(STP_2) Video self-training	STP_2, CP_1	STP_2, CP_2

A factorial design enables the researcher to measure the separate effects of each independent variable working alone. The sales training procedure (STP) effect is calculated similar to that of a completely randomized design but the researcher also can estimate the individual effect of the compensation plans (CP). The individual effects of each independent variable are referred to as the *main effects*. To illustrate the "main effect" concept, hypothetical numbers for online sales performance are used in the above design matrix. The results suggest that regardless of the compensation plan used, the on-the-job training program (STP_1) yields on average \$60,000 more than the video self-training program (STP_2). The main effect of STP_1 is \$60,000. In turn, the main effect of the combination salary plus 4 percent commission plan CP_1, regardless of the type of training program, yields on average \$90,000 more than the straight commission of 9 percent plan (CP_2). The total treatment effect STP_1, CP_2 is \$150,000 (\$60,000 + \$90,000 = \$150,000) and there is no interaction between sales training procedure and compensation plan.

	Compensation Plan (CP)	
Training Procedure (STP)	**(CP_1)** **Combination** **Salary + 4%**	**(CP_2)** **Straight** **Commission**
(STP_1) On-the-job training	\$280,000	\$190,000
(STP_2) Video self-training	\$220,000	\$130,000

The factorial design also allows the researcher to determine the magnitude of an *interaction effect* that may exist between the independent variables (STP and CP). This extra total effect combination of the independent variables working together is often greater than the sum of the variables' individual effects. An interaction effect occurs when the relationship between one of the independent variables, say STP, and the dependent variable (online sales representative performance) is different for different levels of the compensation plan (CP) independent variable. In the Dell Computer example, the relationship between online salespeople's performance and the type of sales training program may vary depending upon which compensation plan is used. The following design matrix illustrates the interaction effect between the independent variables.

	Compensation Plan (CP)	
Training Procedure (STP)	**(CP₁)** **Combination** **Salary + 4%**	**(CP₂)** **Straight** **Commission**
(STP₁) On-the-job training	$280,000	$220,000
(STP₂) Video self-training	$220,000	$130,000

Here the effect of the training procedure depends on the compensation plan used. The on-the-job training program (STP_1) is $60,000 better than video self-training (STP_2) when the combination salary plus 4 percent commission compensation plan (CP_1) is used and $90,000 when the straight commission of 9 percent compensation plan is employed. In turn, the combination of salary plus 4 percent commission (CP_1) is $60,000 better than the straight commission plan (CP_2) when on-the-job training is used and is $90,000 better when video self-training (STP_2) is the training program.

Latin Square Designs

The *Latin Square (LS)* design can be used in field experiment situations where the researcher wants to control the effects of two or more extraneous variables. Latin square designs manipulate one independent variable and control for two additional sources of extraneous variation by restricting randomization with respect to the row and column effects. In order to employ a Latin square experimental design several conditions must be met. First, the number of categories (levels) of each extraneous variable to be controlled must be equal to the number of treatments. For example, let's say management is now interested in three training procedures rather than two and wants to control for the "age of the sales representative" and the "potential dollar sales performances per year." Here STP_1 represents on-the-job training, STP_2 denotes video self-training, and STP_3 represents in-classroom training procedures. Because there are now three treatment groups based on type of training procedure, the researcher has to make sure the selected "age" and "$ sales performance" variables also have only three categorical levels. If this condition is not met, then a Latin square design is not appropriate. In this situation the researcher would use a 3×3 design shown as follows:

	Sales Potential per Year (in thousands)		
Age of Salespersons	**$500–$999**	**$1,000–$3,999**	**$4,000–$6,999**
20–29	STP₁	STP₂	STP₃
30–45	STP₂	STP₃	STP₁
Over 45	STP₃	STP₁	STP₂

Another necessary condition for conducting a Latin Square design is the assignment of treatment levels in the cells of the square. While the assignment is random, each treatment can occur only once in each blocking situation. This means that because each row and column category defines a blocking situation, each type of training program (STP) must appear only once in each row and each column. In conducting this type of experiment, each test subject is exposed to all three treatments in a preset random order.

Considerations in Using Field Experiments

Besides realism and control, there are at least three other issues to consider when deciding whether or not to use a field experiment: time frames, costs, and competitive reactions. Field experiments take longer to complete than laboratory experiments. The planning stage—which can include determining which test market cities to use and which retailers to approach with product experiments, securing advertising time, and coordinating the distribution of the experimental product—adds to the length of time needed to conduct field experiments. Field experiments are more expensive to conduct than laboratory experiments because of the high number of independent variables that must be manipulated. For example, the cost of an advertising campaign alone can increase the cost of the experiment. Other items adding to the cost of field experiments are coupons, product packaging development, trade promotions, and product sampling. Because field experiments are conducted in a natural setting, competitors can learn about the new product almost as soon as it is introduced, and they can respond by using heavy promotional activity or by rushing similar products to market. If secrecy is desired, then laboratory experiments are generally more effective.

Validity Concerns

In deciding whether to use field experiments, researchers should consider the proposed experiment's internal validity and external validity. Although the ideal experiment would be high in both internal and external validity, this is difficult to achieve in a field setting and usually a trade-off must be made. Researchers who want to be able to generalize an experiment's results to other settings might select field experiments. If the lack of control over the independent variables associated with field experiments is a concern, then laboratory experiments are more appropriate to assess true functional relationships.[22] Researchers opting for field experiments can choose from several types depending on the objectives of the experiment and the considerations mentioned above. The next section discusses the most common type of field experiment—test marketing—and includes overviews of six different methods for conducting market tests.

Test Marketing

Test marketing Using controlled field experiments to gain information on specified market performance indicators.

Test marketing is the use of controlled field experiments to gain information on specified market performance indicators. Companies have several options available when choosing a test marketing method. Regardless of the method used, test marketing measures the sales potential of a product and evaluates variables in the product's marketing mix.[23] The cost of conducting test marketing experiments can be high. But with the failure rate of new consumer products estimated to be between 80 and 90 percent, many companies believe the expense of conducting test marketing can help them avoid the more expensive mistake of an unsuccessful product rollout. Exhibit 8.8 presents the six most popular test marketing methods: traditional, controlled, electronic, simulated, Web-based TV, and virtual.[24]

Traditional Test Markets

The most frequently used form of test marketing is a traditional test market. This method tests a product's marketing mix variables through existing distribution channels. Companies select specific cities, or test markets, that have demographic and market characteristics similar to those of the targeted users of the product or service being tested. The most

eXHIBIT 8.8   Different Types of Test Marketing Used in Marketing Research

Types of Test Marketing	Comments
Traditional test markets	Also referred to as "standard" tests, these use experimental design procedures to test a product and/or a product's marketing mix variables through existing distribution channels.
Controlled test markets	Tests that are performed by an outside research firm that guarantees distribution of the test product through prespecified outlets in selected cities.
Electronic test markets	Tests that integrate the use of select panels of consumers who use a special identification card in recording their product-purchasing data.
Simulated test markets	Also referred to as "laboratory tests" or "test market simulations," these are quasi-experiments where test subjects are preselected, then interviewed and observed on their purchases and attitudes toward the test product.
Web-based TV test markets	Similar to electronic test markets, these use broadband interactive TV (iTV) and advances in interactive multimedia communication technologies to conduct the field experiment. Preselected respondents are shown various stimuli and asked questions online through their iTV.
Virtual test markets	Tests that are completely computerized, allowing the test subjects to observe and interact with the product as though they were actually in the test store's environment.

common use of a traditional test is to evaluate consumer acceptance of a new product or a variation of an existing product. For example, Procter & Gamble test-marketed Sunny Delight Smoothies, a blend of Sunny Delight fruit beverage and milk, in Mobile, Alabama, and New Orleans, Louisiana.[25] Test marketing also is used to evaluate the potential of new marketing concepts. Spalding, a major sporting goods manufacturer, test-marketed a women's theme shop in 58 stores of four national sporting goods retailers.[26]

Advantages and Disadvantages of Traditional Test Markets

The primary advantage of traditional tests is they are conducted in actual distribution channels. Other test marketing methods attempt to simulate distribution channels, while traditional test markets place products in actual distribution outlets, typically retail outlets. In addition to measuring consumer acceptance of a product, standard test markets can determine the level of trade support for the tested item. If retailers are reluctant to give a company additional shelf space or displays for the new product, then plans for the product rollout may need to be reevaluated. Even products that have a high level of consumer appeal will have difficulty succeeding if minimum levels of distribution cannot be attained.

The limitations of traditional test markets are cost, time, and exposure to competition. First, traditional test markets are much more expensive compared to laboratory experiments. Expenses incurred during a traditional test market include product development, packaging, distribution, and advertising and promotion. Second, traditional test markets require more time to conduct than other forms of test marketing. Most standard test markets take between 12 and 18 months to complete. Third, because traditional test marketing uses actual distribution channels, other companies are able to observe a competitor's activity and can take action to hurt a test market. The combination of time and competitive pressures has changed the way in which many companies introduce new products. The need to introduce products more quickly than competitors is leading to large-scale rollouts of new products. The traditional approach of beginning with a test market and then increasing

EXHIBIT 8.9 Good Test Market Results Do Not Guarantee New-Product Success

Coors Gives the Cold Shoulder to Wine Coolers[27]

Adolph Coors Company, manufacturer of Coors beer, suffered through a series of new-product disasters in the early 1980s, so when the company made a second attempt to enter the wine cooler market it relied on simulated test marketing to determine consumer acceptance for its new offering.

The company's test marketing woes began in 1978 when it introduced Coors Light. By the time the Coors product reached the market, Miller Lite was firmly entrenched as the number one light beer. The slow rollout did not seem to bother the company. In fact, it was consistent with their philosophy. Pete Coors remarked that his company let other companies do the pioneering work, referring to product development. "Then we'll take what they've done, and do it better," he added. Another product failure, Killian's Irish Red Ale, was introduced in 1982 using traditional test markets. The product stalled in the test marketing phase before national rollout could happen. Perhaps the worst experience was with Herman Josephs, a new beer positioned as a premium-priced beer that was supposed to compete with Michelob and Löwenbräu. Once again, Coors relied on traditional test marketing, planning to iron out bugs in the product and marketing mix before introducing the product in all markets. The test marketing for Herman Josephs began in 1981. Coors abandoned the product in 1989 after years of remaining in the test market phase.

Coors had made a previous attempt to enter the wine cooler market with its Colorado Chiller coolers. The failure of Colorado Chiller was attributed in part to failure to get input from consumers about the product. Coors sought to correct this mistake when another cooler product, Crystal Springs Cooler, was tested in 1986. The company used simulated test marketing (STM) to find out how consumers would respond to the new product. Results of the STM were encouraging. Approximately 63 percent of cooler drinkers surveyed were interested in purchasing Crystal Springs Cooler, and 74 percent said they would buy the product after sampling it. Sales projections for Crystal Springs exceeded 300,000 barrels per year, which would have been Coors's third-largest product. In 1987, the company decided to discontinue its plans for Crystal Springs Cooler. Undoubtedly, its past new-product failures left Coors with little confidence about rolling out a new product like Crystal Springs Cooler despite strong test marketing results.

distribution region by region is being replaced by introducing a product in multiple regions simultaneously. In addition, test marketing does not always mean success, as illustrated in Exhibit 8.9, which describes the problems experienced by Coors.

Controlled Test Markets

Controlled test market
A field experiment that guarantees the distribution of the test product through limited prespecified outlets in selected test cities.

A second type of test market is a controlled test market. A **controlled test market** is performed by an outside firm that guarantees distribution of the test product through outlets in selected cities. AC Nielsen and Audits & Surveys are two firms that offer controlled test marketing services. These companies provide financial incentives to distributors to allow the test product to be added to the product line. The outside firm handles all distribution functions for its client during the test market, including inventory, stocking, pricing, and billing. Sales data are gathered by the research firm. UPC scanner data and consumer surveys are used to compile information on trial and repeat rates, market penetration, and consumer characteristics.

Advantages and Disadvantages of Controlled Test Markets

Controlled test markets overcome many of the disadvantages of traditional test markets. First, distribution of the test product is assured by the outside firm handling the test market. Second, the cost of a controlled test market is less than that of a traditional test market. Third, competitive monitoring of a controlled test market is somewhat difficult compared with traditional test markets, given the level of control that can be implemented.

Controlled test markets are not without limits. First, the limited number of markets used makes accurate projections of sales and market penetration difficult. Second, the amount of actual trade support for a test product may be unclear if the research firm provided incentives to retailers to obtain shelf space. Will trade acceptance of the new product be the same without incentives? Third, the effect of a proposed advertising program is difficult to evaluate. Despite these limitations, controlled test markets can be beneficial for marketers. Many companies use controlled test markets to determine whether a product warrants a full-scale standard test market. Also, controlled test markets are used to test such pricing and promotional variables as coupons and displays.

Electronic Test Markets

Electronic test market
A specific type of field experiment that requires the subject to use an electronic identification card and measures test product/service purchase results using universal product code scanner data.

An **electronic test market** gathers data from consumers who agree to carry an identification card they present when buying goods or services at participating retailers. The test is performed by an outside firm such as AC Nielsen or Information Resources, Inc. The advantage of this method is the identification card enables the researcher to collect demographic data on consumers who purchase the test product. A primary disadvantage of this method is the card-carrying consumers probably are not representative of the entire market because they are not chosen at random. In addition, there is a high cost associated with the use of advanced technologies. As a result, small businesses normally cannot afford electronic test marketing.

Simulated Test Markets

Simulated test market
A field experiment that uses computer models to estimate consumer responses to a new marketing program.

Another type of test market that uses computer models to estimate consumer response to a new marketing program is a **simulated test market** (STM). STMs project sales volume and evaluate the planned marketing mix. Some common STM services are Assessor, Bases II, ESP, and Litmus. While each of these methods uses its own approach to sampling, questionnaires, and modeling, the overall process normally includes the following steps:

1. Potential participants are screened to satisfy certain demographic and product usage criteria.

2. Participants are shown commercials or print advertisements for the test product, as well as for other competitive or noncompetitive products.

3. Participants are then allowed to purchase items in a simulated retail store. Regardless of whether the test item is selected, participants receive a free sample.

4. After a usage period, participants are contacted to gather information on the product as well as their repurchase intentions.[28]

Advantages and Disadvantages of Simulated Test Markets

STMs have several advantages. First, STMs offer substantial cost and time savings. STMs can be conducted in four to six months, compared with a year or more for traditional test markets, and they cost approximately 5 to 10 percent of what a traditional test market costs. Second, a simulation can predict product trial rate, repurchase rate, and purchase cycle length with a great deal of accuracy. Third, computer modeling allows several alternative marketing mix plans to be tested for their effect on sales volume. Finally, exposure to competition is minimized because the test market is not conducted in normal channels of distribution.[29]

The isolation of STMs from the real-world environment leads to some weaknesses with this method. Trade acceptance of a new product cannot be measured using STMs—it must be assumed. A traditional test market would be more desirable if a company believes agreement for distribution with the trade will be difficult to secure. For example, Ore-Ida once conducted an STM for a new product in which it assumed a 90 percent distribution rate in the normal channels. However, the actual distribution rate was only 10 percent, making the sales volume projections from the STM impossible to attain. Second, broad-based consumer reaction to a new product is difficult to measure using STMs. A traditional test market allows a larger number of consumers the opportunity to try a new product. In addition, STMs are more effective in estimating trial rates than repurchase rates. However, a good estimate of repurchase intentions is needed to determine a new product's potential for success. Finally, although STMs cost less than traditional test markets, they are still expensive, costing $75,000 to $150,000. Only the largest of companies can afford to use STMs.[30]

STMs are an effective method for testing new products, especially variations of an existing brand or category of consumer package goods. For example, when Reynolds Metal Company introduced Reynolds Crystal Color plastic wrap, a variation of the traditional Reynolds clear plastic wrap, it used an STM to evaluate the potential of the new product. In the STM, 40 percent of the participants indicated they would definitely try it, which is double the average predicted trial rate for new products.[31]

STMs serve two important purposes. First, they can be used as either a substitute or a supplement to traditional test markets. STMs can be used as a substitute when the risk of product failure or cost is less than that for a traditional test market. They can be used as a supplement to test combinations of marketing mix variables prior to a traditional test market introduction, when making changes would be too costly, if not impossible. Second, STMs can serve as a pilot test to determine whether a particular concept or product has the potential for success. If not, the idea can be dropped before further testing increases the cost of the mistake.

Web-Based TV Test Markets

With consumers' growing acceptance of interactive TV (iTV), and the advances in multimedia communication technologies, larger technology-driven online research companies such as HarrisInteractive, Burke, Inc., Lieberman Research Worldwide, M/A/R/C Research, NFO WorldGroup, and smaller specialty research companies, such as Critical Mix, POPULUS, and DataStar, Inc., are investing heavily in the computer hardware and software to bring test marketing capabilities directly into the living rooms of consumers. **Web-based TV test markets** are a test market among consumers through Web-enabled television technology. This type of test market can literally bring consumers, manufacturers, and sponsors together into a convenient "living room" experience rather than a "desk" experience. Basically, iTV computerizes the consumer's TV set with a "set-top" box that has a hard drive for storing large amounts of data (e.g., a 60-second commercial, live or videotaped 30-minute interactive product demonstrations), allowing the consumer to watch at leisure for more in-depth product information.

Web-based TV test market The conducting of a test market among consumers through Web-enabled television technology.

Advantages and Disadvantages of Web-Based TV Test Markets

All the advantages associated with Web research practices are available through iTV. The big differences are the comfort of having the process delivered on a large screen versus the small PC screen, using larger fonts, bigger graphics, and having interactive products, ads, and other test stimuli delivered in a digital format. For now, applications of this alternative have been limited to advertising copy testing and some infomercials of consumer-oriented products.

Several factors are slowing the acceptance and use of iTV test markets. The most pressing are slow demand for iTV technology in the home, costs of the required hardware and software, and uncertainty among cable operators in supplying iTV services. Because iTV is still in its infancy, many consumers lack full knowledge of the technologies. Without knowledge, acceptance of iTV will remain low. For example, Microsoft's MSN TV service subscriber base is only about 1 million after more than four years in the market.[32] AOL Time Warner Inc. has its version of iTV called AOLTV, which was tested more than four years ago among 4,000 selected households in Orlando, Florida—but has not yet been introduced because of low consumer demand. Although iTV service is comparatively inexpensive, its acceptance may be slow because iTV technology is still an expensive investment to many consumer segments.

Finally, this new technology is a difficult sell to many companies unfamiliar with Web-based TV test marketing. Complicating this situation is the fact that many cable providers have been slow to offer iTV services beyond just an interactive program guide. For example, the former AT&T Broadband dropped plans to introduce an advanced set-top box for its 16 million U.S. cable subscribers. Some experts feel the problem is the iTV industry has been built around the premise that the primary method of iTV distribution is the set-top boxes provided by cable operators. Nevertheless, this form of test marketing is expected to grow in the next few years to the point where it will overtake electronic test marketing activities.

Virtual Test Markets

Virtual test market A high tech–driven field experiment that allows the subjects to manipulate different aspects of the test environment on a computer screen.

In **virtual test markets,** not only can different marketing mixes be evaluated using computer modeling, but even the simulated store itself appears on a computer screen. Using this method, participants can view store shelves stocked with many different kinds of products. The shoppers can pick up an item by touching its image on the monitor, and they can examine the product by moving a tracking ball device that rotates the image. Items are purchased by placing them in a shopping cart which appears on the screen. Information collected during this process includes the amount of time the consumer spends shopping in each product category, the time the consumer spends examining each side of a package, the quantity of product purchased, and the order of items purchased.[33]

Advantages and Disadvantages of Virtual Test Markets

Although virtual test markets are similar to simulated test markets, they do have some unique advantages. First, the "stores" that appear in virtual test markets more closely resemble actual stores than the ones created in simulated test markets. Second, researchers can make changes in the stores rather quickly. Different arrays of brands, pricing, packaging, promotions, and shelf-space allocations can appear in a matter of minutes. Third, virtual test markets can be used for different purposes. They can be used to test entirely new concepts or products as well as to test for changes in existing products. Finally, as with simulated test markets, virtual test markets allow for these tests to be conducted without exposure to competition.

The disadvantages of virtual test markets are similar to those of simulated test markets. The primary concern for many companies is whether consumers will shop in virtual stores using the same patterns they use in actual stores. However, research into this concern suggests there is a high degree of correlation between virtual store and actual store sales. For example, a study in which 300 consumers took six trips through a virtual store and an actual store to purchase cleaning and health-and-beauty-aid products revealed similar market shares. Correlations were .94 for the cleaning product and .90 for the health-and-beauty-aid product. Another concern is the cost of the computer hardware and software needed to conduct virtual test markets. While the cost is still prohibitive for many companies, improvements in technology should lower it in the future. Finally, in a virtual store, consumers cannot feel, smell, or touch a product. Items that involve special handling from consumers

A Closer Look at Research

Goodyear Steps Out of Its Own Stores[35]

Goodyear Tire and Rubber Company used virtual test marketing to evaluate a major change in distribution strategy. For many years, the company sold its tires through its own retail outlets. The new strategy was to sell Goodyear tires through general merchandise stores and still maintain the current system of Goodyear stores. While such a move would no doubt allow Goodyear to reach more consumers, the new strategy would place Goodyear tires in direct competition with other brands in the general merchandise stores. Goodyear questioned whether this increased competition would dictate a change in marketing strategy. Specifically, the company needed to determine what the level of brand equity was for its products. Was it strong enough to be able to charge a premium over other brands, or would it be forced to reduce prices and/or extend warranties to be competitive with other brands?

Goodyear turned to virtual test marketing to find answers to its questions. The company conducted a

study of 1,000 consumers who had recently bought or planned to purchase passenger tires, high-performance tires, or light-truck tires. Participants shopped several different virtual tire stores, each store offering a different assortment of products, pricing, and warranties. Goodyear believed it achieved brand equity if a consumer purchased a Goodyear product at a higher price than competitors' products, if it captured sales from competitors when Goodyear products were reduced in price, and if it maintained sales levels despite competitors' price cuts.

The results of the study assisted Goodyear in several ways. First, the company determined how shoppers in different product-market segments valued the Goodyear brand compared with competing brands. Second, the virtual market test allowed the company to test many different pricing strategies. This feature allowed Goodyear to evaluate how different prices, both its own and competitors' prices, affected consumer tendencies to switch brands. Third, major competitors were identified. Goodyear is aware of the companies it should consider its major competitors in general merchandise stores.

might not be suited for virtual test marketing. Virtual test markets can be used to study questions such as:

1. What is our brand equity in a new retail channel?

2. Do we offer a sufficient variety of products?

3. How should products be displayed?[34]

The Closer Look at Research box provides an example of how one company used virtual test markets.

Other Issues in Test Marketing

Consumer versus Industrial Test Marketing

Our discussion of test marketing has centered on the evaluation of consumer products. However, test marketing practices are used by manufacturers of industrial products as well, though with different methods. Rather than develop a product for trial in the market, industrial manufacturers seek input from customers to determine the features and technologies needed for new products. Manufacturers develop prototypes based on customers' input, then evaluate and test them using selected customers. The manufacturers receive feedback from customers involved in the product test and use the feedback to make further changes to the product before introducing it to the entire market. As with consumer test markets, industrial test markets can be lengthy. The longer a test market runs, the more likely it is a competitor will learn of the new product and respond by rushing a similar product to market or by becoming more competitive with existing products.

Matching Experimental Method with Objectives

When selecting a test marketing method, researchers should consider the objectives of the experiment. For example, if a company is test marketing an extension of its present product line, maybe a new color or flavor, it would be interested in the consumer acceptance of this new product. Therefore, it will want experiment results that can be generalized to all markets, not just the test markets. Also, it would want to observe how the new product performs in the market relative to the competition or how the trade accepts the new product. The decision for the company would be whether to use a standard test market or use a simulated or virtual test market. This decision is based on factors such as time, cost, and exposure to competition. Regardless of the method chosen, the objective is to project the potential of the new product for the entire market.

Other field experiments may require more control over real-world variables. Consider a company that wants to evaluate the effectiveness of an advertising campaign for a new product. While the ability to generalize the results of the experiment to the entire market is important, the company must try to determine whether a relationship is present between the advertising campaign and customers' acceptance of the new product. In other words, did the promotional campaign influence sales, or did the influence come from other variables, such as pricing or competition? This objective requires that the experiment have high internal validity. An experimental design for this objective might be an electronic test market that can record information about the consumers' television viewing (did they view the advertisement?), and purchase and repurchase behaviors (did they buy the advertised product and, if so, how many times?), and determine whether a relationship exists between the advertising campaign and product sales. Such an experiment might not be generalizable, but the company can determine whether the advertising campaign has the intended effect on a small sample of consumers. If the results are positive, the company might roll out the advertising campaign to other areas or even nationwide. If the results are not positive, the company can make changes in the advertising campaign or drop it completely.

Each test marketing approach possesses certain strengths and weaknesses. The researcher must weigh these strengths and weaknesses with the objectives of the field experiment. Once the researcher identifies the objective of the experiment, he or she can select the method that offers the greatest amount of the desired validity, internal or external. Some of the difficulties associated with standard test markets are leading to new trends in new-product testing. First, companies that do not want to undertake the time and expense of standard test markets could turn to simulated and virtual test markets. Also, the growing resistance of retailers to add thousands of new products may lead more companies to use test marketing methods other than standard test markets. Companies that find the standard test market process difficult but are not willing to try other methods may begin rolling out more products without any test marketing, especially if the risk of product failure is low. Read the Marketing Research in Action to see how the Lee Apparel Company used test marketing procedures to build a unique customer database to successfully launch a new brand of female jeans.

marketing research in action

Riders Fits New Database into Brand Launch

The Initial Launch

A few years ago, the Lee Apparel Company decided to market a new apparel line of jeans under the name *Riders*. The brand's management team seized the opportunity to use market test data from a field experiment to begin building a customer database to help successfully launch the new brand of jeans. Unlike the typical process of building a customer database around promotions, merchandising, and advertising efforts that directly benefit retailers, their goal was to use marketing dollars to build both the brand and the database. The initial launch of the Riders apparel line went well with rollouts in the company's Midwest and Northeast regional markets. The initial positioning strategy called for the products to be priced slightly higher than competitive brands and marketed at mass-channel retailers like Ames, Bradlee's, Caldor, Target, and Venture. During the first year, the communication program emphasized the line's "comfortable fit," and within two years the rollouts went national, using major retail channels like Wal-Mart.

Initially, Riders used a spring promotion called "Easy Money" to generate product trial and to gather name, address, and demographic information about the line's first customers. This data was collected using a rebate card and certificate from the retailer. Upon completing and mailing the rebate card to Riders, the customer was rewarded with a check in the mail. This initial market test provided valuable data on each customer, such as the exact type of product purchased, how much was spent, who they bought for, where they heard of the Riders brand, and their lifestyle interests. As part of the test market, Riders supported the effort with point-of-purchase (POP) displays and promotions in Sunday newspaper circulars. In addition, the management team funded the promotion and handled all development, redemption, and fulfillment in-house. Results of the first test market were as follows: a total of $1.5 million in certificates were distributed yielding a 2.1 percent response, or just over 31,000 customer names. About 20 percent of the buyers bought more than one item.

Another part of the test market design was the follow-up phone survey among new customers three months after the initial promotion. Of the customers surveyed, 62 percent had purchased Riders products. The survey provided detailed information to salespeople and consumers. Riders then repeated the test market design adding a postcard mailing to existing database names. The promotional effort netted over 40,000 new customer names and information for the database. It also proved the responsiveness of database customers—3.8 percent of the database customers who received the postcard promotion came into the store to make a purchase, compared to a 2.8 percent response to the POP and circular ads.

To build a successful customer database from test market designs, the critical first step is figuring out the most efficient way to gather names. Then comes the question of how you want to use the information with customers, prospects, and retailers. Finally, you begin the process of testing and evaluating the relationships, and applying what you have learned to build customer loyalty.

Focus on Retail Partnerships

The main goal of the Riders test marketing was to create valuable information that could be used to build relationships with Riders consumers and those retail accounts Riders depended on for distribution. The growing philosophy within the Riders brand management team was "The more we know about our customers, the better the decisions we'll be able to make in dealing both with them and with our retailers." Moreover, the detailed information such as hard dollar results of each promotion as well as the demographic profiles was shared with retailers, as was the research showing the consumer behavior benefits. For example, a tracking study found that purchase intent of database customers was twice that of nondatabase customers in a given trade area. Unaided brand awareness likewise was high (100 percent, compared to 16 percent of the general population), and awareness of Riders advertising was 53 percent compared to 27 percent.

The Riders team believed so strongly in tying database information with promotion efforts that they insisted that a database component be part of any chain-specific promotions. Management hoped to convince the retailers that build their own database capabilities to share their information. For example, retail account information can identify more product and promotion opportunities. Riders believed the real payoff comes when both manufacturer and retailer use data, from either source, to do a better job of attracting and keeping the key assets for both channel members—the customers. Riders must continue convincing retailers that putting Riders merchandise on their shelves is bringing people into their stores. From test marketing to creating complete customer databases, the Riders team has begun to put a major part of its marketing investment into image-building advertising strategies focused on print and television media.

For instance, they say, "The more we know about our customers and their preferences, the better we'll be able to hone our advertising messages and media buys, pinpoint what kind of promotions work best, and understand what new products we ought to be developing. As competitive pressures continue to mount, Riders expects detailed customer information to become more valuable in helping define the brand position clearly. Defining ourselves and what's different about Riders products is going to be an increasingly important element in drawing customers who have a great many choices to stores where Riders products are on the shelves. Although it initially began with test markets guiding the development of a complete customer database program, it's now the databases that are guiding the inclusion of key elements in our test market research. Riders' ultimate goal is creating a tool that is going to make its products more attractive to retailers and to consumers."

Hands-On Exercise

Using your knowledge about market tests from reading the chapter and the above discussion of the launch of Riders jeans, answer each of the following questions:

1. What was Lee Apparel Company's overall goal for conducting such an extensive test market of its new line of jeans under the brand name *Riders?* In your opinion did the company achieve its goal? Why or why not?

2. Identify and explain the strengths and weaknesses associated with the test market process used by the Lee Apparel Company.

3. In your opinion, should the company give consideration to the development and implementation of Web-based test marketing strategies? Why or why not?

Summary of Learning Objectives

■ **Discuss the characteristics, benefits, and weaknesses of observational techniques, and explain how these techniques are used to collect primary data.**
Observation techniques can be used by researchers in all types of research designs (exploratory, descriptive, causal). In addition to the general advantages of observation, major benefits are the accuracy of collecting data on actual behavior, reduction of confounding factors, and the amount of detailed behavioral data that can be recorded. The unique limitations of observation methods are lack of generalizability of the data, inability to explain current behaviors or events, and the complexity of observing the behavior.

■ **Describe and explain the importance of and differences between the variables used in experimental research designs.**
To conduct causal research, the researcher must understand the four key types of variables in experimental designs (independent, dependent, extraneous, control) as well as randomization of test subjects and the role theory plays in creating experiments. The most important goal of any experiment is to determine which relationships exist among different variables (independent, dependent). Functional (cause-effect) relationships require systematic change in one variable as another variable changes.

■ **Explain the theoretical importance and impact of internal, external, and construct validity measures in experiments and interpreting functional relationships.**
Experimental designs are developed to control for contamination, which may confuse the true relationship being studied. Internal, external, and construct validity are the main types of contamination to evaluate. Internal validity refers to the accuracy of conclusions the researcher draws about a demonstrated functional relationship. The question is, "Are the experimental results truly due to the experimental variables?" External validity is concerned with the interaction of experimental variables with extraneous factors causing a researcher to question the generalizability of the results to other settings. Construct validity is important in the process of correctly identifying and understanding both the independent and the dependent variables in an experimental design. Several techniques unique to experimental designs are used to control for problems of internal and external validity. These techniques center on the use of control groups, pre-experimental measures, exclusion of subjects, matching subjects into groups, and randomization of group members. These dimensions, built into the experimental design, provide true power for controlling contamination.

■ **Discuss the three major types of experimental designs used in marketing research. Explain the pros and cons of using causal designs as a means of assessing relationship outcomes.**
Pre-experimental designs do not meet internal validity criteria due to a lack of group comparisons. Despite this weakness, three designs are used quite frequently in marketing research: the one-shot study; the one-group pretest-posttest design; and the static group comparison. True experimental designs ensure equivalence between experimental and control groups by random assignment of subjects into groups. Three forms of true experimental designs exist: pretest-posttest control group; posttest-only control group; and the Solomon Four Group. Quasi-experimental designs are appropriate when the researcher can control some of the variables but cannot establish true randomization of groups. While a multitude of these designs exist, two of the most common forms are the nonequivalent control group and the separate-sample pretest-posttest.

■ **Explain what test markets are, the importance and difficulties of executing this type of research design, and how the resulting data structures are used by researchers and marketing practitioners.**
Test markets are a specific type of field experiment commonly conducted in natural field settings. Most common in the marketing research field are traditional test markets, controlled test markets, electronic test markets, simulated test markets, Web-based TV test markets, and virtual test markets. Data gathered from test markets provide both researchers and practitioners with invaluable information concerning customers' attitudes, preferences, purchasing habits/patterns, and demographic profiles. This information can be useful in predicting new product/service acceptance levels and advertising and image effectiveness, as well as in evaluating current marketing mix strategies.

Key Terms and Concepts

Review Questions

1. List the four types of experimental design variables and provide an explanation of each.

2. Identify the significant variables a consumer would consider when purchasing a computer.

3. Using college students as subjects for experimental studies is a common occurrence in marketing research. What possible problems could arise from this practice?

4. Identify the tests used for (a) pre-experimental testing and (b) true experimental testing. What advantages and disadvantages are associated with each?

5. Explain the difference between internal validity and external validity. Discuss the problems associated with each type of validity.

6. When field experiments are used, what factors are detrimental to the observational techniques that could be used as a control aspect?

7. What are the major advantages and disadvantages of observation studies relative to surveys?

8. Discuss how you might combine the observation technique of data collection with a focus group interview.

9. Discuss why disguised observation is an appropriate data collection technique for investigating how parents discipline their children when shopping at a supermarket.

10. Comment on the ethics of the following situations:
    a. You are unaware that a marketing researcher goes around on garbage day in your neighborhood and collects your trash prior to the trash person's arrival. The purpose is to determine your alcohol consumption behavior during the past month.
    b. You are invited by a researcher to be a test user for a new food item at a mall testing site and the researcher plans to secretly videotape your actions and reactions from behind a one-way mirror.

Discussion Questions

1. Which of the six types of test marketing are gaining acceptance with America's top advertisers? Why is this taking place?

2. Why do you feel that Adolph Coors Company has encountered so many problems in the past two decades concerning new-product introductions? What would you recommend that Coors do to solve these problems?

3. What type of observational technique and experimental design would you suggest for each of the following situations and why?
   a. The research and development director at Calvin Klein suggests a new type of cologne for men that could be promoted by a sports celebrity like Michael Jordan.
   b. The director of on-campus housing at your university proposes some significant style changes to the physical configuration of the current on-campus dorm rooms for freshmen and new transfer students.
   c. The vice president of marketing in charge of new store locations for Home Depot must decide on the best location for a new store in your hometown.
   d. The senior design engineer for DaimlerChrysler wants to identify meaningful design changes for the 2008 Jeep.
   e. A retail supermarket manager would like to know the popularity of a new brand of cereal that is produced by General Mills.

4. **EXPERIENCE THE INTERNET.** Go to the home page for the AC Nielsen research company: www.acnielsen.com. Examine the tools, procedures, and techniques the company uses for conducting test markets. Provide a brief explanation of the goals and objectives the company provides for its clients regarding test marketing.

5. Identify a restaurant situation and develop and execute a "mystery shopper" method that will allow you to collect observational data to answer the research questions below. Write a brief (one or two pages) summary report of your findings.
   a. How well do the restaurant servers and staff interact with their customers?
   b. How friendly are the restaurant's servers and staff to the customers?
   c. How courteous are the restaurant's servers and staff to the customers?
   d. How helpful are the restaurant's servers and staff in meeting customers' needs and wants?
   e. What is the level of product/service knowledge exhibited by the restaurant's servers and staff?
   f. How satisfying or dissatisfying was the restaurant experience?

6. The store manager of a local I.G.A. grocery store thought that customers might stay in the store longer if slow, easy-to-listen-to music were played over the store's intercom system. After some thought, the manager considered whether he should hire a marketing researcher to design an experiment to test the influence of music tempo on shoppers' behaviors. Answer the following questions:
   a. How would you operationalize the independent variable?
   b. What dependent variables do you think might be important in this experiment?
   c. Develop a hypothesis for each of your dependent variables.

7. Recall the continuing case about the Santa Fe Grill Mexican Restaurant from earlier chapters. The owners are interested in increasing the weekly sales of their Mexican chicken wings. Currently customers have three options for ordering these wings (10 wings for $6.00, 20 wings for $9.00, or 50 wings for $15.00). Management would like to know what impact various promotional incentives would have on the weekly sales of their Mexican chicken wings. The two experimental treatment incentives are offering a 25%-off coupon to customers versus a 25-cent wing (with a 15 wing minimum order) coupon. On the advice of a marketing research expert, a control group would need to be included in the experiment, and thus there would be three treatment groups involved: (1) 25%-off coupon, (2) 25-cent wing (minimum 15 wing order) coupon, and (3) no coupon. Design an experiment that would determine the impact of the proposed promotional incentives on the weekly sales of Mexican chicken wings at the Santa Fe Grill restaurant. Make sure you address each of the following items:
   a. Identify and diagram your experiment.
   b. Indicate how you would conduct the experiment.
   c. Assess the internal and external validity of your experiment.
   d. What, if any, extraneous factors will you have to deal with?

Go to the book's Web site at www.mhhe.com/hair06 for more examples of review and discussion questions.

part 4

Gathering and Collecting Accurate Data

chapter 9

Sampling: Theory and Design

Learning Objectives

After reading this chapter, you will be able to

1. Discuss the concept of sampling and list reasons for sampling.

2. Identify and explain the different roles of sampling in the overall information research process.

3. Demonstrate the basic terminology used in sampling decisions.

4. Understand the concept of error in the context of sampling.

5. Discuss and calculate sampling distributions, standard errors, and confidence intervals and how they are used in assessing the accuracy of a sample.

6. Discuss the factors that must be considered when determining sample size.

7. Discuss the methods of calculating appropriate sample sizes.

Sampling Design Decisions: American Airlines

Recently, the executive vice president of marketing for American Airlines (AA) received an end-of-quarter cost report indicating the costs of operating the airline's routes from California to New York and Washington, D.C., were increasing and the company was losing money. In an attempt to better understand the situation, the vice president discussed alternative plans of action with the manager of capacity planning. One of the problems AA was experiencing was the models used to estimate the number of passengers on AA flights did not include passengers' attitudes or intentions. While the price of airline tickets and past passenger load records were important factors in predicting future route loads, the models did not currently incorporate the possible effects of consumers' attitudes toward flying as a mode of transportation, particularly following 9/11. Customers' feelings of satisfaction toward in-flight services as well as their beliefs about American Airlines' ability to provide high-quality passenger services also played an important role in their airline selection process and future purchase intentions. It was clear that AA needed to collect some primary data from its known customer markets as well as from the general flying public.

A research proposal outlining the processes needed to capture the necessary primary data was prepared and presented to AA's vice president of marketing. The proposal discussed the information problems and research objectives, then turned to the methods for collecting the data. A self-administered survey using a multistage sampling plan appeared to be the most cost-efficient approach. At this point the vice president of marketing asked, "What is the real purpose behind such a complex-sounding sampling plan?" The response was it was needed to guarantee the quality of the data. Given that AA had flown over 40 million people in the past 12 months, it would be impossible to contact and interview each of those customers. Therefore, a sample would have to be taken and it would be critically important to ensure that the sample represented the company's total customer base. In addition, it was pointed out that AA's customer base had very different flying patterns. For example, some of the people choose the airline significantly more often than others, and some fly first class and others business class or economy class, and some are business travelers and others nonbusiness travelers. These groups of customers would have to be appropriately represented in any survey to ensure that the collected data portrayed a true picture of customers' attitudes and feelings toward flying AA. The results could then be used to generalize about the attitudes and behavior intentions of AA's total customer base. It was also noted that deciding who should be included in the study would affect the questions to be asked, development of the scale measurements, and the design of the questionnaire and support materials.

Because the airline's total customer population had different types of travelers, the use of a multistage stratified sampling plan was proposed. In such a plan it would be necessary not only to define each stratum very carefully but also to determine the appropriate sample size for each. Sample sizes become critical in determining the overall cost of collecting the required primary data, the accuracy or representativeness of the data, and the data that should be included in the company's current forecasting models. At this point, the costs of collecting the data could only be estimated because the actual sample sizes were not yet determined. Given the nature of management's immediate concerns with certain routes, it was suggested that the proposed research be a "pilot study." Depending on the results, the research could be expanded over time to include all AA routes. As a pilot study, the costs of data collection would be significantly less.

At the end of the presentation, tentative approval was given for budgeting $50,000 for the pilot study. One condition attached was that more specific cost figures would be offered prior to management's final approval. At this point, a complete sampling plan would have to be prepared. The Marketing Research in Action at the end of this chapter describes the sampling plan that was used.

Value of Sampling in Marketing Research

Sampling Selection of a small number of elements from a larger defined target group of elements and expecting that the information gathered from the small group will allow judgments to be made about the larger group.

Sampling is an important concept that we practice in our everyday activities. Consider, for example, going on a job interview. We have been taught that making a good first impression in a job interview is extremely important, because after that initial exposure (i.e., sample) many times people will make judgments about the type of person we are. People sit in front of their TV with a remote control in their hand and rapidly flip through a number of different channels, stopping a few seconds to take a sample of the program on each channel until they find a program worth watching. Next time you have a free moment, go to a bookstore like Barnes and Noble and observe sampling at its best. People at a bookstore generally pick up a book or magazine, look at its cover, and then read a few pages to get a feel for the author's writing style and the content before deciding whether to buy the book. When people go automobile shopping, they want to test-drive a particular car for a few miles to see how that car feels and performs before deciding whether to buy it. One commonality in all these situations is that a decision is based on the assumption that the smaller portion, or sample, is representative of the larger population. From a general perspective, **sampling** involves selecting a relatively small number of elements from a larger defined group of elements and expecting that the information gathered from the small group will enable accurate judgments about the larger group.

Sampling as a Part of the Research Process

Census A research study that includes data about every member of the defined target population.

Sampling is often used when it is impossible or unreasonable to conduct a census. With a **census** primary data is collected from *every* member of a defined target population. The best example of a census is the U.S. census, which takes place every 10 years.

Intuitively, it is easy to see that sampling is less time-consuming and less costly than conducting a census. For example, let's say the management of Delta Airlines wants to find out what business travelers like and dislike about flying Delta. Gathering data from about 2,000 Delta business travelers would be much less expensive and time-consuming than surveying several million travelers. No matter what type of research design is used to collect data, the time and money factors of research projects are usually critical to decision makers. For researchers, shorter projects are more likely to fit the decision maker's time frames.

The concept of sampling also plays an important role in the process of *identifying, developing,* and *understanding* new marketing concepts that need to be investigated. Consider a researcher helping the owner of a local doctor's walk-in clinic to understand the concept of service quality in medical practices. The researcher must identify the concepts that might make up service quality. By using exploratory research methods, a set of attributes representing the service quality construct can be developed. Another area in which sampling plays a significant role is *developing the scale measurements* used to collect primary data. When creating a scale, the researcher must have some idea of who the intended respondents are so the appropriate words and phrases are included in the design. In addition, the scale's reliability and validity must be assessed. These design activities require the researcher to administer the scale measurement to a representative subset of the proposed target population.

Samples also play an important indirect role in *designing questionnaires.* Depending on the research problem and the target population, sampling decisions will affect decisions regarding the type of research design, the survey instrument, and the actual questionnaire. For example, by having some general idea of the target population and the key characteristics that will be used to draw the sample of respondents, researchers can customize the questionnaire to ensure that the questionnaire is of interest to prospective respondents and provides high-quality data.

In cases where the process of measurement results in the destruction of the elements being studied, sampling may be the only alternative. For example, if every Ruffles potato chip that came off Frito-Lay's production line were tested for salt, oil, color, and so on, none would be left to package and sell. Although this reason for sampling is usually thought of in terms of quality control, it can be applied to many marketing problems that require primary research in the testing of new products or ideas. As these examples illustrate, there are different reasons for the use of sampling in research. The main objective is to enable researchers to make decisions about the target population using limited information. The concept of sampling involves two basic issues: (1) making the right decisions in selecting elements (e.g., people, products, or services), and (2) feeling confident that data from the sample can be transformed into accurate information about the target population.

Finally, this chapter sets the tone for better understanding topics later in the text: *construct development, scale measurement, questionnaire design, coding,* and *data analysis.* We begin the chapter by introducing you to the basics of sampling theory. Then we discuss how to determine appropriate sample sizes for different marketing research projects.

Overview: The Basics of Sampling Theory

Basic Sampling Terminology

Population

Population The identifiable set of elements of interest to the researcher and pertinent to the information problem.

A **population** is an identifiable group of elements (e.g., people, products, organizations) of interest to the researcher and pertinent to the information problem. For example, let's say the Mazda Motor Corporation hired J. D. Power and Associates to measure "customer satisfaction among automobile owners." This wording would suggest that the population of interest would be all people who own automobiles. It is unlikely, however, that J. D. Power and Associates could draw a sample that would be truly representative of such a broad, heterogeneous population—any data collected would probably not be generalizable about customer satisfaction that would be of use to Mazda. This lack of specificity unfortunately is common in marketing research. Most businesses that collect data are not really concerned with total populations, but with a prescribed segment. In this chapter we use a modified definition of population: *defined target population*. A **defined target population** consists of the complete group of elements (people or objects) that are identified for investigation based on the objectives of the research project. A precise definition of the target population is essential and is usually done in terms of *elements, sampling units,* or *time frames.*

Defined target population The complete set of elements identified for investigation.

Element

Element   A person or object from the defined target population from which information is sought.

An **element** is a person or object from which information is sought. Often in research, the element is a particular product or group of individuals. Elements must be unique, countable, and when added together, make up the whole of the target population. Elements can be viewed collectively as the target population frame from which a sample will be drawn. Target population elements might include a particular consumer product (e.g., BMW automobiles); specific groups of people (e.g., females aged 18 to 34, or households with checking accounts); or specific organizations (e.g., Fortune 500 companies). When the initial definition of the target population incorrectly identifies the elements, it creates a bias referred to as target population frame error.

Sampling Units

Sampling units   The target population elements available for selection during the sampling process.

Sampling units are the target population elements available for selection during the sampling process. In a single-stage sample, the sampling units and the population elements may be the same. However, many studies involve complex problems that require the use of a multistage sampling process. Using the Mazda example as a case in point, owners of Mazda cars might be the population elements of interest, but J. D. Power and Associates might be concerned only with owners who have purchased a new Mazda in the last two years. Therefore, the target population would be redefined. Refining the set of population elements with a second factor creates population segments from which to draw a representative sample.

Target population elements also might be identified using a specified time frame (e.g., the year 2005, the month of August 2005, or the period from April 15 to April 30, 2006). For instance, the Mazda Corporation might want customer satisfaction information among only Mazda automobile owners who have purchased new cars in 2005. Consequently, J. D. Power and Associates would have to further refine its definition of the target population, thus reducing the eligible sampling units. Exhibit 9.1 illustrates some hypothetical examples that summarize the impact of these factors on target populations.

Sampling Frame

Sampling frame   The list of all eligible sampling units.

After defining the target population, the researcher develops a list of all eligible sampling units, referred to as a **sampling frame.** Some common sources of sampling frames are lists of registered voters and customer lists from magazine publishers or credit card companies. There also are specialized commercial companies (e.g., Survey Sampling, Inc.; American Business Lists, Inc.; Scientific Telephone Samples) that sell databases containing names, addresses, and telephone numbers of potential population elements. Although the costs of

eXHIBIT 9.1	Hypothetical Examples of the Impact of Elements, Sampling Units, and Time Frames

Mazda Automobiles

Elements	Adult purchasers of automobiles
Sampling unit	New Mazda automobiles
Time frame	January 1, 2005, to September 30, 2005

Nail Polish

Elements	Females between the ages of 18 and 34 who purchased at least one brand of nail polish during the past 30 days
Sampling units	U.S. cities with populations between 100,000 and 1 million people
Time frame	June 1 to June 15, 2005

Retail Banking Services

Elements	Households with checking accounts
Sampling units	Households located within a 10-mile radius of NationsBank's central location in Charlotte, North Carolina
Time frame	January 1 to April 30, 2005

obtaining such sampling lists will vary, a list typically can be purchased for between $100 and $200 per 1,000 names.[1]

Regardless of the source, it often is difficult and expensive to obtain accurate, representative, and current sampling frames. It is doubtful, for example, that a list of individuals who have eaten a taco from a Taco Bell in a particular city in the past six months will be readily available. In this instance, a researcher would have to use an alternative method such as random-digit dialing (if conducting telephone interviews) or a location survey (e.g., a mall-intercept interview) to generate a sample of prospective respondents.

The Main Factors Underlying Sampling Theory

To understand sampling theory, you must know sampling related concepts and symbols. Exhibit 9.2 shows a summary of the basic concepts and their symbols. Descriptions and discussions of these concepts are provided in this chapter and revisited in later chapters.

In many statistics texts, sampling concepts and approaches are discussed for situations where the key population parameters are either known or unknown by the researcher prior to conducting the research project. Discussion here is limited to situations where the researcher does not know the true population parameters. The logic behind this perspective is twofold. First, today's business environments are so complex and rapidly changing that it is highly unlikely business decision makers know the parameters of their target populations. For example, most retailers that recently added online shopping alternatives for consumers are scrambling to identify and describe the people who are now making their retail purchases over the Internet rather than at traditional "brick and mortar" stores. Today, experts estimate that the world's online population exceeds 400 million people,[2] but the actual number of online retail shoppers is anyone's guess. One of the major goals of researching small, yet representative, samples of assumed members of a defined target population is that of using sample results to either predict or estimate what the true population parameters are within a certain degree of confidence.

EXHIBIT 9.2   Concepts and Symbols Used in Sampling Theory*

Population Parameters	Symbol	Sample Notations	Symbol
Size	N	Size	n
Mean value	μ	Mean value	$\bar{x}$
Percentage value (population proportion)	P	Percentage value (sample proportion)	$\bar{p}$
	Q or $[1 - P]$		$\bar{q}$ or $[1 - \bar{p}]$
Standard deviation	σ	Estimated standard deviation	$\bar{s}$
Variance	σ^2	Estimated sample	$\bar{s}^2$
Standard error (population parameter)	S_μ or S_P	Estimated standard error (sample statistics)	$S_{\bar{x}}$ or $S_{\bar{p}}$
Other Sampling Concepts			
Confidence intervals	$CI_{\bar{x}}$ or $CI_{\bar{p}}$		
Tolerance level of error	e		
Critical z-value	Z_B		
Confidence levels	CL		
Finite correction factor (the overall square root of $[N - n/N - 1]$ (also referred to as "finite multiplier" or "finite population correction")	fcf		

*For a quick review of these concepts and symbols go to the book's Web site at www.mhhe.com/hair06 and follow the links.

Second, if business decision makers had complete knowledge about their defined target populations, they would have perfect information about the realities of those populations, thus eliminating the need to conduct primary research. Moreover, better than 95 percent of today's marketing problems exist primarily because decision makers lack information about their problem situations and who their customers are, as well as customers' attitudes, preferences, and marketplace behaviors.

An important assumption that underlies sampling theory is that the population elements are randomly distributed. That is, if a researcher were able to do a census of the entire target population elements, then the probability distribution of the population (e.g., actual dollar sales revenue per Home Depot store) would be a normal bell-shaped distribution. Theoretically, this assumption enables the researcher to believe that if repeated random, representative samples of the known sampling elements were taken, then the resulting **sampling distribution** would be a normal distribution.

Sampling distribution
The frequency distribution of a specific sample statistic (e.g., sample mean or sample proportion) from repeated random samples of the same size.

For example, assume researchers are interested in determining the average household income in the state of Florida and there are almost 5 million households in Florida. Moreover, the researchers are able to take 1,000 separate random samples, each the size of 500 households. Assume further that state records show the average household income (μ) of these 4.73 million households is $28,000 and the sampling distribution of average household income ($\bar{x}$) from the 1,000 random samples ranges from $15,500 to $41,000. The frequency distribution of the means ($\bar{x}$) of those samples would be a normal, bell-shaped curve with the population mean (μ) as the mean of the distribution, as shown in Exhibit 9.3.

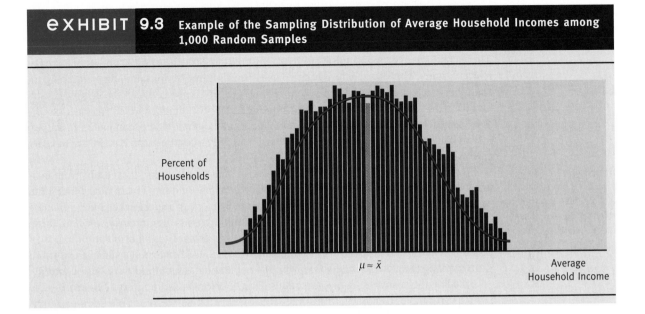

exHIBIT 9.3 Example of the Sampling Distribution of Average Household Incomes among 1,000 Random Samples

Percent of Households

$\mu \approx \bar{x}$

Average Household Income

In reality, it would not be practical to take 1,000 different samples. The idea of a sampling distribution is a theoretical concept. However, it is a fundamental aspect of sampling. To deal with the reality of this sampling factor, researchers rely on the central limit theorem in drawing a representative sample from a target population rather than many repeated samples.

Central Limit Theorem

Central limit theorem (CLT) Theorem that states that for almost all target populations, the sampling distribution of the means ($\bar{x}$) or the percentage ($\bar{p}$) value derived from a simple random sample will be approximately normally distributed provided that the sample size is sufficiently large.

The **central limit theorem (CLT)** is the theoretical backbone of survey research. The CLT is important in understanding the concepts of sampling error, statistical significance, and sample sizes. In brief, the theorem states that for almost all defined target populations, the sampling distribution of the mean ($\bar{x}$) or the percentage ($\bar{p}$) value derived from a simple random sample will be approximately normally distributed, provided the sample size is sufficiently large (i.e., when n is $>$ or $=$ 30). Moreover, the mean ($\bar{x}$) of the random sample with an estimated sampling error ($S_{\bar{x}}$) fluctuates around the true population mean (μ) with a standard error of $\sigma/\sqrt{n}$ and an approximately normal sampling distribution, regardless of the shape of the probability frequency distribution of the overall target population. In other words, there is a high probability that the mean of any sample ($\bar{x}$) taken from the target population will be a close approximation of the true target population mean (μ), as one increases the size of the sample (n). With an understanding of the basics of the central limit theorem, the researcher can

1. Draw representative samples from any target population.

2. Obtain sample statistics from a random sample that serve as accurate estimates of the target population's parameters.

3. Draw one random sample, instead of many, reducing the costs of data collection.

4. Test more accurately the reliability and validity of constructs and scale measurements.

5. Statistically analyze data and transform them into meaningful information about the target population.

Theoretical Tools Used to Assess the Quality of Samples

There are numerous opportunities to make mistakes that result in some type of bias in any research study. This bias can be classified as either sampling or nonsampling error. Random sampling errors could be detected by observing the difference between the sample results and the results of a census conducted using identical procedures. Two difficulties associated with detecting sampling error are (1) a census is very seldom conducted in survey research and (2) sampling error can be determined only after the sample is drawn and data collection is completed.

Sampling error   Any type of bias that is attributable to mistakes in either drawing a sample or determining the sample size.

From a theoretical perspective, **sampling error** is any type of bias that results from mistakes in either the selection process for prospective sampling units or in determining the sample size. Moreover, random sampling error tends to occur because of chance variations in the selection of sampling units. Even if the sampling units are properly selected, those units still might not be a perfect representation of the defined target population, but they generally are reliable estimates. When there is a discrepancy between the statistic estimated from the sample and the actual value from the population, a sampling error has occurred.

Based on the central limit theorem, the sampling error can be reduced by increasing the size of the sample. Exhibit 9.4 illustrates the relationship between sample sizes and sampling error.

The results show that doubling the size of the sample does not reduce the sampling error by the same factor. In fact, the sampling error can become so small that it raises questions concerning the overall costs involved with data collection. In short, increasing the sample size primarily to reduce the standard error may not be worth the cost.

Nonsampling error   A bias that occurs in a research study regardless of whether a sample or census is used.

Nonsampling errors occur in a study regardless of whether a sample or a census is used. These errors can occur at any stage of the research process. For example, the target population may be inaccurately defined causing population frame error; inappropriate question/scale measurements can result in measurement error; a questionnaire may be poorly designed causing response error; or there may be other errors in gathering and recording data or when raw data are coded and entered for analysis. In general, the more extensive a study the greater the potential for nonsampling errors. Unlike sampling error, there are no statistical procedures to assess the impact of nonsampling errors on the quality of the data collected. Nonsampling errors usually are related to the accuracy of the data, whereas sampling errors relate to the representativeness of the sample to the defined target population.

Statistical Precision

Critical level of error The observed difference between a sample statistical value and the corresponding true or hypothesized population parameter.

Knowing the sampling distributions and their shapes enables the researcher to make estimates of the target population. The critical level of error (i.e., allowable margin of error) is specified prior to doing a research study. This critical level of error (e) represents general precision (S) with no specific confidence level or precise precision $[(S)(Z_{B, CL})]$ when a specific level of confidence is required. The **critical level of error** is the amount of observed difference between a sample statistical value (e.g., $\bar{x}$ or $\bar{p}$) and the true target population parameter (e.g., μ or P).

General precision   The amount of general sampling error associated with raw data.

General precision can be viewed as the amount of general sampling error associated with the sample data. **Precise precision** represents the amount of sampling error associated with the data at a specified level of confidence. When attempting to measure the precision of data, researchers must incorporate the theoretical aspects of sampling distributions, the central limit theorem, and the estimated standard error in order to calculate the necessary confidence intervals.

Precise precision   The amount of sampling error at a specified level of confidence.

еXHIBIT 9.4 Theoretical Example of the Relationship of Sample Sizes to Estimates of Sampling Error

In this example, the researcher is interested in better understanding the impact of sample size on predicted estimates of sampling error. Using the estimated standard error for a sample percentage where $(S_{\bar{p}})$ equals the overall square root of $(\bar{p})(\bar{q})/n$ and $\bar{p}$ is held constant at 50%, the researcher calculates the predicted estimated standard error as the sample is doubled holding all other factors constant. The results would be as follows:

Sample Results ($\bar{p}$)	Sample Size	Estimated Standard Error ($S_{\bar{p}}$)	Change in $S_{\bar{p}}$
50%	10	±15.8%	—
50	20	±11.2	4.6%
50	40	±7.9	3.3
50	80	±5.6	2.3
50	160	±4.0	1.6
50	320	±2.8	1.2
50	640	±2.0	0.8

Graphically displaying the results:

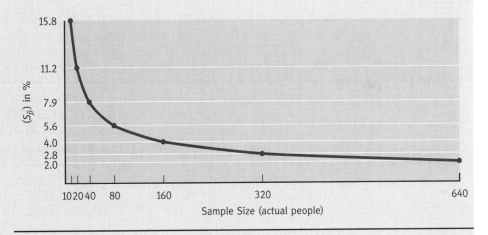

Estimated Standard Error

Estimated standard error, also referred to as general precision, is a measure of the sampling error and an indication of how far the sample result lies from the actual target population parameter. The formula to compute the estimated standard error of a sample mean $(S_{\bar{x}})$ is

$$S_{\bar{x}} = \bar{s}/\sqrt{n}$$

where $\bar{s}$ = Estimated standard deviation of the sample mean

   n = Sample size

For example, suppose Burger King conducts a survey among the general population to determine how many hamburgers the average household in America consumes in a typical 30-day period. A sample of 950 telephone numbers is randomly selected from the corporation's newly purchased telephone-number database, which consists of over 95 million residential telephone numbers. The survey results show the average number of hamburgers consumed per household in the given period is 36 (i.e., $\bar{x} = 36$), and the estimated sample standard deviation is 12.5 hamburgers. Using the above formula, the researcher calculates the estimated standard error of the sample to be $\pm.406$ hamburgers. Now assume the researcher had randomly sampled only 400 households and the average number of hamburgers and estimated standard deviation values were found to be the same as before. In this case, the calculated general sampling error associated with the study increases to $\pm.625$ hamburgers. Without considering a confidence factor, the results suggest there is a greater chance of sampling error when the sample size is reduced. This further illustrates the inherent inverse relationship between sample size (n) and the estimated standard error of a sample mean ($S_{\bar{x}}$).

We can also find the estimated standard error of a sample percentage value ($S_{\bar{p}}$) by using the following formula:

$$S_{\bar{p}} = \sqrt{\frac{[(\bar{p})(\bar{q})]}{n}}$$

where

$\bar{p}$ = The percentage of the sample possessing a specific characteristic

$\bar{q}$ = The percentage of the sample not possessing the characteristic or $(1 - \bar{p})$

n = Sample size

Bank of America, for example, conducts a survey of customers with checking accounts and finds that 65 percent of those sampled have a savings account in addition to a checking account (i.e., $\bar{p} = 65\%$). The results are from a random sample of 489 currently known Bank of America customers. Using the above $S_{\bar{p}}$ formula for sample percentages, the estimated standard error associated with the sample percentage would be ± 2.16 percentage points.

The estimated standard error is a measure of variability since it measures the range the actual value of the target population can be expected to fall within. The more spread out the data, the greater the variability and the larger the estimated standard error. The more similar the survey results, the less the variability. The estimated standard error can be used to construct a confidence interval in which the actual target population's parameter is expected to fall. To see more examples of how estimated standard errors are used in determining statistical precision, visit the book's Web site at www.mhhe.com/hair06 and follow the links.

Confidence Interval

Confidence interval

The statistical range of values within which the true value of the defined target population parameter is expected to lie.

A **confidence interval** represents a statistical range of values within which the true value of the target population parameter is expected to lie. The endpoints of a confidence interval (upper and lower values) are determined on the basis of the sample's results. The following formulas can be used to establish a confidence interval for a population's mean value (μ) and a population's proportion value (P). The confidence interval formula for a population mean parameter is

$$\text{CI}_{\mu} = \bar{x} \pm (S_{\bar{x}})(Z_{\text{B, CL}})$$

where

CI_{μ} = Confidence interval for a target population mean parameter

$\bar{x}$ = Sample mean value

$S_{\bar{x}}$ = Estimated standard error of the sample mean

$Z_{\text{B, CL}}$ = Level of confidence expressed in z-values (which are standardized)

The confidence interval formula for a population proportion parameter is

$$CI_P = \bar{p} \pm (S_{\bar{p}})(Z_{B, CL})$$

where

CI_P = Confidence interval for a target population propotion parameter

$\bar{p}$ = Sample proportion value

$S_{\bar{p}}$ = Estimated standard error of the sample proportion

$Z_{B, CL}$ = Level of confidence expressed in z-values (which are standardized)

In theory there are an infinite number of confidence levels, ranging from almost zero to almost 100 percent. But the most commonly used confidence levels are the 90, 95, and 99 percent levels. Since the central limit theorem enables researchers to assume a normal distribution, researchers can apply their knowledge of basic statistics regarding normal distributions and use a critical z-value of 1.65 for a 90 percent level of confidence, 1.96 for a 95 percent level of confidence, and 2.58 for a 99 percent level of confidence. Since these are the standardized z-values, their values are the only ones represented for their respective confidence levels and do not change when calculating confidence intervals.

To use the above Bank of America example, if the researcher wants to construct a 95 percent confidence interval for the bank survey results, the above formula for a population proportion confidence interval could be used by incorporating the estimated standard error previously calculated, as shown below.

$$CI_P = 65\% \pm (2.16)(1.96)$$
$$= 65\% \pm 4.23\%$$
$$= (65\% - 4.23\%), (65\% + 4.23\%)$$
$$= 60.77\% \leq P \leq 69.23\%$$

In interpreting the confidence interval, we are 95 percent confident that the actual percentage of Bank of America customers that have a checking account and a savings account will fall between 60.77 and 69.23 percent. Stated another way, if the researcher had drawn repeated random samples of Bank of America checking account customers, then 95 percent of the time (19 out of 20 times, or 95 out of 100 times), the true percentage of customers holding both checking and savings accounts with Bank of America would be somewhere between 60.77 and 69.23 percent.

The value generated by multiplying the estimated standard error by the critical z-value determines the amount of sampling error that occurs due to the sampling process. This is the precise precision at a given level of confidence. To see more examples of calculating confidence intervals, visit our Web site at www.mhhe.com/hair06 and follow the links.

Probability Sampling and Sample Sizes

Determining the sample size is not an easy task. The researcher must consider how precise the estimates must be and how much time and money are available to collect the required data, since data collection is generally one of the most expensive components of a study. Three factors play an important role in determining sample sizes:

1. **The variability of the population characteristic under investigation (σ_μ or σ_P).**
   The greater the variability of the characteristic the larger the sample size necessary.

2. **The level of confidence desired in the estimate (CL).** The higher the level of confidence desired the larger the sample size needed.

3. **The degree of precision desired in estimating the population characteristic (e).** The more precise the required sample results (i.e., the smaller the e) the larger the sample size.

As with confidence intervals, there are separate formulas for determining sample size based on a predicted population mean (μ) and a population proportion (P). The formulas are used to estimate the sample size for a simple random sample. When the situation involves estimating a population mean, the formula for calculating the sample size would be

$$n = (Z^2_{B,CL})\left(\frac{\sigma^2}{e^2}\right)$$

where

$Z_{B,CL}$ = The standardized z-value associated with the level of confidence

σ_μ = Estimate of the population standard deviation (σ) based on some type of prior information

e = Acceptable tolerance level of error (stated in percentage points)

In situations where estimates of a population proportion are of concern, the standardized formula for calculating the needed sample size would be

$$n = (Z^2_{B,CL})\left(\frac{[P \times Q]}{e^2}\right)$$

where

$Z_{B,CL}$ = The standardized z-value associated with the level of confidence

P = Estimate of expected population proportion having a desired characteristic based on intuition or prior information

Q = $[1 - P]$, or the estimate of expected population proportion not holding the characteristic of interest

e = Acceptable tolerance level of error (stated in percentage points)

The formulas for determining the sample size are an extension of the standard formula for calculating the standard error of the population parameter, either S_μ or S_P, at a particular confidence level. Several general relationships are apparent between the formulas and the size of a sample. For example, when using the population mean formula, as the variability (σ_μ) of the probability distribution of the population mean (μ) increases, holding the other factors constant, the larger the required sample size. Fundamentally, this relationship holds because (σ_μ) is part of the numerator of the equation. In contrast, when the situation requires the use of a population proportion (P), any population proportion other than 50 percent (e.g., $P = 70\%$ or $P = 30\%$), holding the other factors constant, will result in a decrease in the required sample size.

There is a direct relationship between the desired level of confidence (e.g., 90 percent, 95 percent, 99 percent) and the required sample size. Confidence levels are directly associated with corresponding critical z-values (i.e., 90% CL $\approx$ 1.65; 95% CL $\approx$ 1.96; 99% CL $\approx$ 2.58). The higher the level of confidence required the larger the required number in the sample.

The last key consideration is the acceptable critical level of error (e). It is the amount of statistical precision specified by the researcher. This value is normally stated as a percentage (e.g., 2% [.02], 5% [.05], or 10% [.10]), but it can be expressed as a mean value. The lower the percentage, the more precise the estimate and therefore the larger the required sample size.

The following example shows how to calculate the sample size where population parameter estimates from a pilot study are used. Assume you are the research analyst for LDS Technologies, a long-distance telephone service provider located in Chicago, Illinois. Three months ago, LDS conducted a pilot study in San Diego, California, among 200 households using a variety of long-distance telephone services. The results suggested that 50 percent of the households could be classified as regular users of long-distance telephone services. LDS has decided to do a larger study so it can predict potential long-distance telephone usage patterns as well as understand people's criteria for choosing long-distance telephone services in the West Coast market. Management wants data precision to be ±3 percent with a 99 percent confidence level. To determine the sample size, use the standard formula for a population proportion:

$$n = (Z^2_{B,CL})\left(\frac{[P \times Q]}{e^2}\right)$$

where

$Z_{B,CL}$ = 2.58, the standardized z-value associated with the 99% confidence level

P = 50%, the estimated proportion of LDS's potential customer base who are regular users of long-distance telephone services

Q = 50%, $[1 - P]$ or the estimated proportion of LDS's potential customer base who are not regular users of long-distance telephone services

e = ±3.0%, the acceptable critical level of error (stated in percentage points)

Thus,

$$n = 2.58^2 \frac{(50 \times 50)}{3.0^2}$$

$$= 6.6564 \frac{(2.500)}{9.0}$$

$$= 6.6564 \,(277.8) = 1,849.15, \text{ or } 1,850 \text{ households}$$

LDS will have to randomly select and survey a sample of 1,850 households in the West Coast market for the research results to meet the desired ±3.0 percent critical level of error at a 99 percent confidence level. For more examples of calculating sample sizes, visit the Web site at www.mhhe.com/hair06.

Sample Size and Small Finite Populations

Finite correction factor (fcf) An adjustment factor to the sample size that is made in those situations where the drawn sample is expected to be equal to 5% or more of the defined target population. fcf is equal to the overall square root of [$N - n/N - 1$].

The population size does not impact the sample size. There is often a misconception that a larger population requires a larger sample. But the size of the population is not a direct factor in determining sample size. If the sample size is large relative to the population, a **finite correction factor (fcf),** should be used to determine the sample size. Research industry standards suggest that sample size is considered large if it is more than 5 percent of the population. The formula for the finite correction factor is:

$$\sqrt{\frac{N-n}{N-1}}$$

where

N = Known (or given) defined target population size

n = Calculated sample size using the original sample size formula

Using the finite correction factor is a two-step process. First, we determine whether the sample size is more than 5 percent of the population by taking the calculated sample size and dividing it by the target population size. Second, if it is more than 5 percent, we calculate the appropriate finite correction factor and multiply the originally calculated sample size by it to adjust the required sample size. To illustrate how the finite correction factor affects estimates of sample sizes, let's use the above LDS example.

Initially not knowing how many households actually make up LDS's West Coast market, the researcher estimates that 1,850 randomly selected households would have to be included in the study, with data precision of ±3 percent and a 99 percent confidence level. Now let's assume that LDS learns the initial target population size of the West Coast market is expected to be about 15,000 households. To determine whether the initial sample size needs to be adjusted, the researcher would first determine if the initial sample size was greater than 5 percent of the total defined target population size. This is achieved simply by dividing the estimated sample size (n = 1,850 households) by the target population size (N = 15,000 households). The results of this first step show the initial estimated sample size represents about 12.33 percent of the defined target population. Therefore, the finite correction factor should be applied to adjust the sample size estimate.

Using the above formula, the correction factor is .93634. Now multiplying the initial sample-size estimate (1,850 households) by the correction factor, LDS learns that the number of households needed in the larger study is only 1,733, a reduction of 117 households. When appropriately used, the single biggest benefit of the finite correction factor is that it reduces the overall costs of collecting data. Visit our Web site www.mhhe.com/hair06 for more examples.

When the defined target population size in a consumer study is 500 elements or less, the researcher should consider doing a census of the population rather a sample. The logic behind this is based on the theoretical notion that at least 384 sampling units need to be included in most studies to have a 95 percent confidence level and a sampling error of ±5 percentage points. Read the nearby Closer Look at Research box to learn how some companies have used consumer profile databases to reduce the need for costly customized random sampling designs.

Sample sizes in business-to-business studies present a different problem than in consumer studies where the population almost always is very large. With business-to-business studies the population frequently is only 200 to 300 individuals. What then is an acceptable sample size? In such cases an attempt is made to contact and complete a survey from all individuals in the population. An acceptable sample size may be as small as 30 percent or so but the final decision would be made after examining the profile of the respondents. For example, you could look at position titles to see if you have a good cross section of respondents from all relevant categories. You likely also will determine what proportion of the firm's annual business is represented in the sample to avoid having only smaller firms (or accounts) that do not provide a representative picture of the firm's customers. Whatever approach you use, in the final analysis you must have a good understanding of who has responded so you can accurately interpret the study's findings.

Nonprobability Sampling and Sample Size

Sample size formulas cannot be used for nonprobability samples. Determining the sample size for nonprobability samples is usually a subjective, intuitive judgment made by the researcher based on either past studies, industry standards, or the amount of resources

A Closer Look at Research

Dannon Yogurt Eliminates the Need for Costly Customized Random Sampling Designs[3]

The Dannon Yogurt Company is the market leader for yogurt in the United States. Increased competition convinced Dannon it needed a better understanding of the features that differentiate its brand of yogurt from the competition. Dannon worked with Grey Advertising Inc. (www.grey.com) and two other partners, Ambrosino Research and Marketplace Measurement World-wide, to develop the Dannon con-sumer tracking system. Designed to monitor the yogurt market, the system relied on a 300-member yogurt consumer database. Rather than having to periodically develop expensive random samples of yogurt users to collect data, the database enabled Grey Advertising to conduct quarterly telephone interviews among all 300 database members to assess consumers' category, brand, and advertising awareness; brand usage; and attitudes toward Dannon and competitors' brands.

Using three waves of interviews combined ($n = 900$), the data were analyzed with Competitive Leverage Analysis. The findings indicated that consumers liked Dannon Yogurt because of the company's commitment to quality and purity in

its ingredients and because of its packaging. "Consumers felt a strong emotional attachment to buying Dannon, a sense of nurturing self and family." From the findings, Grey developed a new ad campaign slogan—"Taste Why It's Dannon"—to emphasize the care Dannon takes to use high-quality ingredients and suggest this care is evident in the yogurt's taste. Measurement of the campaign's impact on Dannon's sales was partially tracked using supermarket scanner data from Information Resources Inc. (IRI). Results showed Dannon's yogurt sales were growing at a faster pace than the yogurt category itself. An interesting side effect of this research approach was that not only did the new ad campaign help stimulate Dannon sales to new heights, but Grey Advertising, Dannon, Ambrosino Research, and Marketplace Measurement Worldwide received the prestigious Advertising Research Foundation (ARF) David Ogilvy Award in recognition of the effective use of research to develop advertising.

Consumer profile databases enable researchers to develop effective alternative sampling approaches to data collection rather than using more costly random sampling.

available. Regardless of the method, the sampling results cannot be used to make statistical inferences about the true population parameters. The best that can be offered is directional ideas about the target population.

Sample Sizes versus Usable Observations

An issue of concern in estimating sample sizes that is rarely discussed but should be considered is which observations are actually usable. Researchers can estimate the number of sampling units that must be surveyed. But often not all the initial responses are usable. Reasons for this include inactive mailing addresses, telephone numbers no longer in service, incomplete responses, and so forth.

A question can be raised concerning the sample-size value that is incorporated into many of the statistical formulas used to estimate the defined target population's parameters from a survey's sample statistics. For example, if in the sampling process researchers estimate that one sample size—say, 1,850—is needed but fewer sampled units—say, 1,500—are available for data analysis, then what sample size should be used in the statistical models to calculate and test estimates of the target population—1,850 or 1,500? The difference of 350 sampling units can have a significant impact on the relative magnitudes of the sample statistics.

How specifically the target population is defined (i.e., the number of qualifying factors) will affect the researcher's ability to obtain a representative list of all the sampling units that can be effective in locating the sampling units. While there are a number of factors that can make any list less than 100 percent usable, the list's reachable rate and overall incidence rate, combined with the study's expected completion rate and the estimated sample size, are key in determining the actual number of contacts (e.g., telephone calls, initial mall-intercepts, or mailings) necessary to obtain the required data from a sample. The total number of contacts will directly affect the overall cost of data collection. The reachable rate (RR) will reflect the quality of the sampling frame. For example, in a direct mail survey, the mailing list that serves as the sampling frame may be dated, with some of the listed addresses no longer active. Typically, the percentage of active addresses on a mailing list serves as the reachable rate.

The overall incidence rate (OIR) is the percentage of the defined target population elements that qualify for inclusion in the survey. For example, assume researchers are doing a telephone survey for Time Warner Cable on people's TV viewing habits. Assume further the needed sample size is estimated to be 1,500 people. In addition, Time Warner decides that to qualify for the survey, individuals must meet the following set of requirements:

- Be between the ages of 20 and 60.

- Have a cable TV set.

- Do not work for a telecommunication company, marketing research firm, or TV station, or have anyone in their immediate household who does.

- Have not participated in a marketing research study in the past six months.

The more qualifying requirements placed on prospective respondents, the greater the chance an individual will not qualify. A rule of thumb is that as more qualifying factors are used in locating prospective respondents, the overall incidence rate significantly decreases.

In the research industry, the expected completion rate (ECR) reflects the percentage of prospective respondents who will follow through and complete the survey. This factor is also referred to as the anticipated response rate. In the Time Warner example, let's say the reachable rate was determined to be 90 percent, the overall incidence rate was estimated to be 55 percent, and the expected completion rate for telephone interviews of this nature was 85 percent. Using the following formula,

$$\text{Number of contacts} = \frac{n}{(\text{RR}) \times (\text{OIR}) \times (\text{ECR})}$$

$$= \frac{1{,}500}{.90 \times .55 \times .85}$$

$$= \frac{1{,}500}{.421} = 3{,}562.95, \text{ or } 3{,}563 \text{ people}$$

To ensure the estimated sample size of 1,500 will be obtained, this number must be adjusted by the reachable, overall incidence, and expected completion rates. Consequently, this means that Time Warner Cable must contact about 3,563 people in order to ensure the sample size of 1,500 people is obtained. Prior to conducting the study, Time Warner will have to consider the cost of contacting an extra 2,063 people in order to base the results on the needed 1,500 respondents.

marketing research in action

Sampling Design Decisions in Providing Meaningful Primary Data

American Airlines

This illustration is a continuation of the American Airlines research and sampling problem in the chapter opener. You should review that situation before continuing here.

Using both AA's existing marketing research and route load databases, the number of passengers who flew on American Airlines routes over a three-year period from California to New York and Washington, D.C., was determined. The route load records indicated that on average, 2.73 million people (i.e., 30 daily flights $\times$ 7 days $\times$ 52 weeks $\times$ 250 passengers [83.3 percent average load factor]) boarded flights having a final destination of New York and another 1.92 million people (i.e., 22 daily flights $\times$ 7 days $\times$ 52 weeks $\times$ 240 passengers [80.0 percent average load factor]) boarded flights with their final destination being Washington, D.C. On average, 18 of the daily flights to New York (60 percent) were direct flights, and AA averaged 11 daily direct flights (50 percent) to Washington, D.C. Based on total passengers to the two destinations, total passenger population was estimated to be about 4.85 million people per year, with a little over 60 percent going to New York airports and about 40 percent to airports in Washington, D.C.

A complicating factor involved "indirect" flights in which passengers might not have New York or Washington, D.C., as their final destination, and new passengers that might have boarded the flight at one of the intermediate stops. Consequently, the known percentage values of direct flights to each final destination were used to initially calculate the needed sample sizes for the segment of passengers flying to New York ($P = 60\%$) and those to Washington, D.C. ($P = 50\%$). Furthermore, a 99 percent confidence level was used and a sampling error tolerance level of ± 2.5 percentage points because the data would be used as input for route load forecasting models.

Using the standard formulas for calculating sample size from known population parameter values $\left[n = (Z^2_{99\%\text{CL}})(P^*Q)/e^2 \right]$, it was estimated the sample sizes should be 2,556 passengers flying to New York and 2,663 people going to Washington, D.C. Then the question became one of how to select the actual people from each of the respective target populations. Thoughts of using direct mail surveys, personal interviews, or telephone interviews were eliminated on the basis of a combination of time factors, high interviewing costs, low response rates, and survey design costs. Instead, an "in-flight" self-administered survey approach was used. With the knowledge that AA flew 126 direct routes (averaging 31,500 passengers) to New York and 77 (averaging 18,480 passengers) to Washington, D.C., per week, specific flights could be randomly selected over either the entire year, month, week, or day to obtain the needed number of surveys. AA's marketing research department reported the usual response rate for in-flight surveys was about 50 percent. This rate accounted for the possibility that not all passengers would participate in surveys and that some passengers are children. Using this response factor, it was determined that passengers on 21 direct flights to New York and 23 direct flights to Washington, D.C., would be needed for the study.

Since the project was being viewed as a pilot study, the overall time frame for collecting the data was cut to one week. The new sampling frame from which flights for the study would be randomly selected was reduced to 126 for the New York passengers and 77 for those traveling to Washington, D.C. For each of the flights selected, there was a possibility that more passengers than expected might fill out the survey. This would create the possibility of oversampling for each segment of prospective respondents. Using the flight route load database, a week was selected so that route loads would be consistent across each day of the week. In addition, the time to develop the survey had to be considered and materials for the surveys needed to be prepared. The third week in August was selected as the target date for data collection. That left a month to get everything completed.

The information assembled made an accurate estimate of the data collection costs possible. Taking into consideration the cost of questionnaire development, reproduction of 10,800 surveys, cover letters, and other required materials as well as a 50 percent response rate, cost per completed survey would be $5.15, or $26,878 in total. This cost and the other research costs in the initial proposal brought the total cost for the project to $42,550. This estimate was within management's tentative budget allocation of $50,000. Consequently, the project was given final approval and the research began the following day.

Hands-On Exercise

1. What major points does this example bring to your attention about sampling?

2. How could this sampling design be improved?

Summary of Learning Objectives

■ **Discuss the concept of sampling and list reasons for sampling.**

Sampling uses a portion of the population to make estimates about the entire population. The fundamentals of sampling are used in many of our everyday activities (e.g., selecting a TV program to watch, test-driving a car before deciding whether to purchase it, determining if our food is too hot or if it needs some additional seasoning). The term *target population* is used to identify the complete group of elements (e.g., people or objects) that are identified for investigation. The researcher selects sampling units from the target population and uses the results obtained from the sample to make conclusions about the target population. The sample must be representative of the target population if it is to provide accurate estimates of population parameters.

Sampling is frequently used in marketing research projects instead of a census because sampling can significantly reduce the amount of time and money required in data collection. When data collection destroys or contaminates the elements being studied, sampling usually is the only alternative.

■ **Identify and explain the different roles of sampling in the overall information research process.**

Sampling is necessary when there are short time frames for gathering the needed information. Sampling is useful in identifying, developing, and understanding new marketing constructs, as well as in developing the scales used to collect primary data. Decisions concerning sampling indirectly affect the process of designing questionnaires.

■ **Demonstrate the basic terminology used in sampling decisions.**

A population is an identifiable group of elements (e.g., people, products, organizations, physical entities) of interest to the researcher and relevant to the information problem. An element is a person or object from which information is sought. Sampling units are the target population elements available for selection during the sampling process. After defining the target population, the researcher must assemble a list of eligible sampling units, referred to as a sampling frame.

■ **Understand the concept of error in the context of sampling.**

Sampling error is any type of bias that is attributable to mistakes made either in the selection process for sampling units or in determining the sample size. Moreover, random sampling error tends to occur because of chance variations in the scientific selection of the needed sampling units. Nonsampling errors occur in a research study regardless of whether a sample or a census is used.

■ **Discuss and calculate sampling distributions, standard errors, and confidence intervals and how they are used in assessing the accuracy of a sample.**

A sampling distribution is the frequency distribution of a sample statistic (e.g., sample mean $[\bar{x}]$ or sample proportion $[\bar{p}]$ that would result if we took repeated random samples of the same size). The central limit theorem suggests there is a high probability the mean of any random sample taken from a target population will closely approximate the actual population mean as the sample size increases. Formulas are used to compute the estimated standard error of a sample mean ($\bar{x}$) and the estimated standard error of a sample percentage ($\bar{p}$). The estimated standard error $S_{\bar{x}}$ or $S_{\bar{p}}$ gives us an indication of how far the sample data results lie from the actual population parameters.

Confidence intervals are based on the researcher's specified level of confidence and a given degree of sampling error for which estimates of the true value of the population parameter could be expected to fall.

■ **Discuss the factors that must be considered when determining sample size.**

Several factors must considered when determining the appropriate sample size. The amount of time and money available often affect this decision. In general, the larger the sample, the greater the amount of resources required to collect data. Three factors that are of primary importance in the determination of sample size are (1) the variability of the population characteristic under consideration (σ_μ or σ_p), (2) the level of confidence desired in the estimate (CL), and (3) the degree of precision desired in estimating the population characteristic (*e*). The greater the variability of the characteristic under investigation, the higher the level of confidence required. Similarly, the more precise the required sample results the larger the necessary sample size.

■ **Discuss the methods of calculating appropriate sample sizes.**

Statistical formulas are used to determine the required sample size in probability sampling. Sample sizes for nonprobability sampling designs are determined using subjective methods such as industry standards, past studies, or the intuitive judgments of the researcher. The size of the defined target population does not affect the size of the required sample unless the population is small relative to the sample size. Sample sizes are not the same as usable observations for data analysis. Having fewer observations than desired will affect the accuracy of the data. Researchers must therefore consider reachable rates, overall incidence rates, and expected completion rates on the number of prospective respondent contacts necessary to ensure sample accuracy.

Key Terms and Concepts

Census   308

Central limit theorem (CLT)   313

Confidence interval   316

Critical level of error   314

Defined target population   310

Element   310

Finite correction factor (fcf)   319

General precision   314

Nonsampling error   314

Population   309

Precise precision   314

Sampling   308

Sampling distribution   312

Sampling error   314

Sampling frame   310

Sampling units   310

Review Questions

1. Why do many of today's research situations place heavy emphasis on correctly defining a target population rather than a total population?

2. Why is so much importance placed on the central limit theorem in survey research designs?

3. Identify, graph, and explain the relationship between sample sizes and estimated standard error measures. What does the estimated standard error really measure in survey research?

4. The vice president of operations at Busch Gardens knows that 70 percent of the patrons like roller-coaster rides. He wishes to have an acceptable margin of error of no more than ±2 percent and wants to be 95 percent confident about the attitudes toward the "Gwazi" roller coaster. What sample size would be required for a personal interview study among on-site patrons?

5. What factors must be considered in determining sample size?

6. How does the number of usable responses impact the estimated sample size?

Discussion Questions

1. Summarize why a current telephone directory is not a good source from which to develop a sampling frame for most research studies.

2. Why do researchers find it necessary to calculate confidence intervals? In a telephone survey of 700 people, 45 percent responded positively to liking cats. Calculate a

confidence interval, at the 95 percent confidence level, that will reveal the interval estimate for the proportion of people who like cats within a target population of 60,000 people. How would you interpret the results?

3. You work for the tourist commission in Fort Lauderdale, Florida. You are doing a survey on beer consumption and beer prices during spring break at Fort Lauderdale Beach. Last year, the average price per six-pack of beer was $3.75, with a standard deviation of $.30, and average daily consumption of beer was 12 cans per person, with a deviation of 3.5 cans. Your survey requires a 90 percent confidence level and allowable errors of $.10 on the price of six-packs and 1.5 cans on beer consumption. Calculate the needed sample size for doing this year's survey among college students at Fort Lauderdale Beach during spring break.

4. **EXPERIENCE THE INTERNET.** Go to www.surveysampling.com and select from the menu "the frame." Once there, select "archive" and go to a particular year (i.e., 2004) and review the articles available on the topic of sampling. Select two articles and write a brief summary on how sampling affects the ability to conduct accurate market research.

5. What are the disadvantages of using exit interviews as a sampling method for the Santa Fe Grill customer survey?

6. How could you improve the sampling approach for a Santa Fe Grill survey? Why is your method better?

chapter 10

Sampling: Methods and Planning

Learning Objectives

After reading this chapter, you will be able to

1. Distinguish between probability and nonprobability sampling methods.

2. Understand the advantages and disadvantages of probability sampling designs.

3. Understand the advantages and disadvantages of nonprobability sample designs.

4. Illustrate the factors necessary for determining the appropriate sample design.

5. Understand the steps in developing a sampling plan.

Technology and Sampling Procedures—Can the Two Ever Co-Exist?

Some pollsters say the Internet allows them to collect public attitudes more quickly and cheaply than the telephone. But others say surveys done strictly online don't measure up. They say Internet polling fails to survey people who don't have computers—people who tend to have lower income and less education, people more likely to be minorities. And they say it ignores some basic principles of survey research, especially the concept of random sampling. They raise the specter of 1936, when a famous survey miscalled the presidential election because it relied on lists of people who owned telephones and cars—at a time when those were luxuries.

As for Internet polling, Mike Traugott, president of the American Association for Public Opinion Research, said, "Clearly, the Internet is the wave of the future. The turmoil running through the industry is similar to the anxiety faced by pollsters when they began to make the switch from face-to-face to telephone questioning." Traugott also said the number of American adults who go online, roughly half, is not high enough yet to provide a cross-section of the population. And no one has figured out how to draw a random sample of computer users the way traditional pollsters draw a probability sample of the population. Pollsters are working hard to figure out how to harness the speed, power, and efficiency of the Internet. Two differing approaches are being debated.

InterSurvey of Menlo Park, California, is blending the methods of traditional research with the Internet, starting by drawing a panel of respondents using a telephone poll. Anyone in the panel who doesn't have Internet access is given interactive television, at InterSurvey's expense, to file responses. When InterSurvey wants to conduct a poll, it contacts the respondents by lighting the boxes on top of their televisions, a technique less disruptive than a dinnertime phone call. "You don't have to abandon scientific sampling to poll on the Internet," said Doug Rivers, chief executive of the company. Traditional pollsters and major media outlets have used InterSurvey to get quick reaction on events such as the State of the Union address.

Another wave in Internet research is the collection of panels of potential respondents like those put together by Harris Interactive of Rochester, New York; Greenfield Online Inc.; and other firms. Harris Interactive has built up a panel of 6.2 million people, most of whom volunteer through Web sites.

As one supporter noted, "If they used unweighted data, their results would not be nearly so good. But by weighting data by demographics and the 'propensity' of people to be on the Internet, they stand by their surveys." Harris Interactive says its political polls have been largely successful, but traditional pollsters say they're worried about offers of inexpensive research they feel isn't scientific. "My view is that it's an enormous threat," said pollster Warren Mitofsky, an early proponent of telephone use in surveys. "There are too many unsophisticated people willing to pay and this kind of bad research is going to drive out some good research."[2]

The Value of Sampling Methods in Marketing Research

As illustrated in the opening example, developing an accurate sampling method is an important issue when designing a study that uses interviewing or surveys for data collection. Overall, there are two basic sampling designs: probability and nonprobability. Exhibit 10.1 lists the different types of both sampling methods.

Probability sampling A technique of drawing a sample in which each sampling unit has a known probability of being included in the sample.

In **probability sampling,** each sampling unit in the defined target population has a known probability of being selected for the sample. The actual probability of selection for each sampling unit may or may not be equal depending on the type of probability sampling design used. Specific rules for selecting members from the population for inclusion in the sample are determined at the beginning of a study to ensure (1) unbiased selection of the sampling units and (2) proper sample representation of the defined target population. Probability sampling enables the researcher to judge the reliability and validity of data collected by calculating the probability that the sample findings are different from the defined target population. The observed difference can be partially attributed to the existence of sampling error. The results obtained by using probability sampling designs can be generalized to the target population within a specified margin of error.

Nonprobability sampling A sampling process where the probability of selecting each sampling unit is unknown.

In **nonprobability sampling,** the probability of selecting each sampling unit is not known. Therefore, sampling error is not known either. Selection of sampling units is based on some type of intuitive judgment or knowledge of the researcher. The degree to which the sample may or may not be representative of the defined target population depends on

---

EXHIBIT 10.1   Types of Probability and Nonprobability Sampling Methods

Probability Sampling Methods	Nonprobability Sampling Methods
Simple random sampling	Convenience sampling
Systematic random sampling	Judgment sampling
Stratified random sampling	Quota sampling
Cluster sampling	Snowball sampling

	Summary of Comparative Differences of Probability and Nonprobability Sampling Methods

EXHIBIT 10.2

Comparison Factors	Probability Sampling	Nonprobability Sampling
List of the Population Elements	Complete List Necessary	None Necessary
Information about the Sampling Units	Each Unit Identified	Need Detail on Habits, Activities, Traits, etc.
Sampling Skill Required	Skill Required	Little Skill Required
Time Requirement	Time-Consuming	Low Time Consumption
Cost per Unit Sampled	Moderate to High	Low
Estimates of Population Parameters	Unbiased	Biased
Sample Representativeness	Good, Assured	Suspect, Undeterminable
Accuracy and Reliability	Computed with Confidence Intervals	Unknown
Measurement of Sampling Error	Statistical Measures	No True Measure Available

the sampling approach and how well the researcher executes and controls the selection activities. Although there is always a temptation to generalize nonprobability sample data results to the defined target population, for the most part the results are limited to just the people who provided the survey data. Exhibit 10.2 provides a comparison of probability and nonprobability sampling methods based on selected sampling factors.

Types of Probability Sampling Designs

Simple Random Sampling

Simple random sampling (SRS) A probability sampling procedure that ensures every sampling unit in the target population has a known and equal chance of being selected.

Simple random sampling (SRS) is a probability sampling procedure. With this approach, every sampling unit has a known and equal chance of being selected. For example, let's say an instructor decided to draw a sample of 10 students ($n = 10$) from among all the students in a marketing research class that consisted of 30 students ($N = 30$). The instructor could write each student's name on a separate, identical piece of paper and place all of the names in a jar. Each student would have an equal, known probability of selection for a sample of a given size that could be expressed by the following formula:

$$\text{Probability of selection} = \frac{\text{Size of sample}}{\text{Size of population}}$$

Here, each student in the marketing research class would have a 10/30 (or .333) chance of being randomly selected in the sample.

When the defined target population consists of a larger number of sampling units, a more sophisticated method is used to randomly draw the sample. One of the procedures commonly used in marketing research is to have a computer-generated table of random numbers to select the sampling units. A table of random numbers is just what its name

e X H I B I T 10.3	A Partial Table of Random Numbers		
31 25	81 44	54 34	67 03
14 96	99 80	14 54	30 74
49 05	49 56	35 51	68 36
99 67	57 65	14 46	92 88
54 14	95 34	93 18	78 27
57 50	34 89	99 14	57 37
98 67	78 25	06 90	39 90
40 99	00 87	90 42	88 18
20 82	09 18	84 91	64 80
78 84	39 91	16 08	14 89

Source: M. G. Kendall and B. Babington Smith, "Table of Random Sampling Numbers," *Tracts for Computers* 24 (Cambridge, England; Cambridge University Press, 1946), p. 33.

implies—a table that lists randomly generated numbers (see Exhibit 10.3). Many of today's computer programs can generate a table of random numbers.

Using the marketing research students again as the target population, a random sample could be generated (1) by using the last two digits of the students' social security numbers or (2) by assigning each student a unique two-digit code ranging from 01 to 30. With the first procedure, we would have to make sure that no two students have the same last two digits in their social security number; the range of acceptable numbers would be from 00 to 99. Then we could go to the table of random numbers and select a starting point, which can be anywhere on the table. Using Exhibit 10.3, let's say we select the upper-left-hand corner of the table (31) as our starting point. We would then begin to read down the first column (or across the first row) and select those two-digit numbers that matched the numbers within the acceptable range until 10 students had been selected. Reading down the first column, we would start with 31, then go to 14, 49, 99, 54, and so on.

If we had elected to assign a unique descriptor (01 to 30) to each student in class, we would follow the same selection procedure from the random number table, but use only those random numbers that matched the numbers within the acceptable range of 01 to 30. Numbers that fell outside the acceptable range would be disregarded. Thus, we would select students with numbers 14, 20, 25, 05, 09, 18, 06, 16, 08, and 30. If the overall research objectives call for telephone interviews, drawing the necessary sample can be achieved using a random-digit dialing (RDD) technique.

Advantages and Disadvantages

Simple random sampling has several noteworthy advantages. The technique is easily understood and the survey's results can be generalized to the defined target population with a prespecified margin of error *e*. Another advantage is that simple random samples allow the researcher to obtain unbiased estimates of the population's characteristics. This method guarantees that every sampling unit has a known and equal chance of being selected, no matter the actual size of the sample, resulting in a valid representation of the defined target population. The primary disadvantage of simple random sampling is the difficulty of obtaining a complete and accurate listing of the target population elements. Simple random sampling requires that all sampling units be identified. For this reason, simple random sampling often works best for small populations or those where computer-derived lists are available.

Systematic Random Sampling

Systematic random sampling (SYMRS) A probability sampling technique that requires the defined target population to be ordered in some way.

Systematic random sampling (SYMRS) is similar to simple random sampling but requires that the defined target population be ordered in some way, usually in the form of a customer list, taxpayer roll, or membership roster. In research practices, SYMRS has become a popular alternative probability method of drawing samples. Compared to simple random sampling, systematic random sampling is less costly because it can be done relatively quickly. When executed properly, SYMRS can create a sample of objects or prospective respondents that is very similar in quality to a sample drawn using SRS.

To employ systematic random sampling, the researcher must be able to secure a complete listing of the potential sampling units that make up the defined target population. But unlike SRS, there is no need to give the sampling units any special code prior to drawing the sample. Instead, sampling units are selected according to their position using a skip interval. The skip interval is determined by dividing the number of potential sampling units in the defined target population by the number of units desired in the sample. The required skip interval is calculated using the following formula:

$$\text{Skip interval} = \frac{\text{Defined target population list size}}{\text{Desired sample size}}$$

For instance, if the researcher wants a sample of 100 to be drawn from a defined target population of 1,000, the skip interval would be 10 (1,000/100). Once the skip interval is determined, the researcher would then randomly select a starting point and take every 10th unit until he or she had proceeded through the entire target population list. Exhibit 10.4 displays the steps that a researcher would take in drawing a systematic random sample.

There are two important considerations when using systematic random sampling. First, the natural order of the defined target population list must be unrelated to the characteristic being studied. Second, the skip interval must not correspond to a systematic change in the target population. For example, if a skip interval of 7 was used in sampling daily sales or invoices from a retail store like Bloomingdale's, and Tuesday was randomly selected as the starting point, we would end up with data from the same day every week. We would not want to draw conclusions regarding overall sales performance based only on what happens every Tuesday.

Advantages and Disadvantages

Systematic sampling is frequently used because it is a relatively easy way to draw a sample while ensuring randomness. The availability of lists and the shorter time required to draw a sample versus simple random sampling makes systematic sampling an attractive, economical method for researchers. The greatest weakness of systematic random sampling is the potential for there to be hidden patterns in the data that are not found by the researcher. This could result in a sample that is not truly representative of the defined target population. Nonetheless, the potential small loss in overall representativeness of the target population is usually offset by larger savings in time, effort, and cost. Another difficulty is that the researcher must know exactly how many sampling units make up the defined target

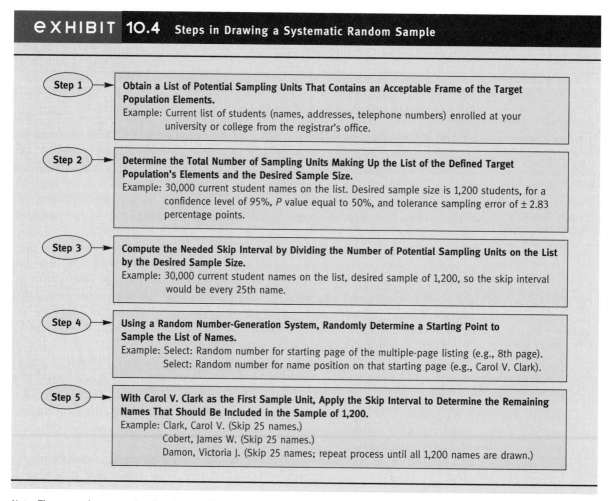

eXHIBIT 10.4 Steps in Drawing a Systematic Random Sample

Step 1 → **Obtain a List of Potential Sampling Units That Contains an Acceptable Frame of the Target Population Elements.**
Example: Current list of students (names, addresses, telephone numbers) enrolled at your university or college from the registrar's office.

Step 2 → **Determine the Total Number of Sampling Units Making Up the List of the Defined Target Population's Elements and the Desired Sample Size.**
Example: 30,000 current student names on the list. Desired sample size is 1,200 students, for a confidence level of 95%, *P* value equal to 50%, and tolerance sampling error of ± 2.83 percentage points.

Step 3 → **Compute the Needed Skip Interval by Dividing the Number of Potential Sampling Units on the List by the Desired Sample Size.**
Example: 30,000 current student names on the list, desired sample of 1,200, so the skip interval would be every 25th name.

Step 4 → **Using a Random Number-Generation System, Randomly Determine a Starting Point to Sample the List of Names.**
Example: Select: Random number for starting page of the multiple-page listing (e.g., 8th page). Select: Random number for name position on that starting page (e.g., Carol V. Clark).

Step 5 → **With Carol V. Clark as the First Sample Unit, Apply the Skip Interval to Determine the Remaining Names That Should Be Included in the Sample of 1,200.**
Example: Clark, Carol V. (Skip 25 names.)
Cobert, James W. (Skip 25 names.)
Damon, Victoria J. (Skip 25 names; repeat process until all 1,200 names are drawn.)

Note: The researcher must visualize the population list as being continuous or "circular"; that is, the drawing process must continue past those names that represent the Z's and include names representing the A's and B's so that the 1,200th name drawn will basically be the 25th name prior to the first drawn name (i.e., Carol V. Clark).

population. When the size of the target population is extremely large or unknown, identifying the true number of units is difficult, and estimates may not be accurate.

Stratified Random Sampling

Stratified random sampling (STRS) A probability sampling method in which the defined target population is divided into groups, called strata, and samples are selected from each stratum.

Stratified random sampling (STRS) involves the separation of the target population into different groups, called *strata,* and the selection of samples from each stratum. Stratified random sampling is useful when the divisions of the target population are skewed or when extremes are present in the probability distribution of the target population. The goal in stratifying is to minimize the variability within each stratum and maximize the differences between strata. STRS is similar to segmentation of the defined target population into smaller, more homogeneous sets of elements. Depending on the problem situation, there are cases in which the defined target population does not portray a normal symmetric distribution of its elements.

To ensure that the sample maintains the required precision, representative samples must be drawn from each of the smaller population groups (each stratum). Drawing a stratified random sample involves three basic steps:

1. Dividing the target population into homogeneous subgroups or strata.

2. Drawing random samples from each stratum.

3. Combining the samples from each stratum into a single sample of the target population.

As an example, if researchers are interested in the market potential for home security systems in a specific geographic area, they may wish to divide the homeowners into several different strata. The subdivisions could be based on such factors as assessed value of the homes, household income, population density, or location (e.g., sections designated as high- and low-crime areas).

Proportionate stratified sampling A stratified sampling method in which each stratum is dependent on its size relative to the population.

Disproportionate stratified sampling A stratified sampling method in which the size of each stratum is independent of its relative size in the population.

Two common methods are used to derive samples from the strata: *proportionate* and *disproportionate*. In **proportionate stratified sampling,** the sample size from each stratum is dependent on that stratum's size relative to the defined target population. Therefore, the larger strata are sampled more heavily because they make up a larger percentage of the target population. In **disproportionate stratified sampling,** the sample size selected from each stratum is independent of that stratum's proportion of the total defined target population. This approach is used when stratification of the target population produces sample sizes for subgroups that differ from their relative importance to the study. For example, stratification of manufacturers based on number of employees will usually result in a large segment of manufacturers with fewer than 10 employees and a very small proportion with, say, 500 or more employees. The obvious economic importance of those firms with 500 or more employees would dictate taking a larger sample from this stratum and a smaller sample from the subgroup with fewer than 10 employees than indicated by the proportionality method.

An alternative type of disproportionate stratified method is *optimal allocation*. In this method, consideration is given to the relative size of the stratum as well as the variability within the stratum. The basic logic underlying optimal allocation is that the greater the homogeneity of the prospective sampling units within a particular stratum, the fewer the units that have to be selected to accurately estimate the true population parameter (μ or P) for that subgroup. In contrast, the opposite would hold true for any stratum that has considerable variance among its sampling units or that is perceived as heterogeneous. Exhibit 10.5 displays the basic steps a researcher would take in drawing a proportionately stratified random sample.

Advantages and Disadvantages

Dividing the defined target population into homogeneous strata provides several advantages, including: (1) the assurance of representativeness in the sample; (2) the opportunity to study each stratum and make comparisons between strata; and (3) the ability to make estimates for the target population with the expectation of greater precision and less error. The primary difficulty encountered with stratified sampling is determining the basis for stratifying. Stratification is based on the target population's characteristics of interest. Secondary information relevant to the required stratification factors might not be readily available, therefore forcing the researcher to use less than desirable surrogate variables as the factors for stratifying the target population. Usually, the larger the number of relevant strata the more precise the results. However, the inclusion of irrelevant strata will waste time and

eXHIBIT 10.5 Steps in Drawing a Stratified Random Sample

Step 1 → **Obtain a List of Potential Sampling Units That Contains an Acceptable Frame of the Defined Target Population Elements.**
Example: List of known performance arts patrons (names, addresses, telephone numbers) living in a three-county area from the current database of the Asolo Performing Arts Centre. Total number of known patrons on the current database is 10,500.

Step 2 → **Using Some Type of Secondary Information or Past Experience with the Defined Target Population, Select a Stratification Factor for Which the Population's Distribution Is Skewed (Not Bell-Shaped) and Can Be Used to Determine That the Total Defined Target Population Consists of Separate Subpopulations of Elements.**
Example: Using attendance records and county location, identify strata by county and number of events attended per season (i.e., regular, occasional, or rare). Total: 10,500 patrons with 5,900 "regular" (56.2%); 3,055 "occasional" (29.1%); and 1,545 "rare" (14.7%) patrons.

Step 3 → **Using the Selected Stratification Factor (or Some Other Surrogate Variable), Segment the Defined Target Population into Strata Consistent with Each of the Identified Separate Subpopulations. That is, use the stratification factor to regroup the prospective sampling units into their mutually exclusive subgroups. Then determine both the actual number of sampling units and their percentage equivalents for each stratum.**
Example: County A: 5,000 patrons with 2,500 "regular" (50%); 1,875 "occasional" (37.5%); and 625 "rare" (12.5%) patrons.
County B: 3,000 patrons with 1,800 "regular" (60%); 580 "occasional" (19.3%); and 620 "rare" (20.7%) patrons.
County C: 2,500 patrons with 1,600 "regular" (64%); 600 "occasional" (24%); and 300 "rare" (12%) patrons.

Step 4 → **Determine Whether There Is a Need to Apply a Disproportionate or Optimal Allocation Method to the Stratification Process; Otherwise, Use the Proportionate Method and Then Estimate the Desired Sample Sizes.**
Example: Compare individual county strata percentage values to overall target population strata values. Let's assume a proportionate method and a confidence level of 95% and a tolerance for sampling error of ±2.5 percentage points. Estimate the sample size for total target population with no strata needed and assuming $P = 50\%$. The desired sample size would equal 1,537 people. Then proportion that size by the total patron percentage values for each of the three counties determined in step 2 (e.g., County A = 5,000/10,500 [47.6%]; County B = 3,000/10,500 [28.6%]; County C = 2,500/10,500 [23.8%]). New sample sizes for each county would be: County A = 732; County B = 439; County C = 366. Now for each county sample size, proportion the sample sizes by the respective within-county estimates for "regular," "occasional," and "rare" strata percentages determined in step 3.

Step 5 → **Select a Probability Sample from Each Stratum, Using either the SRS or SYMRS Procedure.**
Example: Use the procedures discussed earlier for drawing SRS or SYMRS samples.

money without providing meaningful results. Read the Ethics box to learn about ethical issues that could impact stratified sampling methods.

Cluster Sampling

Cluster sampling is similar to stratified random sampling, but is different in that the sampling units are divided into mutually exclusive and collectively exhaustive subpopulations, called clusters, rather than individually. Each cluster is assumed to be representative of the heterogeneity of the target population. Examples of possible divisions for cluster sampling

Cluster sampling A probability sampling method in which the sampling units are divided into mutually exclusive and collectively exhaustive subpopulations, called clusters.

Sampling Methods

U.S. Census Bureau Misleads Congress

The U.S. government is interested in gaining public support for its idea of investing budget surpluses in the stock market as the approach to ensure the stability of the country's ailing Social Security Program in the future. The administration believes that members of the U.S. Congress respond in a predictable manner when they have American public opinion results in front of them. Government officials decide on using a quick telephone survey to ask the American people their opinions about three possible approaches: (1) invest a significant portion of government budget surpluses in the stock market; (2) use the surpluses to reduce overall income taxes of all Americans; or (3) use the surpluses to pay down the national debt. To conduct this study, the administration requests that U.S. Census Bureau researchers develop a sampling plan for the telephone survey to be administered to 5,000 randomly selected Americans that ensures representation across four age groupings described as (a) 20 to 35, (b) 36 to 50, (c) 51 to 65, and (d) 66 and older. Reminded of the importance of the study's main objective, the researchers choose to develop a disproportionate stratified random sampling plan that would place heavier emphasis

on those Americans in the 36 to 50 and 51 to 61 age groupings than on those people in the other two groupings. To help ensure the desired outcome, interviewers would be encouraged to "work hard" on getting responses from respondents between ages 36 and 65. It was further determined that no matter the actual within-age-grouping response rates, only the study's overall response rate and normal error factor would be released to Congress, the media, and the general public.

- Is it ethical to conduct a study that knowingly misrepresents the true defined population for purposes of seeking a predetermined outcome?
- Is it ethical to encourage the interviewers to make disproportionate efforts to obtain completed interviews from less than all the defined sampled strata?
- Is it ethical to report only the overall response rate and error factor when a disproportionate stratified random sampling method is used to collect the data?
- Is it ethical not to report these facts to Congress, the media, and the general public, thereby causing these groups to misinterpret the results?
- Would it be more ethical to use a proportionately stratified random sampling approach?

include customers who patronize a store on a given day, the audience for a movie shown at a particular time (e.g., the matinee), or the invoices processed during a specific week. Once the cluster has been identified, the prospective sampling units are selected for the sample by either using a simple random sampling method or canvassing all the elements (i.e., a census) within the defined cluster.

Area sampling A form of cluster sampling in which the clusters are formed by geographic designations.

In marketing research, a popular form of cluster sampling is **area sampling.** In area sampling, the clusters are formed by geographic designations. Examples include metropolitan statistical areas (MSAs), cities, subdivisions, and blocks. Any geographical unit with identifiable boundaries can be used. When using area sampling, the researcher has two additional options: the one-step approach or the two-step approach. When deciding on a one-step approach, the researcher must have enough prior information about the various geographic clusters to believe that all the geographic clusters are basically identical with regard to the specific factors that were used to initially identify the clusters. By assuming that all the clusters are identical, the researcher can focus his or her attention on surveying the sampling units within one designated cluster and then generalize the results to the population. The probability aspect of this particular sampling method is executed by randomly selecting one geographic cluster and performing a census on all the sampling units in that cluster.

As an example, assume the corporate vice president of merchandising for Dillard's Department Stores (www.dillards.com) wants to better understand shopping behaviors of people who shop at the 36 Dillard's stores located in Florida. Given budget constraints and a review of customer profile information in the database at corporate headquarters, the vice president assumes the same types of customers shop at Dillard's regardless of the store's geographic location or day of the week. The new Dillard's store located in University Mall in Tampa, Florida, is randomly selected as the store site for conducting in-store personal interviews, and 300 interviews are scheduled to be conducted on Wednesday, February 17, 2006.

The vice president's logic of using one store (a one-step cluster sampling method) to collect data on customers' shopping behaviors has several weaknesses. First, his assumption that customers at the University Mall store are similar to customers that shop at the other 35 stores in Florida might well be unfounded. Second, to assume that geographic differences in stores and consumers do not exist is a leap of faith. Limiting the sampling to only Wednesday also can create problems. To assume that consumers' attitudes and shopping behaviors (i.e., traffic flow patterns) toward Dillard's Department Stores are the same on a weekday as they are on the weekend is likely to be very misleading.

Another option is to use a two-step cluster sampling approach. First, a set of clusters could be randomly selected and then a probability method could be used to select individuals within each of the selected clusters. Usually, the two-step approach is preferable over the one-step approach, because there is a strong possibility a single cluster will not be representative of all other clusters. To illustrate the basics of the two-step cluster sampling approach, let's use the Dillard's Department Store example. In reviewing Dillard's database on customer profiles, assume the 36 stores can be clustered on the basis of annual sales revenue into three groups: (1) store type A (stores with gross sales under $2 million), (2) store type B (stores with gross sales between $2 million and $5 million), and (3) store type C (stores with over $5 million in gross sales). The result for the 36 stores operating in the Florida market is 6 stores can be grouped as being type A, another 18 stores as type B, and 12 stores as type C. In addition, sales were significantly heavier on weekends than during the week. Exhibit 10.6 shows the steps to take in drawing a cluster sample for the Dillard's situation.

Advantages and Disadvantages

Cluster sampling is widely used in marketing research because of its cost-effectiveness and ease of implementation, especially in area sampling situations. In many cases, the only representative sampling frame available to researchers is one based on clusters (e.g., states, counties, MSAs, census tracts). These lists of geographic regions, telephone exchanges, or blocks of residential dwellings usually can be easily compiled, thus avoiding the need of compiling lists of all the individual sampling units making up the target population. Clustering methods tend to be a cost-efficient way of sampling and collecting data from a defined target population.

Cluster sampling methods have several disadvantages. A primary disadvantage of cluster sampling is that the clusters often are homogeneous. The more homogeneous the cluster, the less precise the sample estimates. Ideally, the people in a cluster should be as heterogeneous as those in the population. When several sets of homogeneous clusters are uniquely different on the basis of the clustering factor (i.e., Dillard's store types A, B, and C), this problem may be lessened by randomly selecting and sampling a unit from each of the cluster groups. Exhibit 10.6 illustrates how a researcher can overcome this problem of different homogeneous clusters within a defined target population.

Another concern with cluster sampling methods—one that is rarely addressed—is the appropriateness of the designated cluster factor used to identify the sampling units within clusters. Again let's use the Dillard's example to illustrate this potential weakness. Dillard's vice president of merchandising used a single geographic cluster designation factor (i.e., state of Florida) to derive one cluster consisting of 36 stores. By assuming that there was

EXHIBIT 10.6   Steps in Drawing a Two-Step Cluster Sample

Step 1 ▸ **Fully Understand the Information Problem Situation and Characteristics That Are Used to Define the Target Population. Then Determine the Clustering Factors to Be Used to Identify the Clusters of Sampling Units.**
Example: Initial sampling units would be the 36 known Dillard's stores located throughout Florida. Using secondary data of stores' annual gross sales revenue, establish the cluster categories (i.e., store types A, B, and C) and weekday versus weekend dollar sales figures.

Step 2 ▸ **Determine the Number of Sampling Units That Make Up Each Cluster, Obtain a List of Potential Sampling Units for Each Cluster, and Assign Them with a Unique Designation Code.**
Example: 6 type A stores—(01) Jacksonville; (05) Fort Lauderdale; (03) Gainesville; etc.
18 type B stores—(01) Tampa; (16) Sarasota; (07) Vero Beach; etc.
12 type C stores—(10) Miami; (02) West Palm Beach; (07) Orlando; etc.
Weekday sales—(01) through (52).
Weekend sales—(01) through (52).

Step 3 ▸ **Determine Whether to Use a One-Step or Two-Step Cluster Sampling Method.**
Example: Given that both *store type* and *weekday/weekend sales* factors are being used to designate the clusters, a two-step clustering approach will be used to draw the sampling units.

Step 4 ▸ **Determine How Many Sampling Units in Each Cluster Need to Be Sampled to Be Representative of That Cluster.**
Example: Given the perceived homogeneity within each cluster group of stores and cost considerations, let's assume that the researcher feels comfortable in sampling only one store in each store type over two weekday periods and four weekend periods.

Step 5 ▸ **Using Random Numbers, Select the Sampling Unit (i.e., Store) within Each Cluster and the Weekday and Weekend Time Frames to Be Sampled.**
Example: For store type A: (01) Jacksonville; weekday periods for weeks (10) and (34); weekend periods for weeks (03), (14), (26), and (41).
For store type B: (12) Lakeland; weekday periods for weeks (33) and (45); weekend periods for weeks (09), (24), (29), and (36).
For store type C: (10) Miami; weekday periods for weeks (22) and (46); weekend periods for weeks (04), (18), (32), and (37).

Step 6 ▸ **Determine the Needed Sample Sizes for Each Cluster by Weekday/Weekend Time Frames.**
Example: Let's assume a desired confidence level of 95% and a tolerance for sampling error of ±2.5 percentage points. Estimate the desired sample size for total target population with no cluster grouping needed and assuming $P = 50\%$. The desired sample size would equal 1,537 people. Then proportion that size by the percentage values for each type of store to total number of stores making up the defined target population frame (i.e., store type A = 6/36 [16.7%]; store type B = 18/36 [50.0%]; store type C = 12/36 [33.3%]). New sample sizes for each store type would be: store type A = 257; store type B = 769; store type C = 512. Now for each store type sample size, proportion the sample sizes by the respective within weekday and weekend estimates, determined in step 4. As a result, the required sample sizes by store type by weekday/weekend time frames would be:
Store type A: Weekday periods 43 people in week (10), 43 people in week (34); Weekend periods 43 people in week (03) and the same number for weeks (14), (26), and (41).
Store type B: Weekday periods 43 people in week (33), 43 people in week (45); Weekend periods 43 people in week (09) and the same number for weeks (24), (29), and (46).
Store type C: Weekday periods 43 people in week (22), 43 people in week (46); Weekend periods 43 people in week (04) and the same number for weeks (18), (32), and (37).

Step 7 ▸ **Select a Probability Sampling Method for Selecting Customers for In-Store Interviews.**
Example: Randomize the weekday interviews (i.e., Monday, Tuesday, Wednesday, and Thursday) as well as the weekend interviews (i.e., Friday, Saturday, and Sunday) so that the data are represented across shopping days and store operating hours.

equal heterogeneity among all Dillard's shoppers, regardless of the store location, he randomly sampled one store to conduct the necessary in-store interviews. Then by changing the designated cluster factor to "annual gross sales revenue," he determined there were three different sets of store clusters (i.e., stores types A, B, and C) among the same 36 Dillard's stores located within Florida. This clustering method required a more complex sampling technique to ensure that the data collected would be representative of the defined target population of all Dillard's customers. The point is that while the defined target population remains constant, the subdivision of sampling units can be modified depending on the selection of the designation factor used to identify the clusters. This points out that caution must be used in selecting the factor to determine clusters in area sampling situations.

Types of Nonprobability Sampling Designs

Convenience Sampling

Convenience sampling
A nonprobability sampling method in which samples are drawn at the convenience of the researcher.

Convenience sampling is a method in which samples are drawn based on convenience. For example, mall-intercept interviewing of individuals at shopping malls or other high-traffic areas is a common method of generating a convenience sample. The assumption is that the target population is homogeneous and the individuals interviewed at the shopping mall are similar to the overall defined target population with regard to the characteristic being studied. In reality, it is difficult to accurately assess the representativeness of the sample. Given self-selection and the voluntary nature of participating in the data collection, researchers should consider the impact of nonresponse error.

Advantages and Disadvantages

Convenience sampling enables a large number of respondents (e.g., 200–300) to be interviewed in a relatively short time. For this reason, it is commonly used in the early stages of research (i.e., construct and scale measurement development as well as pretesting of questionnaires). But using convenience samples to development constructs and scales can be risky. For example, assume the researcher is developing a measure of service quality and in the preliminary stages uses a convenience sample of 300 undergraduate business students. While college students are consumers of services, serious questions should be raised about whether they are truly representative of the general population. By developing and refining constructs and scales using data from a convenience sample of college students, the construct's measurement scale might later prove to be unreliable when used in investigations of other defined target populations. Another major disadvantage of convenience samples is that the data are not generalizable to the defined target population. The representativeness of the sample cannot be measured because sampling error estimates cannot be calculated.

Judgment Sampling

Judgment sampling A nonprobability sampling method in which participants are selected according to an experienced individual's belief that they will meet the requirements of the study.

In **judgment sampling,** sometimes referred to as purposive sampling, sample respondents are selected because the researcher believes they meet the requirements of the study. In many industrial sales studies, the regional sales manager will survey sales representatives rather than customers to determine whether customers' wants and needs are changing or to assess the firm's product or service performance. Many consumer packaging manufacturers (e.g., Procter & Gamble) regularly select a sample of key accounts believed to be able to provide information about consumption patterns and changes in demand for selected products (e.g., Crest toothpaste, Cheer laundry detergent). The underlying assumption is that the opinions of a group of perceived experts are representative of the target population.

Advantages and Disadvantages

If the judgment of the researcher is correct, the sample generated by judgment sampling will be better than one generated by convenience sampling. However, as with all nonprobability sampling procedures, you cannot measure the representativeness of the sample. At best, the data collected from judgment sampling should be interpreted cautiously.

Quota Sampling

Quota sampling A nonprobability sampling method in which participants are selected according to prespecified quotas regarding demographics, attitudes, behaviors, or some other criteria.

Quota sampling involves the selection of prospective participants according to prespecified quotas for either demographic characteristics (e.g., age, race, gender, income), specific attitudes (e.g., satisfied/dissatisfied, liking/disliking, great/marginal/no quality), or specific behaviors (e.g., regular/occasional/rare customer, product user/nonuser). The purpose of quota sampling is to assure that prespecified subgroups of the target population are represented on relevant sampling factors. Moreover, surveys frequently use quotas that have been determined by the nature of the research objectives. For example, if a research study is conducted about fast-food restaurants, the researcher may establish quotas using an age factor and the patronage behavior of prospective respondents as follows:

Age	Patronage Behavior
[1] Under 25	[1] Patronize a fast-food establishment an average of once a month or more
[2] 25 to 54	[2] Patronize fast-food establishments less frequently than once a month
[3] 55 and over	

Using these demographic and patronage behavior factors, the researcher identifies six different subgroups of people to be included in the study. Determining the quota size for each of the subgroups is a somewhat subjective process. The researcher might use sales information to determine the percentage size of each subgroup according to how much each has contributed to the firm's total sales. This ensures that the sample will contain the desired number in each subgroup. Once the individual percentage sizes for each quota are established, the researcher segments the sample size by those percentage values to determine the actual number of prospective respondents to include in each of the prespecified quota groups. Let's say, for example, that a fast-food restaurant wanted to interview 1,000 people and, using both industry-supplied sales reports and company sales records, determined that individuals aged 25 to 54 who patronize fast-food restaurants at least once a month make up 50 percent of its total sales. The researcher would probably want that subgroup to make up 50 percent of the total sample. Let's further assume that company records indicated that individuals aged 25 to 54 who frequent fast-food restaurants less than once a month make up only 6 percent of sales. This particular subgroup should consist of only 6 percent of the total sample size.

Advantages and Disadvantages

The greatest advantage of quota sampling is that the sample generated contains specific subgroups in the proportions desired by researchers. In research projects that require interviews, the use of quotas ensures that the appropriate subgroups are identified and included in the survey. Also, quota sampling should reduce selection bias by field workers. An inherent limitation of quota sampling is that the success of the study will again be dependent on subjective decisions made by the researchers. Since it is a nonprobability sampling method, the representativeness of the sample cannot be measured. Therefore, generalizing the results beyond the sampled respondents is questionable.

Snowball Sampling

Snowball sampling involves identifying and qualifying a set of initial prospective respondents who can, in turn, help the researcher identify additional people to include in the study. This method of sampling is also called *referral sampling,* because one respondent refers other potential respondents. Snowball sampling typically is used in situations where (1) the defined target population is small and unique, and (2) compiling a complete list of sampling units is very difficult. Consider, for example, researching the attitudes and behaviors of people who volunteer their time to charitable organizations like the Children's Wish Foundation. While traditional sampling methods require an extensive search effort (both in time and cost) to qualify a sufficient number of prospective respondents, the snowball method yields better results at a much lower cost. Here the researcher interviews a qualified respondent, then solicits his or her help to identify other people with similar characteristics. While membership in these types of social circles might not be publicly known, intracircle knowledge is very accurate. The underlying logic of this method is that rare groups of people tend to form their own unique social circles.

Advantages and Disadvantages

Snowball sampling is a reasonable method of identifying respondents who are members of small, hard-to-reach, uniquely defined target populations. As a nonprobability sampling method, it is most useful in qualitative research practices. But snowball sampling allows bias to enter the study. If there are significant differences between people who are known in certain social circles and those who are not, there may be problems with this sampling technique. Like all other nonprobability sampling approaches, the ability to generalize the results to members of the target population is limited.

Determining the Appropriate Sampling Design

Selection of the most appropriate sampling design should consider the seven factors displayed in Exhibit 10.7.

Research Objectives

An understanding of the research problem and objectives provides the initial guidelines for determining the appropriate sampling design. If the research objectives include the desire to generalize the sample results to the target population, then the researcher must likely use some type of probability sampling method rather than a nonprobability sampling method. In addition, the stage of the research project and type of research (e.g., exploratory, descriptive, causal) influence the selection of the sampling method.

Degree of Accuracy

The degree of accuracy required will vary from project to project, especially when cost savings or other considerations are evaluated. If the researcher wants to make predictions about members of the defined target population, then a probability sampling method must be used. In contrast, if the researcher is interested only in preliminary insights about the target population, nonprobability methods might be as appropriate.

eXHIBIT 10.7 Critical Factors in Selecting the Appropriate Sampling Design

Selection Factors	Questions
Research objectives	Do the research objectives call for the use of qualitative or quantitative research designs?
Degree of accuracy	Does the research call for making predictions or inductive inferences about the defined target population, or only preliminary insights?
Resources	Are there tight budget constraints with respect to both dollars and human resources that can be allocated to the research project?
Time frame	How quickly does the research project have to be completed?
Knowledge of the target population	Are there complete lists of the defined target population elements? How easy or difficult is it to generate the required sampling frame of prospective respondents?
Scope of the research	Is the research going be international, national, regional, or local?
Statistical analysis needs	To what extent are accurate statistical projections and/or testing of hypothesized differences in the data structures required?

Resources

If financial and human resources are limited, they most certainly will eliminate some of the more time-consuming, complex probability sampling methods. If the budget is a substantial limitation, then a nonprobability sampling method likely will be used rather than conducting no research at all.

Time Frame

Researchers with short deadlines will be more likely to select a simple, less time-consuming sampling method rather than a more complex method. For example, researchers tend to use convenience sampling to gather data to test the reliability of a newly developed construct. While data from this sampling method might provide preliminary insights about the defined target population, there is no way to assess the representativeness of the results.

Knowledge of the Target Population

In many cases, a list of the population will not be available. Therefore, a preliminary study may be needed to develop a sampling frame for the study. To do so, the researcher must have a clear understanding of who is in the target population. Review the nearby Closer Look at Research box on using the Internet to gain valuable information on sampling using databases.

Scope of the Research

The scope of the research project, whether international, national, regional, or local, will influence the choice of the sampling method. The geographic proximity of the defined target population will influence not only the ability to compile lists of sampling units, but also the selection design. When the target population elements are known or unequally distributed geographically, a cluster sampling method may be more attractive than other methods. Generally, the broader the geographical scope of the research project, the more complex the sampling method becomes to ensure proper representation of the target population.

A Closer Look at Research

The Internet Can Provide Invaluable Intelligence Information

As more businesses turn to online and database marketing research to solve marketing problems, sampling issues and procedures will play an increasing role in the success of obtaining the right information in a timely fashion. Advanced technologies used in creating and maintaining company-owned customer profile databases afford many businesses the opportunity to improve their capability to identify, understand, target, reach, and monitor customers. Increased availability of information from various online databases has enhanced the value of geodemographic segmentation and mapping practices. Business owners seeking to expand their markets can use the Internet to locate resources like Hoovers (www.hoovers.com), GeoPlace (www.geoplace.com) and the University of Virginia

Using Technology

(http://fisher.lib.virginia.edu) to gain access to geodemographic information. For example, a business could use these resources to begin the process of determining where to expand and whether expansion would be economically feasible. Population size, demographic composite and lifestyle characteristics, competitive situation, media coverage and efficiency, media isolation, self-contained trading areas, and availability of scanner data all could be used to evaluate prospective target markets. The resulting information would be useful in assessing the feasibility of expansion as well as determining the appropriate marketing strategy for expansion. In addition, online geodemographic information provides opportunities for digital mapping, store location planning, demographic customer profiling, and gravity modeling activities.

Statistical Analysis Needs

The need for statistical projections based on the sample results is often a criterion. Only probability sampling techniques enable the researcher to use statistical analysis for estimates beyond the immediate set of sampled respondents. While statistical analysis methods can be performed on data obtained from nonprobability samples, the ability to generalize the findings to the target population is suspect. Another important topic in deciding on the appropriateness of any proposed sample design is determining the sample size. Sample size has a direct impact on data quality, statistical precision, and generalizability of findings.

Steps in Developing a Sampling Plan

Sampling plan The blueprint or framework needed to ensure that the data collected are representative of the defined target population.

Sampling is much more than just finding some people to participate in a research study. Researchers must consider a number of different concepts and procedures to successfully gather data from a group of people that can, in turn, be used to make inferential predictions about a larger target population. After understanding the key components of sampling theory, the methods of determining sample sizes, and the various designs available, the researcher is ready to use them to develop a *sampling plan*. A **sampling plan** is the blueprint to ensure that the data collected are representative of the target population. A good sampling plan includes the following steps: (1) define the target population, (2) select the

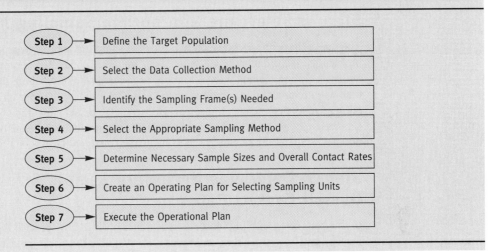

e X H I B I T 10.8 Steps Involved in Developing a Sampling Plan

Step 1 → Define the Target Population

Step 2 → Select the Data Collection Method

Step 3 → Identify the Sampling Frame(s) Needed

Step 4 → Select the Appropriate Sampling Method

Step 5 → Determine Necessary Sample Sizes and Overall Contact Rates

Step 6 → Create an Operating Plan for Selecting Sampling Units

Step 7 → Execute the Operational Plan

data collection method, (3) identify the sampling frames needed, (4) select the appropriate sampling method, (5) determine necessary sample sizes and overall contact rates, (6) create an operating plan for selecting sampling units, and (7) execute the operational plan.

Exhibit 10.8 presents the logical steps that make up a sampling plan, as well as some of the key activities involved in each step. You are encouraged to revisit earlier parts of the chapter for more details of these activities.

Step 1: Define the Target Population

In any sampling plan, the first task of the researcher is to determine the group of people or objects that should be investigated. With the information problem and research objectives as guidelines, the target population should be identified using descriptors that represent the characteristics of the elements of the target population's frame. These elements become the sampling units from which a sample will be drawn. Clear understanding of the target population will help the researcher successfully draw a representative sample.

Step 2: Select the Data Collection Method

Using the information problem definition, the data requirements, and the research objectives, the researcher chooses a method for collecting the data from the target population elements. Choices include some type of interviewing approach (e.g., personal or telephone) or a self-administered survey. The method of data collection guides the researcher in identifying and securing the necessary sampling frame(s) to conduct the research.

Step 3: Identify the Sampling Frame(s) Needed

After deciding who or what should be investigated, the researcher must assemble a list of eligible sampling units. The list should contain enough information about each prospective sampling unit so the researcher can successfully contact them. Having an incomplete sampling frame decreases the likelihood of drawing a representative sample. Sampling frame lists can be created from a number of different sources (e.g., customer lists from a company's internal database, random-digit dialing, an organization's membership roster).

Step 4: Select the Appropriate Sampling Method

The researcher chooses between two types of sampling approaches: probability and nonprobability. If the data will be used to estimate target population parameters, using a probability sampling method will yield more accurate information about the target population than will nonprobability sampling methods. In determining the appropriateness of the sampling method, the researcher must consider seven factors: (1) research objectives, (2) desired accuracy, (3) availability of resources, (4) time frame, (5) knowledge of the target population, (6) scope of the research, and (7) statistical analysis needs.

Step 5: Determine Necessary Sample Sizes and Overall Contact Rates

In this step of a sampling plan, the researcher decides how precise the sample estimates must be and how much time and money are available to collect the data. To determine the appropriate sample size, decisions have to be made concerning (1) the variability of the population characteristic under investigation, (2) the level of confidence desired in the estimates, and (3) the precision required. The researcher also must decide how many completed surveys are needed for data analysis, recognizing that sample size often is not equal to the usable observations.

At this point the researcher must consider what impact having fewer surveys than initially desired would have on the accuracy of the sample statistics. An important question is "How many prospective sampling units will have to be contacted to ensure the estimated sample size is obtained, and at what additional costs?" To answer this, the researcher must be able to calculate the reachable rates, overall incidence rates, and expected completion rates for the sampling situation.

Step 6: Create an Operating Plan for Selecting Sampling Units

In this step, the researcher must determine how to contact the prospective respondents who were drawn in the sample. Instructions should be clearly written so that interviewers know what to do and how to handle any problems contacting prospective respondents. For example, if the study data will be collected using mall-intercept interviews, then instructions on how to select respondents and conduct the interviews must be given to the interviewer.

Step 7: Execute the Operational Plan

In some research projects, this step is similar to collecting the data (e.g., calling prospective respondents to do a telephone interview). The important thing in this stage is to maintain consistency and control.

marketing research in action

Continuing Case Study

Developing a Sampling Plan for a New Menu Initiative Survey for Santa Fe Grill

Owners of the Santa Fe Grill Mexican Restaurant realize that in order to remain competitive in the restaurant industry, new menu items need to be introduced periodically to provide variety for current customers and attract new customers. Recognizing this, the owners of the restaurant believe three issues need to be addressed using marketing research. One, should the menu be changed to include items beyond the traditional Southwestern cuisine? For example, should items be added that would be considered American, Italian, or European cuisine? Two, regardless of the cuisine to be explored, how many new items (i.e. appetizers, entries, desserts, etc.) should be included on the survey? And, three, what type of sampling plan should be developed for selecting respondents, and who should those respondents be (current customers, new customers, old customers, etc.)?

Understanding the importance of sampling and the impact it will have on the validity and accuracy of the research results, the owners have asked the local university if a marketing research class could assist them in this project. Specifically, the owners have posed the following questions that need to be addressed:

- How many questions should the survey contain to adequately address all possible new menu items, including the notion of assessing the desirability of new cuisines? In short, how can it be determined that all necessary items will be included on the survey without the risk of ignoring menu items that may be desirable to potential customers?

- How should the potential respondents be selected for the survey? Should patrons be interviewed while they are dining? Should patrons be asked to participate in the survey upon exiting the restaurant? Or should a mail or telephone approach be used to collect information from patrons/nonpatrons?

Hands-On Exercise

Based on the above questions, your task is to develop a procedure to address the following issues:

a. From the total domain of possible new items to include on the menu, how many items can be put on the survey? Remember, all menu possibilities should be assessed but you must have a manageable number of questions so the survey can be performed in a timely and reasonable manner. Specifically, from a list of all possible menu items that can be included on the survey, what is the optimal number of menu items that should be used? Is there a sampling procedure one can use to determine the maximum number of menu items to place on the survey?

b. Determine the appropriate sample design. Develop a sample design proposal for the Santa Fe Grill that addresses the following: Should a probability or nonprobability sample be used? Given your answer, what type of sampling design should be employed (simple random, stratified, convenience, etc.)? Given the sample design suggested, how will potential respondents be selected for the study? Finally, determine the necessary sample size and create an operating plan for selecting the sampling units.

Summary of Learning Objectives

■ **Distinguish between probability and nonprobability sampling methods.**

In probability sampling, each sampling unit in the defined target population has a known probability of being selected for the sample. The actual probability of selection for each sampling unit may or may not be equal depending on the type of probability sampling design used. In nonprobability sampling, the probability of selection of each sampling unit is not known. The selection of sampling units is based on some type of intuitive judgment or knowledge of the researcher.

■ **Understand the advantages and disadvantages of probability sampling designs.**

Probability sampling enables the researcher to judge the reliability and validity of data collected by calculating the probability that the findings based on the sample will differ from the defined target population. This observed difference can be partially attributed to the existence of sampling error. Each probability sampling method—simple random, systematic random, stratified, and cluster—has its own inherent advantages and disadvantages.

■ **Understand the advantages and disadvantages of nonprobability sample designs.**

In nonprobability sampling, the probability of selection of each sampling unit is not known. Therefore, potential sampling error cannot be accurately known either.

Although there may be a temptation to generalize nonprobability sample results to the defined target population, for the most part the results are limited to the people who provided the data in the survey. Each nonprobability sampling method—convenience, judgment, quota, and snowball—has its own inherent advantages and disadvantages.

■ **Illustrate the factors necessary for determining the appropriate sample design.**

Selection of the most appropriate sampling design should incorporate the seven factors. These factors include: research objectives, degree of accuracy, availability of resources, time frame, advanced knowledge of the target population, scope of the research, and statistical analysis needs.

■ **Understand the steps in developing a sampling plan.**

A sampling plan is the blueprint or framework needed to ensure that the data collected are representative of the defined target population. A good sampling plan will include, at least, the following steps: (1) define the target population, (2) select the data collection method, (3) identify the sampling frames needed, (4) select the appropriate sampling method, (5) determine necessary sample sizes and overall contact rates, (6) create an operating plan for selecting sampling units, and (7) execute the operational plan.

Key Terms and Concepts

Area sampling 337

Cluster sampling 336

Convenience sampling 340

Disproportionate stratified sampling 335

Judgment sampling 340

Nonprobability sampling 330

Probability sampling 330

Proportionate stratified sampling 335

Quota sampling 341

Sampling plan 344

Simple random sampling (SRS) 331

Snowball sampling 342

Stratified random sampling (STRS) 334

Systematic random sampling (SYMRS) 333

Review Questions

1. Briefly discuss the differences between probability and nonprobability samples.

2. Explain the advantages and disadvantages of the following sampling methods:
   a. Simple random sampling
   b. Systematic random sampling
   c. Cluster sampling
   d. Convenience sampling

3. Identify the major steps involved in developing a two-step cluster sample.

4. Discuss the critical factors necessary for determining the appropriate sample design.

5. Briefly discuss the seven steps involved in developing a sampling plan.

Discussion Questions

1. **EXPERIENCE THE INTERNET.** Log on to the Internet and go to VACATION RENTALS by owners at www.vrbo.com/. This Web site consists of thousands of vacation rentals worldwide. After getting to this Web site, select and click on "Colorado." First, how many vacation rentals are available in each of the following towns (Breckenridge, Copper Mountain, Dillon, Frisco, Keystone, and Silverthorne)? Then using a systematic random sampling design, draw a representative sample of those vacation rentals within the six designated towns.

2. **EXPERIENCE THE INTERNET.** Go to the U.S. Census Bureau's home page at www.census.gov. Once there, select the population and housing option. Within this area, view all of the metropolitan areas (MSAs). Using a stratified random sampling approach, develop a sample of MSAs that could be used for distributing a survey on snowmobiles.

3. Many state lotteries require individuals to pick numbers between 1 and 10. Over the past ten weeks, the number "9" was a winning number 40 percent of the time. If you pick a number for the upcoming week, and you select the number "9," will you be more or less likely to win the lottery? How would you explain your answer based on the concept of simple random sampling?

4. Outline the step-by-step process used to determine the following:
   a. A systematic random sample of 200 students at your university.
   b. A convenience sample of 150 shoppers at a local mall.
   c. A stratified random sample of 50 lawyers, 40 doctors, and 60 dentists who subscribe to your local newspaper.

5. A national cellular phone company is interested in determining the heavy users of cell phones (airtime). What type of sampling method would be best suited for this situation? Why?

chapter 11

Overview of Measurement: Construct Development and Scale Measurement

Learning Objectives

After reading this chapter, you will be able to

1. Explain what constructs are, how they are developed, and why they are important to measurement and scale designs.

2. Discuss the integrated validity and reliability concerns underlying construct development and scale measurement.

3. Explain what scale measurement is, and describe how to correctly apply it in collecting raw data from respondents.

4. Identify and explain the five basic levels of scales, and discuss the amount of information they can provide a researcher or decision maker.

5. Discuss the hybrid ordinally-interval scale design and the types of information it can provide researchers.

6. Discuss the components of scale development and explain why they are critical to gathering primary data.

> "Success in predicting consumer sales for new Burger King stores came about after we understood how to better measure location site criteria using information research practices."
>
> —C. MICHAEL POWELL
> **Former Director of Financial Analysis**
> **Burger King Corporation**

Fast Food, Side by Side: A Prediction of Store Location and Loyalty Success

One of the most critical problems facing the Burger King Corporation is selecting sites for new restaurants that will attract sufficient customer loyalty for the new store to be profitable. Since the company has many more major competitors today than just McDonald's or Wendy's, Burger King's initial strategy to locate its stores no closer than about three miles to a McDonald's, on streets with high traffic, in neighborhoods with schools, and in areas of predominantly middle-income families has proven to be no longer feasible. This traditional location strategy was based on management's early belief that these locations would produce the greatest probability of success.

Unfortunately, the decision-making process did not include any organized marketing research data or a clear understanding of the significance of customer loyalty, but rather relied heavily on the experience and knowledge of the Burger King senior management team. After years of using this site-location model, it became increasingly difficult to meet these criteria and new stores' sales forecasts often were inaccurate. To correct the problem, management has begun to seek a new formula for site location. Burger King's marketing research department added interview and survey data from customers to complement its use of traditional sales and geographic data from existing Burger King stores. New research objectives included measuring customer loyalty and its impact on the relationship between the site-location criteria and sales, and then seeking any other criteria that would predict sales more accurately. To gain a better understanding of customer loyalty, Burger King turned to Burke's (www.burke.com) Customer Satisfaction Division and its Customer Loyalty Index measures. New research quickly showed that while traffic density was a significant indicator of sales, neither the proximity of schools nor income levels of the surrounding area were good indicators. Moreover, customers preferred places where several fast-food establishments were clustered together so that more choice was available. The study also found that customer loyalty toward new Burger King restaurants directly influenced the accuracy of sales potential estimates by store location. In the process, management learned that customer loyalty was a complex construct that required better understanding of consumers' satisfaction, positive word-of-mouth recommendations, and different levels of behavioral intentions.

Several insights about the importance of construct and measurement developments can be gained from the Burger King Corporation experience. First, not knowing the critical criteria for locating a business can lead to intuitive guesswork and counterproductive results. Second, making accurate location decisions requires identifying and precisely defining the patronage constructs (e.g., attitudes, emotions, behavioral factors) that consumers deem important to creating customer loyalty. Be sure to read the Marketing Research in Action at the end of this chapter to see how Burke, Inc., defines and measures customer loyalty.

Value of Measurement within Information Research

Measurement is an integral part of the modern world, yet the beginnings of measurement lie in the distant past. Before a farmer could sell his corn, potatoes, or apples, both he and the buyer had to decide on units of measurement. Over time this particular measurement became known as a bushel or four pecks or, more precisely, 2,150.42 cubic inches. In the early days, measurement was simply achieved by using a basket or container of standard size that everyone agreed was a bushel.

From such simple everyday devices as the standard bushel basket, we have progressed in the physical sciences to such an extent that we are now able to measure the rotation of a distant star, the altitude of a satellite in microinches, or time in picoseconds (1 trillionth of a second). Today, such precise physical measurement is critical to airline pilots flying through dense fog or physicians controlling a surgical laser.

In most marketing situations, however, the measurements are applied to things that are much more abstract than altitude or time. For example, most decision makers would agree that information about whether or not a firm's customers are going to like a new product is critically important prior to introducing that product. In many cases, such information has made the difference between business success and failure. Yet, unlike time or altitude, people's preferences can be very difficult to measure accurately. As we described earlier, the Coca-Cola Company introduced New Coke after inadequately measuring consumers' preferences, and thereby suffered substantial losses. In a similar fashion, such inadequate measurements of consumer attitudes quite often lead to the early cancellation of many television series, the withdrawal of new products, and sometimes the failure of entire companies.

Since accurate measurement of constructs is essential to effective decision making, the purpose of this chapter is to provide you with a basic understanding of the importance of measuring customers' attitudes and behaviors, and other marketplace phenomena. We describe the measurement process and the central decision rules for developing scale measurements. The focus here is on basic measurement issues, construct development, and scale measurements. Chapter 12 continues the topic of measurement and discusses several popular attitudinal, emotional, and behavioral intention scales.

Overview of the Measurement Process

Measurement is the process of determining the amount (or intensity) of information about persons, events, ideas, and/or objects of interest and their relationship to a business problem or opportunity. In other words, researchers use the measurement process by assigning either *numbers* or *labels* to (1) people's thoughts, feelings, behaviors, and characteristics;

Measurement An integrative process of determining the intensity (or amount) of information about constructs, concepts, or objects.

(2) the features or attributes of objects; (3) the aspects of ideas; or (4) any type of phenomenon or event using specific rules to represent quantities and/or qualities of the factors being investigated. For example, to gather data that will offer insight about people who shop for automobiles online (a marketing phenomenon), a researcher collects information on the demographic characteristics, attitudes, perceptions, past online purchase behaviors, and other relevant factors associated with these people.

Critical to the process of collecting primary data is the development of well-constructed measurement procedures. The measurement process consists of two distinctly different development processes: *construct development* and *scale measurement*. To achieve the overall goal of collecting high-quality data, researchers must understand what they are attempting to measure before developing the appropriate scale measurements. The goal of the construct development process is to precisely identify and define *what is to be measured*. In turn, the goal of the scale measurement process is to determine *how to precisely measure each construct*. We will begin with construct development then move to scale measurements.

Object Refers to any tangible item in a person's environment that can be clearly and easily identified through his or her senses.

Researchers interpret and use the terms objects and constructs in several ways. First, the term **object** refers to any tangible item in a person's environment that can be clearly and easily identified through the senses (sight, sound, touch, smell, taste). Remember that researchers do not measure the object per se but rather the elements that make up the object. Any object has what is called *objective properties* or features that are used to identify and distinguish it from another object. These properties represent attributes that make up an object of interest and are directly observable and measurable, such as the physical and demographic characteristics of a person (age, sex, income, occupation status, color of eyes, etc.), or the actual number of purchases made of a particular product, or the tangible features of the object (horsepower, style, color, stereo system of an automobile, etc.), to name a few.

Construct A hypothetical variable made up of a set of component responses or behaviors that are thought to be related.

In turn, any object can also have *subjective properties* that are abstract, intangible characteristics that cannot be directly observed or measured because they are the mental images a person attaches to an object, such as attitudes, feelings, perceptions, expectations, or expressions of future actions (e.g., purchase intentions). Researchers refer to these intangible, subjective properties as abstract **constructs.** Measurement of constructs requires researchers to ask people to translate these mental features onto a continuum of intensity using carefully designed questions.

Construct Development

The necessity for precise definitions in marketing research may appear to be obvious, but it frequently is the area where problems arise. Precise definition of marketing constructs begins with defining the purpose of the study and providing clear expressions of the research problem. Without a clear initial understanding of the research problem before the study begins, the researcher can end up collecting irrelevant or inaccurate data, thereby wasting a great deal of time, effort, and money. Misguided research endeavors have contributed many mistakes being made in such industries as music, fashion, and food. Take the U.S. auto industry as a case in point. Even after the first Volkswagens were introduced into the United States, most U.S. manufacturers continued to invest in factories designed to produce large, inefficient automobiles. They ignored studies that suggested that increasing fuel prices, highway congestion, and pollution controls favored more modest vehicles. As a result, hundreds of millions of dollars in auto sales were lost to foreign competitors. Such cases show that a very careful definition of the purpose of the study is essential.

Construct development An integrative process in which researchers determine what specific data should be collected for solving the defined research problem.

Construct development is an integrative process in which researchers identify the subjective properties for which data should be collected to solve the defined research problem. Identifying properties to investigate requires knowledge and understanding of constructs and their dimensionality, validity, and operationalization.

Abstractness of the Construct

At the heart of construct development is the need to determine exactly what is to be measured. The objects that are relevant to the research problem are identified first. Then the objective and subjective properties of each object are specified. In cases where data are needed only about the concreteness of an object, the research focus is limited to measuring the object's objective properties. But when data are needed to understand an object's subjective properties, the researcher must identify measurable subcomponents that can be used to clarify the abstractness associated with the object's subjective properties.

For instance, a hammer can easily be thought of as a concrete object. Researchers can easily measure a hammer's physical characteristics: the hardness of its head, its length and weight, the composition of the handle, and so on. Yet the hammer can also have a set of subjective properties, such as its quality and performance that are created from people's attitudes, emotions, and judgments toward the hammer. Due to level of abstractness associated with the hammer's intangible quality and performance features, there are no physical instruments that can directly measure these constructs. Exhibit 11.1 provides some examples of objects and their concrete, tangible properties and abstract, intangible construct properties, as well as some specific examples of marketing constructs. A rule of thumb is that if an object's features can be directly measured using physical instruments, then that feature is not a construct.

Determining Dimensionality of the Construct

In determining exactly what is to be measured, researchers must keep in mind the need to acquire relevant, high-quality data to support management's decisions. For example, if the purpose is to assess the service quality of an automobile dealership, then what exactly should be measured? Since dealer service quality is an abstract construct, perhaps the most appropriate way to begin to answer this question is to indirectly identify those dealership attributes that are important to customers.

Domain of observables
The set of identifiable and measurable components associated with an abstract construct.

Researchers in this case can use a variety of qualitative data collection methods (e.g., focus groups or in-depth interviews) to develop preliminary insights into service quality and its **domain of observables,** which is the set of identifiable and measurable components associated with an abstract construct.[1] To illustrate this point, researchers interested in identifying the domain of measurable components that represent the service quality construct conducted two different types of exploratory research, a secondary literature review of past research on service quality and several focus groups. The results suggested that the service quality construct can be indirectly represented by the domain of a service provider's ability to (1) *communicate* and *listen* to consumers; (2) demonstrate *excellent interpretative skills;* (3) *sincerely empathize* with consumers in interpreting their needs and wants; (4) be *tactful in responding* to customers' questions, objections, and problems; (5) create an impression of *reliability in performing* the services; (6) create an *image of credibility* by keeping promises; (7) demonstrate *sufficient technical knowledge* and *competence;* and (8) exhibit *strong interpersonal skills* in dealing with consumers. In turn, this preliminary information could then be used as a guideline for collecting data from a larger, more representative sample of customers about important service quality attributes. During the discovery process, the researcher must be careful to include in the qualitative procedures people who are representative of the defined target population. It is also necessary to evaluate the extent to which the actions taken as a result of the preliminary insights fit the organization's goals and objectives. For instance, most customers usually desire lower service prices. Yet, if the dealership is price-competitive in the marketplace, then it may not be in the best interests of the dealership to reduce prices.

e X H I B I T   **11.1**   **Examples of Concrete Features and Abstract Constructs of Objects**

Objects

Airplane
Concrete properties: Number of engines, height, weight, length, seating capacity, physical characteristics of seats, type of airplane, etc.

Abstract constructs: Quality of in-flight cabin service, comfortability of seating, smoothness of takeoff and landing, etc.

Consumer
Concrete properties: Age, sex, marital status, income, brand last purchased, dollar amount of purchase, types of products purchased, color of eyes and hair, etc.

Abstract properties: Attitudes toward a product, brand loyalty, high-involvement purchases, emotions (love, fear, anxiety), intelligence, personality, risk taker, etc.

Organization
Concrete properties: Name of company, number of employees, number of locations, total assets, Fortune 500 rating, computer capacity, types and numbers of products and service offerings, type of industry membership, etc.

Abstract properties: Competence of employees, quality control, channel power, competitive advantages, company image, consumer-oriented practices, etc.

Marketing Constructs

Brand loyalty
Concrete properties: A particular purchase pattern exhibited toward a specific brand-name product or service, the number of times a particular brand is purchased, the frequency of purchases of a particular brand, amount of time needed to select a brand.

Abstract properties: The degree a person likes/dislikes a particular brand, the degree of satisfaction expressed toward a brand, a person's overall attitude toward the brand.

Customer satisfaction
Concrete properties: Identifiable attributes that make up a product, service, or experience.

Abstract properties: The degree that a person is "delighted" with a specific experience; liking/disliking of the individual attributes making up the experience, product, or service; expressions of positive feelings toward the product, service, or experience.

Service quality
Concrete properties: Identifiable attributes (or dimensions) that make up a service encounter or experience. (i.e., level of interaction, personal communications, service provider's knowledge, etc.)

Abstract properties: Expectations held about each identifiable attribute, evaluative judgment of performance.

Advertising recall
Concrete properties: Factual properties of the ad (i.e., message, symbols, movement, models, text, etc.), aided and unaided recognition of the facts.

Abstract properties: Interpretations of the factual elements in the ad, favorable/unfavorable judgments, degree of affective attachment to ad.

Assessing Construct Validity

Content validity The subjective yet systematic assessment of how well a construct's measurable components represent that construct.

Convergent validity When the researcher's measures of a construct are highly correlated with known existing measures of the same construct.

Another important activity is assessing the validity of the construct, especially if the construct is believed to be multidimensional. It is important to note that assessing the validity of a construct is actually an after-the-fact activity because the process requires the researcher to create a set of scale measurements for each of the construct's domain components and collect data on each of those components. The researcher then needs to perform statistical analyses to test for content validity, convergent validity, and discriminant validity.[2] **Content validity** (sometimes referred to as *face validity*) is the systematic assessment of how well a construct's measurable components represent that construct. **Convergent validity** focuses on how well the construct's measurement positively correlates with different measurements of the same construct. For researchers to be able to evaluate convergent validity, they must use several different measurement approaches to evaluate the construct. For **discriminant validity,** researchers must determine whether the construct being investigated differs significantly from other constructs that are different. Finally, in

Discriminant validity
The existence of a negative correlation between the measurement of one construct and those measures of another construct.

Nomological validity
Assessment of how well one construct theoretically fits within a network of other established constructs that are related yet different.

Direct cognitive structural analysis
A data analysis technique that assesses how well the identifiable attributes of a construct reflect that construct and their importance to it.

some cases, **nomological validity** allows researchers to evaluate how well one particular construct theoretically compares with other established constructs that are related yet different.

Usually one of two approaches is used to collect data for assessing construct validity. If there are enough resources, researchers will conduct a pilot study among 50 or so people who are believed to be representative of the defined target population. In situations where resources are not available for a pilot study, researchers will attempt to approximate content validity by having a panel of experts independently judge the dimensionality of the construct. While these approaches have become common measurement practices, they contain several weaknesses.

Inappropriate Scale Measurement Formats

When after-the-fact data are used to assess construct validity, the scale point descriptors used in collecting the data can cause inaccuracies.[3] That is, using untested or inappropriate scale measurement indicators to measure the construct can create measurement artifacts that lead to misinterpretations of the true components as well as the true dimensionality traits of the construct. In this situation, the raw data are driving the researcher's theoretical framework instead of theory driving the measurement process. A procedure that can be used to overcome this type of weakness is **direct cognitive structural analysis,** in which respondents are simply asked to determine whether an attribute is part of the construct and, if so, how important it is to that construct.[4]

Another element that impacts the assessment of construct validity but focuses more on scale measurement is *scale reliability*. Here the researcher determines the extent to which the scale used to measure the construct consistently measures what it was intended to measure. While reliability of scale measurements is a necessary but not, by itself, a sufficient condition for accurately determining construct validity, scale reliability remains an important element in the process of collecting high-quality data.

Inappropriate Set of Respondents

In academic research settings, for example, researchers too often rely on college students' input in their process of determining the components of the construct being investigated. Although college students are consumers and may have some knowledge and experience with certain products and services, in most cases their attitudes and buying behaviors are not representative of the general population or of many specifically defined target populations. A second problem that relates to using college students in construct development is that student samples typically are drawn using a convenience sampling approach. Convenience sampling does not guarantee true representation of a college student population, let alone a larger defined target population. As a consequence, the components originally thought to make up the construct may be different when the study is extended to a larger sample of subjects from the target population. The Closer Look at Research box offers an example of this problem as it occurred in a banking study.

Construct Operationalization

Operationalization
Explaining a construct's meaning in measurement terms by specifying the activities or operations necessary to measure it.

Operationalization is when the researcher explains a construct's meaning in measurement terms by specifying the activities or operations necessary to measure it. The process focuses on the design and use of questions and scale measurements to gather the needed data. Since many constructs, such as satisfaction, preferences, emotions, quality images, and brand loyalty cannot be directly observed or measured, the researcher attempts to indirectly measure them through operationalization of their components.

For example, one researcher developed over 100 questions to determine if customers were satisfied with their recent automobile purchase and the dealer's service.[6] Using a

A Closer Look at Research

Problem in Construct Development

A marketing researcher wanted to identify the areas people might use in their process of judging banking service quality. The researcher conducted several focus groups among both undergraduate students in a basic marketing course and graduate students in a marketing management course to identify the service activities and offerings that might represent service quality. The researcher's rationale for using these groups was that they did have experience in conducting bank transactions, they were consumers, and the researcher had easy access to them for their opinions. The preliminary results of the focus group interviews revealed that the students used four dimensions for judging a bank's service quality: (1) interpersonal social skills of bank staff, (2) reliability of bank statements, (3) convenience of ATM delivery systems, and (4) diagnostic competence of bank tellers.

A month later, the researcher conducted four focus groups among known customers of one of the large banks in Charlotte, North Carolina. The preliminary results clearly suggested those customers used seven dimensions for judging a

In the Field

bank's service quality. Those dimensions were identified as the bank's ability to (1) communicate with and listen to consumers; (2) demonstrate diagnostic competence in understanding the customer's banking needs and wants; (3) elicit sincere empathy by showing concern for how consumers interpret their requirements; (4) be tactful in responding to customers' questions, objections, or problems; (5) create an impression of reliability and credibility inherent in a bank service encounter; (6) demonstrate sufficient technological competence in handling the critical aspects of bank transactions; and (7) exhibit strong positive interpersonal social skills in conducting bank transactions.

The researcher was in a tentative position of not knowing for sure whether people perceive bank service quality as having four or seven critical components. Which qualitative source of information should be used to better understand the construct of bank service quality? Which preliminary information should the researcher rely on to conduct the empirical survey on bank service quality? These issues would directly affect the operationalization of construct development.[5]

variety of different measurement formats, customers were asked to rate a number of components, including the salesperson's listening skills; the reliability of the service; the appearance of the service facilities; and the serviceperson's interpersonal skills. They were also asked about attributes of the vehicle purchased, including road-holding ability, overall comfort, cost of routine maintenance, overall durability, overall exterior styling, visibility, steering precision, security features, fuel economy, and overall power. Exhibit 11.2 illustrates two different measurement approaches used to capture data about the construct of automobile dealership service satisfaction.

The examples in Exhibit 11.2 suggest that assessing what appears to be a simple construct of service satisfaction can be more involved than it might seem at first. Here, the researcher was trying to fully capture information on all dimensions that may affect a customer's service satisfaction. Certainly this approach will give dealerships a more accurate basis for evaluating how successful they have been in satisfying customers. Moreover, this type of in-depth analysis provides a business with better opportunities to pinpoint areas of concern and take corrective actions. With only a single-question approach, corrective action would be very difficult if not impossible since the researcher would not be able to determine the exact problem area. After constructs and their possible traits have been adequately identified and understood, the researcher then needs to create appropriate scale measurements.

---

exHIBIT 11.2 Selected Question/Scales Used to Measure Service Satisfaction with Auto Dealerships

---

Example 1:

Now with all the knowledge, opinions, feelings, and personal experiences you have acquired as a customer with your *primary* automobile service provider (ASP), I would like to know how satisfied or dissatisfied you are concerning several service features.

Using the scale described below, where:

6 = Completely satisfied	4 = Somewhat satisfied	2 = Definitely dissatisfied
5 = Definitely satisfied	3 = Somewhat dissatisfied	1 = Completely dissatisfied

please write a number from 1 to 6 in the space provided that best expresses how satisfied or dissatisfied you are with **each listed** service feature.

____ Convenience of ASP's location	____ ASP's communication skills
____ Flexibility in ASP's operating hours	____ Availability of quality service offerings
____ Service provider's personal social skills	____ Overall reputation of your primary ASP
____ Personnel's understanding of customer needs	____ ASP's concern of putting its customers "first"
____ Reliability/credibility of ASP's service providers	____ ASP's listening skills
____ Service provider's technical knowledge/competence	____ Quality of the ASP's products (or services)

Example 2:

Using the educational letter grading system of "A," "B," "C," "D," and "F," please **circle** the one "letter grade" that best expresses the overall grade that you would give each of the following listed service factors at your primary ASP.

a. The communication skills of the service people at my primary ASP are . . .	A	B	C	D	F
b. The listening capabilities of the service people at my primary ASP are . . .	A	B	C	D	F
c. The ability of the service staff to understand my various repair/maintenance service needs are . . .	A	B	C	D	F
d. The ability of service employees to demonstrate understanding of my auto service needs (or requirements) from my point of view are . . .	A	B	C	D	F
e. The service personnel's ability to respond quickly to my objections (or problems, questions) are . . .	A	B	C	D	F
f. The reliability (or credibility) demonstrated by the service representatives are . . .	A	B	C	D	F
g. The technical knowledge (or understanding) demonstrated by the service personnel are . . .	A	B	C	D	F
h. The personal social skills used by the employees in dealing with me are . . .	A	B	C	D	F
i. The facilities/equipment/personnel all demonstrate that it is a "professional" organization to deal with . . .	A	B	C	D	F

Basic Concepts of Scale Measurement

Types of Data Collected in Research Practices

Regardless of whether the researcher wants to collect secondary or primary data, all information is drawn from responses to questions that focus on verifiable facts, mental thoughts or feelings, past or current actions, or planned future actions of people, organizations, objects, or phenomena. As such, any response can be classified as being one of four basic states of nature: verifiable facts, mental thoughts/emotional feelings, past or current behaviors, and planned future behavior intentions. To simplify discussion of these different states of nature, we will refer to verifiable facts as *state-of-being data,* mental thoughts and emotional feelings as *state-of-mind data,* past and current behaviors as *state-of-behavior data,* and planned future behavior intentions as *state-of-intention data.*

State-of-Being Data (Verifiable Facts)

State-of-being data

The physical and/or demographic or socio-economic characteristics of people, objects, and organizations.

When the problem requires the researcher to collect responses that are relevant to the physical, demographic, or socioeconomic characteristics of individuals, objects, or organizations, the resulting data are considered verifiable facts, or state-of-being data. **State-of-being data** represent factual characteristics that can be verified through sources other than the person providing the responses. For example, a researcher can directly ask respondents their sex, age, income level, education level, marital status, number of children, occupation, height, weight, color of eyes, and telephone number—or the researcher could obtain these data through secondary sources such as birth certificates, loan applications, income tax returns, driver's licenses, public documents at a county courthouse, the telephone company, and so on. For organizations, data on total dollar/unit sales, computer capacity, number of employees, total assets, number and types of stores, and so on, often can be obtained through secondary sources, eliminating the need to ask direct questions about them. The same holds true for the physical characteristics of many objects. The main point to remember about state-of-being data is that the researcher is not limited to collecting the raw data by only asking questions.

State-of-Mind Data (Mental Thoughts or Emotional Feelings)

State-of-mind data

The mental attributes or emotional feelings of people.

State-of-mind data represent the mental attributes or emotional feelings of individuals that are not directly observable or available through some type of external source. State-of-mind data exist only within the minds of people. To collect such data, the researcher has to ask a person to respond to questions. Verification through secondary or external sources is all but impossible. Some examples of state-of-mind data would be a person's personality traits, attitudes, feelings, perceptions, beliefs, cognitive decision processes, product/service preferences, awareness levels, and images. Therefore, data quality and accuracy are limited to the degree of honesty of the person providing the responses to the researcher's questions.

State-of-Behavior Data (Past and Current Behaviors)

State-of-behavior data

A person's or organiza-tion's current observ-able or recorded actions or reactions.

State-of-behavior data represent an individual's or organization's current observable actions or recorded past actions. The researcher has several options available to obtain state-of-behavior data. A person can be asked questions about current or past behavior. For example, a person could be asked to respond to questions such as "In the past six months, how many times have you purchased dry cereal for your household?" or "In a typical week, how often do you go shopping at a mall?" To obtain current behavior, a person could be asked to respond to such questions as "Are you currently enrolled in college?" or "How many courses are you currently taking in marketing?"

Another option is to use either a trained observer or some type of mechanical/electronic device to observe and record current behavior. For example, a disguised observer or hidden camera can be used to selectively observe and record customers' frozen-food selections at the local Winn-Dixie supermarket. Such behavioral data might include length of time in the frozen-food section of the store, the specific brands or types of frozen food inspected or selected, or the number of units of a product that were placed in the shopping cart, and so on.

A third option useful for collecting data on past behavior is to find records of previously conducted behavior. For example, a researcher could examine a restaurant's charge-card receipts over a specified period to determine how often a selected individual came in and ate at that particular restaurant. There are limitations to the quality and accuracy of data using this option. But in general verification of an individual's past behaviors through any type of external, secondary source is a difficult process in terms of time, effort, and accuracy. This method places heavy emphasis on the existence of well-documented behaviors.

State-of-Intention Data (Planned Future Behaviors)

State-of-intention data
A person's or organization's expressed plans of future behavior.

State-of-intention data represent an individual's or organization's expressed plans of future behavior. State-of-intention data can be collected only by asking a person to respond to questions about behaviors that are yet to take place. For instance, a researcher can ask such questions as "How likely are you to purchase a new Mazda in the next six months?" or "Do you plan to come and visit the Museum of Science and Industry next time you are in Chicago?" or "How likely would you be to buy Tide next time you need laundry detergent?" Like state-of-behavior data, state-of-intention data are very difficult to verify through external, secondary sources, but verification sometimes is possible.

The Nature of Scale Measurement

Scale measurement
The process of assigning descriptors to represent the range of possible responses to a question about a particular object or construct.

To be successful in generating primary information for addressing business problems, the researcher must be able to gather the appropriate data. The quantity and quality of the responses associated with any question or observation technique depend directly on the scale measurements used by the researcher. **Scale measurement** is the process of assigning a set of descriptors to represent the range of possible responses to a question about a particular object or construct.[7]

Scale points Designated degrees of intensity assigned to the responses in a given questioning or observation method.

Within this process, the focus is on measuring the existence of various characteristics of a person's response. Scale measurement directly determines the amount of raw data that can be obtained from a given questioning or observation method. Scale measurement attempts to assign designated degrees of intensity to the responses. These degrees of intensity are commonly referred to as **scale points.** For example, a retailer might want to know how important a preselected set of store or service features is to consumers in deciding where to shop. The level of importance attached to each store or service feature would be determined by the researcher's assignment of a range of intensity descriptors (scale points) to represent the possible degrees of importance (e.g., definitely, moderately, slightly, not at all important) associated with each feature.

Properties of Scale Measurements

There are four properties a researcher can use in developing scales: assignment, order, distance, and origin (see Exhibit 11.3).

Assignment

Assignment property
The employment of unique descriptors to identify each object in a set.

The **assignment property,** also referred to as *description* or *category property,* is where the researcher uses unique descriptors, or labels, to identify each object within a set.[8] This property enables a researcher to categorize the responses into mutually exclusive groups, each with its own identity. Any descriptor can be used for a response. Some examples are the use of numbers (22, 34, 45, etc.) to identify the players on a basketball team so the scorekeeper can correctly record points scored or fouls committed; yes and no responses to the question "Are you going to purchase a new automobile within the next six months?"; the use of colors (red, green, blue, etc.) to identify cars, clothes, or bathroom towels; and the use of size indicators (large, medium, small, etc.) to identify the quantity of soft drinks, or fitting of clothes, or amount of pizza people might purchase.

e X H I B I T 11.3	Four Scaling Properties: Description and Examples

Scaling Properties	Description and Examples
Assignment property	The employment of unique descriptors to identify an object in a set.
	Examples: The use of numbers (10, 38, 44, 18, 23, etc.); the use of colors (red, blue, green, pink, etc.); yes and no responses to questions that identify objects into mutually exclusive groups.
Order property	Establishes "relative magnitudes" between the descriptors, creating hierarchical rank-order relationships among objects.
	Examples: 1st place is better than a 4th-place finish; a 5-foot person is shorter than a 7-foot person; a regular customer purchases more often than a rare customer.
Distance property	Allows the researcher and respondent to identify, understand, and accurately express absolute (or assumed) differences between objects.
	Examples: Family A with six children living at home, compared to family B with three children at home, has three more children than family B; differences in income ranges or age categories.
Origin property	A unique scale descriptor that is designated as being a "true natural zero" or "true state of nothing."
	Examples: Asking a respondent his or her weight or current age; the number of times one shops at a supermarket; or the market share of a specific brand of hand soap.

Order

Order property The relative magnitude assigned to each scale point descriptor.

The **order property** is the relative magnitude between the descriptors used as scale points.[9] Relative magnitude between descriptors is based on the relationships between two or more descriptors. For example, there are only three relationships between responses A and B: A can be *greater than* B; A can be *less than* B; or A can be *equal to* B. When respondents can identify and understand a "greater than" or a "less than" relationship between two or more objects or responses, the order scaling property is established and a meaningful rank order can be identified among the reported responses. Some examples of the order property include the following: 1 is less than 5; "extremely satisfied" is more intense than "somewhat satisfied"; "very important" has more importance than "slightly important"; "somewhat disagree" involves less disagreement than "definitely disagree"; and a person holding a master of business administration (MBA) degree has more formal years of education than a person holding an associate of arts (AA) degree. When the order scaling property is included in a set of scale points, it enables the researcher to establish either a "highest to lowest" or a "lowest to highest" rank order among the raw responses. It is important to remember that the order scaling property, by itself, identifies only the relative differences between raw responses and not the absolute differences.

Distance

Distance property The measurement scheme that expresses the exact (or absolute) difference between each of the descriptors, scale points, or raw responses.

The **distance property** expresses the absolute difference between each of the descriptors or scale points.[10] In other words, the distance property shows that the researcher knows the absolute magnitude that exists between each response to a question. For example, family A drives two cars, and family B drives four cars. Thus, family A has two fewer cars than family B. A student who has to travel 20 miles to school drives twice as many miles as a student who drives only 10 miles to the same school. The distance scaling property is restricted to situations where the responses represent some type of natural numerical answer.

In many cases researchers believe the scales associated with collecting state-of-mind data activate the distance property. This is a myth that causes misunderstanding of particular types of data and their structures. For example, some researchers believe that "extremely spicy" is one unit of spiciness away from "very spicy," or that "strongly agree" is two units of agreement away from "somewhat agree," or that "extremely important" is four units of importance away from "only slightly important." In all these examples, there is no way a researcher could statistically verify that the assumed absolute relationship between those scale descriptors exists. This measurement problem is discussed later in this chapter.

Origin

Origin property   Having a unique starting point in a set of scale point descriptors that is designated as a true zero.

The **origin property** refers to the use of a unique starting point in a set of scale points that is designated as being a "true natural zero" or true state of nothing. The origin property relates to a numbering system where zero is the displayed starting point in a set of possible responses. It must be noted that a response of "don't know," "no opinion," "neither agree nor disagree," "don't care," "not at all important," "no response," and so on, to a question does not represent the zero origin property.[11] Rather, these responses are appropriate for questions like current age; income; number of dependent children living at home; number of miles one travels to go shopping at a supermarket; and the number of times a person purchases a specific product or service in a week.

When developing scale measurements, the more scaling properties that can be simultaneously activated in a scale design, the more complete the collected data. Note that each scaling property builds on the previous one. This means that any scale will have the assignment property. A scale that includes the order property automatically possesses the assignment property. If the researcher designs a scale with the distance property, the scale also has assignment and order. Scales that are built with the origin property also have assignment, order, and distance properties.

Basic Levels of Scales

While scaling properties determine the amount of data obtained from any scale design, all scale measurements can be logically and accurately classified as one of five basic scale levels: nominal, ordinal, true class interval, hybrid ordinally-interval, or ratio. There are specific relationships between the level of scale and which scaling properties are activated within the scale (see Exhibit 11.4).

EXHIBIT 11.4   Relationships between Levels of Scales and Scaling Properties

Level of Scale	Scaling Properties			
	Assignment	Order	Distance	Origin
Nominal	Yes	No	No	No
Ordinal	Yes	Yes	No	No
True Class Interval	Yes	Yes	Yes	No
Hybrid Ordinally-Interval	Yes	Yes	Yes	No
Ratio	Yes	Yes	Yes	Yes

e X H I B I T 11.5 Examples of Nominal Scale Structures

Example 1:

Please indicate your current marital status.

___ Married   ___ Single   ___ Separated   ___ Divorced   ___ Widowed

Example 2:

Do you like or dislike chocolate ice cream?

___ Like   ___ Dislike

Example 3:

Please check those information and HCP service areas in which you have had a face-to-face or telephone conversation with a representative of your main HCP in the past six months. (Check as many as apply.)

___ Appointments   ___ Treatment at home   ___ Referral to other HCP

___ Prescriptions   ___ Medical test results   ___ Hospital stay

Some other service area(s); Please specify _____

Example 4:

Please indicate your gender:

___ Female   ___ Male

Example 5:

Which of the following supermarkets have you shopped at in the last 30 days? (Please check all that apply)

___ Albertson   ___ Winn-Dixie   ___ Publix   ___ Safeway   ___ Kash&Karry   ___ I.G.A.

Nominal Scales

Nominal scale The type of scale in which the questions require respondents to provide only some type of descriptor as the raw response.

A **nominal scale** is the most basic of scale designs. In this level of scale, the questions require respondents to provide only some type of descriptor as the response. The response does not contain any level of intensity. Therefore, it is impossible to establish any form of rank order among the set of given responses. That is, nominal scales provide data that cannot be arranged in a "greater than/less than" or "bigger than/smaller than" hierarchical pattern. Nominal scales allow the researcher only to categorize the responses into mutually exclusive subsets that do not illustrate distances between them.[12] Some examples of nominal scales are given in Exhibit 11.5.

Ordinal Scales

Ordinal scale A scale that allows a respondent to express relative magnitude between the answers to a question.

An **ordinal scale** has both assignment and order scaling properties. This level of scale enables respondents to express relative magnitude between the answers to a question. The raw responses can be rank ordered into a hierarchical pattern.[13] Thus, it is easy to determine "greater than/less than," "higher than/lower than," "more often/less often," "more important/less important," or "less agreement/more agreement" types of relationships between the responses. But ordinal scales do not enable the researcher to determine the absolute difference in any of the ordinal relationships. In reality, almost all state-of-mind data responses are collected using ordinal scales. Exhibit 11.6 provides several examples of ordinals.

exHIBIT **11.6** **Examples of Ordinal Scale Structures**

Example 1:

Which category best describes your knowledge about the services offered by your main health care provider?

(Please check just one category.)

___ Complete knowledge of services

___ Good knowledge of services

___ Basic knowledge of services

___ Little knowledge of services

___ No knowledge of services

Example 2:

The following list of library services, activities, and resources may or may not be important to you when using a library. Using the scale provided below, for each listed item please check the response that best expresses how important you feel it is that a library provides **each of the listed items.**

Services, Activities, Resources	Extremely Important	Definitely Important	Somewhat Important	Not at All Important
Loans of books, CDs, videos, etc.	___	___	___	___
Availability of current magazines	___	___	___	___
Children's programs	___	___	___	___
Adult programs	___	___	___	___
Computer classes or assistance	___	___	___	___
Reference material for business	___	___	___	___
Online catalog of resources in region	___	___	___	___
General reference material	___	___	___	___

Example 3:

We would like to know your preferences for actually using different banking methods. Among the methods listed below, please indicate your top three preferences using a "1" to represent your first choice, a "2" for your second preference, and a "3" for your third choice of methods.

(Please write the numbers on the lines next to your selected methods.)

_____ Inside the bank   _____ Bank by mail

_____ Drive-in (Drive-up) windows   _____ Bank by telephone

_____ 24-hour ATM   _____ Internet Banking

Example 4:

For each pair of retail discount stores, circle the store you would be more likely to patronize:

Kmart or Target   Target or Wal-Mart   Wal-Mart or Kmart

Example 5:

Which one statement best describes your opinion of the quality of an Intel Pentium processor?

(Please check just one statement.)

____ Higher than AMD's Athlon processor

____ About the same as AMD's Athlon processor

____ Lower than AMD's Athlon processor

True Class Interval Scales

True class interval scale
A scale that demonstrates absolute differences between each scale point.

A **true class interval scale** has not only assignment and order scaling properties but also the distance property. Scales with the distance property can be used to measure absolute differences between each scale point. Also, because of the distance property, more powerful statistical techniques can be used to analyze the data.[14] With true class interval scale structures, researchers can identify not only the hierarchical order in the data but also the specific differences between the data. Also, it is possible to calculate means and standard deviations by using the mid-point of the scale categories. True class interval scales are most appropriate when the researcher wants to collect state-of-behavior, state-of-intention, or certain types of state-of-being data. Exhibit 11.7 illustrates some examples of true class interval scale formats.

Hybrid Ordinally-Interval Scales

Hybrid ordinally-interval scale   An ordinal scale that is artificially transformed into an interval scale by the researcher.

There are many situations in marketing research where it is useful to transform ordinal scaled data into what is generally assumed to be interval scaled data. To achieve this, researchers employ what are referred to as **hybrid ordinally-interval scale** designs. Ordinally-interval scales are ordinal but have an *assumed distance* scaling property so the

---

e X H I B I T   11.7   Examples of True Class Interval Scales

Example 1:
Approximately, how many charges for overdrawn checks (NSF checks) has "your" bank imposed on you in the past year?
_____ None   _____ 1–2   _____ 3–7   _____ 8–15   _____ 16–25   _____ More than 25

Example 2:
Approximately how long have you lived at your current address?
_____ Less than 1 year   _____ 4 to 6 years   _____ 10 to 12 years
_____ 1 to 3 years   _____ 7 to 9 years   _____ Over 12 years

Example 3:
In which one of the following categories does your current age fall?
_____ Under 18   _____ 26 to 35   _____ 46 to 55   _____ Over 65
_____ 18 to 25   _____ 36 to 45   _____ 56 to 65

Example 4:
Into which of the following categories does your total (approximate) current family income, before taxes, fall?
_____ Under $10,000   _____ $25,000 to $29,999
_____ $10,000 to $14,999   _____ $30,000 to $50,000
_____ $15,000 to $19,999   _____ Over $50,000
_____ $20,000 to $24,999

Example 5:
In a typical week (7-day period), how often do you access the Internet from a home computer?
(Please check the most appropriate response category)
_____ More than 20 times   _____ 11 to 15 times   _____ 1 to 5 times
_____ 16 to 20 times   _____ 6 to 10 times   _____ Do not access it

researcher can perform some type of advanced statistical analysis.[15] The transformation is achieved by the researcher assuming that the original scale point descriptors activated the distance scaling property.[16] Strictly speaking, this transformation is a researcher artifact that does not meet the four scaling properties.[17] But it is a widely accepted practice in marketing research.

Primary scale point descriptors The set of narratively expressed scale point descriptors used in creating an ordinally-interval scale.

Secondary scale point descriptors The set of cardinal numbers (whole integers) used as scale point expressions in an ordinally-interval scale design.

To create an ordinally-interval scale, the researcher uses two sets of scale point descriptors. The first set consists of narratively expressed indicators, referred to as **primary scale point descriptors.** The second set consists of whole integer numbers that are assigned to the primary set of descriptors and are referred to as **secondary scale descriptors.** Let's take, for example, a situation in which the researcher originally develops an ordinal scale to collect general opinions from respondents. The original set of narrative scale points might range from "definitely agree" to "definitely disagree" (i.e., "definitely agree," "generally agree," "slightly agree," "slightly disagree," "generally disagree," and "definitely disagree"). These scale point indicators would be considered the primary descriptors, and the complete scale measurement might look as follows (example of an initial ordinal scale design):

For each of the following statements, please check the response that best expresses the extent to which you either agree or disagree with that statement.

Statements	Definitely Agree	Generally Agree	Slightly Agree	Slightly Disagree	Generally Disagree	Definitely Disagree
It is good to have charge accounts.	—	—	—	—	—	—
I buy many things with a bank (or credit) card.	—	—	—	—	—	—
I like to pay cash for everything at department stores.	—	—	—	—	—	—
I wish my family had a lot more money.	—	—	—	—	—	—

Cardinal numbers Any set of consecutive whole integers.

One option a researcher has is to redefine those scale points to include the distance property by assigning a secondary set of number descriptors to represent each of the original primary scale descriptors. Usually the researcher will use a set of **cardinal numbers** as the secondary set of descriptors. In the simplest form, cardinal numbers are any set of consecutive whole integers (1, 2, 3, 4, 5, 6, 7, etc.). Because numerical descriptors are elements of a ratio-based numbering system, the distance and origin scaling properties are automatically activated on the scale. By combining the primary and secondary sets of descriptors, the researcher creates a relationship between the original scale descriptors so that "definitely agree" = 6, "generally agree" = 5, "slightly agree" = 4, "slightly disagree" = 3, "generally disagree" = 2, and "definitely disagree" = 1. By using these secondary numerical values to represent the original scale points, the researcher can now apply higher levels of data analysis techniques to the responses. This first approach would make the scale measurement appear something like the following (example of hybrid ordinally-interval design using full range of primary and secondary scale point descriptors):

For each of the following statements, please circle the response that best expresses the extent to which you either agree or disagree with that statement.

Statements	Definitely Agree	Generally Agree	Slightly Agree	Slightly Disagree	Generally Disagree	Definitely Disagree
It is good to have charge accounts.	6	5	4	3	2	1
I buy many things with a bank (or credit) card.	6	5	4	3	2	1
I like to pay cash for everything at department stores.	6	5	4	3	2	1
I wish my family had a lot more money.	6	5	4	3	2	1

Another option used quite frequently by marketing researchers involves having primary descriptors identify the extreme end points of a set of secondary cardinal numbers that make up the range of raw scale descriptors. This approach leaves the interpretation of what the in-between numerical scale descriptors truly represent up to the imagination of the respondent. Again, such a method assumes there is a known distance property between each of the scale point descriptors.[18] Using the above example, this second approach would make the scale measurement appear something like the following (example of hybrid ordinally-interval scale design using primary scale point descriptors as only extreme end points):

For each of the following statements, please circle the number that best expresses the extent to which you either agree or disagree with that statement.

Statements	Definitely Agree					Definitely Disagree
It is good to have charge accounts.	6	5	4	3	2	1
I buy many things with a bank (or credit) card.	6	5	4	3	2	1
I like to pay cash for everything at department stores.	6	5	4	3	2	1
I wish my family had a lot more money.	6	5	4	3	2	1

In this second approach, the absolute difference between a response of "definitely agree" and that of "generally agree" is assumed to be one unit of agreement. The assumption of an absolute difference of one unit cannot be confirmed. Therefore, researchers must be careful in interpreting findings obtained from hybrid scale designs. Additional examples of hybrid ordinally-interval type scales are provided in Exhibit 11.8.

Ratio Scales

Ratio scale A scale that allows the researcher not only to identify the absolute differences between each scale point but also to make comparisons between the raw responses.

A **ratio scale** is the only level of scale that activates all four scaling properties. A ratio scale is the most sophisticated scale because it enables the researcher not only to identify the absolute differences between each scale point but also to make absolute comparisons between the responses.[19] For instance, in collecting data about how many cars are

---

EXHIBIT 11.8 Examples of Hybrid Ordinally-Interval Scale Structures

---

Example 1:

For each of the brands of soft drinks listed below, please circle the number that best expresses your overall performance judgment of that brand.

Soft Drink Brands	Very Poor						Outstanding
Coke	1	2	3	4	5	6	7
Pepsi	1	2	3	4	5	6	7
Mountain Dew	1	2	3	4	5	6	7
A&W Root Beer	1	2	3	4	5	6	7
Sprite	1	2	3	4	5	6	7
Seven-Up	1	2	3	4	5	6	7

Example 2:

Using the scale provided below, select the number that best describes how important each of the listed attributes were in your deciding which restaurant to eat at. **(Please place your numerical response on the line provided next to each attribute.)**

Importance Scale

1 = Not at all important   3 = Somewhat important   5 = Definitely important
2 = Only slightly important 4 = Important   6 = Extremely important

Restaurant Attributes

____ Quality of the food   ____ Dining atmosphere   ____ Convenience of location
____ Wide variety in selection ____ Speed of service   ____ Offers a no-smoking section
____ Allows reservations   ____ Reasonably-priced entrees ____ Valet parking

Example 3:

Concerning the different banking methods you may or may not use, we would like to know your feelings toward these methods. Next to each of the listed banking methods, please circle the number that best describes the degree to which you like or dislike using that method.

Banking Methods	Very Much Dislike Using									Very Much Like Using
Inside the bank	1	2	3	4	5	6	7	8	9	10
Drive-up window	1	2	3	4	5	6	7	8	9	10
24-hour ATM	1	2	3	4	5	6	7	8	9	10
Bank by mail	1	2	3	4	5	6	7	8	9	10
Bank by phone	1	2	3	4	5	6	7	8	9	10
Bank by Internet	1	2	3	4	5	6	7	8	9	10

---

driven by households in Atlanta, Georgia, a researcher knows that the difference between driving one car and driving three cars is always going to be two. Furthermore, when comparing a one-car family to a three-car family, the researcher can assume that the three-car family will have significantly higher total car insurance and maintenance costs than the one-car family.

---

eXHIBIT 11.9   Examples of Ratio Scale Structures

Example 1:

Please circle the number of children under 18 years of age currently living in your household.

   0   1   2   3   4   5   6   7   (If more than 7, please specify: _____.)

Example 2:

In the past seven days, how many times did you go shopping at a retail shopping mall?

_____ # of times

Example 3:

In whole years, what is your current age?

_____ # of years old

Example 4:

When buying soft drinks for your household, approximately how many 12-ounce six-packs do you normally buy of each of the following listed brands?

____ Regular Pepsi	____ Regular Coke	____ Orange Crush
____ Diet Pepsi	____ Diet Coke	____ Sprite
____ A&W Root Beer	____ Mountain Dew	____ 7UP

Example 5:

In a typical 12-month period, how many miles do you drive your automobile and/or truck for personal activities?

____ # of miles driven in your car   ____ # of miles driven in your truck

---

Remember that ratio scale structures are designed to enable a "true natural zero" or "true state of nothing" response to be a valid raw response to the question. Normally, ratio scales request that respondents provide a specific numerical value as their response, regardless of whether or not a set of scale points is used. Exhibit 11.9 shows several examples of ratio scales. For more examples of the various types of scales go to www.mhhe.com/hair06 and follow the links.

Development and Refinement of Scaling Measurements

The keys to designing high-quality scales are (1) understanding the defined problem, (2) establishing detailed data requirements, (3) identifying and developing the constructs, and (4) understanding that a complete measurement scale consists of three critical components (the question, the attributes, and the scale point descriptors). After the problem and data requirements are understood, the researcher must develop constructs. Next, the appropriate scale format (e.g., nominal, ordinal, interval, ordinally-interval, or ratio) must be selected. For example, if the problem requires interval data, but the researcher asks the questions using a nominal scale, the wrong level of data will be collected and the final information that can be generated will not be helpful in resolving the initial problem. To

EXHIBIT 11.10 Example of the Five Basic Types of Question Phrasings

---

Information requirement: To determine how often cusumer purchases pizza from Papa John's.

NOMINAL QUESTION PHRASING:

When you are in the mood for pizza, do you usually purchase a pizza from Papa John's?

The logical raw response to this question would be a simple **Yes** or **No.**

ORDINAL QUESTION PHRASING:

When you are in the mood for pizza, how often do you purchase a pizza from Papa John's? (**Check only one response.**)

The logical raw responses might be as follows:

___ Never   ___ Seldom   ___ Occasionally   ___ Usually   ___ Every time

TRUE CLASS INTERVAL QUESTION PHRASING:

Thinking about your pizza purchases over the past six months, approximately how often have you purchased a pizza from Papa John's? (**Check the one appropriate response.**)

The logical raw responses might be as follows:

___ Less than 3 times   ___ 7 to 9 times   ___ Over 12 times (Please specify: ___)

___ 4 to 6 times   ___ 10 to 12 times

HYBRID ORDINALLY-INTERVAL QUESTION PHRASING:

Thinking about your pizza purchases over the past six months, please circle the number that best expresses how often have you purchased a pizza from each of the listed pizza chains.

The logical raw responses might be as follows:

Pizza Chains	Never							Every Time
Papa John's	0	1	2	3	4	5	6	7
Pizza Hut	0	1	2	3	4	5	6	7
Little Caesars	0	1	2	3	4	5	6	7
Lenny & Vinny's	0	1	2	3	4	5	6	7
Windy City	0	1	2	3	4	5	6	7

RATIO QUESTION PHRASING:

In the past twelve (12) months, how many times did you purchase a pizza from Papa John's? (**Write the # of times on the line provided.**)

_____ # of times

---

illustrate this point, Exhibit 11.10 offers examples of the different levels of data that are obtained on the basis of how the question is phrased to a respondent. These examples show that how the questions are phrased will directly affect the amount of raw data collected. It should be clear that nominal scale questions provide the least amount of raw data and ratio scale questions provide the most specific data.

Some Criteria for Scale Development

Once the importance of question phrasing is understood, the researcher can now focus on developing the most appropriate scale descriptors to be used as the primary scale point elements. While there is no one agreed-on set of criteria for establishing the actual scale point descriptors, we offer several criteria in Exhibit 11.11.

eXHIBIT 11.11 Key Criteria in Scale Development

Scale Development Criteria	Description
Intelligibility of the questions	Use language in the questions and responses that is familiar to the respondents' to ensure clarity and understanding.
Appropriateness of primary scale descriptors	Make sure that the narrative scale point descriptors accurately reflect the type of data being sought in the setup part of the scale measurement.
Discriminatory power of the scale descriptors	Make sure that each scale point descriptor used can be understood by the respondent as being mutually exclusive from each of the other scale point descriptors as well as the use of the appropriate number of descriptors to accurately represent the intended intensity levels of the descriptors.
Reliability of the scale	Use of pretest procedures to ensure that each scale measure meets, at least, a desired minimum level of reproducible results in repeated trials.
Balancing positive/negative scale descriptors	In those cases where a "symmetrical" scale design is required, objectivity must be maintained by assuring equal inclusion of both positive and negative response opportunities.
Inclusion of a neutral response choice	When attempting to capture state-of-mind or certain types of behavior-intention raw data, consideration must be given toward including or excluding "neutral" or "not applicable" scale responses.
Measures of central tendency and dispersion	Consideration must be given to the desired statistics and data analysis that will be used after the raw data are collected from respondents and understanding how different levels of scales activate the fundamental sample statistics (i.e., modes, medians, means, frequency distributions, ranges, and standard deviations).

Intelligibility of the Questions

The researcher must consider the intellectual capacity and language ability of those to whom the scale will be administered. The researcher should assume that prospective respondents do not know the research project's information requirements. That is, researchers should not automatically assume that respondents understand the questions being asked or the response choices. The **intelligibility** criterion is the degree to which questions are understood by respondents. Appropriate language must be used in both the questions and the answer choices.

Intelligibility The degree to which the questions on a scale are understood by the respondents.

The researcher should try to eliminate guessing by respondents. Moreover, respondents should be able to understand what types of data are being asked for and how to respond. Refer back to scale example 3 in Exhibit 11.8. Suppose that in the setup portion of that scale the researcher had used only the first sentence ("Concerning the different banking methods you may or may not use, we would like to know your feelings toward these methods"). This would suggest that the researcher assumed the respondents would automatically understand how to complete the scale question. Without the second sentence (the exact instructions), respondents may not know what to do. Such assumptions on the part of the researcher could easily increase the likelihood of missing responses. The intelligibility factor thus promotes the use of "respondent instructions" in scale measurement designs, especially in self-administered surveys. For in-person or telephone interviews, it is quite possible that "interviewer instructions" will also have to be included in the question/setup portion of the scale measurements.

Appropriateness of Primary Scale Descriptors

Researchers must make sure the scale descriptors match the type of raw data they are seeking. Therefore, another criterion is the researcher must consider the **appropriateness of the descriptors.** That is, the adjectives or adverbs used to indicate the relative magnitudes must be related to the scale descriptors. Let's say, for example, that the researcher wants to find out respondents' opinions about whether or not the I.G.A. supermarket has "competitive meat prices." The task becomes one of determining which scale descriptors best represent the notion of "competitive prices."

Appropriateness of descriptors The extent to which the scale point elements match the data being sought.

There are several creative ways of representing competitive prices. First, if the researcher designs the question/setup to ask the respondents to agree or disagree that "I.G.A. has competitive meat prices," then the appropriate set of scale descriptors would be levels of agreement/disagreement (e.g., "strongly agree," "agree," "neither agree nor disagree," "disagree," "strongly disagree"). Stating the question in terms of competitiveness would require an ordinal set of descriptors such as "extremely competitive," "definitely competitive," "generally competitive," "only slightly competitive," and "not at all competitive." In contrast, it would be inappropriate to try to represent respondents' opinions about "competitive prices" using a performance-oriented set of descriptors like "excellent," "very good," "good," "average," "fair," and "poor."

Discriminatory Power of the Scale Descriptors

This scale criterion relates to those situations when either (1) the problem requires the inclusion of relative magnitudes to the set of possible responses or (2) the researcher decides to establish sizes of differences between the scale points. The **discriminatory power** of a scale is the scale's ability to significantly differentiate between the categorical scale responses.[20] Researchers must decide how many scale points are necessary to represent the relative magnitudes of a response scale. Remember, the more scale points the greater the discriminatory power of the scale.

Discriminatory power The scale's ability to significantly differentiate between the categorical scale responses.

There is no clear rule about the number of scale points that should be used in creating a scale. But some researchers believe that scales should be between three and seven points[21] because some respondents find it difficult to make a choice when there are more than seven levels. To illustrate this point, suppose Marriott International is interested in determining which hotel features patrons consider important in their process of choosing a hotel. In developing an "importance" scale to capture the relative magnitude of importance attributed to each hotel feature, the researcher must subjectively decide how many recognizable levels of importance exist in the minds of travelers. The researcher must first understand that the basic dichotomous scale descriptors are simply "important" and "not important." Second, the researcher must decide how detailed or how varied the raw importance data responses have to be to address the initial information problem.[22] For example, an importance scale can consist of five different levels of importance. The five differential degrees usually are expressed as "extremely," "definitely," "generally," "somewhat," and "only slightly" important. But an importance scale can also use seven points and sometimes more. The more scale points you have the greater the opportunity there is for variability in the data—an important consideration in data analysis. But one must always consider respondents' ability to discriminate when more scale points are used.

By understanding the makeup of the importance scale, the researcher can include variations that may better fit the specific information requirements of different situations. When developing an importance scale, remember the scale descriptors are not simply "important" and "unimportant." In reality, most human beings *do not think or express* their "not at all important" feelings in degrees of "unimportant" (e.g., "extremely unimportant," "definitely unimportant," "generally unimportant"). In addition, there are times when attempting to incorporate too many degrees of relative magnitude into the scale can decrease discriminatory power. Suppose in the above Marriott hotel example the researcher designs an importance scale that consists of 15 scale descriptors and presents the scale as follows:

IMPORTANCE SCALE

Not at All Important 1 2 3 4 5 6 7 8 9 10 11 12 13 14 15 Extremely Important

While this scale denotes "not at all important" as being a 1 and "extremely important" as being a 15, it is very unlikely that either the researcher or the respondent can attach any meaningful, differential descriptor interpretations to the scale points of 2 through 14. This potential discriminatory power problem can exist in any type of scale design.

Reliability of the Scale

Scale reliability The extent to which a scale can produce the same measurement results in repeated trials.

Test-retest A technique of measuring scale reliability by administering the same scale to the same respondents at two different times or to two different samples of respondents under similar conditions.

Scale reliability refers to the extent to which a scale can reproduce the same measurement results in repeated trials. Random error produces inconsistency in scale measurements that leads to lower scale reliability. Two of the techniques that can help researchers assess the reliability of scales are test-retest and equivalent form.

First, the **test-retest** technique involves repeating the scale measurement with either the same sample of respondents at two different times or two different samples of respondents from the same defined target population under as nearly the same conditions as possible. The idea behind this approach is simply that if random variations are present, they will be revealed by variations in the scores between the two sampled measurements.[23] If there are very few differences between the first and second administrations of the scale, the measuring scale is viewed as being stable and therefore reliable. For example, assume that determining the teaching effectiveness associated with your marketing research course involved the use of a 28-item scale designed to measure the degree to which respondents agree or disagree with each item. To gather the data on teaching effectiveness, your professor administers this scale to the class after the 7th week of the semester and again after the 12th week. Using a mean analysis procedure on the items for each measurement period, the professor then runs correlation analysis on those mean values. If the correlations between the mean value measurements from the two assessment periods are high, the professor concludes that the reliability of the 28-item scale is high.

There are several potential problems with the test-retest approach. First, some of the students who completed the scale the first time might be absent for the second administration of the scale. Second, students might become sensitive to the scale measurement and therefore alter their responses in the second measurement. Third, environmental or personal factors may change between the two administrations, thus causing changes in student responses in the second measurement.

Equivalent form A technique to establish scale reliability by measuring and correlating the measures of two equivalent scaling instruments.

Some researchers believe that the problems associated with test-retest reliability technique can be avoided by using the **equivalent form** technique. In this technique, the researcher creates two similar yet different (e.g., equivalent) scale measurements for the given construct (e.g., teaching effectiveness) and administers both forms to either the same sample of respondents or two samples of respondents from the same defined target population.[24] In the marketing research course "teaching effectiveness" example, the professor would construct two 28-item scales whose main difference would lie in the wording of the item statements, not the agree/disagree scaling points. Although the specific wording of the statements would be changed, their meaning would remain constant. After administering each of the scale measurements, the professor calculates the mean values for each item and then runs correlation analysis. Equivalent form reliability is assessed by measuring the correlations of the scores on the two scale measurements. High correlation values are interpreted as meaning high scale measurement reliability.

There are two potential drawbacks with the equivalent form reliability technique. First, if the testing process suggests that equivalence can be achieved, it might not be worth the time, effort, and expense of determining that two similar yet different scales can be used to measure the same construct. Second, it is very difficult and perhaps impossible to create two totally equivalent scale measurements. Questions may be raised as to which scale measurement is the most appropriate to use in measuring teaching effectiveness.

When investigating multidimensional constructs, summated scale measurements tend to be the most appropriate scales. In this type of scale, each dimension represents some aspect of the construct. Thus, the construct is measured by the entire scale, not just one component. **Internal consistency** refers to the degree to which the various dimensions of a multidimensional construct correlate with the scale. That is, the set of items that make up the scale must be internally consistent. There are two popular techniques used to assess internal consistency: split-half tests and coefficient alpha, also referred to as *Cronbach's alpha.* In a **split-half test,** the items in the scale are divided into two halves (odd versus even attributes, or randomly) and the resulting halves' scores are correlated against one another. High correlations between the halves indicate good (or acceptable) internal consistency. A **coefficient alpha** takes the average of all possible split-half measures that result from different ways of splitting the scale items.[25] The coefficient value can range from 0 to 1, and, in most cases, a value of less than 0.6 would typically indicate marginal to low (unsatisfactory) internal consistency.

Researchers need to remember that just because their scale measurement designs prove to be reliable, the data collected are not necessarily valid. Separate validity assessments must be made on the constructs being measured.

Balancing Positive/Negative Scale Descriptors

This scale development criterion relates to the researcher's decision to maintain objectivity in a scale that is designed to capture both positive and negative raw responses. To maintain scale objectivity, the researcher must design both positive and negative descriptors as scale points. For example, let's assume that J. D. Power and Associates wants to add to its "New Vehicle Survey" a single-item scale that measures a purchaser's satisfaction with his or her new vehicle's overall performance. Since most people would consider the feeling of satisfaction to be positive and the feeling of dissatisfaction to be negative, J. D. Power and Associates would need to decide whether or not the scale measurement should be "objective" and not bias the respondent's feelings one way or the other. By having equal relative magnitudes of satisfaction (positive) and dissatisfaction (negative), the scale measure would maintain a level of objectivity. Such a balanced scale measurement design might look like the following (example of a balanced scale measurement design):

Based on your experiences with your new vehicle since owning and driving it, to what extent are you presently satisfied or dissatisfied with the overall performance of the vehicle?

(PLEASE CHECK THE ONE APPROPRIATE RESPONSE)

____Completely satisfied (no dissatisfaction)	____Slightly dissatisfied (some satisfaction)
____Definitely satisfied	____Generally dissatisfied
____Generally satisfied	____Definitely dissatisfied
____Slightly satisfied (some dissatisfaction)	____Completely dissatisfied (no satisfaction)

Internal consistency
The degree to which the various dimensions of a multidimensional construct correlate with the scale.

Split-half test A technique used to evaluate the internal consistency of scale measurements that have multiple dimensions.

Coefficient alpha A technique of taking the average of all possible split-half coefficients to measure the internal consistency of multidimensional scales.

With a balanced scale measurement, objectivity is maintained in both the question/setup portion of the scale and the descriptors.[26]

Now let's assume that J. D. Power and Associates is primarily interested in assessing new-vehicle purchasers' satisfaction with their vehicle's overall performance and that dissatisfaction data are not that important. This type of data requirement might be better met by using an unbalanced scale measurement[27] that placed heavier emphasis on the positive (satisfaction) scale descriptors than on the negative (dissatisfaction) ones. The unbalanced scale measurement design might look like the following (example of an unbalanced scale measurement):

Based on your experiences with your new vehicle since owning and driving it, to what extent are you presently satisfied with the overall performance of the vehicle?

(PLEASE CHECK THE ONE APPROPRIATE RESPONSE)

___Completely satisfied   ___Generally satisfied   ___Dissatisfied

___Definitely satisfied   ___Slightly satisfied

It is important to remember that with an unbalanced scale measurement, objectivity is lower in both the question/setup portion of the scale and the descriptors.

Inclusion of a Neutral Response Choice

In scale measurement design, the number of scale point descriptors becomes an important criterion only if the data requirements call for capturing either state-of-mind data or specific types of state-of-intention data that focus on positive/negative continuum ranges. The issue involves offering the respondent the opportunity to express a neutral response.[28] Having an even number of positive/negative scale descriptors tends to force the respondent to select either a positive or a negative answer only.

Forced-choice scale A symmetrically designed polar scale that does not include a neutral response category.

Free-choice scale A symmetrically designed polar scale that does include a neutral response category.

A symmetrical scale that does not have a neutral descriptor to divide the positive and negative domains is referred to as a **forced-choice scale** measurement. In contrast, a symmetrical scale that includes a center neutral response is referred to as a **free-choice scale** measurement. Exhibit 11.12 presents several different examples of both "even-point, forced-choice" and "odd-point, free-choice" descriptors.

Some experts believe that scales used to collect state-of-mind data should be designed as "odd-point, free-choice" scale measurements[29] since not all respondents will have enough knowledge or experience with the given topic to be able to accurately assess their thoughts or feelings. If those respondents are forced to choose, the scale may produce lower-quality data than the researcher desires. In free-choice scale designs, however, the so-called neutral scale point offers respondents an easy way to express their feelings about the given topic.

Many researchers believe there is no such thing as a neutral attitude or feeling—that these mental aspects almost always have some degree of a positive or negative orientation attached to them. A person either has an attitude or does not have an attitude about a given object. Likewise, a person will either have a feeling or not have a feeling. An alternative approach to handling situations, in which respondents may feel uncomfortable about expressing their thoughts or feelings about a given object because they have no knowledge of or experience with it, would be to incorporate a "not applicable" response choice that would not be part of the actual scale measurement. The following example illustrates the *not applicable* (NA) response:

Based on your experiences with your new vehicle since owning and driving it, to what extent are you presently satisfied or dissatisfied with the overall performance of the vehicle? If you feel that you lack

EXHIBIT 11.12   Examples of "Even-Point" (Forced-Choice) and "Odd-Point" (Free-Choice) Scale Descriptors

---

"Even-Point, Forced-Choice" Itemized Rating Scale Descriptors

PURCHASE INTENTION (BUY/NOT BUY)

___ Definitely will buy   ___ Probably will buy   ___ Probably will not buy   ___ Definitely will not buy

PERSONAL BELIEFS/OPINIONS (AGREEMENT/DISAGREEMENT)

Definitely agree	Generally agree	Slightly agree	Slightly disagree	Generally disagree	Definitely disagree
___	___	___	___	___	___

MODERNITY (MODERN/OLD-FASHIONED)

___ Very modern   ___ Somewhat modern   ___ Somewhat old-fashioned   ___ Very old-fashioned

COST (EXPENSIVE/INEXPENSIVE)

Extremely expensive	Definitely expensive	Somewhat expensive	Somewhat inexpensive	Definitely inexpensive	Extremely inexpensive
___	___	___	___	___	___

"Odd-Point, Free-Choice" Itemized Rating Scales

PURCHASE INTENTION (BUY/NOT BUY)

Definitely will buy	Probably will buy	Neither will nor will not buy	Probably will not buy	Definitely will not buy
___	___	___	___	___

PERSONAL BELIEFS/OPINIONS (AGREEMENT/DISAGREEMENT)

Definitely agree	Generally agree	Slightly agree	Neither agree nor disagree	Slightly disagree	Generally disagree	Definitely disagree
___	___	___	___	___	___	___

MODERNITY (MODERN/OLD-FASHIONED)

Very modern	Somewhat modern	Neither modern nor old-fashioned	Somewhat old-fashioned	Very old-fashioned
___	___	___	___	___

COST (EXPENSIVE/INEXPENSIVE)

Definitely expensive	Somewhat expensive	Neither expensive nor inexpensive	Somewhat inexpensive	Definitely inexpensive
___	___	___	___	___

---

enough experience with your vehicle or that the statement is not pertinent to you, please check the "NA" (Not Applicable) response.

(PLEASE CHECK THE ONE APPROPRIATE RESPONSE)

____Completely satisfied (no dissatisfaction)	____Generally dissatisfied
____Definitely satisfied	____Definitely dissatisfied
____Generally satisfied	____Completely dissatisfied (no satisfaction)
____Slightly satisfied (some dissatisfaction)	____NA (Not Applicable)
____Slightly dissatisfied (some satisfaction)	

This approach allows the researcher to sort all the "NA" responses out of the raw data and ensures that only quality data will be included in the data analysis.

Desired Measures of Central Tendency and Dispersion

In determining what levels of scale measurements should be developed, the researcher must consider the data analysis that will be used after the data are collected from respondents. The researcher must therefore have an understanding of the measures of central tendency and the measures of dispersion associated with different types of scale measurement designs. **Measures of central tendency** refer to the basic sample statistics that are generated through analyzing the collected data; these are the mean, the median, and the mode. The *mean* is nothing more than the arithmetic average of all the raw data responses. The *median* represents the sample statistic that splits the raw data into a hierarchical pattern where half the raw data are above the statistic value and half are below. The *mode* is the raw response that is the most frequently given among all of the respondents.

Measures of dispersion relate to how the data are dispersed around a central tendency value. These sample statistics allow the researcher to report the diversity of the raw responses to a particular scale measurement. They include the frequency distribution, the range, and the estimated sample standard deviation. A *frequency distribution* is a summary of how many times each possible response to a scale question/setup was recorded by the total group of respondents. This distribution can be easily converted into percentages or histograms for ease of comparison between raw data responses. The *range* represents the grouping of responses into mutually exclusive subgroups, each with an identifiable lower and upper boundary. The *sample standard deviation* is the statistical value that specifies the degree of variation in the data responses in such a way that allows the researcher to translate the variations into normal curve interpretations (e.g., 99 percent of the responses fall between the mean value plus or minus 3 standard deviations).

Given the important role that these six basic sample statistics play in data analysis procedures, understanding how different levels of scales influence the use of a particular statistic becomes critical in scale measurement design. Exhibit 11.13 displays these

Measures of central tendency The basic sample statistics that are generated through analyzing raw data; these are the mode, the median, and the mean.

Measures of dispersion The sample statistics that allow a researcher to report the diversity of the raw data collected from scale measurements; they are the frequency distribution, the range, and the estimated sample standard deviation.

exhibit 11.13 Relationships between Scale Levels and Measures of Central Tendency and Dispersion

Measurements	Five Basic Levels of Scales				
	Nominal	Ordinal	True Class Interval	Hybrid Ordinally-Interval	Ratio
Central Tendency					
Mode	**Appropriate**	Appropriate	Appropriate	Appropriate	Appropriate
Median	*Inappropriate*	**More Appropriate**	Appropriate	Appropriate	Appropriate
Mean	*Inappropriate*	*Inappropriate*	**Most Appropriate**	**Most Appropriate**	**Most Appropriate**
Dispersion					
Frequency Distribution	**Appropriate**	Appropriate	Appropriate	Appropriate	Appropriate
Range	*Inappropriate*	**More Appropriate**	Appropriate	Appropriate	Appropriate
Estimated Standard Deviation	*Inappropriate*	*Inappropriate*	**Most Appropriate**	**Most Appropriate**	**Most Appropriate**

A Closer Look at Research

Macro Consulting, Inc.[30]

Deciding on a market segmentation strategy can be a very difficult task for any manager or business owner. For small-business owners, the choice can be especially daunting. Macro Consulting, Inc., realizes that small-business owners and managers are forced to make most decisions with very little input or outside help. To provide guidance in this area, Macro Consulting publishes articles on its World Wide Web page (www.macroinc.com/articles/imageq.htm) that promote, among other options, innovative market segmentation strategies. Below is an excerpt from Macro Consulting's Internet page that describes ImageQ, a unique approach to measuring customer segmentation. By using Macro Consulting's Web site, small-business owners and managers have access to many innovative marketing ideas.

For example, ImageQ offers several advantages over other methods: (1) consumers are grouped together based not on how each of them perceive various brands but rather on which brand imagery attributes are most important to their individual purchase decisions; (2) the most important brand perceptions (as well as the least important) are clearly identified for each consumer segment; (3) brand imagery importance data do not need to be collected; and (4) virtually any existing brand imagery data can serve as the basis for this segmentation approach, making expensive data collection unnecessary.

These technical advantages of ImageQ provide marketers, advertisers, and anyone else needing to communicate to his or her customers several key benefits: (1) a completely new insight into the target market's motivations; (2) a customer-focused foundation for developing communications strategies; (3) a fresh perspective on how to best define the primary and secondary market segments; and (4) a new and deeper understanding of how brand imagery affects sales to specific market segments. The approach involves a unique and proprietary analytic protocol. It is an ideal tool for secondary analysis of existing data sets.

ImageQ uses McCullough's correlation measures (MCM), a family of nonparametric correlations that measure the relationships between a battery of brand imagery attributes and purchase interest at the individual respondent level. For virtually any data set that contains brand imagery data and some purchase interest or preference measure, one of these correlations can be calculated. MCMs reflect the importance of each brand imagery attribute to the purchase interest of all brands tested for each respondent in the sample. Cluster analysis is then conducted, using an MCM as its basis. Typically, several cluster solutions are examined and evaluated. The solution that offers the most interpretable and actionable results is selected for profiling and further analysis. The resulting segmentation provides a unique look at brand imagery-based market dynamics, on a segment-by-segment basis.

This is the only method that we are aware of that can segment the marketplace based on the relevance of various brand imagery attributes to individual consumers. In a dynamic marketplace it is essential to gather information and make decisions as quickly as possible. Getting the right message to the right consumer quickly is critical to success. This approach gleans additional and powerful information from existing data sets, saving time and money, while providing insights unattainable with other approaches or measures.

Using Technology

relationships. Remember that data collected through a nominal scale can be analyzed only by using modes and frequency distributions. For ordinal scales, you can analyze the data using medians and ranges as well as modes and frequency distributions.

For interval or ratio scale measurements, the most appropriate analysis procedures would be those that involve means and standard deviations as the sample statistics. In addition, interval and ratio data can also be appropriately analyzed using modes, medians, frequency distributions, or ranges.

Now that we have presented the basics of construct development as well as the rules surrounding scale measurements, we are ready to move forward to the popular attitudinal, emotional, and behavior scales used by marketing researchers.

Chapter 12 focuses on more advanced scales. The Closer Look at Research box shows how a consulting firm integrates advanced technology to create high-quality segmentation measures.

marketing research in action

Part 1

What You Can Learn from a Customer Loyalty Index

This application is presented in a two-part format. In Part 1, you will read how researchers at Burke Customer Satisfaction Associates (www.burke.com), a commercial research firm that specializes in customer satisfaction measurement and management programs, defines customer loyalty and how this construct is operationalized into a measurable index called the *Secure Customer Index*. The second part is presented in the Marketing Research in Action at the end of Chapter 12 and will focus on how this construct is actually measured by Burke Customer Satisfaction Associates.

The idea that loyal customers are especially valuable is not new to today's business managers. Loyal customers repeatedly purchase products or services. They recommend a company to others. And they stick with a business over time. Loyal customers are worth the special effort it may take to keep them. But how can you provide that special treatment if you don't know your customers and how their loyalty is won and lost?

Understanding loyalty—what makes your customers loyal and how to measure and understand loyal customers—enables your company to improve customer-driven quality. A customer loyalty index provides management with an easily understood tool that helps focus the organization toward improving satisfaction and retention, for a positive impact on the bottom line.

What Customer Loyalty Is and Isn't

To better understand the concept of customer loyalty, let's first define what customer loyalty is not. Customer loyalty is not customer satisfaction. Satisfaction is a necessary component of loyal or secure customers. However, the mere aspect of being satisfied with a company does not necessarily make customers loyal. Just because customers are satisfied with your company today does not mean they will continue to do business with you in the future.

Customer loyalty is not a response to trial offers or incentives. If customers suddenly begin buying your product or service, it may be the result of a special offer or incentive and not necessarily a reflection of customer loyalty. These same customers may be just as quick to respond to your competitors' incentives.

Customer loyalty is not strong market share. Many businesses mistakenly look at their sales numbers and market share and think, "Those numbers are surrogates for direct measures of customer loyalty. After all, we wouldn't be enjoying high levels of market share if our customers didn't love us." However, this may not be true. Many other factors can drive up market share, including poor performance by competitors or pricing issues. And high share doesn't mean low churn (the rate at which existing customers leave you—possibly to patronize your competition—and are replaced by new customers).

Customer loyalty is not repeat buying or habitual buying. Many repeat customers may be choosing your products or services because of convenience or habit. However, if they learn about a competitive product that they think may be less expensive or better quality, they may quickly switch to that product. Habitual buyers can defect; loyal customers usually don't.

Now that we know what does not constitute customer loyalty, we can talk about what does. Customer loyalty is a composite of a number of qualities. It is driven by customer

⊖XHIBIT **11.14** **The Secure Customer Index (i.e., Customer Loyalty Index)**

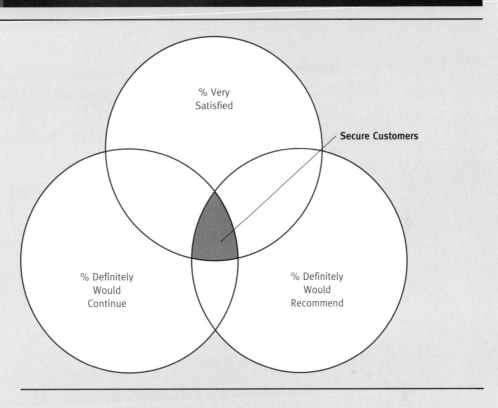

satisfaction, yet it also involves a commitment on the part of the customer to make a sustained investment in an ongoing relationship with a brand or company. Finally, customer loyalty is reflected by a combination of attitudes and behaviors. These attitudes include:

- The intention to buy again and/or buy additional products or services from the same company.
- A willingness to recommend the company to others.
- A commitment to the company demonstrated by a resistance to switching to a competitor.

Customer behaviors that reflect loyalty include:

- Repeat purchasing of products or services.
- Purchasing more and different products or services from the same company.
- Recommending the company to others.

Any one of these attitudes or behaviors in isolation does not necessarily indicate loyal customers. However, by recognizing how these indicators work together in a measurement system, we can derive an index of customer loyalty or, in a broader sense, customer security. Burke Customer Satisfaction Associates has developed a Secure Customer Index (SCI) using three major components to measure customer loyalty: overall customer satisfaction, likelihood of repeat business, and likelihood to recommend the company to others. Other elements may be included in the index depending upon the industry. In their experience, however, these three components are the core of a meaningful customer loyalty index.

Hands-On Exercise

Using the material from the chapter and the above information, answer each of the following questions:

1. Identify and provide a meaningful definition of each of the three constructs that researchers at Burke Customer Satisfaction Associates believe are the driving forces behind measuring the concept of customer loyalty.

2. What is the dimensionality of each of these three constructs? That is, are the constructs unidimensional or multidimensional? For each of those constructs that you believe is multidimensional, identify the possible domain of subcomponents that would be representative of that construct. Also, explain why you feel your proposed domain set represents that construct.

3. In your judgment, what level of scale design would be the most appropriate in creating the necessary scale measurements for collecting primary data on each construct?

4. For each construct, design an example of the actual scale measurement that could be used by Burke Customer Satisfaction Associates to collect the data.

Source: www.burke.com. Accessed June 2004.

Summary of Learning Objectives

■ **Explain what constructs are, how they are desveloped, and why they are important to measurement and scale designs.**

Within the overall process of creating meaningful information for resolving both today's and future business/marketing problems, researchers must be able to develop appropriate questions and record the raw responses to those questions. Next to correctly defining the information problem, determining what type of data should be collected is the second most critical aspect in information research. Gaining access to raw data responses is achieved by the scale measurement incorporated into the questioning process. A construct can be viewed as any object that cannot be directly observed and measured by physical devices. Within the development process, researchers must consider the abstractness of the construct, its dimensionality, assessments of validity, and its operationalization. Not knowing exactly what it is that one needs to measure makes it difficult to design the appropriate scale measurements.

■ **Discuss the integrated validity and reliability concerns underlying construct development and scale measurement.**

Regardless of the method used for data collection, researchers must strive to collect the most accurate data and information possible. Data accuracy depends heavily on the validity of the constructs and the reliability of the measurements applied to those constructs. Constructs can be assessed for content, convergent, discriminant, and nomological validity. Testing for reliability of constructs is indirectly achieved by testing the reliability of the scale measurements used in data collection. Scale reliability test methods available to researchers include test-retest, equivalent form, and internal consistency. Although scale measurements may prove to be reliable, reliability alone does not guarantee construct validity.

■ **Explain what scale measurement is, and describe how to correctly apply it in collecting raw data from respondents.**

Scale measurement is the process of assigning a set of descriptors to represent the range of possible responses that a person gives in answering a question about a particular object, construct, or factor. This process aids in determining the amount of raw data that can be obtained from asking questions, and therefore indirectly impacts the amount of primary information that can be derived from the data. Central to the amount of data issue is understanding that there are four basic scaling properties (i.e., assignment, order, distance, and origin) that can be activated through scale measurements. The rule of thumb is that as a researcher simultaneously activates more properties within the question/answering process, the greater the amount of raw data that can be gathered from people's responses. All raw data can be classified into one of four mutually exclusive types: state-of-being, state-of-mind, state-of-behavior, and state-of-intention. Understanding the categorical types of data that can be produced by individuals' responses to questions improves the researcher's ability in determining not only what questions should be asked, but also how to ask those questions.

■ **Identify and explain the five basic levels of scales, and discuss the amount of information they can provide a researcher or decision maker.**

The five basic levels of scales are nominal, ordinal, true class interval, hybrid ordinally-interval, and ratio. Nominal scales are the most basic and provide the least amount of data. They activate only the "assignment" scaling property; the raw data do not exhibit relative magnitudes between the categorical subsets of responses. The main data structures (or patterns) that can be derived from nominal raw data are in the form of modes and frequency distributions. Nominal scales would ask respondents about their religious affiliation, gender, type of dwelling, occupation, or last brand of cereal purchased, and so on. The questions require yes/no, like/dislike, or agree/disagree responses.

Ordinal scales require respondents to express their feelings of relative magnitude about the given topic. Ordinal scales activate both the assignment and order scaling properties and allow researchers to create a hierarchical pattern among the possible raw data responses (or scale points) that determine "greater than/less than" relationships. Data structures that can be derived from ordinal scale measurements are in the forms of medians and ranges as well as modes and frequency distributions. An example of a set of ordinal scale descriptors would be "complete knowledge," "good knowledge," "basic knowledge," "little knowledge," and "no knowledge." While the ordinal scale measurement is an excellent design for capturing the relative magnitudes in respondents' raw responses, it cannot capture absolute magnitudes.

A true class interval scale activates not only the assignment and order scaling properties but also the distance property. This scale measurement allows the researcher to build into the scale elements that demonstrate the existence of absolute differences between each scale point. Normally, the raw scale descriptors will represent a distinct set of numerical ranges as the possible responses to a given question (e.g., "less than a mile," "1 to 5 miles," "6 to 10 miles," "11 to 20 miles," "over 20 miles"). With interval scaling designs, the distance between each scale point or response does not have to be equal. Disproportional scale descriptors (e.g., different-sized numerical ranges) can be used. With interval raw data, researchers can develop a number of more meaningful data structures that are based on means and standard deviations, or create data structures based on mode, median, frequency distribution, and range.

Ratio scales are the only scale measurements that simultaneously activate all four scaling properties (i.e., assignment, order, distance, and origin). Considered the most sophisticated scale design, they allow researchers to identify absolute differences between each scale point and to make absolute comparisons between the respondents' raw responses. Ratio question/scale structures are designed to allow "true natural zero" or "true state of nothing" responses. Normally, though, the respondent is requested to choose a specific singular numerical value. The data structures that can be derived from ratio scale measurements are basically the same as those for interval scale measurements. It is important to remember that the more scaling properties simultaneously activated, the greater the opportunity to derive more detailed and sophisticated data structures and therefore more information. Interval and ratio scale designs are most appropriate to use when researchers want to collect state-of-behavior or state-of-intention or certain types of state-of-being data.

■ **Discuss the hybrid ordinally-interval scale design and the types of information it can provide researchers.**

Some researchers misidentify certain types of ordinal scales as being interval scales. They take an ordinal scale design and assume that the scale has activated the distance and origin scaling properties. This assumption comes about when the researcher assigns a secondary set of numerical scale descriptors (e.g., consecutive whole integers) to the original primary set of ordinal descriptors. There are two main approaches to developing an ordinally-interval scale measurement: (1) using a secondary set of cardinal number descriptors and redefining the complete set of primary scale descriptors (1 = definitely agree, 2 = generally agree, 3 = slightly agree, 4 = slightly disagree, 5 = generally disagree, and 6 = definitely disagree); or (2) using primary descriptors to identify only the extreme end points of a set of secondary cardinal numbers that make up the range of raw scale descriptors or scale points (definitely agree 1 2 3 4 5 6 definitely disagree). Regardless of the method used, for the researcher to believe that the absolute difference between a respondent's response of "definitely agree" and another respondent's response of "generally agree" is one unit of agreement is to some extent a leap of faith. Researchers should be careful how they interpret the data structures generated from this hybrid scale design.

■ **Discuss the components of scale development and explain why they are critical to gathering primary data.**

In developing high-quality scale measurements, there are three critical components to any complete scale measurement: question/setup; dimensions of the object, construct, or behavior; and the scale point descriptors. Some of the criteria for scale development are the intelligibility of the questions, the appropriateness of the primary descriptors, the discriminatory power of the scale descriptors, the reliability of the scale, the balancing of positive/negative scale descriptors, the inclusion of a neutral response choice, and desired measures of central tendency (mode, median, and mean) and dispersion (frequency distribution, range, estimated standard deviation). If the highest-quality raw data are to be collected to transform into useful primary information, researchers and practitioners alike must have an integrated understanding of construct development and scale measurement.

Key Terms and Concepts

Appropriateness of descriptors 372

Assignment property 360

Cardinal numbers 366

Coefficient alpha 374

Construct 353

Construct development 353

Content validity 355

Convergent validity 355

Direct cognitive structural analysis 356

Discriminant validity 356

Discriminatory power 372

Distance property 361

Domain of observables 354

Equivalent form 373

Forced-choice scale 375

Free-choice scale 375

Hybrid ordinally-interval scale 365

Intelligibility 371

Internal consistency 374

Measurement 353

Measures of central tendency 377

Measures of dispersion 377

Nominal scale 363

Nomological validity 356

Object 353

Operationalization 356

Order property 361

Ordinal scale 363

Origin property 362

Primary scale point descriptors 366

Ratio scale 367

Scale measurement 360

Scale points 360

Scale reliability 373

Secondary scale point descriptors 366

Split-half test 374

State-of-behavior data 359

State-of-being data 359

State-of-intention data 360

State-of-mind data 359

Test-retest 373

True class interval scale 365

Review Questions

1. How does activating scaling properties determine the amount of data and information that can be derived from scale measurement designs?

2. Among the five basic levels of scale measurements, which one provides the researcher with the most data and information? Why is this particular scale the least used in research practices? Explain the main differences between interval and ratio scale measurements.

3. What are hybrid ordinally-interval scale measurements? Why do researchers insist on creating them to measure or gather state-of-mind data from respondents? Make sure you discuss their strengths and weaknesses in your answer.

4. Identify and explain the components that make up any level of scale measurement. What are the interrelationships between these components?

5. When developing the scale point descriptors for a scale measurement, what rules of thumb should the researcher follow?

6. Why should researchers complete construct development activities prior to actually designing a complete scale measurement?

7. What is scale measurement? In your response, explain the difference between an object's, such as a wireless cell phone's, "concrete" properties and "abstract" properties.

8. In construct/scale measurement development, how does discriminant validity differ from convergent validity? Make sure you include definitions for each of these terms.

9. What are the major differences between ordinal, true interval, and ordinally-interval designed scale measures? In your response include an example of each type of scale design (for the topic or construct).

10. Identify and discuss the differences between the four scaling properties that are used in scale measurement design. Include a solid example illustrating each property.

Discussion Questions

1. What are some of the weaknesses of using college students as respondents when developing constructs like "retail store loyalty," "telecommunication service quality," or "attitudes toward kids' advertisements"?

2. For each of the listed scale measurements (A, B, and C), answer the following questions:
   a. What type of raw data is being collected?
   b. What level of scale measurement is being used?
   c. What scaling properties are being activated in the scale?
   d. What is the most appropriate measure of central tendency?
   e. What is the most appropriate measure of variation (or dispersion)?
   f. What weakness, if any, exists with the scale?

   A.   How often do you travel for business or pleasure purposes?

For Business	**For Pleasure**
___ 0–1 times per month	___ 0–1 times per year
___ 2–3 times per month	___ 2–3 times per year
___ 4–5 times per month	___ 4–5 times per year
___ 6 or more times per month	___ 6 or more times per year

   B.   How do you pay for your travel expenses?

___ Cash	___ Company charge
___ Check	___ Personal charge
___ Credit card	___ Other _____

   C.   Please check the one category that best approximates your total family annual income, before taxes. (Please check only one category.)

___ Under $10,000	___ $30,001–$40,000	___ $60,001–$70,000
___ $10,000–$20,000	___ $40,001–$50,000	___ $70,001–$100,000
___ $20,001–$30,000	___ $50,001–$60,000	___ Over $100,000

3. For each of the listed concepts or objects, design a scale measurement that would allow you to collect data on that concept/object.
   a. An excellent long-distance runner.
   b. A person's favorite Mexican restaurant.
   c. Size of the listening audience for a popular country and western radio station.
   d. Consumers' attitudes toward the Colorado Rockies professional baseball team.
   e. The satisfaction a person has toward his or her automobile.
   f. Purchase intentions for a new tennis racket.

4. **EXPERIENCE THE INTERNET.** Using a browser of your choice, log on to the Internet and go to American Demographics' home page at www.demographics.com. Now surf the "hot spots" until you come across one of their segmentation questionnaires. Take the first five question/scales that appear on the questionnaire and evaluate each of them for the following five questions:
   a. What type of data is being sought?
   b. What level of scale measurement is being employed?
   c. What scaling properties are being activated?
   d. What would be the most appropriate measure of central tendency for analyzing the data?
   e. What would be the most appropriate measure of dispersion?

5. Identify and discuss the key issues a researcher should consider when choosing a scale measurement for capturing consumers' expressions of satisfaction?

6. AT&T is interested in capturing the evaluative judgments of its new wireless cell phone services. Determine and justify what service attributes should be used to capture the *performance* of its wireless cell phone service. Then design two scale measurements (one as an *ordinal* and the second scale as an *ordinally-interval*) that would allow AT&T to accurately capture the necessary performance data.

7. The local Ford Dealership is interested in collecting data to answer the following information research question: "How likely are young adults to purchase a new automobile within a year after graduating from college?" Design a nominal, ordinal, true class interval, hybrid ordinally-interval, and ratio scale measurement that will allow the dealership to collect the required data. In your opinion, which one of your designs would be most useful to the dealership? And why?

8. Recall our continuing case about the Santa Fe Grill Mexican Restaurant. Management would like to capture some data/information from current customers that would help address the following set of research questions: (a) What type of Mexican-oriented food items do customers prefer? (b) How often do customers dine out at Mexican theme restaurants per month? (c) How important are food prices, food quality, restaurant atmosphere, and service in customers' process of selecting a restaurant to dine at? and (d) How many people make up their current household? Using your understanding of scale measurements, develop the following scale measurements:
   a. Develop an *ordinal* scale measurement that would capture data for addressing "What type of Mexican-oriented food items do customer prefer?"
   b. Develop a *true class interval* scale measurement that would capture data for addressing "How often do customers dine out at Mexican theme restaurants per month?"
   c. Develop a *hybrid ordinally-interval* scale measurement that would capture data for addressing "How important are food prices, food quality, restaurant atmosphere, and service in selecting a restaurant to dine at?"
   d. Develop a *ratio* scale measurement that would provide the data to address the research question concerning "current household size."

chapter 12

Attitude Scale Measurements Used in Marketing Research

Learning Objectives

After reading this chapter, you will be able to

1. Discuss what an attitude is and its three components.

2. Design Likert, semantic differential, and behavior intention scales, and explain their strengths and weaknesses.

3. Discuss the differences between noncomparative and comparative scale designs as well as the appropriateness of rating and ranking scale measurements.

4. Identify and discuss the critical aspects of consumer attitudes and other marketplace phenomena that require measurement to allow us to make better decisions.

5. Discuss the overall rules of measurement and explain the differences between single versus multiple measures of a construct as well as direct versus indirect measures.

Attitude Measurements and Meaningful Diagnostic Marketing Research Information

Aca Joe, Inc., had been operating for three years in the Tampa Bay metropolitan area. Prior to opening the business, the owner decided to present the image of Aca Joe as being a specialty men's casual-wear store that was conveniently located, with a good reputation of offering a wide selection of high-quality, fashionable men's casual apparel at competitive prices. In addition, the owner wanted Aca Joe to be known as having very knowledgeable sales associates and store staff who were committed to providing outstanding customer service and satisfaction.

The owner created and implemented marketing strategies to ensure that this image was communicated to actual and potential customers. Three years later, however, the sales and profit figures were lower than expected, causing the owner to question the effectiveness of the store's current marketing strategies. The owner was not sure how consumers viewed the store.

Realizing that help was needed, Aca Joe's owner consulted a marketing research expert. After several preliminary discussions, it was decided that a store

image study should be conducted to gain insights into how Aca Joe's image compared to several competitors'. The ensuing information research process combined both qualitative and quantitative research methods in a two-phase study. First, using qualitative research practices, the researcher completed several in-depth interviews with Aca Joe's owner and sales associates as well as a review of the retail literature; and four focus group sessions among known customers were conducted to identify the dimensions and store-service features that were most closely related to the store's desired image. The results from the qualitative stage suggested that customers viewed seven dimensions (quality; assortment; style of the merchandise; prices; store's location; store's overall reputation; and knowledge of sales staff) with 18 store-service features as being relevant to Aca Joe's image. Once the critical store image dimensions and features were identified, the researcher had to determine the appropriate scale measurements needed to collect data on those factors. Guided by the information research problem, the established list of information needs, and the understanding of the different types of scale measurements that could be used, the researcher developed a seven-point semantic differential scale to measure the seven recognized dimensions and a modified four-point, self-rating importance scale for the store-service features. These scale measurements were included in an eight-page store image questionnaire.

Using quantitative information research practices to collect the necessary data, the scales were developed, tested, and administered to a randomly selected sample of 300 known Aca Joe customers using a direct mail survey. Interpretation of the findings from the semantic differential data structures revealed that customers perceived Aca Joe as having a good reputation as a retail men's specialty store that offered high-quality, stylish/fashionable merchandise, but that it had only an average assortment of items that were somewhat high priced. In addition, customers viewed the store as being only somewhat conveniently located but the sales staff as generally knowledgeable and very helpful.

When cross-matched to the owner's desired store image, the image information created from the quantitative data structures identified several areas of concern. The results suggested that Aca Joe's overall desired store image was being compromised by the store's current merchandising and pricing strategies. The owner needed to further evaluate these particular strategies and be willing to modify them to change the current image held by customers toward the store's merchandise selection and prices.

Value of Attitude Measurement in Information Research

In today's business world, more and more marketers are attempting to better understand their customers' attitudes and feelings toward their products, services, and delivery systems, as well as those of their direct competitors. This chapter continues the discussion of scale measurement begun in Chapter 11 and builds on the concepts discussed in earlier chapters. The chapter focuses on scales used to collect attitudinal, emotional, and behavior intention responses. These scales have a common link in that they are typically used to collect state-of-mind and state-of-intention data from respondents. They include noncomparative rating and comparative ranking scales.

In addition, there are several fundamental principles from earlier chapters that you need to think about as you read this chapter: (1) raw data, data structures, and information are not the same things—they are unique concepts with different origins and uses (Chapter 2); (2) raw data are a given set of responses to a stated question (Chapters 2, 8, and 9); and (3) a complete scale measurement consists of three components: the question, the scale dimensions and attributes, and the scale point descriptors (Chapter 11). The importance of the last principle cannot be overstated. If the overall goal is to collect high-quality data to transform into useful primary information, researchers and practitioners alike must have a full understanding of the relationships that exist among the three components.

The Nature of Attitudes and Marketplace Behaviors

Many businesses today are attaching more importance to identifying their customers' attitudes and feelings as a way to determine their strengths and weaknesses. Attitudes are useful in understanding consumers' and industrial buyers' observable marketplace behaviors. Yet measuring attitudes and their components is a difficult process that uses less precise scales than those found in the physical sciences. Complete treatment of the theory of attitudes goes well beyond the scope of this chapter. For those who wish additional information, we suggest that you go to a consumer behavior textbook or to the *Handbook of Consumer Behavior* by T. S. Robertson and H. H. Kassarjian[1] or *Readings in Attitude Theory and Behavior* by Martin Fishbein.[2]

Attitude A learned predisposition to react in a consistent positive or negative way to a given object, idea, or set of information.

An **attitude** is a learned predisposition to act in a consistent positive or negative way to a given object, idea, or set of information. Attitudes are state-of-mind constructs that are not directly observable. The true structure of an attitude lies in the mind of the individual holding that attitude. To accurately capture customers' attitudes, the researcher must be able to understand the dimensions of the construct.

Components of Attitudes

Attitudes can be thought of as having three components: cognitive, affective, and behavioral. Marketing researchers and decision makers need to understand all three components.

Cognitive Component

Cognitive component The part of an attitude that represents a subject's beliefs, perceptions, and knowledge about a specified object.

The **cognitive component** of an attitude is the person's beliefs, perceptions, and knowledge about an object and its attributes. For example, as a college student you may believe that your university

- Is a prestigious place to get a degree.

- Has excellent professors.

- Is a good value for the money.

- Needs more and better computer labs.

These beliefs represent the cognitive component of your attitude toward your university. Your beliefs may or may not be true, but they represent reality to you. The more positive beliefs you have of your university and the more positive each belief is, the more favorable the overall cognitive component is assumed to be.

Affective Component

Affective component The part of an attitude that represents the person's emotional feelings held toward the given object.

The **affective component** of an attitude is the person's emotions or feelings toward a given object. This component is the one most frequently expressed when a person is asked to verbalize his or her attitude toward some object, person, or phenomenon. For example, if you claim you "love your university" or "your university has the best athletes or smartest students" you are expressing your emotions or feelings. These emotions or feelings are the affective component of your attitude about your university. Your overall feelings about your university may be based on years of observing it, or they may be based on little actual knowledge. Your attitude could change as you are exposed to more information (e.g., from your freshman to your senior year), or it may remain essentially the same. Finally, two individuals may have different affective responses to the same experience (e.g., one student may like a particular professor's teaching approach while another one may hate it).

Behavioral Component

Behavioral (conative) component The part of an attitude that represents a person's intended or actual behavioral response to the given object.

The **behavioral component,** also sometimes referred to as a *conative* component, is a person's intended or actual behavioral response to an object. For example, your decision to return to your university for the sophomore year is the behavioral component of your attitude. The behavioral component is an observable outcome driven by the interaction of a person's cognitive component (beliefs) and affective component (strength of beliefs) as they relate to a particular object. The behavioral component may represent future intentions (e.g., your plan to get an MBA degree after you finish your BA), but it usually is limited to a specific time period. Recommendations also represent a behavioral component (e.g., recommending that another student take a class from a particular professor).

Attitudes are a complex area to understand fully. For those who wish to learn more we have included an Appendix 12.A at the end of this chapter with more complete coverage. In the next section we discuss the different scales used to measure attitudes and behaviors.

Scales to Measure Attitudes and Behaviors

Although the information problem and research objectives dictate which type of scale measurement a researcher should use, there are several types of attitudinal scaling formats that have proven to be useful in many different situations. The following section discusses three attitude scale formats: Likert scales, semantic differential scales, and behavior intention scales. Exhibit 12.1 shows the general steps in the construct development/ scale measurement process.

Likert scale An ordinal scale format that asks respondents to indicate the extent to which they agree or disagree with a series of mental belief or behavioral belief statements about a given object.

Likert Scale

A **Likert scale** asks respondents to indicate the extent to which they either agree or disagree with a series of mental or behavioral belief statements about a given object. Usually the scale format is balanced between agreement and disagreement scale descriptors. Named after its original developer, Rensis Likert, this scale typically has five scale descriptors:

⊖XHIBIT 12.1 A General Construct Development/Scale Measurement Process

Process Steps	Key Activities
1. Identify and Define the Construct	Determine Dimensionality of Construct
2. Create Initial Pool of Attribute Items	Determine Theory, Secondary Data, Qualitative Research
3. Assess and Select a Reduced Set of Items	Perform Structural Analysis and Qualitative Judgments
4. Construct Initial Measurements and Pretest	Conduct Pilot Study, Collect Data from Pretest Sample
5. Do Appropriate Statistical Data Analysis	Conduct Construct Validity and Scale Reliability Tests
6. Refine and Purify Scale Measurements	Eliminate Irrelevant Attribute Items
7. Collect More Data on Purified Scale	Select New Sample of Subjects from Defined Target Population
8. Statistically Evaluate Scale Measurements	Conduct Reliability, Validity, Generalizability Tests
9. Perform Final Scale Measurement	Include Scale Measurement in Final Questionnaire

"strongly agree," "agree," "neither agree nor disagree," "disagree," "strongly disagree." A series of hierarchical steps is followed in developing a Likert scale:

Step 1: Identify and understand the concept to be studied; let's assume the concept is voting in Florida.

Step 2: Assemble a large number of belief statements (e.g., 50 to 100) concerning the general public's sentiments toward voting in Florida.

Step 3: Subjectively classify each statement as having either a "favorable" or an "unfavorable" relationship to the specific attitude under investigation. Then, the entire list of statements is pretested (e.g., through a pilot test) using a sample of respondents.

Step 4: Respondents decide the extent to which they either agree or disagree with each statement, using the intensity descriptors "strongly agree," "agree," "not sure," "disagree," "strongly disagree." Each response is then given a numerical weight, such as 5, 4, 3, 2, 1. For assumed favorable statements, a weight of 5 would be given to a "strongly agree" response; for assumed unfavorable statements, a weight of 5 would be given to a "strongly disagree" response.

Step 5: A respondent's overall-attitude score is calculated by the summation of the weighted values associated with the statements rated.

Step 6: Only statements that appear to discriminate between the high and low total scores are retained in the analysis. One possible method is a simple comparison of the top (or highest) 25 percent of the total mean scores with the bottom (or lowest) 25 percent of total mean scores.

Step 7: In determining the final set of statements (normally 20 to 25), statements that exhibit the greatest differences in mean values between the top and bottom total scores are selected.

Step 8: Using the final set of statements, steps 3 and 4 are repeated in a full study.

By using the summation of the weights associated with all the statements, the researcher can tell whether a person's attitude toward the object is positive or negative. For example, the maximum favorable score on a 25-item scale would be 125 ($5 \times 25 = 125$). Therefore a person scoring 110 would be assumed to hold a positive (favorable) attitude. Another respondent who scores 45 would be assumed to hold a negative attitude toward the object. The total scores do not identify any of the possible differences that might exist on an individual statement basis between respondents.

The Likert scale has been extensively modified by marketing researchers over the years. Today, the modified Likert scale expands the original five-point format to either a six-point forced-choice format with such scale descriptors as "definitely agree," "generally agree," "slightly agree," "slightly disagree," "generally disagree," "definitely disagree" or a seven-point free-choice format with these same descriptors plus "neither agree nor disagree" in the middle. In addition, many researchers treat the Likert scale format as an interval scale.

Regardless of the actual number of scale descriptors that are used, Likert scales have several other useful characteristics. First, the Likert scale is the only summated rating scale that uses a set of agreement/disagreement scale descriptors. A Likert scale collects only cognitive-based or specific behavioral beliefs. Despite the popular notion that Likert scales can measure a person's complete attitude, they can capture only the cognitive components of a person's attitude and are therefore only partial measures. They also do not capture the different possible intensity levels of expressed affective or behavioral components of a

---

EXHIBIT 12.2 Example of a Partial Modified Likert Scale

For each of the listed statements, please check the one response that best expresses the extent to which you agree or disagree with that statement.

Statements	Definitely Agree	Generally Agree	Slightly Agree	Slightly Disagree	Generally Disagree	Definitely Disagree
I buy **many things** with a credit card.	——	——	——	——	——	——
I wish we had **a lot more** money.	——	——	——	——	——	——
My friends **often come** to me for advice.	——	——	——	——	——	——
I am **never influenced** by advertisements.	——	——	——	——	——	——

---

person's attitude. This misunderstanding of a Likert scale's capability might account for the scale's weak interpretive results in situations where identifying and measuring respondents' attitudes are critical to solving the information problem.

Likert scales are best for research designs that use self-administered surveys, personal interviewers, or most online methods to collect the data. It is difficult to administer a Likert scale over the telephone because respondents have trouble visualizing and remembering the relative magnitudes of agreement and disagreement that make up the scale descriptors. Exhibit 12.2 illustrates an example of a partial modified Likert scale in a self-administered survey.

To point out the interpretive difficulties associated with the Likert scale, we have used boldface in each of the statements in Exhibit 12.2 for the words that indicate a single level of intensity. For example, in the first statement (I buy many things with a credit card), the main belief focuses on **many things.** If the respondent checks the "generally disagree" response, it would be a leap of faith for the researcher to interpret that response to mean that the respondent buys only a few things with a credit card. In addition, it would be a speculative guess on the part of the researcher to assume that the respondent's attitude toward purchasing products or services with a credit card is unfavorable. The intensity level assigned to the agree/disagree scale point descriptors does not truly represent the respondent's feelings associated with the belief response. The intensity levels used in a Likert scale identify only the extent to which the respondent thinks the statement represents his or her own belief about credit card purchases.

Let's take the last statement in Exhibit 12.2 (I am never influenced by advertisements) as another example. The key words in this statement are **never influenced.** If the respondent checks "definitely disagree," it would again be the researcher's subjective guess that the response means that the respondent is very much influenced by advertisements. In reality, all that the "definitely disagree" response indicates is that the statement is not one that the respondent would make. No measure of feeling can be attached to the statement.

Likert scales can also be used to identify and assess personal or psychographic (lifestyle) traits of individuals. To see how international marketing research companies, like the Gallup Organization, use attitude and psychographic scale measurements to profile consumers across Latin American countries, visit the book's Web site at www.mhhe.com/hair06 and follow the links.

Semantic differential scale A unique bipolar ordinal scale format that captures a person's attitudes or feelings about a given object.

Semantic Differential Scale

Another rating scale used quite often in information and marketing research endeavors is the **semantic differential scale.** This type of scale is unique in its use of bipolar adjectives and adverbs (good/bad, like/dislike, competitive/noncompetitive, helpful/unhelpful, high quality/low quality, dependable/undependable, etc.) as the endpoints of a symmetrical continuum. Usually there will be one object and a related set of factors, each with its own set of bipolar adjectives to measure either a cognitive or an affective element. Because the individual scale descriptors are not identified, each bipolar scale appears to be a continuum. In most cases, semantic differential scales will use between five and seven scale descriptors, though only the endpoints are identified. Respondents are asked to select the point on the continuum that expresses their thoughts or feelings about the given object.

In most cases a semantic differential scale will use an odd number of scale points, thus creating a so-called neutral response that symmetrically divides the positive and negative poles into two equal parts. An interpretive problem that arises with an odd-number scale point format comes from the natural neutral response in the middle of the scale. In many cases a neutral response has little or no diagnostic value to the researcher or decision maker. Sometimes it is interpreted as meaning "no opinion," "don't know," "neither/nor," or "average." None of these interpretations gives much information to the researcher. To overcome this problem, the researcher can use an even-point (or forced-choice) format and incorporate a "not applicable" response out to the side of the bipolar scale.

A semantic differential scale is one of the few attitudinal scale formats that enables the researcher to collect both cognitive and affective data for any given factor. But both types of data cannot be collected at the same time. For a given factor, a bipolar scale can be designed to capture either a person's feelings or cognitive beliefs. Although some researchers believe a semantic differential scale can be used to measure a person's complete attitude about an object or behavior, this scale type is best for identifying a "perceptual image profile" about the object or behavior of concern.

The actual design of a semantic differential scale can vary from situation to situation. To help you understand the benefits and weaknesses associated with design differences, we present three different formats and discuss the pros and cons of each. In the first situation, the researcher is interested in developing a credibility scale that can be used by Nike to assess the credibility of Tiger Woods as a spokesperson in TV or print advertisements for Nike brands of personal grooming products. The researcher determines that the credibility construct consists of three factors—(1) expertise, (2) trustworthiness, and (3) attractiveness—with each factor measured using a specific set of five bipolar scales (see Exhibit 12.3).

Randomization of the Positive and Negative Pole Descriptors

While the semantic differential scale format in Exhibit 12.3 appears to be correctly designed, there are several technical problems that may create response bias. First, notice that all the positive pole descriptors are arranged on the left side of each scale and the negative pole descriptors are all on the right side. This approach can cause a **halo effect bias**.[3] That is, it tends to lead the respondent to react more favorably to the positive poles on the left side than to the negative poles on the right side. To prevent this problem, the researcher should randomly mix the positions of the positive and negative pole descriptors.[4]

Halo effect bias A generalization from the perception of one outstanding factor, attribute, or trait to an overly favorable evaluation on the whole object or construct.

Lack of Extreme Magnitude Expressed in the Pole Descriptors

A second response problem with the scale format displayed in Exhibit 12.3 is that the descriptors at the ends of each scale do not express the extreme intensity associated with end poles. The respondent is asked to check one of seven possible lines to express his or her opinion, but only the two end lines are given narrative meaning. The researcher can only guess how the respondent is interpreting the other positions between the two endpoints. Let's take, for example, the "dependable/undependable" scale for the trustworthiness dimension. Notice the extreme left scale position represents "dependable" and the

---

EXHIBIT 12.3 **Example of a Semantic Differential Scale Format for Tiger Woods as a Credibility Spokesperson[5]**

Now with respect to Tiger Woods as the spokesperson for Nike golf apparel, we would like to know your opinions about the expertise, trustworthiness, and attractiveness that you believe he brings to the advertisement. Each dimension has five factors that may or may not represent your opinion. For each listed factor, **please check the line that best expresses your opinion about that factor.**

Expertise:

Knowledgeable	____	____	____	____	____	____	____	Unknowledgeable
Expert	____	____	____	____	____	____	____	Not an Expert
Skilled	____	____	____	____	____	____	____	Unskilled
Qualified	____	____	____	____	____	____	____	Unqualified
Experienced	____	____	____	____	____	____	____	Inexperienced

Trustworthiness:

Reliable	____	____	____	____	____	____	____	Unreliable
Sincere	____	____	____	____	____	____	____	Insincere
Trustworthy	____	____	____	____	____	____	____	Untrustworthy
Dependable	____	____	____	____	____	____	____	Undependable
Honest	____	____	____	____	____	____	____	Dishonest

Attractiveness:

Sexy	____	____	____	____	____	____	____	Not Sexy
Beautiful	____	____	____	____	____	____	____	Ugly
Attractive	____	____	____	____	____	____	____	Unattractive
Classy	____	____	____	____	____	____	____	Not Classy
Elegant	____	____	____	____	____	____	____	Plain

---

extreme right scale position represents "undependable." Because dependable and undependable are natural dichotomous phrase descriptors, the scale design does not allow for any significant magnitudes to exist between them. The logical question is what do the other five scale positions represent, which in turn raises the question of whether or not the scale truly is a continuum ranging from dependable to undependable. This problem can be corrected by attaching a narratively expressed extreme magnitude to the bipolar descriptors (e.g., "extremely" or "quite" dependable, and "extremely" or "quite" undependable).

Use of Non-bipolar Descriptors to Represent the Poles

A third response problem that occurs in designing semantic differential scales relates to the inappropriate narrative expressions of the scale descriptors. In a good semantic differential scale design, the individual scales should be truly bipolar so that a symmetrical scale can be designed. Sometimes the researcher will express the negative pole in such a way that the positive one is not really its opposite. This creates a skewed scale design that is difficult for the respondent to interpret correctly.

Take, for example, the "expert/not an expert" scale in the "expertise" dimension in Exhibit 12.3. While the scale is dichotomous, the words "not an expert" do not allow the respondent to interpret any of the other scale points as being relative magnitudes of that phrase. Other than that one endpoint being described as "not an expert," all the other scale points would have to represent some intensity of "expert," thus creating a skewed scale toward the positive pole. In other words, interpreting "not an expert" as really meaning "extremely" or "quite" not an expert makes little or no diagnostic sense.

Researchers must be careful when selecting bipolar descriptors to make sure the words or phrases are truly extreme bipolar in nature and they allow for creating symmetrical scale designs. For example, the researcher could use pole descriptors such as "complete expert" and "complete novice" to correct the above-described scale point descriptor problems.

Matching Standardized Intensity Descriptors to Pole Descriptors

The scale design used by Bank of America in a bank image study in Exhibit 12.4 eliminates the three problems we discussed in the example in Exhibit 12.3, as well as a fourth—it gives narrative expression to the intensity level of each scale point. Notice that all the separate poles and scale points in between them are anchored by the same set of intensity descriptors ("very," "moderately," "slightly," "neither one nor the other," "slightly," "moderately," "very"). In using standardized intensity descriptors, however, the researcher must be extra careful in determining the specific phrases for each pole— each phrase must fit the set of intensity descriptors in order for the scale points to make complete sense to the respondent. Take, for example, the "makes you feel at home/makes you feel uneasy" scale in Exhibit 12.4. The intensity descriptor of "very"

ᕮXHIBIT | 12.4   Example of a Semantic Differential Scale Used by Bank of America That Expresses Each Scale Descriptor

For each of the following banking traits/features, please check the one line that best expresses your impression of that feature as it relates to Bank of America. **Make sure you give only one response for each listed feature.**

	Very	Moderately	Slightly	Neither One nor the Other	Slightly	Moderately	Very	
Courteous Employees	___	___	___	___	___	___	___	Discourteous Employees
Helpful Staff	___	___	___	___	___	___	___	Unhelpful Staff
Unattractive Exterior	___	___	___	___	___	___	___	Attractive Exterior
Competitive Rates	___	___	___	___	___	___	___	Noncompetitive Rates
Limited Service Offerings	___	___	___	___	___	___	___	Wide Variety of Service Offerings
Good Operating Hours	___	___	___	___	___	___	___	Bad Operating Hours
High-Quality Service	___	___	___	___	___	___	___	Low-Quality Service
Unreliable	___	___	___	___	___	___	___	Reliable
Successful Bank	___	___	___	___	___	___	___	Unsuccessful Bank
Makes You Feel at Home	___	___	___	___	___	___	___	Makes You Feel Uneasy

---

eXHIBIT 12.5 Example of a Semantic Differential Scale for Midas Auto Systems Experts

---

From your personal experiences with Midas Auto Systems' service representatives, please rate the performance of Midas on the basis of the following listed features. Each feature has its own scale ranging from "one" (1) to "six" (6). **Please circle the response number that best describes how Midas has performed on that feature.** For any feature(s) that you feel is (are) not relevant to your evaluation, please circle the (NA)—Not applicable—response code.

Cost of Repair/Maintenance Work	(NA)	Extremely High	6	5	4	3	2	1	Very Low, Almost Free
Appearance of Facilities	(NA)	Very Professional	6	5	4	3	2	1	Very Unprofessional
Customer Satisfaction	(NA)	Totally Dissatisfied	6	5	4	3	2	1	Truly Satisfied
Promptness in Delivering Service	(NA)	Unacceptably Slow	6	5	4	3	2	1	Impressively Quick
Quality of Service Offerings	(NA)	Truly Terrible	6	5	4	3	2	1	Truly Exceptional
Understands Customer's Needs	(NA)	Really Understands	6	5	4	3	2	1	Doesn't Have a Clue
Credibility of Midas	(NA)	Extremely Credible	6	5	4	3	2	1	Extremely Unreliable
Midas's Keeping of Promises	(NA)	Very Trustworthy	6	5	4	3	2	1	Very Deceitful
Midas Services Assortment	(NA)	Truly Full Service	6	5	4	3	2	1	Only Basic Services
Prices/Rates/Charges of Services	(NA)	Much Too High	6	5	4	3	2	1	Great Rates
Service Personnel's Competence	(NA)	Very Competent	6	5	4	3	2	1	Totally Incompetent
Employee's Personal Social Skills	(NA)	Very Rude	6	5	4	3	2	1	Very Friendly
Midas's Operating Hours	(NA)	Extremely Flexible	6	5	4	3	2	1	Extremely Limited
Convenience of Midas's Locations	(NA)	Very Easy to Get to	6	5	4	3	2	1	Too Difficult to Get to

---

does not make much sense when applied to that scale (i.e., "very makes you feel at home" or "very makes you feel uneasy"). Thus, including standardized intensity descriptors in a semantic differential scale design may force the researcher to limit the types of bipolar phrases used to describe or evaluate the object or behavior of concern. This can only raise questions about the appropriateness of the data collected using this type of scale design.

The fundamentals discussed in Chapter 11 can help the researcher learn how to correctly develop customized scales to collect the most appropriate attitudinal or behavioral data for the given information problem. To illustrate this point, Exhibit 12.5 shows a semantic differential scale used by Midas Auto Systems Experts to collect attitudinal data about the performance of Midas. Notice that each of the 14 different features that make up Midas's service profile has its own bipolar scale communicating the intensity level for the positive and negative poles. This reduces the possibility the respondent will misunderstand the scale's continuum range. This example also illustrates the use of an "NA"—not applicable—response as a replacement for the more traditional midscale neutral response. After the data are collected from this scale format, the researcher could calculate aggregate mean values for each of the 14 features, plot those mean values on each of their respective scale lines, and graphically display the results using "profile" lines. The result is an overall profile that depicts Midas's service performance patterns (see Exhibit 12.6). In addition, the researcher could use the same scale and collect raw data on several competing automobile service providers (e.g., Firestone

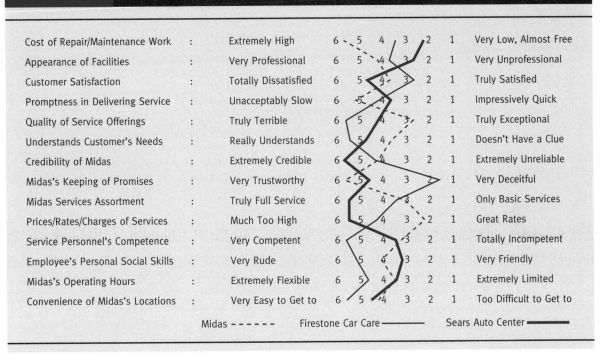

EXHIBIT 12.6 Example of Midas Auto Systems' Performance Profile Compared with Two Competitors

Car Care and Sears Auto Center), then show each of the semantic differential profiles on one display.

Behavior Intention Scale

Behavior intention scale
A special type of rating scale designed to capture the likelihood that people will demonstrate some type of predictable behavior intent toward purchasing an object or service in a future time frame.

One of the most widely used scale formats in commercial marketing research is the **behavior intention scale.** In using this scale the decision maker is attempting to obtain some idea of the likelihood that people will demonstrate some type of predictable behavior regarding the purchase of a product or service. In general, behavior intent scales have been found to be good predictors of consumers' choices of frequently purchased and durable consumer products.[6]

Behavior intention scales (e.g., purchase intent, attendance intent, shopping intent, usage intent) are easy to construct. Consumers are asked to make a subjective judgment on their likelihood of buying a product or service, or taking a specified action. The scale descriptors typically used with a behavior intention scale are "definitely would," "probably would," "not sure," "probably would not," and "definitely would not." For example, for Vail Valley Foundation's interest in identifying how likely it is that people will attend a variety of performing arts events at its new outdoor Ford Amphitheater in Vail, Colorado, see Exhibit 12.7, which illustrates the behavior intention scale the Vail Valley Foundation management team used to collect the raw intention data. Note that this scale uses a forced-choice design

EXHIBIT 12.7 Example of Behavior Intention Scale for Determining Attendance at Performing Arts Events In Vail, Colorado

Now with respect to the next six months, we would like to know the extent to which you would consider attending various types of entertainment/performing arts events if they were held in the Vail Valley area.

Next to each type of event, please check the one box that best expresses the extent to which you would consider attending within the next six months.

(PLEASE CHECK ONLY ONE BOX FOR EACH EVENT)

Type of Event	Definitely Would Consider Attending	Probably Would Consider Attending	Probably Would Not Consider Attending	Definitely Would Not Consider Attending
I. Music Concerts				
Popular Music	❏	❏	❏	❏
Jazz Music	❏	❏	❏	❏
Country Music	❏	❏	❏	❏
Bluegrass Music	❏	❏	❏	❏
Classical Music	❏	❏	❏	❏
Chamber Music	❏	❏	❏	❏
II. Theatrical Productions				
Drama	❏	❏	❏	❏
Comedy	❏	❏	❏	❏
Melodrama	❏	❏	❏	❏
Musical	❏	❏	❏	❏
III. Dance Productions				
Classical Dance	❏	❏	❏	❏
Modern Dance	❏	❏	❏	❏
Jazz	❏	❏	❏	❏
Folk Dance	❏	❏	❏	❏

by not including the middle logical scale point of "not sure." It is important to remember that when designing a behavior intention scale, you should include a specific time frame (e.g., "would consider attending in the next six months") in the question/setup portion of the scale. Without an expressed time frame, you increase the possibility that the respondents will bias their response toward the "definitely would" or "probably would" scale categories.

To increase the clarity of the scale point descriptors, the researcher can attach a percentage equivalent expression to each one. To illustrate this concept, let's assume that Sears is interested in knowing how likely it is that customers will shop at certain types of retail stores for men's casual clothing. The following set of scale points could be used to obtain the intention data: "definitely would shop at (90% to 100% chance)"; "probably would shop at (50% to 89% chance)"; probably would not shop at (10% to 49% chance)"; and

EXHIBIT 12.8 Retail Store: Shopping Intention Scale for Men's Casual Clothes

When shopping for men's casual wear for yourself or someone else, how likely are you to shop at each of the following types of retail stores? **(Please check one response for each store type.)**

Type of Retail Store	Definitely Would Shop At (90–100% chance)	Probably Would Shop At (50–89% chance)	Probably Would Not Shop At (10–49% chance)	Definitely Would Not Shop At (less than 10% chance)
Giant Retail Stores (e.g., Sears, JCPenney)	❏	❏	❏	❏
Department Stores (e.g., Burdine's, Dillard's Marshall Field)	❏	❏	❏	❏
Discount Department Stores (e.g., Marshall's, TG&Y, Kmart, Target)	❏	❏	❏	❏
Retail Mall Outlets (e.g., Orlando Mall Outlet)	❏	❏	❏	❏
Men's Clothing Specialty Shops (e.g., Wolf Brothers, Surrey's George Ltd.)	❏	❏	❏	❏
Men's Casual Wear Specialty Stores (e.g., The Gap, Banana Republic, Aca Joe's)	❏	❏	❏	❏

definitely would not shop at (less than 10% chance)." Exhibit 12.8 shows what the complete shopping intention scale might look like.

For more examples of Likert, semantic differential, and behavior intention types of scale designs visit the book's Web site at www.mhhe.com/hair06 and follow the links.

Strengths and Weaknesses of Attitude and Behavior Intention Scale Measurements

Information researchers and marketing practitioners alike must realize that no matter what type of scale measurements are used to capture people's attitudes and behaviors, there often is no one best or guaranteed approach. While there are proven scale measurements for capturing the components that make up people's attitudes as well as behavioral intentions, the data provided from these scale measurements should not be interpreted as being facts about a given object or behavior. Instead, the raw data and any derived structures should be viewed as insights into what might be reality. For example, if the information problem involves predicting some type of shopping, purchase, or consumption behavior, then developing and administering behavioral intention scales might well be the best approach. Unfortunately, knowledge of an individual's attitudes often is not a good predictor of behavior. Intentions are better than attitudes at predicting behavior, but the strongest predictor of actual behavior is past behavior.[7] Researchers have

A Closer Look at Research

Instant On-Site Customer Satisfaction Feedback

Most small-business owners are constantly in search of different methods to evaluate customer satisfaction. An integral component of any small business, positive customer satisfaction is vital in building long-term relationships with valuable customers. Below is an excerpt taken from Direct Network Access, Inc.'s Web site (www.opinionmeter.com) that describes a tool small-business owners can use to quickly and efficiently evaluate customer satisfaction. We recommend browsing through some of the "hot links" to reveal other technologically advanced products that will improve small-business operations.

The Opinionmeter is a flexible, easy-to-use interactive survey system designed to collect customer satisfaction feedback at point-of-service. No more paper surveys or data entry—the Opinionmeter instantly tabulates responses and provides immediate on-site access to survey results. When placed in a business lobby, customers interact with the freestanding battery-operated Opinionmeter to self-administer their own surveys, anonymously.

Opinionmeter takes advantage of customers' waiting time and captures feedback while opinions are still fresh. In addition, on-site surveying sends a powerful message about a company's commitment to customer satisfaction.

EASY TO USE Now you can have the questionnaire customized, the machine programmed, the data collected, and the formal report completed in a single day. Opinionmeter's unique questionnaire display system permits questions and answers printed in any language to be displayed in the easy-to-read Questionnaire Holder. Reprogramming for a new questionnaire takes only 2–3 minutes.

QUICK RESULTS Respondent answers are screened and tallied, and results made instantly available after any survey. Results can be called up on the screen, hard-copied by a handheld infrared printer or transmitted via serial cable to your PC for in-depth analysis using Opinionmeter's Opinion Analyzer statistical software package. Full cross-tabulations are available, including date and time bracketing of data.

made significant advances in their predictive models using attitudes and intentions, but there is still much room for improvement.

In contrast, if the information problem is that of better understanding why consumers or customers behave or respond as they do in the marketplace, the researcher needs something other than a basic measurement of their buying intentions. Behavior can be explained, directly or indirectly, by measuring both the cognitive and affective elements of the consumers' attitudes. Read the nearby Closer Look at Research box to see how small-business owners might use the Internet and Opinionmeters to measure their customers' satisfaction.

Other Types of Comparative and Noncomparative Scale Formats

Besides the rating scales discussed earlier, several variations, both comparative and noncomparative, remain popular among commercial marketing research firms. Unfortunately, the terms used to identify these different scale formats vary from one researcher

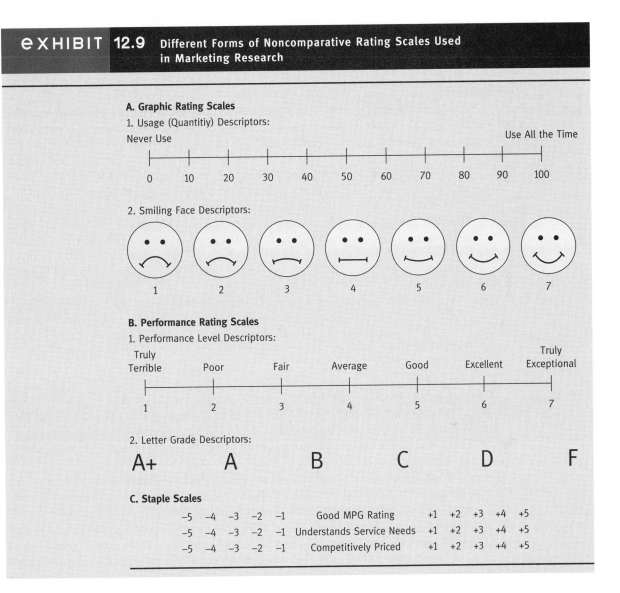

eXHIBIT 12.9 Different Forms of Noncomparative Rating Scales Used in Marketing Research

A. Graphic Rating Scales

1. Usage (Quantitiy) Descriptors:

Never Use — Use All the Time

0   10   20   30   40   50   60   70   80   90   100

2. Smiling Face Descriptors:

1   2   3   4   5   6   7

B. Performance Rating Scales

1. Performance Level Descriptors:

| Truly Terrible | Poor | Fair | Average | Good | Excellent | Truly Exceptional |

1   2   3   4   5   6   7

2. Letter Grade Descriptors:

A+   A   B   C   D   F

C. Staple Scales

−5	−4	−3	−2	−1	Good MPG Rating	+1	+2	+3	+4	+5
−5	−4	−3	−2	−1	Understands Service Needs	+1	+2	+3	+4	+5
−5	−4	−3	−2	−1	Competitively Priced	+1	+2	+3	+4	+5

Noncomparative rating scale A scale format that requires a judgment without reference to another object, person, or concept.

Comparative rating scale A scale format that requires a judgment comparing one object, person, or concept against another on the scale.

to the next. For example, some researchers refer to a *performance* rating scale format (e.g., example B in Exhibit 12.9) as an *itemized* rating scale format. Other researchers refer to a similar format as a *numerical* scale, or maybe a *monadic* scale, or a *composite* scale, or a *category* scale. For now, to avoid confusion it is easiest to classify any type of rating or ranking scale format as being either comparative or noncomparative in nature.

Overall, a **noncomparative rating scale** is used when the objective is to have a respondent express his or her attitudes, emotions, actions, or intentions about a specific object (or person, or phenomenon) or its attributes without making reference to another object or its attributes. In contrast, a scale format is **comparative rating** in nature when the objective is to have a respondent express his or her attitude, feelings, or behaviors about an object (or person, or phenomenon) or its attributes on the basis of some other object or its attributes. Within the "family" of noncomparative scale descriptor designs, we describe the three types—*graphic rating* scales, *performance rating* scales, and *staple* scales—frequently used by researchers in their efforts to create noncomparative scales. Exhibit 12.9 provides a few examples that illustrate these types of scale descriptor designs. Additional examples can be viewed by visiting the book's Web site at www.mhhe.com/hair06 and following the links.

Graphic rating scales

A scale measure that uses a scale point format that presents the respondent with some type of graphic continuum as the set of possible raw responses to a given question.

Graphic rating scales (also referred to as *continuous* rating scales) use a scaling descriptor format that presents a respondent with a graphic continuum as the set of possible responses to a question. For example, the first graphic rating scale (usage or quantity descriptors) displayed in Exhibit 12.9 is used in situations where the researcher wants to collect "usage behavior" data about an object (or person, or phenomenon). Let's say Yahoo wants to determine how frequently Internet users employ its search engine without making reference to any other available search engine alternatives (e.g., Google or AltaVista). In using this type of scale design, the respondents would simply place an "X" along the graphic "usage" line where the extreme endpoints of the line have narrative descriptors (Never Use and Use all the Time) and numerical descriptors (0 and 100), while the remainder of the line is sectioned and described in equal-appearing numerical intervals (10, 20, 30, etc.).

Another popular type of graphic rating scale descriptor design is the "Smiling Faces." The smiling faces are arranged in a particular order and depict a continuous range from "very sad" to "very happy" without providing narrative meaning of the two extreme positions. Typically, the design uses a symmetrical format having equal numbers of happy and unhappy faces with a "neutral" face in the middle position. This type of visual graphic rating design can be used to collect a variety of attitudinal and emotional data. It is most popular in collecting data from children. For example, let's say Mattel, Inc., the toy manufacturer, is product testing several new toys among children aged 6 to 10 years. Researchers can have the children play with the toys, then ask them questions about their likes and dislikes. The child answers by pointing to the face that best expresses his or her feelings about the particular toy.

Graphic rating scales can be constructed easily and are simple to use. They allow the identification of fine distinctions between responses, assuming the respondents have adequate discriminatory abilities. Overall, graphic rating scales are most appropriate in self-administered surveys (both online and offline) or personal interviews and are difficult to use in telephone interviews.

Performance rating scales A scale measure that uses an evaluative scale point format that allows the respondent to express some type of postdecision or behavior evaluative judgment about an object.

Performance rating scales are a type of itemized rating scale that uses a scale point format that allows respondents to express some type of postdecision or evaluative judgment about the object under investigation. Although these scale descriptor designs have the initial appearance of being very similar to a graphic rating scale, the primary difference is that each scale point included is given narrative meaning and sometimes additional numerical meaning as well. The examples in part B of Exhibit 12.9 illustrate two design possibilities among many a researcher could use. When using performance-level descriptors, the researcher asks respondents to select the response among a prelist of possible responses that best expresses their evaluative judgment toward the object or attribute of interest. The second design in Exhibit 12.9 illustrates the letter-grade descriptor design. With this design, the researcher asks the respondent to express his or her performance judgment using a letter-grade scheme used in the United States. This type of design has an inherent flexibility factor in that researchers could easily expand the 6-point format as displayed in Exhibit 12.9 to a 13-point scale ranging from A+ down to F (A+, A, A−, B+, B, B−, C+, C, C−, D+, D, D−, F).

In contrast, this particular scale format has obvious limitations, making its use inappropriate in the conducting of international research studies. Performance rating scales are

EXHIBIT 12.10 Different Forms of Comparative Rating Scales Used in Marketing Research

A. Rank-Order Rating Scales

Thinking about the different types of music, please rank your top three preferences of types of music you enjoy listening to by writing in your first choice, second choice, and third choice on the lines provided below.

First Preference: _____

Second Preference: _____

Third Preference: _____

B. Paired-Comparison Rating Scales

We are going to present you with several pairs of traits associated with a saleperson's on-the-job activities. For each pair, please indicate which trait you feel is more important for being a salesperson.

a. trust	b. competence
a. trust	b. communication skills
a. trust	b. personal social skills
a. competence	b. communication skills
a. competence	b. personal social skills
a. communication skills	b. personal social skills

Note: the researcher would want to scramble and reverse the order of these paired comparisons to avoid possible order bias.

C. Constant Sums Rating Scales

Below is a list of seven banking features. Please allocate 100 points among those features such that the allocation represents the importance each feature was to you in your selecting "your" bank. The more points you assign to a feature, the more important that feature was to your selection process. If the feature was "not at all important" in your process, you should not assign it any points. When you have finished, please double-check to make sure your total adds to 100.

Banking Features	Number of Points
Convenience/location	_____
Banking hours	_____
Good service charges	_____
The interest rates on loans	_____
The bank's reputation	_____
The interest rates on savings	_____
Bank's promotional advertising	_____
	100 points

excellent for use in self-administered questionnaires or personal interviews, and generally poor for any type of telephone interview, unless the number of scale point descriptors is kept to three or four. An exception to this latter point would be the shorter form of the letter-grade design. Because of the inherent acceptance and understanding of this particular design, letter-grade descriptors are fairly easy to administer in both traditional and computer-assisted telephone interviews.

Turning now to comparative rating scales, Exhibit 12.10 illustrates some of the scales associated with rank-order, paired comparisons, and constant sums scale formats. A common characteristic among all types of comparative scale designs is that the scaling objective is to collect data that enable the researcher to identify and directly compare similarities and differences between *objects* (e.g., Mercedes versus Lexus cars), *people* (e.g., George W. Bush versus John Kerry), *marketing phenomena* (e.g., shopping online versus shopping offline), *concepts* (e.g., customer satisfaction versus service quality), or any of the *attributes* that underline objects, people, or phenomena (e.g., importance of salespeople's traits). In addition, comparative scale designs can be used to collect any type of data (e.g., state of being, mind, behavior, or intentions).

Rank-order scales

Rank-order scales
These allow respondents to compare their own responses by indicating their first, second, third, and fourth preferences, and so forth, until all the desired responses are placed in a rank order.

Rank-order scales use a scale format that enables respondents to compare their own responses by indicating the first preference, second preference, third preference, and so forth, until all the desired responses are placed in either a "highest to lowest" or a "lowest to highest" rank order. For example, consider the rank-order scale design in Exhibit 12.10. Music.com, a new online music retailer, could use this rank-order scale design in an Internet user survey to determine the types of music prospective customers would most likely purchase online. This format allows for easy comparison of each possible response (e.g., type of music) that holds high importance or positive emotional feelings to the respondents.

Rank-order scales are easy to use in personal interviews and all types of self-administered surveys. Use of rank-order scales in traditional or computer-assisted telephone interviews may be difficult, but it is possible as long as the number of items being compared is kept to four or five. When respondents are asked to rank an object's attributes, problems can occur if the respondent's preferred attributes are not part of the prelisted set of attributes being measured. Another limitation is that only ordinal data can be obtained using rank-order scales. Also, the researcher cannot learn anything about the reasoning used by the respondents in making their ranking choices.

Paired-comparison scales This format creates a preselected group of traits, product characteristics, or features that are paired against one another into two groups; respondents are asked to select which in each pair is more important to them.

Paired-comparison scales use a group of traits, product or service characteristics, or features that are paired against one another into two groups. Respondents are asked to select which trait, characteristic, or feature in each pair is more important to them. Consequently, respondents make a series of paired judgments between the attributes (features). It is important to remember that the number of paired comparisons increases geometrically as a function of the number of features being evaluated. For example, the paired-comparison scale shown in Exhibit 12.10 is one of several scales that Procter & Gamble's (P&G) recruiting team administers to new college graduates seeking employment in its consumer-products sales division. Here, P&G is concerned with the traits of communication skills, competence, and trust among its sales associates. By asking a prospective applicant to make a series of paired judgments between these traits, the results are then compared with Procter & Gamble's standards to determine how well the applicant matches P&G's desired profile of a sales associate. A potential weakness of this type of scale design is that respondent fatigue can set in if too many attributes and paired choices are included.

Constant sums scales
Require the respondent to allocate a given number of points, usually 100, among several attributes or features based on their importance to the individual; this format requires a person to evaluate each separate attribute or feature relative to all the other listed ones.

Constant sums scales require the respondent to allocate a given number of points, usually 100, among several attributes or features based on their importance or some other emotional feeling. This format requires the respondent to determine the value of each separate feature relative to all the other listed features. The resulting value assignments indicate the relative magnitude of importance (or emotional feeling) that each feature has to the respondent. This scaling format requires that the individual values must add up to 100. Take, for example, the constant sums scale displayed in Exhibit 12.10. Bank of America can use this type of scale design to identify which banking attributes are more important to customers in influencing their decision of where to bank. This type of comparative scale design is most appropriate for use in self-administered surveys and to a much lesser extent in personal interviews. Caution must be used with constant sums scales when too many (e.g., more than seven) attributes are included for evaluation, since this design requires a lot of mental energy on the part of the respondent.

For more examples of comparative and noncomparative scale designs, log on to the book's Web site at www.mhhe.com/hair06 and follow the links.

Comments on Single-Item and Multiple-Item Scales

Before we conclude our discussion of advanced scale measures used, it is worthwhile to make several comments about when and why researchers use single-item and multiple-item scaling formats. First, a scale design can be characterized as being a **single-item scale design** when the data requirements focus on collecting data about only one attribute of the object or construct being investigated. An easy example to remember is collecting age data. Here the object is "a person" and the single attribute of interest is that person's "age." Only one measure is needed to collect the required age data. The respondent is asked a single question about his or her age and supplies only one possible response to the question. In contrast, most marketing research projects that involve collecting attitudinal, emotional, and behavioral data require some type of **multiple-item scale design.** Basically, when using a multiple-item scale to measure the object or construct of interest, the researcher will have to measure several items simultaneously rather than measuring just one item. Most advanced attitude, emotion, and behavior scales are multiple-item scales.

The decision to use a single-item versus a multiple-item scale is made in the construct development stage. Two factors play a significant role in the process. First, the researcher must assess the dimensionality of the construct under investigation. Any construct that is viewed as consisting of several different, unique subdimensions will require the researcher to measure each of those subcomponents. Second, researchers must deal with the reliability and validity issues of the scales used to collect data. Consequently, researchers are forced to measure each subcomponent using a set of different scale items. To illustrate these two points, consider the Tiger Woods as a spokesperson example in Exhibit 12.3. Here the main construct of interest was "credibility as a spokesperson." Credibility was made up of three key subcomponents (expertise, trustworthiness, and attractiveness). Each of the subcomponents was measured using five different seven-point scale items (e.g., expertise—knowledgeable/unknowledgeable, expert/not expert, skilled/unskilled, qualified/unqualified, experienced/inexperienced).

Another point to remember about multiple-item scales is that there are two types of scales: formative and reflective. A **formative composite scale** is used when each of the individual scale items measures some part of the whole construct, object, or phenomenon. For example, to measure the *overall image* of a 2005 Hummer H2, the researchers would have to measure the different attributes that make up that automobile's image, such as performance, resale value, gas mileage, styling, price, safety features, sound system, and craftsmanship. By creating a scale that measures each pertinent attribute, the researcher can sum the parts into a complete (e.g., formative) whole that measures the overall image held by respondents toward the 2005 Hummer.

With a **reflective composite scale** design, researchers use multiple items to measure an individual subcomponent of a construct, object, or phenomenon. For example, in isolating the investigation to the *performance* dimension of the 2005 Hummer H2, the researcher can use a common performance rating scale and measure those identified attributes (e.g., trouble-free, MPG rating, comfort of ride, workmanship, overall quality, dependability, responsiveness) which make up the performance dimension. Each of

Single-item scale design A scale format that collects data about only one attribute of an object or construct.

Multiple-item scale design A scale format that simultaneously collects data on several attributes of an object or construct.

Formative composite scale A scale format that uses several individual scale items to measure different parts of the whole object or construct.

Reflective composite scale A scale format that uses multiple scale items to measure one component of an object or construct.

these attributes reflects performance and an average of the reflective scale items can be interpreted as a measure of performance.

Recap of Key Measurement Design Issues

The main design issues related to both construct development and scale measurement are reviewed below.

Construct Development Issues

Researchers should clearly define and operationalize constructs before they attempt to develop their scales. For each construct being investigated, the researcher must determine its dimensionality traits (i.e., single versus multidimensional) before developing appropriate scales. In a multidimensional construct, all relevant dimensions must be identified as well as their related attributes.

Avoid creating *double-barreled dimensions*. That is, do not present two different dimensions of a construct as if they are one. For example, when investigating consumers' perceptions of service quality, do not attempt to combine the service provider's technological competence and diagnostic competence as one dimension. Within a singular dimension, avoid using double-barreled attributes. For example, avoid asking a respondent to rate two attributes simultaneously (e.g., "indicate to what extent you agree or disagree that Martha Stewart perjured herself and should have been indicted"). For a multidimensional construct, use scale designs in which multiple attribute items are used separately to measure each dimension independently from the other dimensions (see the Tiger Woods example in Exhibit 12.3). Construct validity assessments should always be performed prior to creating the final scales.

Scale Measurement Issues

When phrasing the question/setup element of a scale, use clear wording and avoid ambiguity. Also avoid using "leading" words or phrases in any scale measurement's question/setup.

Regardless of the data collection method (e.g., personal, telephone, or computer-assisted interviews, or any type of offline or online self-administered survey), all necessary instructions for both respondent and interviewer should be part of the scale measurement's setup. All instructions should be kept simple and clear. When using multiattribute items, make sure the items are phrased *unidimensionally* (e.g., avoid double-barreled item phrases). When determining the appropriate set of scale point descriptors, make sure the descriptors are relevant to the type of data being sought. Use only scale descriptors and formats that have been pretested and evaluated for scale reliability and validity. Scale descriptors should have adequate discriminatory power, be mutually exclusive, and make sense to the respondent.

Screening Questions

Screening questions (also referred to as *screeners* or *filter questions*) should always be used in any type of interview. Their purpose is to identify qualified prospective respondents and prevent unqualified respondents from being included in the study. It is difficult to use screening questions in many self-administered questionnaires, except for computer-assisted surveys. Screening questions need to be separately administered before the beginning of the main interview.

Skip Questions

Skip questions (also referred to as *conditional* or *branching* questions) should be avoided if at all possible. If they are needed, the instructions must be clearly communicated to the respondent or interviewer. Skip questions can appear anywhere within the questionnaire and are used if the next question (or set of questions) should be responded to only by a respondent who meets a previous condition. A simple expression of a skip command might be: "If you answered "yes" to Question 5, skip to Question 9." Skip questions help ensure that only specifically qualified respondents answer certain items.

Ethical Responsibility of the Researcher

In the development of scale measurements, the researcher should use the most appropriate scales possible. Intentionally using scale measurements to produce biased information raises questions about the professional ethics of the researcher. To illustrate, let's revisit the Aca Joe example at the beginning of the chapter.

Any set of scale point descriptors used to frame a noncomparative rating scale can be manipulated to bias the results in any direction. Inappropriate scale descriptors to collect brand-image data can be used to create a positive view of one brand or a negative view of a competitor's brand, which might not paint a true picture of the situation. To illustrate this point, let's assume that in creating the seven-point semantic differential scale used to collect the image data for the seven dimensions of Aca Joe's store image (i.e., quality, assortment, style/fashion, prices of merchandise, store's location, overall reputation, and knowledgeability of sales staff), the researcher decided not to follow many of the process guidelines for developing accurate scale measurements, including no pretesting of the scales. Instead, he just used his intuitive judgment of what he thought the owner of Aca Joe was hoping for. Consequently, the following semantic differential scale measurement was developed:

For each of the following attributes, please circle the number that best expresses how you would rate that attribute for the Aca Joe retail store.

Quality of Merchandise	Truly Terrible	1	2	3	4	5	6	7	Outstanding
Merchandise Assortment	Limited	1	2	3	4	5	6	7	Extremely Wide
Style of Merchandise	Very Stylish	1	2	3	4	5	6	7	Not Stylish
Merchandise Prices	Extremely High	1	2	3	4	5	6	7	Reasonable
Overall Store Reputation	Very Good	1	2	3	4	5	6	7	Extremely Poor
Store's Location	Very Inconvenient	1	2	3	4	5	6	7	Definitely Convenient
Sales Staff	Very Professional	1	2	3	4	5	6	7	Very Unprofessional

Now, select a retail store of your choice, assume it to be Aca Joe, and rate that store using the above scale. Interpret the image profile that you create and compare it to Aca Joe's desired and actual images described in the chapter opener. What differences do you detect? How objective were your ratings? Did you find yourself rating your store positively like Aca Joe? What problems did you encounter on each dimension? Using the above scale, a researcher can negatively bias evaluations of competitors' image by providing mildly negative descriptors against strong descriptors or vice versa. Ethically, it is important to use balanced scales with comparable positive and negative descriptors. In addition, when a researcher does not follow scale development guidelines, responses can be biased. This example also points out the need to pretest and establish scale measurements that have adequate reliability, validity, and generalizability. Remember, scales that are unreliable are invalid, or lack generalizability to the defined target population, will provide misleading findings (garbage in, garbage out).

MARKETING RESEARCH IN ACTION

Part 2

Scale Measurements Used in Creating a Customer Loyalty Index[8]

This is the second part of the Marketing Research in Action that began at the end of Chapter 11. Recall that researchers at Burke Customer Satisfaction Associates measured the three main components (i.e., overall customer satisfaction, likelihood of repeat business, and likelihood to recommend the company) making up their construct of Secure Customer Index (SCI).

Measuring Customer Loyalty

At Burke Customer Satisfaction Associates, these three components (i.e., overall customer satisfaction, likelihood of repeat business, and likelihood to recommend the company) are measured by looking at the combined scores of three survey questions. For example, in examining the overall satisfaction of restaurant customers, we ask, "Overall, how satisfied were you with your visit to this restaurant?" To examine their likelihood to recommend: "How likely would you be to recommend this restaurant to a friend or associate?" And finally, to examine the likelihood of repeat purchases, we ask, "How likely are you to choose to visit this restaurant again?"

With these three components, and the appropriate scales for each, secure customers would be defined as those giving the most positive responses across all three components. All other customers would be considered vulnerable or at risk of defecting to a competitor. The degree of vulnerability can be determined from responses to these questions.

When we interpret a company's SCI, we typically compare it to other relevant SCI scores, such as the company's SCI score in past years, the SCI scores of competitors, and the SCI scores of "best-in-class" companies. While a company should always strive for higher scores, understanding how "good" or "bad" a given score might be is best done in comparative terms.

Customer Loyalty and Market Performance

Increasingly, we are able to link customer satisfaction and customer loyalty to bottom-line benefits. By examining customer behaviors over time and comparing them to SCI scores, we see a strong connection between secure customers and repeat purchasing of products or services. For example, we examined the relationship between customer satisfaction survey data and repeat purchasing levels in the computer industry. Secure customers in this industry were twice as likely to renew contracts than were vulnerable customers. Secure customers also were twice as likely to expand their business with their primary vendor.

As we've continued to look at cases across customer and industry types, we've found other compelling illustrations that show a connection between the index scores and financial or market performance. These findings demonstrate the value of examining index scores not only across an industry but also over time within the same company to determine changes in the proportion of secure customers.

Competition, Customers, and Surveys

As with any measurement, a customer loyalty index may be influenced by other factors depending on the industry, market characteristics, or research methods. These factors should be considered when interpreting the meaning of any loyalty index. Industries with more than one provider of services tend to produce higher customer satisfaction scores than industries with limited choices. For example, the cable industry, which in many markets still tends to be monopolistic, generally has lower customer satisfaction scores in comparison to other industries. The notion that competition breeds more opportunities clearly affects customer satisfaction as well.

A second factor that may contribute indirectly to a customer loyalty index score is the type of market being examined. In specialty markets where the product is tailored or customized for the customer, loyalty index scores tend to be higher than in general or non-customized markets. For example, index scores for customers of a specialized software or network configuration would likely be higher than scores for customers of an airline.

The type of customer being measured also may influence the index scores. For example, business-to-business customers may score differently than general consumers. Again, the type of industry involved also will influence the type of customers being examined.

Finally, the data collection method may influence the customer's response. Researchers have long recognized that the different methods used to collect information, such as live interviews, mail surveys, and telephone interviews, may produce varying results.

Recognizing these factors is important not only in collecting information but also in interpreting an index. Learning how to minimize or correct these influences will enhance the validity or true "reading" of a customer loyalty index.

Using Data to Evaluate Your Own Efforts

Businesses committed to customer-driven quality must integrate the voice of the customer into their business operations. A customer loyalty index provides actionable information by demonstrating the ratio of secure customers to vulnerable customers. An index acts as a baseline or yardstick for management to create goals for the organization, and helps to focus efforts for continuous improvement over time. And as changes and initiatives are implemented in the organization, the index's score may be monitored as a way of evaluating initiatives.

Using a customer loyalty index helps companies better understand their customers. By listening to customers, implementing change, and continuously monitoring the results, companies can focus their improvement efforts with the goal of winning and keeping customers.

Hands-On Exercise

Using your knowledge from the chapter and the information provided in this illustration, answer each of the following questions. Make sure you can defend your answers.

1. What are several weaknesses associated with how Burke Customer Satisfaction Associates measured its Secure Customer Index (SCI)? Make sure you clearly identify each weakness and explain why you feel it is a weakness.

2. If you were the head researcher, what types of scale measurement designs would you have used to collect the needed data for calculating SCI? Why? Design a sample of the scale measurements that you would use.

3. Do you agree or disagree with the Burke Associates' interpretation of the value they provide their clients using the Customer Loyalty Index? Support your response.

Summary of Learning Objectives

■ **Discuss what an attitude is and its three components.**
An *attitude* is a learned predisposition to act in a consistent positive or negative way to a given object, idea, or set of information. Attitudes are state-of-mind constructs that are not directly observable. Attitudes can be thought of as having three components: cognitive, affective, and behavioral. Marketing researchers and decision makers need to understand all three components. The *cognitive component* of an attitude is the person's beliefs, perceptions, and knowledge about an object and its attributes. The *affective component* of an attitude is the person's emotional feelings toward a given object. This component is the one most frequently expressed when a person is asked to verbalize his or her attitude toward some object, person, or phenomenon. The *behavioral component,* also sometimes referred to as a *conative component,* is a person's intended or actual behavioral response to an object.

■ **Design Likert, semantic differential, and behavior intention scales, and explain their strengths and weaknesses.**
Likert scale designs uniquely employ a set of agreement/disagreement scale descriptors to capture a person's attitude toward a given object or behavior. Contrary to popular belief, a Likert scale format does not measure a person's complete attitude, only the cognitive structure. Semantic differential scale formats are exceptional in capturing a person's perceptual image profile about a given object or behavior. This scale format is unique in that it uses a set of bipolar scales to measure several different yet interrelated factors (both cognitive and affective) of a given object or behavior.

Multiattribute affect scales use scale point descriptors that consist of relative magnitudes of an attitude (e.g., "very important," "somewhat important," "not too important," "not at all important," or "like very much," "like somewhat," "neither like nor dislike," "dislike somewhat," "dislike very much"). With respect to behavior intention scale formats, the practitioner is interested in obtaining some idea of the likelihood that people (e.g., actual or potential consumers, customers, buyers) will demonstrate some type of predictable behavior toward purchasing an object or service. The scale point descriptors like "definitely would," "probably would," "probably would not," and "definitely would not" are normally used in an intentions scale format. If

the information objective is that of collecting raw data that can directly predict some type of marketplace behavior, then behavior intention scales should be used in the study. In turn, if the objective is understanding the reasons that certain types of marketplace behavior take place, then it is necessary to incorporate scale measurement formats that capture both the person's cognitive belief structures and feelings.

■ **Discuss the differences between noncomparative and comparative scale designs as well as the appropriateness of rating and ranking scale measurements.**
The main difference is that comparative scale measurements require the respondent to do some type of direct comparison between the attributes of the scale from the same known reference point, whereas noncomparative scales rate each attribute independently of the other attributes making up the scale measurement. The data from comparative scales must be interpreted in relative terms and only activate the assignment and order scaling properties. Noncomparative scale data are treated as interval or ratio, and more advanced statistical procedures can be employed in analyzing the data structures. One benefit of comparative scales is that they allow for identifying small differences between the attributes, constructs, or objects. In addition, their comparative scale designs require fewer theoretical assumptions and are easier for respondents to understand and respond to than are many of the noncomparative scale designs. However, noncomparative scales provide opportunity for greater insights into the constructs and their components.

■ **Identify and discuss the critical aspects of consumer attitudes and other marketplace phenomena that require measurement to allow us to make better decisions.**
In order for organizations to make informed decisions regarding their suppliers, customers, competitors, employees, or organizational members, they must gather detailed, accurate information. The selection of a supplier may rest partially on their history of on-time delivery, reputation for quality, and experience within the industry. Information concerning the preferences, purchase behavior, shopping patterns, demographics, and attitudes of consumers can be vital to the success or failure of an organization.

Similarly, in-depth profiles of competitors may reveal opportunities or challenges facing the company and can lead to coherent plans designed to create a significant competitive advantage. If consumers prefer a competitor's product, then it would be quite valuable to understand through the use of proper measurement techniques why such preferences exist.

■ Discuss the overall rules of measurement and explain the differences between single versus multiple measures of a construct as well as direct versus indirect measures.

No single set of rules exists for all measurements; however, certain standards can be applied to the measurement process. For example, the rules for correctly using a thermometer to measure the temperature of water would be quite different from the rules for the use of a telescope to measure the distance to a star. Even so, the rules must be explicit and detailed so as to allow consistent application of the instrument.

Key Terms and Concepts

Affect global approach   424

Affective component   391

Attitude   391

Behavioral (conative) component   391

Behavior intention scale   399

Cognitive component   391

Comparative rating scale   403

Constant sums scales   406

Formative composite scale   407

Graphic rating scales   404

Halo effect bias   395

Likert scale   392

Multiple-item scale design   407

Noncomparative rating scale   403

Paired-comparison scales   406

Performance rating scales   404

Rank-order scales   406

Reflective composite scale   407

Semantic differential scale   394

Single-item scale design   407

Trilogy approach   416

Review Questions

1. Conceptually, what is an attitude? Is there one best method of measuring a person's attitude? Why or why not?

2. Explain the major differences between "rating" and "ranking" scales. Which is a better scale measurement technique for collecting attitudinal data on salesforce performance of people who sell commercial laser printers? Why?

3. When collecting importance data about the features business travelers use to select a hotel, should a researcher use a balanced or an unbalanced scale measurement? Why?

4. Explain the main differences between using "even-point" and "odd-point" scale measurement designs for collecting purchase intention data. Is one approach better than the other? Why?

5. If a semantic differential has eight attribute dimensions, should all the positive pole descriptors be on the left side and all the negative pole descriptors be on the right side of the scale continuum? Why or why not?

6. What are the benefits and limitations of comparative scale measurements? Design a paired-comparison scale that will allow you to determine brand preference between Bud Light, Miller Lite, Coors Light, and Old Milwaukee Light beers.

7. What are the weaknesses associated with the use of a Likert scale design to measure customers' attitudes toward the purchasing of products at Wal-Mart?

Discussion Questions

1. Develop a semantic differential scale that can identify the perceptual profile differences between Outback Steakhouse and Longhorn Steakhouse restaurants.

2. Explain the differences between a Likert summated scale format and a numeric rating scale format. Should a Likert scale ever be considered an interval scale? Why or why not? Now develop a forced-choice Likert scale measurement that can be used to measure consumers' perceptions about the movie *Titanic*.

3. Design a behavior intention scale that can answer the following research question: "To what extent are college students likely to purchase a new automobile within six months after graduating?" Discuss the potential shortcomings of your scale design.

4. Develop an appropriate set of attitudinal scales that would allow you to capture the cognitive and affective components of college students' overall attitude concerning the United States' involvement in rebuilding the country of Iraq.

5. **EXPERIENCE THE INTERNET.** One company that relies heavily on asking Americans about their attitudes and values is SRI International. It has developed a unique segmentation technique that uses VALS-type data to classify people into different lifestyle categories. Get on the Internet and go to SRI's Web site at www.future.sri.com:/valshome.html. Take their short survey to determine your VALS (Values and Lifestyles) type. While you are taking the survey, evaluate what scale measurements are being used. What type of possible design bias might exist?

6. What are the main differences between the Fishbein modeling approaches of "attitude-toward-object" and "attitude-toward-behavior"? (See Appendix 12.A discussions.) Discuss in which situations each of these two modeling approaches would be more appropriate than trying to employ the "affect global" approach in investigating consumers (commercial customers) attitudes.

7. The results from two focus groups conducted on restaurant characteristics among 20 known customers suggested that the following features were thought about during their dining experiences: (1) friendly employees, (2) fun place to eat at, (3) size of portions served, (4) freshness of food, (5) prices, (6) attractiveness of interior, (7) food taste, (8) employees' knowledge, (9) food quality, and (10) speed of service. With these insights, the owners of the Santa Fe Grill Mexican Restaurant want to gain clearer insight into the following three questions: "How important are those restaurant features to known and prospective customers when selecting a Mexican themed restaurant to eat at?" "How well does the Santa Fe Grill perform on those features?" and "What is the likelihood that people will revisit the restaurant within the next 30 days?" To help the owners answer these three research questions, develop a specific scale measurement (attitudinal, affective, or behavioral) that could be used to capture the needed data for each of the stated research questions. (Make sure that each of your scale measurements include all three components of a scale measurement, i.e., question/setup, specific attributes/dimensions, scale point descriptors.)

appendix 12.A

Trilogy and Affect Global Approaches

This appendix provides an overview of the theoretical trilogy and affect global approaches to explaining the structure of an attitude. The discussion illustrates how different attitude scaling formats yield different results about the same attitude construct.

The Trilogy Approach

Trilogy approach The theoretical viewpoint that a person's overall attitude consists of the interaction between three specific components: the person's (1) beliefs (cognitive), (2) feelings (affect), and (3) outcome behavior (conative).

The **trilogy approach** suggests that understanding of a person's complete attitude toward an object, a person, or a phenomenon requires an understanding of the *cognitive, affective, and conative* components that make up that attitude. It is the integration of these three components that allows a person to create an overall perception of a given object. Exhibit 12.A.1 illustrates the integrative nature of these components.

The *cognitive component* of an attitude represents the person's beliefs, perceptions, and knowledge about the specified object and its attributes. These aspects are the key elements and outcomes of learning. For example, think back to the 39 days that followed the U.S. presidential election on November 7, 2000. Let's consider the notion that George W. Bush stole the election with the help of his younger brother Jeb, then governor of Florida. Many people held a variety of different beliefs about this, which they developed as they learned

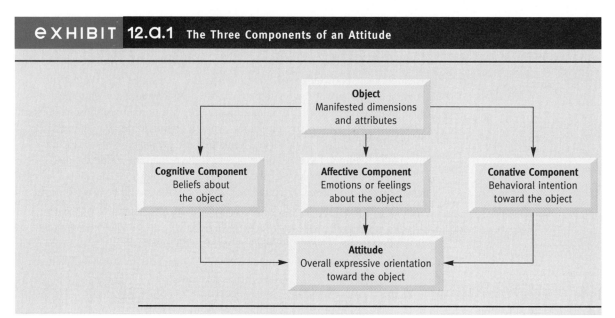

EXHIBIT 12.A.1 The Three Components of an Attitude

Object
Manifested dimensions and attributes

Cognitive Component
Beliefs about the object

Affective Component
Emotions or feelings about the object

Conative Component
Behavioral intention toward the object

Attitude
Overall expressive orientation toward the object

more about the situation. Here is a sample of those beliefs:

- Al Gore received more votes in Florida than did George W. Bush.
- Florida did not count all the votes that were cast by its citizens.
- Florida's voting process disenfranchised a significant number of key voters.
- Al Gore and the Democratic Party were outmaneuvered by the Republicans.
- George W. Bush won the state in accordance with Florida voting laws.
- People in Florida cannot count ballots.

These statements are selected beliefs about some of the attributes that people formed regarding the Florida voting phenomenon. Although any one of these beliefs by itself would provide a poor representation of the people's attitude concerning Bush's stealing the U.S. presidency from Gore, in combination they form the basis for identifying people's overall attitude on the vote–recount phenomenon. A key point to remember here is that most state-of-mind objects or constructs investigated by researchers will most likely have a multidimensional aspect requiring researchers to include sets of attributes in their scale measurement designs. In reality, people have hundreds of beliefs about many different items, attributes, and objects that make up their everyday environment.

An attitude's *affective component* represents the person's emotions or feelings toward the given object. This is the component most frequently expressed when a person is asked to verbalize his or her attitude toward some object, person, or phenomenon. A simple way to view this affective component is to think of it as being the amount of emotion or feeling a person attaches to each of his or her individual beliefs. This component serves as a mechanism that enables a person to create some type of hierarchical order among a set of beliefs about an object or behavior. For example, a person considering the purchase of a new 2005 Acura 3.2 TL might identify several common factors about cars that in general are important in the selection process. The affective component of that person's attitude toward the Acura allows him or her to decide which of the car's attributes (engine power, safety system, sport option package, fuel economy, price, etc.) hold more importance (or less importance) with regard to that specific car. At this point, remember that people's emotions or feelings toward an object are anchored to a set of recognizable beliefs about that object.

The *conative component* of an attitude relates to the person's intended or actual behavioral response to the given object. The conative component is also referred to as the *behavioral component.* This part of an attitude tends to be an observable outcome driven by the interaction of a person's cognitive component (beliefs) and affective component (emotional strength of those beliefs) as they relate to the given object. In the Acura example, the person's purchase intention decision to buy (conative component) a gold-colored 2005 Acura 3.2 TL with leather and wood interior, an antilock braking system, cruise control, automatic seat and side mirror adjustment, a high-performance six-cylinder engine, dual airbags, and a high-tech DVD sound system would be directly influenced by the set of beliefs (cognitive components) and the emotional feelings of importance (affective components) attached to those beliefs concerning each of the listed options that are part of the Acura car.

The key point to remember about the trilogy approach is that the complete measurement of attitudes cannot be achieved using a single-item or multiple-item global scale design but rather requires the development of some type of multiplicative-additive model. The fundamental reasons behind the need for a model are that most objects are really nothing more than a composite of many different parts (or attributes). People have the capability of developing a separate attitude toward each attribute, and attitudes themselves tend to consist of distinguishable components. In other words, to measure attitudes, researchers must collect several types of data (cognitive, affective, and conative) about the object and its attributes of interest and then, through a modeling process, derive a composite attitude score. Several types of multiplicative-additive model have been developed within the trilogy framework, but we will limit our discussion to two of the most frequently used models: attitude-toward-object and attitude-toward-behavior.

Attitude-toward-Object Model

One popular attitudinal model is Fishbein's *attitude-toward-object model,* which is normally presented in the form of the following equation:[9]

$$Attitude_O = \sum_{i=1}^{k} b_i e_i$$

where $Attitude_O$ is a separate, indirectly derived composite measure (sometimes considered a global measure) of a person's combined thoughts and feelings for or against the given object (e.g., product, service, brand, manufacturer, retail establishment); b_i is the strength of the belief that the person holds toward the ith attribute of the object (e.g., the 2005 Acura 3.2 TL has a satisfactory mileage rating); e_i is the person's affect evaluation (expressed feeling or importance) of the belief toward that ith attribute of the object (e.g., it is very important that my car has an excellent mileage rating); and Σ indicates that there are k salient attributes making up the object over which the multiplicative combinations of b_i and e_i for those attributes are summated.

To illustrate the development processes for the scales researchers use to collect the data to capture a person's overall attitude toward an object through the attitude-toward-object modeling approach, we expand the 2005 Acura 3.2 TL example. Let's say the overall research objective is to collect data that will enable management to better understand the attitudes owners hold toward the *performance* of a 2005 Acura 3.2 TL. Acura's marketing experts worked with J. D. Power and Associates to develop a two-phase research plan that includes both qualitative and quantitative research activities to create the different scale measurements needed to collect the cognitive components (b_i) and corresponding affective components (e_i) that relate to assessing respondents' attitudes toward the performance of an automobile. First, using qualitative research practices, several general focus group interviews were conducted among a cross section of people who were known to have purchased a new automobile within the past 12 months. One topic of those interviews was the elements people use to judge the performance of automobiles. This part of the research discovered and identified the following seven attributes:

1. The perception of the car as *trouble-free.*

2. The actual *miles per gallon (MPG) rating* of the automobile.

3. The *comfort* of the ride provided by the car.

4. The *craftsmanship* (or workmanship) built into the automobile.

5. The *overall quality* of the automobile.

6. The *dependability* (or reliability) of the automobile.

7. The *responsiveness* of the car in different weather conditions.

To validate these seven attributes as meaningful subfactors people use to assess their attitudes toward the performance of automobiles, the researchers conducted a pilot study where 300 randomly selected respondents were given a survey that included these seven attributes and were asked to judge them using a four-point scale scheme where 4 = "definitely a factor of performance," 3 = "generally a factor of performance," 2 = "only somewhat a factor of performance," and 1 = "not at all a factor of performance." The researchers then analyzed the data collected from the pilot study using direct cognitive structural (DCS) analysis. The results demonstrated that all seven attributes were considered factors people used in assessing the performance of automobiles, all having mean values of 3.5 or higher.

Using the information generated from the first phase of the research project, researchers planned and executed the second phase by conducting a more elaborate quantitative study where surveys were administered to 1,500 known Acura 3.2 TL owners who were randomly selected from Acura (Honda America) Corporation's customer data bank. To capture these respondents' emotional importance (e_i) associated with each of the seven performance attributes, the affective scale measurement displayed in Exhibit 12.A.2 was

---

exhibit 12.a.2 Scale Measurements Used in Determining the Attitude toward the *Performance* of a 2005 Acura 3.2 TL

AFFECTIVE (IMPORTANCE) SCALE MEASUREMENT

Using the scale below, please write a number from one (1) to six (6) in the space provided that best expresses how emotionally important you feel each listed attribute is to you in assessing the performance of an automobile.

Not at all Important	Only Slightly Important	Somewhat Important	Important	Definitely Important	Extremely Important
(1)	(2)	(3)	(4)	(5)	(6)

ATTRIBUTES

____ The perception of the car as trouble-free (or practically defect-free).

____ The actual miles per gallon (MPG) rating of the automobile.

____ The comfort (or smoothness) of the ride provided by the car.

____ The craftsmanship (or workmanship) built into the automobile.

____ The overall quality of the automobile.

____ The dependability (or reliability) of the automobile.

____ The responsiveness of the car in different weather conditions.

COGNITIVE (BELIEF) SCALE MEASUREMENT

Thinking about all experiences with driving your 2005 Acura 3.2 TL, we would like to know your opinion about each of the following factors. For each factor, please circle the number that best expresses how you believe your 2005 Acura 3.2 TL has performed on that factor. For any factor(s) that are not relevant to your assessment, please circle the "zero" (0), which means "not applicable" (N/A).

2005 Acura 3.2 TL	Truly Terrible	Fair	Average	Good	Excellent	Truly Exceptional	(N/A)
Trouble- (practically defect-) free	1	2	3	4	5	6	0
Miles per gallon (MPG) rating	1	2	3	4	5	6	0
Comfort (smoothness) of the ride	1	2	3	4	5	6	0
Craftsmanship (or workmanship)	1	2	3	4	5	6	0
Overall quality	1	2	3	4	5	6	0
Dependability (or reliability)	1	2	3	4	5	6	0
Responsiveness (or handling)	1	2	3	4	5	6	0

developed and tested for reliability (internal consistency). Using this scale measurement, respondents were asked to write a number from 1 to 6 in the space provided that best expressed how emotionally important they felt each listed factor was to them in assessing the performance of a new automobile. In contrast, the six-point cognitive scale measurement displayed in the exhibit was developed, tested for reliability (internal consistency), and used to capture the respondents' evaluative performance beliefs (b_i) about the 2005 Acura 3.2 TL. In applying the cognitive scale measurement, respondents were asked to circle a number from 1 to 6 that best expressed how well their 2005 Acura 3.2 TL performed on each listed factor. In those cases where a particular factor might not be relevant in their assessment, respondents were instructed to circle the zero (0) response, which meant "not applicable" (N/A).

After collecting the cognitive (b_i) and corresponding affective (e_i) data on the seven attributes, researchers can apply the multiplicative-additive model to determine a respondent's overall composite attitude toward the performance of the 2005 Acura 3.2 TL or the respondent's individual attitudes for each of the separate seven attributes. To see how researchers can determine a respondent's individual attitude toward a particular attribute, let's use attribute 1, perception of the car *as being a trouble-free* automobile. We simply multiply the respondent's raw belief score (b_i) assigned to this factor by the corresponding raw importance score (e_i), resulting in a possible score range of 1 ($1 \times 1 = 1$) to 36 ($6 \times 6 = 36$). The score would be interpreted to mean that the lower the value, the weaker the attitude and the higher the value, the stronger the attitude. In determining a respondent's overall attitude toward the *performance* of the 2005 Acura 3.2 TL, the researchers would take each of the individually derived attitude scores for each factor and simply add them together into one composite score that could range between 7 (7 attributes $\times 1 = 7$) on the low end and 252 (7 attributes $\times 36 = 252$) at the high end. Again, interpretation of the composite scores would be that the lower the composite value, the weaker the overall attitude and the higher the score, the stronger the attitude.

This modeling approach also allows the researchers to determine the average attitudes held by all the respondents included in the study for each attribute as well as the comprehensive performance attitude held toward the 2005 Acura 3.2 TL. To analyze the group attitude toward a particular attribute, the researchers with the use of a computer would calculate the 1,500 individual attitude scores for that attribute, then add those scores together, then divide that total by the total number of respondents who contributed in deriving that total score. The average group attitude score for any of the individual attributes would range between 1 and 36 and be interpreted similarly to an individual attitude score. A similar procedure would be used to determine the group's overall composite performance attitude toward the 2005 Acura 3.2 TL. Researchers would have the computer calculate the individual composite scores for each of the seven attributes among the 1,500 respondents, add those scores together, then divide that total by the sample size of respondents used to derive the total attitude score. Interpretation of the group's average composite attitude score would be the same as the interpretation of an individual's composite score described earlier.

It is important to remember that in this measurement approach, equal emphasis is given to measuring both a person's beliefs (cognitive) and a person's feelings (affective) toward the attributes of the object under investigation. This modeling approach provides researchers and decision makers with a lot of diagnostic insight into the components that make up the consumer's attitude. Decision makers can learn how and what the customer used to evaluate either the potential or actual performance of a given object (e.g., a 2005 Acura 3.2 TL).

e X H I B I T 12.a.3 **Scale Measurements Used in Determining the Attitude toward** *Purchasing* **a 2005 Acura 3.2 TL**

In this example, both qualitative and quantitative research activities were employed to create the different scale measurements needed to collect both the cognitive components (b_i) and the affective components (a_i) that relate to assessing respondents' attitude toward the purchasing of automobiles (attitude-toward-behavior).

I. Qualitative research activities

A. Several general focus group interviews were conducted among a cross section of people who were known to be considering the purchasing of a new automobile within the next six months. One of the topics of those interviews was the elements people deemed as factors in purchasing a new automobile. The study discovered and identified the following 15 factors.

1. The car is viewed as being a trouble-free (or practically defect-free) automobile.
2. The car's miles per gallon (MPG) rating.
3. The comfort (or smoothness) in the car's ride.
4. The craftsmanship (or workmanship) built into the car.
5. The overall quality of the car.
6. The dependability (or reliability) of the car.
7. The car will have responsiveness in different weather conditions.
8. The car's potential resale value.
9. The warranty guarantee program associated with the car.
10. The car must have the styling features (or options) I want.
11. The car's price is affordable.
12. Overall reputation of the dealership.
13. Reputation of the dealer's service department.
14. The car's safety features.
15. The quality reputation of the manufacturer.

B. To validate the 15 factors as the meaningful items that people consider in their purchasing of a new automobile, 250 randomly selected respondents were given a survey that included those 15 factors and were asked to express the degree to which each one was a factor of consideration they would use in purchasing a new automobile, using the following five-point scale: (5) "a critical factor"; (4) "definitely a factor"; (3) "generally a factor"; (2) "only somewhat of a factor"; (1) "not at all a factor." With direct cognitive structural (DCS) analysis, the results demonstrated that all 15 factors were reasonable elements of consideration that people used in their process of purchasing a new automobile, all having mean values of 3.5 or higher.

[Importance Scale]

Not at all Important	Only Slightly Important	Somewhat Important	Generally Important	Definitely Important	Extremely Important
(1)	(2)	(3)	(4)	(5)	(6)

Buying a car . . .

___ that is *trouble- (or practically defect-) free.*

___ with an *acceptable miles per gallon (MPG) rating.*

___ that provides a *comfortable (or smooth) ride.*

___ that has the *craftsmanship (or workmanship)* built into it.

___ that is built with *overall quality.*

___ that is *dependable (or reliable).*

___ that will have *responsiveness* in different weather conditions.

___ that keeps its *resale value.*

___ that is backed by a solid *warranty (or guarantee) program.*

___ that has the *styling features (or options)* I want.

___ that has a *price that is affordable.*

___ from a dealership having *overall reputation excellence.*

___ from a dealership whose service department is *reputable.*

___ that has the *safety features* I want.

___ that is made by a manufacturer with a *quality reputation.*

(continued)

eXHIBIT 12.a.3 Scale Measurements Used in Determining the Attitude toward *Purchasing* a 2005 Acura 3.2 TL, *continued*

II. Quantitative research activities

A. To capture respondents' emotional importance (a_i) associated with each of the 15 purchasing attributes, the following scale measurement was developed and tested for internal consistency.

Using the affective (importance) scale below, please write a number from 1 to 6 in the space provided that best expresses how emotionally important you feel each listed factor is to you in purchasing a new automobile.

B. To capture respondents' evaluative expectation beliefs (b_i) about the 2005 Acura 3.2 TL being able to meet the individual's needs/wants, the following scale measurement was developed and tested for internal consistency.

Regarding all your expectations about a new car, we would like to know your opinions about each of the following factors as they relate to the 2005 Acura 3.2 TL. For each factor please circle the number that best expresses the extent to which you agree or disagree that buying a 2005 Acura 3.2 TL will meet that factor. For any factor(s) that are not relevant to your assessment, please circle "zero" (0), which means "not applicable" (NA).

Buying a 2005 Acura 3.2 TL Will . . .	Definitely Agree	Generally Agree	Slightly Agree	Slightly Disagree	Generally Disagree	Definitely Disagree	(NA)
	(6)	(5)	(4)	(3)	(2)	(1)	(0)
Give me a *trouble-free (or practically defect-free)* mode of transportation	6	5	4	3	2	1	0
Give me a car with acceptable *miles per gallon (MPG) rating*	6	5	4	3	2	1	0
Allow me a *comfortable smooth) ride*	6	5	4	3	2	1	0
Give me a car with *great craftsmanship*	6	5	4	3	2	1	0
Give me a car with the *overall quality* I was looking for	6	5	4	3	2	1	0
Give me a car that is *dependable (reliable)*	6	5	4	3	2	1	0
Give me a car that has *responsiveness* in different weather conditions	6	5	4	3	2	1	0
Give me a car that keeps its *resale value*	6	5	4	3	2	1	0
Give me a solid *warranty (guarantee) program*	6	5	4	3	2	1	0
Give me a car that has the *styling features (or options)* I want	6	5	4	3	2	1	0
Give me a car I can *afford*	6	5	4	3	2	1	0
Give me a car from a dealership with an *overall reputation of excellence*	6	5	4	3	2	1	0
Give me a car from a dealership whose service department is *reputable*	6	5	4	3	2	1	0
Give me a car that has the *safety features* I want	6	5	4	3	2	1	0
Be a car made by a manufacturer with a *quality reputation*	6	5	4	3	2	1	0

Attitude-toward-Behavior Model

Another popular multiplicative-additive attitude model is Fishbein's *attitude-toward-behavior model.*[10] This model captures a person's attitude toward his or her *behavior* with a given object rather than the attitude toward the object itself. One benefit of this approach is that it gives researchers a picture that more closely demonstrates the actual behavior of individuals than does the attitude-toward-object model. Normally, the attitude-toward-behavior model is presented by the following equation:

$$Attitude_{(beh)} = \sum_{i=1}^{n} b_i a_i$$

where *Attitude*$_{(beh)}$ is a separate, indirectly derived composite measure (sometimes considered an overall or global measure) of a person's combined thoughts and feelings for or against carrying out a specific action or behavior (e.g., the purchasing and driving of an Acura 3.2 TL); b_i is the strength of the person's belief that the ith specific action will lead to a specific outcome (e.g., that driving a 2005 Acura 3.2 TL will increase the person's social standing in the community); a_i is the person's expressed feeling (affect) toward the ith action outcome (e.g., the "favorableness feeling" of knowing friends admire the 2005 Acura 3.2 TL); and Σ indicates that there are n salient action outcomes making up the behavior over which the multiplicative combinations of b_i and a_i for those outcomes are summated.

Exhibit 12.A.3 illustrates the scales and procedures that might be used in an attitude-toward-behavior model to capture a person's overall attitude toward *purchasing* a 2005 Acura 3.2 TL. The key thing to remember here is that behavior-oriented beliefs are used and that greater emphasis is placed on measuring the person's affective evaluation of the behavioral outcome. This approach can help the researcher or decision maker understand why customers might behave as they do toward a given object. For example, collecting this type of attitudinal data offers the researcher insights into how and why customers judge the "service quality" construct associated with purchasing a new automobile.

From a scale measurement perspective, deciding which affective or cognitive scale point descriptors to use for an attitudinal scale measurement can be difficult. To help make that decision a little easier, we advocate the following *rules for deciding the use of a cognitive or affective based scale measurement:*

1. If the measurement objective is one of collecting data that enable you to describe *how the respondent is thinking,* then the focus should be on using scale descriptors that emphasize the *cognitive component.*

2. If the measurement objective is one of collecting data that enable you to identify *how the respondent is feeling,* then the focus should be on using scale descriptors that reflect the *affective component.*

The Affect Global Approach

In contrast to the trilogy approach to attitude measurement, the **affect global approach** maintains that an attitude is nothing more than a person's global (or overall) expression of favorable or unfavorable feelings toward a given object. The idea here is that a person's

Affect global approach
The theoretical approach of viewing the structure of a person's attitude as nothing more than the overall (global) expression of his or her favorable or unfavorable feeling toward a given object or behavior.

feelings can have dominant influence on his or her overall judgment of a given object. In other words, affect equals attitude. Within this approach, heavy emphasis is placed on capturing a person's global evaluative feeling of an object as being either positive or negative (i.e., liking/disliking, good/bad, satisfied/dissatisfied). Rating scale formats use a set of affective scale descriptors to capture the necessary responses. A limitation to the affect global approach is that it does not give the researcher insights into what beliefs contribute to the formation of the overall attitude. At best, the researcher can only speculate about the beliefs underlying the expressed emotional ratings. Exhibit 12.A.4 displays several affect-based attitude scale formats.

---

e X H I B I T 12.a.4   Examples of Affect Scale Formats for Measuring Attitudes

Example 1:

For each of the following listed items, please *fill in* the box that best expresses the extent to which you were satisfied or dissatisfied with that item at the time you purchased or leased your vehicle.

Items	Very Satisfied	Somewhat Satisfied	Somewhat Dissatisfied	Very Dissatisfied
Availability of parts and service	❑	❑	❑	❑
Trouble-free operation	❑	❑	❑	❑
Quality of workmanship	❑	❑	❑	❑
Reputation of manufacturer	❑	❑	❑	❑
Low purchase price	❑	❑	❑	❑
High resale value	❑	❑	❑	❑

Example 2:

Now we would like you to think about your driving experiences, then read each of the following statements and *fill in* the box that best expresses your feelings about that statement.

Statement	Like Very Much	Like Somewhat	Neither Like nor Dislike	Dislike Somewhat	Dislike Very Much
Selecting option for my car	❑	❑	❑	❑	❑
Changing the oil myself	❑	❑	❑	❑	❑
Driving on an extended trip	❑	❑	❑	❑	❑
Letting someone else do the driving	❑	❑	❑	❑	❑
Observing the speed limit at all times	❑	❑	❑	❑	❑

Example 3:

Overall, how angry or happy were you with the outcome of the 2004 Presidential election results? **(Please check only one response.)**

Very Angry	Somewhat Angry	Neither Angry nor Happy	Somewhat Happy	Very Happy
❑	❑	❑	❑	❑

Overview of the Links between Measurements of Cognitive, Affective, and Actual or Intended Behavior

Researchers tend to have mixed feelings about the strength of the relationships between the cognitive and affective components as they are used to explain or predict marketplace behaviors. Some researchers have found that when people's beliefs toward an object (e.g., the 2005 Acura 3.2 TL) coincide with their associated feelings, then attitude consistency exists and behavior is more likely to be predictable.[11] Yet others have found only limited relationships among the three components.[12] Today's marketers should be aware of several factors that can operate to reduce the consistency between measures of beliefs, feelings, and observations of marketplace behavior:[13] Elements that might create attitude measurement bias are:

1. A favorable attitude requires a need or motive before it can be translated into action.

2. Translating favorable beliefs and feelings into ownership requires ability.

3. Some attitude scales measure only one concept, construct, or object at a time.

4. If the cognitive and affective components are weakly held when the consumer obtains additional information in the shopping process, then the initial attitudes may give way to new ones.

5. Researchers typically measure attitudes of an isolated member of the family and the other members may affect purchase behavior.

6. Researchers generally measure brand attitudes independent of the purchase action.

7. In reality, it is difficult to measure all of the relevant aspects of an attitude.

chapter 13

Questionnaire Design and Issues

Learning Objectives

After reading this chapter, you will be able to

1. Identify and discuss the critical factors that can contribute to directly improving the accuracy of surveys, and explain why questionnaire development is not a simple process.

2. Discuss the theoretical principles of questionnaire design, and explain why a questionnaire is more than just asking a respondent some questions.

3. Identify and explain the communication roles of questionnaires in the data collection process.

4. Explain why the type of information needed to address a decision maker's questions and problems will substantially influence the structure and content of questionnaires.

5. List and discuss the 11 steps in the questionnaire development process, and tell how to eliminate some common mistakes in questionnaire designs.

6. Discuss and employ the "flowerpot" approach in developing scientific questionnaires.

7. Discuss the importance of cover letters, and explain the guidelines to help eliminate common mistakes in cover letter designs.

The Value of a Survey Instrument in Creating Meaningful Diagnostic Information

a major university in the Southeast decided it needed to prepare a marketing plan for a comprehensive on-campus housing program. The marketing plan would directly influence the quality of the students' living experiences at the university over the next 15 years. Administrators implemented a "Residence Life" program to identify, investigate, and gain insights into the factors on-campus students needed to enrich their academic and social experiences while attending the institution.

Some of their short-term goals evolved around the idea that high-quality on-campus living facilities and programs could help attract new students to the university. Other concerns focused on developing marketing strategies that could (1) aid the university in increasing the occupancy rate of its current housing facilities to 100 percent; (2) improve retention levels of students, thus increasing the likelihood that students would renew their on-campus housing contracts for multiple years; and (3) predict renovation, redevelopment, and new construction needs of on-campus housing facilities

regarding style of structures, lifestyle configurations, rent prices, amenities, and integrative learning programs.

After clarifying the objectives of the Residence Life program, the project director realized that information was needed to address the objectives. Consequently, the MPC Consulting Group, Inc., a firm that specializes in the assessment of on-campus housing programs, was retained to advise and oversee the project. This firm was not known for conducting primary information marketing research. After several consultations with university administrators, MPC's representatives determined that the appropriate method for collecting the needed information would require the development of a self-administered survey instrument. The survey would be administered through the existing student e-mail system at the university. The rationale for an e-mail approach was that all 28,000 university students had access to and used e-mail, and this method would save time and costs.

Given the project's multiple objectives, the consulting team brainstormed a list of 59 questions to be asked of both on-campus and off-campus students currently enrolled at the university. A variety of questions focused on housing attitudes and preferences (state-of-mind data); importance of different housing structures, lifestyle configurations, rent prices, amenities, and integrative learning programs (state-of-mind data); likelihood of selecting on-campus housing or off-campus housing based on amenities, prices, and availability (state-of-intention data); and approximately 17 demographic/socioeconomic characteristics (state-of-being data).

Now the task at hand for the consultants was to create a questionnaire that could be sent to students via e-mail. Not having strong understanding of scientific survey instruments, the consulting firm prepared the initial questionnaire, which began by asking about personal demographic characteristics, followed by some questions concerning students' current housing situations and an assessment of those conditions. The survey then asked questions about the importance of a list of preselected housing characteristics, followed by questions designed to capture the student's intention of living in on-campus versus off-campus housing facilities and the reasons for those intentions. After a few more questions concerning marital status and number of young children, questions were asked on the types of housing structures and amenities most desired by students. The survey ended with personal thoughts about the need for child care services.

When placed on the computer for access by e-mail, the questionnaire was 12 pages long with six different "screener" questions having the respondents skipping back and forth between computer screens depending on how they responded to the screening questions. After three weeks of having the survey in the field, only 17 students had responded, and 8 of those surveys were incomplete. University officials asked three simple but critical questions: (1) Why such a low response rate? (2) Was the survey a good or bad instrument for collecting the needed primary information? and (3) Is there any diagnostic value of the data for addressing the given objectives?

On the basis of your knowledge and understanding of good information research practices to this point, can you give some answers to these three questions? Take a few moments to write down the potential problems that were created by the consulting firm's process described above. Then, after reading this chapter, return here and see if you would answer these questions any differently.

Value of Questionnaires in Information Research

The chapter opener example shows that designing a single questionnaire for collecting a specific type of data is different from taking a set of scale measurements and creating a good scientific questionnaire. A researcher's ability to design a good scale is, by itself, not enough to guarantee that the appropriate data will automatically be collected.

This chapter focuses on developing a clear understanding of the importance of questionnaire designs and the process that should be undertaken in the development of most data collection instruments. Understanding questionnaire designs will require you to integrate many of the concepts discussed in earlier chapters.

As a future marketing or business decision maker, you may never personally design a questionnaire, but most certainly you will be in a client's position of determining whether a survey is good or bad. Therefore, you should know about the considerations, preliminary activities, and processes that are undertaken in designing scientific questionnaires.

Much of the primary data necessary to create new information for resolving business and marketing problems requires the researcher to ask people questions and record their responses. If business problems were simple and required only one bit of raw data, questionnaires would not be necessary. A researcher could develop a single question measurement and administer it to a sample of respondents, collect the data, analyze it, and derive meaningful information from the data structure. For example, let's say a retailer like Target wanted to know if having a "50 percent off" sale on Saturday, January 8, 2005, would increase sales revenues that day. A researcher could develop the following question: "If Target had a storewide 50 percent off sale on all merchandise Saturday, January 8, 2005, would you come to Target and buy at least one item? ___YES ___NO." Then the researcher could administer the question to 1,000 consumers representative of the general population. Let's assume that 650 people said yes (65 percent) and 350 people said no (35 percent) to the question, and the researcher interpreted the results as being "the majority (65 percent) of shoppers would come to Target and buy merchandise." By having this one bit of information, would Target have enough information to decide whether or not to hold the sale?

In reality, it is highly unlikely that this one bit of information would be a good predictor of actual shopping behavior. Some of the other factors that might also directly affect a person's decision to shop at Target might be (1) attitude toward Target and its merchandise, (2) other obligations or activities the day of the sale, (3) lack of a means of transportation on that particular day, or (4) limited financial resources. The point is that many business situations or problems are not unidimensional, and therefore a single piece of information about a problem often is not sufficient to resolve it.

Questionnaire A formalized framework consisting of a set of questions and scales designed to generate primary raw data.

A **questionnaire** is a formalized framework consisting of a set of questions and scales designed to generate primary data. Questionnaire construction involves taking established sets of scale measurements and formatting them into an instrument for collecting raw data from respondents. Prior to discussing questionnaire designs, there are several key insights about questionnaires worth noting. First, the purpose of designing a "good" survey instrument is to increase the probability of collecting high-quality primary data that can be transformed into reliable and valid information for marketing managers and/or researchers. Actual construct and scale measurement reliability and validity issues should be addressed and assessed during the construct development stage by researchers prior to finalizing the questionnaire. The *layout* of the scale measurements used to collect primary data can influence any particular measurement's ability to provide reliable and valid data. Second, advancements in communication systems, the Internet, and computer software programs have impacted the methods of asking questions and recording responses. Yet the critical decisions and processes that underlie the construction of good questionnaires basically remain unchanged. That is, whether designing a survey instrument for "online" methods (i.e., CATI, Internet, Web survey) or "offline" methods (i.e., personal, telephone, direct mail), the rules and process steps researchers need to follow in designing questionnaires are essentially the same. Finally, questionnaires are the key instruments used in collecting raw data, regardless of the type of research (i.e., exploratory, descriptive, causal) study.

Theoretical Principles of Questionnaire Design

One of the great weaknesses of questionnaire design today is that many researchers still do not understand the theory behind questionnaire development. Many researchers believe that designing questionnaires is an art rather than a science. While there is some creativity in designing questionnaires, the process itself should be a scientific one that integrates established rules of logic, objectivity, and systematic procedures.[1] Everyone understands that words go into questions and that questions go into questionnaires, but not everyone understands that writing questions does *not* give you a questionnaire.

Theoretical Components of a Questionnaire (or Data Collection Instruments)

Theoretically, a questionnaire consists of several components—words, questions, formats, and hypotheses—that are integrated into a recognizable, hierarchical layer system.[2]

Words

The most obvious component is words. Researchers must carefully consider which words to use in creating the questions and scales for collecting raw data from respondents. A few examples of wording problems include ambiguity, abstraction, and connotation. The words selected by the researcher can influence a respondent's answer to a given question. The following examples illustrate this point:

1. Do you think anything *could* be done to make it more convenient for students to register for classes at your university or college?

2. Do you think anything *should* be done to make it more convenient for students to register for classes at your university or college?

3. Do you think anything *might* be done to make it more convenient for students to register for classes at your university or college?

The different answers each of these questions would generate show how "word phrasing" variations can become significant in questionnaire designs. Slight changes in wording can introduce different concepts or emotional levels into the questionnaire.

Questions/Setups

The next component is the question/setup used in a particular scale to collect raw data from the respondent. Two important issues relating to question phrasing that have a direct impact on survey designs are (1) the type of question format (unstructured or structured) and (2) the quality of the question (good or bad).[3]

Unstructured questions
Open-ended questions formatted to allow respondents to reply in their own words.

Unstructured questions are open-ended questions that allow respondents to reply in their own words. There is no predetermined list of responses available to aid or limit the respondents' answers. This type of question requires more thinking and effort on the part of respondents. In most cases, a trained interviewer asks follow-up probing questions. If administered correctly, unstructured questions can provide the researcher with a rich array of information. The actual format of open-ended questions might vary depending on the data collection method (e.g., personal interviews, traditional, and computer-assisted telephone interviews, or online and offline self-administered surveys). Exhibit 13.1 provides several examples to illustrate these format differences.

Structured questions
Closed-ended questions that require the respondent to choose from a predetermined set of responses or scale points.

Structured questions are closed-ended questions that require the respondent to choose a response from a predetermined set of responses or scale points. This question format reduces the amount of thinking and effort required by respondents. In general, structured questions are more popular than unstructured ones. Interviewer bias is eliminated because either (1) the interviewer simply checks a box or line, circles a category, hits a key on a keyboard, points and clicks a computer mouse, or records a number or (2) the respondents themselves check a box or line, circle a category, hit a key on a keyboard, point and click a computer mouse, or record a number that best represents their response to the question.[4]

e X H I B I T 13.1 **Examples of Unstructured Question Setup Designs**

Personal or Telephone Interviews

What toppings, if any, do you usually add to a pizza other than cheese when ordering a pizza for yourself from Pizza Hut? **(Interviewer: Record all mentioned toppings in the space provided below. Make sure you probe for specifics and clarity of responses.)**

_____

_____

_____

or

What toppings, if any, do you usually add to a pizza other than cheese when ordering a pizza for yourself from Pizza Hut? **(Interviewer: DO NOT read the listed toppings; just record the toppings by checking the box next to the mentioned toppings below. Make sure you probe for specifics and clarity of responses.)**

❏ anchovies   ❏ bacon   ❏ barbecue beef

❏ black olives   ❏ extra cheese   ❏ green olives

❏ green peppers   ❏ ground beef   ❏ ham

❏ hot peppers   ❏ mushrooms   ❏ onions

❏ pepperoni   ❏ sausage   ❏ some other topping: _____

Self-Administered Survey (Online or Offline)

In the space provided below, please write the types of toppings, if any, that you usually add to a pizza other than cheese when ordering a pizza for yourself from Pizza Hut. **(Please indicate as many toppings as apply.)**

_____

_____

_____

_____

In many ways, structured formats give the researcher greater opportunities to control the thinking respondents must do in order to answer a question. Exhibit 13.2 shows some examples.

Bad questions are any questions _that prevent or distort the fundamental communication between the researcher and the respondent._ A researcher may think an excellent question has been written because it accurately conveys a point of view or interest to the respondent, but if the respondent cannot answer it in a meaningful way, it is a bad question. Some examples of bad questions are those that are:

1. _Incomprehensible_ to the respondent because the wording, the concept, or both cannot be understood. An example would be "What is your attitude about the linkage between the 2004 war on the terrorists of al-Quaida in Afghanistan and the Democrats decrying of sexual McCarthyism toward improving the environment in Arizona?"

2. _Unanswerable_ either because the respondent does not have access to the information needed or because none of the answer choices apply to the respondent. An example would be "What was your parents' exact annual income two years ago?"

Bad questions Any questions that prevent or distort the fundamental communication between the researcher and the respondents.

---

e X H I B I T 13.2 Examples of Structured Question/Setup Designs

---

Personal Interview

(HAND RESPONDENT CARD.) Please look at this card and tell me the letters that indicate what toppings, if any, you usually add to a pizza other than cheese when ordering a pizza for yourself from Pizza Hut. **(Interviewer: Record all mentioned toppings by circling the letters below, and make sure you probe for any other toppings.)**

[a] anchovies	[b] bacon	[c] barbecue beef
[d] black olives	[e] extra cheese	[f] green olives
[h] green peppers	[i] ground beef	[j] ham
[k] hot peppers	[l] mushrooms	[m] onions
[n] pepperoni	[o] sausage	[p] some other topping: _____

Telephone Interview (Traditional or Computer Assisted)

I'm going to read you a list of pizza toppings. As I read each one, please tell me whether or not that topping is one that you usually add to a pizza when ordering a pizza for yourself from Pizza Hut. **(Interviewer: Read each topping category slowly and record all mentioned toppings by circling their corresponding letter below, and make sure you probe for any other toppings.)**

[a] anchovies	[b] bacon	[c] barbecue beef
[d] black olives	[e] extra cheese	[f] green olives
[h] green peppers	[i] ground beef	[j] ham
[k] hot peppers	[l] mushrooms	[m] onions
[n] pepperoni	[o] sausage	[p] some other topping: _____

Self-Administered Survey (Online or Offline)

Among the pizza toppings listed below, what toppings, if any, do you usually add to a pizza other than cheese when ordering a pizza for yourself from Pizza Hut?

(Please check as many boxes as apply.)

❑ anchovies	❑ bacon	❑ barbecue beef
❑ black olives	❑ extra cheese	❑ green olives
❑ green peppers	❑ ground beef	❑ ham
❑ hot peppers	❑ mushrooms	❑ onions
❑ pepperoni	❑ sausage	❑ some other topping: _____

---

3. *Leading (or loaded)* in that the respondent is forced or directed into a response that would not ordinarily be given if all possible response categories or concepts were provided, or if all the facts of the situation were provided. An example of this would be "Do you believe that Republicans who loved George W. Bush agreed he did a good job as president of the United States?"

4. *Double-barreled* in that they ask the respondent to address more than one issue at a time. An example would be "To what extent do you agree or disagree that Monica Lewinsky *and* Representative Henry Hyde, R-Ill., were responsible for the impeachment vote against President Clinton?"

For more examples of bad questions go to the book's Web site at www.mhhe.com/hair06 and follow the links.

Questionnaire Format

This component does not directly relate to the process of developing the individual questions but rather the layout of sets of questions or scale measurements into a systematic instrument. The questionnaire's format should allow for clear communication. Later in the chapter, we will discuss in detail the "flowerpot" approach to designing scientific questionnaires, which improves the researcher's ability to collect accurate data.

Hypothesis Development

This final component focuses on the notion that questionnaires are designed for collecting meaningful data to test a **hypothesis** rather than merely to gather facts. Theoretically, each of the questions used in a questionnaire should either directly or indirectly relate to a research hypothesis that is relevant to the research objectives. Hypotheses can relate to

Hypothesis A formalized statement of a testable relationship between two or more constructs or variables.

1. The nature of the respondent.
2. The relationship between the expressed attitudes and behavior of the respondent (e.g., motivation).
3. The sociological structures and their influence on the respondent.
4. The meaning of words and the respondent's grasp of language and/or concepts.
5. The relationships among a respondent's knowledge, attitudes, and marketplace behaviors.
6. The descriptive and predictive capabilities of attributes of the constructs (e.g., customer satisfaction, product or service quality, and behavioral intentions).[5]

By identifying the hypothesis associated with each of the questions on a questionnaire, researchers can improve their ability to determine which measurements are necessary for collecting primary data and which ones are nice but not necessary. Collecting "nice but not necessary" data only increases the length of the questionnaire and the likelihood of bias. Exhibit 13.3 displays some examples of different types of hypotheses a researcher can develop about the questions on a questionnaire.

Description versus Prediction

While all good questionnaires are systematically structured, most surveys are designed to be descriptive or predictive.[6] A descriptive design allows the researcher to collect raw data that can be turned into facts about a person or object. For example, the U.S. Census Bureau uses questionnaire designs that collect primarily state-of-being or state-of-behavior data that can be translated into facts about the U.S. population (e.g., income levels, marital status, age, occupation, family size, usage rates, consumption quantities). In contrast, predictive questionnaires force the researcher to collect a wider range of state-of-mind and state-of-intention data that can be used in predicting changes in attitudes and behaviors as well as in testing hypotheses.

Accuracy versus Precision

Accuracy The degree to which the data obtained from a questionnaire provide the researcher with a description of the true state of affairs.

Another theoretical principle that should guide the design of questionnaires is that of accuracy. This means a true report is obtained of the respondent's attitudes, preferences, beliefs, feelings, intentions, and/or actions. Questions and scales must be used that enable the researcher to gain an overall picture rather than just a fragment.[7] **Accuracy** refers to the degree to which the data provide the researcher with a description of the true state of

EXHIBIT 13.3 Examples of Different Types of Hypotheses Used in Information Research

Null Hypothesis

There is **no significant difference** between the preferences toward specific banking methods exhibited by white-collar customers and blue-collar customers.

No significant differences will be found to exist in the requests for specific medical treatments from emergency medical walk-in clinics between users and nonusers of annual physical preventive health care progams.

Nondirectional Hypothesis

Significant differences do exist in the sexual behavior profiles of academically strong and weak male and female students.

There is a **significant difference** in the satisfaction levels among 2002 Mazda Millenia owners according to how much they have driven the car.

Inverse (Negative) Directional Hypothesis

Those students who exhibit **high levels** of self-confidence and knowledge toward the topic and **positive** overall study habits will demonstrate **low profiles** of introverted social behavior.

The **greater the amount** of outside-classroom studying done by marketing majors, the **less chance** there is that they will turn to cheating to improve their grades.

Direct (Positive) Directional Hypothesis

Positive study habits are related **positively** to GPA.

College students who tend to **worry a lot about** what other students think of them will tend to be **more conservative** in their overall classroom and social behavior than those students who don't worry much about their self-image.

Questionnaire design precision The extent to which a questionnaire design can reproduce similar results over repeated usages.

affairs. In contrast, **questionnaire design precision** focuses on whether questions or scales are narrowly defined.

The Value of a Good Survey Instrument

The value of a well-constructed questionnaire cannot be overestimated by researchers and marketing practitioners. How a survey instrument is developed is a critical component in the process of creating information that can be used to solve business problems. The main function of a questionnaire is to capture people's true thoughts and feelings about different issues or objects. Data collected through a questionnaire can be viewed as the key to unlocking understanding and truth about a problem situation.[8]

In contrast, a bad questionnaire can be costly in terms of time, effort, and money. It produces nothing more than "garbage" data that, if used by decision makers, results in inappropriate or incorrect marketing actions.[9] New technologies are providing alternatives for designing good questionnaires. Read the nearby Closer Look at Research box for a discussion of computerized questionnaire designs. For examples of "good" and "bad" questionnaires visit the book's Web site at www.mhhe.com/hair06 and follow the links.

A Closer Look at Research

Computerized Questionnaires

"Smart" questionnaires are a very important development in marketing research. These questionnaires are structured with a mathematical logic that enables the computer to customize them for each respondent as the interview progresses. Through the use of interactive software, the computer constantly evaluates new information and presents the respondent with a new decision to make. In this type of survey, different respondents taking the same questionnaire would answer different sets of questions, each custom-designed to provide the most relevant data.

For global corporations with diverse product lines, computerized questionnaires can provide information related to each product line. Before computerized questionnaires, corporations had to rely on survey data that used scripted questions that often did not provide relevant data. However, with computerized questionnaires, the information obtained is relevant to the needs of the organization.

Important advantages of computerized questionnaires over pen-and-paper surveys include increased ease of participation, decreased time requirements, and a reduction in resources needed to conduct the survey, thereby reducing the overall cost of survey administration. For corporations faced with constantly increasing time demands, computerized questionnaires are a natural choice for meeting their data collection needs.

The Flowerpot Approach to Questionnaire Designs

The process researchers follow to develop a questionnaire is systematic. While the specific steps may vary, most researchers follow established rules. Exhibit 13.4 shows a set of steps for developing survey instruments. Note that some of the activities in each step are critically necessary but not part of the actual layout. For example, some questionnaires call for the development of separate screening questions that are used to qualify the prospective respondents. Other activities are pertinent to the actual design task.

With all these steps to understand, the development process can seem overwhelming at first. To simplify the questionnaire development process, we present the **flowerpot approach.** This scientific approach involves a series of activities that have a logical, hierarchical order.[10] The "flowerpot" notion is symbolically derived from the natural shape associated with a clay pot used for growing flowers. The shape is wide at the top and narrower at the bottom—symbolizing a natural flow of data from general to specific. Although this approach is primarily used to create a good questionnaire structure, it has direct impact on steps 1 and 3 of the development process outlined in Exhibit 13.4. The flowerpot approach helps the researcher make decisions regarding (1) construct development, (2) attributes of objects, (3) various question/scale formats, (4) wording of questions, and (5) scale points. In situations where there are multiple research objectives, each objective will have its own pot of data. To reduce the likelihood of creating biased data, the size and width of the data requirements must be determined for each objective, with the most general data requirements going into the biggest flowerpot and the next most general set of data going into a smaller pot. As illustrated in Exhibit 13.5, when multiple pots are stacked,

Flowerpot approach
A specific framework for integrating sets of question/scale measurements into a logical, smooth-flowing questionnaire.

eXHIBIT **13.4**   **Steps in the Development of Survey Instruments**

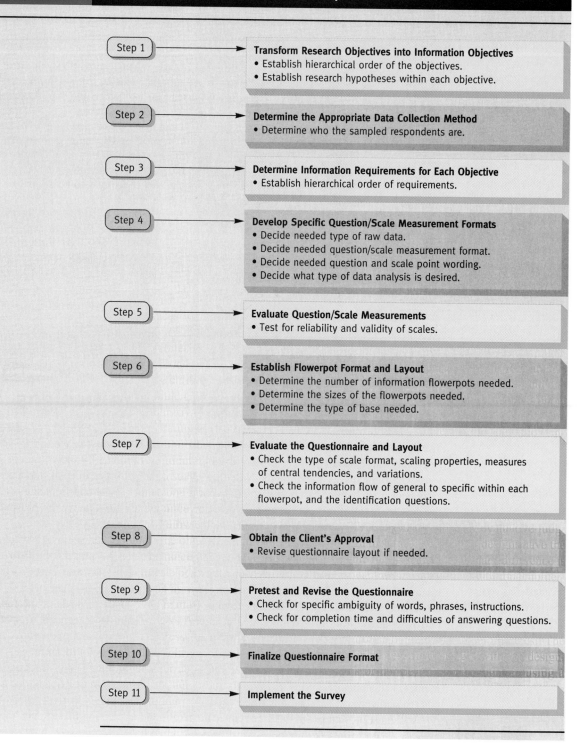

Step 1

Transform Research Objectives into Information Objectives
- Establish hierarchical order of the objectives.
- Establish research hypotheses within each objective.

Step 2

Determine the Appropriate Data Collection Method
- Determine who the sampled respondents are.

Step 3

Determine Information Requirements for Each Objective
- Establish hierarchical order of requirements.

Step 4

Develop Specific Question/Scale Measurement Formats
- Decide needed type of raw data.
- Decide needed question/scale measurement format.
- Decide needed question and scale point wording.
- Decide what type of data analysis is desired.

Step 5

Evaluate Question/Scale Measurements
- Test for reliability and validity of scales.

Step 6

Establish Flowerpot Format and Layout
- Determine the number of information flowerpots needed.
- Determine the sizes of the flowerpots needed.
- Determine the type of base needed.

Step 7

Evaluate the Questionnaire and Layout
- Check the type of scale format, scaling properties, measures of central tendencies, and variations.
- Check the information flow of general to specific within each flowerpot, and the identification questions.

Step 8

Obtain the Client's Approval
- Revise questionnaire layout if needed.

Step 9

Pretest and Revise the Questionnaire
- Check for specific ambiguity of words, phrases, instructions.
- Check for completion time and difficulties of answering questions.

Step 10

Finalize Questionnaire Format

Step 11

Implement the Survey

eXHIBIT 13.5   Illustrative Diagram of the Flowerpot Approach

This diagram illustrates the overall flowerpot design of a questionnaire that fits a research survey that has two defined information objectives and calls for an identification base that contains both psychographic and demographic-socioeconomic traits about the respondent.

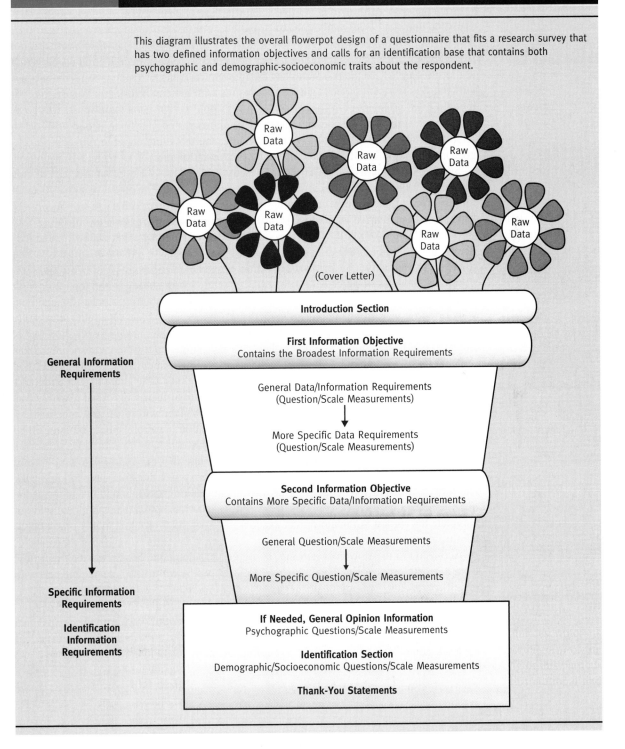

General Information
Requirements

Specific Information
Requirements

Identification
Information
Requirements

Raw Data

(Cover Letter)

Introduction Section

First Information Objective
Contains the Broadest Information Requirements

General Data/Information Requirements
(Question/Scale Measurements)
↓
More Specific Data Requirements
(Question/Scale Measurements)

Second Information Objective
Contains More Specific Data/Information Requirements

General Question/Scale Measurements
↓
More Specific Question/Scale Measurements

If Needed, General Opinion Information
Psychographic Questions/Scale Measurements

Identification Section
Demographic/Socioeconomic Questions/Scale Measurements

Thank-You Statements

the larger pot is always placed on top of a smaller pot to ensure that the overall general-to-specific flow of data is maintained.

Someone just learning to develop a scientific-based questionnaire might raise this fundamental question: *Why should the questioning layout in the overall questionnaire as well as individual flowerpots always create a directional flow from general to more specific information?* The answer is threefold. First, logic has to be used in collecting primary data in the situation where the researcher (or the interviewer) and respondent begin the process as "strangers" to each other. A survey that begins with general information questions promotes the development of the necessary "comfort zone" between the two parties. This comfort zone is similar to the one that has to be established in either focus group or in-depth interviews. When respondents feel comfortable, the question/answer exchange process goes more smoothly and respondents are more thoughtful and honest with their responses.

Second, data quality is critical in any research study. Researchers run the risk of collecting low-quality data by asking respondents questions about an object or construct in an illogical order. For example, expecting respondents to be able to honestly or accurately express their evaluative judgments toward the performance of a particular object (e.g., an Apple iPod) is illogical if they have no knowledge of or personal experience with that particular object. A more general question about MP3 ownership or experience must be asked prior to the evaluative performance question. In some cases, asking a specific question about the attributes or purchasing behaviors associated with an object and then following up with more general questions about the object can cause ambiguity, confusion, and possibly response bias. For example, let's say the researcher, in conducting a retail store study in Chicago, asks several questions concerning the respondent's *intentions* of shopping at Marshall Field's for children's clothes, then asks a question about what the respondent likes or dislikes about shopping at Marshall Field's. Further let's assume the respondent indicated he or she *definitely plans to shop* at Marshall Field's the next time shopping for children's clothing is necessary. The respondent's answer here could influence his or her response pattern to the liking/disliking question in that the responses given will justify the intentions-to-shop response. What a respondent likes and dislikes about the store should be established prior to finding out the respondent's intentions to shop at that store.

Finally, the general-to-specific sequence helps ensure that the appropriate sequence of questions will be maintained so the respondent or interviewer does not have to jump back and forth between different pages of the instrument in order to respond to questions. If the questionnaire appears to be complex, there is a greater chance that the respondent will not complete the survey. An inappropriate response is a potential problem in any type of self-administered questionnaire.

According to the flowerpot concept, in a good questionnaire design, the data will flow from a general information level, down to a more specific information level, and end with identification data. A questionnaire begins with an *introductory section* that gives the respondent a basic idea of the main topic of the research. This section also includes general instructions for filling out the survey. The introduction's appearance will vary with the desired data collection method (e.g., self-administered or interview). For example, the introduction needed for a self-administered questionnaire in a restaurant study might look as follows:

Thank you for your participation in this study. Your participation will aid us in determining what people in our community think about the present products and services offered by restaurants. The results of the study will provide the restaurant industry with insights into how to better serve the needs of people in the Cincinnati metropolitan community.

Your attitudes, preferences, and opinions are important to this study; they will be kept strictly confidential.

DIRECTIONS: Please read each question carefully. Answer the question by checking the appropriate box(es) that represent your response or responses.

In contrast, an introduction for a Hillsborough County housing survey using computer-assisted telephone interviews might look as follows:

Hillsborough County Housing Study

Verified   Phone # _____

By: _____   Call Back Date: _____ Time: _____

Date: _____   Time Started: _____ (a.m.) (p.m.)

                                     Serial # _____

MARKETS: [1] NW Hillsborough   [2] NE Hillsborough   [3] Brandon

INTERVIEWER: Ask to speak with the man of the house. If not available or none, ask for the lady of the house.

Hello, I'm (Your Name) representing the Marketing Resources Group here in Tampa. Today, we are conducting an interesting study on housing in Hillsborough County and would like to include your opinions in it.

As it was explained in the letter mailed to your residence about a week ago, we are not interested in selling you anything. We are only interested in your honest opinions about housing structures in the Hillsborough area.

Notice how the two introductions differ. The computer-assisted telephone interview requires specific interviewer instructions.

Next, the researcher must determine how many different information objectives there are (i.e., the number of flowerpots needed to construct the questionnaire) and the true breadth and depth of the information requirements (i.e., the different pot sizes).

First working with the largest flowerpot (i.e., most general information), the researcher must identify the specific information requirements and arrange them from general to more specific. Then, going to the next largest flowerpot, the researcher again arranges the information requirements from general to specific. Because stacking the larger pots on top of smaller pots tends to create an unstable, top-heavy structure, a good questionnaire design will also end with demographic and socioeconomic questions about the respondent to form a solid identification base. All questionnaires produced by the flowerpot approach will end with a thank-you statement.

The reasons underlying the placement of demographic and socioeconomic characteristics at the end of a questionnaire are twofold. First, in most research studies, the primary information research objectives focus on collecting attitudinal, emotional, and/or behavioral data about objects, people, and marketing phenomena. Demographic, socioeconomic, and physical characteristics about people and organizations, although important, are collected to add a "face" to those attitudes, feelings, and behaviors. In most cases that require a cover letter or letter of introduction, seldom if ever is the purpose of the research expressed in terms of wanting to obtain demographic information about people. Demographic and socioeconomic factors are neither the stated primary objective nor directly used to achieve a person's willingness to participate in the study. Second, these types of characteristics are direct facts about a respondent often of a personal nature. In general, people are initially unwilling to provide these facts to strangers (e.g., researcher or interviewer). This unwillingness stems from the fact that most respondents do not understand their relevancy to the study's main information objectives and view them as inappropriate. Until the "comfort zone" is established between the interviewer and respondent, asking personal questions could easily bring the interviewing process to a halt. To illustrate this point, suppose when you leave this class a student you don't know stops you and begins asking questions relating to your age, income, family members, occupation, marital status, and so on. How would you react? Without knowing why this stranger was asking these types of questions and how the information was going be used, this awkward situation would create uneasy feelings for you—powerful reasons for not responding and for ending the question/answer process.

The Flowerpot Approach's Impact on Questionnaire Development

Although the flowerpot approach is primarily used to determine the appropriate sequential order of the questions and scale measurements, it has a direct impact on several of the other development activities.

Determining the Information Objectives

After transforming the research objectives into information objectives, the researcher must evaluate each information objective for its broadness. This activity achieves two things for the researcher. First, it helps the researcher decide which information objectives truly represent a flowerpot of information. Second, it helps the researcher to determine how many flowerpots, and in what sizes, will need to be stacked up in the questionnaire design.

Determining the Information Requirements

Rather than using general brainstorming techniques to develop all the data requirements for the information objectives, the flowerpot approach focuses on one information topic at a time. This decreases the likelihood of generating irrelevant or "nice but not necessary" data. It also enhances the researcher's ability to determine the necessary order (e.g., general to specific) among the data requirements within a given pot.

Development of a Flowerpot-Designed Questionnaire

This section describes how the flowerpot approach influences the activities in the survey instrument development process described in Exhibit 13.4. It is important to remember that the flowerpot approach to questionnaire designs is very workable regardless of the method used to collect primary data. The discussion is based on an actual study conducted for American Bank and Trust.

The Situation

The American Bank and Trust Company was located in Baton Rouge, Louisiana. The primary goal of the survey was to provide the marketing team with relevant information regarding banking habits and patterns, as well as demographic and lifestyle characteristics of the bank's current customers.

Transform Research Objectives into Information Objectives

In the initial phase of the development process, the flowerpot approach guides the researcher not only in transforming the research objectives into information objectives but also in determining how many information objectives to include (the number of pots), along with parts of the base stand and those objectives which represent testable hypotheses. The order of the information objectives (the size of the pots) also is determined. The initial research objectives (in bold) were rewritten into information objectives (in italics) as follows:

1. **To obtain a demographic profile of American Bank's current customers.** *(To collect data on selected demographic characteristics that can be used to create a profile of people who are current American Bank customers.)*

2. **To obtain a partial lifestyle profile of people who currently bank with American Bank, with particular emphasis on financial dimensions.** *(To collect data on selected financial-oriented lifestyle dimensions that can be used to create a profile that further identifies people who currently bank at American Bank.)*

3. **To determine banking habits and patterns of these customers.** *(To collect data to identify and describe desired and actual banking habits and patterns exhibited by customers, as well as their selected attitudes and feelings toward those banking practices.)*

4. **To investigate the existence of possible differences between the psychological and demographic dimensions associated with customers' perceptions of being either a blue-collar or white-collar person.** *(To collect data that will enable the researcher to (1) classify customers as being either "blue collar" or "white collar" and (2) test for significant demographic and lifestyle profile differences between these two social classes.)*

5. **To determine the various geographic markets now being served by American Bank on the basis of customers' length of residence in the area.** *(To collect selected state-of-being data that will enable the researcher to identify and describe existing geographic service markets.)*

After transforming the research objectives into information objectives, the researcher determined that objectives 1 and 2 directly related to data that would be part of the questionnaire's basic structure. Objective 3 represents an information flowerpot. In contrast, objectives 4 and 5 do not represent information flowerpots but rather hypotheses about data structures that will be derived from data obtained within either the basic structure or the identified information flowerpot. Although there were five initial information objectives, the actual structure consists of only one information flowerpot and its base.

Determine the Appropriate Data Collection Method

On the basis of the information objectives and target population (i.e., American Bank's own current customers), bank management and the researcher jointly decided that a direct mail survey approach would be the most efficient method of collecting data from the randomly selected respondents. This step has a direct influence on creating the individual questions and scales, although these are designed only after the specific information items are determined for each objective.

Determine Information Requirements for Each Objective

The flowerpot approach has a significant impact on this step of the development process. Here the researcher interacts with bank management to determine what specific data requirements are needed to achieve each of the information objectives as well as the respondent classification information. The researcher must establish the general-to-specific order among the identified data requirements. The study's data requirements and flow are detailed as follows:

1. *Flowerpot 1* (third objective): To collect data that can identify and describe desired and actual banking habits and patterns exhibited by customers as well as their selected attitudes and feelings toward those banking practices.
   a. Consideration toward the bank patronized most often.
   b. Bank characteristics deemed important in selecting a bank (e.g., convenience/location, banking hours, good service charges, interest rates on savings accounts, knew a person at the bank, bank's reputation, bank's promotional advertisements, interest rates on loans).
   c. Considerations toward having personal savings accounts at various types of financial institutions.
   d. Preference considerations toward selected banking methods (e.g., inside the bank, drive-up window, 24-hour ATM, electronic banking, bank by mail, bank by phone).
   e. Actual usage considerations toward various banking methods (e.g., inside the bank, drive-up window, 24-hour ATM, electronic banking, bank by mail, bank by phone).
   f. Frequency of balancing a checkbook as well as the number of not-sufficient-funds (NSF) charges.

2. *Flowerpot base—lifestyle dimensions* (second objective): To collect data on selected financial-oriented lifestyle dimensions that can be used to create a descriptive profile that further identifies people who currently bank at American Bank.

   Belief statements that will classify the customer's lifestyle as being financial optimist, financially dissatisfied, information exchanger, credit card user, advertising viewer, family oriented, price conscious, blue/white-collar oriented.

3. *Flowerpot base—demographic characteristics* (first objective): To collect data on selected demographic characteristics that can be used to create a descriptive profile identifying people who are current American Bank customers. Include characteristics of gender, years in area, years at current residence, present employment status, present marital status, spouse's current employment status, number of dependent children, education level, age, occupation, nature of work, union membership, income level, and zip code.

Notice that the fourth and fifth objectives have no direct bearing on determining the data requirements because they include factors that are covered either in the information flowerpot or its base. Therefore, the researcher does not have to integrate them into this particular aspect of the development process.

Develop Specific Question/Scale Measurement Formats

The flowerpot approach does not impact the activities that take place in this part of the development process. Nevertheless, these activities remain a critical part of questionnaire design. Researchers must use their construct and scale measurement knowledge to develop appropriate scales (e.g., question/setup, dimension/attributes, scale points/responses) for each individual data requirement. To do so, the researcher must make three key decisions: (1) the type of data (e.g., state of being, mind, behavior, intention); (2) question/scale format (e.g., open-ended or closed-ended format and nominal,

EXHIBIT 13.6 Consumer Banking Opinion Survey: Baton Rouge, Louisiana

THANK YOU for your participation in this interesting study. Your participation will aid us in determining what people in our community think about the present products and services offered by banks. The results will provide the banking industry with additional insights on how to better serve the needs of people in the Baton Rouge community. Your attitudes, preferences, and opinions are important to this study; they will be kept strictly confidential.

DIRECTIONS: PLEASE READ EACH QUESTION CAREFULLY. ANSWER THE QUESTION BY FILLING IN THE APPROPRIATE BOX(ES) THAT REPRESENT YOUR RESPONSE OR RESPONSES.

I. GENERAL BANKING HABITS SECTION

1. Which one of the following banks would you consider the one that you use most often in conducting banking or financial transactions? **(PLEASE FILL IN THE ONE APPROPRIATE BOX)**

   ❑ American Bank   ❑ Capital Bank   ❑ Fidelity National Bank
   ❑ Baton Rouge Bank   ❑ City National Bank   ❑ Louisiana National Bank
   ❑ Some other bank; please specify: _____

2a. To what extent were each of the following bank items an important consideration to you in selecting your bank mentioned in Q.1 above? **(PLEASE BE SURE TO FILL IN ONLY ONE RESPONSE FOR EACH BANK ITEM.)**

Bank Items	Extremely Important	Important	Somewhat Important	Not at All Important
Convenience of location	❑	❑	❑	❑
Banking hours	❑	❑	❑	❑
Good service charges	❑	❑	❑	❑
Interest rates on savings	❑	❑	❑	❑
Personally knew someone at the bank	❑	❑	❑	❑
Bank's reputation	❑	❑	❑	❑
Bank's promotional advertising	❑	❑	❑	❑
Interest rate on loans	❑	❑	❑	❑

2b. If there was some other reason (or bank item) you deemed important in selecting your bank mentioned in Q.1, please write it in the space below.

3. At which of the following financial institutions do you or some member of your immediate household have a personal savings account? **(PLEASE FILL IN AS MANY OR AS FEW AS ARE NECESSARY.)**

Financial Institutions	Both You and Some Other Member	Some Other Member	Yourself
A credit union	❑	❑	❑
Savings & loan	❑	❑	❑
American Bank	❑	❑	❑
Baton Rouge Bank	❑	❑	❑
Capital Bank	❑	❑	❑
City National Bank	❑	❑	❑
Fidelity National Bank	❑	❑	❑
Louisiana National Bank	❑	❑	❑
Another institution: _____	❑	❑	❑
(Please Specify)			

continued

EXHIBIT 13.6 Consumer Banking Opinion Survey: Baton Rouge, Louisiana, *continued*

---

4. Concerning the different banking methods which you may or may not use, we would like to know your feeling toward these methods. For each listed banking method, please fill in the appropriate response that best describes your desire for using that method. **(PLEASE FILL IN ONE RESPONSE FOR EACH BANKING METHOD)**

Banking Methods	Definitely Like Using	Somewhat Like Using	Somewhat Dislike Using	Definitely Dislike Using
Inside the bank	❑	❑	❑	❑
Drive-in (Drive-up)	❑	❑	❑	❑
24-hour machine	❑	❑	❑	❑
Bank by phone	❑	❑	❑	❑
Bank by mail	❑	❑	❑	❑
Electronic banking	❑	❑	❑	❑
Third-person banking	❑	❑	❑	❑

5. Now we would like to know to what extent you actually use each of the following banking methods. **(PLEASE FILL IN THE APPROPRIATE RESPONSE FOR EACH LISTED BANKING METHOD.)**

Banking Methods	Usually	Occasionally	Rarely	Never
Inside the bank	❑	❑	❑	❑
Drive-in (Drive-up)	❑	❑	❑	❑
24-hour machine	❑	❑	❑	❑
Bank by phone	❑	❑	❑	❑
Bank by mail	❑	❑	❑	❑
Electronic banking	❑	❑	❑	❑
Third-person banking	❑	❑	❑	❑

6. Thinking about your monthly bank statement, approximately how often do you balance your checkbook with the aid of your statement?

❑ Always (every statement)   ❑ Rarely (once or twice a year)
❑ Occasionally (every 2 or 3 months)   ❑ Never

7. Approximately how many overdrawn charges on your checking account (NSF checks) has your bank imposed on your account in the past year?

❑ None   ❑ 1–2   ❑ 3–7   ❑ 8–15   ❑ 16–25   ❑ More than 25

II. GENERAL OPINION SECTION

In this section, there is a list of general opinion statements for which there are no right or wrong answers. As such, the statements may or may not describe you or your feelings.

8. Next to each statement, please fill in the one response box that best expresses the extent to which you agree or disagree with the statement. Remember, there are no right or wrong answers—we just want your opinions.

Statements	Definitely Agree	Generally Agree	Somewhat Agree	Somewhat Disagree	Generally Disagree	Definitely Disagree
I often seek out the advice of my friends regarding a lot of different things.	❑	❑	❑	❑	❑	❑
I buy many things with credit cards.	❑	❑	❑	❑	❑	❑

eXHIBIT 13.6 *continued*

Statements	Definitely Agree	Generally Agree	Somewhat Agree	Somewhat Disagree	Generally Disagree	Definitely Disagree
I wish we had a lot more money.	❑	❑	❑	❑	❑	❑
Security for my family is most important to me.	❑	❑	❑	❑	❑	❑
I am definitely influenced by advertising.	❑	❑	❑	❑	❑	❑
I like to pay cash for everything I buy.	❑	❑	❑	❑	❑	❑
My neighbors or friends often come to me for advice on many different matters.	❑	❑	❑	❑	❑	❑
It is good to have charge accounts.	❑	❑	❑	❑	❑	❑
I will probably have more money to spend next year than I have now.	❑	❑	❑	❑	❑	❑
A person can save a lot of money by shopping around for bargains.	❑	❑	❑	❑	❑	❑
For most products or services, I try the ones that are most popular.	❑	❑	❑	❑	❑	❑
Unexpected situations often catch me without enough money in my pocket.	❑	❑	❑	❑	❑	❑
Five years from now, the family income will probably be a lot higher than it is now.	❑	❑	❑	❑	❑	❑
Socially, I see myself more as a blue-collar person rather than a white-collar one.	❑	❑	❑	❑	❑	❑

III. CLASSIFICATION DATA SECTION

Now just a few more questions so that we can combine your responses with those of the other people taking part in this study.

9. Please indicate your gender. ❑ Female ❑ Male

10. Please fill in the one response that best approximates how long you have lived in the Baton Rouge area.
   ❑ Less than 1 year   ❑ 4 to 6 years   ❑ 11 to 20 years
   ❑ 1 to 3 years   ❑ 7 to 10 years   ❑ Over 20 years

11. Approximately how long have you lived at your current address?
   ❑ Less than 1 year   ❑ 4 to 6 years   ❑ 11 to 20 years
   ❑ 1 to 3 years   ❑ 7 to 10 years   ❑ Over 20 years

12. Please indicate your current employment status.
   ❑ Employed full-time   ❑ Employed part-time   ❑ Not currently employed   ❑ Retired

continued

EXHIBIT 13.6   Consumer Banking Opinion Survey: Baton Rouge, Louisiana, *continued*

13. Please indicate your current marital status.

☐ Married   ☐ Single (widowed, divorced, or separated) ⟶ **PLEASE SKIP TO Q.15**

☐ Single (never married) ⟶ **PLEASE SKIP TO Q.15**

14. **IF MARRIED,** please indicate your spouse's current employment status.

☐ Employed full-time   ☐ Employed part-time   ☐ Not currently employed   ☐ Retired

15. **IF YOU HAVE CHILDREN,** please indicate the number of children under 18 years of age in your household.

0	1	2	3	4	5	6	7	8	More than 8; please specify: _____	☐ Do not have children
☐	☐	☐	☐	☐	☐	☐	☐	☐		

16. Which one of the following categories best corresponds with your last completed year in school?

☐ Post-graduate studies or advanced degree   ☐ Completed high school

☐ Graduate studies or degree   ☐ Some high school

☐ Completed college (4-year degree)   ☐ Completed grammar school

☐ Some college or technical school   ☐ Some grammar school

17. Into which one of the following categories does your current age fall?

☐ Under 18   ☐ 26 to 35   ☐ 46 to 55   ☐ 66 to 70

☐ 18 to 25   ☐ 36 to 45   ☐ 56 to 65   ☐ Over 70

18. What is your occupation; that is, in what kind of work do you spend the major portion of your time?

_____

19. Which one of the following categories best describes the nature of your work?

☐ Government (Fed., State, City)   ☐ Legal   ☐ Financial   ☐ Insurance

☐ Petrochemical   ☐ Manufacturing   ☐ Transportation   ☐ Consulting

☐ Educational   ☐ Medical   ☐ Retailing   ☐ Wholesaling

☐ Some other area, please specify: _____

20. Are you a non-union or union worker?   ☐ Non-union worker   ☐ Union worker

21. Into which of the following categories does your total (approximate) family income, before taxes, fall?

☐ Under $10,000   ☐ $30,001 to $50,000

☐ $10,000 to $15,000   ☐ $50,001 to $75,000

☐ $15,001 to $20,000   ☐ $75,001 to $100,000

☐ $20,001 to $30,000   ☐ Over $100,000

22. What is your residence address five-digit zip code?   ☐ ☐ ☐ ☐ ☐

Thank you very much for participation in this study! Your time and opinions are greatly and deeply appreciated.

ordinal, interval, or ratio structure); and (3) the question and specific scale point wording.

The flowerpot approach advocates that when designing the specific question/scale measurements, researchers should act as if they are two different people, one thinking like a technical, logical researcher and the other like a respondent. The results of this step can be seen in the final questionnaire displayed in Exhibit 13.6.

eXHIBIT 13.7 Guidelines for Evaluating the Adequacy of Questions

1. Questions should be *simple* and *straightforward* whenever possible.
2. Questions should be *expressed clearly* whenever possible.
3. Questions should *avoid qualifying phrases* or *extraneous references*, unless they are being used as a qualifying (screening) factor.
4. *Avoid descriptive words* unless absolutely necessary.
5. The question/setups, attribute statements, and data response categories should be *unidimensional*, except when there is a need for a multiple-response question.
6. Raw data response categories (scale points) should be *mutually exclusive*.
7. The question/setups and the response categories should be *meaningful to the respondent*.
8. Question/scale measurement formats should *avoid arrangement* of response categories *that might bias* the respondent's answer.
9. Unless called for, question/setups should *avoid undue stress* of particular words.
10. Question/setups should *avoid double negatives*.
11. Question/scale measurements should *avoid technical* or *sophisticated language*, unless necessary.
12. Where possible, question/setups should be phrased in a *realistic setting*.
13. Question/scale measurements should be designed to *read logically*.
14. Question/scale measurements should always *avoid the use of double-barreled items*.

Note: For examples, go to the book's Web site (www.mhhe.com/hair06) and follow the links.

Evaluate Question/Scale Measurements

The flowerpot approach also does not impact the activities that take place in this aspect of the development process. Prior to laying out the actual survey instrument, the researcher should have already examined each question and scale measurement for reliability and validity. Now the focus is on evaluating any needed instructions and revisions. See Exhibit 13.7 for a summary of the guidelines for evaluating the adequacy of questions.

Establish Flowerpot Format and Layout

The activities undertaken here are at the center of the flowerpot approach to questionnaire designs. Taking all the individual questions and scales previously developed and tested, the researcher must present them in a specific, logical order. After creating a title for the questionnaire, the researcher must include a brief introductory section and any general instructions prior to asking the first question. The questions that make up the first information flowerpot must be asked in a natural general-to-specific order to reduce the potential for sequence bias.

In any type of research design that uses questioning as the data collection method (i.e., personal interviews, computer-assisted or regular telephone interviews, or self-administered questionnaires), all instructions should be included within each question or scale, where appropriate. After completing the information flowerpot, the researcher must stabilize the structure by building a base. In the American Bank example, there is a two-part base. The lifestyle belief (i.e., general opinions or psychographics) section is presented first, and then the more standardized classification section (i.e., demographics). The final part of any base is the thank-you statement.

At the beginning of the classification section is this statement: "Now just a few more questions so that we can combine your answers with those of the other people taking part in this study." This is a "transition phrase," which serves three basic purposes. First, it communicates to the respondents that a change in their thinking process is about to take place. No longer do they have to think about their specific belief structures. They can clear their mind before thinking about their personal data. Second, it hints that the task of completing the survey is almost over. Third, it assures the respondent that the information she or he gives will be used only in aggregate combinations—that is, it will be blended with information from other respondents participating in the survey.

Evaluate the Questionnaire and Layout

After drafting the questionnaire, but before submitting it to the management team for approval, the researcher should review the layout to make sure the questionnaire meets all the information objectives. Normally, the researcher would focus on determining whether each question is necessary and whether the overall length is acceptable. In contrast, the flowerpot approach would give more attention to (1) checking whether the instrument meets the overall objectives; (2) checking the scale format and scaling properties; and (3) checking general-to-specific order.

An easy method of evaluating any questionnaire design is to answer the following five questions for each question or scale measurement:

1. What types of raw data (state of being, mind, behavior, or intention) are being sought in the question, and for what purpose?

2. What types of questions or scale measurements (nominal, ordinal, true class interval, hybrid ordinally-interval, ratio) are being used?

3. What scaling properties (assignment, order, distance, origin) are being activated in the scale measurement?

4. What is the most appropriate measure of central tendency (mode, median, mean)?

5. What is the most appropriate measure of dispersion (frequency distribution, range, standard deviation)?

Obtain the Client's Approval

The flowerpot concept does not impact this aspect of the overall development process. Copies of the questionnaire draft should be made and distributed to all parties that have authority over and interest in the project. Realistically, the client may step in at any time in the design process to express a need for some type of modification.

Nevertheless, it is important to get final approval of the questionnaire prior to pretesting it. The logic behind client approval is that it commits management to the body of data and eventually to the information that will result from the specific questionnaire design. In addition, it helps reduce unnecessary surprises and saves time and money. If changes are necessary, this is where they should occur. The researcher must make sure that any changes adhere to the design requirements.

Pretest and Revise the Questionnaire

While fine-tuning the questionnaire can take place via discussions between the researcher and client, the final evaluation should come from people representing the individuals who will be asked to actually fill out the survey. Remember, pretesting the questionnaire does not mean that one researcher administers the questionnaire to another researcher, or to the client's management or staff. Furthermore, it does not mean that the pretest is done with college students unless they are representative of the study's target population.

An appropriate pretest involves a simulated administration of the survey to a small, representative group of respondents. How many respondents should be included in a pretest is open to debate. Some researchers will use as few as 10 respondents, while others might use as many as 50 depending on the purpose of the pretest, the method of administering the survey, and how the survey was developed. For example, if the questions were not properly tested for reliability and validity during the construct/scale measurement development process, then the pretest should include at least 50 respondents so that the researcher addresses reliability and validity issues.[11] In contrast, if the main purpose of the pretest is to check for specific wording problems, then only about 10 respondents are needed in the pretest.[12] In a pretest respondents are asked to pay attention to such elements as words, phrases, instructions, and question flow patterns and point out anything they feel is confusing, difficult to understand, or otherwise a problem.

When using the flowerpot approach, the researcher should find no reliability/validity or wording issues at this point, since those issues should have been addressed in earlier development procedures. Rather, the pretest should help the researcher determine how much time respondents will need to complete the survey, whether to add any instructions, and what to say in the cover letter. If any problems or concerns arise in the pretest, modifications must be made and approved by the client prior to moving to the next step. The American Bank study questionnaire was pretested on 25 randomly selected bank customers and revealed no surprises.

Finalize the Questionnaire Format

Here, the questionnaire is placed in final format. Decisions are made about typing instructions, spacing, numbers for questions and pages, folding, and stapling—all of which relate to the professional appearance of the questionnaire. Quality in appearance is more important in self-administered surveys than in personal or telephone interviews. Reproduction considerations of documents also comes into play here. Any support materials—such as interviewer instructions, cover letters, rating cards, mailing and return envelopes—are finalized and reproduced for distribution.

Another set of decisions relates to the precoding of the response categories used to represent the scaling points. In the American Bank study, the questionnaire was formatted as a four-page booklet with a separate cover letter and a self-addressed, stamped return envelope. (See Exhibit 13.10 on p. 457 for the cover letter used by American Bank.)

Implement the Survey

The focus here is on the processes that must be followed to begin the collection of the required raw data. These will vary based on the data collection method. Although the American Bank example illustrates how the flowerpot approach plays a useful role in the development process of survey instruments, no single study can exemplify all of the numerous factors researchers must consider when designing a questionnaire. We offer a general summary of the major considerations in questionnaire designs in Exhibit 13.8. Firms are also faced with new challenges as they expand into global markets. One question they must address is whether the research techniques they used in their own country can be directly applied in foreign countries. To illustrate this point log on to the book's Web site (www.mhhe.com/hair06), follow the links to the Global Insight, read the Holiday Inn Resort example, and answer the questions.

EXHIBIT 13.8 Summary of Important Considerations in Questionnaire Designs

1. Determine the *information objectives* and the *number of information flowerpots* required to meet those objectives.

2. Determine the *specific data requirements* (i.e., the size) for each information flowerpot, and stack the pots from *largest to smallest*.

3. Introduction section should include a *general description* of what the study is pertaining to; this may well be in a *disguised format*.

4. All types of *instructions*, if necessary, should be given *clear expression*.

5. Perhaps most important, the *question/scale measurements* have to follow some *logical order*—that is, an order that appears logical to the respondent rather than to the researcher or practitioner.

6. Begin an interview or questionnaire with *simple questions* that are easy to respond to, and then *gradually lead up* to the more difficult questions. *Create a general-to-specific data flow.*

7. Postpone *highly personal questions* (state-of-being data) *until late* in the interview or survey (i.e., place in the base after the last information flowerpot).

8. Place questions that *involve psychological tests* (i.e., lifestyle beliefs) toward *the end* of the interview or survey, but before the identification base.

9. *Do not ask too many questions of the same measurement format* (i.e., nominal, ordinal, interval, ratio scale formats) in sequence.

10. *Taper off* an interview or survey with a *few relatively simple questions* that do not require extensive thoughts or expressions of feelings (i.e., the demographic data questions are very appropriate here).

11. Always *end the interview* or survey with the *appropriate thank-you statement.*

Development of Cover Letters

The Role of a Cover Letter

Cover letter A separate written communication to a prospective respondent designed to enhance that person's willingness to complete and return the survey in a timely manner.

A critical aspect associated with good questionnaire design is the development of an appropriate cover letter. Many marketing research textbooks offer little discussion of cover letter development. Usually, a **cover letter** is viewed as a letter accompanying a self-administered questionnaire that explains the nature of the survey. With personal or telephone interviews, researchers might not think to use a cover letter. However, cover letters play several important roles in the successful collection of primary raw data, regardless of the data collection method. A cover letter is neither the same as the introductory section on the actual questionnaire nor the same as a screener.

The main role of the cover letter should be that of winning over the respondent's cooperation and willingness to participate in the research project. In other words, the cover letter should help persuade a prospective respondent to fill out the questionnaire and return it in a timely fashion. With self-administered surveys, many times a research project falls short of its goal because the response rate is very low (e.g., 25 percent or less). Usually when the response rate is low, the researcher can only guess at why. With either telephone or personal interviewing, similar problems occur when large numbers of prospective respondents decline to participate.

Secondary roles of a cover letter include (a) introducing the respondent to the research project and the researcher, (b) informing the respondent of the importance of the study, and (c) communicating the study's legitimacy and other particulars such as the deadline for returning the completed survey, and where to return it.[13]

Having a standardized cover letter that will fit all survey or interviewing situations is highly unlikely, but there are several factors that should be included in any cover letter. Exhibit 13.9 presents guidelines for developing cover letters. Each of these is discussed in the next section.

EXHIBIT 13.9 Guidelines for Developing Cover Letters

Factors	Description
1. Personalization	Cover letter should be addressed to the specific prospective respondent; use research firm's professional letterhead stationery.
2. Identification of the organization doing the study	Clear identification of the name of the research firm conducting the survey or interview; decide on disguised or undisguised approach of revealing the actual client (or sponsor) of the study.
3. Clear statement of the study's purpose and importance	Describe the general topic of the research and emphasize its importance to the prospective respondent.
4. Anonymity and confidentiality	Give assurances that the prospective respondent's name will not be revealed. Explain how the respondent was chosen, and stress that his or her meaningful input is important to the study's success.
5. General time frame of doing the study	Communicate the overall time frame of the survey or interview.
6. Reinforcement of the importance of the respondent's participation	Where appropriate, communicate the importance of the prospective respondents' participation.
7. Acknowledgment of reasons for nonparticipation in survey or interview	Point out "lack of leisure time," "surveys classified as junk mail," and "forgetting about survey" reasons for not participating, and defuse them.
8. Time requirements and compensation	Clearly communicate the approximate time required to complete the survey; discuss incentive program, if any.
9. Completion date and where and how to return the survey	Communicate to the prospective respondent all instructions for returning the completed questionnaire.
10. Advance thank-you statement for willingness to participate	Thank the prospective respondent for his or her cooperation.

Guidelines for Developing Cover Letters

Regardless of a research project's method of data collection, the researcher should include a well-developed cover letter that relates to the survey instrument. For self-administered questionnaires, a separate cover letter should be sent with the questionnaire. For most telephone surveys and some types of personal interviews, a cover letter should be mailed to each prospective respondent before the initial contact by the interviewer.

Prior mailing of cover letters in interviewing situations is not a common practice among researchers, but this procedure can increase respondents' willingness to participate.[14] The reason for this comes from an understanding of human behavior. For example, the prospective respondent and interviewer are strangers to each other. People are more hesitant to express their opinions or feelings about a topic to a stranger than to someone they know, even to a limited extent. Mailing a cover letter to prospective respondents enables the researcher to break the ice prior to the actual interview.

The cover letter should introduce the potential respondent to the research project, stress its legitimacy, encourage participation, and let respondents know that a representative will be contacting them in the near future. Using a cover letter in interviewing situations increases the initial cost of data collection, but the resulting increase in the response rate can reduce the overall cost of the project.

While the exact wording of a cover letter will vary from researcher to researcher and from situation to situation, any cover letter should include the factors displayed in Exhibit 13.9.

Factor 1: Personalization

Whenever possible, the cover letter should be addressed to the person who was randomly selected as a prospective respondent. The cover letter should be typed on a professional letterhead that represents the research organization's affiliation, not the client's.

Factor 2: Identification of the Organization Doing the Study

The first comments should identify the research company conducting the survey but not necessarily the sponsor. If the sponsor wants or needs to be identified, then the researcher can choose one of two options: an undisguised or a disguised approach. With an undisguised approach, the actual sponsor's name will appear as part of the introduction statement. For example, the opening statement might read as follows:

> The Nationwide Opinion Research Company in New York is conducting a study for Verizon on people's cell phone practices.

In contrast, a disguised approach would not divulge the sponsor's identity to the respondent and would appear like this:

> The Nationwide Opinion Company in New York is conducting a study on people's cell phone habits and would like to include your opinions.

Which sponsorship approach to use will be determined by the overall research objectives or a mutual agreement between the researcher and client regarding the possible benefits and drawbacks of revealing the sponsor's name to the respondent. One reason for using a disguised approach is that it prevents competitors from finding out about the survey.[15]

Factor 3: Clear Statement of the Study's Purpose and Importance

One or two statements must be included in any cover letter to describe the general nature or topic of the survey and emphasize its importance. In the American Bank survey example, the researcher might use the following statements:

> Consumer banking practices are rapidly changing in 2005. With more bank locations, many new bank services, new technologies, the growth of credit unions, and the increased complexity of people's financial needs and wants, financial institutions are indeed changing. These changes are having important effects on you and your family. We would like to gain insights into these changes and their impact from the consumer's perspective by better understanding your opinions about different banking services, habits, and patterns. We think you will find the survey interesting.

When you state the purpose of the study, it is important that you introduce the general topic of the survey in an interesting manner using words that are familiar to most members of the target audience. The purpose of the study should be followed by a statement that conveys the importance of the respondent's opinions on the topic. Some researchers like to follow up the purpose by adding a disclaimer that strongly emphasizes (1) that the company is not trying to sell anything and (2) that the respondent's name will not be added to any type of mailing list.

Factor 4: Anonymity and Confidentiality

After describing the purpose of the survey, the researcher must let the respondent know how and why people were selected for the study. The researcher can use a statement like this:

> Your name was one of only 2,000 names randomly selected from a representative list of people living in the Chicago area. Because the success of the survey depends upon the cooperation of all people who were selected, we would especially appreciate your willingness to help.

The phrasing should emphasize the importance of the respondent's participation to the success of the study and indirectly suggest that the respondent is special.

If the researcher and client decide that assurances about anonymity and confidentiality are necessary, those factors should be incorporated at this point. **Anonymity** assures that the respondent's name or any identifiable designation will not be associated with his or her responses. Among the different data collection methods, anonymity statements are most appropriately associated with self-administered questionnaires. The researcher might use the following as an anonymity statement:

Anonymity The assurance that survey respondents will in no way be matched to their responses.

> The information obtained from the survey will in no way reflect the identities of the people participating in the study.

When an interview is used to collect data, an anonymity statement can appear in the letter of introduction that is mailed prior to the interviewer's initial contact with a prospective respondent.

A statement of **confidentiality** assures the prospective respondent that his or her name, while known to the researcher, will not be divulged to a third party, especially the client. Regardless of the data collection method, a confidentiality statement should always be included in a cover letter. A confidentiality statement might be phrased as follows:

Confidentiality The assurance that the respondent's identity will not be divulged to a third party, including the client of the research.

> Your cooperation, attitudes, and opinions are very important to the success of the study and will be kept strictly confidential. Your opinions and responses will only be used when grouped with those of the other people participating in the survey.

Once the prospective respondent is promised confidentiality, it is the researcher's responsibility to keep that promise.

Factor 5: Time Frame

The cover letter should identify the general time frame for the survey. To encourage a prospective respondent to participate, it should state the actual completion time and any compensation that might be offered. When using an interview, for example, the researcher would include a statement or phrase like the following:

> In the next couple of days, one of our trained representatives will be contacting you by phone . . . The survey will only take a few moments of your time.

The key consideration with this factor is not to use a question format that requires a simple yes or no response. For example, "May I have one of our trained representatives contact you in the next couple of days?" or "May we have a few moments of your time?" If prospective respondents can answer "no" to a question asked in the cover letter, they are less likely to participate in the study.

Factor 6: Reinforcement of the Importance of the Respondent's Participation

The researcher can incorporate simple phrases into any part of the cover letter to reinforce the point that the respondent's participation is critical to the success of the study. Such phrases should be worded positively, not negatively.

Factor 7: Acknowledgment of Reasons for Not Participating in the Study

People offer numerous reasons when declining the role of being a respondent in a survey. Research among a variety of different groups has identified three of the most common reasons for not participating in a survey: (1) not having enough time, (2) seeing surveys as junk mail, and (3) forgetting about the survey.

First, people treasure their leisure time and feel they do not have enough of it. Therefore, when they receive a survey or telephone call or are asked on the spot to answer a few questions, potential respondents tend to use "do not have the time" as a reason not to participate. Since people are more likely to take the time to answer questions from someone they know, or are at least aware of, than from a stranger, the researcher has to acknowledge the time factor in the cover letter. To do this, a researcher should use a statement like this:

> We realize that to most of us in the community our leisure time is scarce and important and that we do not like to spend it filling out a questionnaire for some unknown person's or organization's study. Please remember that you are among a few being asked to participate in this study and your opinions are very important to the success of it.

This type of statement can easily be combined with statements about time requirements and compensation to effectively negate the time objection. Second, many people have the tendency to classify surveys received through regular mail or e-mail as "junk mail" or a telephone interviewer's call as an attempt to sell them something they do not need or want. To acknowledge this, something like the following statement could be used:

> We realize that many of us in the community receive a lot of things through regular mail or e-mail which we classify as "junk mail" and not important to respond to, but please do not consider the attached survey as being "junk mail." Your opinions, attitudes, and viewpoints toward each question are very important to us as well as the success of this study.

And for regular telephone interviews or CATI, the researcher should incorporate a statement like the following:

> We realize that many of us in the community receive a lot of phone calls from strangers trying to sell us some product or service that we neither need nor want. Let me assure you that I am not trying to sell you anything. I would just like to get your honest opinions on several questions pertaining to your banking habits and preferences; they are important to the success of this study.

Third, the issue of forgetting the survey primarily relates to direct mail or e-mail surveys. To help eliminate this problem, the researcher should incorporate a statement in the cover letter something like this:

> Past research has suggested that many questionnaires received through the mail or e-mail, if not completed and returned within the first 36 hours, have a tendency to get misplaced or forgotten about. Upon receiving this survey, please take the time to complete it. Your opinions are very important to us.

By taking away these three main reasons for not participating in a research study, the researcher significantly improves the likelihood that the prospective respondent will complete and return the direct mail, e-mail, or Web survey or cooperate in a telephone interview.

Factor 8: Time Requirements and Compensation

In an effort to win over a prospective respondent, the researcher might emphasize in the cover letter that the survey will not take much time or effort. For a self-administered survey, the researcher can incorporate statements like the following:

> We have designed the questionnaire to include all the directions and instructions necessary to complete the survey without the assistance of an interviewer. The survey will take approximately 15 minutes to complete. Please take your time in responding to each question. Your honest responses are very important to the success of the study.

For any type of interview, the researcher could incorporate the following statement into the letter of introduction: "The interview will take approximately 15 minutes to complete."

This type of statement reinforces the notion that the survey will not take up much of the person's time.

The researcher and client may decide that some form of compensation is needed to encourage the respondent's participation. The type of compensation will depend on the study's topic and the data collection method. A token dollar amount (e.g., $1 or $5) can be offered to each prospective respondent and included in the questionnaire packet. The idea is that giving respondents a reward up front for participating will make them feel obligated to complete the survey and return it as requested.[16] Experience with this method, however, suggests that people tend to assign a higher price than $1 or even $5 to their time. In other situations, nonmonetary incentives (e.g., a sample product, tickets to a movie, a certificate redeemable for specific products or services) might be used to encourage a respondent's participation.

Lottery incentive approach The pooling of individual incentive offerings into a significantly larger offering for which those people who participate have an equal chance of receiving the incentive.

An alternative to the individual reward system is the **lottery incentive approach** in which the incentive money forms a significantly larger dollar amount and everyone who completes and returns the survey has a chance of receiving the incentive. A significant reward is most likely to increase the response rate. The lottery approach is not, however, restricted to direct monetary rewards. Alternative rewards might be the chance to win an expense-paid trip somewhere. For example, the JP Hotel Corporation has used a "three-day, two-night all-expenses-paid weekend stay for two people" at one of its luxury hotel complexes as the incentive for respondents who completed and returned their questionnaire by the specified date.

Among the different incentive programs available to the researcher, the lottery incentive system is advocated whenever possible. When a lottery is used, extra effort is required by the researcher to develop and include a separate identification form in the questionnaire packet that can be filled out and returned with a respondent's completed questionnaire. This incentive system tends to be most appropriate for self-administered surveys. Comments concerning incentives in a cover letter might be phrased as follows:

> To show our appreciation for your taking the time to participate in this study, we are going to hold a drawing for $500 among those who complete this survey. The drawing procedure has been designed in such a way that everyone who completes and returns the questionnaire will have an equal opportunity to receive the appreciation gift of $500.

Factor 9: Completion Date and Where and How to Return the Survey

In studies that collect data using a self-administered mail method, the researcher must give the respondent instructions for how, where, and when to return their completed survey. The how and where instructions can be simply expressed through the following type of statement:

> After completing all the questions in the survey, please use the enclosed stamped, addressed envelope to return your completed survey and appreciation gift card.

To deal with the return deadline date, the researcher should include a statement like this:

> To help us complete the study in a timely fashion, we need your cooperation in returning the completed questionnaire and incentive drawing card by no later than **Friday, June 24, 2005.**

For cover letters used with e-mail or Internet-based surveys, the researcher must communicate the notion that after completing the survey the respondent only needs to click the "submit" button to send the completed survey to the researcher.

Factor 10: An Advanced Thank You

Prior to closing the cover letter with a thank-you statement, the researcher might want to include a final reassurance that she or he is not trying to sell the prospective respondent anything. In addition, the legitimacy of the study can be reinforced by supplying a name

A Closer Look at Research

MARKETING RESOURCES GROUP
2305 Windsor Oaks Drive, Suite 1105
Baton Rouge, Louisiana 70814

CONSUMER BANKING OPINION STUDY
BATON ROUGE, LOUISIANA
(June 10, 2005)

In the Field

If you have a bank account—

We need your opinion.

With more bank locations, new banking services, and the growth of credit unions and savings and loans, financial institutions are indeed changing. These changes will have an effect on you and your family, and that's why your opinion is important.

Your name has been selected in a sample of Baton Rouge residents to determine what people in our community think about the present products and services offered by banks. Your individual opinions in this survey can never be traced back to you, and all results will be held strictly confidential. The results of the study will provide the banking industry with insight into how to better serve the needs of its customers.

The brand-new quarter enclosed with this letter is not enough to compensate you for your time, but it may brighten the day of a youngster you know.

Thank you for your assistance.

Sincerely,

Thomas L. Kirk
MRG Project Director

P.S. Please return no later than June 24, 2005. A postage-paid envelope is enclosed.

---

and telephone number if there are any concerns or questions, as follows:

> Again, let me give you my personal guarantee that we are not trying to sell you something. If you have any doubts, concerns, or questions about this survey, please give me a call at (504) 974-6236. Thank you in advance. We appreciate your cooperation in taking part in our study.

The researcher should sign the cover letter and include his or her title.

A good cover letter entails as much thought, care, and effort as the questionnaire itself. While the actual factors will vary from researcher to researcher, these 10 are standard elements of any good cover letter. The specific examples given above should not be viewed as standardized phrases that must be included in all cover letters, but they do show how a researcher might increase a prospective respondent's willingness to participate in a given study. To see how these factors fit together in a cover letter, see Exhibit 13.10. The bold number inserts in the cover letter refer to the guidelines listed in Exhibit 13.9 of the chapter.

Cover Letter Length

A rarely discussed design question that affects the development of a cover letter is "How long should the cover letter be?" There is no simple answer that is correct in all situations, and in fact there are two opposing views. First, many researchers believe that the cover letter should be simple, to the point, and no longer than one page. The nearby Closer Look at Research box illustrates a hypothetical cover letter for the American Bank and Trust survey that follows the direct, one-page approach.

EXHIBIT 13.10 Cover Letter Used with the American Bank Survey

MARKETING RESOURCES GROUP
2305 Windsor Oaks Drive, Suite 1105
Baton Rouge, Louisiana 70814

June 10, 2005

[1]

Ms. Caroline V. Livingstone
873 Patterson Drive
Baton Rouge LA 70801

Dear Ms. Livingstone:

[2]We at Marketing Resources Group here in Baton Rouge are conducting an interesting study this month on people's banking habits and services [5]this month and would like to include your opinions.

[3]As you know, consumer banking practices are rapidly changing in the new millennium. With more bank locations, many new bank services, new technologies, the growth of credit unions and savings and loans, and the increased complexity of people's financial needs and wants, financial institutions are indeed changing. These changes are having important effects on you and your family. We would like to gain insights into these changes and their impact from the consumer's perspective by better understanding your opinions about different banking services, habits, and patterns.

We think you will find the survey interesting.

[4]Your name was one of only 600 names randomly selected from a representative list of people currently living in the Baton Rouge community. [6]Because the success of the survey depends upon the cooperation of all the people who were selected, we would especially appreciate your willingness to help us in this study.

[4]The information obtained from the survey will in no way reflect the identities of the people participating. Your cooperation, attitudes, and opinions are very important to the success of the study and will be kept strictly confidential. Your response will only be used when grouped with those of the other people taking part in the study.

[7]We realize that many of us in the community receive a lot of things through the mail which we classify as "junk mail" and not important to respond to, but please do not consider the attached survey as being "junk mail." [6]Your opinions, attitudes, and viewpoints toward each question are very important to us.

[7]To most of us in the community our leisure time is scarce and important, and we do not like to spend it filling out a questionnaire for some unknown organization's survey. Please remember that you are among a few being asked to participate in this study and [6]your opinions are very important to the success of it. [8]We have designed the questionnaire to include all the directions and instructions necessary to complete the survey without the assistance of an interviewer. You will find that the survey will take only about 15 minutes of your time. Please take your time in responding to each question. [6]Your honest responses are what we are looking for in the study.

[8]To show, in part, our appreciation for your taking the time to participate in this important study, we are going to hold a drawing for $500 among those of you who donate some of your leisure time to help us in completing this survey. The drawing procedure has been designed in such a way that everyone who completes and returns the questionnaire will have an equal opportunity to receive the appreciation gift of $500.

[7]Past research has suggested that many questionnaires that are received through the mail, if not completed and returned within the first 36 hours, have a tendency to be misplaced or forgotten about. Upon receiving this survey, please take the time to complete it. [6]Your opinions are very important to us.

[9]After completing all the questions in this survey, please use the enclosed stamped and addressed envelope to return your completed survey and appreciation gift card. To help us complete the study in a timely fashion, we need your cooperation in returning the survey and gift card by **no later than Friday, June 24, 2005.**

Again, let me give you my personal guarantee that we are not trying to sell you something. If you have any doubts, concerns, or questions about this survey, please give me a call at (504) 974-6236.

[10]Thank you in advance. We deeply appreciate your cooperation in taking part in our study.

Sincerely,

Thomas L. Kirk
MRG Project Director

eТHICS

Telephone Survey Goes Sour

In the Spring of 2004, the Quality A-1 Rainbow Rug Cleaners, a new franchised carpet cleaning business, began operations in San Diego, California. This company was a member of San Diego's chamber of commerce. The owners of this franchised carpet cleaning business were struggling to get customers. They turned to a telemarketing firm for help. After several conversations with the telemarketing experts, a joint decision was made to use a disguised approach to solicit prospective customers by phone. The telemarketing firm developed what it called a telephone survey that would capture the necessary information to identify people in need of carpet cleaning services. Upon determination of the need, the survey was designed for the telephone interviewer to activate the customized sales pitch for Quality A-1 Rainbow Rug Cleaners' services. The survey started out by informing prospective respondents that they were randomly selected to participate in a short survey about cleaning

products. Once it was determined that the individual qualified, the survey became a sales pitch, telling the qualified prospective customers that Quality A-1 Rainbow Rug Cleaners would be in their neighborhood that week and asking when would they like to schedule an appointment. Those unsuspecting respondents who agreed were scheduled on the spot by the telemarketing interviewer. The telemarketing firm convinced the owners that the survey process should run for one month at a cost of $4,000. Two weeks into the project, Quality A-1 Rainbow's owners received a call from San Diego's chamber of commerce notifying them that it had received about 100 calls from residents complaining about unwanted sales solicitations for Quality A-1 Rainbow's carpet cleaning services. Identify the ethical problems Quality A-1 Rainbow Rug Cleaners created for itself through their research program. How might the cleaning company have avoided those problems?

While the one-page cover letter includes some of the factors we have discussed for influencing a prospective respondent's willingness to participate, it tends to lack the intensity level and clarity needed to win over a stranger. Still, many researchers go with a one-page design because of the cost factor and because they believe people do not like to read correspondence from unknown commercial organizations like a research company. It is true that it costs less to develop, reproduce, and mail a one-page cover letter than a multiple-page letter, but if the one-page cover letter does not produce an adequate response rate, the study will cost more in the long run. The notion that people do not like to read correspondence from unknown commercial senders is basically true and is one of the reasons people use to justify not participating in a survey.

The contrasting view focuses on the need to deliver an emotion-laden story that compels the prospective respondent to cooperate. If a cover letter is well crafted and interesting, the prospective respondent will read not only the first page but the complete cover letter and move on to the questionnaire.

As always, the researcher should keep in mind the importance of ethical behavior. The Ethics box discusses a carpet cleaning company's misuse of a telephone survey to gain new sales.

Supplemental Documents Associated with Survey Instrument Designs

Although the main focus of this chapter is the development process and flowerpot approach to designing questionnaires, several supplemental documents required to execute the field-work activities in marketing research are worthy of discussion. When the decision is made to collect data by means of either personal, CATI, or telephone interviews, there is a need to develop good supervisor and interviewer instructions as well as screening forms, rating cards, and call record sheets. These types of documents help ensure that the process of collecting high-quality data will be successful. We discuss the highlights of each of these forms in this section.

Supervisor Instructions

Supervisor instruction form A form that serves as a blueprint for training people on how to execute the interviewing process in a standardized fashion; it outlines the process by which to conduct a study that uses personal and telephone interviewers.

Many commercial research companies collect much of their data using interviews that are conducted by specialty field interviewing companies located in selected geographic test markets. These companies are the production line for collecting raw data within the research industry. Usually, this type of company completes the interviews and sends them to the research company for processing. A **supervisor instruction form** serves as a blueprint for training people on how to complete the interviewing process in a standardized fashion. The instructions outline the process for conducting the study and are vitally important to any research project that utilizes personal or telephone interviews. They include detailed information about the nature of the study, start and completion dates, sampling instructions, number of interviewers required, equipment and facility requirements, reporting forms, quotas, and validation procedures. Exhibit 13.11 displays a sample page from a set of supervisor instructions for a retail banking study that uses trained student interviewers to administer personal interviews for collecting the data.

EXHIBIT 13.11 Example of Supervisor Instructions for a Retail Bank Study Using Personal Interviews

Purpose:	To determine from students their banking practices and attitudes toward bank service quality across several different types of financial institutions.
Number of interviewers:	A total of 90 trained student interviewers (30 interviewers per class, three different classes).
Location and time of interviews:	Interviews will be conducted over a two-week period beginning October 10 and ending October 24, 2005. They will be conducted between the hours of 8:00 A.M. and 9:00 P.M., Monday through Friday. The locations of the interviews will be outside the campus buildings housing the 14 colleges making up the university plus the Library and Student Union. There will be three shifts of interviewers, 30 interviewers per shift, working the time frames of 8:00 A.M. to 12:00 noon or 12:01 P.M. to 5:00 P.M. or 5:01 P.M. to 9:00 P.M.
Quota:	Each interviewer will conduct and complete 30 interviews, with a maximum of 5 completed interviews for each of the following named retail banks: Bank of America, Sun Trust Bank, Citicorp, Capital One, First Union, and any five "Other Banks." All the completed interviews should come from their assigned location and time period.
	For each shift of 30 interviewers, there will be a minimum of 150 completed interviews for each of the five named banks in the study and maximum of 150 completed interviews representing the set of "Other Banks."
Project materials:	For this study, you are supplied with the following materials: 2,701 personal questionnaires, 91 interviewer instruction-screening-quota forms, 91 sets of "Rating Cards" with each set consisting of six different rating cards, 91 "Verification of Interview" forms, and 1 interviewer scheduling matrix form.
Preparation:	Using your set of materials, review all material for complete understanding. Set a two-hour time frame for training your 90 student interviewers on how they should select a prospective respondent, screen for eligibility, and conduct the interviews. Make sure each interviewer understands the embedded "interviewer's instructions" in the actual questions making up the survey. In addition, assign each interviewer to a specified location and time frame for conducting the interviews, making sure all locations and time frames are appropriately covered.

Interviewer Instructions

Interviewer instructions The vehicle for training the interviewer on how to select prospective respondents, screen them for eligibility, and conduct the actual interview.

To ensure data quality, the interviewing process must be consistent. Thus, it is very important to train the people who will actually be conducting the interviews. **Interviewer instructions** serve as the vehicle for training the interviewers to (1) correctly select a prospective respondent for inclusion in the study, (2) screen prospective respondents for eligibility, and (3) properly conduct the actual interview. Although these instructions cover many of the same points found in the supervisor's instructions, they are designed to be pertinent to the actual interview. The instructions include detailed information about the nature of the study; start and completion dates; sampling instructions; screening procedures; quotas; number of interviews required; guidelines to asking questions, using rating cards, and recording responses; reporting forms; and verification form procedures. Exhibit 13.12 displays a sample page from a set of interviewer instructions for a retail banking study that used personal interviews to collect the data.

Although not explicitly displayed in Exhibit 13.12, many interviewer instructions list separately each general instruction as well as those within each question of the survey. In addition, the instructions include specific comments on procedures for asking each question and recording responses. The primary purpose of interviewer instructions is to ensure that all the interviews are conducted in basically the same fashion. It is critical for all interviewers to read each survey question as it was written, with no modifications. The interviewer instructions constitute a training tool to enhance the likelihood that all interviews will be conducted in the same manner, thus reducing the possibility that potential interviewer bias will enter the study and negatively impact the quality level of the data.

Screening Forms

Screening forms A set of preliminary questions that are used to determine the eligibility of a prospective respondent for inclusion in the survey.

Although screening forms are not involved in all surveys, when used they play an important role in ensuring that the sampled respondents of a study are representative of the defined target population. Determining the eligibility of a prospective respondent up front increases the likelihood that the resulting data will be of high quality. **Screening forms** are a set of preliminary questions used to determine the *eligibility* of a prospective respondent for inclusion in the survey. Normally, the researcher and the client group determine the set of special characteristics a person must have in order to be included into the pool of prospective respondents. Almost any characteristics of an individual can be used as a screener. For example, a person's age, marital status, education level, number of purchases in a given time frame, or level of satisfaction toward a product or service might serve as a useful screener in a particular survey.

Screening forms should also be used to ensure that certain types of respondents are *not* included in the study. This means there are many marketing situations where it is desirable to have a good cross section of individuals, yet within the cross section there are particular types of individuals that should be excluded from the group. This occurs most frequently when a person's direct occupation or a family member's occupation in a particular industry would eliminate the person from inclusion in the study. For example, let's assume that J. D. Power and Associates was hired to conduct a study among the general population on the impact of advertising on perceived quality of automobiles manufactured by the Ford Motor Company. To ensure objectivity in the results, J. D. Power and Associates would want to automatically exclude people who themselves or whose immediate family members work for a marketing research firm, an advertising firm, the Ford Motor Company, or an automobile dealership that sold Ford vehicles. The reason behind excluding people who have an association with these particular types of occupations is that they normally hold inherent biases toward Ford vehicles or they have knowledge about the advertising industry.

EXHIBIT 13.12 **Example of Interviewer Instructions for a Retail Bank Study Using Personal Interviews**

Purpose:	To determine from students their banking practices and attitudes toward bank service quality across several different types of financial institutions.
Method:	All interviewing will be conducted in person at your assigned designated locations within your assigned interviewing time frames. These locations and times will be assigned to you by your supervisor.
Location and time of interviews:	Your interviews will be conducted over a two-week period beginning October 10 and ending October 24, 2005. You will conduct the interviews during your assigned shift between the hours of 8:00 A.M. and 9:00 P.M., Monday through Friday. The locations of the interviews will be outside the campus buildings assigned to you by your supervisor.
Number of interviews/quota:	You will conduct and complete 30 interviews, with a maximum of 5 completed interviews for each of the following named retail banks: Bank of America, Sun Trust Bank, Citicorp, Capital One, First Union and any five "Other Banks." All your completed interviews should come from your assigned location and time period.
Project materials:	For this study, you are supplied with the following materials: 30 personal questionnaires, 1 interviewer instruction-screening-quota form, 1 set of "Rating Cards" consisting of six different rating cards, 1 "Verification of Interview" form, and 1 interviewer scheduling matrix form.
Sampling procedure:	Once you are at your assigned location during your assigned interviewing shift (e.g., College of Education, 8:00 A.M. to 12:00 noon), randomly select a person in that area and follow the "introduction" instructions on your *Introduction-Screening-Quota* sheet. (First, politely walk up to that individual and introduce yourself. Then, politely explain to the person that: [read the given introduction statement on your *Introduction-Screening-Quota* sheet].) Follow the exact instructions. If the person is willing to be interviewed, continue to ask the "screening" questions to determine that person's eligibility and quota requirements. Follow the instructions on your *Introduction-Screening-Quota* sheet. If the person qualifies, begin the actual survey. If you determine that the person is not eligible, follow the instructions for terminating the interview and selecting your next prospective respondent. All interviewer instructions will be denoted in **FULL CAPS** on your *Introduction-Screening-Quota* sheet.
Screening factors:	Prospective respondents will be eligible if: 1. They are a current university student this current fall semester. 2. They have not already participated in this survey. 3. They are needed to fill any of the designated "quotas" for the five specific named banks or the "Other Banks" group.
Guidelines for actual interview:	Once the prospective respondent is determined eligible, you should begin the actual survey starting with question 1. Make sure you read each question as it is written on the questionnaire. All your instructions will appear in **FULL CAPS**; follow them carefully. After completing the interview, you must have the respondent fill out the required information on the "Verification of Interview" form. Then randomly select your next prospective respondent and follow the procedures and instructions on your *Introduction-Screening-Quota* sheet.
Preparation:	Using your set of materials, review all material for complete understanding. Prior to beginning the actual interviews, do at least three practice interviews to become familiar with the procedures for selecting a prospective respondent, screening for eligibility, and conducting the interviews. Make sure you understand the embedded "interviewer instructions" in the actual questions making up the survey.

Thus, their opinions, attitudes, and feelings about the impact of advertising and/or quality of Ford vehicles *are not representative* of the people who make up the general population.

Screening forms tend to be used mainly with personal or telephone interviews rather than with self-administered surveys. The reason for this is that the researcher needs a human being to control the screening process and make the final judgment about eligibility.

Self-administered questionnaires prevent this type of control. This does not mean that screening of prospective respondents is not possible in self-administered surveys. But it does require an additional process prior to administering the questionnaires. This process involves conducting a separate screening procedure either by telephone or with a personal interviewer before the prospective respondent receives his or her questionnaire. An exception to the need for a human being to serve as the control mechanism would be a survey that is self-administered through a computer or a television network (e.g., a hotel-guest survey that is programmed on the TV in a guest's room). In these methods, the questionnaire can be preprogrammed to automatically terminate the survey depending upon how respondents themselves answered the prelisted screening questions. Exhibit 13.13 illustrates the screening form used in the retail banking study among college students.

---

e X H I B I T   13.13   **Example of an Introduction-Screening-Quota Sheet for a Retail Bank Study Using Personal Interviews**

INTRODUCTION-SCREENING-QUOTA SHEET
FOR THE UNIVERSITY STUDENT BANKING OPINION SURVEY

Approach to Randomly Selecting a Student

A. Politely walk up to an individual and introduce yourself.

B. Politely explain to the person that:

Your Marketing Research class is conducting an interesting class project this semester on students' banking attitudes and habits and you would like to include their opinions in the study.

- IF THEY SAY **"NO"** or **"DON'T WANT TO PARTICIPATE,"** politely thank them and move on to randomly select another person and repeat steps A and B.
- IF THEY ARE WILLING TO BE INTERVIEWED, ASK:

Q1. **Are you currently a university student this semester?**

If **YES,** continue with Q2.

If **NO,** thank them and **DISCONTINUE** the survey.

Q2. **Have you already participated in this survey?**

If **YES,** thank them and **DISCONTINUE** the survey.

If **NO,** continue with Q3.

Q3. **Thinking about the various banking systems which you may or may not use, please tell me the name of the <u>one</u> bank that you would generally consider as being <u>"YOUR"</u> primary bank.**

(CHECK TO SEE IF THE RESPONDENT'S CHOICE FITS YOUR NEEDED QUOTA OF BANK TYPES BELOW)

Quota		Possible "Other" Banks	
1 2 3 4 5	Bank of America	❑	Beneficial Savings
1 2 3 4 5	Sun Trust Bank	❑	Glendale Federal
1 2 3 4 5	Citicorp	❑	USF Credit Union
1 2 3 4 5	Capital One	❑	Southeast Bank
1 2 3 4 5	First Union	❑	Wells Fargo
1 2 3 4 5	Some Other Bank ⟶	❑	Write In _____

- IF THE ANSWER **<u>FITS</u>** A NEEDED QUOTA AREA,

(a) cross out one of the respective quota counts, and

(b) record the answer in Question 1 of the survey and continue with Question 2 of the survey.

- IF THE ANSWER **DOES NOT FIT** A NEEDED QUOTA AREA,

(a) politely thank them and **DISCONTINUE** the survey, and

(b) go back and repeat Steps A and B.

Quota Sheets

In any type of research study there are situations when the researcher and client decide the prospective respondents should automatically represent specifically defined subgroups or categories of prespecified sizes (or quotas). **Quota sheets** are a simple tracking form that enhances the interviewer's ability to collect data from the right type of respondents. This form ensures that the identifiable respondent groups meet the prespecified requirements. Quotas also help an interviewer determine who is eligible for inclusion in the study. When a particular quota for a subgroup of respondents is filled, it indicates to the interviewer that although a respondent might qualify on the basis of all the screening factors, she or he is not needed for the specific subgroup of respondents. Therefore, the interview would be terminated at that point.

In the retail banking example, it was noted that 90 interviewers were used to collect the data for the study. Each interviewer was required to complete 30 interviews, for a total of 2,700 interviews. Among that total, overall quotas of 16.67 percent were established for Bank of America, Sun Trust Bank, Citicorp, Capital Bank, and First Union as well as for "Other Banks." Once the quota was reached for a particular bank, let's say Capital One, any prospective respondent who qualified on the screening questions but indicated that Capital One was his or her primary bank would be terminated from the survey. Exhibit 13.13 illustrates how the quota system worked for the retail banking survey.

Rating Cards

When collecting data by means of personal interviews, the researcher needs to develop another type of support document, referred to as a rating card. These cards serve as a tool to help the interviewer and respondent speed up the process of asking and answering the questions that make up the actual survey instrument. A **rating card** represents a reproduction of the set of actual scale points and their descriptions for specific questions on the survey. Whenever there is a question that asks the respondent to express some degree of intensity as part of the response, the interviewer provides the respondent with a rating card that reflects the possible scale responses. Before asking the survey question, the interviewer would hand the respondent the rating card and explain how to use the information on the card to respond to the question. Then the interviewer would read the question and each prelisted attribute to the respondent and record the person's response. Typically, the respondent's answer would be in the form of a letter or numerical descriptor that was specifically assigned to represent each response on the card. Exhibit 13.14 offers a specific example of a question and the appropriate rating card used in a retail banking survey administered using personal interviews.

Call Record Sheets

Call record sheets, also referred to as either *reporting or tracking sheets*, are used to help the researcher estimate the efficiency of interviewers' performance. While there is no one best format for designing a call record sheet, the form usually indicates some basic summary information regarding the number of contacts (or attempts) made by each interviewer and the results of those attempts. Typically, record sheets are used in data collection methods that require the use of an interviewer. Examples of the types of information gathered from a call record sheet would include number of calls or contacts made per hour, number of contacts per completed interview, length of time of the interview, completions by quota categories, number of terminated interviews, basic reasons for termination, and number of callback attempts (see Exhibit 13.15).

exHIBIT 13.14 Example of the Question/Scale Format and Rating Card Used in Collecting Raw Data in a Retail Banking Survey

RATING CARD A
(IMPORTANCE SCALE FOR Q2)

Rating Numbers	Description
6____	**Extremely Important** Consideration to Me
5____	**Definitely Important** Consideration to Me
4____	**Generally Important** Consideration to Me
3____	**Somewhat Important** Consideration to Me
2____	**Only Slightly Important** Consideration to Me
1____	**Not At All Important** Consideration to Me

Q2 Let's begin. I am going to read to you some bank features which may or may not have been important to you in selecting "YOUR" bank.

Using this rating card **(HAND RESPONDENT RATING CARD A),** please tell me the number that best describes how important you feel the bank feature was to you in helping select "YOUR" bank.

To what extent was **(READ FIRST FEATURE)** an important consideration to you in selecting "YOUR" bank?

(INTERVIEWER: MAKE SURE YOU READ AND RECORD THE ANSWER FOR ALL LISTED FEATURES)

Rating Number	Features	Rating Number	Features
____	Convenience of branch locations	____	Competitive minimum service charges
____	Flexibility of banking hours	____	Free checking availability
____	Friendly/courteous bank personnel	____	Interest rates on saving type accounts
____	No minimum balance requirement	____	Competitive interest rates on loans
____	Availability of credit card services	____	Credibility of the bank's reputation
____	Availability of ATM services	____	Bank's promotional advertisements

(UPON COMPLETION TAKE BACK RATING CARD A)

A researcher or supervisor can examine the information in an effort to assess an interviewer's efficiency in gathering the required data or to identify potential problem areas in the data collection process. For example, if the supervisor notices that an interviewer's number of contacts per completed survey is significantly above the average of all interviewers, he or she should investigate the reasons behind it. Perhaps the interviewer was not appropriately trained or is not using the proper approach in securing the prospective respondents' willingness to participate. From a cost perspective, the researcher might find that the high cost per interview associated with a particular field service operation was due to a larger number of contacts needed to get a completed interview. Further investigation might indicate that the field service company did a poor job in either selecting the needed interviewers or provided inadequate training.

Your understanding of the activities needed to develop a scientific-based survey instrument completes the third phase of the information research process—gathering and collecting accurate data—and prepares you to journey into the last phase—data preparation and analysis. Chapter 14 will focus on the activities involved with coding, editing, and preparing data for analysis.

е X H I B I T 13.15 An Example of an Interviewer's Call Record Sheet

Interviewer Code Number 076	Date 10/11	Date 10/13	Date 10/16	Date 10/18	Date 10/19	Date 10/20	Date 10/23
Total Contact Attempts	20	22	24	18	14	20	8
Number of initial attempts	8	12	10	8	12	14	4
Number of callbacks	12	10	14	10	2	6	4
Total Number of Noncontacts	4	2	5	0	6	2	2
No answer	1	—	1	—	—	—	—
Reached a recording	2	—	1	—	3	—	1
Wrong phone number	—	1	—	—	1	—	—
Phone no longer in service	1	—	3	—	—	1	1
Specific person not available	—	—	—	—	2	—	—
Other reasons	—	1	—	—	—	1	—
Total Number of Actual Contacts	4	10	5	8	6	12	2
Number of Completed Interviews	4	8	5	6	3	2	2
Bank of America	2	1	—	1	1	—	—
Sun Trust Bank	—	2	1	2	—	—	—
Citicorp	1	1	2	—	—	1	—
Capital One	1	1	—	3	—	—	—
First Union	—	3	—	—	1	—	1
Other Banks	—	—	2	—	1	1	1
Contacts per Completed Interview	1	1.25	1	1.3	2	6	0
Number of Terminated Interviews	0	2	0	2	3	10	0
Screening ineligibility	—	—	—	—	1	2	—
Refused participation	—	—	—	1	—	1	—
Respondent break-off	—	1	—	1	—	—	—
Quota requirement filled	—	—	—	—	3	7	—
Language/hearing problems	—	1	—	—	—	—	—
Some other reason	—	—	—	—	—	—	—
Interviewing hours	4	4	4	5	4	4	4

Training hours	2
Travel hours	4.5
Mileage to interviewing center	35

But before leaving this chapter, you are encouraged to revisit the chapter's opening example and reassess your original answers to the university officials' three critical questions:

1. Why such a low response rate (i.e., 9 completed surveys out of a possible 28,000)?

2. Was the survey a "good" or "bad" instrument for collecting the needed primary information?

3. Is there any diagnostic value of the data for addressing the given objectives?

In addition, remember to visit the book's Web site (www.mhhe.com/hair06) for more useful information and examples pertinent to questionnaire designs.

mαRKeTInG ReseαRcH In αcTIOn

Continuing Case Study

Designing a Questionnaire to Assess the Dining Habits and Patterns of the Santa Fe Grill's Customers

This illustration extends the chapter discussions on questionnaire development via the flowerpot approach. Read through this restaurant example, and using the actual Screening Questions and questionnaire (Exhibit 13.16), answer the questions at the end.

Background of the Situation

In early 2004, two recent college business graduates (one majored in finance and the other in management) came together with a new restaurant concept for a Southwestern casual dining experience that focused on a Mexican theme with a variety of good food items and a friendly family-oriented atmosphere. After six months of planning and creating detailed business and marketing plans, the two entrepreneurs were able to get the necessary capital to build and open their restaurant—calling it the Santa Fe Grill Mexican Restaurant.

After the initial six months of success, they noticed that revenues, traffic flow, and sales were declining and realized that they knew only the basics about their patrons. Neither of the owners had taken any marketing courses beyond basic marketing in college, so they turned to a friend who worked in marketing for some advice. Initially they were advised to hire a marketing research firm to collect some primary data about people's dining out habits and patterns. Looking into marketing research consulting firms, they quickly found out that these firms wanted too much money to conduct the research. So they went to a Barnes & Noble bookstore and purchased a practitioner's book on how to do marketing research studies. Using their new understanding of how to do research and design questionnaires, the owners decided to use an experience intercept research design (randomly stopping customers as they were leaving the Santa Fe Grill), with trained interviewers to qualify the respondents using a set of three screening questions (see Exhibit 13.16), and a 35-question, self-administered survey to actually collect the needed data. Several followup questions the interviewers were to ask are also shown. In addition, the following six research objectives were used to guide the design of their survey instrument shown in Exhibit 13.16.

Research Objectives

1. To identify the factors people deem important in making casual dining restaurant choice decisions.

2. To determine the characteristics that customers use to describe the Santa Fe Grill Mexican Restaurant.

3. To develop a psychographic/demographic profile of Santa Fe Grill's customer base.

4. To determine the patronage and positive word of mouth advertising patterns toward the Santa Fe Grill Mexican Restaurant.

5. To assess the likelihood of the customer's willingness to return to the Santa Fe Grill in the future.

6. To assess the degree to which the customer is satisfied with their Santa Fe Grill restaurant experience.

EXHIBIT 13.16   The Santa Fe Grill Questionnaire

Below are the screening and follow-up questions asked and completed by the interviewer for each respondent.

_____

Hello. My name is _____ and I work for DSS Research. We are talking to individuals today/tonight about dining out habits.

"Do you regularly eat out at casual dining restaurants?"   __ Yes   __ No

"Have you eaten at other Mexican restaurants in the last six months?"   __ Yes   __ No

"Is your gross annual household income $15,000 or more?"   __ Yes   __ No

If respondent answers 'Yes' to all three questions, then say:

We would like you to answer a few questions about your experience today/tonight at the Santa Fe Grill restaurant, and we hope you will be willing to give us your opinions. The survey will only take a few minutes and it will be very helpful to management in better serving its customers.

If the person says yes, give them a clipboard with the questionnaire on it, briefly explain the questionnaire, and show them where to complete the survey.

_____

When the respondent returns the questionnaire, check it for completeness and if there are missing items try to get the individual to complete them.

Look closely at the answers to questions 22, 23, and 24. If the respondent answers 1, 2, or 3 ask the following questions.

You indicated you are not too satisfied with the Santa Fe Grill. Could you please tell me why?

Record answer here:

_____

You indicated you are not likely to return to the Santa Fe Grill. Could you please tell me why?

Record answer here:

_____

You indicated you are not likely to recommend the Santa Fe Grill. Could you please tell me why?

Record answer here:

_____

Could I please have your name and phone number for verification purposes?

_____   _____

Name   **Phone #**

I hereby attest that this is a true and honest interview and complete to the best of my knowledge. I guarantee that all information relating to this interview shall be kept strictly confidential.

_____   _____

Interviewer's Signature   **Date and Time completed**

The following is the actual survey completed by respondents.

DINING OUT SURVEY

Please read all questions carefully. If you do not understand a question, ask the interviewer to help you. In the first section a number of statements are given about interests and opinions. Using a scale from

continued

EXHIBIT 13.16 The Santa Fe Grill Questionnaire, *continued*

1 to 7, with 7 being "Strongly Agree" and 1 being "Strongly Disagree," please indicate the extent to which you agree or disagree a particular statement describes you. Circle only one number for each statement.

Section 1: Life Style Questions

1. I often try new and different things.

   Strongly Disagree   Strongly Agree
   1 2 3 4 5 6 7

2. I like parties with music and lots of talk.

   Strongly Disagree   Strongly Agree
   1 2 3 4 5 6 7

3. People come to me more often than I go to them for information about products.

   Strongly Disagree   Strongly Agree
   1 2 3 4 5 6 7

4. I try to avoid fried foods.

   Strongly Disagree   Strongly Agree
   1 2 3 4 5 6 7

5. I like to go out and socialize with people.

   Strongly Disagree   Strongly Agree
   1 2 3 4 5 6 7

6. Friends and neighbors often come to me for advice about products and brands.

   Strongly Disagree   Strongly Agree
   1 2 3 4 5 6 7

7. I am self-confident about myself and my future.

   Strongly Disagree   Strongly Agree
   1 2 3 4 5 6 7

8. I usually eat balanced, nutritious meals.

   Strongly Disagree   Strongly Agree
   1 2 3 4 5 6 7

9. When I see a new product in stores, I often buy it.

   Strongly Disagree   Strongly Agree
   1 2 3 4 5 6 7

10. I am careful about what I eat.

    Strongly Disagree   Strongly Agree
    1 2 3 4 5 6 7

11. I often try new brands before my friends and neighbors do.

    Strongly Disagree   Strongly Agree
    1 2 3 4 5 6 7

Section 2: Perceptions Measures

Listed below is a set of characteristics that could be used to describe the Santa Fe Grill Mexican Restaurant. Using a scale from 1 to 7, with 7 being "Strongly Agree" and 1 being "Strongly Disagree," to what extent do you agree or disagree the Santa Fe Grill:

12. Has friendly employees

    Strongly Disagree   Strongly Agree
    1 2 3 4 5 6 7

eXHIBIT 13.16 *continued*

13. Is a fun place to eat

Strongly Disagree   1 2 3 4 5 6 7   Strongly Agree

14. Has large size portions

Strongly Disagree   1 2 3 4 5 6 7   Strongly Agree

15. Has fresh food

Strongly Disagree   1 2 3 4 5 6 7   Strongly Agree

16. Has reasonable prices

Strongly Disagree   1 2 3 4 5 6 7   Strongly Agree

17. Has an attractive interior

Strongly Disagree   1 2 3 4 5 6 7   Strongly Agree

18. Has excellent food taste

Strongly Disagree   1 2 3 4 5 6 7   Strongly Agree

19. Has knowledgeable employees

Strongly Disagree   1 2 3 4 5 6 7   Strongly Agree

20. Serves food at the proper temperature

Strongly Disagree   1 2 3 4 5 6 7   Strongly Agree

21. Has quick service

Strongly Disagree   1 2 3 4 5 6 7   Strongly Agree

Section 3: Relationship Measures

Please indicate your view on each of the following questions:

22. How satisfied are you with the Santa Fe Grill?

Not Satisfied At All   1 2 3 4 5 6 7   Very Satisfied

23. How likely are you to return to the Santa Fe Grill in the future?

Definitely Will Not Return   1 2 3 4 5 6 7   Definitely Will Return

24. How likely are you to recommend the Santa Fe Grill to a friend?

Definitely Will Not Recommend   1 2 3 4 5 6 7   Definitely Will Recommend

25. How often do you patronize the Santa Fe Grill?

1 = Occasionally (Less than once a month)
2 = Frequently (1–3 times a month)
3 = Very Frequently (4 or more times a month)

Section 4: Selection Factors

Listed below are some factors (reasons) many people use in selecting a restaurant where they want to dine. Think about your visits to casual dining restaurants in the last three months and please rank each

continued

e X H I B I T 13.16   The Santa Fe Grill Questionnaire, *continued*

attribute from 1 to 4, with 1 being the most important reason for selecting the restaurant and 4 being the least important reason. There can be no ties so make sure you rank each attribute with a different number.

Attributes	Ranking
26. Prices	
27. Food Quality	
28. Atmosphere	
29. Service	

Section 5: Classification Questions

Please circle the number that classifies you best.

30. Distance Driven

1 Less than 1 mile
2 1–3 miles
3 More than 3 Miles

31. Do your recall seeing any advertisements in the last 60 days for the Santa Fe Grill?

0 No
1 Yes

32. Your Gender

0 Male
1 Female

33. Number of Children at Home

1 None
2 1–2
3 More than 2 children at home

34. Your Age in Years

1 18–25
2 26–34
3 35–49
4 50–59
5 60 and Older

35. Your Annual Gross Household Income

1 $15,000–$30,000
2 $30,001–$50,000
3 $50,001–$75,000
4 $75,001–$100,000
5 More than $100,000

Thank you very much for your help. Please return your completed questionnaire to the interviewer.

Hands-On Exercise

Using your knowledge and understanding of the material in Chapter 13, prepare answers to each of the following questions:

1. Based on the research objectives, does the owners' self-administered questionnaire, in its current form, correctly illustrate the "flowerpot" survey design approach? Please explain why or why not.

2. Overall, is the current survey design able to capture the required data needed to address all the stated research objectives? Why or why not? If changes are needed, how would you change the survey's design?

3. Evaluate the "screener" used to qualify the respondents. Are there any changes needed? Why or why not?

4. Redesign questions 26–29 on the survey as "ordinal rating" scales that will enable you to capture the "degree of importance" that a customer might attach to each of the four listed attributes in selecting a restaurant to dine at.

Summary of Learning Objectives

■ **Identify and discuss the critical factors that can contribute to directly improving the accuracy of surveys, and explain why questionnaire development is not a simple process.**

Questionnaire development is much more than just writing a set of questions and asking people to answer them. Designing good surveys goes beyond just developing reliable and valid scales. A number of design factors, systematic procedural steps, and rules of logic must be considered in the development process. In addition, the process requires knowledge of sampling plans, construct development, scale measurement, and types of data. It is important to remember that a questionnaire is a set of questions/scales designed to generate enough raw data to allow the researcher and decision maker to develop information to solve the business problem.

■ **Discuss the theoretical principles of questionnaire design, and explain why a questionnaire is more than just asking a respondent some questions.**

Many researchers, unaware of the underlying theory, still believe that questionnaire design is an art rather than a science. Questionnaires are, however, hierarchical structures consisting of four different components: words, questions, formats, and hypotheses. Most surveys are descriptive instruments that rely heavily on the collection of state-of-being or state-of-behavior data. Others are predictive instruments that focus on collecting state-of-mind and state-of-intention data that allow for predicting changes in people's attitudes and behaviors as well as testing hypotheses.

■ **Identify and explain the communication roles of questionnaires in the data collection process.**

Good questionnaires enable researchers to gain a true report of the respondent's attitudes, preferences, beliefs, feelings, behavioral intentions, and actions/reactions in a holistic manner, not just a fragment. Through carefully worded questions and clear instructions, a researcher has the ability to control a respondent's thoughts and ensure objectivity. By understanding good communication principles, researchers can avoid bad questioning procedures that might result in unrealistic information requests, unanswerable questions, or leading questions that prohibit or distort the meaning of a person's responses.

■ **Explain why the type of information needed to address a decision maker's questions and problems will substantially influence the structure and content of questionnaires.**

Once research objectives are transformed into information objectives, determining the specific information requirements plays a critical role in the development of questionnaires. For each information objective, the researcher must be able to determine the types of data (state of being, mind, behavior, or intentions); types of question/scale formats (nominal, ordinal, interval, or ratio); types of question structures (open-ended and closed-ended); and the appropriate selection of scale point descriptors. Researchers must be aware of the impact that different data collection methods (personal, telephone, self-administered, computer-assisted, etc.) have on the wording of both questions and response choices.

■ **List and discuss the 11 steps in the questionnaire development process, and tell how to eliminate some common mistakes in questionnaire designs.**

Using their knowledge of construct development and scale measurement development (Chapter 11) and attitude measurement (Chapter 12), researchers can follow an 11-step process to develop scientific survey instruments. Refer back to Exhibit 13.4 (on p. 436) which lists these steps.

■ **Discuss and employ the "flowerpot" approach in developing scientific questionnaires.**

The flowerpot approach serves as a unique framework for integrating different sets of questions and scales into a scientific structure for collecting high-quality data. This ordered approach helps researchers make critical decisions regarding (1) construct development, (2) the appropriate dimensions and attributes of objects, (3) question/scale formats, (4) wording of actual questions and directives, and (5) scale points and descriptors. Following the flowerpot approach assures that the data flow will correctly move from a general information level to a more specific level.

■ **Discuss the importance of cover letters, and explain the guidelines to help eliminate common mistakes in cover letter designs.**

While the main role of any cover letter should be winning over a prospective respondent, a set of secondary roles ranges from initial introduction to communicating the legitimacy and other important factors about the study. Ten critical factors should be included in most, if not all, cover letters. Including these will help the researcher counteract the three major reasons prospective respondents use to avoid participating in self-administered surveys and personal interviews. A lottery-based compensation system can significantly improve a prospective respondent's willingness to participate.

Key Terms and Concepts

Accuracy 433

Anonymity 453

Bad questions 431

Call record sheets 463

Confidentiality 453

Cover letter 450

Flowerpot approach 435

Hypothesis 433

Interviewer instructions 460

Lottery incentive approach 455

Questionnaire 429

Questionnaire design precision 434

Quota sheets 463

Rating card 463

Screening forms 460

Structured questions 430

Supervisor instruction form 459

Unstructured questions 430

Review Questions

1. Discuss the advantages and disadvantages of using unstructured (open-ended) and structured (closed-ended) questions in developing an online, self-administered survey instrument.

2. Explain the role of a questionnaire in the information research process. What should be the role of the client during the questionnaire development process?

3. Identify and discuss the guidelines available for deciding the form and layout of a questionnaire. Discuss the advantages and disadvantages of using the flowerpot approach in developing survey instruments.

4. What are the factors that constitute bad questions in questionnaire design? Develop three examples of bad questions. Then, using the information in Exhibit 13.7, rewrite your examples so they could be judged as good questions.

5. Discuss the value of a good questionnaire design.

6. Discuss the main benefits of including a brief introductory section in questionnaires.

7. Unless needed for screening purposes, why shouldn't classification questions be presented up front in most questionnaire designs?

8. Discuss the critical issues involved in pretesting a questionnaire.

Discussion Questions

1. Identify and discuss the guidelines for developing cover letters for a survey research instrument. What are some of the advantages of developing good cover letters? What are some of the costs of a bad cover letter?

2. Using the five specific questions that should be asked in evaluating any questionnaire design (see p. 448), evaluate the Santa Fe Grill Mexican Restaurant questionnaire at the end of this chapter. Write a one-page assessment report.

3. **EXPERIENCE THE INTERNET.** Using any browser of your choice, go to www.open-text.com and type in the search phrase "questionnaire design." Browse the various listings until you find a questionnaire of your liking. Evaluate the extent to which your selected questionnaire follows the flowerpot approach and write a two-page summary of your findings. (Make sure you include in your report the exact Web site address used for reaching your selected questionnaire.)

4. **EXPERIENCE THE INTERNET.** Get on the Net and go to Visual Research's Web site at www.vrcinc.com. Browse through the site and evaluate the various new technologies being offered for conducting surveys via the Internet. Write a one-page summary that focuses on the advantages and disadvantages associated with collecting survey data through the Internet.

part 5

Data Preparation, Analysis, and Reporting the Results

chapter 14

Coding, Editing, and Preparing Data for Analysis

Learning Objectives

After reading this chapter, you will be able to

1. Illustrate the process of preparing data for preliminary analysis.
2. Demonstrate the procedure for assuring data validation.
3. Describe the process of editing and coding data obtained through survey methods.
4. Acquaint the user with data entry procedures.
5. Illustrate a process for detecting errors in data entry.
6. Discuss techniques used for data tabulation and data analysis.

"The rapid proliferation of computer technology has made the procedure for raw data entry appear almost second nature for many data analysts. Yet everyone in this field understands the fundamental concept behind this task—GIGO: garbage in, garbage out."[1]

—ROBERT W. KNEEN
Senior Systems Analyst
Union Bancorporation

Wal-Mart and Scanner Technology

each item you purchase in almost any retail store is scanned into a computer. The bar code enables each store to know exactly what products are selling and when. Store managers can also keep accurate control of inventory, so they can easily order more products when they run low. Probably the ultimate example of scanning use is at Wal-Mart, where scanners have been vital. Wal-Mart does not own the products on its shelves; they remain there on consignment by the manufacturers. With its scanning system, however, Wal-Mart always knows what is there, what is selling, and what needs replenishment. The scanner has pushed back the law of diminishing returns and made it possible to build and manage larger inventories than would have been possible a few years ago.

The same equipment that scans product codes can also scan a bar-coded customer card so the customer is associated with his or her purchase in a central database. This process takes a second or two per transaction and requires only that the customer produce the card at purchase time.

Scanner technology is widely used in the marketing research industry. Questionnaires can be prepared through any of a number of word processing software packages and printed on a laser printer. Respondents can complete the questionnaire with any type of writing instrument. With the appropriate software and scanning device, the researcher can scan the completed questionnaires and the data are checked for errors, categorized, and stored within a matter of seconds. When a researcher expects to receive 400 to 500 completed surveys, scanner technology can be worth its weight in gold.[2]

Value of Preparing Data for Analysis

Converting information from a questionnaire so it can be transferred to a data warehouse is referred to as data preparation. This process usually follows a four-step approach, beginning with data validation, then editing and coding, followed by data entry and data tabulation. Error detection begins in the first phase and continues throughout the process. The purpose of data preparation is to take data in its raw form and convert it to establish meaning and create value for the user.

The process of data preparation and analysis starts after the data is collected. Several interrelated tasks must be completed to ensure the data is accurately reported. The stages of data preparation and analysis are shown in Exhibit 14.1. This chapter discusses the data preparation process and Chapters 15, 16, and 17 provide an overview of data analysis.

EXHIBIT 14.1 **Overview of the Stages of Data Preparation and Analysis**

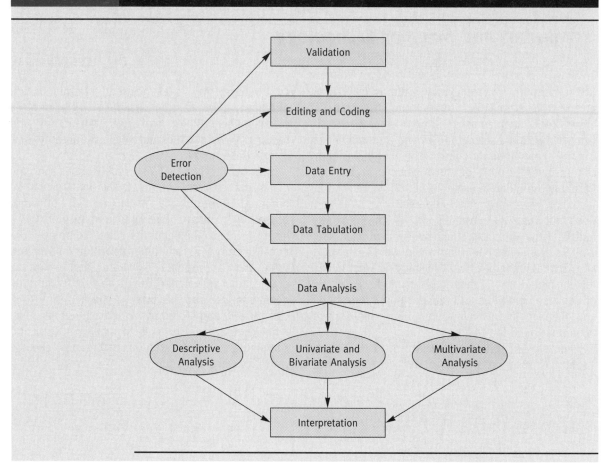

Data Validation

Data validation The process of determining, to the extent possible, whether a survey's interviews or observations were conducted correctly and are free of fraud or bias.

Curbstoning Cheating or falsification in the data collection process.

Data validation is concerned with determining, to the extent possible, if surveys, interviews, or observations were conducted correctly and free of bias. In many data collection approaches it is not always convenient to closely monitor the data collection process. To facilitate accurate data collection, each respondent's name, address, and phone number may be recorded. While this information is not used for analysis, it does enable the validation process to be completed.

Curbstoning is a term used in the marketing research industry to indicate falsification of data. As the name implies, **curbstoning** is when interviewers find an out-of-the-way location, such as a curbstone, and fill out the survey themselves rather than follow the procedure with an actual respondent. Because of the potential for such falsification, data validation becomes a necessary step in the data acquisition process.

Most marketing research professionals will target between 10 and 30 percent of completed interviews for "callbacks." Specifically for telephone, mail, and personal interviews, a certain percentage of respondents from the completed interviews will be recontacted by the research firm to make sure the interview was conducted correctly. Normally through telephone recontact, respondents will be asked several short questions as a way of validating the returned interview. Generally, the process of validation covers five areas:

1. *Fraud.* Was the person actually interviewed, or was the interview falsified? Did the interviewer contact the respondent simply to get a name and address, and then proceed to fabricate responses? Did the interviewer use a friend to obtain the necessary information?

2. *Screening.* Many times an interview must be conducted only with qualified respondents. To ensure accuracy of the data collected, many respondents will be screened according to some preselected criteria, such as household income level, recent purchase of a specific product or brand, or even sex or age. For example, the interview procedure may require that only female heads of households with an annual household income of $25,000 or more be interviewed. In this case, a validation callback would verify each of these factors.

3. *Procedure.* In many marketing research projects it is critical that the data be collected according to a specific procedure. For example, many customer exit interviews must occur in a designated place as the respondent leaves a certain retail establishment. In this particular example a validation callback may be necessary to ensure the interview took place at the proper setting, not some social gathering area like a party or a park.

4. *Completeness.* In order to speed through the data collection process, an interviewer may ask the respondent only a few of the requisite questions. In such cases, the interviewer asks the respondent a few questions from the beginning of the interview form and then skips to the end, omitting questions from other sections. The interviewer may then make up answers to the remaining questions. To determine if the interview is valid, the researcher could recontact a sample of respondents and ask about questions from different parts of the interview form.

5. *Courtesy.* Respondents should be treated with courtesy and respect during the interviewing process. Situations can occur, however, where the interviewer may inject a

tone of negativity into the interviewing process. To ensure a positive image, respondent callbacks are common to determine whether the interviewer was courteous. Other aspects of the interviewer checked during callbacks include appearance, pleasantness, and proper personality.

Data Editing and Coding

Editing   The process whereby the raw data are checked for mistakes made by either the interviewer or the respondent.

After being validated, the data must be edited for mistakes. **Editing** is the process where raw data are checked for mistakes made by either the interviewer or the respondent. By scanning each completed interview, the researcher can check several areas of concern: (1) asking the proper questions, (2) accurate recording of answers, (3) correct screening of respondents, and (4) complete and accurate recording of open-ended questions.

Asking the Proper Questions

One aspect of the editing process especially important to interviewing methods is to make certain the proper questions were asked of the respondent. As part of the editing process, the researcher will check to make sure all respondents were asked the proper questions. In cases where they were not, respondents are recontacted to obtain a response to omitted questions.

Accurate Recording of Answers

Completed questionnaires sometimes have missing information. The interviewer may have accidentally skipped a question or not recorded it in the proper location. With a careful check of all questionnaires, these problems can be identified. In such cases, respondents are recontacted and the omitted responses recorded.

Correct Screening Questions

The first three items on the questionnaire in Exhibit 14.2 are actually screening questions that determine whether the respondent is eligible to complete the survey. During the editing phase, the researcher will make certain that only qualified respondents were included.

It is also critical in the editing process to establish that the questions were asked and (for self-administered surveys) answered in the proper sequence. If the proper sequence is not followed, the respondent must be recontacted to ensure the accuracy of the recorded data.

Responses to Open-Ended Questions

Responses to open-ended questions often provide very meaningful data. Open-ended questions provide greater insight into the research questions than forced-choice questions. A major part of editing the answers to open-ended questions is interpretation.

e X H I B I T 14.2 The Santa Fe Grill Questionnaire

Below are the screening and follow-up questions asked and completed by the interviewer for each respondent.

_____

Hello. My name is _____ and I work for DSS Research. We are talking to individuals today/tonight about dining out habits.

"Do you regularly eat out at casual dining restaurants?"	___ Yes	___ No
"Have you eaten at other Mexican restaurants in the last six months?"	___ Yes	___ No
"Is your gross annual household income $15,000 or more?"	___ Yes	___ No

If respondent answers "Yes" to all three questions, then say:

We would like you to answer a few questions about your experience today/tonight at the Santa Fe Grill restaurant, and we hope you will be willing to give us your opinions. The survey will only take a few minutes and it will be very helpful to management in better serving its customers.

If the person says yes, give them a clipboard with the questionnaire on it, briefly explain the questionnaire, and show them where to complete the survey.

_____

When the respondent returns the questionnaire, check it for completeness and if there are missing items try to get the individual to complete them.

Look closely at the answers to questions 22, 23 and 24. If the respondent answers 1, 2, or 3 ask the following questions.

You indicated you are not too satisfied with the Santa Fe Grill. Could you please tell me why?

Record answer here:

_____

You indicated you are not likely to return to the Santa Fe Grill. Could you please tell me why?

Record answer here:

_____

You indicated you are not likely to recommend the Santa Fe Grill. Could you please tell me why?

Record answer here:

_____

Could I please have your name and phone number for verification purposes?

_____   _____
        Name   **Phone #**

I hereby attest that this is a true and honest interview and complete to the best of my knowledge. I guarantee that all information relating to this interview shall be kept strictly confidential.

_____   _____
  Interviewer's Signature   **Date and Time completed**

The following is the actual survey completed by respondents.

DINING OUT SURVEY

Please read all questions carefully. If you do not understand a question, ask the interviewer to help you. In the first section a number of statements are given about interests and opinions. Using a scale from

continued

ЄXHIBIT 14.2 The Santa Fe Grill Questionnaire, *continued*

1 to 7, with 7 being "Strongly Agree" and 1 being "Strongly Disagree," please indicate the extent to which you agree or disagree a particular statement describes you. Circle only one number for each statement.

Section 1: Life Style Questions

1. I often try new and different things.

Strongly Disagree 1 2 3 4 5 6 7 Strongly Agree

2. I like parties with music and lots of talk.

Strongly Disagree 1 2 3 4 5 6 7 Strongly Agree

3. People come to me more often than I go to them for information about products.

Strongly Disagree 1 2 3 4 5 6 7 Strongly Agree

4. I try to avoid fried foods.

Strongly Disagree 1 2 3 4 5 6 7 Strongly Agree

5. I like to go out and socialize with people.

Strongly Disagree 1 2 3 4 5 6 7 Strongly Agree

6. Friends and neighbors often come to me for advice about products and brands.

Strongly Disagree 1 2 3 4 5 6 7 Strongly Agree

7. I am self-confident about myself and my future.

Strongly Disagree 1 2 3 4 5 6 7 Strongly Agree

8. I usually eat balanced, nutritious meals.

Strongly Disagree 1 2 3 4 5 6 7 Strongly Agree

9. When I see a new product in stores, I often buy it.

Strongly Disagree 1 2 3 4 5 6 7 Strongly Agree

10. I am careful about what I eat.

Strongly Disagree 1 2 3 4 5 6 7 Strongly Agree

11. I often try new brands before my friends and neighbors do.

Strongly Disagree 1 2 3 4 5 6 7 Strongly Agree

Section 2: Perceptions Measures

Listed below is a set of characteristics that could be used to describe the Santa Fe Grill Mexican restaurant. Using a scale from 1 to 7, with 7 being "Strongly Agree" and 1 being "Strongly Disagree," to what extent do you agree or disagree the Santa Fe Grill

12. Has friendly employees

Strongly Disagree 1 2 3 4 5 6 7 Strongly Agree

e X H I B I T 14.2 *continued*

13. Is a fun place to eat

Strongly Disagree 1 2 3 4 5 6 7 Strongly Agree

14. Has large size portions

Strongly Disagree 1 2 3 4 5 6 7 Strongly Agree

15. Has fresh food

Strongly Disagree 1 2 3 4 5 6 7 Strongly Agree

16. Has reasonable prices

Strongly Disagree 1 2 3 4 5 6 7 Strongly Agree

17. Has an attractive interior

Strongly Disagree 1 2 3 4 5 6 7 Strongly Agree

18. Has excellent food taste

Strongly Disagree 1 2 3 4 5 6 7 Strongly Agree

19. Has knowledgeable employees

Strongly Disagree 1 2 3 4 5 6 7 Strongly Agree

20. Serves food at the proper temperature

Strongly Disagree 1 2 3 4 5 6 7 Strongly Agree

21. Has quick service

Strongly Disagree 1 2 3 4 5 6 7 Strongly Agree

Section 3: Relationship Measures

Please indicate your view on each of the following questions:

22. How satisfied are you with the Santa Fe Grill?

Not Satisfied At All 1 2 3 4 5 6 7 Very Satisfied

23. How likely are you to return to the Santa Fe Grill in the future?

Definitely Will Not Return 1 2 3 4 5 6 7 Definitely Will Return

24. How likely are you to recommend Santa Fe Grill to a friend?

Definitely Will Not Recommend 1 2 3 4 5 6 7 Definitely Will Recommend

25. How often do you patronize the Santa Fe Grill?

1 = Occasionally (Less than once a month)
2 = Frequently (1–3 times a month)
3 = Very Frequently (4 or more times a month)

Section 4: Selection Factors

Listed below are some factors (reasons) many people use in selecting a restaurant where they want to dine. Think about your visits to casual dining restaurants in the last three months and please rank each attribute from 1 to 4, with 1 being the most important reason for selecting the restaurant and 4 being the least important reason. There can be no ties so make sure you rank each attribute with a different number.

continued

EXHIBIT 14.2 The Santa Fe Grill Questionnaire, *continued*

Attribute	Ranking
26. Prices	
27. Food Quality	
28. Atmosphere	
29. Service	

Section 5: Classification Questions

Please circle the number that classifies you best.

30. Distance Driven
- 1 Less than 1 mile
- 2 1–3 miles
- 3 More than 3 Miles

31. Do your recall seeing any advertisements in the last 60 days for the Santa Fe Grill?
- 0 No
- 1 Yes

32. Your Gender
- 0 Male
- 1 Female

33. Number of Children at Home
- 1 None
- 2 1–2
- 3 More than 2 children at home

34. Your Age in Years
- 1 18–25
- 2 26–34
- 3 35–49
- 4 50–59
- 5 60 and Older

35. Your Annual Gross Household Income
- 1 $15,000–$30,000
- 2 $30,001–$50,000
- 3 $50,001–$75,000
- 4 $75,001–$100,000
- 5 More than $100,000

Thank you very much for your help. Please return your completed questionnaire to the interviewer.

Exhibit 14.3 shows some typical responses to an open-ended question and thus points to problems associated with interpreting these questions. For example, one response to the question "Why are you eating at the Santa Fe Grill more often?" is simply "They have good service." This answer by itself is not sufficient to determine what the respondent means by "good service." The interviewer needs to probe for a more specific response. For example, are the employees friendly, helpful, courteous? Do they appear neat and clean? Do they smile when taking an order? Probes such as these would enable the researcher to better interpret the "good service" answer. In cases such as these, the individual doing the editing must use judgment in classifying responses. At some point the responses must be placed in standardized categories. Answers that are incomplete are categorized as useless.

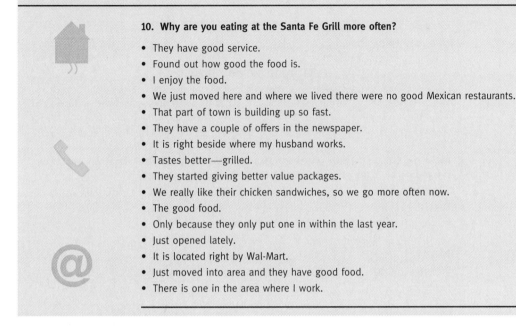

EXHIBIT 14.3 Responses to an Open-Ended Question

10. Why are you eating at the Santa Fe Grill more often?

- They have good service.
- Found out how good the food is.
- I enjoy the food.
- We just moved here and where we lived there were no good Mexican restaurants.
- That part of town is building up so fast.
- They have a couple of offers in the newspaper.
- It is right beside where my husband works.
- Tastes better—grilled.
- They started giving better value packages.
- We really like their chicken sandwiches, so we go more often now.
- The good food.
- Only because they only put one in within the last year.
- Just opened lately.
- It is located right by Wal-Mart.
- Just moved into area and they have good food.
- There is one in the area where I work.

The Coding Process

Coding Grouping and assigning value to various responses from the survey instrument.

Data **coding** involves grouping and assigning values to responses to the questions on the survey instrument. Specifically, coding is the assignment of numerical values to each individual response for each question on the survey. Typically, the codes are numerical—a number from 0 to 9—because numbers are quick and easy to input and computers work better with numbers than alphanumerical values. Like editing, coding can be tedious if certain issues are not addressed prior to collecting the data. A well-planned and constructed questionnaire can reduce the amount of time spent on coding and increase the accuracy of the process if it is incorporated into the design of the questionnaire. Exhibit 14.2 shows the Santa Fe Grill questionnaire that has built-in coded responses for all questions except the open-ended ones asked by the interviewer. In the "Life Style Questions," for example, a respondent has the option of responding from 1 to 7, based on his or her level of agreement or disagreement with a particular statement. Thus, if the respondent circled "5" as his or her choice, then the value of "5" would become the coded value for a particular question.

In questionnaires that do not use such simple coded responses, the researcher will establish a master code on which the assigned numeric values are shown for each response. Exhibit 14.4 provides an example of such a form. Question 1 in Exhibit 14.4 illustrates all the coded values for responses to "fast-food establishments visited in the past two months." These values range from 01 to 13, with Taco Bell having the value of 01, Hardee's 02, Kentucky Fried Chicken 03, and so on. An additional statement in question 1, "Other, please specify," has different coding properties. "Other, please specify" will have a separate set of codes based on all possible answers that may have been provided by the respondents. For example, a respondent may have specified "White Castle" in this response

---

e X H I B I T **14.4** An Illustration of a Master Code Form

Master Code Form   **Questionnaire Identification**
                                                  Number 000 (1–3)

FAST-FOOD OPINION SURVEY

This questionnaire pertains to a project being conducted by a marketing research class at The University of Memphis. The purpose of this project is to better understand the attitudes and opinions of consumers toward fast-food restaurants. The questionnaire will take only 10–15 minutes to complete, and all responses will remain strictly confidential. Thank you for your help on this project.

1. **Below is a listing of various fast-food restaurants. How many of these restaurants would you say you visited in the past two months? Check as many as may apply.**

Taco Bell	01	Church's Fried Chicken	08
Hardee's	02	McDonald's	09
Kentucky Fried Chicken	03	Burger King	10
Wendy's	04	Back Yard Burgers	11 ✓
Rally's	05	Arby's	12
Popeye's Chicken	06	Sonic	13
Krystal's	07	Other, please specify →	see code sheet.
		Have not visited any of these establishments	20

2. **In a typical month, how many times would you say you visit a fast-food restaurant, such as the ones indicated above? (X ONE BOX)**

One ❑	Two ❑	Three ☑	Four ❑	Five ❑	Six ❑	Seven or more ❑
1	2	3	4	5	6	7

3. **On your last visit to a fast-food restaurant, what was the dollar amount you spent on food and beverages?**

Under $2	❑ 1	$8.01–$10.00	❑ 5
$2.01–$4.00	❑ 2	$10.01–$12.00	❑ 6
$4.01–$6.00	☑ 3	More than $12	❑ 7
$6.01–$8.00	❑ 4	Don't remember	❑ 8

---

category. Since "White Castle" is not on the list of possible responses for question 1, a separate and unique value will have to be coded for "White Castle" that is different from the other values in question 1. Such coded values are normally stored and listed on a separate code sheet identified as "code sheets for 'Other' responses."

Another example of a coded response can be seen in question 3. In this case, if the respondent checked "$4.01–$6.00" in question 3, the coder would assign the value of 3 to that response. If a respondent checked "more than $12," the coder would assign a value of 7 to the category. Such closed-ended questions as these are normally precoded at the time of questionnaire design. The use of a master code is an additional safeguard to ensure that the coding sequence is followed correctly.

In contrast, open-ended questions pose unique problems to the coding process. Open-ended questions do not allow for an exact list of potential responses. Therefore the data they provide are not easy to prepare. Yet in most cases, the value of the information obtained from open-ended questions outweighs the problems of coding the responses.

e X H I B I T 14.5 **Illustration of Response Consolidation Using Open-Ended Questions**

Q10a. Why are you dining less frequently at the _____ restaurant?

Respondent # 72113

- (I'm a) state employee. I look for bargains. (Need) more specials.
- Because I'm no longer close to a _____.

Respondent # 72114

- I do not like their food.

Respondent # 72116

- They never get my order right.
- I got tired of the hamburgers. I don't like the spices.
- Prices (are) too high. Family doesn't like it. My husband didn't like the way the burgers tasted. They should give more with their combos than they do. More fries.
- Because they always got our orders wrong and they are rude.
- The order is never right.
- Health reasons.
- I work longer hours, and don't think about food.
- Cannot eat the food.
- We started using _____.
- The location of my work moved so I am not near a _____.

Researchers typically use a four-step process to develop codes for responses. The procedure begins by generating a list of as many potential responses as possible. These responses are then assigned values within a range determined by the actual number of separate responses identified. As the researcher begins to edit the responses to the open-ended questions, he or she simply attaches a value from the developed response list. For responses that do not appear on the list, the researcher adds a new response and corresponding value to the list or places the response into one of the existing categories.

Consolidation of responses is actually the second phase of the four-step process. Exhibit 14.5 illustrates several actual responses to the question "Why are you dining less frequently at the _____ restaurant?" Four of these—related to not liking the food—can be consolidated into a single response category because they all have the same shared meaning. The development of consolidated categories is a subjective decision that should be made only by an experienced research analyst with input from the project's sponsor.

The third step of the process is to assign a numerical value as a code. While at first this may appear to be a simple task, the structure of the questionnaire and the number of responses per question need to be considered. For example, if a question has more than 10 responses, then double-digit codes need to be used, such as "01," "02," . . . "12." Another good practice is to assign higher-value codes to positive responses than to negative responses. For example, "no" responses are coded 0 and "yes" responses coded 1; "dislike" responses are coded as 1 and "like" responses coded as 5. Coding of this nature makes subsequent analysis easier. For example, the researcher will find it easier to interpret means or averages if higher values occur as the average moves from "dislike" to "like."

If the researcher is going to use correlation or regression in data analysis, then for categorical data there is another consideration. The researcher may wish to create "dummy" variables in which the coding is "0" and "1."

Assigning a coded value to missing data is very important. If, for example, a respondent completes a questionnaire except for the very last question and a recontact is not possible, how do you code the response to the unanswered question? A good practice in this situation is to first consider how the response is going to be used in the analysis phase. In certain types of analysis, if the response is left blank and has no numerical value, the entire questionnaire (not just the individual question) will be deleted. The best way to handle the coding of omitted responses is first to check on how your data analysis software will handle missing data. This should be the guide for determining whether omissions are coded or left blank.

The fourth step in the coding process is to assign a coded value to each response. This is probably the most tedious process because it is done manually. Unless an optical scanning approach is being used to enter the data, this task is almost always necessary to guard against problems in the data entry phase.

First, each questionnaire needs to be assigned a numerical value. The numerical value typically is a three-digit code if there are fewer than 1,000 questionnaires to code, and a four-digit code if there are 1,000 or more. For example, if 452 completed questionnaires were returned, the first would be coded 001, the second 002, and so on, finishing with 452. Questionnaire coding will be discussed again when we cover data entry.

Immediately following each questionnaire code, a numbered reference should be included in parentheses next to the code. This informs the data entry operator to place the questionnaire code in the corresponding data fields of the data record. It is important to realize that throughout the questionnaire the numbers in parentheses indicate the data field where each coded response will be added on the data record. The researcher should proceed through the entire questionnaire, assigning the appropriate numerical codes to each response.

Data Entry

Data entry Those tasks involved with the direct input of the coded data into some specified software package that ultimately allows the research analyst to manipulate and transform the raw data into useful information.

Data entry follows validation, editing, and coding. **Data entry** is the procedure used to enter the data into the computer for subsequent data analysis. Data entry includes those tasks involved with the direct input of the coded data into a software package that enables the research analyst to manipulate and transform the raw data into useful information.

There are several ways of entering coded data into a computer. The most popular option is the personal computer (PC). But other labor-saving devices are available for data entry. Some terminals have touch-screen capabilities that allow the analyst to simply touch an area of the terminal screen to enter a data element. A similar technique uses a light pen—a handheld electronic pointer that enters data through the terminal screen.

Improved scanning technology has facilitated another approach to data entry. Questionnaires prepared on any form of Microsoft Windows software and printed on a laser printer can be readily scanned through optical scanning. Exhibit 14.6 shows a questionnaire that has been designed for optical character recognition. This approach allows the computer to read alphabetic, numeric, and special character codes through a scanning device. On the questionnaire in Exhibit 14.6, the respondent would use a number two pencil to fill in his or her responses, which would then be scanned directly into a computer.

Online surveys are becoming increasingly popular for completing marketing research studies. Not only are they often faster to complete, but they eliminate entirely the data entry process.

One critical task of data entry personnel is to ensure that the data entered are correct and error free. Specialized software prevents errors by making it impossible for data entry personnel to make certain types of mistakes.

e X H I B I T 14.6 Example of Optical Character Recognition Questionnaire

WELLNESS ASSESSMENT QUESTIONNAIRE

Risk Assessment Systems, Inc.
5846 Distribution Drive
Memphis, Tennessee 38141

INSTRUCTIONS

To ensure an accurate Personal Wellness Assessment, please answer all of the following questions as accurately and completely as possible.

USE A NO. 2 PENCIL ONLY   Example: ▭ ▭ ▬ ▭ ▭   Erase completely to change

Name _____

Street address _____

City _____

State _____

Phone # (___) ___

Zip Code

Social Security Number

PHYSICAL DATA/CURRENT HEALTH STATUS

Sex | Date of Birth: Month – Day – Year | Height: ft. in. | Weight: lbs. | Blood Pressure: If you know your Blood Pressure, enter it here ----> | Systolic (High) | Diastolic (Low) | If not, which best describes it?

☐ Male
☐ Female

☐ High
☐ Normal or Low
☐ Don't Know

1. In general, would you say your current state of health is:
☐ Excellent   ☐ Very Good   ☐ Good   ☐ Fair   ☐ Poor

2. During the past 12 months, how many days of work have you missed due to your own injury or sickness?
☐ None   ☐ 1 to 3   ☐ 4 to 6   ☐ 7 or more   ☐ Does not apply

PERSONAL/FAMILY MEDICAL HISTORY

3. How often are you given a routine physical examination by a physician?
☐ More than once a year   ☐ Once a year   ☐ Once every 2 years   ☐ Every 3 years or longer   ☐ Never had one

4. How long has it been since your last electrocardiogram (EKG)?
☐ Less than 1 year ago   ☐ 1 to 2 years ago   ☐ 2 to 3 years ago   ☐ 3 or more years ago   ☐ Never had one

5. Have you or has anyone in your family (parents, grandparents, brother or sister) had any of the following health problems? If so, please mark the corresponding box. (Please mark all that apply.)

	Self	Brother	Sister	Father	Mother	Father's side Grandfather	Father's side Grandmother	Mother's side Grandfather	Mother's side Grandmother
Heart disease before age 55	☐	☐	☐	☐	☐	☐	☐	☐	☐
Heart disease age 55 to 64	☐	☐	☐	☐	☐	☐	☐	☐	☐
Heart disease age 65 or later	☐	☐	☐	☐	☐	☐	☐	☐	☐
High blood pressure	☐	☐	☐	☐	☐	☐	☐	☐	☐
Stroke	☐	☐	☐	☐	☐	☐	☐	☐	☐
Diabetes	☐	☐	☐	☐	☐	☐	☐	☐	☐
Breast cancer	☐	☐	☐	☐	☐	☐	☐	☐	☐
Colon cancer	☐	☐	☐	☐	☐	☐	☐	☐	☐
Cancer (except breast/colon)	☐	☐	☐	☐	☐	☐	☐	☐	☐
Kidney disease	☐	☐	☐	☐	☐	☐	☐	☐	☐
Tuberculosis	☐	☐	☐	☐	☐	☐	☐	☐	☐
Mental illness	☐	☐	☐	☐	☐	☐	☐	☐	☐
Suicide	☐	☐	☐	☐	☐	☐	☐	☐	☐
Drug/alcohol addiction	☐	☐	☐	☐	☐	☐	☐	☐	☐

Continued on Page 2

1

© 1992 Risk Assessment Systems, Inc. 11/92

SCANTRON FORM NO. F-5414-RAS

P4 3593-C C1520- 5 4 3 2

Error Detection

The first step in error detection is to determine whether the software used for data entry and tabulation will allow the researcher to perform "error edit routines." These routines identify the wrong type of data. For example, say that for a particular field on a given data record, only the codes of 1 or 2 should appear. An error edit routine can display an error message on the data output if any number other than 1 or 2 has been entered. Such routines can be quite thorough. For example, a coded value can be rejected if it is too large or too small for a particular scaled item on the questionnaire. In some instances, a separate error edit routine can be established for every item on the questionnaire.

Another approach to error detection is for the researcher to review a printed representation of the entered data. Exhibit 14.7, for example, shows the coded values for observations 398–427 in the Santa Fe Grill database. In this example the top row indicates the variable names assigned to each data field (i.e., "id" is the label for the questionnaire number, "x_s1" represents the first screening question, x1 is the first question on the survey after the three screening questions, etc.). The numbers in the columns are the coded values that were entered. The dots indicate missing responses. While the process is somewhat tedious, the analyst can view the actual entered data for accuracy and can tell exactly where any errors occurred.

The final approach to error detection is to produce a data/column list for the entered data. A sample data/column list is shown in Exhibit 14.8. The rows of this output indicate the fields of the data record. The columns indicate the frequency of responses for each

EXHIBIT 14.7 SPSS Data View of Coded Values for Santa Fe Grill Observations

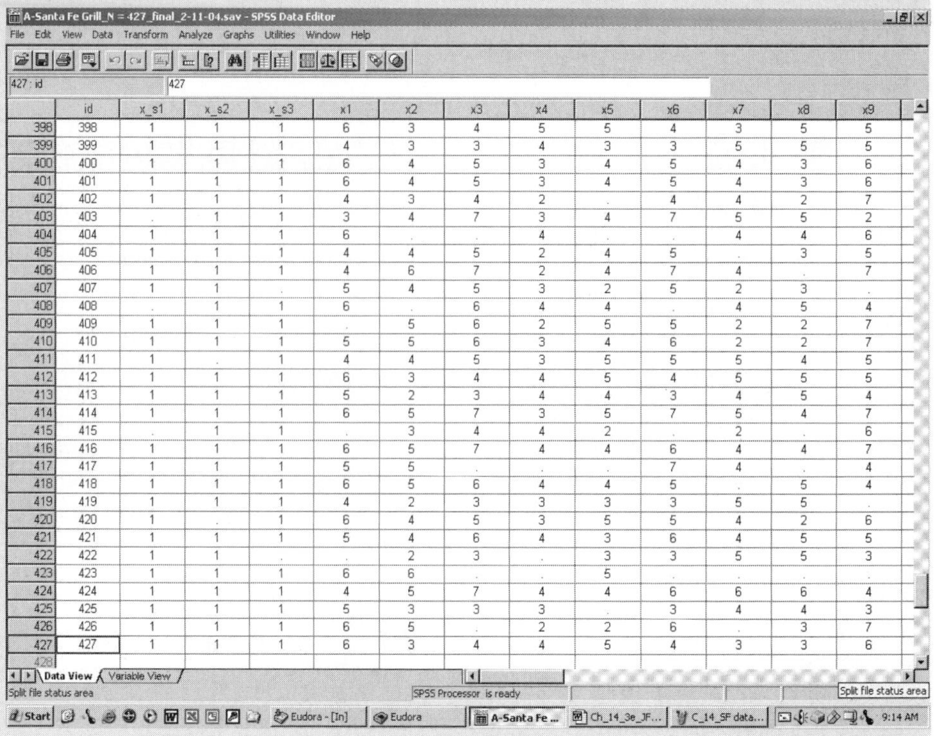

	id	x_s1	x_s2	x_s3	x1	x2	x3	x4	x5	x6	x7	x8	x9
398	398	1	1	1	6	3	4	5	5	4	3	5	5
399	399	1	1	1	4	3	3	4	3	3	5	5	5
400	400	1	1	1	6	4	5	3	4	5	4	3	6
401	401	1	1	1	6	4	5	3	4	5	4	3	6
402	402	1	1	1	4	3	4	2	.	4	4	2	7
403	403	.	1	1	3	4	7	3	4	7	5	5	2
404	404	1	1	1	6	.	.	4	.	.	4	4	6
405	405	1	1	1	4	4	5	2	4	5	.	3	5
406	406	1	1	1	4	6	7	2	4	7	4	.	7
407	407	1	1	.	5	4	5	3	2	5	2	3	.
408	408	.	1	1	6	.	6	4	4	.	4	5	4
409	409	1	1	1	.	5	6	2	5	5	2	2	7
410	410	1	1	1	5	5	6	3	4	6	2	2	7
411	411	1	.	1	4	4	5	3	5	5	5	4	5
412	412	1	1	1	6	3	4	4	5	4	5	5	5
413	413	1	1	1	5	2	3	4	4	3	4	5	4
414	414	1	1	1	6	5	7	3	5	7	5	4	7
415	415	.	1	1	.	3	4	4	2	.	2	.	6
416	416	1	1	1	6	5	7	4	4	6	4	4	7
417	417	1	1	1	5	5	.	.	.	7	4	.	4
418	418	1	1	1	6	5	6	4	4	5	.	5	4
419	419	1	1	1	4	2	3	3	3	3	5	5	.
420	420	1	.	1	6	4	5	3	5	5	4	2	6
421	421	1	1	1	5	4	6	4	3	6	4	5	5
422	422	1	1	.	.	2	3	.	3	3	5	5	3
423	423	1	1	1	6	6	.	.	5	.	.	.	.
424	424	1	1	1	4	5	7	4	4	6	6	6	4
425	425	1	1	1	5	3	3	3	.	3	4	4	3
426	426	1	1	1	6	5	.	2	2	6	.	3	7
427	427	1	1	1	6	3	4	4	5	4	3	3	6
428													

A Closer Look at Research

Data Collection Should Not Be Manual Labor

With the computerization of survey design and dissemination, manual questionnaires have become a thing of the past. Computer-based surveys can accommodate vast and complex arrays of data, greatly increasing the capacity for data collection and substantially reducing confusion and errors by interviewers and respondents. Three of the major benefits are as follows:

In the Field

1. **Encoding data without transcribing from paper.** The interviewer or respondent can enter encoded data directly into a computer database. Numerous hours of tedious effort can be eliminated by avoiding transcription from paper surveys.

2. **Minimizing errors in data.** Errors in data are less likely with computer data collection than with manual transcriptions of paper surveys. Researchers no longer have to decipher illegible interviewer or respondent handwriting.

3. **Speeding up data collection and coding.** Computer surveys can speed the process of gathering data at any or all of five points in the data collection process: (*a*) getting the questions to the respondent, (*b*) asking questions of the respondent, (*c*) recording the respondent's answers, (*d*) getting the answers back to the researcher, and (*e*) entering the answers into a computer database. Clearly, all of these add up to time savings and potential cost savings.

particular field. In data field 40, for example, 50 responses of 1 were entered, 20 responses of 2 were entered, and so on. A quick viewing of this data/column list procedure can indicate to the analyst whether inappropriate codes were entered into the data fields. The analyst can then find the corresponding questionnaire and correct the error as needed.

By initiating error edit routines, scanning actual raw data input, and producing a data/column list table, the researcher should be confident of error-free data entry. At this point the data should be ready for preliminary tabulation and data analysis. The Closer Look at Research box addresses additional issues of error detection.

EXHIBIT 14.8 Example of Data/Column List Procedure

Data Field	1	2	3	4	5	6	7
40	50	20	33	81	0	2	1
41	5	9	82	77	36	8	0
42	10	12	11	15	0	0	0
43	15	16	17	80	1	3	5
44	0	0	7	100	2	11	0
45	17	42	71	62	1	3	5
46	100	2	5	18	16	2	12
47	22	25	62	90	10	30	15
48	0	0	25	18	13	17	35
49	61	40	23	30	18	22	17
50	10	11	62	73	10	21	0
51	7	11	21	17	52	47	5
52	82	46	80	20	30	6	7

Data Tabulation

Tabulation is a simple process of counting the number of observations (cases) that are classified into certain categories. Two common forms of data tabulation are used in marketing research projects: one-way tabulations and cross-tabulations. A one-way tabulation is the categorization of single variables in the study. In most cases, a one-way tabulation shows the number of respondents who gave each possible answer to each question on the questionnaire. The actual number of one-way tabulations is directly related to the number of variables being measured in the study.

Cross-tabulation simultaneously compares two or more variables in the study. It categorizes the number of respondents who have responded to two or more questions. For example, a cross-tabulation could involve the number of respondents who spent more than $7.00 eating at McDonald's versus those who spent less.

The use and purpose of tabulations ranges from further validation of the accuracy of the data to the reporting of research results. Since each tabulation procedure serves its own unique purpose in the research study, each will be treated separately in our discussion.

One-Way Tabulation

One-way tabulations serve several purposes in the research project. First, they can be used to determine the amount of nonresponse to individual questions. Based on the coding scheme used for missing data, **one-way tabulations** identify the actual number of respondents who did not answer various questions on the questionnaire. Second, one-way tabulations can be used to locate simple blunders in data entry.

If a specific range of codes has been established for a given response to a question, say 1 through 5, a one-way tabulation can illustrate if an inaccurate code was entered, say, a 7 or 8. It does this by providing a list of all responses to the particular question. In addition, means, standard deviations, and related descriptive statistics often are determined from a one-way tabulation. Finally, one-way tabulations are also used to communicate the results of the research project. One-way tabulations can profile sample respondents, identify characteristics that distinguish between groups (i.e., heavy users versus light users), and show the percentage of respondents who respond differently to different situations, e.g., the percentage of people who purchase fast food from drive-thru windows versus those who use dine-in facilities.

The most basic way to illustrate a one-way tabulation is to construct a one-way frequency table. A one-way frequency table shows the number of respondents who answered each possible response to a question given the available alternatives. An example of this type of table is shown in Exhibit 14.9, which shows which Mexican restaurants the respondents dined at in the last 30 days. The information indicates that 99 individuals (20.1 percent) ate at Superior Grill in the last 30 days, 74 (15.0 percent) ate at Mamacita's, 110 (22.3 percent) ate at Ninfa's, and so on. Typically, a computer printout will be prepared with one-way frequency tables for each question on the survey. In addition to listing the absolute number of responses, one-way frequency tables also identify missing data, valid percentages, and summary statistics.

1. *Indications of missing data.* One-way frequency tables show the number of missing responses for each question. As shown in Exhibit 14.10, a total of 27 respondents, or 6.3 percent of the sample, did not respond to how frequently they

EXHIBIT 14.9   Example of One-Way Frequency Distribution

Output19 - SPSS Viewer

File Edit View Insert Format Analyze Graphs Utilities Window Help

Restaurant

		Frequency	Percent	Valid Percent	Cumulative Percent
Valid	Superior Grill	99	20.1	20.1	20.1
	Mamacitas	74	15.0	15.0	35.1
	Ninfa's	110	22.3	22.3	57.4
	Moe's southwestern Grill	47	9.5	9.5	66.9
	Santa Fe Grill	38	7.7	7.7	74.6
	Jose's	36	7.3	7.3	81.9
	Papacita's	32	6.5	6.5	88.4
	Other	24	4.9	4.9	93.3
	None	23	4.7	4.7	98.0
	Don't Remember	10	2.0	2.0	100.0
	Total	493	100.0	100.0	

EXHIBIT 14.10   One-Way Frequency Table Illustrating Missing Data

Output3 - SPSS Viewer

File Edit View Insert Format Analyze Graphs Utilities Window Help

→ Frequencies

Statistics

X25 -- Frequency of Patronizing Santa Fee Grill

N	Valid	400
	Missing	27
Mean		2.00
Median		2.00
Mode		2
Std. Deviation		.746

X25 -- Frequency of Patronizing Santa Fee Grill

		Frequency	Percent	Valid Percent	Cumulative Percent
Valid	Occasionally (less than once a month)	111	26.0	27.8	27.8
	Frequently (1 - 3 times a month)	178	41.7	44.5	72.3
	Very Frequently (4 or more times a month)	111	26.0	27.8	100.0
	Total	400	93.7	100.0	
Missing	System	27	6.3		
Total		427	100.0		

patronized the Santa Fe Grill. It is important to recognize the actual number of missing responses when estimating percentages from a one-way frequency table. In order to establish valid percentages, missing responses must be removed from the calculation.

2. *Determining valid percentages.* To determine valid percentages one must remove incomplete surveys or particular questions. For example, the one-way frequency table in Exhibit 14.10 actually constructs valid percentages (the third column). While the total number of responses for this particular question was 427, only 400 are used to develop the valid percentage of response across categories because the 27 missing responses were subtracted.

3. *Summary statistics.* Finally, one-way frequency tables also can illustrate a variety of summary statistics. In Exhibit 14.10 the summary statistics for question X25 are the mean, median, mode, and standard deviation. These statistics help the researcher better understand the average responses. For example, the mean of 2.0 indicates that many respondents are frequent patrons of the Santa Fe Grill.

Cross-Tabulation

Cross-tabulation Simultaneously treating two or more variables in the study; categorizing the number of respondents who have answered two or more questions consecutively.

After we examine a one-way frequency table, the next logical step in data analysis is to perform cross-tabulation. Cross-tabulation is extremely useful when the analyst wishes to study relationships between variables. The purpose of **cross-tabulation** is to determine whether certain variables differ when compared among various subgroups of the total sample. In fact, cross-tabulation is the primary form of data analysis in some marketing research projects. Two key elements of cross-tabulation are how to develop the cross-tabulation and how to interpret the outcome.

Exhibit 14.11 shows a simple cross-tabulation between gender and recall of Santa Fe Grill ads. The cross-tabulation shows frequencies and percentages, with percentages

EXHIBIT 14.11 Example of a Cross-Tabulation: Gender by Ad Recall

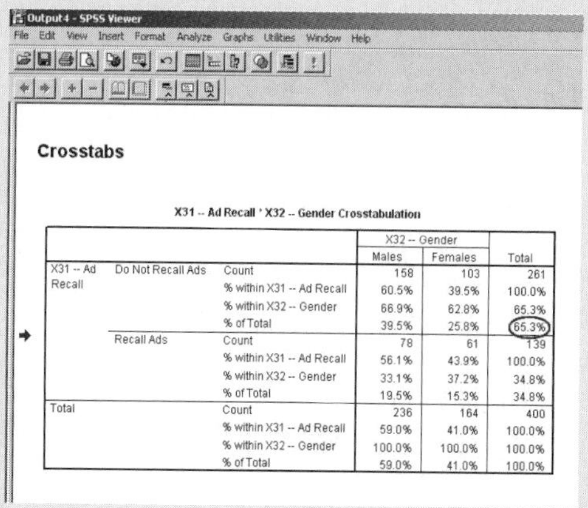

X31 -- Ad Recall * X32 -- Gender Crosstabulation

			X32 -- Gender		
			Males	Females	Total
X31 -- Ad Recall	Do Not Recall Ads	Count	158	103	261
		% within X31 -- Ad Recall	60.5%	39.5%	100.0%
		% within X32 -- Gender	66.9%	62.8%	65.3%
		% of Total	39.5%	25.8%	65.3%
	Recall Ads	Count	78	61	139
		% within X31 -- Ad Recall	56.1%	43.9%	100.0%
		% within X32 -- Gender	33.1%	37.2%	34.8%
		% of Total	19.5%	15.3%	34.8%
Total		Count	236	164	400
		% within X31 -- Ad Recall	59.0%	41.0%	100.0%
		% within X32 -- Gender	100.0%	100.0%	100.0%
		% of Total	59.0%	41.0%	100.0%

existing for both rows and columns. A simple way to interpret this table, for example, would be to isolate those individuals who do not recall ads for Santa Fe Grill. These individuals represent 65.3 percent of the sample, with 39.5 percent being male and 25.8 percent female.

Several issues must be considered in developing and interpreting cross-tabulation tables. Looking at Exhibit 14.11, note that percentages are calculated for each cell of the cross-tabulation table. The top number within each cell represents the absolute frequency of responses for each variable or question (e.g., 158 male respondents do not recall ads). Below the absolute frequency is the row percentage per cell. For example, the 158 male respondents who do not recall Santa Fe ads represent 60.5 percent of the total in the do not recall category (261). The cell also shows the total percentage of respondents within cells based on the total sample. So, for example, with a total sample of 400, 39.5 percent of the sample are males who do not recall ads, and 19.5 percent are males who do recall ads.

When constructing the cross-tabulation table, the marketing researcher selects the variable to use when examining relationships. As always, the selection of variables should be based on the objectives of the research project. Paired variable relationships are selected on the basis of whether they answer the specific research questions in the research project.

Demographic variables or lifestyle/psychographic characteristics typically are the starting point in developing cross-tabulations. These variables usually are the columns of the cross-tabulation table, and the rows are variables like purchase intention, usage, or actual sales data. Cross-tabulation tables such as these calculate percentages on the basis of column variable totals. In turn, this allows the researcher to make comparisons of the relationship between behaviors and intentions with predictor variables such as income, sex, and marital status. Preliminary analysis of this nature is especially useful if the researcher wants to determine subgroup differences in relation to certain actions.

As a preliminary technique, cross-tabulation provides the research analyst with a powerful tool to summarize survey data. It is easy to understand and interpret and can provide a valid description of both aggregate and subgroup data. Yet the simplicity of this technique can create problems. Some survey approaches can result in an endless variety of cross-tabulation tables. In developing these tables, the analyst must always keep in mind both the project objectives and specific research questions the study will attempt to answer. The analyst should construct cross-tabulations that accurately reflect information relevant to the objectives of the project.

A variety of software and statistical packages can be used to generate cross-tabulation tables. Spreadsheets such as Excel, Access, and Quattro Pro, along with statistical packages like SAS and SPSS, can all generate effective cross-tabulations. Chapter 15 will discuss various statistical techniques often used with cross-tabulation, as well as tests of association, significant differences, and measures of central tendency.

Descriptive Statistics

Descriptive statistics are used to summarize and describe the data obtained from a sample of respondents. Two types of measures are often used to describe data. One of those is measures of central tendency and the other is measures of dispersion. Both are described in detail in the next chapter. For now we refer you to Exhibit 14.12 which provides an overview of the major types of descriptive statistics used by marketing researchers.

eXHIBIT 14.12 Overview of Descriptive Statistics

To clarify descriptive statistics, we use a simple data set to illustrate each of the major ones. Assume that data has been collected from ten students about satisfaction with their MP3 player. Satisfaction is measured on a 7-point scale with the end points labeled "Highly Satisfied = 7" and "Not Satisfied at All = 1." The results of this survey are shown below by respondent.

Respondent	Satisfaction Rating
1	7
2	5
3	6
4	4
5	6
6	5
7	7
8	5
9	4
10	5

DESCRIPTIVE STATISTICS

Frequency = the number of times a number (raw response) is in the data set.

To compute it, count how many times the number is in the data set. For example, the number 7 is in the data set twice.

Frequency distribution = a summary of how many times each possible raw response to a question appears in the data set.

To develop a frequency distribution, count how many times each number appears in the data set and make a table that shows the results. For example, create a chart like the one shown below:

Satisfaction Rating	Count
7	2
6	2
5	4
4	2
3	0
2	0
1	0
Total	10

Percentage distribution = the result of converting a frequency distribution into percentages.

To develop a percentage distribution, divide each frequency count for each rating by the total count.

Satisfaction Rating	Count	Percentage
7	2	20%
6	2	20
5	4	40
4	2	20
3	0	0
2	0	0
1	0	0
Total	10	100%

Cumulative percentage distribution = each individual percentage added to the previous to get a total.

To develop a cumulative percentage distribution, arrange the percentages in descending order and sum the percentages one at a time and show the result.

Satisfaction Rating	Count	Percentage	Cumulative Percentage	
7	2	20%	20	
6	2	20	40	
5	4	40	80	← median
4	2	20	100%	
3	0	0		
2	0	0		
1	0	0		
Total	10	100%		

Mean = the arithmetic average of all the raw responses.

To calculate the mean, add up all the values of a distribution of responses and divide the total by the number of valid responses.

The mean is: $(7 + 5 + 6 + 4 + 6 + 5 + 7 + 5 + 4 + 5) = 54 / 10 = 5.4$

Median = the descriptive statistic that splits the raw data into a hierarchical pattern where half the raw data is above the median value and half is below.

To determine the median, look at the cumulative percentage distribution and find either where the cumulative percentage is equal to 50 percent or where it includes 50 percent. The median is marked in the table above.

Mode = the most frequently occurring raw response in the set of responses to a given set of questions.

To determine the mode, find the number which has the largest frequency (count). In the responses above, the number 5 has the largest count and is the mode.

Range = a statistic that represents the spread of the data and is the distance between the largest and the smallest values of a frequency distribution.

To calculate the range, subtract the lowest rating point from the highest rating point and the difference is the range. For the above data, the maximum number is 7 and the minimum number is 4 so the range is $7 - 4 = 3$.

Standard deviation = the measure of the average dispersion of the values in a set of responses about their mean. It provides an indication of how similar or dissimilar the numbers are in the set of responses.

To calculate the standard deviation, subtract the mean from the square of each number and sum them. Then divide that sum by the total number of responses minus one, and then take the square root of the result.

Graphical Illustration of Data

The next logical step following the construction of one-way frequency and cross-tabulation tables is to translate them into graphical illustrations. Graphical illustrations, as opposed to tables, can be very powerful for communicating key research results generated from preliminary data analysis to the client. Given the importance of this topic, a more detailed discussion will be provided in Chapters 15 through 17.

mARKETInG RESEARCH In ACTIOn

Data Analysis Case

Deli Depot

In this chapter we have shown you simple approaches for examining data. In later chapters, we focus on using more advanced statistical techniques to analyze data. The most important consideration in deciding how to analyze data is keep in mind your underlying purpose—for instance, to enable businesses to use data to make better business decisions. To help students more easily understand the best ways to examine data, we have prepared several databases that can be applied to various research problems. This case is about Deli Depot, a sandwich restaurant. The database is available at www.mhhe.com/hair06.

Deli Depot sells cold and hot sandwiches, soup and chili, yogurt, and pies and cookies. The restaurant is positioned in the fast-food market to compete directly with Subway and similar sandwich restaurants. Its competitive advantages include special sauces on sandwiches, supplementary menu items like soups and pies, and quick delivery within specified zones. As part of their marketing research class, students conducted a survey for the owner of a local restaurant near their campus.

The students obtained permission to conduct interviews with customers inside the restaurant. Information was collected for 17 questions. Customers were first asked their perceptions of the restaurant on six factors (variables X1–X6) and then asked to rank the same six factors in terms of their importance in selecting a restaurant where they wanted to eat (variables X12–X17). Finally, respondents were asked how satisfied they were with the restaurant, how likely they were to recommend it to a friend, how often they eat there, and how far they drove to eat a meal at Deli Depot. Interviewers recorded the sex of the respondents without asking it. The variables, sample questions, and their coding are shown below.

Performance Perceptions Variables

The performance perceptions were measured as follows. Listed below is a set of characteristics that could be used to describe Deli Depot. Using a scale from 1 to 10, with 10 being "Strongly Agree" and 1 being "Strongly Disagree," to what extent do you agree or disagree? Deli Depot has:

X1—Friendly employees

X2—Competitive prices

X3—Competent employees

X4—Excellent food quality

X5—Wide variety of food

X6—Fast service

If a respondent chose a 10 on "friendly employees," this would indicate strong agreement that Deli Depot has friendly employees. On the other hand, if a respondent chose a 1 for "fast service," this would indicate strong disagreement and the perception that Deli Depot offers very slow service.

ΕΧΗΙΒΙΤ 14.13 Deli Depot Questionnaire

SCREENING AND RAPPORT QUESTIONS

Hello. My name is _____ and I work for Decision Analyst, a market research firm in Dallas, Texas. We are talking to people today/tonight about eating out habits.

1. "How often do you eat out?" __ Often __ Occasionally __ Seldom

2. "Did you just eat at Deli Depot?" __ Yes __ No

3. "Have you completed a restaurant questionnaire on Deli Depot before?" __ Yes __ No

If respondent answers "Often or Occasionally" to the first question, "Yes" to the second question, and "No" to the third question, then say:

We would like you to answer a few questions about your experience today/tonight at Deli Depot, and we hope you will be willing to give us your opinions. The survey will only take a few minutes and it will be very helpful to management in better serving its customers. We will pay you $5.00 for completing the questionnaire.

If the person says yes, give them a clipboard with the questionnaire on it, briefly explain the questionnaire, and show them where to complete the survey.

DINING OUT SURVEY

Please read all questions carefully. If you do not understand a question, ask the interviewer to help you.

Section 1: Perceptions Measures

Listed below is a set of characteristics that could be used to describe Deli Depot. Using a scale from 1 to 10, with 10 being "Strongly Agree" and 1 being "Strongly Disagree," to what extent do you agree or disagree that Deli Depot has (Circle the correct response)?

1. Friendly employees

   Strongly Disagree Strongly Agree

   1 2 3 4 5 6 7 8 9 10

2. Competitive prices

   Strongly Disagree Strongly Agree

   1 2 3 4 5 6 7 8 9 10

3. Competent employees

   Strongly Disagree Strongly Agree

   1 2 3 4 5 6 7 8 9 10

4. Excellent food quality

   Strongly Disagree Strongly Agree

   1 2 3 4 5 6 7 8 9 10

5. Wide variety of food

   Strongly Disagree Strongly Agree

   1 2 3 4 5 6 7 8 9 10

6. Fast service

   Strongly Disagree Strongly Agree

   1 2 3 4 5 6 7 8 9 10

Section 2: Classification Variables

Circle the response that describes you.

7. Your Gender 1 Male

   0 Female

8. How likely are you to recommend Deli Depot to a friend?

   Definitely Not Recommend Definitely Recommend

   1 2 3 4 5 6 7

continued

EXHIBIT 14.13 Deli Depot Questionnaire, *continued*

9. How satisfied are you with Deli Depot?

Not Very   Highly
Satisfied   Satisfied
1   2   3   4   5   6   7

10. How often do you patronize Deli Depot?

1 = eat at Deli Depot 2 or more
     times each week.
0 = eat at Deli Depot fewer than
     2 times each week.

11. How far did you drive to get to Deli Depot?

1 = came from within one mile
2 = 1–3 miles
3 = came from more than 3 miles

Section 3: Selection Factors

Listed below is a set of attributes (reasons) many people use when selecting a fast-food restaurant to eat at. Regarding your visits to fast-food restaurants in the last 30 days, please rank each attribute from 1 to 6, with 6 being the most important reason for selecting the restaurant and 1 being the least important reason. There can be no ties so make sure you rank each attribute with a different number.

Attribute	Ranking
12. Friendly employees	
13. Competitive prices	
14. Competent employees	
15. Excellent food quality	
16. Wide variety of food	
17. Fast service	

Thank you very much for your help. Please give your questionnaire to the interviewer and you will be given your $5.00.

Classification Variables

Data for the classification variables was asked at the end of the survey, but in the database it is recorded as variables X7–X11. Responses were coded as follows:

X7—Gender (1 = Male; 0 = Female)

X8—Recommend to friend (7 = Definitely recommend; 1 = Definitely not recommend)

X9—Satisfaction level (7 = Highly satisfied; 1 = Not very satisfied)

X10—Usage level (1 = Heavy user [eats at Deli Depot 2 or more times each week]; 0 = Light user [eats at Deli Depot fewer than 2 times a week])

X11—Market area (1 = Came from within 1 mile; 2 = Came from 1–3 miles; 3 = Came from more than 3 miles)

Selection Factor Rankings

Data for the selection factors were collected as follows. Listed below is a set of attributes (reasons) many people use when selecting a fast-food restaurant to eat at. Regarding your visits to fast-food restaurants in the last 30 days, please rank each attribute from 1 to 6, with

6 being the most important reason for selecting the fast-food restaurant and 1 being the least important reason. There can be no ties, so make sure you rank each attribute with a different number.

X12—Friendly employees

X13—Competitive prices

X14—Competent employees

X15—Excellent food quality

X16—Wide variety of food

X17—Fast service

Hands-On Exercise

1. How would you improve the Deli Depot survey and questionnaire?

2. What are the competitive advantages and disadvantages of Deli Depot over Subway?

Summary of Learning Objectives

■ **Illustrate the process of preparing data for preliminary analysis.**

The value of marketing research is its ability to provide decision-making information to the user or client. To accomplish this, the raw data must be converted into usable information. After collecting data through the appropriate method, the task becomes one of ensuring that the data will provide meaning and value. Data preparation is the first part of the process of transforming raw data into usable information. This process takes into account five steps: (1) data validation, (2) editing and coding, (3) data entry, (4) error detection, and (5) data tabulation.

■ **Demonstrate the procedure for assuring data validation.**

Data validation attempts to determine whether surveys, interviews, or observations were conducted correctly and are free from fraud. In recontacting select respondents, the researcher asks whether the interview (1) was falsified, (2) was conducted with a qualified respondent, (3) took place in the proper procedural setting, (4) was completed correctly and accurately, and (5) was accomplished in a courteous manner.

■ **Describe the process of editing and coding data obtained through survey methods.**

The editing process involves the manual scanning of interviews or questionnaire responses to determine whether the proper questions were asked, proper answers recorded, and proper screening questions employed, as well as whether open-ended questions were recorded accurately. Once edited, all questionnaires are coded by

assigning numerical value to all responses. Coding is the process of providing numeric labels to the data so they can be entered into a computer for subsequent statistical analysis.

■ **Acquaint the user with data entry procedures.**

There are four principal methods of entering coded data into a computer. First is the keyboard terminal or PC keyboard. Data may also be entered through terminals having touch-screen capabilities, or through the use of a handheld electronic pointer or light pen. Finally, data from certain questionnaires can be entered through a scanner using optical character recognition.

■ **Illustrate a process for detecting errors in data entry.**

Unfortunately, error detection normally occurs after the data have been entered into computer storage. Entry errors can be detected through the use of error edit routines built or developed into the data entry software. An additional approach is to visually scan the actual data after entry. A data table is one approach for visually scanning entered data.

■ **Discuss techniques used for data tabulation and data analysis.**

Two common forms of data tabulations are used in marketing research. A one-way tabulation indicates the number of respondents who gave each possible answer to each question on a questionnaire. Cross-tabulation provides categorization of respondents by treating two or more variables simultaneously. Categorization is based on the number of respondents who have responded to two or more consecutive questions.

Key Terms and Concepts

Coding　485

Cross-tabulation　494

Curbstoning　479

Data entry　488

Data validation　479

Editing　480

One-way tabulation　492

Tabulation　492

Review Questions

1. Briefly describe the process of data validation. Specifically discuss the issues of fraud, screening, procedure, completeness, and courtesy.

2. What are the differences between data validation, data editing, and data coding?

3. Explain the differences between establishing codes for open-ended questions and for closed-ended questions.

4. What is the role of probing questions and why are they an important part of the research process?

5. Briefly describe the process of data entry. What changes in technology have simplified this procedure?

6. What are the three approaches to error detection? In your discussion be sure to describe the data/column list procedure.

7. What is the purpose of a simple one-way tabulation? How does this relate to a one-way frequency table?

8. What is the advantage of cross-tabulation over one-way tabulation?

Discussion Questions

1. **EXPERIENCE THE INTERNET.** Go to the Web site for the Acxiom Corporation, at www.acxiom.com, and select the topic Case in Point. Once there, select the topic Newsletters and select the newsletter for vol. 2, issue 1. Read the passage on cluster coding systems and comment on how they apply to preliminary data analysis.

2. **EXPERIENCE THE INTERNET.** At the Acxiom Web site select newsletter vol. 2, issue 3. Select the article on data warehousing and comment on how it relates to the coding of marketing data.

3. Obtain a copy of a marketing research questionnaire and on the basis of your knowledge of developing codes, convert the questionnaire into a master code illustrating the appropriate values for each question and corresponding responses.

4. Look back at the quote at the beginning of this chapter. On the basis of what you now know about preparing data for analysis, explain what Robert W. Kneen meant by "garbage in, garbage out."

5. Run several one-way tabulations using either the Deli Depot or Santa Fe Grill databases. Develop tables to present your findings. Write a one-paragraph explanation of your findings for each tabulation.

6. Now run several cross-tabulations using either the Deli Depot or Santa Fe Grill databases. Develop tables to present your findings. Write a one-paragraph explanation of your findings for each cross-tabulation. Discuss the value of cross-tabulations over one-way tabulations.

chapter 15

Data Analysis: Testing for Significant Differences

Learning Objectives

After reading this chapter, you will be able to

1. Understand how to prepare graphical presentations of data.

2. Calculate the mean, median and mode as measures of central tendency.

3. Explain the range and standard deviation of a frequency distribution as measures of dispersion.

4. Understand the difference between independent and related samples.

5. Explain hypothesis testing and assess potential error in its use.

6. Understand univariate and bivariate statistical tests.

7. Apply and interpret the results of the ANOVA and *n*-way ANOVA statistical methods.

8. Utilize perceptual mapping to simplify presentation of research findings.

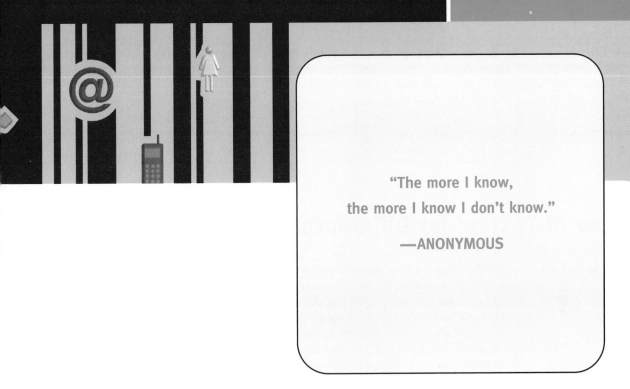

> "The more I know,
> the more I know I don't know."
>
> —ANONYMOUS

Statistical Software Makes Data Analysis Easy

Firms of all sizes increasingly are collecting and storing data relevant to their business activities. These data may come from surveys of customers or be internally generated by sales force contact software and stored in the company's data warehouse. But to be useful for decision making, the data must be organized, categorized, analyzed, and shared among company employees. Tom Peters, in his book *Thriving on Chaos,* said, "We are drowning on information and starved for knowledge." To convert this ocean of information into knowledge, we need user-friendly, powerful software packages. Many software packages can help us accomplish this conversion, including the popular Excel program that is part of Microsoft Windows. But as the amount of information increases exponentially, we need comprehensive, sophisticated packages that are relatively inexpensive and easy to use. Fortunately, at least two are available and can be used with most PCs: SPSS and SAS. Both are very powerful and provide statistical processing capabilities for a variety of tasks, from calculating means and modes to executing neural networking and other sophisticated data mining tasks. Each package is briefly described below. We rely on SPSS in many chapters in this text

to analyze and evaluate data collected in a customer survey of a local restaurant—the Santa Fe Grill.

SPSS

The SPSS, Inc., software package is designed to be user-friendly, even for novice computer users. Released in the Microsoft Windows format and touted as "Real Stats, Real Easy," SPSS delivers easy data access and management, highly customizable output, complete just-in-time-training, and a revolutionary system for working with charts and graphs. The producers of SPSS proudly claim that "you don't have to be a statistician to use SPSS," an important characteristic for individuals who are somewhat afraid of computers and their power. Available in almost any format, SPSS provides immense statistical analysis capability while remaining one of the most user-friendly statistical packages available today. Information concerning SPSS is available online at www.spss.com.

SAS

The SAS (rhymes with class) system provides extensive statistical capabilities, including tools for both specialized and enterprisewide analytical needs.

Research institutes, laboratories, marketing research firms, universities, pharmaceutical companies, government agencies, and banks all take advantage of the statistical capabilities of SAS. From traditional analysis of variance to exact methods of statistical visualization, the SAS system provides the tools required to analyze data and help organizations make the right statistical choices. Many heavy users of statistical software packages feel that SAS offers greater statistical analysis capability than SPSS. However, this increased statistical power is sometimes compromised by applications less user-friendly than those of SPSS. Information concerning SAS is available online at www.sas.com.

Value of Testing for Differences in Data

Once the data have been collected and prepared for analysis, there are some basic statistical analysis procedures the marketing researcher will want to perform. An obvious need for these statistics comes from the fact that almost all data sets are disaggregated. In other words, it's hard to find out what the entire set of responses means because there are "too many numbers" to look at. Consequently, almost every data set needs some summary information developed that describes the numbers it contains. Basic statistics and descriptive analysis were developed for this purpose.

Some of the statistics common to almost all marketing research projects are described in this chapter. The chapter also explains how to graphically display the data so decision makers can understand it. For example, if you conducted a study of people who buy Domino's pizza you would be able to most effectively show who the most frequent purchasers are compared to the least frequent purchasers, and perhaps why.

First, we describe measures of central tendency and dispersion. The advantages and pitfalls of each measure need to be understood so that the distribution of the information can be reasonably well described. Next, we discuss relationships of the sample data. The t distribution and associated confidence interval estimation are discussed in this second section. Third, we describe hypothesis testing, including tests for examining hypotheses related to differences between two sample means, as well as appropriate terminology. Finally, the chapter closes with an introduction to analysis of variance, a powerful technique for detecting differences between three or more sample means.

Guidelines for Graphics

Graphics should be used whenever practical. They help the information user to quickly grasp the essence of the information developed in the research project. Charts also can be an effective visual aid to enhance the communication process and add clarity and impact to research reports. In this section we will show the value of bar charts, pie charts, and line charts. We will use the variable X25—Frequency of Patronizing Santa Fe Grill database to develop the frequency distribution in Exhibit 15.1. Note that 400 respondents indicated how frequently they patronize the Santa Fe Grill using a 3-point scale, with 1 = Occasionally, 2 = Frequently, and 3 = Very Frequently. The total sample was 427, but 27 respondents did not answer this question and therefore are considered missing data. The numbers in the Percent column are calculated using the total sample size of 427, while the numbers in the Valid percent and Cumulative percent columns are calculated using the total sample size minus the number of missing responses to this question ($427 - 27 = 400$).

eXHIBIT 15.1   **Frequency Distribution for Variable X25—Frequency of Patronizing Santa Fe Grill**

Output3 - SPSS Viewer

File Edit View Insert Format Analyze Graphs Utilities Window Help

➜ **Frequencies**

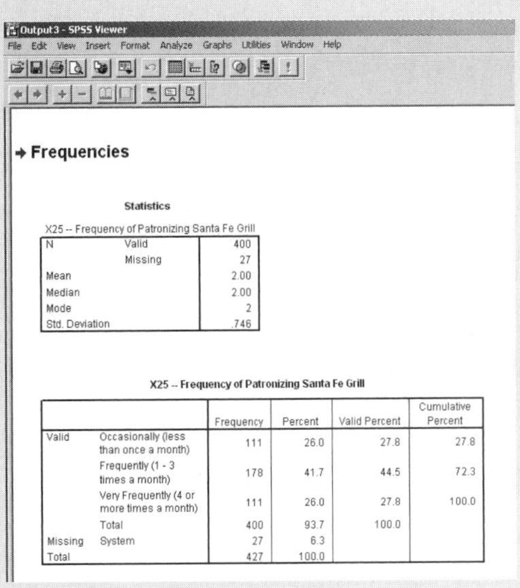

Statistics

X25 -- Frequency of Patronizing Santa Fe Grill

N	Valid	400
	Missing	27
Mean		2.00
Median		2.00
Mode		2
Std. Deviation		.746

X25 -- Frequency of Patronizing Santa Fe Grill

		Frequency	Percent	Valid Percent	Cumulative Percent
Valid	Occasionally (less than once a month)	111	26.0	27.8	27.8
	Frequently (1 - 3 times a month)	178	41.7	44.5	72.3
	Very Frequently (4 or more times a month)	111	26.0	27.8	100.0
	Total	400	93.7	100.0	
Missing	System	27	6.3		
Total		427	100.0		

Bar Charts

A *bar chart* shows the data in the form of bars that may be horizontally or vertically oriented. Bar charts are excellent tools to depict both absolute and relative magnitudes, differences, and change. Exhibit 15.2 is an example of a vertical bar chart that displays the information in Exhibit 15.1. For example, the frequency for the value label of Very Infrequently = 1 (N = 49) is the first vertical bar on the left side of the chart. The remaining bars are developed in the same way. Bar charts also can be displayed horizontally.

A histogram is similar to a bar chart and often there is confusion between the two types of charts. A histogram for variable X22—Satisfaction is shown in Exhibit 15.3. Note the bars in a bar chart have space between them whereas in a *histogram* they do not. An additional feature of the histogram is that a normal line has been drawn over the frequency distribution to provide an indication of whether the data approximates a normal curve. The distribution of X22 is skewed a little to the right but still closely approximates a normal curve.

Line Charts

A *line chart* simply connects a series of data points with a continuous line. Line charts are frequently used to portray trends over several periods of time. In addition, several lines can be displayed on the same chart, allowing for multiple comparisons by the viewer. This can be very useful in explaining comparisons between variables. If multiple lines are used in the same chart, each line needs to have its own label and must be clearly different in

e X H I B I T 15.2 Bar Chart for Variable X25—Frequency of Patronizing Santa Fe Grill

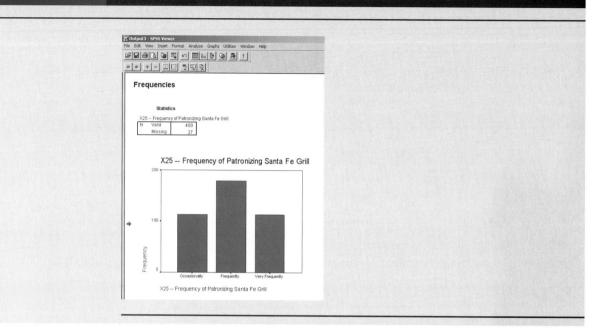

e X H I B I T 15.3 Histogram Showing Distribution of X22 and the Normal Curve

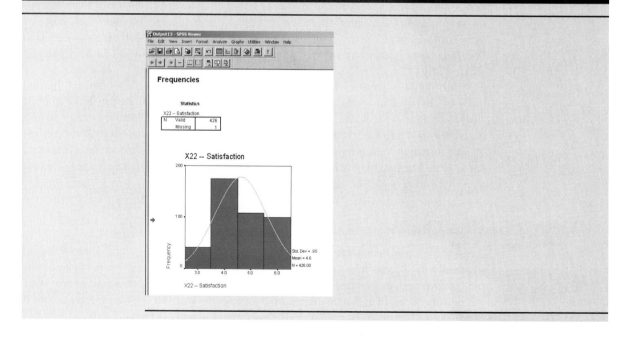

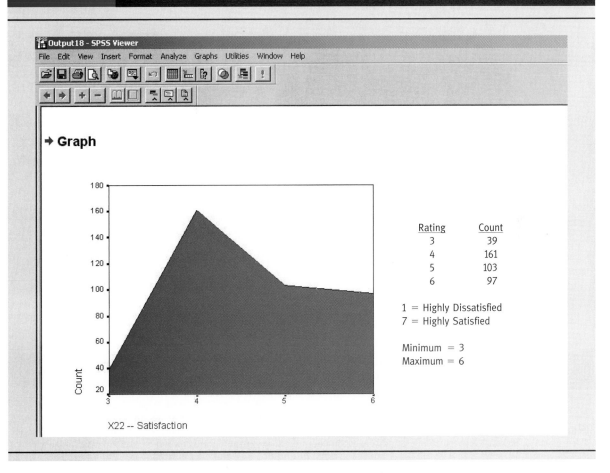

EXHIBIT 15.4 Area Chart for X22—Satisfaction with Santa Fe Grill

form or color to avoid confusing the viewer. Exhibit 15.4 is a special form of a line chart, called an *area chart*. In an area chart, the area below the line is filled in to dramatically display the information.

Pie or Round Charts

Pie charts are excellent for displaying relative proportions. Each section of the pie is the relative proportion, as a percentage of the total area of the pie, associated with the value of a specific variable. The relative proportions of X25—Patronizing Santa Fe Grill were used to create the chart in Exhibit 15.5. Pie charts are not useful for displaying comparative information between several variables or changes over time. Generally, seven sections are considered the practical maximum in a pie chart.

Marketing researchers need to exercise caution when using charts and figures to explain data. It is possible to misinterpret information in a chart and lead marketing research information users to inappropriate conclusions. See Exhibit 15.6 for a discussion of this pitfall.

EXHIBIT 15.5 Pie Chart for X25—Frequency of Patronizing Santa Fe Grill

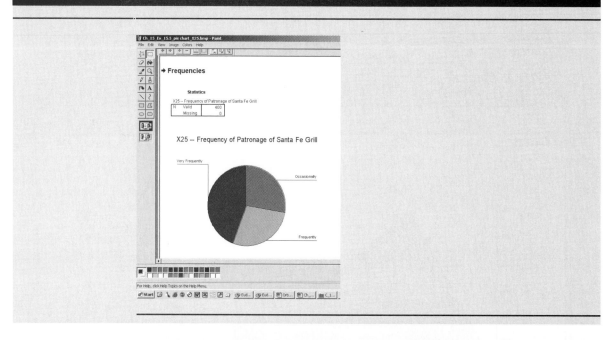

EXHIBIT 15.6 A Good Picture Is Worth a Thousand Words

Many people panic when confronted with mounds of statistics, but they are quick to rely on charts and graphs. The old saying "A picture is worth a thousand words" seems especially appropriate when applied to charts intended to simplify tables of numbers. The problem is, however, that the saying lacks one very important qualifier: a good picture is worth a thousand words. A bad picture is worth very little.

Unfortunately, we are all exposed to many charts that are bad pictures. A chart may be colorful, artistic, eye-catching, and even accurate but can still fail in its mission. Charts are supposed to dramatize the facts, but some—called "gee-whiz" charts—overstate the facts.

Gee-whiz chart is a term coined by Darrell Huff in his book *How to Lie with Statistics*. No doubt Huff intended his book to help readers recognize misleading representations of data, though some readers may have misappropriated it as a primer for data muddling instead. Politicians, economists, marketing researchers, and many others with an ax to grind or a cause to promote have used gee-whiz charts to overdramatize their point.

It is simple to make a gee-whiz chart. Draw the chart correctly and cut off the bottom part. Insert a little jog in the vertical scale on the left to indicate that the scale is incomplete and you have created a chart that overdramatizes any trend, up or down, and makes it appear to be much more impressive.

Suppose annual sales of a brand of toothpaste dropped from 420 tons to 295 tons, a 30 percent decline. A good picture will show a 30 percent decline, but a gee-whiz chart would show something that looked like a 90 percent decline. While close examination of the numbers will reveal the actual decline to be 30 percent, the picture creates a stronger, and thus misleading, impression. The numbers tell, the picture shows—a sort of twisted version of a children's show-and-tell exercise.

Thomas Semon, a research consultant, bemoans the fact that he has seen many gee-whiz charts in research presentations. He notes that it is very unlikely that a marketing researcher would deliberately distort the actual results when expressed in numbers, yet some will distort the results visually in charts. A misleading chart is disinformation according to Semon. It is a deliberate attempt to create an erroneous impression or to make a trend appear more dramatic and noteworthy.

He suggests the following experiment. Look closely at every chart you see in the newspaper and magazines for the next week. Imagine what they would look like if they were correctly drawn. If many of the trends appear insignificant, it may be because the trend is insignificant. This is a useful thought to keep in mind when interpreting information.

As a final note, Semon says that while a lot of news is hype, research shouldn't be.[1]

e X H I B I T 15.7 SPSS Dialog Boxes for Graphics with Bar Charts

SPSS Applications—How to Develop Graphics

Graphics like the ones we just showed you are easy to develop using SPSS. The SPSS "click-through" sequence is ANALYZE → DESCRIPTIVE STATISTICS → FREQUENCIES. Highlight variable X25 from the list of variables on the left-hand side of the screen and move it into the Variable(s): box. If you want only the frequency table as shown in Exhibit 15.1, then click OK now. Note on the lower left side of the dialog box that "Display frequency tables" is already checked. If you do not want a frequency table you can uncheck it here. If you want charts, click on this button at the bottom of the dialog box. This sequence will take you to the dialog box shown in the lower portion of Exhibit 15.7. You could also select pie charts or histograms from this sequence.

Measures of Central Tendency

As described above, frequency distributions can be useful for examining the different values for a given variable. Frequency distribution tables are easy to read and provide a great deal of basic information. There are times, however, when the amount of detail is just too much. In such situations the researcher needs a way to summarize and condense all the information in order to get at the underlying meaning. Descriptive statistics are commonly used to accomplish this task. The mean, median, and mode are measures of central tendency. These measures locate the center of the distribution. For this reason, the mean, median, and mode are sometimes also called *measures of location.*

Mean

Mean The arithmetic average of the sample; all values of a distribution of responses are summed and divided by the number of valid responses.

The **mean** is the average value within the distribution, and is the most commonly used measure of central tendency. The mean tells us, for example, the average number of cups of coffee the typical student may drink during finals to stay awake. The mean can be calculated when the data scale is either interval or ratio. Generally, the data will show some degree of central tendency, with most of the responses distributed close to the mean.

The mean is a very robust measure of central tendency. It is fairly insensitive to data values being added or deleted. The mean can be subject to distortion, however, if extreme values are included in the distribution. For example, suppose you ask four students how many cups of coffee they drink in a single day. Respondent answers are as follows: Respondent A = 1 cup; Respondent B = 10 cups; Respondent C = 5 cups; and Respondent D = 6 cups. Let's also assume that we know that respondents A and B are males and respondents C and D are females and we want to compare consumption of coffee between males and females. Looking at the males first (Respondents A and B), we calculate the mean number of cups to be 5.5 (1 + 10 = 11/2 = 5.5). Similarly, looking at the females next (Respondents C and D), we calculate the mean number of cups to be 5.5 (5 + 6 = 11/2 = 5.5). If we look only at the mean number of cups of coffee consumed by males and females, we would conclude there are no differences in the two groups. Looking at the underlying distribution, however, we must conclude there are some differences and the mean in fact distorts our understanding of coffee consumption patterns of males and females.

Mode

Mode The most common value in the set of responses to a question; that is, the response most often given to a question.

The **mode** is the value that appears in the distribution most often. For example, the average number of cups of coffee students drink per day during finals may be 5 (the mean), while the number of cups of coffee that most students drink is only 3 (the mode). The mode is the value that represents the highest peak in the distribution's graph. The mode is especially useful as a measure for data that have been somehow grouped into categories. The mode of the data distribution in Exhibit 15.1 is Occasionally (Coded 3) because when you look in the Frequency column you will note that the largest number of responses is 111 for the "Occasionally" value label, which has a value of 3.

Median

Median The middle value of a rank-ordered distribution; exactly half of the responses are above and half are below the median value.

The **median** is the middle value of the distribution when the distribution is ordered in either an ascending or a descending sequence. For example, if you interviewed a sample of students to determine their coffee-drinking patterns during finals, you might find that the median number of cups of coffee consumed is 4. The number of cups of coffee consumed above and below this number would be the same (the median number is the exact middle of the distribution). If the number of data observations is even, the median is generally considered to be the average of the two middle values. If there are an odd number of observations, the median is the middle value. The median is especially useful as a measure of central tendency for ordinal data.

Each measure of central tendency describes a distribution in its own manner, and each measure has its own strengths and weaknesses. For nominal data, the mode is the best measure. For ordinal data, the median is generally best. For interval or ratio data, the mean is generally used. If there are extreme values within the interval or ratio data, however, the mean can be distorted. In those cases, the median and the mode should be considered. SPSS and other statistical software packages are designed to perform such types of analysis.

SPSS Applications—Measures of Central Tendency

The Santa Fe Grill database can be used with the SPSS software to calculate measures of central tendency. The SPSS "click-through" sequence is ANALYZE → DESCRIPTIVE STATISTICS → FREQUENCIES. Let's use X25—Frequency of Patronage of Santa Fe Grill as a variable to examine. Click on X25 to highlight it and then on the arrow box for the Variables box to use in your analysis. Next open the Statistics box and click on Mean, Median, and Mode, and then Continue and OK. Recall that if you want to create charts open the Charts box. Your choices are Bar, Pie, and Histograms. For the Format box we will use the defaults, so click on OK to execute the program. The dialog boxes for this sequence are shown in Exhibit 15.8.

ⓔXHIBIT 15.8 **Dialog Boxes for Calculating the Mean, Median, and Mode**

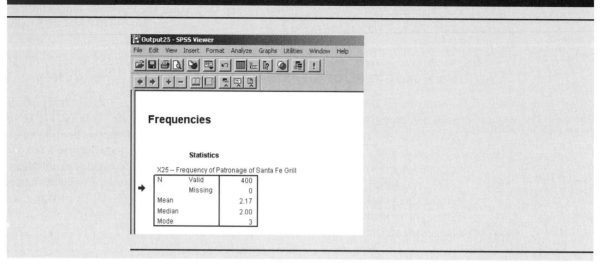

EXHIBIT 15.9 Output for Mean, Median, and Mode for X25—Frequency of Patronage

Let's look at the output for the measures of central tendency shown in Exhibit 15.9. In the Statistics table we see the mean is 2.17, the median is 2.00, the mode is 3, and there is no missing data. Recall that this variable is measured on a 3-point scale, with 1 = Occasionally and 3 = Very Frequently. The three measures of central tendency can all be different within the same distribution, as described above in the coffee-drinking example, and as they are here. But it also is possible that all three measures can be the same.

Measures of Dispersion

Often measures of central tendency cannot tell the whole story about a distribution of responses. For example, if data have been collected about consumers' attitudes toward a new brand of a product, you could find out the mean, median, and mode of the distribution of answers, but you might also want to know if most of the respondents had similar opinions. One way to answer this question would be to examine the measures of dispersion associated with the distribution of responses to your questions. Measures of dispersion describe how close to the mean or other measure of central tendency the rest of the values in the distribution fall. Two measures of dispersion used to describe the variability in a distribution of numbers are the *range* and the *standard deviation*.

Range

Range The distance between the smallest and largest values in a set of responses.

The **range** defines the spread of the data. It is the distance between the smallest and largest values of the variable. Another way to think about it is that the range identifies the end-points of the distribution of values. For variable X25—Frequency of Patronizing the Santa Fe Grill, the range is the difference between the response category 3 (largest value) and response category 1 (smallest value); that is, the range is 2. In this example, since we defined the response categories to begin with, the range doesn't tell us much. However, if we asked people questions, such as how often in a month they rent DVDs, or how much they would pay to buy a DVD player that also records songs, the range would be more informative. In this case, the respondents, not the researchers, would be defining the range by their answers. For this reason, the range is more often used to describe the variability of such open-ended questions as our DVD example.

For variable X25—Frequency of Patronizing the Santa Fe Grill, the range is calculated as the distance between the largest and smallest values in the set of responses and equals 2 (3 − 1 = 2).

Standard Deviation

Standard deviation
The average distance of the distribution values from the mean.

The **standard deviation** describes the average distance of the distribution values from the mean. The difference between a particular response and the distribution mean is called a *deviation.* Since the mean of a distribution is a measure of central tendency, there should be about as many values above the mean as there are below it (particularly if the distribution is symmetrical). Consequently, if we subtracted each value in a distribution from the mean and added them up, the result would be close to zero (the positive and negative results would cancel each other out).

The solution to this difficulty is to square the individual deviations before we add them up (squaring a negative number produces a positive result). Once the sum of the squared deviations is determined, it is divided by the number of respondents minus 1. The number 1 is subtracted from the number of respondents to help produce an unbiased estimate of the standard deviation. The result of dividing the sum of the squared deviations is the average squared deviation. To get the result back to the same type of units of measure as the mean, we simply take the square root of the answer. This produces the estimated standard deviation of the distribution. Sometimes the average squared deviation is also used as a measure of dispersion for a distribution. The average squared deviation, called the **variance,** is used in a number of statistical processes that analyze collected data.

Variance   The average squared deviation about the mean of a distribution of values.

Since the estimated standard deviation is the square root of the average squared deviations, it represents the average distance of the values in a distribution from the mean. If the estimated standard deviation is large, the responses in a distribution of numbers do not fall very close to the mean of the distribution. If the estimated standard deviation is small, you know that the distribution values are close to the mean.

Another way to think about the estimated standard deviation is that its size tells you something about the level of agreement among the respondents when they answered a particular question. For example, in the Santa Fe Grill database, respondents were asked to rate the restaurant on the friendliness and knowledge of its employees (X12 and X19). We will use the SPSS program later to examine the standard deviations for these questions. The formula for calculating the estimated standard deviation is available on the book's Web site, www.mhhe.com/hair06.

Together with the measures of central tendency, these descriptive statistics can reveal a lot about the distribution of a set of numbers representing the answers to an item on a questionnaire. Often, however, marketing researchers are interested in more detailed questions that involve more than one variable at a time. The next section, on hypothesis testing, provides some ways to analyze those types of questions.

SPSS Applications—Measures of Dispersion

The Santa Fe Grill database can be used with the SPSS software to calculate measures of dispersion, just as we did with the measures of central tendency. The SPSS click-through sequence is ANALYZE → DESCRIPTIVE STATISTICS → FREQUENCIES. Let's use

e X H I B I T 15.10 **Output for Measures of Dispersion**

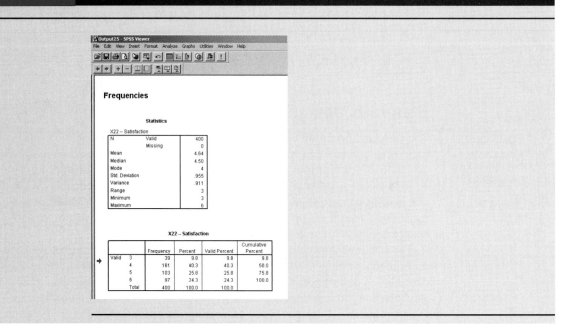

X22—Satisfaction as a variable to examine. Click on X22 to highlight it and then on the Arrow box to move X22 to the Variables box. Next open the Statistics box, go to the Dispersion box in the lower-left-hand corner, and click on Standard deviation, Variance, Range, Minimum and Maximum, and then Continue. If you would like to create charts, then open the Charts box—your choices are Bar, Pie, and Histograms. For the Format box we will use the defaults, so click on OK to execute the program.

Let's look at the output for the measures of dispersion shown in Exhibit 15.10 for variable X22. First, the highest response on the 7-point scale is 6 (maximum) and the lowest response is 3 (minimum). The range is 3 ($6 - 3 = 3$), the standard deviation is .955, and the variance is .911. A standard deviation of .955 on a 7-point scale tells us the responses are dispersed fairly closely around the mean of 4.64.

Hypothesis Testing

Hypothesis An empirically testable though yet unproven statement developed in order to explain phenomena.

Frequency distributions and measures of central tendency are very useful to marketing researchers. In most cases, however, the researcher will have some preconceived notion of the relationships the data should present. The preconception should be based on marketing theory or other research. The preconception is called a **hypothesis.** An example of a hypothesis would be "The average number of cups of coffee students consume during finals will be greater than the average they consume at other times." In this section of the chapter, we introduce the concept of hypothesis testing, explain some related terms, and discuss some types of possible errors.

Independent versus Related Samples

Independent samples

Two or more groups of responses that are tested as though they may come from different populations.

Often the marketing researcher will want to compare the means of two groups. There are two possible situations when means are compared. The first is when the means are from **independent samples,** and the second is when the samples are related. An example of independent samples would be the results of interviews with male and female coffee drinkers. The researcher may want to compare the average number of cups of coffee consumed per day by male students with the average number of cups of coffee consumed by female students. An example of the second situation, **related samples,** is when the researcher compares the average number of cups of coffee consumed per day by male students with the average number of soft drinks consumed per day by the same sample of male students.

Related samples

Two or more groups of responses that originated from the sample population.

In the related-sample situation, the marketing researcher must take special care in analyzing the information. Although the questions are independent, the respondents are the same. This is called a *paired sample.* When testing for differences in related samples the researcher must use what is called a *paired samples* t-*test.* The formula to compute the *t* value for paired samples is not presented here; the student is referred to more advanced texts for the actual calculation of the *t* value for related samples. The SPSS package contains options for both the related-samples and the independent-samples situations.

Developing Hypotheses

The first step in testing a hypothesis is, of course, to develop the hypothesis itself. As we have said in earlier chapters, hypotheses are developed not only prior to the collection of data but also as a part of the research plan. Hypotheses allow the researcher to make comparisons between two groups of respondents and to determine if there are important differences between the groups. For example, if the average number of cups of coffee consumed by female students per day during finals is 6.1, and the average number of cups of coffee consumed by males is 4.7, is this finding meaningful?

The groups compared in developing hypotheses may be from two different surveys or they may be different subsets of the total sample. In effect, the research is conducted under the assumption that the two groups potentially are from separate populations.

To illustrate, let's consider the fast-food industry. Suppose you have conducted research on fast-food restaurant patronage and find that of the 1,000 people surveyed this year, 18 percent say they visit fast-food establishments at least 15 times per month (in the United States this is a typical percentage for "heavy users" of fast food). But in a survey conducted last year, only 12 percent said they visited fast-food restaurants at least 15 times per month. In this example, the samples are independent. The question is whether or not the difference in the number of visits per month is meaningful. Stated another way, "Did the percentage of persons eating at fast-food restaurants 15 times per month increase from 12 percent last year to 18 percent this year?"

The answer appears to be straightforward, but as we have previously pointed out, some type of sampling error could have distorted the results enough so there may not be any real differences between this year's percentage of heavy users of fast-food restaurants and last year's. If the difference between the percentages is very large, one would be more confident that there is in fact a true difference between the groups. However, there would still be some uncertainty as to whether the difference is meaningful. In this instance we have intuitively factored in one of the most important components in determining whether important differences exist between two sample means: the magnitude of the difference between the

A Closer Look at Research

SPSS and SAS

Small-business owners and managers can use information from the SPSS and SAS Web sites for a variety of marketing research purposes. The sites provide a wealth of information that can lead to idea generation for marketing research opportunities. (See the chapter opener for their addresses.)

In many small businesses, owners and managers possess limited statistical ability in terms of computer application. SPSS and SAS offer a variety of suggestions for how small-

business owners can use statistical analysis to benefit their business. Examples include uncovering trends in a particular niche market, identifying potential outliers (companies not following the standard path in that particular market), graphical representations of all market participants (which allows for easy visual comparison of competitors), and a host of additional techniques. With this technology, small-business owners can build sophisticated statistical networks within their organization one small step at a time.

Null hypothesis A statement that asserts the status quo; that is, that any change from what has been thought to be true is due to random sampling error.

Alternative hypothesis A statement that is the opposite of the null hypothesis; that is, that the difference exists in reality and is not simply due to random error.

means. But another important component to consider is the size of the sample used to calculate the means.

In hypothesis development, the **null hypothesis** states that there is no difference between the group means in the comparison. In this case, the null hypothesis states there is no difference between the 12 percent visiting fast-food restaurants an average of 15 times a month last year and the 18 percent found this year. The null hypothesis is the one that is always tested by statisticians and market researchers. Another hypothesis, called the **alternative hypothesis,** states that there is a true difference between the group means. If the null hypothesis is accepted, there is no change to the status quo. If the null hypothesis is rejected, we automatically accept the alternative hypothesis and conclude that there has been a change in opinions or actions.

A null hypothesis refers to a population parameter, not a sample statistic. The data will show that either there is a meaningful difference between the two groups (reject the null hypothesis) or there is not a large enough difference between the groups to conclude that the groups are different (fail to reject the null hypothesis). In the latter case, the researcher would not be able to detect any significant differences between the groups. It is important to bear in mind that failure to reject the null hypothesis does not necessarily mean that the null hypothesis is true. This is because data from another sample from the same population could produce different results.

In marketing research the null hypothesis is developed in such a way that its rejection leads to an acceptance of the desired situation. In other words, the alternative hypothesis represents the condition desired. Using the visits at the fast-food establishments as an example, the null hypothesis is that there is no difference between the patronage levels this year and last year. The alternative hypothesis is that this year's fast-food patronage is different from last year's. Usually, the null hypothesis is notated as H_0 and the alternative hypothesis is notated as H_1. If the null hypothesis (H_0) is rejected, then the alternative hypothesis (H_1) is accepted. The alternative hypothesis always bears the burden of proof.

Small businesses need to test hypotheses just as large ones do. SPSS and SAS can help them do this, as shown in the nearby Closer Look at Research box.

Statistical Significance

Whenever the marketing researcher draws an inference regarding a population, there is a risk that the inference may be incorrect. That is, in marketing research, error can never be completely avoided. Thus, the test the marketing researcher performs in order to decide whether or not to reject the null hypothesis may produce incorrect results.

Type I error The error made by rejecting the null hypothesis when it is true; the probability of alpha.

There are two types of error associated with hypothesis testing that the marketing researcher needs to be aware of when forming conclusions based on the data analysis. The first type of error is termed Type I. **Type I error** is associated with rejecting the null hypothesis and accepting the alternative hypothesis in error. This type of error, frequently called *alpha* (α), occurs when the sample data lead to rejection of a null hypothesis that is in fact true. The probability of such an error is termed the **level of significance.** The level of significance is equivalent to the amount of risk regarding the accuracy of the test that the researcher is willing to accept. In other words, the level of significance is the probability that the rejection of the null hypothesis is in error. Usually, marketing researchers accept a level of significance of .10, .05, or .01, depending on the research objectives. This means that the researcher is willing to accept some risk of incorrect rejection of the null hypothesis, but that level of risk is prespecified.

Level of significance The amount of risk regarding the accuracy of the test that the researcher is willing to accept.

Type II error The error of failing to reject the null hypothesis when the alternative hypothesis is true; the probability of beta.

The second type of error, termed **Type II error,** is the error that occurs when the sample data produce results that fail to reject the null hypothesis when in fact the null hypothesis is false and should be rejected. Type II error is frequently called *beta* (β). Unlike α, which is specified by the researcher, β depends on the actual population parameter.

Sample size can help control Type I and Type II errors. Generally, the researcher will select an α and the sample size in order to increase the power of the test and β. However, in some research situations, the researcher may want to manage the type of risk (α or β) to help achieve the best results. For example, if a new drug is being tested with potentially serious side effects, the researcher would probably want to minimize the α error to minimize the possibility of concluding that the drug is effective (i.e., to reject the null hypothesis) when in fact the drug is not effective.

Analyzing Relationships of Sample Data

Once the researcher has developed hypotheses and calculated the means of the groups, the next step is to actually analyze the relationships of the sample data. In this section we will discuss the methods used to test hypotheses. We will introduce the *t* distribution and describe its function for testing hypotheses. This requires a review of some basic statistical terminology.

Sample Statistics and Population Parameters

The purpose of inferential statistics is to make a determination about a population on the basis of a sample from that population. As we explained in Chapter 9, a sample is a subset of all the elements within the population. For example, if we wanted to determine the average number of cups of coffee consumed per day by students during finals at your university, we would not interview all the students. This would be costly, take a long time, and might be impossible since we may not be able to find them all or some would decline to participate. Instead, if there are 16,000 students at your university, we may decide that a sample of 200 females and 200 males is sufficiently large to provide accurate information about the coffee-drinking habits of all 16,000 students.

Sample statistics are measures obtained directly from the sample or calculated from the data in the sample. A population parameter is a variable or some sort of measured characteristic of the entire population. Sample statistics are useful in making inferences regarding the population's parameters. Generally, the actual population parameters are unknown since the cost to perform a true census of almost any population is prohibitive.

A frequency distribution displaying the data obtained from the sample is commonly used to summarize the results of the data collection process. When a frequency distribution displays a variable in terms of percentages, then this distribution is representing proportions within a population. For example, a frequency distribution showing that 40 percent of the people patronize Burger King indicates the percentage of the population that meets the criterion (eating at Burger King). The proportion may be expressed as a percentage, a decimal value, or a fraction.

Univariate Tests of Significance

In many situations a marketing researcher will form hypotheses regarding population means based on sample data. This involves going beyond the simple tabulations incorporated in a frequency distribution and calculation of averages. In these instances, the researcher may conduct univariate tests of significance. Univariate tests of significance involve hypothesis testing using one variable at a time.

Suppose a marketing researcher has agreed to help Santa Fe Grill's owners determine whether customers think their menu prices are reasonable. Respondents have answered this question using a 7-point scale on which 1 = "Strongly Disagree" and 7 = "Strongly Agree." The scale is assumed to be an interval scale, and previous research using this measure has shown the responses to be approximately normally distributed.

The researcher must perform a couple of tasks before attempting to answer the question posed above. First, the hypotheses to be compared (the null and alternative hypotheses) have to be developed. Then the level of significance for rejecting the null hypothesis and accepting the alternative hypothesis must be selected. At that point, the researcher can conduct the statistical test and determine the answer to the research question.

In this example, the owners think the customers consider the prices of food at the Santa Fe Grill to be average. That means responses to the question on reasonable prices will have a mean of 4 (approximately halfway between 1 and 7 on the response scale). The null hypothesis is that the mean of the X16—Reasonable Prices will not be significantly different from 4. Recall that the null hypothesis asserts the status quo: any difference from what is thought to be true is due to random sampling. The alternative hypothesis is that the mean of the answers to X16—Reasonable Prices will not be 4: there is in fact a true difference between the sample mean we find and the mean we think it is (4).

t-test A hypothesis test that utilizes the t distribution; used when the sample size is smaller than 30 and the standard deviation is unknown.

z-test A hypothesis test procedure that utilizes the z distribution; used when the sample size is larger than 30 and the standard deviation is unknown.

Assume also the owners want to be 95 percent certain the mean is not 4. Therefore, the significance level will be set at .05. Using this significance level means that if the survey of Santa Fe Grill customers is conducted many times, the probability of incorrectly rejecting the null hypothesis when it is true would be less than 5 times out of 100 (.05).

Two tests could be used to examine this hypothesis—the z-test and the t-test. A **t-test** utilizes the t distribution; it is most appropriate when the sample size is smaller than 30 and the standard deviation is unknown. In contrast, a **z-test** utilizes the z distribution. This test is used when the sample size is larger than 30 and the standard deviation is unknown. Use of the z-test assumes the data have a normal distribution and should be used if the sample size is larger than 30. But if the sample size is 30 or less the assumption of a normal distribution is not valid and the t-test should be used. Fortunately, in most situations we do not have to deal with this issue. Most computerized software such as SPSS or SAS is set up to compute the correct statistic. That is, the software determines whether the z or t is appropriate and calculates the correct one. In SPSS you should know, however, that the statistic is always referred to as a t-test. But if the sample is larger than 30 a z-test has been used.

SPSS Application—Univariate Hypothesis Test

Using the SPSS software, you can test the responses in the Santa Fe Grill database to find the answer to the research question posed above. The click-through sequence is: ANALYZE → COMPARE MEANS → ONE-SAMPLE T-TEST. When you get to the dialog box, click on X16—Reasonable Prices to highlight it. Then click on the arrow to move X16 into the Test Variables box. In the box labeled Test Value, enter the number 4. This is the number you want to compare the respondents' answers against. Click on the Options box and enter 95 in the confidence interval box. This is the same as setting the significance level at .05. Then, click on the Continue button and OK to execute the program.

The SPSS output is shown in Exhibit 15.11. The top table is labeled One-Sample Statistics and shows the mean, standard deviation, and standard error for X16—Reasonable Prices (a mean of 4.34 and standard deviation of 1.228). The One-Sample Test table below shows the results of the t-test for the null hypothesis that the average response to X16 is 4 (Test Value = 4). The t-test statistic is 5.537, and the significance level is .000. This means that the null hypothesis can be rejected and the alternative hypothesis accepted with a high level of confidence from a statistical perspective.

From a practical standpoint, in terms of the Santa Fe Grill, the results of the univariate hypothesis test mean respondents perceived that menu prices were somewhat reasonable. The mean of 4.34 is somewhat higher than the mid-point of 4 on the 7-point scale (7 = "Strongly Agree" prices are reasonable). Thus, the Santa Fe Grill owners can conclude

---

EXHIBIT 15.11 Univariate Hypothesis Test Using X16—Reasonable Prices

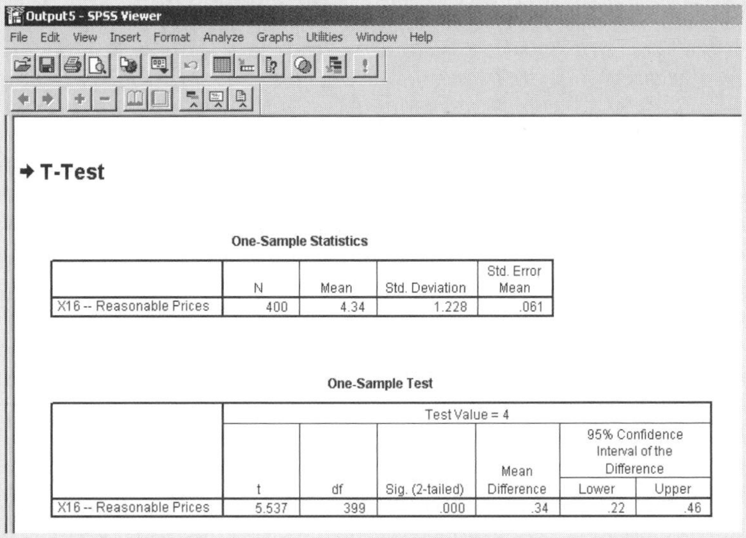

→ T-Test

One-Sample Statistics

	N	Mean	Std. Deviation	Std. Error Mean
X16 -- Reasonable Prices	400	4.34	1.228	.061

One-Sample Test

	Test Value = 4					
					95% Confidence Interval of the Difference	
	t	df	Sig. (2-tailed)	Mean Difference	Lower	Upper
X16 -- Reasonable Prices	5.537	399	.000	.34	.22	.46

that their prices are not perceived as unreasonable. But, on the other hand, there is a lot of room to improve between the mean of 4.34 on the 7-point scale and the highest value of 7. This is definitely an area that needs to be examined. The owners also need to know if the price perceptions are based on reality or incorrect perceptions.

Bivariate Hypotheses Tests

In many instances the marketing researcher will want to test hypotheses that compare the mean of one group with the mean of another group. For example, the marketing researcher may be interested in determining whether there is any difference between older and younger new car purchasers in terms of the importance of a DVD player. In situations where more than one group is involved, bivariate tests are needed. In the following section we describe two bivariate hypothesis tests: the t-test (to compare two means) and analysis of variance (a method to compare three or more group means).

In nearly all cases the null hypothesis is that there is no difference between the group means. This null hypothesis is specifically stated as follows:

$$\mu_1 = \mu_2 \text{ or that } \mu_1 - \mu_2 = 0$$

Using the t-Test to Compare Two Means

Just as with the univariate t-test, the bivariate t-test requires interval or ratio data. Also, the t-test is especially useful when the sample size is small ($n < 30$) and when the population standard deviation is unknown. Unlike the univariate test, however, we assume that the samples are drawn from populations with normal distributions and that the variances of the populations are equal.

Essentially, the t-test for differences between group means can be conceptualized as the difference between the means divided by the variability of random means. The t value is a ratio of the difference between the two sample means and the standard error. The t-test tries to provide a rational way of determining if the difference between the two sample means occurred by chance. The formula for calculating the t value is:

$$Z = \frac{\overline{X}_1 - \overline{X}_2}{S\overline{x}_1 - \overline{x}_2}$$

where

$\overline{x}_1$ = mean of sample 1

$\overline{x}_2$ = mean of sample 2

$S\overline{x}_1 - \overline{x}_2$ = standard error of the difference between the two means

SPSS Application—Independent Samples t-Test

To illustrate the use of a t-test for the difference between two group means, let's turn to the Santa Fe Grill database. Santa Fe Grill's owners want to find out if there are differences in the level of satisfaction between male and female customers. To do that we can use the SPSS Compare Means program.

The SPSS click-through sequence is ANALYZE → COMPARE MEANS → INDEPEN-DENT-SAMPLES t-Test. When you get to this dialog box click variable X22—Satisfaction into the Test Variables box and variable X32—Gender into the Grouping Variable Box. For variable X32 you must define the range in the Define Groups box. Enter

EXHIBIT 15.12 Using the Independent-Samples *t*-Test to Compare Two Means

Output1 – SPSS Viewer
File Edit View Insert Format Analyze Graphs Utilities Window Help

→ **T-Test**

Group Statistics

	X32 -- Gender	N	Mean	Std. Deviation	Std. Error Mean
X22 -- Satisfaction	Males	236	4.83	.966	.063
	Females	164	4.38	.874	.068

Independent Samples Test

		Levene's Test for Equality of Variances		t-test for Equality of Means						
									95% Confidence Interval of the Difference	
		F	Sig.	t	df	Sig. (2-tailed)	Mean Difference	Std. Error Difference	Lower	Upper
X22 -- Satisfaction	Equal variances assumed	3.572	.059	4.789	398	.000	.45	.094	.267	.638
	Equal variances not assumed			4.875	371.443	.000	.45	.093	.270	.635

a 0 for Group 1 and a 1 for Group 2 (males were coded 0 in the database and females were coded 1) and then click Continue. For the Options we will use the defaults, so just click OK to execute the program.

Results are shown in Exhibit 15.12. The top table shows the Group Statistics. Note that 236 male customers and 164 female customers were interviewed. Also, the mean satisfaction level for males was a bit higher at 4.83, compared with 4.38 for the female customers. The standard deviation for females was somewhat smaller (.874) than for the males (.966).

To find out if the two means are significantly different, we look at the information in the Independent Samples Test table. The statistical significance of the difference in two means is calculated differently if the variances of the two means are equal versus unequal. The Levene's test for equality of variances is reported on the left side of the table. In this case the test shows the two variances are equal (Sig. value of .059), but almost significantly different. In all cases where this value is < .05 you would use the "Equal variances not assumed" test. In the column labeled Sig. (2-tailed) and you will note that the two means are significantly different (< .000), whether we assume equal or unequal variances. Thus, there is no support for the null hypothesis that the two means are equal, and we conclude that male customers are significantly more satisfied than female customers.

There is other information in this table, but we do not need to concern ourselves with it at this time. As a researcher, however, you must always interpret statistical findings

Accurate reporting of research results is considered to be so important that it is specifically addressed in the American Marketing Association's *Marketing Research Code of Ethics.* However, the way preelection poll results are reported might be misleading and give rise to criticism of marketing survey research. At least one person, Thomas S. Gruca, a marketing professor at the University of Iowa, thinks that one potential source of error in election polls is the focus on the point spread between the candidates. Professor Gruca's research supports the notion that the point spread between candidates is a dubious portrayal of survey research. The problem with focusing on the point spread arises from the segment of voters who report themselves as undecided in the so-called trial-heat election polls. Research in the 1980s showed an interesting pattern in the disposition of undecided voters in incumbent reelections. In a study of 155 polls primarily from 1986 and 1988, it was shown that in most cases, most of the undecided vote appeared to go to the challenger. This finding, dubbed the "incumbent rule," has important implications for the analysis and interpretation of trial-heat election poll reporting.

Suppose an incumbent is facing a single challenger. The results of a trial-heat poll show that 48 percent of voters are for the incumbent and 40 percent for the challenger, with a margin of error of 2 percent. One could report the results of such a poll as an 8-point lead for the incumbent, or one could report the percentages. While the two reporting methods may seem equivalent, they are not.

Consider the following real election examples. In the 1993 New Jersey governor's race and the 1994 New York governor's race, the incumbents were leading in the preelection polls just a few days before the elections. The polls were conducted by prestigious organizations such as the Gallup Organization, *The New York Times,* Louis Harris and Associates, and others. Both incumbents lost.

In each case newspaper articles appeared trying to explain the surprising results in terms of late media blitzes, voter attitude swings, and other factors. Yet the real reason, according to Professor Gruca, was that the focus on the point spread missed the obvious. The polls may have been right, but assuming the point spread would hold through election day ignored the incumbency rule.

In effect, the focus on only point spread misleads readers in several ways. First, the actual election results will probably be closer than the poll suggests because the undecided vote will not be spread equally. Any lead by an incumbent is probably less than it appears. Focusing on only the point spread between candidates masks this phenomenon.

Second, incumbents leading a single challenger but having less than a 50 percent share of the vote usually end up losing the election. This is a direct result of the opponent's receiving the majority of the undecided voters ballots in the actual election. It appears that the incumbent's chances of actually winning depend on how far under 50 percent he is and how close the race is.

Third, many polls that at first appear to be in error may actually be correct. The problem is the interpretation of the undecided vote. Given the name recognition and other advantages enjoyed by most incumbents, the fact that a voter is undecided close to election day is not necessarily good news.

Professor Gruca suggests that it is clear that caution must be used when reporting preelection poll results. The polls may be good at gauging an incumbent's support, but they are less good at projecting the final election results. Professor Gruca thinks that every polling story should incorporate a simple statement about the trend for undecided voters to swing to the challenger on election day.[2]

cautiously before drawing conclusions. Exhibit 15.13 provides an example of why such caution is needed.

SPSS Application—Paired Samples *t*-Test

Sometimes marketing researchers want to test for differences in two means for variables in the same sample. For example, the owners of the Santa Fe Grill noticed in their survey that the taste of their food was rated 5.31 while the food temperature was rated only 4.57. Since the two food variables are obviously related, they want to know if the ratings for taste really are significantly higher (more favorable) than for temperature. To examine this, we use the paired samples test for the difference in two means. This test examines whether two means from two different questions using the same scaling and answered by the same respondents are significantly different. The null hypothesis is the mean ratings for the two food variables (X18 and X20) are equal.

EXHIBIT 15.14 Paired Samples *t*-Test

Output52 - SPSS Viewer

File Edit View Insert Format Analyze Graphs Utilities Window Help

T-Test

Paired Samples Statistics

		Mean	N	Std. Deviation	Std. Error Mean
Pair 1	X18 -- Excellent Food Taste	5.31	400	1.088	.054
	X20 -- Proper Food Temperature	4.57	400	1.104	.055

Paired Samples Test

		Paired Differences							
					95% Confidence Interval of the Difference				
		Mean	Std. Deviation	Std. Error Mean	Lower	Upper	t	df	Sig. (2-tailed)
Pair 1	X18 -- Excellent Food Taste - X20 -- Proper Food Temperature	.74	.841	.042	.66	.83	17.649	399	.000

To test this hypothesis we use the SPSS paired-samples *t*-test. The click-through sequence is ANALYZE → COMPARE MEANS → PAIRED-SAMPLES *t*-Test. When you get to this dialog box, highlight both X18—Food Taste and X20—Food Temperature and then click on the arrow button to move them into the Paired Variables box. For the Options we will use the defaults, so just click OK to execute the program.

Results are shown in Exhibit 15.14. The top table shows the Paired Samples Statistics. The mean for food taste is 5.31 and for food temperature is 4.57. The *t* value for this comparison is 17.649 (see Paired Samples Test table) and it is significant at the .000 level. Thus we can reject the null hypothesis that the two means are equal and conclude that Santa Fe Grill customers definitely have more favorable perceptions of food taste than food temperature.

Analysis of Variance (ANOVA)

Analysis of variance (ANOVA) A statistical technique that determines whether three or more means are statistically different from each other.

Analysis of variance (ANOVA) is used to determine the statistical difference between three or more means. For example, if a sample finds that the average number of cups of coffee consumed per day by freshmen during finals is 3.7, while the average number of cups of coffee consumed per day by seniors and graduate students is 4.3 cups and 5.1 cups, respectively, are these observed differences statistically significant? The ability to make such comparisons can be quite useful for the marketing researcher.

While the name ANOVA can be disconcerting to many students, the technique is really quite straightforward. In this section we shall describe a one-way ANOVA. The term *one-way* is used since there is only one independent variable. ANOVA can be used in cases where multiple independent variables are considered, and it allows the analyst to estimate both their individual and their joint effects on the dependent variable.

Multiple dependent variables can be analyzed together using a related procedure called *multivariate analysis of variance (MANOVA)*. The objective in MANOVA is identical to that in ANOVA—to examine group differences in means—only the comparisons are considered for a group of dependent variables. While a detailed discussion is beyond the scope of this text, a brief description of MANOVA is included at the end of this chapter.

An example of an ANOVA problem may be to compare light, medium, and heavy drinkers of Starbucks coffee on their attitude toward a particular Starbucks advertising campaign. In this instance there is one independent variable—consumption of Starbucks coffee—but it is divided into three different levels. Our earlier *t* statistics won't work here, since we have more than two groups to compare.

ANOVA requires that the dependent variable, in this case the attitude toward the Starbucks advertising campaign, be metric. That is, the dependent variable must be either interval or ratio scaled. A second data requirement is that the independent variable, in this case the coffee consumption variable, be categorical.

The null hypothesis for ANOVA always states that there is no difference between the ad campaign attitudes of the groups of Starbucks coffee drinkers. In specific terminology, the null hypothesis would be

$$\mu_1 = \mu_2 = \mu_3$$

The ANOVA technique focuses on the behavior of the variance within a set of data. If you remember the earlier discussion of measures of dispersion, the variance of a variable is equal to the average squared deviation from the mean of the variable. The logic of the ANOVA technique says that if we calculate the variance between the groups and compare it with the variance within the groups, we can make a rational determination as to whether the means (attitudes toward the advertising campaign) are significantly different.[3]

Determining Statistical Significance in ANOVA

F-test The test used to statistically evaluate the differences between the group means in ANOVA.

In ANOVA, the **F-test** is used to statistically evaluate the differences between the group means. For example, suppose the heavy users of Starbucks coffee rate the advertising campaign 4.4 on a five-point scale, with 5 = Very favorable. The medium users of Starbucks coffee rate the campaign 3.9, and the light users of Starbucks coffee rate the campaign 2.5. The *F*-test in ANOVA tells us if these observed differences are meaningful.

The total variance in a set of responses to a question can be separated into between-group and within-group variance. The *F* distribution is the ratio of these two components of total variance and can be calculated as follows:

$$F \text{ ratio} = \frac{\text{Variance between groups}}{\text{Variance within groups}}$$

The larger the difference in the variance between groups, the larger the *F* ratio. Since the total variance in a data set is divisible into between and within components, if there is more variance explained or accounted for by considering differences between groups than there is within groups, then the independent variable probably has a significant impact on the dependent variable. Larger *F* ratios imply significant differences between the groups. The larger the *F* ratio, the more likely it is that the null hypothesis will be rejected.

ANOVA, however, is able to tell the researcher only that statistical differences exist somewhere between the group means. The technique cannot identify which pairs of means are significantly different from each other. In our example of Starbucks coffee drinkers' attitudes toward the advertising campaign, we could conclude that differences in attitudes toward the advertising campaign exist among light, medium, and heavy coffee drinkers, but we would not be able to determine if the differences are between light and medium, or between light and heavy, or between medium and heavy, and so on. We would be able to say only that there are significant differences somewhere among the groups. Thus, the marketing researcher is still saddled with the task of determining where the mean differences lie. Follow-up tests have been designed for just that purpose.

Follow-up test A test that flags the means that are statistically different from each other; follow-up tests are performed after an ANOVA determines there are differences between means.

There are several **follow-up tests** available in statistical software packages such as SPSS and SAS, including comparison tests by Tukey, Duncan, and Dunn. All of these methods involve multiple comparisons, or simultaneous assessment of confidence interval estimates of differences between the means. All means are compared two at a time. The differences between the techniques lie in their ability to control the error rate. We shall briefly describe the Scheffé procedure, although a complete discussion of these techniques is well beyond the scope of this book. Relative to the other follow-up tests mentioned, however, the Scheffé procedure is a more conservative method of detecting significant differences between group means.

The Scheffé follow-up test essentially establishes simultaneous confidence intervals, which holds the entire experiment's error rate to a specified α level. The test exposes differences between all pairs of means to a high and low confidence interval range. If the difference between each pair of means falls outside the range of the confidence interval, then we reject the null hypothesis and conclude that the pairs of means falling outside the range are statistically different. The Scheffé test might show that one, two, or all three pairs of means in our Starbucks example are different. The Scheffé test is equivalent to simultaneous two-tailed hypothesis tests, and the technique holds the specified analysis significance level. Because the technique holds the experimental error rate to α, the confidence intervals tend to be wider than in the other methods, but the researcher has more assurance that true mean differences exist.

n-Way ANOVA

The entire discussion of ANOVA to this point has been devoted to one-way ANOVA. In a one-way ANOVA there is only one independent variable. In the foregoing examples, the usage category (consumption of Starbucks coffee) was the independent variable. However, it is not at all uncommon for the researcher to be interested in several independent variables simultaneously. In that case an *n*-way ANOVA would be used.

Often, however, the market researcher may be interested in the region of the country where a product is sold as well as consumption patterns. Using multiple independent factors allows for an interaction effect, or the effects of the multiple independent factors acting in concert to affect group means. For example, heavy consumers of Starbucks coffee in the Northeast may have different attitudes about advertising campaigns than heavy consumers of Starbucks coffee in the West, and there may be still further differences between the various coffee-consumption-level groups, as shown earlier.

Another situation that may require *n*-way ANOVA is the use of experimental designs, where the researcher provides different groups in a sample with different information to see how their responses change. For example, a marketer may be interested in finding out whether consumers prefer a humorous ad to a serious one and whether that preference varies across gender. Each type of ad could be shown to different groups of customers (both male and female). Then, questions about their preferences for the ad and the product it advertises could be asked. The primary difference between the groups would be the difference in ad execution (humorous or nonhumorous) and customer gender. An *n*-way ANOVA could be used to find out whether the ad execution differences helped cause differences in ad and product preferences, as well as what effects might be attributable to customer gender.

From a conceptual standpoint, *n*-way ANOVA is very similar to one-way ANOVA, but the mathematics are more complex. However, statistical packages such as SPSS will conveniently allow the marketing researcher to perform *n*-way ANOVA.

SPSS Application—ANOVA

To help you further understand the basic ideas involved in using ANOVA techniques to answer research questions, we will use the Santa Fe Grill database to answer a typical question. The owners want to know first whether customers who come to the restaurant from greater distances differ from customers who live nearby in their willingness to recommend the restaurant to a friend. Second, they also want to know whether that difference in willingness to recommend, if any, is influenced by the gender of the customers. The database variables are X24—Likely to Recommend, measured on a 7-point scale, with 1 = "Definitely Will Not Recommend" and 7 = "Definitely Recommend"; X30—Distance Driven, where 1 = "Less than 1 mile," 2 = "1–3 miles," and 3 = "More than 3 miles"; and X32—Gender, where 0 = male and 1 = female.

On the basis of informal comments from customers, the owners think customers who come from more than 3 miles will be more likely to recommend the restaurant. Moreover, they believe female customers will be more likely to recommend the restaurant than males. The null hypotheses were there would be no difference between the mean ratings for X24—Likely to Recommend for customers who traveled different distances to come to the restaurant (X30) and between females and males (X32).

The purpose of the ANOVA analysis is to see if the differences that do exist are statistically significant. To examine the differences, an *F* ratio is used. The bigger the *F* ratio, the bigger the difference among the means of the various groups with respect to their likelihood of recommending the restaurant.

SPSS can help you conduct the statistical analysis to test the null hypotheses. The best way to analyze the Santa Fe Grill data to answer the owner's questions is to use a factorial model. A factorial model is a type of ANOVA in which the individual effects of each independent variable on the dependent variable are considered separately and then the combined effects (an interaction) of the independent variables on the dependent variable are analyzed. The click-through sequence is ANALYZE → GENERAL LINEAR MODEL → UNIVARIATE. Highlight the dependent variable X24—Likely to Recommend by clicking on it and move it to the Dependent Variable box. Next, highlight X30—Distance Driven and X32—Gender, and move them to the Fixed Factors box. Click OK, since we don't need to specify any other options for this test.

The SPSS output for ANOVA is shown in Exhibit 15.15. The Tests of Between-Subjects Effects table shows that the *F* ratio for X30—Distance Driven is 80.452, which is statistically significant at the .000 level. This means that customers who come from different distances to eat at the restaurant vary in their likelihood of recommending the restaurant. The *F* ratio for X32—Gender is 49.421, which also is statistically significant at the .000 level. This means the gender of customers influences their likelihood of recommending the restaurant.

We now know that both X30—Distance Driven and X32—Gender influence likelihood of recommending the Santa Fe Grill. But we do not know how. To answer this question we

eXHIBIT 15.15 ANOVA for X24—Likely to Recommend, X30—Distance Driven, and X32—Gender

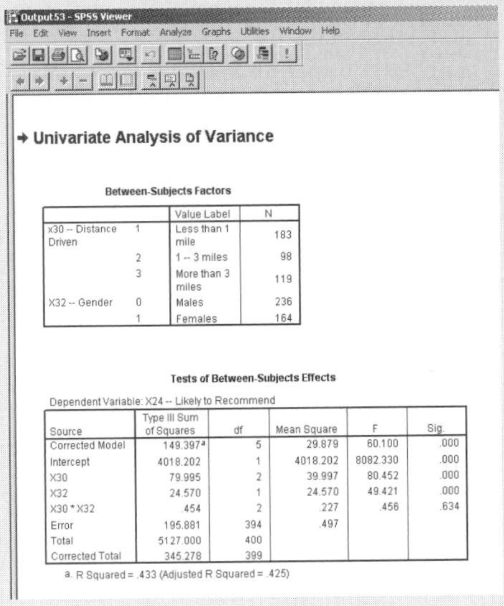

Univariate Analysis of Variance

Between-Subjects Factors

		Value Label	N
x30 -- Distance Driven	1	Less than 1 mile	183
	2	1 -- 3 miles	98
	3	More than 3 miles	119
X32 -- Gender	0	Males	236
	1	Females	164

Tests of Between-Subjects Effects

Dependent Variable: X24 -- Likely to Recommend

Source	Type III Sum of Squares	df	Mean Square	F	Sig.
Corrected Model	149.397[a]	5	29.879	60.100	.000
Intercept	4018.202	1	4018.202	8082.330	.000
X30	79.995	2	39.997	80.452	.000
X32	24.570	1	24.570	49.421	.000
X30 * X32	.454	2	.227	.456	.634
Error	195.881	394	.497		
Total	5127.000	400			
Corrected Total	345.278	399			

a. R Squared = .433 (Adjusted R Squared = .425)

must look at the means for these two variables. The SPSS means program helps us to do this. The click-through sequence is ANALYZE → COMPARE MEANS → MEANS. Highlight the dependent variable X24—Likely to Recommend by clicking on it and move it to the Dependent List box. Next, highlight X30—Distance Driven and X32—Gender and move them to the Independent List. Then click OK. The results are shown in Exhibit 15.16.

eXHIBIT 15.16 Comparison of Likely to Recommend for Male and Female Customers Who Drove Different Distances to Dine at the Santa Fe Grill

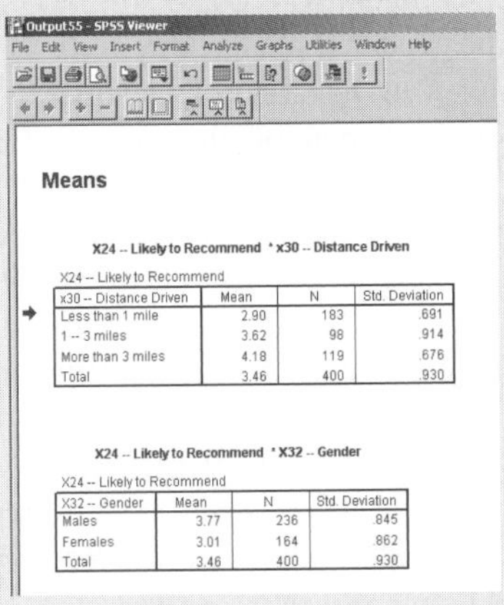

Means

X24 -- Likely to Recommend * x30 -- Distance Driven

X24 -- Likely to Recommend

x30 -- Distance Driven	Mean	N	Std. Deviation
Less than 1 mile	2.90	183	.691
1 -- 3 miles	3.62	98	.914
More than 3 miles	4.18	119	.676
Total	3.46	400	.930

X24 -- Likely to Recommend * X32 -- Gender

X24 -- Likely to Recommend

X32 -- Gender	Mean	N	Std. Deviation
Males	3.77	236	.845
Females	3.01	164	.862
Total	3.46	400	.930

Best Western

Best Western is the world's biggest hotel chain, with some 3,300 independently owned hotels. By using marketing research, Best Western has been able to identify its market segments. The hotel chain has discovered that business travelers tend to shy away from unknown, less-expensive brands of hotels in favor of consistent-quality brands, such as Best Western. The first table here shows the composition of the worldwide hotel market, and the second shows the source of business (domestic or foreign) by world region.

Composition of Business Traveler Market

Source of Business	Worldwide	Africa/ Middle East	Asia/ Australia	North America	Europe
Domestic	50.7%	24.6%	35.0%	84.6%	47.3%
Foreign	49.3	75.4	65.0	15.4	52.7
Total	100.0	100.0	100.0	100.0	100.0

Composition of Worldwide Hotel Market

Market Segment Group	Percent of Total Market
Business travelers	36.0%
Individual travelers	24.5
Tour groups	13.5
Conference participants	12.7
Other groups	9.2
Government officials	4.1

Using marketing research to uncover facts about its market segments such as the ones above, Best Western has been able to focus its marketing strategy on business travelers. In addition, the hotel chain emphasizes domestic business in North America; focuses on both domestic and foreign business in Europe; and targets foreign business in Africa, Asia, Australia, and the Middle East.[5]

Look at the table under the Mean heading on the SPSS output and you will see that the average likelihood of recommending the Santa Fe Grill to a friend increases as the Distance Driven by the respondent increases. In short, customers who come from within 1 mile of the Santa Fe Grill show an average likelihood to recommend of 2.90, compared with a 3.62 and 4.18 average likelihood for customers who come from 1–3 and more than 3 miles away, respectively. We examine the gender results next.

The Santa Fe Grill's owners also were interested in whether there is a difference in the likelihood of males versus females recommending the Santa Fe Grill. The F ratio for gender is again quite large (49.421; see Exhibit 15.15) and statistically significant (.000). Looking at the means of the customer groups based on gender (see Exhibit 15.16), we see that indeed males are more likely to recommend the Santa Fe Grill (mean = 3.77) as compared to females (mean = 3.01). The null hypothesis is rejected, and we conclude there is a difference in the average likelihood of male and female customers to recommend the Santa Fe Grill.

The comparison of the interaction between distance traveled and gender has an F ratio of .456, with a probability level of .634, meaning that the difference in the likelihood of recommendation when both independent variables are considered together is very small. This means there is no interaction between distance driven, gender, and likelihood of recommending the Santa Fe Grill.

MANOVA

A related technique, MANOVA, was mentioned earlier in this chapter. MANOVA is designed to examine multiple dependent variables across single or multiple independent variables. The technique considers the mean differences for a group of dependent measures. For example, a researcher might want to measure customers' use of several types of related products, such as golf balls, golf shoes, golf clubs, and golf clothing. Since use of one of these types of products is probably related to use of the others, MANOVA would be a good choice for examining the effect of independent variables like income or gender on use of the entire group of golf-related products. The statistical calculations for MANOVA are similar to n-way ANOVA and are typically included in the statistical software packages (such as SAS and SPSS) mentioned earlier.[4]

Statistical techniques are used globally as well as in the United States. The Global Insights box explains how.

Perceptual Mapping

Perceptual mapping A process that is used to develop maps showing the perceptions of respondents. The maps are visual representations of respondents' perceptions of a company, product, service, brand, or any other object in two dimensions.

Perceptual mapping is a process that is used to develop maps that show the perceptions of respondents. The maps are visual representations of respondents' perceptions of a company, product, service, brand, or any other object in two dimensions. A perceptual map typically has a vertical and a horizontal axis that are labeled with descriptive adjectives. Possible adjectives for our restaurant example might be food temperature and/or freshness, speed of service, good value for the money, and so on.

Several different approaches can be used to develop perceptual maps. These include rankings, mean ratings, and multivariate techniques discussed in Chapter 17. To illustrate perceptual mapping, data from an example involving ratings of fast-food restaurants are presented in Exhibit 15.17. Customers are given a set of six fast-food restaurants and asked to express how they perceive each restaurant. The perceptions of the respondents are then plotted on a two-dimensional map using two of the adjectives, freshness of food and food temperature. Inspection of the map, shown in Exhibit 15.18, illustrates that Wendy's and Back Yard Burgers were perceived as quite similar to each other, as were McDonald's and Burger King. Arby's and Hardee's were also perceived as somewhat similar, but not as favorable as the other restaurants. However, Back Yard Burgers and McDonald's were perceived as very dissimilar.

EXHIBIT 15.17 Ratings of Six Fast-Food Restaurants

	Food Freshness	Food Temperature
McDonald's	1.8	3.7
Burger King	2.0	3.5
Wendy's	4.0	4.5
Back Yard Burger	4.5	4.8
Arby's	4.0	2.5
Hardee's	3.5	1.8

Key: Food temperature, 1 = Warm, 5 = Hot; Food freshness, 1 = Low, 5 = High.

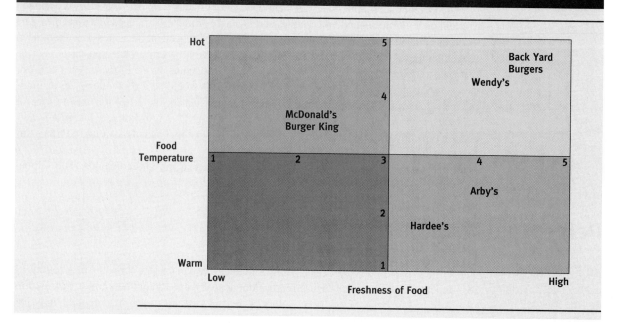

exhibit 15.18   Perceptual Map of Six Fast-Food Restaurants

Perceptual Mapping Applications in Marketing Research

While our fast-food example illustrates how perceptual mapping grouped pairs of restaurants together based on perceived ratings, perceptual mapping has many other important applications in marketing research. Other applications include

- *New-product development.* Perceptual mapping can identify gaps in perceptions and thereby help to position new products.

- *Image measurement.* Perceptual mapping can be used to identify the image of the company to help to position one company relative to the competition.

- *Advertising.* Perceptual mapping can assess advertising effectiveness in positioning the brand.

- *Distribution.* Perceptual mapping could be used to assess similarities of brands and channel outlets.

mARKETING RESEARCH IN ACTION

Examining Restaurant Image Positions

Remington's Steak House

About three years ago, John Smith opened Remington's Steak House, a retail theme restaurant located in a large midwestern city. Smith's vision for his restaurant was for customers to perceive his restaurant as being a unique, theme-oriented specialty restaurant with an excellent reputation for offering a wide assortment of high-quality yet competitively priced entrees and services, and having knowledgeable employees who understood customers' needs and placed heavy emphasis on satisfying the customer.

Smith used this vision to guide the development and implementation of his restaurant's positioning and marketing strategies. Although Smith knew how to deliver dining experiences, he did not know much about developing, implementing, and assessing marketing strategies.

Recently, Smith began asking himself some fundamental questions about his restaurant's operations and the future of his business. Smith expressed these questions to an account representative at a local marketing research firm and, as a result, decided to do some research to better understand his customers' attitudes and feelings. More specifically, he wanted to gain some information and insights into the following set of questions:

1. What are the major factors customers use when selecting a restaurant to dine at, and what is the relative importance of each of these factors?

2. What image do customers have of Remington's and its two major competitors?

3. Is Remington's providing quality and satisfaction to its customers?

4. Do any of Remington's current marketing strategies need to be changed, and if so in what ways?

To address Smith's questions, the account representative recommended completing an image survey using an Internet panel approach. Initial contact was made with potential respondents using a random digit dialing telephone survey to screen for individuals who were patrons of Remington's as well as customers of similar restaurants (i.e., Remington's main competitors: Outback Steakhouse and Longhorn Steak House) within the market area. Respondents had to have a minimum annual household income of $20,000 and be familiar enough with one of the three restaurant competitors to accurately rate them. If an individual correctly answered the screening questions, she or he was directed to a Web site to complete the survey.

Since this was the first time Smith had conducted any marketing research, it was considered exploratory and the consultant recommended a sample size of 200. She said that if the results of the initial 200 surveys were helpful, then increasing the sample size would be evaluated to increase the precision of the findings. The questionnaire collected data on the importance ratings of restaurant selection factors, perceptions of the images of the three restaurant competitors on the same factors, and selected classification information on the respondents. When the quota of 200 usable completed questionnaires was reached, the sample included 86 respondents most familiar with Outback, 65 most familiar with Longhorn, and 49 most familiar with Remington's. This last criterion was used to determine which restaurant competitor a respondent evaluated.

e X H I B I T   15.19   Importance Ratings for Restaurant Selection Factors

Output7 - SPSS Viewer

File   Edit   View   Insert   Format   Analyze   Graphs   Utilities   Window   Help

→ Frequencies

Statistics

		X1 -- Large Portions	X2 -- Competent Employees	X3 -- Food Quality	X4 -- Speed of Service	X5 -- Atmosphere	X6 -- Reasonable Prices
N	Valid	200	200	200	200	200	200
	Missing	0	0	0	0	0	0
Mean		4.95	3.12	6.09	5.99	4.74	5.39

e X H I B I T   15.2O   One-Way ANOVA for Three Restaurant Competitors

Output3 - SPSS Viewer

File   Edit   View   Insert   Format   Analyze   Graphs   Utilities   Window   Help

Descriptives

		N	Mean	Std. Deviation	Std. Error	95% Confidence Interval for Mean		Minimum	Maximum
						Lower Bound	Upper Bound		
X7 -- Large Portions	Outback	86	3.57	.805	.087	3.40	3.74	2	4
	Longhorn	65	2.77	.880	.109	2.55	2.99	1	4
	Remington's	49	3.39	.862	.123	3.14	3.64	1	4
	Total	200	3.27	.910	.064	3.14	3.39	1	4
X8 -- Competent Employees	Outback	86	5.15	.623	.067	5.02	5.28	4	6
	Longhorn	65	3.25	.919	.114	3.02	3.47	2	5
	Remington's	49	2.49	.617	.088	2.31	2.67	2	4
	Total	200	3.88	1.355	.096	3.69	4.07	2	6
X9 -- Food Quality	Outback	86	6.42	.659	.071	6.28	6.56	5	7
	Longhorn	65	5.12	.839	.104	4.92	5.33	4	7
	Remington's	49	6.86	.354	.051	6.76	6.96	6	7
	Total	200	6.11	.969	.069	5.97	6.24	4	7
X10 -- Speed of Service	Outback	86	4.35	.943	.102	4.15	4.55	3	6
	Longhorn	65	3.02	.857	.106	2.80	3.23	2	5
	Remington's	49	2.27	.670	.096	2.07	2.46	1	3
	Total	200	3.41	1.216	.086	3.24	3.57	1	6
X11 -- Atmosphere	Outback	86	6.09	.890	.096	5.90	6.28	4	7
	Longhorn	65	4.35	.799	.099	4.16	4.55	3	6
	Remington's	49	6.59	.537	.077	6.44	6.75	5	7
	Total	200	5.65	1.210	.086	5.48	5.82	3	7
X12 -- Reasonable Prices	Outback	86	5.50	.763	.082	5.34	5.66	4	6
	Longhorn	65	5.00	.810	.100	4.80	5.20	4	6
	Remington's	49	5.49	.767	.110	5.27	5.71	4	6
	Total	200	5.34	.810	.057	5.22	5.45	4	6

ᴇXHIBIT 15.21 **One-Way ANOVA of Differences in Restaurant Perceptions Variables**

→ **Oneway**

ANOVA

		Sum of Squares	df	Mean Square	F	Sig.
X7 -- Large Portions	Between Groups	24.702	2	12.351	17.349	.000
	Within Groups	140.253	197	.712		
	Total	164.955	199			
X8 -- Competent Employees	Between Groups	259.779	2	129.889	242.908	.000
	Within Groups	105.341	197	.535		
	Total	365.120	199			
X9 -- Food Quality	Between Groups	98.849	2	49.425	110.712	.000
	Within Groups	87.946	197	.446		
	Total	186.795	199			
X10 -- Speed of Service	Between Groups	150.124	2	75.062	102.639	.000
	Within Groups	144.071	197	.731		
	Total	294.195	199			
X11 -- Atmosphere	Between Groups	169.546	2	84.773	136.939	.000
	Within Groups	121.954	197	.619		
	Total	291.500	199			
X12 -- Reasonable Prices	Between Groups	10.810	2	5.405	8.892	.000
	Within Groups	119.745	197	.608		
	Total	130.555	199			

Note: A database for the questions in this case is available in SPSS format at www.mhhe.com/hair06. The name of the database is C_15_Remingtons MRIA_3e.sav. A copy of the questionnaire is in the appendix at the end of this chapter.

The initial analysis of the data focused on the importance ratings for the restaurant selection factors. The importance ratings were variables X1–X6 in the Remington's database. Exhibit 15.19 shows that food quality and speed of service were the two most important factors. To derive this exhibit, the click-through sequence is ANALYZE → DESCRIPTIVE STATISTICS → FREQUENCIES. Highlight variables X1–X6 and move them to the Variable(s) box. Then go to the Statistics box and check Mean, and then click Continue and OK. The least important factor was competent employees (mean = 3.12). This does not mean employees aren't important. It simply means they are relatively less important compared to the other factors respondents were asked about in the survey. In sum, these respondents wanted good food, fast service, and reasonable prices.

The next task was to examine the perceptions of the three restaurant competitors. Using the restaurant image factors, the consultant conducted an ANOVA to see if there were any differences in the perceptions of the three restaurants (Exhibits 15.20 and 15.21). To derive

e XHIBIT   15.22   Summary of ANOVA Findings from Exhibits 15.19, 15.20, and 15.21

Attributes	Rankings[a]	Competitor Means			Sig.
		Outback	Longhorn	Remington's	
X7—Large portions	4	3.57	2.77	3.39	.000
X8—Competent employees	6	5.15	3.25	2.49	.000
X9—Food quality	1	6.42	5.12	6.86	.000
X10—Speed of service	2	4.35	3.02	2.27	.000
X11—Atmosphere	5	6.09	4.35	6.59	.000
X12—Reasonable prices	3	5.50	5.00	5.49	.000
N = 200 total		86	65	49	.000

[a]Rankings are based on mean importance ratings.

these exhibits, the click-through sequence is ANALYZE → COMPARE MEANS → ONE-WAY ANOVA. Highlight variables X1–X6 and move them to the Dependent List box, and then highlight variable X22 and move it to the Factor Box. Next go to the Options box and check Descriptive, and then click Continue and OK.

Results are shown in Exhibits 15.20 and 15.21. An overview of the findings presented in Exhibits 15.19, 15.20, and 15.21 is provided in Exhibit 15.22.

The findings of the survey were quite revealing. On the most important factor (food quality), Remington's rated the highest (mean = 6.86; see Exhibit 15.20), but Outback was

e XHIBIT   15.23   Importance Performance Chart for Remington's Steak House

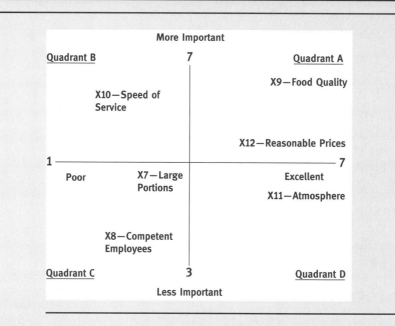

a close second (mean = 6.42). Remington's was also rated the highest on atmosphere (mean = 6.59) but that factor was fifth most important. For speed of service (second most important) and competent employees (least important) Remington's was rated the lowest of the three competitors.

An easy way to convey the results of an image analysis is to prepare an importance performance chart (IPC). An IPC has quadrants (A–D) that are described as follows:

Quadrant A: Modifications are needed.

Quadrant B: Good job—no need to modify.

Quadrant C: Don't worry—low priority.

Quadrant D: Rethink—a possible overkill.

The IPC for Remington's Steak House is shown in Exhibit 15.23. The chart shows that in terms of food quality and prices, Remington's is doing well. But there are several areas for improvement, particularly in comparison to the competition.

Hands-On Exercises

1. What are other areas of improvement for Remington's?

2. Run post hoc ANOVA tests between the competitor groups. What additional problems or challenges does this reveal?

3. What new marketing strategies would you suggest?

Summary of Learning Objectives

■ **Understand how to prepare graphical presentations of data.**

Distributions of numbers can be illustrated by several different types of graphs. Histograms and bar charts display data in either horizontal or vertical bars. Line charts are good choices for communicating trends in data, while pie charts are well suited for illustrating relative proportions.

■ **Calculate the mean, median, and mode as measures of central tendency.**

The mean is the most commonly used measure of central tendency and describes the arithmetic average of the values in a sample of data. The median represents the middle value of an ordered set of values. The mode is the most frequently occurring value in a distribution of values. All these measures describe the center of the distribution of a set of values.

■ **Explain the range and standard deviation of a frequency distribution as measures of dispersion.**

The range defines the spread of the data. It is the distance between the smallest and largest values of the distribution. The standard deviation describes the average distance of the distribution values from the mean. A large standard deviation indicates a distribution in which the individual values are spread out and are relatively farther away from the mean.

■ **Understand the difference between independent and related samples.**

In independent samples the respondents come from different populations, so their answers to the survey questions do not affect each other. In related samples, the same respondent answers several questions, so comparing answers to these questions requires the use of a paired-samples t-test. Questions about mean differences in independent samples can be answered by using a student t-test statistic.

■ **Explain hypothesis testing and assess potential error in its use.**

A hypothesis is an empirically testable though yet unproven statement about a set of data. Hypotheses allow the researcher to make comparisons between two groups of respondents and to determine whether there are important differences between the groups.

Hypothesis tests have two types of error connected with their use. The first type of error (Type I error) is the risk of rejecting the null hypothesis on the basis of your sample data when it is, in fact, true for the population from which the sample data were selected. The second type of error (Type II error) is the risk of not detecting a false null hypothesis. The level of statistical significance (alpha) associated with a statistical test is the probability of making a Type I error.

■ **Understand univariate and bivariate statistical tests.**

t statistics are tests of mean values that should be used when the sample size is small (less than 30) and the standard deviation of the population is unknown; z-tests are statistical tests of mean values best used when sample sizes are above 30 and the standard deviation of the population is known. Both tests involve the use of the sample mean, a t or z value selected from the respective distribution, and the standard deviation of either the sample or the population.

Tests of the differences between two groups require the use of t-tests for small samples (less than 30) and unknown population standard deviations. For larger samples and known population standard deviations, either the t-test or z-test can be used.

■ **Apply and interpret the results of the ANOVA and n-way ANOVA statistical methods.**

ANOVA is used to determine the statistical significance of the difference between two or more means. The ANOVA technique calculates the variance of the values between groups of respondents and compares it with the variance of the responses within the groups. If the between-group variance is significantly greater than the within-group variance as indicated by the F ratio, the means are significantly different.

The statistical significance between means in ANOVA is detected through the use of a follow-up test. The Scheffé test is one type of follow-up test. The test examines the differences between all possible pairs of sample means against a high and low confidence range. If the difference between a pair of means falls outside the confidence interval, then the means can be considered statistically different.

■ **Utilize perceptual mapping to simplify presentation of research findings.**

Perceptual mapping is used to develop maps that show perceptions of respondents visually. These maps are graphic representations that can be produced from the results of several multivariate techniques. The maps provide a visual representation of how companies, products, brands, or other objects are perceived relative to each other on key attributes such as quality of service, food taste, and food preparation.

Key Terms and Concepts

Review Questions

1. Why are graphic approaches to reporting marketing research better than simply reporting numbers?

2. Explain the difference between the mean, the median, and the mode.

3. Why do we use hypothesis testing?

4. Why and how would you use t- and z-tests in hypothesis testing?

5. Why and when would you want to use ANOVA in marketing research?

6. What will ANOVA tests not tell you, and how can you overcome this problem?

Discussion Questions

1. The measures of central tendency discussed in this chapter are designed to reveal information about the center of a distribution of values. Measures of dispersion provide information about the spread of all the values in a distribution around the center values. Assume you were conducting an opinion poll on voters' approval ratings of the job performance of the mayor of the city where you live. Do you think the mayor would be more interested in the central tendency or the dispersion measures associated with the responses to your poll? Why?

2. If you were interested in finding out whether or not young adults (21–34 years old) are more likely to buy products online than older adults (35 or more years old), how would you phrase your null hypothesis? What is the implicit alternative hypothesis accompanying your null hypothesis?

3. The level of significance (alpha) associated with testing a null hypothesis is also referred to as the probability of a Type I error. Alpha is the probability of rejecting the null hypothesis on the basis of your sample data when it is, in fact, true for the population you are interested in. Since alpha concerns the probability of making a mistake in your analysis, should you always try to set this value as small as possible? Why or why not?

4. Analysis of variance (ANOVA) allows you to test for the statistical difference between two or more means. Typically, there are more than two means tested. If the ANOVA results for a set of data reveal that the four means that were compared are significantly different from each other, how would you find out which individual means were statistically different from each other? What statistical techniques would you apply to answer this question?

5. **EXPERIENCE THE INTERNET.** Nike, Reebok, and Converse are strong competitors in the athletic shoe market. The three use different advertising and marketing strategies to appeal to their target markets. Use one of the search engines on the Internet to identify information on this market. Go to the Web sites for these three companies (www.Nike.com; www.Reebok.com; www.Converse.com). Gather background information on each, including its target market and market share. Design a questionnaire based on this information and survey a sample of students. Prepare a report on the different perceptions of each of these three companies, their shoes, and related aspects. Present the report in class and defend your findings.

6. **SPSS EXERCISE.** Form a team of three to four students in your class. Select one or two local franchises to conduct a survey on, such as Subway or McDonald's. Design a brief survey (10–12 questions) including questions like ratings on quality of food, speed of service, knowledge of employees, attitudes of employees, and price, as well as several demographic variables such as age, address, how often individuals eat there, and day of week and time of day. Obtain permission from the franchises to interview their customers at a convenient time, usually when they are leaving. Assure the franchiser you will not bother customers and that you will provide the franchise with a valuable report on your findings. Develop frequency charts, pie charts, and similar graphic displays of findings, where appropriate. Use statistics to test hypotheses, such as "Perceptions of speed of service differ by time of day or day of week." Prepare a report and present it to your class; particularly point out where statistically significant differences exist and why.

7. **SPSS EXERCISE.** Using SPSS and the Santa Fe Grill database, provide frequencies, means, modes, and medians for the relevant variables on the questionnaire. The actual questionnaire is presented in Chapter 14. In addition, develop bar charts and pie charts where appropriate for the data you analyzed. Run an ANOVA using the lifestyle and restaurant perceptions variables to identify any group differences that may exist. Be prepared to present a report on your findings.

8. **SPSS EXERCISE.** Review the Marketing Research in Action case for this chapter. There were three restaurant competitors—Remington's, Outback, and Longhorn. Results for a one-way ANOVA of the restaurant image variables were provided. Now run post hoc ANOVA follow-up tests to see where the group differences are. Make recommendations for new marketing strategies for Remington's compared to the competition.

appendix 15.A

The Remington's Steak House Questionnaire

SCREENING AND RAPPORT QUESTIONS

Hello. My name is _____ and I work for DSS Research. We are talking to individuals today/tonight about dining out habits.

1. "Do you regularly dine at casual dining restaurants?" __ Yes __ No
2. "Have you eaten at other casual restaurants in the last six months?" __ Yes __ No
3. "Is your gross annual household income $20,000 or more?" __ Yes __ No
4. There are three casual steakhouse restaurants in you neighborhood—Outback, **Longhorn**, and Remington's. Which of these restaurants are you most familiar with?
   a. Outback __
   b. Longhorn __
   c. Remington's __
   d. None __

If respondent answers "Yes" to first three questions, and is familiar with one of the three restaurants, then say:

We would like you to answer a few questions about your recent dining experiences at Outback/ Longhorn/Remington's restaurant. The survey will only take a few minutes and it will be very helpful in better serving restaurant customers in this area.

If the person says yes, give them instructions on how to access the Web site and complete the survey.

DINING OUT SURVEY

Please read all questions carefully. If you do not understand a question, stop the survey and e-mail us so we can help you to understand it.

In the first section a number of factors are listed that people use in selecting a particular restaurant to dine at. Using a scale from 1 to 7, with 7 being "Very Important" and 1 being "Very Unimportant," please indicate the extent to which a particular selection factor is important or unimportant. Circle only one number for each selection factor.

Section 1: Importance Ratings

How important is/are the following in selecting a particular restaurant to dine at?

1. Large portions

Very Unimportant						Very Important
1	2	3	4	5	6	7

2. Competent employees

Very Unimportant						Very Important
1	2	3	4	5	6	7

3. Food quality

Very Unimportant						Very Important
1	2	3	4	5	6	7

4. Speed of service

Very Unimportant						Very Important
1	2	3	4	5	6	7

5. Atmosphere

	Very Unimportant					Very Important
1	2	3	4	5	6	7

6. Reasonable prices

	Very Unimportant					Very Important
1	2	3	4	5	6	7

Section 2: Perceptions Measures

Listed below is a set of characteristics that could be used to describe Outback/Longhorn/Remington's. Using a scale from 1 to 7, with 7 being "Strongly Agree" and 1 being "Strongly Disagree," to what extent do you agree or disagree that Remington's—Outback—Longhorn's: (a particular restaurant's name appears on the screen based on the familiarity question on the telephone screening question)

7. Has large portions

	Strongly Disagree					Strongly Agree
1	2	3	4	5	6	7

8. Has competent employees

	Strongly Disagree					Strongly Agree
1	2	3	4	5	6	7

9. Has excellent food quality

	Strongly Disagree					Strongly Agree
1	2	3	4	5	6	7

10. Has quick service

	Strongly Disagree					Strongly Agree
1	2	3	4	5	6	7

11. Has a good atmosphere

	Strongly Disagree					Strongly Agree
1	2	3	4	5	6	7

12. Reasonable prices

	Strongly Disagree					Strongly Agree
1	2	3	4	5	6	7

Section 3: Relationship Measures

Please indicate your view on each of the following questions:

13. How satisfied are you with _____?

	Not Satisfied At All					Very Satisfied
1	2	3	4	5	6	7

14. How likely are you to return to _____ in the future?

	Definitely Will Not Return					Definitely Will Return
1	2	3	4	5	6	7

15. How likely are you to recommend _____ to a friend?

	Definitely Will Not Recommend					Definitely Will Recommend
1	2	3	4	5	6	7

16. Frequency of Patronage
How often do you eat at _____?

1 = Occasionally (Less than once a month)
2 = Frequently (1–3 times a month)
3 = Very Frequently (4 or more times a month)

Section 4: Classification Questions

Please circle the number that classifies you best.

17. Number of children at home

1 None
2 1–2
3 More than 2 children at home

18. Do your recall seeing any advertisements in the last 60 days for Outback/Longhorn/Remington's?

0   No
1   Yes

19. Your gender

0   Male
1   Female

20. Your age in years

1   18–25
2   26–34
3   35–49
4   50–59
5   60 and older

21. Your annual gross household income

1   $20,000–$35,000
2   $35,001–$50,000
3   $50,001–$75,000
4   $75,001–$100,000
5   More than $100,000

22. Competitors: most familiar with _____?

1   Outback
2   Longhorn
3   Remington's

Thank you very much for your help. Click on the submit button to exit the survey.

chapter 16

Data Analysis: Testing for Association

Learning Objectives

After reading this chapter, you will be able to

1. Understand and evaluate the types of relationships between variables.

2. Explain the concepts of association and covariation.

3. Discuss the differences in chi-square, Pearson correlation, and Spearman correlation.

4. Explain the concept of statistical significance versus practical significance.

5. Understand when and how to use regression analysis.

Data Analysis Improves Marketing Strategies

Businesses generally pursue three overall marketing objectives—to get customers, to keep customers, and to grow customers. The major difference is the marketing strategies and tactics they use. Increasingly, businesses are using information technology and CRM as part of their marketing approach. CRM programs help businesses to find and attract new customers, to keep current customers happy, and to grow customers to maximize their lifetime value to the company.

EATEL, a regional telecommunications company located in Gonzales, Louisiana, uses CRM to improve its marketing programs. EATEL is a diversified company whose major products are local and long-distance phone service, the Sunshine Pages, and Web site development and enhancement. They compete directly with BellSouth for phone service and the Sunshine Pages, which is an alternative to BellSouth's Yellow Pages Directory. Several local and national companies are competing for their Web site development and enhancement services. EATEL focuses on two major market segments—residential customers for local and long-distance phone service, and commercial customers for phone service and Web site development and enhancement.

EATEL uses statistical analysis on the data in its data warehouse to develop best customer models for both its residential and business market segments. The objective of the best residential model is to acquire new customers from the Sunshine Pages and other prospect lists, and to enhance cross selling to current residential customers. The objective of the best business model is to identify the best small and medium-size business prospects for EATEL's new customer acquisition campaigns.

Statistical models with high predictive capability have been developed and validated for both the residential and business segments. The predictive power of the residential model is based on factors such as purchasing power, length of residence, age, Nielsen county ranking, and so on. The predictive power of the commercial model is based on factors such as population, size of business, gender of contact person, SIC code, and so forth. Initial marketing campaigns using these statistical models have attracted new customers. In the future they hope to improve the models to maximize the lifetime value of customers. To learn more about EATEL go to www.eatel.com.

Relationships between Variables

Relationship A consistent and systematic link between two or more variables.

Relationships between variables can be described in several ways, including presence, direction, strength of association, and type. We will describe each of these concepts in turn.

The first issue, and probably the most obvious, is whether two or more variables are related at all. If a systematic relationship exists between two or more variables, this is referred to as the presence of a relationship. To measure whether a relationship is present, we rely on the concept of statistical significance. If we test for statistical significance and find that it exists, then we say that a relationship is present. Stated another way, we say that knowledge about the behavior of one variable allows us to make a useful prediction about the behavior of another. For example, if we found a statistically significant relationship between the perceptions of the quality of Santa Fe Grill food and satisfaction, we would say a relationship is present and that perceptions of the quality of the food will tell us what the perceptions of satisfaction are likely to be.

If a relationship is present between two variables, it is important to know the direction. The direction of a relationship can be either positive or negative. Using the Santa Fe Grill example, we could say that a positive relationship exists if respondents who rate the quality of the food high also are highly satisfied. Similarly, a negative relationship exists if respondents say the speed of service is slow (low rating) but they are still satisfied (high rating).

An understanding of the strength of association also is important. We generally categorize the strength of association as nonexistent, weak, moderate, or strong. If a consistent and systematic relationship is not present, then the strength of association is nonexistent. A weak association means there is a low probability of the variables having a relationship. A strong association means there is a high probability a consistent and systematic relationship exists.

A fourth concept that is important to understand is the type of relationship. If we say that two variables can be described as related, then we would pose this as a question: "What is the nature of the relationship?" How can the link between Y and X best be described? There are a number of different ways in which two variables can share a relationship. Variables Y and X can have a **linear relationship,** which means that the strength and nature of the relationship between them remains the same over the range of both variables, and can best be described using a straight line. Conversely, Y and X could have a **curvilinear relationship,** which would mean that the strength and/or direction of their relationship changes over the range of both variables (perhaps Y's relationship with X first gets stronger as X increases, but then gets weaker as the value of X continues to increase).

Linear relationship A relationship between two variables whereby the strength and nature of the relationship remains the same over the range of both variables.

Curvilinear relationship A relationship between two variables whereby the strength and/or direction of their relationship changes over the range of both variables.

It may occur to you that a linear relationship would be much simpler to work with than a curvilinear relationship, and that is true. That is, if we know the value of variable X, then we can apply the formula for a straight line ($Y = a + bX$) to determine the value of Y. But when two variables have a curvilinear relationship, the formula that best describes that linkage will be more algebraically complex and possibly hard to determine. For these reasons, most marketing researchers tend to work with relationships that they believe are linear, or are close approximations. In fact, many of the statistics you learned about in preceding chapters are based on the assumption that a linear relationship is an efficient way to describe the link between two variables under investigation.

We have suggested that marketers are very often interested in describing the relationship between two variables they think make a difference in purchases of their product(s). There are three basic questions to ask about a possible relationship between two variables. First, "Is there a relationship between the two variables we are interested in?" Interest in questions two and three depend upon the answer to the first. If there is a relationship, then one would be interested in knowing "How strong is that relationship?" and "How can that relationship be best described?" What we need now is an efficient way to answer these questions.

Using Covariation to Describe Variable Relationships

Covariation The amount of change in one variable that is consistently related to the change in another variable of interest.

Since we are interested in finding out whether two variables describing our customers are related, the concept of covariation is a very useful idea. **Covariation** is defined as the amount of change in one variable that is consistently related to a change in another variable of interest. For example, if we know that DVD purchases are related to age, then we want to know the extent to which younger persons purchase more DVDs, and ultimately which types of DVDs. Another way of stating the concept of covariation is that it is the degree of association between two items (e.g., the change in the attitude toward Starbucks coffee advertising campaigns as it varies between light, medium, and heavy consumers of Starbucks coffee). If two variables are found to change together on a reliable or consistent basis, then we can use that information to make predictions as well as decisions on advertising and marketing strategies.

Scatter diagram A graphic plot of the relative position of two variables using a horizontal and a vertical axis to represent the values of the respective variables.

One easy way of visually describing the covariation between two variables is with the use of a **scatter diagram.** A scatter diagram plots the relative position of two variables using a horizontal and a vertical axis to represent the values of the respective variables. Exhibits 16.1 through 16.4 show some examples of possible relationships between two variables that might show up on a scatter diagram. In Exhibit 16.1, the best way to describe the visual impression left by the collection of dots representing the values of each variable is probably a circle. That is, there is no particular skewness or direction to the collection of dots. Thus, if you take two or three sample values of variable *Y* from the scatter diagram and look at the values for *X,* there is no predictable pattern to the values for *X.* Knowing the values of *Y* or *X* would not tell you very much (maybe nothing at all) about the possible values of the other variable. Exhibit 16.1 suggests that there is no systematic relationship between *Y* and *X* and that there is very little or no covariation shared by the two variables. If we measured the amount of covariation shared by these two variables (something you will learn how to do in the next section), it would be very close to zero.

eXHIBIT 16.1 No Relationship between *X* and *Y*

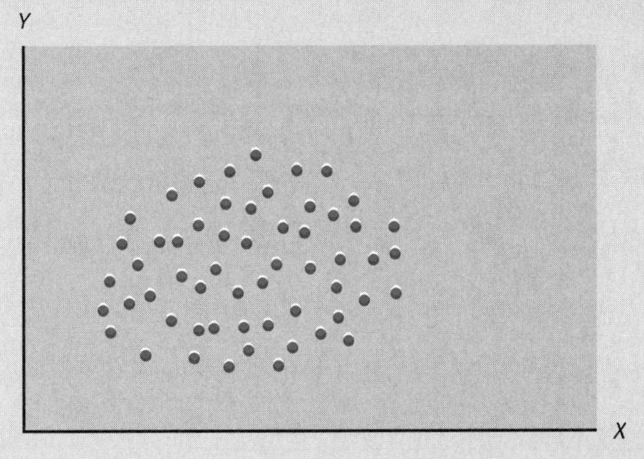

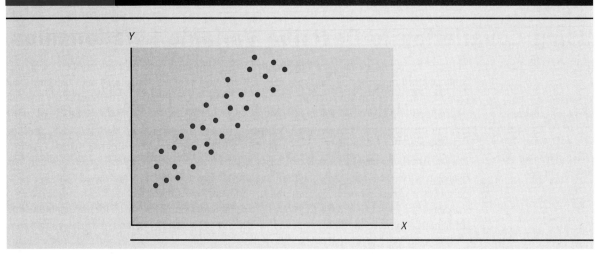

eXHIBIT 16.2 Positive Relationship between *X* and *Y*

In Exhibit 16.2, the two variables present a very different picture from that of Exhibit 16.1. There is a distinct pattern to the dots. As the values of *Y* increase, so do the values of *X*. This pattern could be very effectively described using the idea of a straight line or an ellipse (a circle that has been stretched out from both sides). We could also describe this relationship as positive, because increases in the value of *Y* are associated with increases in the value of *X*. That is, if we know the relationship between *Y* and *X* is a linear, positive relationship, we would know that the values of *Y* and *X* change in the same direction. As the values of *Y* increase, so do the values of *X*. Similarly, if the values of *Y* decrease, the values of *X* should decrease as well. If we try to measure the amount of covariation shown by the values of *Y* and *X*, it would be relatively high. Thus, changes in the value of *Y* are systematically related to changes in the value of *X*.

Exhibit 16.3 shows the same type of distinct pattern between the values of *Y* and *X*, but the direction of the relationship is opposite the one in Exhibit 16.2. There still seems to be

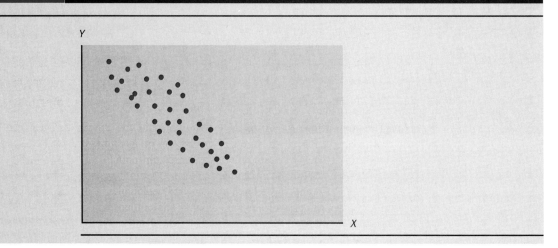

eXHIBIT 16.3 Negative Relationship between *X* and *Y*

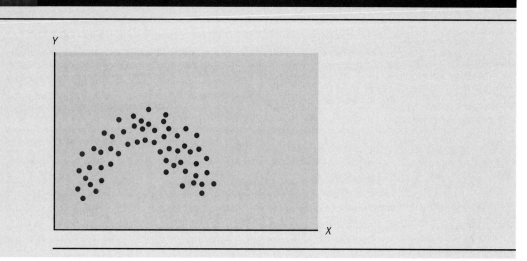

the same linear pattern, but now increases in the value of *Y* are associated with decreases in the values of *X*. The values of *Y* and *X* change in the opposite direction. This type of relationship is known as a negative relationship. The amount of covariation shared between the two variables is still high, because *Y* and *X* still change together, though in a direction opposite from that shown in Exhibit 16.2. The concept of covariation refers to the amount of shared movement, not the direction of the relationship between two variables.

Finally, Exhibit 16.4 shows a more complicated type of relationship between the values of *Y* and *X*. This pattern of dots can be described as *curvilinear*. That is, the relationship between the values of *Y* and the values of *X* is different for different values of the variables. In the case of Exhibit 16.4, part of the relationship is positive (increases in the small values of *Y* are associated with increases in the small values of *X*), but then the relationship becomes negative (increases in the larger values of *Y* are now associated with decreases in the larger values of *X*).

This pattern of dots could not easily be described as a linear relationship. An additional complication comes from the fact, noted earlier, that many of the statistics marketing researchers use to describe association assume the two variables have a linear relationship. These statistics don't perform very effectively when used to describe a curvilinear relationship. In Exhibit 16.4, we can still say the relationship is strong, or that the covariation exhibited by the two variables is strong. However, now we can't talk very easily about the direction (positive or negative) of the relationship, because the direction changes. To make matters more difficult, many statistical methods of describing relationships between variables cannot be effectively applied to situations where you suspect the relationship is curvilinear. The Closer Look at Research box provides some insight on how correlations can be used in small businesses.

Chi-Square Analysis

As noted earlier in the text, marketing researchers often analyze data collected in surveys by means of one-way frequency counts and cross tabulations. One purpose of cross tabulations is to study relationships among variables. The research question, then, is "Do the

A Closer Look at Research

Correlation Does Not Identify Causation

Situations often arise where many small-business owners and managers collect data from two relevant samples yet do not know how to statistically compare the two measures. When this occurs, the most frequently used statistical technique available to the small-business owner is correlation analysis.

Correlation analysis describes the degree of relationship between the two variables, often stated as an absolute value score between 0 and 1. The higher the correlation score, the stronger the relationship between the two variables. Through the use of correlation procedures, small-business owners can identify trends in their particular market.

A brief description of correlation analysis in action is described below. This example is only one of a variety of possible applications of correlation analysis.

A small-business owner might have information on the exact number of hours worked by salespeople in his company last year and the amount of advertising sold by each sales representative that year. After initial graphical representation, the two measures would appear to be highly correlated. In other words, as the number of hours worked by salespeople increased, the amount of advertisements sold per individual would also increase.

While this brief example shows the possible inferences from correlation analysis, a common mistake in interpreting the correlation score for two variables is to assume that a high correlation score implies causation. No such conclusion is automatic. In the previous example, although the number of hours worked and sales productivity are highly correlated, other factors—such as territory or number of representatives in that area—play an important role in analyzing correlation. Assuming causation based solely on these two factors might ignore other important variables.

Therefore, small-business owners should use correlation analysis to analyze potential relationships but should be careful in attempting to determine causal relationships between two variables.

---

numbers of responses that fall into different categories differ from what is expected?" For example, the owners of the Santa Fe Grill might believe there is no difference in the percentage of men and women who recall ads about their restaurant. Thus, the null hypothesis would be that the number of men and women customers who recall Santa Fe Grill ads is the same. This question and similar ones could be answered by using chi-square analysis.

Chi-square (X²) analysis
Assesses how closely the observed frequencies fit the pattern of the expected frequencies and is referred to as a "goodness-of-fit" test.

Chi-square (X^2) analysis permits us to test for significance between the frequency distributions for two (or more) nominally scaled variables in a cross-tabulation table to determine if there is any association. Categorical data from questions about gender, education, or other nominal variables can be examined to provide tests of hypotheses of interest. Chi-square analysis compares the observed frequencies (counts) of the responses with the expected frequencies. The expected frequencies are based on our ideas about the population distribution or our predicted proportions. Chi-square analysis assumes that no association exists between the nominal-scaled variables being examined. It tests whether or not the observed data are distributed the way we expect them to be. For example, if we observe that women recall ads more so than men, we would compare it with the expected frequency to see if it differs.

The use of the chi-square statistic is very helpful in answering questions about data that are nominally scaled and cannot be analyzed with other types of statistical analysis, such as ANOVA or *t*-tests. One word of caution, however, in using Chi-square. The Chi-square results will be distorted if more than 20 percent of the cells have an expected count of less than 5, or if any cell has an expected count of less than 1. In such cases, you should not use this test. SPSS will tell you if these conditions have been violated. One solution to small counts in individual cells is to collapse them into fewer cells to get larger counts.

Calculating the X^2 Value

To help you to better understand the Chi-square statistic, we will show you how to calculate it. The Chi-square formula is shown below:

$$X^2 = \sum_{i=1}^{n} \frac{(\text{Observed}_i - \text{Expected}_i)^2}{\text{Expected}_i}$$

where

Observed$_i$ = observed frequency in cell i

Expected$_i$ = expected frequency in cell i

n = number of cells

When you apply the above formula to the Santa Fe Grill data shown in Exhibit 16.5, you get the following calculation of Chi-square value:

$$\text{Chi-square value} = \frac{(88 - 108)^2}{108} + \frac{(95 - 75)^2}{75} + \frac{(58 - 57.8)^2}{57.8}$$

$$+ \frac{(40 - 40.2)^2}{40.2} + \frac{(90 - 70.2)^2}{70.2} + \frac{(29 - 48.8)^2}{48.8} = 22.616$$

As you can see from the above equation, the expected frequency is subtracted from the observed frequency and then squared to eliminate any negative values. The resulting value is divided by the expected frequency to take into consideration cell size differences. Then these amounts are summed over all cells to arrive at the Chi-square value. The Chi-square value tells you how far the observed frequencies are from the expected frequencies. The computed Chi-square statistic is compared to a table of Chi-square values to determine if the differences are statistically significant. In general, larger Chi-square values indicate greater differences.

Some marketing researchers call Chi-square a "goodness-of-fit" test. That is, the test evaluates how closely the actual frequencies "fit" the expected frequencies. When the differences between observed and expected frequencies are large, you have a poor fit and you reject your null hypothesis. When the differences are small, you have a good fit.

SPSS Application—Chi-square

Based on their conversations with customers, the owners of the Santa Fe Grill have begun to think that male customers are coming to the restaurant from farther away than are female customers. The Chi-square statistic can be used to determine if this is true. The null hypothesis is that the same proportion of male and female customers would make up each of the response categories for X30—Distance Driven.

To conduct this analysis, the click-through sequence is ANALYZE → DESCRIPTIVE STATISTICS → CROSSTABS. Click on X30—Distance Traveled for the Row variable and on X32—Gender for the Column variable. Click on the Statistics button and the

e X H I B I T 16.5   SPSS Chi-Square Crosstab Example

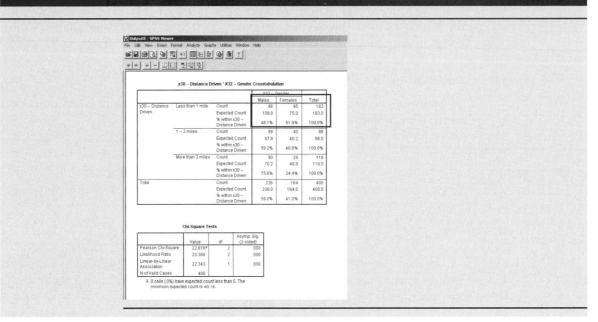

Chi-square box, and then Continue. Next click on the Cells button and on Expected frequencies (Observed frequencies is usually already checked). Then click Continue and OK to execute the program.

The SPSS results are shown in Exhibit 16.5. The top table shows the actual number of responses (count) for males and females for each of the categories of X30—Distance Driven. Also shown in this table are the expected frequencies under the null hypothesis of no difference. For example, 88 males drove a distance of less than 1 mile while 95 females drove from this same distance.

The expected frequencies (count) are calculated on the basis of the proportion of the sample represented by a particular group. For example, the total sample of Santa Fe Grill customers is 400 and 236 are males and 164 are females. This means 59 percent of the sample is male and 41 percent is female. When we look in the Total column for the distance driven category labeled "Less than 1 mile" we see that there are a total of 183 male and female respondents. To calculate the expected frequencies, you multiply the proportion a particular group represents times the total number in that group. For example, with males you calculate 59 percent of 183 and the expected frequency is 107.97. Similarly, females are 41 percent of the sample so the expected number of females = 75.03 (.41 × 183). The other expected frequencies are calculated in the same way.

Look again at the observed frequencies. Note that a higher proportion than expected of male customers of Santa Fe Grill drive farther to get to Santa Fe Grill. That is, we would expect only 70.2 men to drive to the Santa Fe Grill from more than three miles, but actually 90 men drove from this far away. Similarly, there are fewer female customers than expected who drive from more than three miles away (expected = 48.8 and actual only 29).

Information in the Chi-Square Tests table, as displayed in Exhibit 16.5, shows the results for this test. The Pearson Chi-Square value is 22.616 and it is significant at the .000 level. Since this level of significance is much higher than our standard criterion of .05, we can reject the null hypothesis with a high degree of confidence. The interpretation of this finding suggests that there is a high probability that male customers drive from farther away to get to the Santa Fe Grill. There also is a tendency for females to drive shorter distances to get to the restaurant.

Treatment and Measures of Correlation Analysis

The use of a scatter diagram gives us a visual way to describe the relationship between two variables and a sense of the amount of covariation they share. For example, a scatter diagram can tell us that as age increases the average consumption of Starbucks coffee increases too. But even though a picture is worth a thousand words, it is often more convenient to use a quantitative measure of the covariation between two items.

Pearson correlation coefficient A statistical measure of the strength of a linear relationship between two metric variables.

The **Pearson correlation coefficient** measures the degree of linear association between two variables. It varies between -1.00 and 1.00, with 0 representing absolutely no association between two variables, and -1.00 or 1.00 representing a perfect link between two variables. The higher the correlation coefficient, the stronger the level of association between two variables. The correlation coefficient can be either positive or negative, depending on the direction of the relationship between two variables. As we explained earlier, if there is a negative correlation coefficient between Y and X, that means that increases in the value of Y are associated with decreases in the value of X, and vice versa.

The null hypothesis for the Pearson correlation states that there is no association between the two variables in the population and that the correlation coefficient is zero. For example, we may hypothesize that there is no relationship between Starbucks coffee consumption and income levels. If you take measures of two variables (coffee consumption and income) from a sample of the population and estimate the correlation coefficient for that sample, the basic question is "What is the probability that I would get a correlation coefficient of this size in my sample if the correlation coefficient in the population is actually zero?" That is, if you calculate a large correlation coefficient between the two variables in your sample, and your sample was properly selected from the population of interest, then the chances that the population correlation coefficient is really zero are relatively small. Therefore, if the correlation coefficient is statistically significant, the null hypothesis is rejected, and you can conclude with some confidence that the two variables you are examining do share some association in the population. In other words, Starbucks coffee consumption is related to income.

If you remember, earlier in the chapter we stated that the first question of interest was "Does a relationship between Y and X exist?" This question is equivalent to asking whether a correlation coefficient is statistically significant. If this is the case, then you can move on to the second and third questions: "If there is a relationship between Y and X, how strong is that relationship?" and "What is the best way to describe that relationship?"

The size of the correlation coefficient can be used to quantitatively describe the strength of the association between two variables. Many authors have suggested some rules of thumb for characterizing the strength of the association between two variables based on the size of the correlation coefficient.

As Exhibit 16.6 suggests, correlation coefficients between .81 and 1.00 are considered very strong. That is, covariance is shared between the two variables under study. At the other extreme, if the correlation coefficient is between .00 and .20, there is a good chance the null hypothesis won't be rejected (unless you are using a large sample). You should realize that these numbers are only suggestions and other ranges and descriptions of relationship strength are possible.

In addition to the size of the correlation coefficient, we also must consider its significance level. How do we do this? There are published tables that show which correlation

EXHIBIT 16.6   Rules of Thumb about the Strength of Correlation Coefficients

Range of Coefficient	Description of Strength
±.81 to ±1.00	Very strong
±.61 to ±.80	Strong
±.41 to ±.60	Moderate
±.21 to ±.40	Weak
±.00 to ±.20	None

coefficients are significant at various sample sizes. Most statistical software, including SPSS, show you the significance level for a computed correlation coefficient. The SPSS software indicates significance as the probability that the null hypothesis is true and in the output is identified as the "Sig." value. For example, if the null hypothesis is no association between Starbucks coffee consumption and income, and the correlation coefficient is .71 with a statistical significance of .05, then there are only five chances out of 100 that there is not a relationship between the two variables. Thus, we reject the null hypothesis of no association. When we review the SPSS outputs we point out the "Sig." values and discuss how to interpret them.

Pearson Correlation Coefficient

The Pearson correlation coefficient makes several assumptions about the nature of the data you are applying it to. First, we assume the two variables have been measured using interval- or ratio-scaled measures (ordinally-interval are acceptable; See Chapter 11). If this is not the case, there are other types of correlation coefficient that can be computed which match the type of data on hand. More discussion will be devoted to these coefficients after we have described the basic concepts.

A second implicit assumption made by the Pearson correlation coefficient (and most other correlation coefficient measures) is that the nature of the relationship we are trying to measure is linear. That is, a straight line will do a reasonably good job of describing the relationship between the two variables of interest.

Use of the Pearson correlation coefficient also assumes that the variables you want to analyze come from a bivariate normally distributed population. That is, the population is such that all the observations with a given value of one variable have values of the second variable that are normally distributed. This assumption of normal distributions for the variables under study is a common requirement for many statistical techniques used by marketing researchers. Although it is a common assumption, determining whether it holds for the sample data you are working with is sometimes difficult and often taken for granted.

SPSS Application—Pearson Correlation

We can use the Santa Fe Grill database to examine the Pearson correlation. The owners anticipate that the relationship between satisfaction with the restaurant and likelihood to recommend the restaurant would be significant and positive. Looking at the database variables you note that information was collected on Likely to Recommend (variable X24) and Satisfaction Level (variable X22).

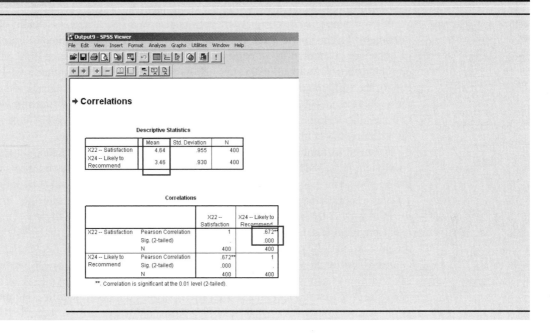

e X H I B I T 16.7 SPSS Pearson Correlation Example

With SPSS for Windows it is easy to compute a Pearson correlation between these two variables and test this assumption. The SPSS click-through sequence is ANALYZE → CORRELATE → BIVARIATE, which leads to a dialog box where you select the variables. Transfer variables X22 and X24 into the Variables box. Note that we will use all three default options shown below: Pearson correlation, two-tailed test of significance, and flag significant correlations. Next go to the Options box, and after it opens click on Means and Standard Deviations and then continue. Finally, when you click on OK at the top right of the dialog box it will execute the Pearson correlation.

The SPSS Pearson correlation results are shown in Exhibit 16.7. As you can see in the Correlations table, the correlation between variable X24—Likely to Recommend and X22—Satisfaction Level is .672. The statistical significance of this correlation is .000. Thus, we have confirmed our assumption that satisfaction is positively related to likely to recommend. When we examine the means of the two variables, we see that satisfaction level (4.64) is somewhat higher than likely to recommend (3.46) but we know the pattern of the responses to these questions is similar. That is, there is covariation between the responses to the two variables. What we also know is there is room for improvement in both measures because they are measured on a 7-point scale and both are near the mid-point.

Substantive Significance of the Correlation Coefficient

When the correlation coefficient is strong and significant, you can be confident that the two variables are associated in a linear fashion. In our Santa Fe Grill example, we can be reasonably confident that likelihood to recommend is in fact related to level of satisfaction. When the correlation coefficient is weak, then two possibilities must be considered: (1) there simply is no consistent, systematic relationship between the two variables in the population you are interested in; or (2) the association exists, but it is not linear, and other types of relationships must be investigated further.

Coefficient of determination (r^2) A number measuring the proportion of variation in one variable accounted for by another. The r^2 measure can be thought of as a percentage and varies from 0.0 to 1.00.

When you square the correlation coefficient, you arrive at the **coefficient of determination,** or r^2. This number ranges from .00 to 1.0 and shows the proportion of variation explained or accounted for in one variable by another. In our Santa Fe Grill example, the correlation coefficient was .672. Thus, the $r^2 = .452$, meaning that approximately 45.2 percent of the variation in likelihood to recommend is associated with satisfaction. The larger the size of the coefficient of determination, the stronger the linear relationship between the two variables being examined. In our example, we have accounted for almost one-half of the variation in likelihood to recommend by relating it to satisfaction.

You need to remember that finding only the statistical significance of a correlation coefficient is not sufficient. You also need to assess the substantive significance (i.e., do the numbers you calculate mean anything useful?). Since the statistical significance procedure for correlation coefficients includes information on the sample size, it is possible to find statistically significant correlation coefficients that are really too small to be of much practical use. For example, if we had compared satisfaction with the likelihood to recommend and the correlation coefficient was .30 (significant at .05 level), the coefficient of determination would be .09. Can we conclude the results are meaningful? To say yes requires much more thought. Remember you must always look at both types of significance (statistical and substantive) before you develop your conclusions. This is particularly important when assessing information from more complex issues and larger markets.

Influence of Measurement Scales on Correlation Analysis

A common occurrence in marketing research studies is that the answers to questions that marketing researchers are most interested in can be measured only with ordinal or even nominal scales. For example, if we are interested in learning more about Starbucks coffee consumption, we might consider consumption patterns of female versus male coffee drinkers. In these cases, applying the Pearson correlation coefficient to the data and assuming these measures of gender have interval or ratio scale properties (when they do not) will possibly produce misleading or overstated results.

Spearman rank order correlation coefficient A statistical measure of the linear association between two variables where both have been measured using ordinal (rank order) scales.

What options are available to the researcher when ordinal scales are used to collect data or when the data simply cannot be measured with an interval scale or better? The **Spearman rank order correlation coefficient** is the recommended statistic to use when two variables have been measured using ordinal scales. If either one of the variables is represented by rank order data, the best approach is to use the Spearman rank order correlation coefficient, rather than the Pearson product moment correlation coefficient. The Spearman rank order correlation coefficient tends to produce the lowest coefficient and is considered a more conservative measure.

In addition to the Spearman rank order correlation coefficient, there are other correlation coefficients that may be used to take into consideration the scale properties inherent in the data. For example, if you think that the gender of your customers makes a difference in the amount of your product they purchase, it would be possible to correlate customer gender (male/female) with product purchases (dollars) to answer your question. To do so, you would use a biserial correlation coefficient to make this calculation. You must use the appropriate statistic to match the characteristics of your data, and there are formulas available to calculate almost any type of correlation coefficient to match the situation.

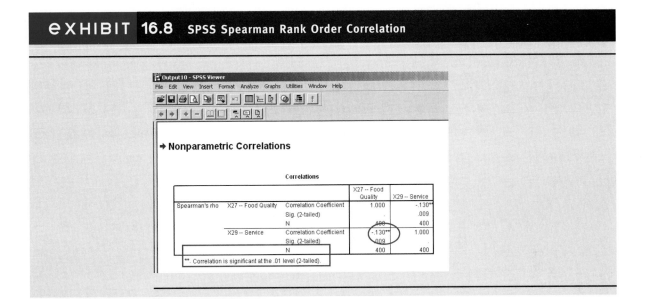

eXHIBIT 16.8 SPSS Spearman Rank Order Correlation

SPSS Application—Spearman Rank Order Correlation

The Santa Fe Grill customer survey collected data that ranked four restaurant selection factors. These data are represented by variables X26 to X29. Management is interested in knowing whether "Food Quality" is a significantly more important selection factor than is "Service." Since these are ordinal (ranking) data, the Pearson correlation is not appropriate. The Spearman correlation is the appropriate coefficient to calculate. Variables X27—Food Quality and X29—Service are the variables we will use.

The SPSS click-through sequence is ANALYZE → CORRELATE → BIVARIATE, which leads to a dialog box where you select the variables. Transfer variables X27 and X29 into the Variables box. You will note that the Pearson correlation is the default along with the two-tailed test of significance, and flag significant correlations. "Unclick" the Pearson correlation and then click on Spearman. Then click on OK at the top right of the dialog box to execute the program.

The SPSS results for the Spearman correlation are shown in Exhibit 16.8. As you can see in the Correlations table, the correlation between variable X27—Food Quality and X29—Service is −.130, and the significance value is .01 (see footnote to Correlations table). Thus, we have confirmed that there is a statistically significant relationship between the two restaurant selection factors. But, the size of the correlation is so small it is not considered substantively significant based on the information in Exhibit 16.6. Also, when we examine the correlation coefficient, we note that it is negative. A negative correlation indicates that a customer who ranks food quality high in importance tends to rank service significantly lower, if a substantive and significant relationship exists.

SPSS Application—Calculating Median Rankings

To better understand the Spearman correlation findings, we need to calculate the median rankings of the four selection factors. To do this, the SPSS click-through sequence is ANALYZE → DESCRIPTIVE STATISTICS → FREQUENCIES. Click on variables X26–X29 to highlight them and then on the arrow box for the Variables box to use them in your analysis. We use all four selection factors because this will enable us to examine the

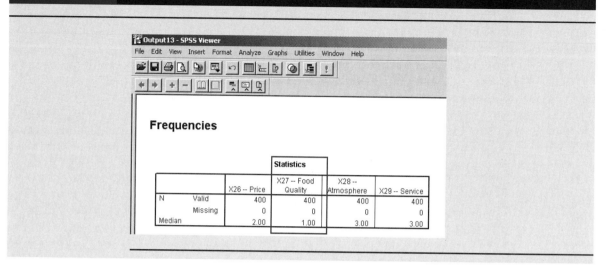

e X H I B I T   **16.9**   SPSS Median Example for Restaurant Selection Factors

overall relative rankings of all the restaurant selection factors. Next, open the Statistics box and click on Median and then Continue. For the Charts and Format options we will use the defaults, so click on OK to execute the program.

The SPSS results for median rankings are shown in the Statistics table in Exhibit 16.9. The variable with the lowest median is ranked the highest and is the most important, and the variable with the highest median is the least important. Recall the four selection factors were ranked from 1 to 4, with 1 = most important, and 4 = least important. Note that food quality is ranked as the most important (median = 1.0) while atmosphere and service are the least important. Our Spearman rank correlation compared food quality (median = 1) with service (median = 3.00). Thus, food quality is a significantly more important restaurant selection factor than is service.

What Is Regression Analysis?

We have discussed correlation as a way of determining the existence of a relationship between two variables. The correlation coefficient also can be used to answer questions about the overall strength of the association and the direction of the relationship between the variables. There are instances, however, when these answers do not provide enough information to the marketing manager. We may still need to know how to describe the relationship between the variables we are examining in greater detail. One method for arriving at these more detailed answers is called *regression analysis.*

Often, a marketing manager may need to make predictions about future sales levels or how a potential price increase will affect the profits or market share of the company. There are a number of ways to make such predictions: (1) extrapolation from past behavior of the variable; (2) simple guesses; or (3) use of a regression equation that compares information about related variables to assist in the prediction. Extrapolation and guesses (educated or otherwise) usually assume that past conditions and behaviors will continue into the future. They do not examine the influences behind the behavior of interest. Consequently, when sales levels, profits, or other variables of interest to a manager differ from those in the past, extrapolation and guessing do not provide any means of explaining why.

Bivariate regression analysis is a statistical technique that uses information about the relationship between an independent or predictor variable and a dependent or criterion variable, and combines it with the algebraic formula for a straight line to make predictions. Particular values of the independent variable are selected, and the behavior of the dependent variable is observed. These data are then applied to the formula for a straight line we discussed earlier. For example, if you wanted to find the current level of your company's sales volume, you would apply the following straight-line formula:

$$\text{Sales volume } (Y) = \$0 + (\text{Price per unit} = b) (\text{Number of units sold} = X)$$

You would not expect any sales volume if nothing were sold. Price per unit (b) determines the amount that sales volume (Y) increases with each unit sold (X). In this example, the relationship between sales volume and number of units sold is linear (i.e., it is consistent over the values of both Y and X).

Once a regression equation has been developed to predict values of Y, we are interested in trying to find out how good that prediction is. An obvious place to begin would be the actual value we collected in our sample. By comparing this actual value Y_i with our predicted value Y_i we can tell how far away our prediction is. In fact, this procedure of comparing actual values from a sample with predicted values from a regression equation is a commonly used method of determining the accuracy of a regression equation.

A couple of points should be made about the assumptions behind regression analysis. First, just like correlation analysis, regression analysis assumes that a linear relationship will provide a good description of the relationship between two variables. If the scatter diagram showing the positions of the values of both variables looks like the scatter plot in Exhibit 16.2 or Exhibit 16.3, this assumption would seem to be a good one. If the plot looks like Exhibit 16.1 or Exhibit 16.4, however, then regression analysis isn't a good choice.

Second, even though the common terminology of regression analysis uses the labels *dependent* and *independent* for the variables, those names don't mean that we can say one variable causes the behavior of the other. Regression analysis uses knowledge about the level and type of association between two variables to make predictions. Statements about the ability of one variable to cause changes in another must be based on conceptual logic or information other than just statistical techniques.

Finally, the use of a simple regression model assumes (1) the variables of interest are measured on interval or ratio scales (except in the case of dummy variables, which we will discuss later); (2) these variables come from a bivariate normal population (the same assumption made by correlation analysis); and (3) the error terms associated with making predictions are normally and independently distributed (we will also talk about this particular assumption and its validation later in this chapter).

Fundamentals of Regression Analysis

A fundamental basis of regression analysis is the assumption of a straight line relationship between the independent and dependent variables. This relationship is illustrated in Exhibit 16.10. The general formula for a straight line is:

$$Y = a + bX + e_i$$

Bivariate regression analysis A statistical technique that analyzes the linear relationship between two variables by estimating coefficients for an equation for a straight line. One variable is designated as a dependent variable and the other is called an independent or predictor variable.

eXHIBIT 16.10 The Straight Line Relationship in Regression

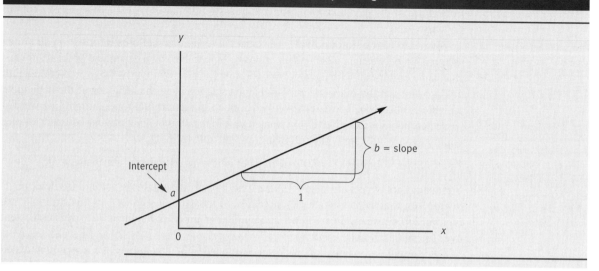

where

Y = the dependent variable

a = the intercept (point where the straight line intersects the y-axis when $X = 0$)

b = the slope (the change in Y for every 1-unit change in X)

X = the independent variable used to predict Y

e_i = the error for the prediction

In applying regression analysis, we examine the relationship between the independent variable X and the dependent variable Y. To do so, we use the known values of X and Y and the computed values of a and b. The calculations are based on the least squares procedure. The *least squares procedure* determines the best-fitting line by minimizing the vertical distances of all the points from the line, as shown in Exhibit 16.11. The best-fitting line is the regression line. Any point that does not fall on the line is unexplained variance. This unexplained variance is called error and is represented by the vertical distance between the regression straight line and the points not on the line. The distances of all the points not on the line are squared and added together to determine the sum of the squared errors, which is a measure of the total error in the regression.

After we compute the values of a and b, we must test their statistical significance. The calculated a (intercept) and b (slope) are sample estimates of the true population parameters α (alpha) and β (beta). The t-test is used to determine whether the computed intercept and slope are significantly different from zero. In the SPSS regression examples discussed later, the significance of these tests is reported in the Sig. column for each of these coefficients. The a is referred to as a "Constant" and the b is associated with each independent variable.

In the case of bivariate regression analysis, we are looking at one independent variable and one dependent variable. Managers frequently want to look at the combined influence of several independent variables on one dependent variable. For example, are DVD purchases related only to age, or are they also related to income, ethnicity, gender, geographic

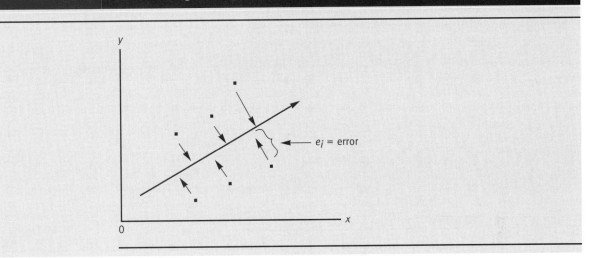

EXHIBIT 16.11   Fitting the Regression Line Using the "Least Squares" Procedure

location, education level, and so on? Similarly, referring to the Santa Fe Grill database, we might ask whether customer satisfaction is related only to perceptions of the restaurant's food taste (X18), or is satisfaction also related to perceptions of friendly employees (X12), reasonable prices (X16), and speed of service (X21)? Multiple regression is the appropriate technique to measure these relationships and is a straightforward extension of bivariate regression. We will go through the mechanics of conducting a bivariate or simple regression analysis before turning to a discussion of multiple regression analysis.

Developing and Estimating the Regression Coefficients

Remember that the regression equation examining the relationship between two variables is derived from the equation for a straight line. The slope coefficient b tells us how much we can expect Y to change, given a 1-unit change in X. Once this equation is developed from sample data, we can use it to make predictions about Y, given different values of X.

At this point, you might be thinking, "Okay, so we use a straight line to describe the relationship between Y and X, but which one? Is it the best line, or the first line the computer program estimates?" It turns out there is a procedure called *ordinary least squares (OLS)* which guarantees that the line it estimates to describe the data is the best one. We said earlier that the best prediction would be one in which the difference between the actual value of Y and the predicted value of Y was the smallest. **Ordinary least squares** is a statistical procedure that results in equation parameters (a and b) that produce predictions with the lowest sum of squared differences between actual and predicted values.

Ordinary least squares A statistical procedure that estimates regression equation coefficients which produce the lowest sum of squared differences between the actual and predicted values of the dependent variable.

Error in Regression

The differences between actual and predicted values of Y are represented by e_i (the error term of the regression equation). If we square these errors for each observation (the difference between actual values of Y and predicted values of Y) and add them up, the total would represent an aggregate or overall measure of the accuracy of the regression equation.

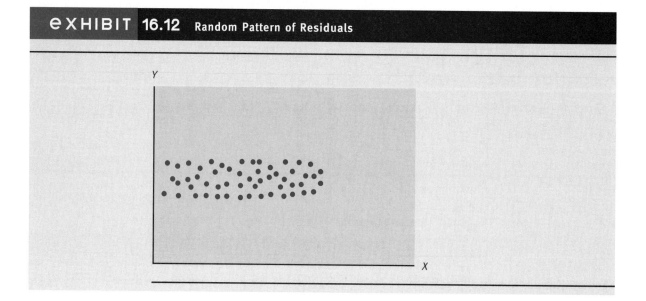

Regression equations calculated through the use of ordinary least squares procedures will always give the lowest squared error totals, and this is why both bivariate and multiple regression analysis are sometimes referred to as *OLS regression*.

Besides allowing the researcher to evaluate the quality of the prediction produced by a regression equation, the error terms also can be used to diagnose potential problems caused by data observations that do not meet the assumptions described above. The pattern of errors produced by comparing actual Y values with predicted Y values can tell you whether the errors are normally distributed and/or have equal variances across the range of X values. Exhibits 16.12, 16.13, and 16.14 show several possible patterns of *residuals* (another term for the error between actual and predicted Y values).

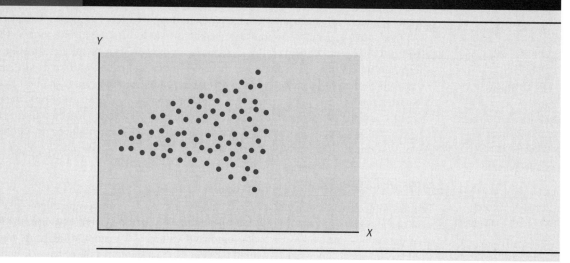

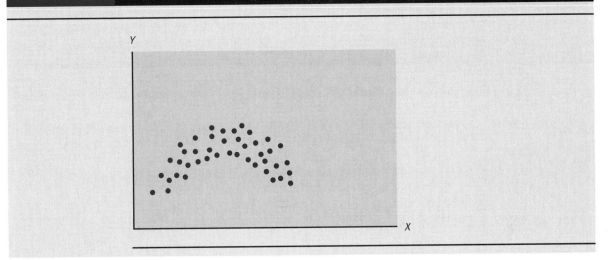

EXHIBIT 16.14 Nonlinear Pattern of Residuals

In Exhibit 16.12, there is no discernible pattern to the error terms when you plot the predicted values against the residuals. In Exhibit 16.13, there is an apparent pattern; the predictions made for small values of Y are more precise than the predictions made for large values of Y. Obviously, our regression equation is more accurate for some values of the independent variable X than for others. There are transformation techniques that can be applied to the data to potentially help this problem.[1]

Exhibit 16.14 portrays a pattern to the error terms that suggests a nonlinear relationship between Y and X. In this case, the researcher's initial assumption that a straight line would be the best way to describe the potential relationship may need to be changed. The best approach may be a nonlinear relationship-based technique.

Examination of the error terms and the pattern obtained by comparing the predicted values of Y against the residuals can tell us whether our initial assumptions about the appropriateness of using regression analysis to examine variable relationships are correct. In addition, this type of evidence can sometimes suggest the next type of analysis to undertake, given the characteristics of the data we have collected. We illustrate the use and value of regression coefficients and residuals in a Santa Fe Grill SPSS multiple regression application later in this chapter.

SPSS Application—Bivariate Regression

An example at this point will help illustrate the procedures for completing a bivariate regression analysis. Suppose the owners of the Santa Fe Grill want to know if more favorable perceptions of their prices are associated with higher customer satisfaction. The obvious answer would be "of course it would." But how much improvement would be expected in customer satisfaction if the owners improved the perceptions of prices? Bivariate regression analysis can provide information to help answer this question.

In the Santa Fe Grill database X22 is a measure of customer satisfaction level, with 1 = Not Satisfied at All and 7 = Highly Satisfied. Variable X16 is a measure of respondents' perceptions of the reasonableness of the restaurant's prices (1 = Strongly Disagree, 7 = Strongly Agree). The null hypothesis in this case is there is no relationship between

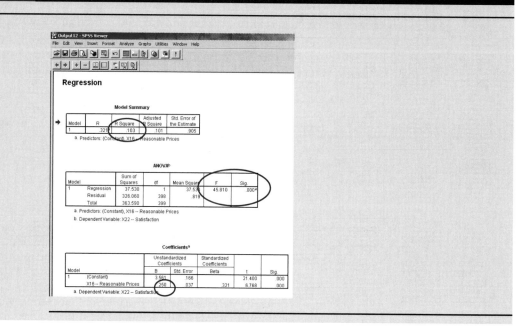

ⓔXHIBIT 16.15 SPSS Results for Bivariate Regression

X22—Satisfaction and X16—Reasonable Prices. The alternative hypothesis is that X22 and X16 are significantly related.

The formulas to calculate the regression equation components are provided in Appendix 16.A. We will use the SPSS program to perform these calculations.

The SPSS click-through sequence is ANALYZE → REGRESSION → LINEAR. Click on X22—Satisfaction and move it to the Dependent Variable box. Click on X16—Reasonable Prices and move it to the Independent Variables box. We will use the defaults for the other options so click OK to run the bivariate regression.

Exhibit 16.15 contains the results of the bivariate regression analysis. The table labeled Model Summary has three types of "Rs" in it. The R on the far left is the correlation coefficient (.321). The R-square is .103; you get it by squaring the correlation coefficient (.321) for this regression. The third R—**Adjusted R-Square**—reduces the R^2 by taking into account the sample size and the number of independent variables in the regression equation. It tells you when the multiple regression equation has too many independent variables. As you recall from our earlier discussion, R-square figures show the percentage of variation in one variable that is accounted for by another variable. In this case, customer perceptions of the Santa Fe Grill's prices accounts for 10.3 percent of the total variation in customer satisfaction with the restaurant.

The final number in the table—Std. Error of the Estimate—is a measure of the accuracy of the predictions of the regression equation. The smaller the standard error of the estimate, the better the fit of the regression line and therefore the better the predictive power of the regression.

The ANOVA table, as displayed in Exhibit 16.15, shows the *F* ratio for the regression model that indicates the statistical significance of the overall regression model. The *F* ratio is calculated the same way for regression analysis as it was for the ANOVA techniques described in Chapter 15. The variance in X22—Customer Satisfaction that is associated

Adjusted R-square
This adjustment reduces the R^2 by taking into account the sample size and the number of independent variables in the regression equation. It tells you when the multiple regression equation has too many independent variables.

Explained variance Is the amount of variation in the dependent construct that can be accounted for by the combination of independent variables.

Unexplained variance Is the amount of variation in the dependent construct that cannot be accounted for by the combination of independent variables.

Regression coefficient An indicator of the importance of an independent variable in predicting a dependent variable. Large coefficients are good predictors and small coefficients are weak predictors.

with X16—Reasonable Prices is referred to as **explained variance.** The remainder of the total variance in X22 that is not associated with X16 is referred to as **unexplained variance.** The F ratio is the result of comparing the amount of explained variance to the unexplained variance. The larger the F ratio the more variance in the dependent variable that is associated with the independent variable. In our example, the F ratio = 45.810. The statistical significance is .000—the "Sig." value on the SPSS output—so we can reject the null hypothesis that no relationship exists between the two variables.

The Coefficients table (See Exhibit 16.15) shows the regression coefficient for X16. The **regression coefficient** is an indicator of the importance of an independent variable in predicting a dependent variable. Large coefficients are good predictors and small coefficients are weak predictors. In bivariate regression, the regression coefficient is considered "unstandardized." The column labeled Unstandardized Coefficients indicates the unstandardized regression coefficient for X16 is .250. The column labeled Sig. shows the statistical significance of the regression coefficient for X16, as measured by the t-test. The t-test examines the question of whether the regression coefficient is different enough from zero to be statistically significant. The t statistic is calculated by dividing the regression coefficient by its standard error (labeled Std. Error in the Coefficients table of Exhibit 16.15). If you divide .250 by .037, you will get a t value of 6.768, which is significant at the .000 level.

The Coefficients table also shows the result for the Constant component in the regression equation. This item is a term in the equation for a straight line we discussed earlier. If the independent variable takes on a value of 0, the dependent measure (X22) would have a value of 3.561. Combining the results of the Coefficients table into a regression equation, we have

Predicted value of X22 = 3.561 + .250 (value of X16) + .905 (avg. error in prediction)

The relationship between customer satisfaction and reasonable prices is positive and moderately strong. The regression coefficient for X16 is interpreted as "For every unit that X16 increases, X22 will increase by .250 units." Recall that the Santa Fe Grill owners asked: "If the prices in our restaurant are perceived as being reasonable, will this be associated with improved customer satisfaction?" The answer is yes, somewhat, because the model was significant at the .000 level and the R-square was .103. How closely are they related? For every unit increase in X16, X22 goes up .250 units.

One additional note must be mentioned. The Coefficients table contained a column labeled Standardized Beta Coefficients. This number is not meaningful in a bivariate regression. However, when multiple independent variables are used, the scales used to measure each one may not always be the same (e.g., using years of age and annual income to predict frequency of dining out). Standardization is a method of removing the units of measure from each variable and placing all the predictors on the same scale. The term "Beta" is another way to refer to the regression coefficient.

Significance

Once the statistical significance of the regression coefficients is determined, we have answered the first question about our relationship: "Is there a relationship between our dependent and independent variable?" In this case, the answer is yes. The second question we wanted to ask was: "How strong is that relationship?" The output of the regression analysis includes the coefficient of determination, or r^2. As we noted earlier, the coefficient of determination describes the amount of variation in the dependent variable associated with the variation in the independent variable. Another way of thinking about it is that the regression r^2 tells you what percentage of the total variation in your dependent variable you can explain by using the independent variable. The r^2 measure varies between .00 and 1.00, and is calculated by dividing the amount of variation you have been able to explain with your regression equation (found by summing the squared differences between your predicted value and the mean of the dependent variable) by the total variation in the dependent variable. In the previous Santa Fe Grill example that examined the relationship between reasonable prices and satisfaction, the r^2 was .107. That means approximately 10.7 percent of the variation in customer satisfaction is associated with the variation in reasonable prices. Remember, we cannot say that reasonable prices cause changes in satisfaction, only that changes in perceived prices tend to be reliably associated with changes in satisfaction.

When examining the substantive significance of a regression equation, you should look at the size of the r^2 obtained for the regression equation and the strength of the regression coefficient. The regression coefficient may be statistically significant, but still relatively small, meaning that your dependent measure won't change very much for a given unit change in the independent measure. In our Santa Fe Grill example, the unstandardized regression coefficient was .254, which is not a very strong relationship. When regression coefficients are significant but small, we say a relationship is present in our population, but that it is weak. In this case, Santa Fe Grill owners need to consider additional independent variables that will help them to better understand and predict customer satisfaction. We tell you how to do that in the next section.

Multiple Regression Analysis

Multiple regression analysis A statistical technique which analyzes the linear relationship between a dependent variable and multiple independent variables by estimating coefficients for the equation for a straight line.

In most practical problems faced by managers, there are several independent variables that need to be examined for their influence on a dependent variable of interest. **Multiple regression analysis** is the appropriate technique to use for these situations. The technique is a straightforward extension of the bivariate regression analysis we just discussed. Multiple independent variables are entered into the same type of regression equation, and for each variable a separate regression coefficient is calculated that describes its relationship with the dependent variable. These coefficients allow the marketing researcher to examine the relative influence of each independent variable on the dependent variable. For example, Santa Fe Grill owners want to examine not only reasonable prices, but also perceptions of employees, atmosphere, service, and so forth. This gives them a more accurate picture of what to focus on in developing marketing strategies to compete more effectively.

The relationship that exists between each independent variable and the dependent measure is still linear. Now, however, with the addition of multiple independent variables we have to think of multiple independent dimensions instead of just a single one. The easiest way to analyze the relationships is to examine the regression coefficients for each independent variable. These coefficients still describe the average amount of change to be expected in Y given a unit change in the value of the particular independent variable you are examining. Moreover, each particular regression coefficient describes the relationship of that independent variable to the dependent variable. For example, assume the dependent variable in a multiple regression is number of cups of Starbucks coffee consumed on a typical day by students during finals. The two independent variables are number of hours studied and number of exams on a particular day. We would expect the regression coefficients for both of these independent variables to be rather large because both are logically related to the number of cups of coffee consumed, assuming the student drinks coffee.

With the addition of more than one independent variable, we have a couple of new issues to consider. One concern is the possibility that each independent variable may be measured using a different scale. For example, let's assume a group of students was asked by the local Canon copier distributor to predict the distributor's annual sales revenue. To predict the dependent variable, sales revenue, we could use size of sales force (X1), amount of advertising budget (X2), and consumer attitude toward the distributor's products (X3). Each of these independent variables is likely to be measured using a different scale, that is, different units. The size of the sales force would be measured by the number of salespeople, the amount of the advertising budget would be in dollars, and the consumer attitude might be measured on a five-point scale from "Very poor" to "Excellent." When multiple independent variables are measured with different scales, it is not possible to make relative comparisons between regression coefficients to see which independent variable has the most influence on the dependent variable.

To solve this problem, we calculate the *standardized regression coefficient.* It is called a **beta coefficient,** and it is calculated from the normal regression coefficient. The regression coefficient is recalculated to have a mean of 0 and a standard deviation of 1. Standardization removes the effects of using different scales of measurement. Beta coefficients will range from .00 to 1.00. Use of the beta coefficient allows direct comparisons between independent variables to determine which variables have the most influence on the dependent measure.

Statistical Significance

After the regression coefficients have been estimated, you still must examine the statistical significance of each coefficient. This is done in the same manner as the bivariate regression case. Each regression coefficient will be divided by its standard error to produce a t statistic, which is compared against the critical value to determine whether the null hypothesis can be rejected. The basic question we are trying to answer is still the same: "What is the probability that we would get a coefficient of this size in our sample if the real regression coefficient in the population were zero?" You should examine the t-test statistics for each regression coefficient. Many times not all the independent variables in a regression equation will be statistically significant. Practically speaking, if a regression coefficient is not statistically significant, that means the independent variable does not have a relationship with the dependent variable and the slope describing that relationship is relatively flat (i.e., the value of the dependent variable does not change at all as the value of the statistically insignificant independent variable changes).

When using multiple regression analysis, it is important to examine the overall statistical significance of the regression model. The amount of variation in the dependent variable that you have been able to explain with the independent measures is compared with the total variation in the dependent measure. This comparison results in a statistic called a **model F statistic.** This measure is compared against a critical value to determine whether or not to reject the null hypothesis. If the F statistic is statistically significant, it means that the chances of the regression model for your sample producing a large r^2 when the population r^2 is actually 0 are acceptably small.

Substantive Significance

Once we have estimated the regression equation describing the relationships between our independent variables and the dependent variable, we need to assess the strength of the association that exists. From an overall perspective, the multiple r^2 or multiple coefficient of determination describes the strength of the relationship between all the independent variables in our equation and the dependent variable. If you recall our discussion of r^2 from the

Beta coefficient An estimated regression coefficient that has been recalculated to have a mean of 0 and a standard deviation of 1. Such a change enables independent variables with different units of measurement to be directly compared on their association with the dependent variable.

Model F statistic A statistic that compares the amount of variation in the dependent measure "explained" or associated with the independent variables to the "unexplained" or error variance. A larger F statistic indicates that the regression model has more explained variance than error variance.

section on correlation analysis, the coefficient of determination is a measure of the amount of variation in the dependent variable associated with the variation in the independent variable. In the case of multiple regression analysis, the r^2 measure shows the amount of variation in the dependent variable associated with (or explained by) all of the independent variables considered together.

The larger the r^2 measure, the more of the behavior of the dependent measure is associated with the independent measures we are using to predict it. For example, if the multiple r^2 in our Canon copier example above were .78, that would mean that we can account for, or explain, 78 percent of the variation in sales revenue by using the variation in sales force size, advertising budget, and customer attitudes toward our copier products. Higher values for r^2 mean stronger relationships between the group of independent variables and the dependent measure. As before, the measure of the strength of the relationship between an individual independent variable and the dependent measure of interest is shown by the regression coefficient or the beta coefficient for that variable.

To summarize, the elements of a multiple regression model to examine in determining its significance include the r^2; the model F statistic; the individual regression coefficients for each independent variable; their associated t statistics; and the individual beta coefficients. The appropriate procedure to follow in evaluating the results of a regression analysis is as follows: (1) assess the statistical significance of the overall regression model using the F statistic and its associated probability; (2) evaluate the obtained r^2 to see how large it is; (3) examine the individual regression coefficients and their t statistics to see which are statistically significant; and (4) look at the beta coefficients to assess relative influence. Taken together, these elements should give you a comprehensive picture of the answers to our basic three questions about the relationships between your dependent and independent variables.

SPSS Application—Multiple Regression

Regression can be used by the marketing researcher to examine the relationship between a single metric dependent variable and one or more metric independent variables. If you examine the Santa Fe Grill database you will note that the first 21 variables are metric independent variables. They are lifestyle variables and perceptions of the restaurant, measured using a 7-point Likert-type rating scale with 7 representing the positive dimension and 1 the negative dimension. Variables X22, X23, and X24 are metric dependent variables measured on a seven-point Likert-type rating scale. Variable X25—Frequency of Patronage, X30—Distance Driven, X31—Ad Recall, and X32—Gender are nonmetric. Variables X26 to X29 also are nonmetric variables because they are ranking data, and cannot therefore be used in regression.

A simple problem to examine with multiple regression would be to see if perceptions of the food in the restaurant are related to satisfaction. In this case, the single metric dependent variable is X22—Satisfaction, and the independent variables would be X15—Fresh Food, X18—Food Taste, and X20—Food Temperature. The null hypothesis would be that there is no relationship between the three food variables and X22. The alternative hypothesis would be that X15, X18, and X20 are significantly related to X22—Customer Satisfaction.

The SPSS click-through sequence to examine this relationship is ANALYZE → REGRESSION → LINEAR. Highlight X22 and move it to the Dependent Variables box. Highlight X15, X18, and X20 and move them to the Independent Variables box. We will use the defaults for the other options so click OK to run the multiple regression.

The SPSS output for the multiple regression is shown in Exhibit 16.16. The Model Summary table shows R-square for this model is .381. This means that 38.1 percent of the

eXHIBIT 16.16 SPSS Multiple Regression Example

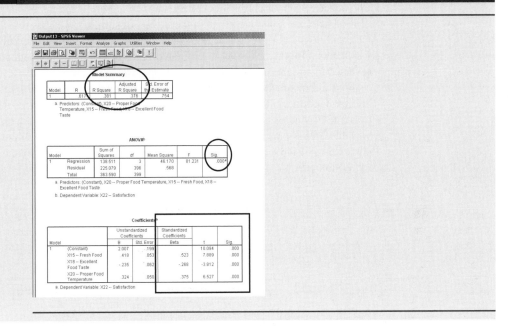

variation in satisfaction (dependent variable) can be explained from the three independent variables. The table also shows the adjusted R-square for the model as .376. Any time another independent variable is added to a multiple regression model, the R-square will increase (even if only slightly). Consequently, it becomes difficult to determine which models do the best job of explaining variation in the same dependent variable. The adjusted R-square does just what its name implies. It adjusts the R-square by the number of predictor variables in the model. This adjustment allows the easy comparison of the explanatory power of models with different numbers of predictor variables. It also helps us decide how many variables to include in our regression model.

The regression model results in the ANOVA table show that the overall model is significantly different from 0 (F ratio = 81.231; probability level ("Sig.") = .000). This probability level means there are .000 chances the regression model results come from a population where the R-square actually is .00. That is, there are zero chances out of 1,000 that the correlation coefficient is .00.

To determine if one or more of the food independent variables are significant predictors of satisfaction we examine the information provided in the Coefficients table. Looking at the Standardized Coefficients Beta column reveals that X15—Fresh Food has a beta coefficient of .523 which is significant (.000). Similarly, X18—Food Taste and X20—Food Temperature have beta coefficients of −0.268 and 0.375, respectively (Sig. level of .000). This means we can reject the null hypothesis that the three food variables are not related to X22—Customer Satisfaction. Thus, this regression analysis tells us that customer perceptions of food in the Santa Fe Grill are a good predictor of the level of satisfaction with the restaurant.

A word of caution is needed at this point regarding the beta coefficients. Recall that the size of the individual coefficients show how strongly each independent variable is related to the dependent variable. The signs (negative or positive) also are important. A positive sign indicates a positive relationship (higher independent variable values are associated with higher dependent variable values). A negative sign indicates a negative relationship. The negative sign of X18—Food Taste suggests, therefore, that less favorable perceptions of food taste are associated with higher levels of satisfaction. This result is clearly not logical, and points out one of the weaknesses of multiple regression. When the independent variables are highly correlated with each other the signs of the beta coefficients may be reversed in a regression model, which happened in this case.

For this reason, the analyst must always examine the logic of the signs for the regression betas when independent variables are highly correlated. If an expected relationship is the opposite of what is anticipated, one must look at a simple bivariate correlation of the two variables. This can be seen in the table below, which clearly shows the true positive correlation of .409. So always be careful in using the beta coefficient signs to interpret regression results.

Correlations		
		X22—Satisfaction
X18—Food Taste	Pearson Correlation	.409*
	Sig. (2-tailed)	.000
	N	400

*Correlation is significant at the 0.01 level (2-tailed).

Examination of the SPSS tables reveals that there is a lot of information provided that we did not discuss. Statistical researchers may use this information, but managers typically do not. One of the challenges for you will be to learn which information to use and which to discard. This becomes more difficult as you use additional kinds of analysis.

At this point we recommend you start simply and learn from there. For example, the next problem you examine may be to change the dependent variable from X22—Satisfaction to X23—Likely to Return, and run the same regression with the food variable independents. Another possibility is to keep X22—Satisfaction as the dependent and use either the lifestyle variables or the other restaurant perceptions as independent variables. By doing this you will learn how to use the SPSS package and also see if any relationships exist between the variables. Have fun!

The Use of Dummy Variables in Multiple Regression

Dummy variables Artificial variables introduced into a regression equation to represent the categories of a nominally scaled variable.

Sometimes the particular independent variables you may want to use to predict a dependent variable are not measured using interval or ratio scales (a basic assumption for the use of regression analysis). It is still possible to include such variables through the use of **dummy variables.** For example, if you wanted to include the gender of customers of the Santa Fe Grill restaurant to help explain their satisfaction with the restaurant, it is obvious your measure for gender would include only two possible values—male or female.

The use of dummy variables involves choosing one category of the variable to serve as a reference category and then adding as many dummy variables as there are possible values of the variable, minus that reference category. The categories are coded as either

0 or 1. In the example above, if you choose the male category as the reference category, you would have one dummy variable for the female category. That dummy variable would be assigned the value of 1 for females and 0 for males. In the Santa Fe Grill database, X32—Gender is already coded as a dummy variable for gender, with males as the reference category.

SPSS Application—Use of Dummy Variables in Regression

To see how multiple regression works with dummy variables, let's use the Santa Fe Grill database responses to investigate the question of whether the satisfaction of customers is related to X15—Fresh Food and X16—Reasonable Prices, and whether this relationship is different for X32, male and female customers. The null hypothesis would be that X22—Customer Satisfaction is not related to X15, X16, or X32.

The SPSS click-through sequence is ANALYZE → REGRESSION → LINEAR. Click on X22—Satisfaction and move it to the Dependent Variables box. Click on X15—Fresh Food, X16—Reasonable Prices, and X32—Gender and move them to the Independent Variables box. Now click OK to run the multiple regression.

The SPSS results are shown in Exhibit 16.17. In the Model Summary table, you can see the R^2 for the model is .392. Thus, approximately 39.2 percent of the total variation in X22 is associated with X15—Fresh Food, X16—Reasonable Prices, and X32—Gender. The ANOVA table indicates the regression model is significant—the "Sig." value indicates a probability level of .000.

The Coefficients table shows that X15—Fresh Food is a significant predictor of satisfaction, with a beta coefficient of .525 (note that in this regression model the beta coefficient for fresh food is positive, indicating that in this case multicollinearity among the independent variables is not a problem). Reasonable prices (X16), with a beta of .193, also is significantly related to customer satisfaction (i.e., probability level of .000). Now, the question of interest is "Does the satisfaction level of Santa Fe Grill customers differ depending on whether they are male or female?" According to the results in the Coefficients table, the beta coefficient of −.156 for X32—Gender is significant (i.e., Sig. level of .000). This means the female and male customers exhibit significantly different levels of satisfaction with the Santa Fe Grill. The negative beta coefficient means that lower numbers for gender are associated with higher values for satisfaction. Since males were coded 0 in our database this means males are more satisfied with the Santa Fe Grill than females.

It is also possible to use categorical independent variables with more than just two categories. Let's say you wanted to use consumers' purchase behavior of Starbucks coffee to help predict their purchase behavior for Maxwell House, and you had separated your sample into nonusers, light users, and heavy users. To use dummy variables in your regression model, you would pick one category as a reference group (nonusers) and add two dummy variables for the remaining categories. The variables would be coded as follows, using 0 and 1:

Category	D_1	D_2
Nonuser	0	0
Light user	1	0
Heavy user	0	1

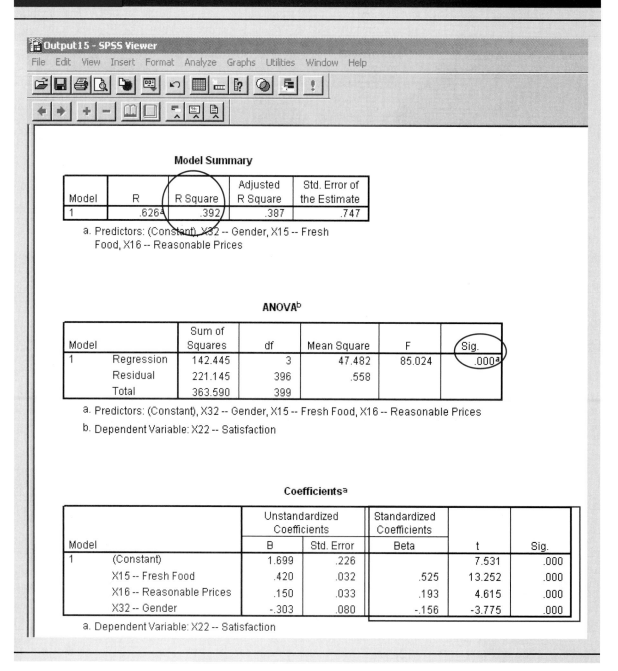

e X H I B I T 16.17 SPSS Multiple Regression with a Dummy Variable

Model Summary

Model	R	R Square	Adjusted R Square	Std. Error of the Estimate
1	.626ᵃ	.392	.387	.747

a. Predictors: (Constant), X32 -- Gender, X15 -- Fresh Food, X16 -- Reasonable Prices

ANOVAᵇ

Model		Sum of Squares	df	Mean Square	F	Sig.
1	Regression	142.445	3	47.482	85.024	.000ᵃ
	Residual	221.145	396	.558		
	Total	363.590	399			

a. Predictors: (Constant), X32 -- Gender, X15 -- Fresh Food, X16 -- Reasonable Prices

b. Dependent Variable: X22 -- Satisfaction

Coefficientsᵃ

Model		Unstandardized Coefficients		Standardized Coefficients	t	Sig.
		B	Std. Error	Beta		
1	(Constant)	1.699	.226		7.531	.000
	X15 -- Fresh Food	.420	.032	.525	13.252	.000
	X16 -- Reasonable Prices	.150	.033	.193	4.615	.000
	X32 -- Gender	-.303	.080	-.156	-3.775	.000

a. Dependent Variable: X22 -- Satisfaction

The use of dummy variables in regression models allows different types of independent variables to be included in prediction efforts. The researcher must keep in mind the difference in the interpretation of the regression coefficient and the identity of the reference category that is represented by the intercept term.

Multicollinearity and Multiple Regression Analysis

Multicollinearity A situation in which several independent variables are highly correlated with each other. This characteristic can result in difficulty in estimating separate or independent regression coefficients for the correlated variables.

One common problem area for marketing researchers involves the situation in which the independent variables are highly correlated among themselves. This characteristic of the data presents a problem and is referred to as **multicollinearity.** The general definition of the regression coefficient that describes the relationship between one independent variable and the dependent variable of interest is that it signifies the average amount of change in the dependent variable associated with a unit change in the independent variable, assuming all other independent variables in the equation remain the same. If several independent variables are highly correlated (say, for example, the education level and annual income of a respondent), then clearly income level is not going to remain the same as the education level of a respondent changes.

The effect of high levels of multicollinearity is to make it difficult or impossible for the regression equation to separate out the independent contributions of the independent or predictor variables. The practical impact of multicollinearity relates to the statistical significance of the individual regression coefficients, as well as their signs (negative or positive). Multicollinearity inflates the standard error of the coefficient and lowers the t statistic associated with it (recall that the regression coefficient is subtracted from the null hypothesis coefficient and divided by its standard error to calculate the t statistic). Therefore, it may be possible, if the multicollinearity is severe enough, for your regression model to have a significant F statistic, a reasonably large r^2, and still have no regression coefficients that are statistically significant from zero.

Multicollinearity problems do not have an impact on the size of the r^2 or your ability to predict values of the dependent variable. As noted above, one impact is on the statistical significance of the individual regression coefficients. But another is multicollinearity may reverse the signs of the individual coefficients on the SPSS output. When results look suspicious, always check the signs using a bivariate correlation procedure.

SPSS Application—Multicollinearity

The SPSS output from the Santa Fe Grill example described earlier provides some results to help you determine whether multicollinearity is a potential problem in the data. Recall that the click-through sequence is ANALYZE → REGRESSION → LINEAR. Highlight X22 and move it to the Dependent Variable box. Highlight X15 and X16 and move them to the Independent Variable box. In the Methods box we will keep Enter, which is the default. Similarly, click on the Statistics button and keep Estimates in the Regression Coefficients box Model Fit as defaults (already checked). Now click Collinearity Diagnostics and then Continue.

The results are shown in Exhibit 16.18. First, the R^2 for this regression model is .37 and it is significant at the .000 level. To assess multicollinearity, look at the columns labeled Tolerance and VIF under the heading Collinearity Statistics on the right side of the Coefficients table. These are both measures of collinearity among the variables (VIF stands for *variance inflation factor*). They tell us the degree to which each independent variable is explained by the other independent variables.

To assess multicollinearity we look at the sizes of the Tolerance and VIF. For the tolerance small values indicate the absence of collinearity. The VIF is the inverse of tolerance, so we look for large values. If the tolerance value is smaller than .10, we conclude that multicollinearity is a problem. Similarly, if the VIF is 5 or larger, then multicollinearity is a problem. In the Santa Fe Grill output, the tolerance between X15 and X16 is .978 and the VIF is 1.022. Since the tolerance value is substantially above .10 and the VIF is much

eXHIBIT 16.18 SPSS Results for Multicollinearity

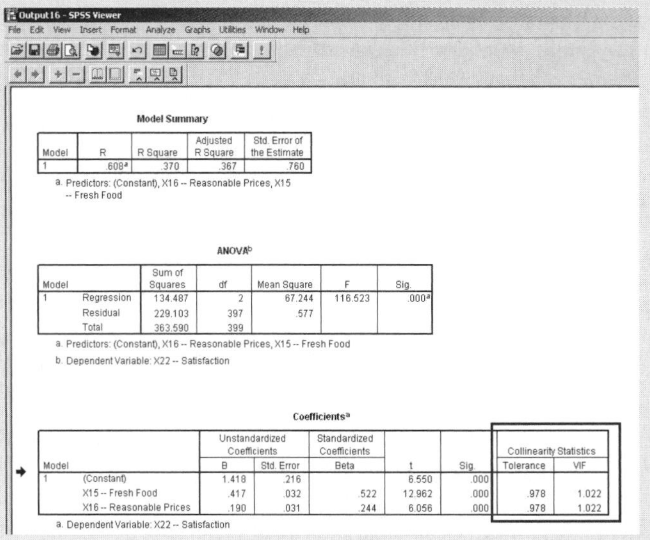

Output16 - SPSS Viewer

File Edit View Insert Format Analyze Graphs Utilities Window Help

Model Summary

Model	R	R Square	Adjusted R Square	Std. Error of the Estimate
1	.608[a]	.370	.367	.760

a. Predictors: (Constant), X16 -- Reasonable Prices, X15 -- Fresh Food

ANOVA[b]

Model		Sum of Squares	df	Mean Square	F	Sig.
1	Regression	134.487	2	67.244	116.523	.000[a]
	Residual	229.103	397	.577		
	Total	363.590	399			

a. Predictors: (Constant), X16 -- Reasonable Prices, X15 -- Fresh Food

b. Dependent Variable: X22 -- Satisfaction

Coefficients[a]

Model		Unstandardized Coefficients		Standardized Coefficients	t	Sig.	Collinearity Statistics	
		B	Std. Error	Beta			Tolerance	VIF
1	(Constant)	1.418	.216		6.550	.000		
	X15 -- Fresh Food	.417	.032	.522	12.962	.000	.978	1.022
	X16 -- Reasonable Prices	.190	.031	.244	6.056	.000	.978	1.022

a. Dependent Variable: X22 -- Satisfaction

smaller than 5, we conclude that multicollinearity among the independent variables is not a problem.

To avoid the problem of multicollinearity in regression, you should examine the correlations between the independent variables ahead of time. If they are too high (> .70), then you should remove one of the highly correlated variables. Another approach to deal with multicollinearity is to submit the variables to a factor analysis. We discuss how to do this in Chapter 17.

marketing Research in action

Customer Satisfaction for a Manufacturing Operation

Employee Perspectives

The plant manager of QualKote Manufacturing is interested in the impact his year-long effort to implement a quality improvement program is having on the satisfaction of his customers. The plant foreman, assembly-line workers, and engineering staff have closely examined their operations to determine which activities have the most impact on product quality and reliability. Together, the managers and employees have worked to better understand how each particular job affects the final delivered quality of the product as the customer perceives it.

To answer his questions about customer satisfaction, the plant manager conducted an internal survey of plant workers and managers using a 7-point Likert scale (endpoints— 1 = Strongly Disagree and 7 = Strongly Agree). His plans are to get opinions from within the company first and then do a customer survey on similar topics. He has collected completed surveys from 57 employees. The following are examples of the topics that were covered in the questionnaire:

- Data from a variety of external sources (customers, competitors, suppliers, etc.) are used in the strategic planning process. Independent variable A10.

- Customers are involved in the product quality planning process. Independent variable A12.

- Customer requirements and expectations of the company's products are used in developing strategic plans and goals. Independent variable A17.

- There is a systematic process to translate customer requirements into new/improved products. Independent variable A23.

- There is a systematic process to accurately determine customers' requirements and expectations. Independent variable A31.

- The company's product quality program has improved the level of customer satisfaction. Dependent variable A36.

- The company's product quality program has improved the likelihood that customers will recommend us. Dependent variable A37.

- Gender of the employee responding: Male = 1; Female = 0. Classification variable A40.

A multiple regression was run using SPSS with responses of the 57 employees as input to the model. The output is shown in Exhibits 16.19 and 16.20. There is an actual database of QualKote employee responses to these questions available in SPSS format at www.mhhe.com/hair06. The database is labeled C_16_Qualkote MRIA.3e.sav.

The results indicate there is a statistically significant relationship between the metric dependent variable (A36—Satisfaction) and the metric independent variables. The R^2 for the relationship is 67.0. This suggests there are favorable perceptions by employees about the implementation of the quality improvement program.

e X H I B I T 16.19 Descriptive Statistics and Correlations for Variables

e X H I B I T 16.20 Multiple Regression of Satisfaction Variables

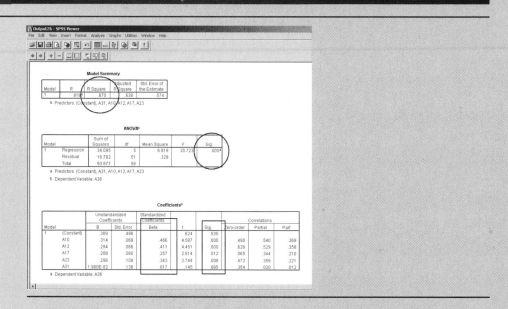

Hands-On Exercises

1. Will the results of this regression model be useful to the QualKote plant manager? If yes, how?

2. Which independent variables are helpful in predicting A36—Customer Satisfaction?

3. What other regression models might be examined with the questions from this survey?

Summary of Learning Objectives

■ **Understand and evaluate the types of relationships between variables.**

Relationships between variables can be described in several ways, including presence, direction, strength of association, and type. Presence tells us whether a consistent and systematic relationship exists. Direction tells us whether the relationship is positive or negative. Strength of association tells us whether we have a weak or strong relationship, and the type of relationship is usually described as either linear or nonlinear.

Two variables may share a linear relationship, in which changes in one variable are accompanied by some change (not necessarily the same amount of change) in the other variable. As long as the amount of change stays constant over the range of both variables, the relationship is termed linear. Relationships between two variables that change in strength and/or direction as the values of the variables change are referred to as curvilinear.

■ **Explain the concepts of association and covariation.**

The terms covariation and association refer to the attempt to quantify the strength of the relationship between two variables. Covariation is the amount of change in one variable of interest that is consistently related to change in another variable under study. The degree of association is a numerical measure of the strength of the relationship between two variables. Both these terms refer to linear relationships.

■ **Discuss the differences in chi-square, Pearson correlation, and Spearman correlation.**

The chi-square statistic permits us to test for significance between the frequency distributions of two or more groups. Categorical data from questions about gender, race, profession, and so forth, can be examined and tested for statistical differences. Pearson correlation coefficients are a measure of linear association between two variables of interest. The Pearson correlation coefficient is used when both variables are measured on an interval or ratio scale. When one or more variables of interest are measured on an ordinal scale, the Spearman rank order correlation coefficient should be used.

■ **Explain the concept of statistical significance versus practical significance.**

Because some of the procedures involved in determining the statistical significance of a statistical test include consideration of the sample size, it is possible to have a very low degree of association between two variables show up as statistically significant (i.e., the population parameter is not equal to zero). However, by considering the absolute strength of the relationship in addition to its statistical significance, the researcher is better able to draw the appropriate conclusion about the data and the population from which they were selected.

■ **Understand when and how to use regression analysis.**

Regression analysis is useful in answering questions about the strength of a linear relationship between a dependent variable and one or more independent variables. The results of a regression analysis indicate the amount of change in the dependent variable that is associated with a one-unit change in the independent variables. In addition, the accuracy of the regression equation can be evaluated by comparing the predicted values of the dependent variable to the actual values of the dependent variable drawn from the sample.

Key Terms and Concepts

Adjusted R-square 564

Beta coefficient 567

Bivariate regression analysis 559

Chi-square (X^2) analysis 550

Coefficient of determination (r^2) 556

Covariation 547

Curvilinear relationship 546

Dummy variables 570

Explained variance 565

Linear relationship 546

Model *F* statistic 567

Multicollinearity 573

Multiple regression analysis 566

Ordinary least squares 561

Pearson correlation coefficient 553

Regression coefficient 565

Relationship 546

Scatter diagram 547

Spearman rank order correlation coefficient 556

Unexplained variance 565

Review Questions

1. Explain the difference between testing for significant differences and testing for association.

2. Explain the difference between association and causation.

3. What is covariation? How does it differ from correlation?

4. Which statistical tests should be used with nominal and ordinal data? Which can be used with interval and ratio data?

5. What are the differences between univariate, bivariate, and multivariate statistical techniques?

6. What is regression analysis? When would you use it? What is the difference between simple regression and multiple regression?

7. How do we use beta coefficients in multiple regression analysis?

8. What is the value of dummy variables in multiple regression analysis?

Discussion Questions

1. Regression and correlation analysis both describe the strength of linear relationships between variables. Consider the concepts of education and income. Many people would say these two variables are related in a linear fashion. As education increases, income usually increases (although not necessarily at the same rate). Can you think of two variables that are related in such a way that their relationship changes over their range of possible values (i.e., in a curvilinear fashion)? How would you analyze the relationship between two such variables?

2. Is it possible to conduct a regression analysis on two variables and obtain a significant regression equation (significant F ratio), but still have a low r^2? What does the r^2 statistic measure? How can you have a low r^2 yet still get a statistically significant F ratio for the overall regression equation?

3. The ordinary least squares (OLS) procedure commonly used in regression produces a line of "best fit" for the data to which it is applied. How would you define best fit in regression analysis? What is there about the procedure that guarantees a best fit to the data? What assumptions about the use of a regression technique are necessary to produce this result?

4. When multiple independent variables are used to predict a dependent variable in multiple regression, multicollinearity among the independent variables is often a concern. What is the main problem caused by high multicollinearity among the independent variables in a multiple regression equation? Can you still achieve a high r^2 for your regression equation if multicollinearity is present in your data?

5. **EXPERIENCE THE INTERNET.** A trend in marketing is to shop for products and services on the Internet. In the last decade or so, traditional retailers have begun selling through catalogs. More recently, they also are selling over the Internet. To learn more about this,

go to www.catalogsite.com. At this site, many retailers are listing their merchandise and hoping to sell it. Review the catalogs. Compare the information on the Web site with traditional catalogs and retail stores. Prepare a questionnaire covering the common elements of these three approaches to selling. Select a retailer students are familiar with. Compile a sample of catalogs that offer similar merchandise. Then ask a sample of students to visit catalogs on the Web site, look at the catalogs you have brought to class, and then complete the questionnaire. Enter the data into a software package and assess your finding statistically. Prepare a report and be able to defend your conclusions.

6. **SPSS EXERCISE.** Choose one or two other students from your class and form a team. Identify the different retailers from your community where DVD players, TVs, and other electronics products are sold. Team members should divide up and visit all the different stores and describe the products and brands that are sold in each. Also observe the layout in the store, the store personnel, and the type of advertising the store uses. In other words, familiarize yourself with each retailer's marketing mix. Use your knowledge of the marketing mix to design a questionnaire. Interview approximately 100 people who are familiar with all the retailers you selected and collect their responses. Analyze the responses using a statistical software package such as SPSS. Prepare a report of your findings, including whether the perceptions of each of the stores are similar or different, and particularly whether the differences are statistically or substantively different. Present your findings in class and be prepared to defend your conclusions and your use of statistical techniques.

7. **SPSS EXERCISE.** In Chapter 15, the Marketing Research in Action example for Remington's Steak House and two competitors included numerous categorical variables. Run a Chi-square analysis to compare the three competitors on the categorical segmentation variables (X16–X21) and prepare a profile of each restaurant's customers. Next, run a multiple regression between the restaurant selection factors and satisfaction. Be prepared to present your findings. A database for the Remington's Steak House case is available in SPSS format at www.mhhe.com/hair06. The database is labeled C_15_Remingtons MRIA.3e.sav.

8. **SPSS EXERCISE.** Santa Fe Grill owners believe one of their competitive advantages is that the restaurant is a fun place to eat. Use the Santa Fe Grill database and run a bivariate correlation analysis between X13—Fun Place to Eat and X22—Satisfaction to test this hypothesis. Could this hypothesis be further examined with multiple regression?

appendix 16.A

Formulas for Calculating Correlation and Regression Issues

Marketing researchers seldom calculate statistics. We provide the formulas below for those who wish to better understand the computational process.

Pearson Product Moment Correlation

$$r_{xy} = \frac{\sum\limits_{i=1}^{n}(x_i - \bar{x})(y_i - \bar{y})}{n s_x s_y}$$

where

X_i = the X values

Y_i = the Y values

$\bar{X}$ = mean of the X values

$\bar{Y}$ = mean of the Y values

n = number of paired cases

$s_x s_y$ = standard deviation of X and Y

Regression

The general equation for regression is:

$$y = a + bx + e_i$$

where

Y = the dependent variable

a = the intercept for the regression line, or constant (point where the straight line intersects the y-axis when $x = 0$)

b = the slope of the regression line, or regression coefficient (the change in y for every 1-unit change in x)

x = the independent variable used to predict y

e_i = the error for the prediction (the difference between the predicted value and the true value)

Values for a and b can be calculated using the following formulas:

The formula for computing the regression parameter b is:

$$b = \frac{n\sum\limits_{i=1}^{n} x_i y_i - \left(\sum\limits_{i=1}^{n} x_i\right)\left(\sum\limits_{i-1}^{n} y_i\right)}{n\sum\limits_{i=1}^{n} x_i^2 - \left(\sum\limits_{i=1}^{n} x_i\right)^2}$$

where

x_i = an x variable value

y_i = a y value paired with each x_i value

n = the number of pairs

The formula for computing the intercept is:

$$a = \bar{y} - b\bar{x}$$

appendix 16.B

Examining Residuals

Earlier in the chapter we discussed the need to examine error terms (residuals) in order to diagnose potential problems caused by data observations that do not meet the assumptions of regression. Remember, residuals are the difference between the observed value of the dependent variable and the predicted value of the dependent variable produced by the regression equation. We can use SPSS to examine the residuals.

The click-through sequence is ANALYZE → REGRESSION → LINEAR. Highlight X22 and move it to the Dependent Variable box. Highlight X15 and X16 and move them to the Independent Variable box. In the Methods box we will keep Enter, which is the default.

This is the same sequence as earlier regression SPSS applications, but now we also must click on the Plots button. To produce plots of the regression residuals to check on potential problems, click on ZPRED and move it to the Y box. Then click on ZRESID and move it to the X box. These two items stand for Standardized Predicted Dependent Variable and Standardized Residual. Comparing these two quantities allows us to determine whether the hypothesized relationship between the dependent variable X22 and the independent variables X15 and X16 is linear, and also whether the error terms in the regression model are normally distributed (one of the basic assumptions of a regression model).

To fully evaluate the regression results, we need to examine two other graphs. To do so, go to the lower left-hand portion of the dialog box where it says Standardized Residual Plots. Click on the Histogram and Normal probability options. Now click on Continue and then OK to run the regression procedure.

The SPSS output is shown in Exhibit 16.B.1. The information in the Model Summary table shows the R-square is .370. From the ANOVA table you can see that this R-square is significant at the .000 level. Finally, in the Coefficients table we see that both independent variables have significant betas and are therefore related to the dependent variable satisfaction.

Now go to the Charts section at the end of the output to evaluate whether the data we used in the regression model violated any of the basic assumptions (linear relationship, normally distributed errors, etc.). Exhibits 16.B.2 to 16.B.4 present information about the distribution of the residuals. If the regression model predicts equally well over the entire range of the independent variables, there should be no discernible pattern or shape to the residuals and their distribution should be normal. The results shown in these residual charts will help you determine whether the residuals produced by our regression analysis conform to this standard.

Exhibit 16.B.2 shows the frequency distribution of the standardized residuals compared to a normal distribution. As you can see, most of the residuals are fairly close to the normal curve. There are some observations at -1.50 and $+1.00$ that exceed the curve, but this result is not of significant concern at this point. Examination of only this table does not suggest there is a problem—but you need to look at all three tables to make a final judgment.

Exhibit 16.B.3 shows the observed standardized residuals compared against the expected standardized residuals from a normal distribution. If the observed residuals are normally distributed, they will fall directly on the 45° line shown on the graph. As you can see, the e X H I B I T   **16.B.1**   **Examining Residuals in Multiple Regression**

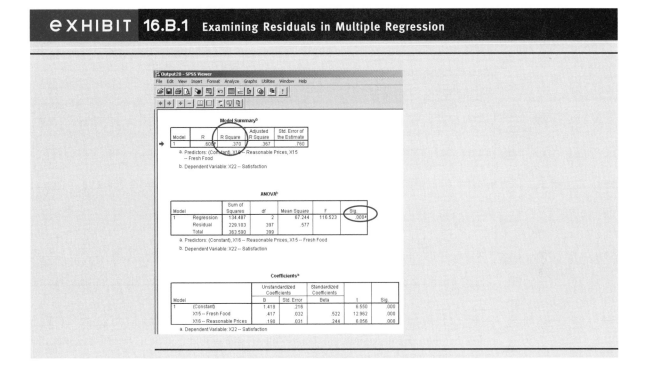

residuals from our regression model are fairly close so there does not seem to be a problem. Finally, Exhibit 16.B.4 compares the standardized predicted values of the dependent variable with the standardized residuals from the regression equation. The scatter plot of residuals shows no large difference in the spread of the residuals as you look from left to right on the chart. Again, this result suggests the relationship we are trying to predict is linear and that the error terms are normally distributed.

e X H I B I T   **16.B.2**   **Standardized Residuals versus Normal Distribution**

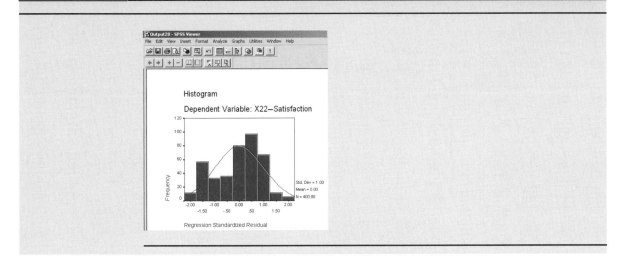

ΘXHIBIT 16.B.3 Observed versus Expected Standardized Residuals

---

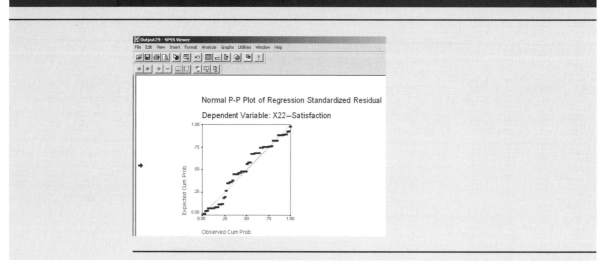

Thus, from an examination of the information presented in all three exhibits we conclude that there are no significant data problems that would lead us to say the assumptions of multiple regression have been seriously violated. As a final note we can say that regression is a robust statistical method and substantial violations of the assumptions are necessary to create problems.

There is one last issue to examine from the printout—the Residual Statistics table (see Exhibit 16.B.5). Note that it includes columns across the top for the minimum, maximum,

---

ΘXHIBIT 16.B.4 Standardized Predicted Values versus Standardized Residuals

---

e X H I B I T 16.B.5 Residual Statistics for Regression

Residuals Statistics[a]

	Minimum	Maximum	Mean	Std. Deviation	N
Predicted Value	3.47	5.48	4.64	.581	400
Residual	-1.68	1.51	.00	.758	400
Std. Predicted Value	-2.030	1.434	.000	1.000	400
Std. Residual	-2.212	1.986	.000	.997	400

a. Dependent Variable: X22 -- Satisfaction

mean, and standard deviation for the predicted value of the dependent variable, X22. Down the left side are references to the predicted value of X22, the residual, the standardized predicted value, and the standardized residual value. Since the standardization process produces scores with a mean of 0 and a standard deviation of 1.00, you should look most closely at the Minimum and Maximum columns. The numbers in these columns will tell you if the data have any distinctive outliers (i.e., individual responses that probably are valid responses, but quite different from the rest of the responses to a particular question). The entries in the Minimum and Maximum columns for the standardized predicted value and standardized residual value represent the number of standard deviations from the mean of 0. For example, the largest value of the standardized predicted value for X22 is −2.030 standard deviations below the mean value of 0. Likewise, the largest value of the standardized residual is −2.212 standard deviations below its mean of 0. The best way to utilize these numbers is to look for minimum and maximum values greater than 3.0. That would mean that some of the predicted values and residuals are further than three standard deviations away from their means and could indicate the presence of outliers in the data.

chapter 17

Data Analysis: Multivariate Techniques for the Research Process

Learning Objectives

After reading this chapter, you will be able to

1. Define multivariate analysis.

2. Understand how to use multivariate analysis in marketing research.

3. Distinguish between dependence and interdependence methods.

4. Define and understand factor analysis and cluster analysis.

5. Define and use discriminant analysis.

Multivariate Methods Impact Our Lives Every Day

The amount of information available for business decision making has grown tremendously over the last decade. Until recently, much of that information just disappeared. It either was not used or was discarded because collecting, storing, extracting, and interpreting it was not economical. Now, decreases in the cost of data collection and storage, development of faster data processors and user-friendly client–server interfaces, and improvements in data analysis and interpretation made possible through data mining enable businesses to convert what had been a "waste by-product" into a great new resource to provide added value to customers and to improve business decisions.

Data mining facilitates the discovery of interesting patterns in databases and data warehouses that are difficult to identify and have a high potential for improving decision making and creating knowledge. It does this first through an automated process involving "machine-learning" methods which emerged mostly from artificial intelligence. Examples include neural networking and genetic algorithms. After this first phase, the identified relationships are confirmed using "human-learning" approaches such as multiple regression, discriminant analysis, and factor analysis. The use of data mining and related approaches will continue to expand because data will increase exponentially, applications will become real-time, the quality of data will improve, and data-mining tools will be more powerful and easier to use.

Multivariate methods are widely used today for commercial purposes. Fair Isaac & Co. (www.fairisaac.com) is a $300-million business built around the commercial use of multivariate techniques. The firm has developed a complex analytical model that can accurately predict who will pay bills on time, who will pay late, who will not pay at all, who will file for bankruptcy, and so on. Its models are useful for both the consumer and the business-to-business markets. Similarly, the IRS uses discriminant analysis to identify which returns to audit and which to pass on. State Farm uses multivariate statistics to decide who to sell insurance to, and Progressive Insurance combines multivariate methods with global positioning technology to identify where and how fast you drive and then to raise your auto insurance premiums if you drive in a hazardous manner.

To make accurate business decisions in today's increasingly complex environment, we must analyze intricate relationships with many intervening variables. Multivariate methods are powerful analytical techniques made for addressing such issues.

Value of Multivariate Techniques in Data Analysis

In recent years we have seen remarkable advances in computer hardware and software. The speed and storage capability of PCs have been doubling every 18 months while prices have tumbled. Statistical software packages with Windows user interfaces have taken many tasks into the "click-and-point" era. We can now analyze large quantities of complex data with relative ease. For many years data came mostly from surveys. Data warehouses are now stocked with mountains of internal data that can be mined to identify valuable relationships about customers and employees. Some of these data can be analyzed using simple statistics like those discussed in earlier chapters. But in many situations we need more complex techniques. Indeed, many market researchers believe that unless we use more complex multivariate techniques we are only superficially examining marketing problems.

Today most of the problems marketing researchers are interested in understanding involve more than two variables and therefore require multivariate statistical techniques. Moreover, business decision makers as well as consumers tend to use a lot of information to make choices and decisions. Consequently, potential influences on consumer behavior and business reactions abound.

Multivariate techniques arose partially out of the need of businesses to address such complexity. The ability to determine the relative influence of different independent variables, as well as to assess the behavior of groups of dependent measures simultaneously, has become an important asset in the marketing researcher's toolbox. In addition, tremendous increases in computing power and portability have encouraged the adoption of multivariate analysis by individuals who were unable to realistically consider such approaches in earlier years.

Multivariate analysis A group of statistical techniques used when there are two or more measurements on each element and the variables are analyzed simultaneously. Multivariate analysis is concerned with the simultaneous relationships among two or more phenomena.

What is multivariate analysis? **Multivariate analysis** refers to a group of statistical procedures that simultaneously analyze multiple measurements on each individual or object being investigated. The multivariate statistical procedures we will highlight in this chapter are extensions of the univariate and bivariate statistical procedures that were discussed in previous chapters. It should be emphasized that we can only provide a very brief overview of some of these techniques in this chapter. The reader is referred to other more advanced texts for a more complete coverage of all the techniques.[1]

Multivariate analysis is extremely important in marketing research because most business problems are multidimensional. Corporations and their customers are seldom described on the basis of one dimension. An individual's decision to visit a fast-food restaurant is often dependent on such factors as the quality, variety, and price of the food; the restaurant's location; and the service. When corporations develop databases to better serve their customers, the database often includes a vast array of information—such as demographics, lifestyles, zip codes, purchasing behavior—on each customer. As marketing researchers become increasingly aware of the power of multivariate analysis, they will use multivariate techniques more and more in solving complex business problems. The Closer Look at Research box illustrates how these techniques can aid the small-business owner.

A Closer Look at Research

XLSTAT

Many small businesses cannot afford the rather expensive statistical packages like SPSS or SAS. XLSTAT is an affordable and user-friendly statistical package designed for small businesses that utilize Microsoft Excel. XLSTAT is an add-on for Excel. It allows the small-business user, working mainly in an Excel worksheet, to transfer stored data into the program for data analysis purposes.

XLSTAT offers more than 40 different functions to empower Excel and make it an everyday

Small Business Implications

statistical solution package for small businesses. The package can perform very simple techniques like box plots, frequencies, and other descriptive statistics. But it also can perform many of the more complex statistical techniques, such as factor analysis, cluster analysis, discriminant analysis, and multiple regression. To see examples of data analyzed, and how XLSTAT performs various statistical analysis functions, consult the XLSTAT Web page at www.xlstat.com.

Classification of Multivariate Methods

One challenge facing marketing researchers is determining the appropriate statistical method for a given problem. Several approaches have been suggested. A useful classification of most multivariate statistical techniques is presented in Exhibit 17.1. The multivariate procedures presented in this text are briefly described in Exhibit 17.2.

eXHIBIT 17.1 Classification of Multivariate Methods

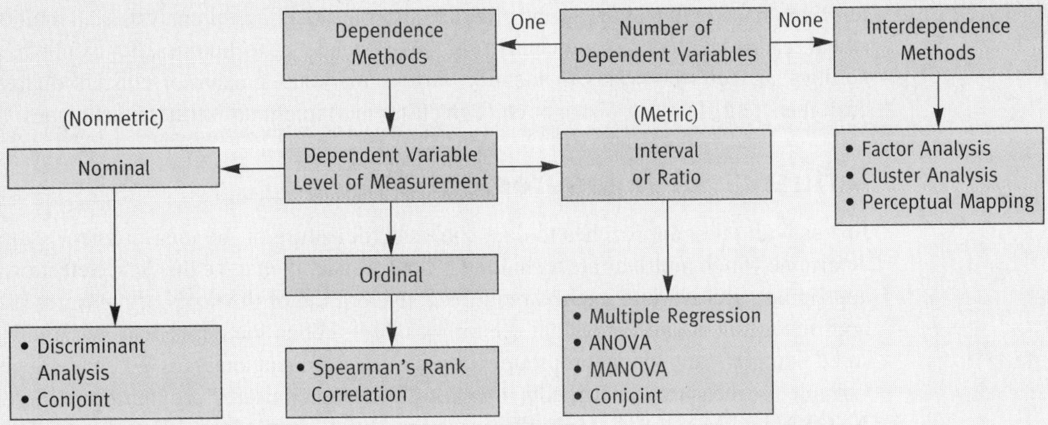

---

e X H I B I T 17.2 Summary of Selected Multivariate Methods

Multiple regression enables the marketing researcher to predict a single dependent metric variable from two or more metrically measured independent variables.

Multiple discriminant analysis can predict a single dependent nonmetric variable from two or more metrically measured independent variables.

Factor analysis is used to summarize the information contained in a large number of variables into a smaller number of subsets called factors.

Cluster analysis is used to classify respondents or objects (e.g., products, stores) into groups that are homogeneous, or similar within the groups but different between the groups.

Conjoint analysis is used to estimate the value (utility) that respondents associate with different product and/or service features, so that the most preferred combination of features can be determined.

Perceptual mapping is used to visually display respondents' perceptions of products, brands, companies, and so on. Several multivariate methods can be used to develop the data to construct perceptual maps.

Dependence or Interdependence Methods?

Dependence method Multivariate technique appropriate when one or more of the variables can be identified as dependent variables and the remaining as independent variables.

If we use multivariate techniques to explain or predict the dependent variable on the basis of two or more independent variables, we are attempting to analyze and understand dependence. A **dependence method** can be defined as one in which a variable is identified as the dependent variable to be predicted or explained by other independent variables. Dependence techniques include multiple regression analysis, discriminant analysis, and MANOVA. For example, many businesses today are very interested in predicting dependent variables like customer loyalty, or high-volume customers versus light users (e.g., heavy vs. light consumers of Starbucks coffee), on the basis of numerous independent variables. Multiple discriminant analysis is a dependence technique that predicts customer usage (frequent beer drinker vs. nondrinker) based on several independent variables, such as how much is purchased, how often it is purchased, and age of purchaser.

Interdependence method Multivariate statistical technique in which the whole set of interdependent relationships is examined.

In contrast, an **interdependence method** is one in which no single variable or group of variables is defined as being independent or dependent. In this case, the multivariate procedure involves the analysis of all variables in the data set simultaneously. The goal of interdependence methods is to group respondents or objects together. In this case, no one variable is to be predicted or explained by the others. Cluster analysis, factor analysis, and multidimensional scaling are the most frequently used interdependence techniques. For example, a marketing manager who wants to identify various market segments or clusters of fast-food customers (e.g., burgers, pizza, or chicken customers) might utilize these techniques.

Influence of Measurement Scales

Just as with other approaches to data analysis, the nature of the measurement scales will determine which multivariate technique is appropriate to analyze the data. Selection of the appropriate multivariate method requires consideration of the types of measures used for both independent and dependent sets of variables. When the dependent variable is measured nonmetrically, the appropriate method is discriminant analysis. When the dependent variable is measured metrically, the appropriate techniques are multiple regression, ANOVA, and MANOVA. Multiple regression and discriminant analysis typically require metric independents, but they can use nonmetric dummy variables. ANOVA and MANOVA are appropriate with nonmetric independent variables. The interdependence techniques of factor analysis and cluster analysis are most frequently used with metrically measured variables, but nonmetric adaptations are possible.

We covered multiple regression in Chapter 16. In this chapter we will consider factor analysis, cluster analysis, and discriminant analysis. These statistical techniques help us to analyze marketing problems that have multiple variables.

Multivariate statistical techniques help marketers make better decisions than is possible with univariate or bivariate statistics. But regardless of which type of technique is selected, the outcome of the analysis is key. Review the Global Insights box to see how outcomes can change across markets.

Interdependence Techniques

We will start our discussion of specific multivariate techniques with an analysis of interdependence methods. The purpose of techniques such as factor analysis and cluster analysis is not to predict a variable from a set of independent variables, but to summarize and better understand a large number of variables or objects.

Factor Analysis

Factor analysis Used to summarize the information contained in a large number of variables into a smaller number of subsets called factors.

Factor analysis is a multivariate statistical technique that is used to summarize the information contained in a large number of variables into a smaller number of subsets or factors. The purpose of factor analysis is to simplify the data. With factor analysis there is no distinction between dependent and independent variables; rather, all variables under investigation are analyzed together to identify underlying factors.

Many problems facing businesses today are often the result of a combination of several variables. For example, if the local McDonald's franchisor is interested in assessing customer satisfaction, many variables of interest must be measured. Variables such as freshness of the food, speed of service, taste, food temperature, cleanliness, and how friendly and courteous the personnel are would all be measured by means of a number of rating questions.

e X H I B I T 17.3 **Example of a Factor Analysis Application to a Fast-Food Restaurant**

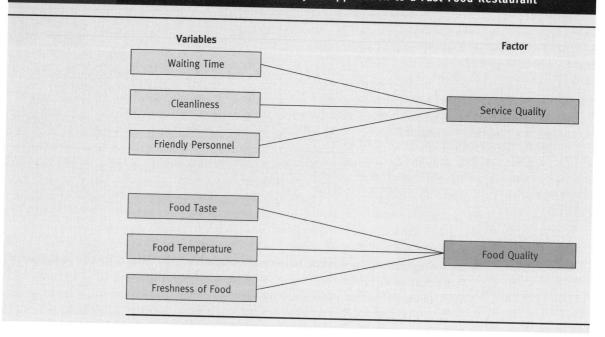

Let's look at an intuitive example of factor analysis. Customers were asked to rate a fast-food restaurant on six characteristics. On the basis of the pattern of their responses, these six measures were combined into two summary measures, or factors: service quality and food quality (see Exhibit 17.3). Marketing researchers use factor analysis to summarize the information contained in a large number of variables into a smaller number of factors. The result is that managers can then simplify their decision making because they have to consider only two broad areas—service quality and food quality—instead of six. Our example has reduced six variables to two factors, but in typical business situations marketing researchers use factor analysis to reduce, for example, 50 variables to only 10 or fewer factors—a much simpler problem to handle.

Factor loading A simple correlation between the variables and the factors.

The starting point in interpreting factor analysis is factor loadings. **Factor loading** refers to the correlation between each of the original variables and the newly developed factors. Each factor loading is a measure of the importance of the variable in measuring each factor. Factor loadings, like correlations, can vary from $+1.0$ to -1.0. If variable A_4 (food taste) is closely associated with factor 2, the factor loading or correlation would be high. The statistical analysis associated with factor analysis would produce factor loadings between each factor and each of the original variables. An illustration of the output of this statistical analysis is given in Exhibit 17.4. Variables A_1, A_2, and A_3 are highly correlated with factor 1 and variables A_4, A_5, and A_6 are highly correlated with factor 2. An analyst would say that variables A_1, A_2, and A_3 have "high loadings" on factor 1, which means that they help define that factor. Similarly, an analyst would say that variables A_4, A_5, and A_6 have "high loadings" on factor 2.

The next step in factor analysis is to name the resulting factors. The researcher examines the variables that have high loadings on each factor. There often will be a certain consistency among the variables that load high on a given factor. For example, the ratings on waiting time (A_1), cleanliness (A_2), and friendly personnel (A_3) all load on the same factor.

eXHIBIT 17.4 Factor Loadings for the Two Factors

| | Correlation with: | |
Variable	Factor 1	Factor 2
A_1 (waiting time)	.79	.07
A_2 (cleanliness)	.72	.10
A_3 (friendly personnel)	.72	.05
A_4 (food taste)	.09	.85
A_5 (food temperature)	.11	.70
A_6 (freshness of food)	.04	.74

We have chosen to name this factor service quality because the three variables deal with some aspect of a customer's service experience with the restaurant. Variables A_4, A_5, and A_6 all load highly on factor 2, which we named food quality. Naming factors is often a subjective process of combining intuition with an inspection of the variables that have high loadings on each factor.

A final aspect of factor analysis concerns the number of factors to retain. While our restaurant example dealt with two factors, many situations can involve anywhere from one factor to as many factors as there are variables. Deciding on how many factors to retain is a very complex process because there can be more than one possible solution to any factor analysis problem. A discussion of the technical aspects of this part of factor analysis is beyond the scope of this book, but we will provide an example of how an analyst can decide how many factors to retain.

An important measure to consider in deciding how many factors to retain is the percentage of the variation in the original data that is explained by each factor. A factor analysis computer program will produce a table of numbers that will give the percentage of variation explained by each factor. A simplified illustration of these numbers is presented in Exhibit 17.5. In this example, we would definitely keep the first two factors, because they explain a total of 96.8 percent of the variability in the five measures. The last three factors combined explain only 3.2 percent of the variation, and each accounts for only a small portion of the total variance. Thus, they contribute little to our understanding of the data and would not be retained. Most marketing researchers stop factoring when additional factors no longer make sense, because the variance they explain often contains a large amount of random and error variance.

eXHIBIT 17.5 Percentage of Variation in Original-Data Explained by Each Factor

Factor	Percentage of Variation Explained
1	50.3%
2	46.5
3	1.8
4	0.8
5	0.6

Factor Analysis Applications in Marketing Research

While our fast-food example illustrated the power of factor analysis in simplifying customer perceptions toward a fast-food restaurant, the technique has many other important applications in marketing research:

- *Advertising.* Factor analysis can be used to better understand media habits of various customers.

- *Pricing.* Factor analysis can help identify the characteristics of price-sensitive and prestige-sensitive customers.

- *Product.* Factor analysis can be used to identify brand attributes that influence consumer choice.

- *Distribution.* Factor analysis can be employed to better understand channel selection criteria among distribution channel members.

SPSS Application—Factor Analysis of Restaurant Perceptions

The value of factor analysis can be demonstrated with our Santa Fe Grill database. When we look at our database we have many variables that are measured metrically. Let's look first at variables X12 to X21, which are customers' perceptions of the Santa Fe Grill on eleven dimensions. The task is to determine if we can simplify our understanding of the perceptions of the restaurant by reducing the number of perceptions variables to fewer than eleven. If this is possible, the owners of the Santa Fe Grill can simplify their decision making by focusing on fewer aspects of their restaurant in developing appropriate marketing strategies.

The SPSS click-through sequence is ANALYZE → DATA REDUCTION → FACTOR, which leads to a dialog box where you select variables X12–X21. After you have put these variables into the Variables box, look at the data analysis options below. First click on the Descriptives box and unclick the Initial Solution box because we do not need it at this point. Now click Continue to return to the previous dialog box. Next go to the Extraction box. In this one you leave the default of principal components and unclick the unrotated factor solution under Display. We will keep the other defaults, so now click the Continue box. Next go to the Rotation box. The default is None. We want to rotate, so click on Varimax as your rotational choice and then Continue. Finally, go to the Options box and click Sorted by Size, and then change the Suppress Absolute Values from .10 to .30. These last choices eliminate unneeded information, thus making the solutions printout much easier to read. We do not need Scores at this point, so we can click on OK at the top of the dialog box to execute the factor analysis. Exhibit 17.6 shows examples of some of the dialog boxes for running this factor analysis.

The SPSS output for a factor analysis of the restaurant perceptions is shown in Exhibit 17.7. The first table you will see on the output is the Rotated Component Matrix table. Labels for the eleven variables analyzed (X12–X21) are shown in the left column. To the right are four columns of numbers containing the factor loadings for the four factors that resulted from the factor analysis of restaurant perceptions. By suppressing loadings under .30 we see only three numbers under column one (Component 1, or factor 1), three numbers under column two (Component 2, or factor 2), and two numbers under columns three and four (Components 3 and 4). For example, X18—Excellent Food Taste has a loading of .910 on factor 1 and X12—Friendly Employees has a loading of .949 on factor 2. We prefer a factor solution in which each original variable loads on only one factor, as in our example. But in many cases this does not happen.

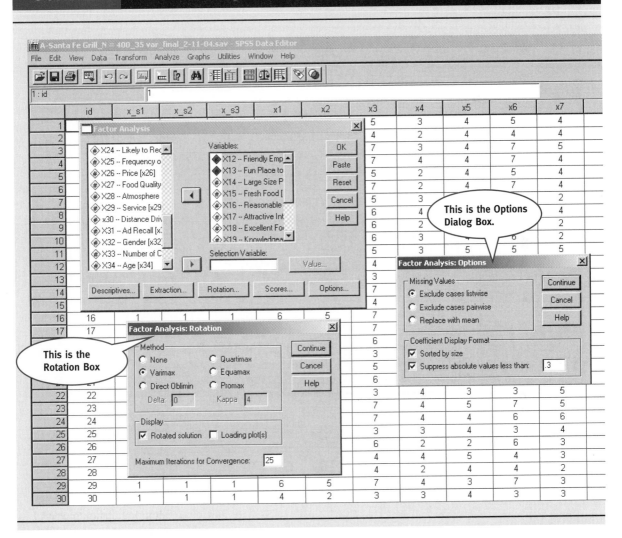

EXHIBIT 17.6   SPSS Dialog Box Examples for Factor Analysis

Before trying to name the factors we must decide if four factors are enough or if we need more. Our objective here is to have as few factors as possible yet account for a reasonable amount of the information contained in the eleven original variables. To determine the number of factors, we look at information in the Total Variance Explained table (bottom of Exhibit 17.7). It shows the four factors accounted for 85.676 percent of the variance in the original eleven variables. This is a substantial amount of the information to account for, and we have reduced the number of original variables by two-thirds, from eleven to four. So let's consider four factors acceptable and see if our factors seem logical.

To determine if our factors are logical, look at the information in the Rotated Component Matrix (Exhibit 17.7). First, examine which original variables combine to make each new factor. Factor 1 is made up of X18—Excellent Food Taste, X15—Fresh Food, and X20—Proper Food Temperature. Factor 2 is made up of X12—Friendly Employees, X21—Speed of Service, and X19—Knowledgeable Employees. Factor 3 is made up of

EXHIBIT 17.7 SPSS Output for Factor Analysis of Restaurant Perceptions

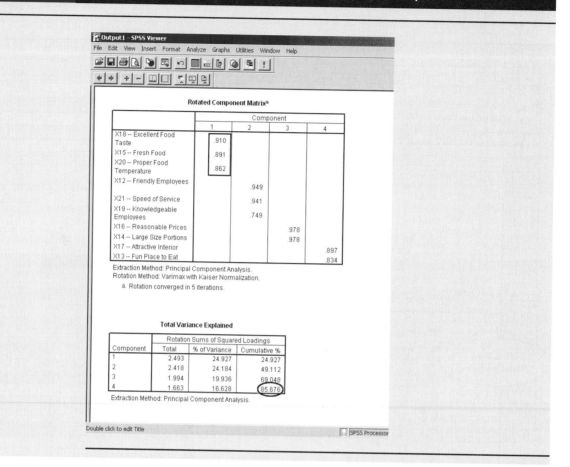

X16—Reasonable Prices and X14—Large Size Portions. Factor 4 is made up of X17—Attractive Interior and X13—Fun Place to Eat. To analyze the logic of the combinations we look at the variables with the highest loadings (largest absolute size). That is why we suppressed loadings less than .30. Factor 1 seems to be related to food, whereas factor 2 is related to service. Similarly, factor 3 seems to be related to value, whereas factor 4 is related to atmosphere. Thus, we have developed a four-factor solution that accounts for a substantial amount of variance and shows logic in the combinations of the original eleven variables. With this four-factor solution, instead of having to think about eleven variables the owners of the Santa Fe Grill can now think about only four variables—food, service, value, and atmosphere—when they are developing their marketing strategies.

Using Factor Analysis with Multiple Regression

Sometimes we may want to use the results of a factor analysis with another multivariate technique, such as multiple regression. This is most helpful when we use factor analysis to combine a large number of variables into a smaller set of variables. We can demonstrate this with the previous example, where we combined the eleven restaurant perceptions into four factors.

Without factor analysis, we must consider customer perceptions on eleven separate characteristics. But if we use the results of our factor analysis we have to consider only the four characteristics (factors) developed in our factor solution. To use the resulting four factors in a multiple regression, we first must calculate factor scores. Factor scores are composite scores estimated for each respondent on each of the derived factors. Return to the SPSS dialog box for the four-factor solution (if you have left the previous factor solution, follow the same instructions as before to get to this dialog box). Looking at the bottom of this dialog box you see the Scores box, which we did not use before. Click on this box and then click Save as Variables. When you do this there will be more options, but just click the Regression option. Now click Continue and then OK and you will calculate the factor scores. The result will be four factor scores for each of the 400 respondents. They will appear at the far right side of your original database and will be labeled fac1_1 (scores for factor 1), fac2_1 (scores for factor 2), and so on. See Exhibit 17.8 to view the factor scores.

Now we want to see if perceptions of the restaurant, as measured by the factors, are related to satisfaction. In this case, the single dependent metric variable is X22—Satisfaction, and the independent variables are the factor scores. The SPSS click-through sequence is ANALYZE → REGRESSION → LINEAR, which leads you to a dialog box where you

---

e X H I B I T 17.8 **Factor Scores for Restaurant Perceptions**

A-Santa Fe Grill_N = 400_35 var_final_2-11-04.sav - SPSS Data Editor

File Edit View Data Transform Analyze Graphs Utilities Window Help

26 :

	x34	x35	fac1_1	fac2_1	fac3_1	fac4_1	var	var
1	2	2	.46421	.28466	-.27729	-.10644		
2	1	1	1.30852	-1.29299	-1.15073	.26942		
3	4	3	-.97928	-2.02664	1.48165	-1.01958		
4	3	2	-.30261	.74131	1.25403	-.27420		
5	4	4	.70139	-.87148	-.21462	-1.20998		
6	2	1	1.04665	-.90447	1.05328	1.05914		
7	3	3	.32109	-.34641	-.17141	-1.26896		
8	4	5	-1.45724	1.00347	.67014	-1.22122		
9	3	1	.87490	.54014	-.14763	.95834		
10	3	1	1.45430	.22163	.41393	-.40605		
11	5	5	-.08915	-1.54190	-.36300	.37756		
12	4	4	-1.12576	.62061	-1.01813	-1.01412		
13	3	2	-1.17848	.67075	-1.60998	-2.02812		
14	3	5	.44661	.53836	1.35752	-.29621		
15	3	3	-.91621	.85576	-1.11377	.19005		
16	3	2	-.26056	1.04960	.86087	-.16072		
17	4	2	-.85045	-.18225	1.28212	.05265		
18	3	5	-1.63443	.86119	.08349	.15703		
19	4	4	-.49301	-1.06102	-2.09185	.60973		
20	4	2	.39983	.80706	-.30311	-.22812		
21	3	1	-1.15387	-.43914	.49507	-.42271		
22	4	2	-1.23499	-.21490	-1.64725	-1.29709		
23	1	2	-1.10750	1.03608	1.18576	1.12128		
24	3	4	-2.21541	-1.64909	.93024	.46322		

e X H I B I T 17.9 SPSS Dialog Boxes for Regression with Factor Scores

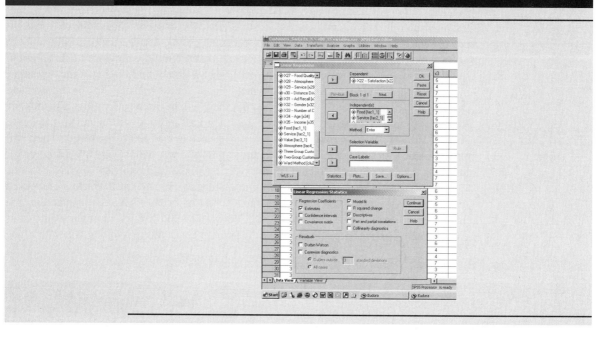

select the variables. You should select X22 as the dependent and fac1_1, fac2_1, fac3_1, and fac4_1 as the independents. Now click on the Statistics button and check Descriptives. There are several additional types of analysis that can be selected, but at this point we will use the program defaults. Click OK at the top right of the dialog box to execute the regression. The dialog boxes for this regression are shown in Exhibit 17.9.

The output for the SPSS regression with factor scores is shown in Exhibit 17.10. The Model Summary table reveals that the R-square is .492 and the ANOVA table indicates it is statistically significant at the .000 level. This means that 49.2 percent of the variation in satisfaction (dependent variable) can be explained from the four independent variables—the factor scores. Footnote a underneath the table tells you that the regression equation included a constant and that the predictor (independent) variables were factor scores for the four variables (Atmosphere, Value, Service, and Food).

To determine if one or both of the factor score variables are significant predictors of satisfaction we must examine the Coefficients table (Exhibit 17.10). Looking at the Standardized Coefficients Beta column reveals that Factor 1—Food is .480, Factor 2—Service is .325, Factor 3—Value is .258, and Factor 4—Atmosphere is .300. The statistical significance is .000 for all four factors. Thus, we know from this regression analysis that perceptions of all restaurant factors are strong predictors of satisfaction, with Factor 1 being somewhat better than the other three factors since the size of the Factor 1 beta is somewhat larger. Furthermore, interpreting only four variables in developing a marketing strategy is much easier for the owners of the Santa Fe Grill than is dealing with the original eleven independent variables.

In this section we have demonstrated how you can use one multivariate technique—factor analysis—with another technique—regression—to better understand your data. It is also possible, however, to use other multivariate techniques in combination. For example, if your dependent variable is nonmetric, such as gender, then you could use discriminant

EXHIBIT 17.10 Output for SPSS Regression with Factor Scores

Output19 - SPSS Viewer

File Edit View Insert Format Analyze Graphs Utilities Window Help

Model Summary

Model	R	R Square	Adjusted R Square	Std. Error of the Estimate
1	.702[a]	.492	.487	.684

a. Predictors: (Constant), Atmosphere, Value, Service, Food

ANOVA[b]

Model		Sum of Squares	df	Mean Square	F	Sig.
1	Regression	179.047	4	44.762	95.809	.000[a]
	Residual	184.543	395	.467		
	Total	363.590	399			

a. Predictors: (Constant), Atmosphere, Value, Service, Food

b. Dependent Variable: X22 -- Satisfaction

Coefficients[a]

Model		Unstandardized Coefficients		Standardized Coefficients	t	Sig.
		B	Std. Error	Beta		
1	(Constant)	4.645	.034		135.914	.000
	Food	.458	.034	.480	13.396	.000
	Service	.310	.034	.325	9.054	.000
	Value	.246	.034	.258	7.189	.000
	Atmosphere	.287	.034	.300	8.374	.000

a. Dependent Variable: X22 -- Satisfaction

analysis in a manner similar to our use of regression. Also, you could use cluster analysis in combination with regression or discriminant analysis. This will be clearer after we have covered these other techniques later in this chapter.

Cluster analysis A multivariate interdependence technique whose primary objective is to classify objects into relatively homogeneous groups based on the set of variables considered.

Cluster Analysis

Cluster analysis is another interdependence multivariate method. As the name implies, the basic purpose of cluster analysis is to classify or segment objects (e.g., customers, products, market areas) into groups so that objects within each group are similar to one another on a variety of variables. Cluster analysis seeks to classify segments or objects such that there

еХHIBIT 17.11 Cluster Analysis Based on Two Characteristics

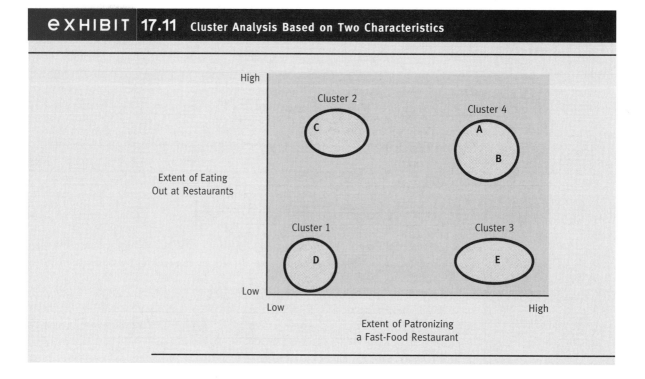

will be as much similarity within segments and as much difference between segments as possible. Thus, this method strives to identify natural groupings or segments among many variables without designating any of the variables as a dependent variable.

We will start our discussion of cluster analysis with this intuitive example. A fast-food chain wants to open an eat-in restaurant in a new, growing suburb of a major metropolitan area. Marketing researchers surveyed a large sample of households in this suburb and collected data on characteristics such as demographics, lifestyles, and expenditures on eating out. The fast-food chain wants to identify one or more household segments that are likely to visit its new restaurant. Once this segment is identified, the firm's advertising and services would be tailored to them.

A target segment can be identified for the company by conducting a cluster analysis of the data it has gathered. Results of the cluster analysis will identify segments, each containing households that have similar characteristics but differs considerably from the other segments. Exhibit 17.11 identifies four potential clusters or segments for our fast-food chain. As our intuitive example illustrates, this growing suburb contains households that seldom visit restaurants at all (cluster 1), households that tend to frequent dine-in restaurants exclusively (cluster 2), households that tend to frequent fast-food restaurants exclusively (cluster 3), and households that frequent both dine-in and fast-food restaurants (cluster 4). By examining the characteristics associated with each of the clusters, management can decide which clusters to target and how best to reach them through marketing communications.

Statistical Procedures for Cluster Analysis

Several cluster analysis procedures are available, each based on a somewhat different set of complex computer programs. The general approach in each procedure is the same, however, and involves measuring the similarity between objects on the basis of their ratings on the various characteristics. The degree of similarity between objects is usually determined through a distance measure. This process can be illustrated with our earlier example involving two variables:

V1 = Frequency of eating out at fancy restaurants

V2 = Frequency of eating out at fast-food restaurants

Data on V1 and V2 are shown on the two-dimensional plot in Exhibit 17.11. Five individuals are plotted with the letters A, B, C, D and E. Each letter represents the position of one consumer with regard to the two variables V1 and V2. The distance between any pair of letters is positively related to how similar the corresponding individuals are when the two variables are considered together. Thus, individual A is more like B than either C, D, or E. As can be seen, four distinct clusters are identified in the exhibit.

This analysis can inform marketing management of the proposed new fast-food restaurant that customers are to be found among who tend to eat at both fancy and fast-food restaurants (cluster 4). To develop a marketing strategy to reach this cluster of households, management would like to identify demographic, psychographic, and behavioral profiles of the individuals in cluster 4.

Clusters are often developed from scatter plots, as we have done with our fast-food restaurant example. This is a complex trial-and-error process. Fortunately, computer algorithms are available, and must be used if the clustering is to be done in an efficient, systematic fashion. While the mathematics are beyond the scope of this chapter, the algorithms are all based on the idea of starting with some arbitrary cluster boundaries and modifying the boundaries until a point is reached where the average distances within clusters are as small as possible relative to the average distances between clusters.

Cluster Analysis Applications in Marketing Research

While our fast-food example illustrated how cluster analysis segmented groups of households, it has many other important applications in marketing research:

- *New-product research.* Clustering brands can help a firm examine its product offerings relative to competition. Brands in the same cluster often compete more fiercely with each other than with brands in other clusters.

- *Test marketing.* Cluster analysis groups test cities into homogeneous clusters for test marketing purposes.

- *Buyer behavior.* Cluster analysis can be employed to identify similar groups of buyers who have similar choice criteria.

- *Market segmentation.* Cluster analysis can develop distinct market segments on the basis of geographic, demographic, psychographic, and behavioral variables.

SPSS Application—Cluster Analysis

The value of cluster analysis can be demonstrated easily with our restaurant database. The task is to determine if there are subgroups/clusters of the 400 respondents to the Santa Fe restaurant survey that are different. In selecting the variables to use in cluster analysis, we must use only variables that are metrically measured and logically related.

There are three logical sets of metric variables to consider for the cluster analysis—the lifestyle questions, the restaurant perceptions questions, and the three relationship questions (question #25 is nonmetric). The owners of the Santa Fe Grill have been asking if

---

eXHIBIT 17.12   SPSS Dialog Boxes for Cluster Analysis

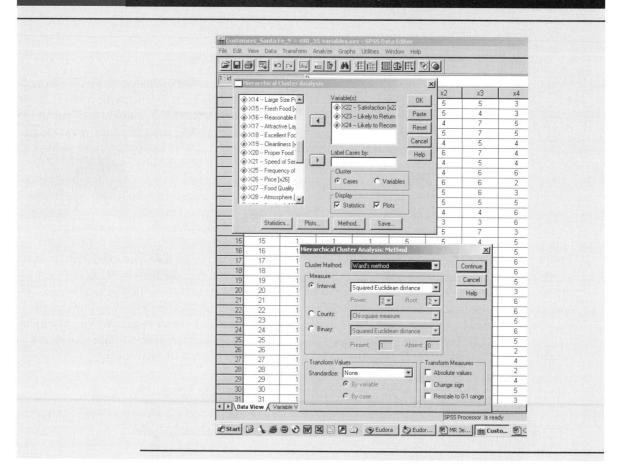

there are subgroups of customers that exhibit different levels of commitment to the restaurant. This question can be answered by applying cluster analysis to variables 22, 23 and 24, all three of which represent measures of customer commitment. The task then is to see if there are clusters of customers that have distinctly different levels of commitment to the restaurant.

The SPSS click-through sequence is ANALYZE → CLASSIFY → HIERARCHICAL CLUSTER, which leads to a dialog box where you select variables X22, X23, and X24. After you have put these variables into the Variables box, look at the other options below. Keep all the defaults that are shown on the dialog box. You should also use the defaults for the Statistics and Plots options below. Click on the Method box and select Ward's under the Cluster Method (you have to scroll to the bottom of the list), but use the default of squared euclidean distances under Measure. We do nothing with the Save option at this point, so you can click OK at the top of the dialog box to execute the cluster analysis. Exhibit 17.12 shows the SPSS dialog boxes for running this cluster.

The SPSS output has a table called Agglomeration Schedule, a portion of which is shown in Exhibit 17.13. This table has lots of numbers in it, but we look only at the numbers in the Coefficients column (middle of table). Go to the bottom of the table and look at the

e X H I B I T 17.13 Cluster Analysis Agglomeration Schedule

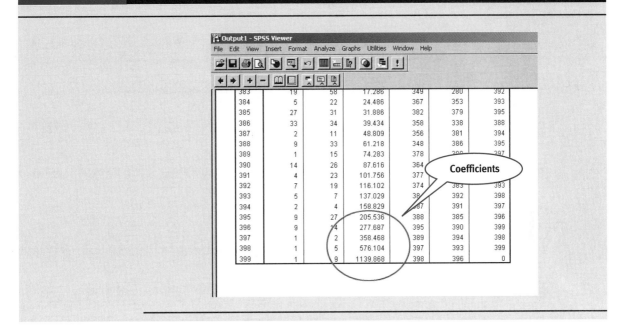

numbers in the Coefficients column (circled in red). The number at the bottom will be the largest, and the numbers get smaller as you move up the table. The bottom number is 1139.868, the one right above it is 576.104, and the next above is 358.468. The coefficients in this column show how much you reduce your error by moving from one cluster to two clusters, from two clusters to three clusters, and so on. As you move from one cluster to two clusters there always will be a large drop (difference) in the coefficient of error, and from two clusters to three clusters another drop. Each time you move up the column the drop (difference) in the numbers will get smaller. What you are looking for is where the difference between two numbers gets substantially smaller. This means that going from, say, three clusters to four clusters has not reduced your error very much. You will note that in this case the change is from 358.468 to 277.687. For this solution, we definitely would choose three clusters over four because the difference between the numbers as you go from three clusters to four clusters is getting much smaller. We might also choose to use only two clusters instead of three. We could do this because the error is reduced a huge amount by going from one to two clusters, and two clusters likely will be easier to understand than three.

Let's focus on the two-cluster solution because it is easier to understand. Before trying to name the two clusters, let's make sure they are significantly different. To do so, you must first create a new variable that identifies which cluster each of the 400 respondents has been assigned to by the cluster analysis. Go back to the Cluster dialog box and click on the Save box. When you do this, you can choose to create a new cluster membership variable for a single solution or for a range of solutions. Choose the single solution, put a 2 in the box, and a group membership variable for the two-group solution will be created when you run the cluster program again. The new group membership variable will be the new variable in your data set at the far-right-hand side of your data labeled clu2_1. It will show a 1 for respondents in cluster 1 and a 2 for respondents assigned to cluster 2, as shown in Exhibit 17.14.

EXHIBIT   17.14   New Cluster Variable To Identify Group Membership

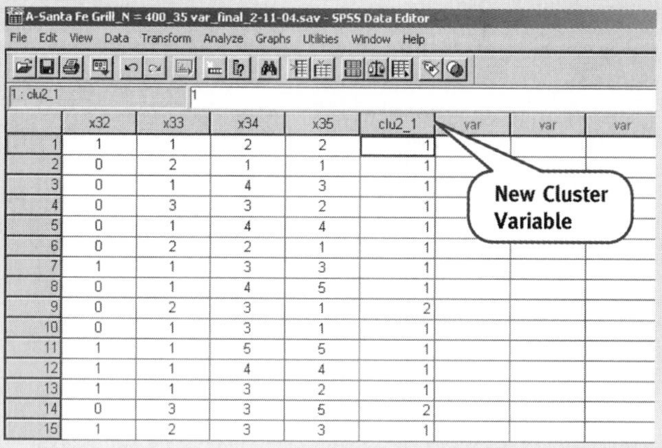

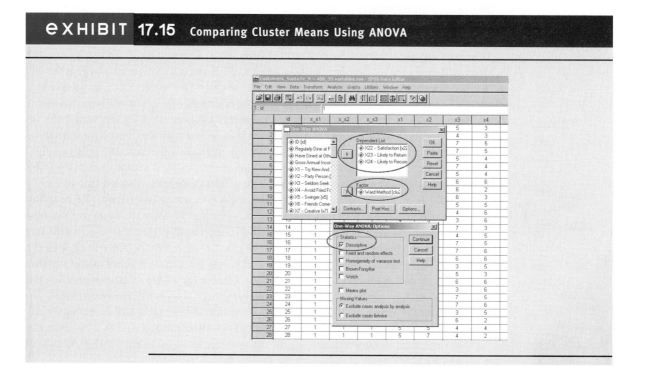

Now you can run a one-way ANOVA between the two clusters to see if they are statistically different. The SPSS click-through sequence is ANALYZE → COMPARE MEANS → ONE-WAY ANOVA. Next you put variables X22, X23, and X24 in the Variables box and the new Cluster Membership variable in the Factor box. This will be the new variable in your data set labeled clu2_1. Next click on the Options box and then on Descriptive under Statistics, and Continue. Now click OK and you will get an output with a Descriptives and an ANOVA table. The dialog boxes for running this procedure are shown in Exhibit 17.15.

EXHIBIT   17.15   Comparing Cluster Means Using ANOVA

eXHIBIT 17.16 SPSS ANOVA Output—Results for Cluster of X22–X24

Output2 - SPSS Viewer

File Edit View Insert Format Analyze Graphs Utilities Window Help

Descriptives

		N	Mean	Std. Deviation	Std. Error	95% Confidence Interval for Mean		Minimum	Maximum
						Lower Bound	Upper Bound		
X22 -- Satisfaction	1	269	4.11	.625	.038	4.04	4.19	3	5
	2	131	5.74	.440	.038	5.66	5.82	5	6
	Total	400	4.64	.955	.048	4.55	4.74	3	6
X23 -- Likely to Return	1	269	3.81	.719	.044	3.73	3.90	2	5
	2	131	5.45	.659	.058	5.34	5.56	4	6
	Total	400	4.35	1.039	.052	4.25	4.45	2	6
X24 -- Likely to Recommend	1	269	3.12	.787	.048	3.02	3.21	2	5
	2	131	4.15	.808	.071	4.01	4.29	3	5
	Total	400	3.46	.930	.047	3.37	3.55	2	5

ANOVA

		Sum of Squares	df	Mean Square	F	Sig.
X22 -- Satisfaction	Between Groups	233.760	1	233.760	716.604	.000
	Within Groups	129.830	398	.326		
	Total	363.590	399			
X23 -- Likely to Return	Between Groups	235.866	1	235.866	481.079	.000
	Within Groups	195.134	398	.490		
	Total	431.000	399			
X24 -- Likely to Recommend	Between Groups	94.138	1	94.138	149.187	.000
	Within Groups	251.140	398	.631		
	Total	345.277	399			

SPSS Processor is ready   H: 17 , W: 720 pt.

Start   Eudora   Eudora   Ch_17_...   Microso...   A-Santa...   C_17_C...   Output...   8:00 AM

The SPSS output for the ANOVA of the cluster solution is shown in Exhibit 17.16. When you look at the Descriptives table you will see the sample sizes for each cluster (N) and the means of each variable for each cluster, as well as a lot of other numbers we will not use. For example, the sample size for cluster 1 is 269 and for cluster 2 it is 131. Similarly, the mean for satisfaction in cluster 1 is 4.11, and in cluster 2 it is 5.74; the mean for likely to return in cluster 1 is 3.81, and in cluster 2 it is 5.45; and the mean for likely to recommend in cluster 1 is 3.12, and in cluster 2 it is 4.15.

We interpret the two clusters by looking at the means of the variables for each of the groups. By looking at the means we see that respondents in cluster 1 are relatively less satisfied, less likely to return, and less likely to recommend (lower mean values). In contrast, cluster 2 respondents are relatively more satisfied, more likely to return, and more likely to recommend the Santa Fe Grill (higher mean values). Thus, cluster 2 has much more favorable perceptions of the restaurant than does group one.

Next look at the ANOVA table to see if the differences between the group means are statistically significant. You will see that for all three variables the differences between the means of the two clusters are highly significant (Sig. = .000) and therefore statistically different. Thus, we have two very different groups of restaurant customers with cluster 2 being moderately committed to the restaurant and cluster 1 only somewhat committed. Based on the mean values and significance levels, we will name cluster 1 "Somewhat Committed" and cluster 2 "Moderately Committed."

Analysis of Dependence

We now focus our discussion on the multivariate techniques that deal with analysis of dependence. The purpose of these techniques is to predict a variable from a set of independent variables. The dependence techniques we cover in this book include multiple regression, discriminant analysis, and conjoint analysis. We covered regression in Chapter 16, and we cover the other techniques in this chapter.

Discriminant Analysis

Discriminant analysis
A technique for analyzing marketing research data when the criterion or dependent variable is categorical and the predictor or independent variables are intervals.

Discriminant analysis is a multivariate technique used for predicting group membership on the basis of two or more independent variables. There are many situations where the marketing researcher's purpose is to classify objects or groups by a set of independent variables. Thus, the dependent variable in discriminant analysis is nonmetric or categorical. In marketing, consumers are often categorized on the basis of heavy versus light users of a product, or viewers versus nonviewers of a media vehicle such as a television commercial. Conversely, the independent variables in discriminant analysis are metric and often include characteristics such as demographics and psychographics. Additional insights into discriminant analysis can be found in the Closer Look at Research box.

Let's begin our discussion of discriminant analysis with an intuitive example. A fast-food restaurant, Back Yard Burgers (BYB), wants to see whether a lifestyle variable such as eating a nutritious meal (X_1) and a demographic variable such as household income (X_2) are useful in distinguishing households visiting their restaurant from those visiting other fast-food restaurants. Marketing researchers gathered data on X_1 and X_2 for a random sample of households that eat at fast-food restaurants, including Back Yard Burgers. Discriminant analysis procedures would plot these data on a two-dimensional graph, as shown in Exhibit 17.17.

The scatter plot in Exhibit 17.17 yields two groups, one containing primarily Back Yard Burgers' customers and the other containing primarily households that patronize other fast-food restaurants. From this example, it appears that X_1 and X_2 are critical discriminators of fast-food restaurant patronage. Although the two areas overlap, the extent of the overlap does not seem to be substantial. This minimal overlap between groups, as in Exhibit 17.17, is an important requirement for a successful discriminant analysis. What the plot tells us is that Back Yard Burgers customers are more nutrition conscious and have relatively higher incomes.

Discriminant function
The linear combination of independent variables developed by discriminant analysis which will best discriminate between the categories of the dependent variable.

Let us now turn to the fundamental statistics of discriminant analysis. Remember, the prediction of a categorical variable is the purpose of discriminant analysis. From a statistical perspective, this involves studying the direction of group differences based on finding a linear combination of independent variables—the **discriminant function**—that shows large differences in group means. Thus, discriminant analysis is a statistical tool for determining linear combinations of those independent variables and using this to predict group membership.

A linear function can be developed with our fast-food example. We will use a two-group discriminant analysis example in which the dependent variable, Y, is measured on a nominal

A Closer Look at Research

Discriminant Analysis—SPSS

Discriminant analysis is used primarily to classify individuals or experimental units into two or more uniquely defined populations. An example of the use of discriminant analysis could include a credit card company that would like to classify credit card applicants into two groups: (1) individuals who are considered good credit risks, and (2) individuals who are considered poor credit risks.

On the basis of this classification, individuals considered good credit risks would be offered credit

Using Technology

cards, while individuals considered poor credit risks would not be offered credit cards. Different factors that could help the credit card company in determining which of the two groups applicants would fall into include salary, past credit history, level of education, and number of dependents. The statistical software package SPSS could be used to determine where the line should be drawn between these two groups.

To learn more about the use of discriminant analysis in SPSS, go to the SPSS Web site at www.spss.com.

scale (i.e., patrons of Back Yard Burgers versus other fast-food restaurants). Again, the marketing manager believes it is possible to predict whether a customer will patronize a fast-food restaurant on the basis of lifestyle (X_1) and income (X_2). Now the researcher must find a linear function of the independent variables that shows large differences in group means. The plots in Exhibit 17.17 show this is possible.

EXHIBIT 17.17   Discriminant Analysis Scatter Plot of Lifestyle and Income Data for Fast-Food Restaurant Patronage

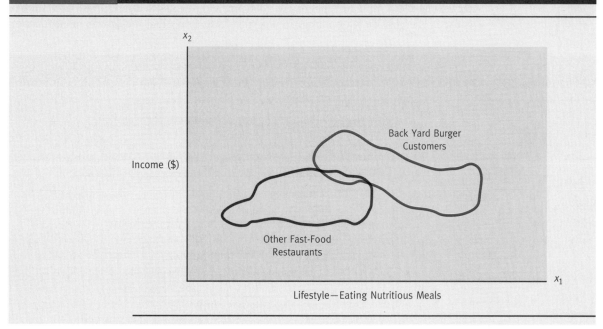

Discriminant score In discriminant analysis, the score of each respondent on the discriminant function.

The **discriminant score,** or the Z score, is the basis for predicting to which group a particular individual belongs and is determined by a linear function. This Z score will be derived for each individual by means of the following equation:

$$Z_i = b_1 X_{1i} + b_2 X_{2i} \cdots + b_n X_{ni}$$

where

Z_i = ith individual's discriminant score

b_n = Discriminant coefficient for the nth variable

X_{ni} = Individual's value on the nth independent variable

Discriminant function coefficients The multipliers of variables in the discriminant function when the variables are in the original units of measurement.

Discriminant weights (b_n), or **discriminant function coefficients,** are estimates of the discriminatory power of a particular independent variable. These coefficients are computed by means of the discriminant analysis software, such as SPSS. The size of the coefficients associated with a particular independent variable is determined by the variance structure of the variables in the equation. Independent variables with large discriminatory power will have large weights, and those with little discriminatory power will have small weights.

Returning to our fast-food example, suppose the marketing researcher finds the standardized weights or coefficients in the equation to be

$$Z = b_1 X_1 + B_2 X_2$$
$$= .32 X_1 + .47 X_2$$

Classification (or prediction) matrix The classification matrix in discriminant analysis that contains the number of correctly classified and misclassified cases.

These results show that income (X_2) with a coefficient of .47 is the more important variable in discriminating between those patronizing Back Yard Burgers and those who patronize other fast-food restaurants. The lifestyle variable (X_1) with a coefficient of .32 also represents a variable with good discriminatory power.

Another important goal of discriminant analysis is classification of objects or individuals into groups. In our example, the goal was to correctly classify consumers into Back Yard Burgers patrons and those who patronize other fast-food restaurants. To determine whether the estimated discriminant function is a good predictor, a **classification (prediction) matrix** is used. The classification matrix in Exhibit 17.18 shows that the discriminant function

ⓔXHIBIT 17.18 **Classification Matrix for BYB Patrons and Nonpatrons**

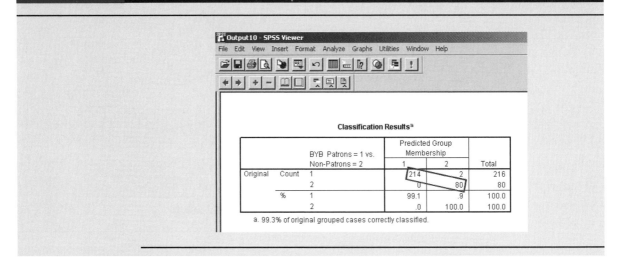

correctly classified 214 of the original BYB patrons (99.1 percent) and 80 of the nonpatrons (100 percent). The classification matrix also shows that the number of correctly classified consumers (216 patrons and 80 nonpatrons) out of a total of 296 equals 99.3 percent correctly classified. This resulting percentage is much higher than would be expected by chance.

Discriminant Analysis Applications in Marketing Research

While our example illustrated how discriminant analysis helped classify users and nonusers of the restaurant based on independent variables, other applications include the following:

- *Product research.* Discriminant analysis can help to distinguish between heavy, medium, and light users of a product in terms of their consumption habits and lifestyles.

- *Image research.* Discriminant analysis can discriminate between customers who exhibit favorable perceptions of a store or company and those who do not.

- *Advertising research.* Discriminant analysis can assist in distinguishing how market segments differ in media consumption habits.

- *Direct marketing.* Discriminant analysis can help in distinguishing characteristics of consumers who respond to direct marketing solicitations and those who don't.

SPSS Application—Discriminant Analysis

The usefulness of discriminant analysis can be demonstrated with our Santa Fe Grill database. Remember that with discriminant analysis the single dependent variable is a nonmetric variable and the multiple independent variables are measured metrically. In the classification variables of the database, variables X30—Distance Driven, X31—Ad Recall, and X32—Gender are nonmetric variables. Variables X31 and X32 are two-group variables and X30 is a three-group variable. We could use discriminant analysis to see if there are differences between perceptions of the Santa Fe Grill by male and female customers or by ad recall, or we could see if the perceptions differ depending on how far customers drove to eat at the Santa Fe Grill.

The Santa Fe Grill recently has been running an advertising campaign emphasizing its fresh, good-tasting food and good service. The owners want to know if the ads have been effective. One way to assess this is to see if recall of the ads influences perceptions of the restaurant. In looking at variables X12–X21, there are three variables associated with food—variables X15, X18, and X20.

The task is to determine if perceptions of Santa Fe Grill's food are different between customers who recall ads and those who do not (X31—Ad Recall). Another way of stating this is, "Can perceptions of Santa Fe Grill's food predict whether or not customers recall ads?" This second question is based on the primary objective of discriminant analysis—to predict group membership. In this case, can the food perceptions predict ad recall groups?

The SPSS click-through sequence is ANALYZE → CLASSIFY → DISCRIMINANT, which leads to a dialog box where you select the variables (see Exhibit 17.19). The dependent, nonmetric variable is X31 and the independent, metric variables are X15, X18, and X20. The first thing you do is transfer variable X31 to the Grouping Variable box at the top, and then click on the Define Range box just below it. You must tell the program what the minimum and maximum numbers are for the grouping variable. In this case the minimum is 0 = Do Not Recall Ads and the maximum is 1 = Recall Ads, so just put these numbers in and click on Continue. Next you must transfer the food perceptions variables into the Independents box (X15, X18, and X20). Then click on the Statistics box at the bottom and

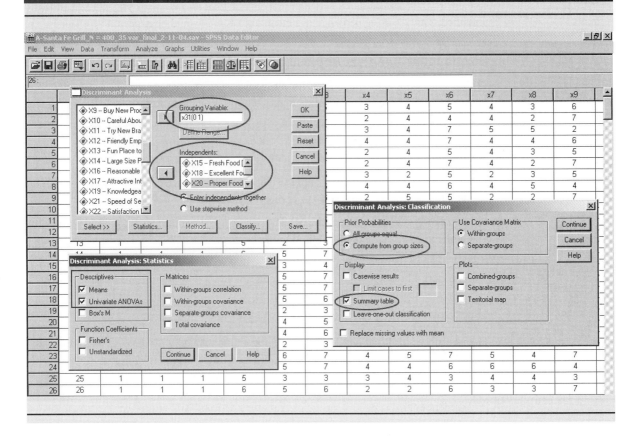

e X H I B I T   17.19   SPSS Screen for Ad Recall Discriminant Analysis

check Means, Univariate ANOVAS, and Continue. The Method default is Enter, and we will use this. Now click on Classify and Compute from group sizes. We do not know if the sample sizes are equal, so we must check this option. You should also click Summary Table and then Continue. We do not use any options under Save, so click OK to run the program. Exhibit 17.19 shows the SPSS screen where you move the dependent and independent variables into their appropriate dialog boxes as well as the Statistics and Classification boxes.

Discriminant analysis is an SPSS program that gives you a lot of output you will not use for a simple analysis like this one. We will look at only five tables from the SPSS output. The first two tables are shown in Exhibit 17.20. The first important information to consider is in the Wilks' Lambda table. The Wilks' Lambda is a statistic that assesses whether the discriminant analysis is statistically significant. If this statistic is significant, as it is in our case (.000), then we next look at the Classification Results table. At the bottom we see that the overall ability of our discriminant function to predict group membership is 77.5 percent. This is good because without the discriminant function we could predict with only 65.5 percent accuracy (our sample sizes are recall ads = 139 and do not recall ads = 261, so if we placed all respondents in the do not recall ads group, we would predict with 65.5 percent accuracy).

To find out which of the independent variables help us to predict group membership we look at the information in two tables shown in Exhibit 17.21. Results shown in the table labeled Tests of Equality of Group Means show which food perceptions variables

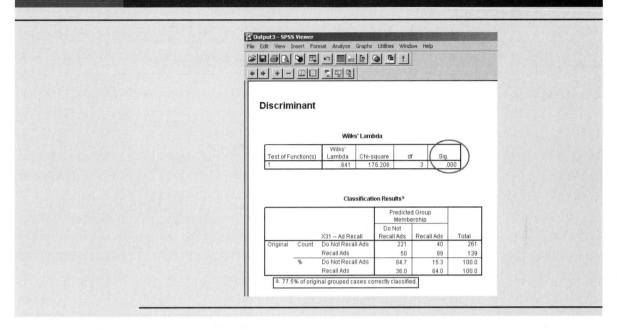

eXHIBIT 17.20 SPSS Discriminant Analysis of X31—Ad Recall

Discriminant

Wilks' Lambda

Test of Function(s)	Wilks' Lambda	Chi-square	df	Sig.
1	.641	176.206	3	.000

Classification Results[a]

		X31 -- Ad Recall	Predicted Group Membership: Do Not Recall Ads	Predicted Group Membership: Recall Ads	Total
Original	Count	Do Not Recall Ads	221	40	261
		Recall Ads	50	89	139
	%	Do Not Recall Ads	84.7	15.3	100.0
		Recall Ads	36.0	64.0	100.0

a. 77.5% of original grouped cases correctly classified.

eXHIBIT 17.21 Discriminant Output for X31—Ad Recall continued

Discriminant

Tests of Equality of Group Means

	Wilks' Lambda	F	df1	df2	Sig.
X15 -- Fresh Food	.700	170.327	1	398	.000
X18 -- Excellent Food Taste	.829	82.117	1	398	.000
X20 -- Proper Food Temperature	.732	145.999	1	398	.000

Structure Matrix

	Function 1
X15 -- Fresh Food	.875
X20 -- Proper Food Temperature	.810
X18 -- Excellent Food Taste	.607

Pooled within-groups correlations between discriminating variables and standardized canonical discriminant functions
Variables ordered by absolute size of correlation within function.

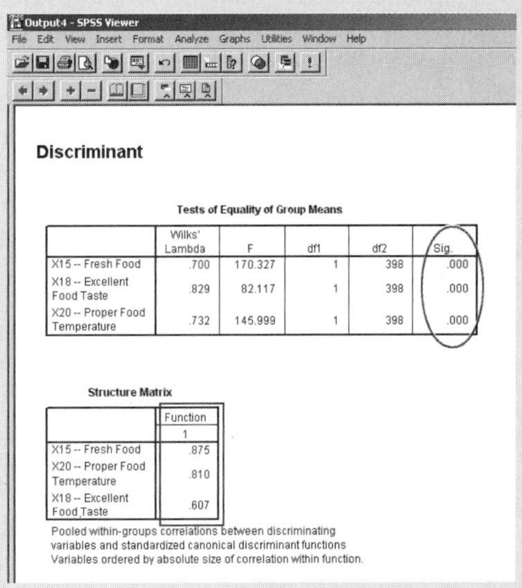

differ between ad recall on a univariate basis. Note that variables X15, X18, and X20 are all highly statistically significant (look at the numbers in the Sig. column). Thus, on a univariate basis all three food perceptions variables differ significantly between the ad recall groups.

eXHIBIT 17.22 Group Means for Discriminant Output for X31—Ad Recall continued

Output5 - SPSS Viewer

File Edit View Insert Format Analyze Graphs Utilities Window Help

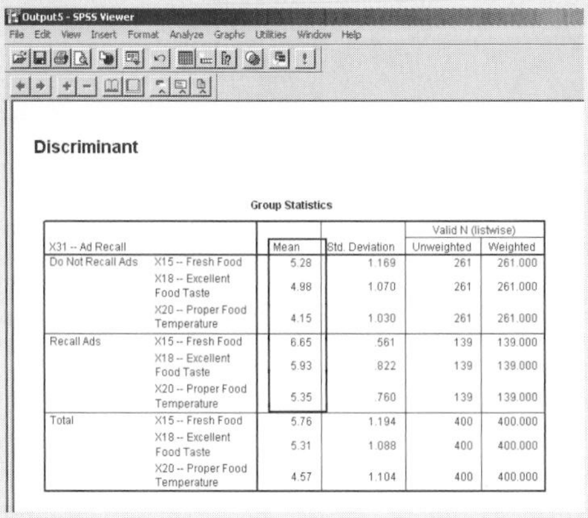

Discriminant

Group Statistics

X31 -- Ad Recall		Mean	Std. Deviation	Valid N (listwise) Unweighted	Valid N (listwise) Weighted
Do Not Recall Ads	X15 -- Fresh Food	5.28	1.169	261	261.000
	X18 -- Excellent Food Taste	4.98	1.070	261	261.000
	X20 -- Proper Food Temperature	4.15	1.030	261	261.000
Recall Ads	X15 -- Fresh Food	6.65	.561	139	139.000
	X18 -- Excellent Food Taste	5.93	.822	139	139.000
	X20 -- Proper Food Temperature	5.35	.760	139	139.000
Total	X15 -- Fresh Food	5.76	1.194	400	400.000
	X18 -- Excellent Food Taste	5.31	1.088	400	400.000
	X20 -- Proper Food Temperature	4.57	1.104	400	400.000

To consider the variables from a multivariate perspective (discriminant analysis), we look at the information in the Structure Matrix table. First we identify the numbers in the Function column that are .30 or higher. This cutoff level is determined in a manner similar to a factor loading. All variables .30 or higher are considered to be helpful in predicting group membership. Like the univariate results, all three food perceptions variables help us to predict ad recall group membership. X15 (.875) and X20 (.810) are very strong predictors while X18 (.607) is a moderately strong predictor.

To further interpret the discriminant function we look at the group means in the Group Statistics table (Exhibit 17.22). For all three variables (X15, X18, and X20) we see that customers who recalled ads had more favorable perceptions of the Santa Fe Grill's food (mean values for recalled ads group all higher). Thus, perceptions of food are significantly more favorable for customers who recall ads versus those who do not. This finding can definitely be used by the owners of the Santa Fe Grill to further develop their advertising campaign.

SPSS Application—Combining Discriminant Analysis and Cluster Analysis

We can easily use discriminant analysis in combination with other multivariate techniques. Remember the cluster analysis example earlier in the chapter in which we identified customer commitment groups using variables X22, X23, and X24. Of the two clusters, cluster 1 respondents were moderately committed while cluster 2 respondents were highly committed to the Santa Fe Grill. We can use the results of this cluster analysis solution as the dependent variable in a discriminant analysis.

Now we must identify which of the database variables we might use as metric independent variables. We have used the restaurant perceptions variables (X12–X21) in an earlier example but we have not used the lifestyle variables (X1–X11). Let's, therefore, see if we can find a relationship between the metric lifestyle variables and the nonmetric customer commitment clusters.

There are 11 lifestyle variables that could be used as independent variables. Three of the variables are related to nutrition—X4—Avoid Fried Foods, X8—Eat Balanced Meals, and X10—Careful about What I Eat. If we use these three variables as independents the objective will be to determine whether nutrition is related to customer commitment. That is, can nutrition predict whether a customer is moderately committed or highly committed?

The SPSS click-through sequence is ANALYZE → CLASSIFY → DISCRIMINANT, which leads to a dialog box where you select the variables. The dependent, nonmetric variable is clu2_1, and the independent, metric variables are X4, X8, and X10. First transfer variable clu2_1 to the Grouping Variable box at the top, and then click on the Define Range box just below it. Insert the minimum and maximum numbers for the grouping variable. In this case the minimum is 1 = cluster 1 and the maximum is 2 = cluster 2, so just put these numbers in and click on Continue. Next you must transfer the food perceptions variables into the Independents box (X4, X8, and X10). Then click on the Statistics box at the bottom and check Means, Univariate ANOVAS, and Continue. The Method default is Enter, and we will use this. Now click on Classify and Compute from group sizes. We do not know if the sample sizes are equal, so we must check this option. You should also click Summary Table and then Continue. We do not use any options under Save, so click OK to run the program.

Remember the SPSS discriminant analysis program gives you a lot of output you will not use for a simple analysis like this. We again will look at only five tables. The first two tables to look at are shown in Exhibit 17.23. Note that the discriminant function is highly significant (Wilks' Lambda of .000) and that the predictive accuracy is very high (86.8 percent correctly classified). Recall that group 1 of our cluster analysis solution had relatively less favorable perceptions of Santa Fe Grill employees than did group 2, which had very favorable perceptions. The overall predictive accuracy of 86.8 percent indicates that this is an excellent predictive function.

To find out which of the independent variables help us to predict group membership we look at the information in two tables (shown in Exhibit 17.24). Results shown in the table labeled Tests of Equality of Group Means show which nutrition lifestyle variables differ on

e X H I B I T   17.23   Discriminant Analysis of Customer Commitment Clusters and Nutrition Lifestyle Variables

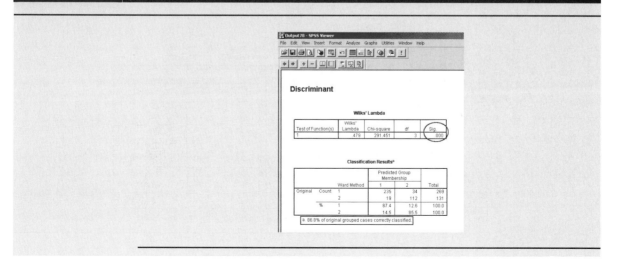

eXHIBIT 17.24 Discriminant Analysis—Customer Commitment Clusters

Output80 - SPSS Viewer

File Edit View Insert Format Analyze Graphs Utilities Window Help

Discriminant

Tests of Equality of Group Means

	Wilks' Lambda	F	df1	df2	Sig.
X4 -- Avoid Fried Foods	.605	259.467	1	398	.000
X8 -- Eat Balanced, Nutritious Meals	.866	61.390	1	398	.000
X10 -- Careful About What I Eat	.689	179.342	1	398	.000

Structure Matrix

	Function 1
X4 -- Avoid Fried Foods	.775
X10 -- Careful About What I Eat	.644
X8 -- Eat Balanced, Nutritious Meals	.377

Pooled within-groups correlations between discriminating variables and standardized canonical discriminant functions
Variables ordered by absolute size of correlation within function.

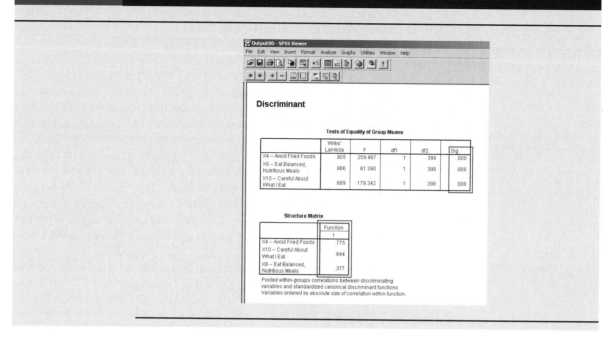

eXHIBIT 17.25 Nutrition Variable Means for Customer Commitment Clusters

Output81 - SPSS Viewer

File Edit View Insert Format Analyze Graphs Utilities Window Help

Discriminant

Group Statistics

Ward Method		Mean	Std. Deviation	Valid N (listwise) Unweighted	Weighted
1	X4 -- Avoid Fried Foods	4.69	1.136	269	269.000
	X8 -- Eat Balanced, Nutritious Meals	4.90	1.155	269	269.000
	X10 -- Careful About What I Eat	4.86	.975	269	269.000
2	X4 -- Avoid Fried Foods	2.94	.721	131	131.000
	X8 -- Eat Balanced, Nutritious Meals	3.96	1.070	131	131.000
	X10 -- Careful About What I Eat	3.55	.787	131	131.000
Total	X4 -- Avoid Fried Foods	4.12	1.308	400	400.000
	X8 -- Eat Balanced, Nutritious Meals	4.60	1.210	400	400.000
	X10 -- Careful About What I Eat	4.43	1.104	400	400.000

a univariate basis. Note that all the predictor variables are highly significant. To consider the variables from a multivariate perspective, use the information from the Structure Matrix table. Identify the numbers in the Function column that are .30 or higher. This cutoff level is determined in a manner similar to a factor loading. All variables .30 or higher are considered to be helpful in predicting group membership. Like the univariate results, all of the variables help us to predict group membership. The strongest nutrition variable is X4 (.775), the second best predictor is X10 (.644), and the least predictive but still helpful is X8 (.377).

To interpret the meaning of the discriminant analysis results we examine the means of the nutrition variables shown in the Group Statistics table of Exhibit 17.25. Looking at the means we see that all the means for the nutrition variables in group 2 are lower than the means in group 1. Moreover, based on the information provided in Exhibit 17.24 we know all of the nutrition variables are significantly different. Thus, customers in group 1 are significantly more "nutrition conscious" than those in group 2.

Recall that cluster 1 was somewhat satisfied with the Santa Fe Grill and cluster 2 (less nutrition conscious) was moderately satisfied. Thus, the results indicate the most satisfied customers are less nutrition conscious. One interpretation of this finding might be that the owners of Santa Fe Grill should consider putting some "Heart Healthy" entrees on the menu to appeal to the somewhat satisfied cluster. These new entrées might also appeal to the moderately satisfied cluster.

marketing research in action

Cluster Analysis and Discriminant

DVD Recorders Replacing VCRs

The latest DVD recorders do a lot more than just record material on DVDs. The latest models let you play and record VHS video, while others include hard drives and programming guides to give you TiVo-like functionality. Stand-alone DVD recorders use the same drive technology as PCs, only they provide a home theater platform. The DVD discs take up less physical space than bulky VHS tapes, plus they have menus that let you easily jump to specific points within a recording. Moreover, the quality is much better than a VCR, with the ability to record up to 700 horizontal lines of resolution compared to only 250 with a VCR.

The DVD market is huge and rapidly getting much larger. No longer limited to home entertainment playback boxes, it is being combined with increasing numbers of consumer electronics products: computers, portable devices, appliances, and industrial systems—DVD is everywhere!

DVDs hit the market in the late 1990s and have enjoyed very fast growth, as evidenced by meteoric U.S. sales since mass-market introduction. Indeed, DVD has enjoyed the most rapid rise of any consumer electronics technology ever introduced. The total market for all types of DVD systems (players, recorders, set-tops, PCs, etc.) is expected to exceed 400 million units by 2006.

DVD players, and more recently player/recorders, have caught the imagination and interest of consumers. DVD set-top box players have boomed in sales due not only to their functionality, but also to their rapidly falling prices. The average selling price fell from about $500 in 1998 to $130 in major retail outlets in early 2003, with some units selling for as low as $40.

The six most popular brands of DVD recorders are: Apex DRX-9000, Panasonic DMR-E60, Philips DVDR80, Pioneer DVR-810H-S, Sharp DV-RW2U, and Sony RDR-GX7. *PC World* recently evaluated these six brands and rated the Sony RDR-GX7 as the best.

Two of the biggest challenges of today's marketers are (1) the successful introduction of new technology-based product innovations into consumer markets, and (2) stimulating the diffusion of those innovations to profitable penetration levels. To meet these challenges, researchers must be able to gain clearer insights into the key factors people might use in deciding whether to adopt technology innovations in consumer electronics.

A study recently was completed to investigate opinions of potential purchasers of DVDs. The study focused on comparing the innovator and early adopter segments with regard to product usage, DVD purchase likelihood, demographics, and related issues. The primary questions addressed were: "Are there attitudinal and behavioral differences between consumers who are innovators versus early adopters?" and "Can these differences be associated with purchase likelihood of DVDs?" A copy of the questionnaire is shown in Exhibit 17.26.

Data was collected using an Internet panel approach from a sample of 200 individuals. The sample frame was consumers with annual household incomes $20,000 or more and ages 18 to 35 years. Data were collected over a two-week period. Participants had to live in North America since the market study was limited to this geographic area. The questionnaire included topics on innovativeness, lifestyles, product and brand image,

EXHIBIT 17.26 Electronics Products Opinion Survey

This is a project being conducted by a marketing research class at The University of Oklahoma. The purpose of this project is to better understand the attitudes and opinions of consumers toward electronics products. The questionnaire will take only a few minutes to complete, and all responses will remain strictly confidential. Thank you for your help on this project.

I. Attitudes

The following questions relate to your attitudes about electronics products, things you like to do, and so forth. On a scale of 1 to 7, with 7 being Strongly Agree, and 1 being Strongly Disagree, please circle the number that best expresses the extent to which you agree or disagree with each of the following statements.

	Strongly Disagree						Strongly Agree
1. The Internet is a good place to get lower prices.	1	2	3	4	5	6	7
2. I don't shop for specials.	1	2	3	4	5	6	7
3. People come to me for advice.	1	2	3	4	5	6	7
4. I often try new brands before my friends and neighbors.	1	2	3	4	5	6	7
5. I would like to take a trip around the world.	1	2	3	4	5	6	7
6. My friends and neighbors come to me for advice and consultation.	1	2	3	4	5	6	7
7. Coupons are a good way to save money	1	2	3	4	5	6	7
8. I seldom look for the lowest price when I shop.	1	2	3	4	5	6	7
9. I like to try new and different things.	1	2	3	4	5	6	7

10. To what extent do you believe you need a DVD player? Please indicate on the scale provided below:

Product I Definitely Do Not Need						Product I Would Like to Try
1	2	3	4	5	6	7

11. How likely are you to purchase a DVD player? Please indicate whether you are moderately likely or highly likely to purchase a DVD player. (Note: respondents who were not likely to purchase a DVD player were screened out of the survey.)

   0 = Moderately Likely
   1 = Highly Likely

II. Classification Information

We need some information for classification purposes. Please tell us a little about yourself.

12. What is the highest level of education you have attained? (Check only ONE box.)
   __ High school graduate
   __ College graduate

13. Electronics Products Ownership. Please indicate the level of electronics products ownership that best describes you.
   __ Own few electronics products
   __ Own a moderate amount of electronics products
   __ Own lots of electronics products

continued

| e X H I B I T | **17.26** | **Electronics Products Opinion Survey,** *continued* |

14. Please check the category that best indicates your total annual household income before taxes. (Check only ONE box.)
    __ $20,000–$35,000
    __ $35,001–$50,000
    __ $50,001–$75,000
    __ $75,001–$100,000
    __ More than $100,000

15. Innovators vs. Early Adopters—this classification was developed using the statistical technique called cluster analysis. In the database, participants were classified as shown below:
    0 = Early Adopters
    1 = Innovators

16. Price Conscious—this classification was developed using questions 1, 2, 7 and 8 from the survey. In the database, participants were classified as shown below:
    0 = Less Price Conscious
    1 = More Price Conscious

Thank you for sharing your opinions with our marketing research class.

and classification questions. Some of the questions were intervally measured while others were nominal and ordinal. There is a database for the questions in this case available in SPSS format at www.mhhe.com/hair06. The database is labeled C_17_DVD Survey MRIA.3e.sav.

To examine the main question, it was necessary to classify respondents as either an innovator or an early adopter. The Innovativeness scale consisted of five variables: X3, X4, X5, X6, and X9. A cluster analysis was run to identify respondents who rated themselves higher on these scales, that is, relatively more innovative. The result was 137 Innovators and 63 Early Adopters. This categorical variable (X15) was then used as the dependent categorical variable in a discriminant analysis. The independent variables were X10—DVD Product Perceptions, X11—Purchase Likelihood, X12—Education, X13—Electronic Products Ownership, X14—Income, and X16—Price Conscious.

The results are shown in Exhibit 17.27. Based on the Wilks' Lambda the discriminant function is highly significant in predicting innovators versus early adopters. Moreover, the Classification Results indicate the predictive accuracy of the discriminant function is 92.0 percent.

The significant independent variable predictors are shown in Exhibit 17.28. On a univariate basis (see Tests of Equality of Group Means table) all of the independent variables are highly significant. Looking at the information in the Structure Matrix table, variables X11, X10, and X14 are the most significant in predicting innovators versus early adopters.

The comparison of group means is shown in Exhibit 17.29. The group means indicate that for all variables except X16—Price Conscious, the means are higher for innovators than they are for early adopters. This can be interpreted as follows. Innovators:

• Have more positive perceptions of DVD player-recorders.

• Are more likely to purchase a DVD player-recorder.

• Are more highly educated.

EXHIBIT 17.27   Discriminant Analysis of Innovators vs. Early Adopters

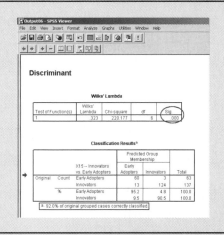

- Own relatively more electronic products.

- Have higher incomes.

The price-conscious mean is lower for innovators than for early adopters (0 = less price conscious; 1 = more price conscious). The interpretation of this is:

- Innovators are less price conscious than early adopters.

EXHIBIT 17.28   Significant Predictors of Innovators vs. Early Adoptors

Tests of Equality of Group Means

	Wilks' Lambda	F	df1	df2	Sig.
X10 -- DVD Product Perceptions	.527	178.053	1	198	.000
X11 -- Purchase Likelihood	.512	188.856	1	198	.000
X12 -- Education	.921	17.006	1	198	.000
X13 -- Electronic Products Ownership	.954	9.505	1	198	.002
X16 -- Price Conscious	.968	6.643	1	198	.011

Structure Matrix

	Function 1
X11 -- Purchase Likelihood	.679
X10 -- DVD Product Perceptions	.660
X12 -- Education	.204
X13 -- Electronic Products Ownership	.152
X16 -- Price Conscious	-.127

Pooled within-groups correlations between discriminating variables and standardized canonical discriminant functions
Variables ordered by absolute size of correlation within function.

EXHIBIT 17.29   Mean Profiles of Innovators vs. Early Adopters

Output3 - SPSS Viewer

File   Edit   View   Insert   Format   Analyze   Graphs   Utilities   Window   Help

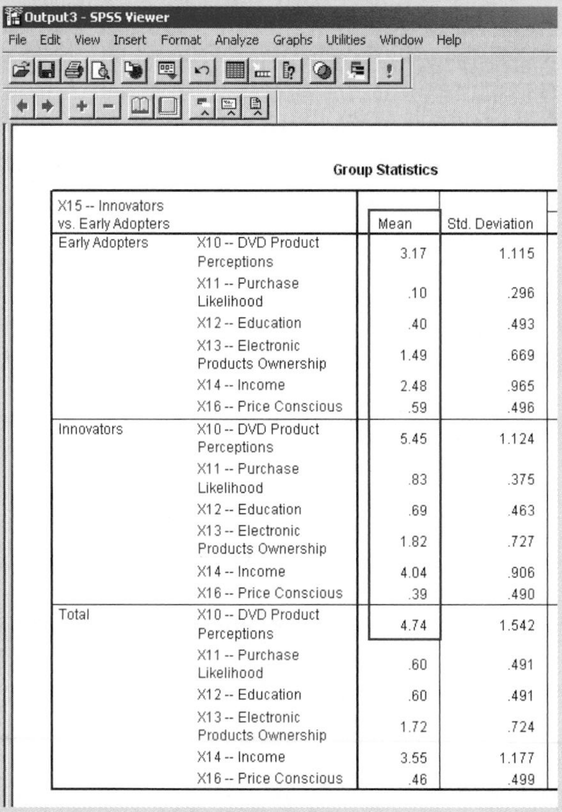

Group Statistics

X15 -- Innovators vs. Early Adopters		Mean	Std. Deviation
Early Adopters	X10 -- DVD Product Perceptions	3.17	1.115
	X11 -- Purchase Likelihood	.10	.296
	X12 -- Education	.40	.493
	X13 -- Electronic Products Ownership	1.49	.669
	X14 -- Income	2.48	.965
	X16 -- Price Conscious	.59	.496
Innovators	X10 -- DVD Product Perceptions	5.45	1.124
	X11 -- Purchase Likelihood	.83	.375
	X12 -- Education	.69	.463
	X13 -- Electronic Products Ownership	1.82	.727
	X14 -- Income	4.04	.906
	X16 -- Price Conscious	.39	.490
Total	X10 -- DVD Product Perceptions	4.74	1.542
	X11 -- Purchase Likelihood	.60	.491
	X12 -- Education	.60	.491
	X13 -- Electronic Products Ownership	1.72	.724
	X14 -- Income	3.55	1.177
	X16 -- Price Conscious	.46	.499

Overall, discriminant analysis can help today's DVD marketers gain a better understanding of their potential market segments. This study demonstrated that DVDs have left the innovation stage of the diffusion process and are making inroads into the early adopter phase. But DVD manufacturers and retail marketers alike must focus on developing strategies that can attract more potential early adopters as well as create awareness and desire among the early majority.

Hands-On Exercises

1. What other issues can be examined with this survey?

2. What problems do you see with the questionnaire? (See Exhibit 17.26)

Summary of Learning Objectives

■ **Define multivariate analysis.**

Multivariate analysis refers to a group of statistical procedures used to simultaneously analyze three or more variables. Factor analysis, cluster analysis, multidimensional scaling, and discriminant analysis are commonly used multivariate statistical techniques.

■ **Understand how to use multivariate analysis in marketing research.**

Multivariate analysis is extremely important in marketing research because most business problems are multidimensional. Marketing managers are often concerned with various aspects of the consumer (e.g., demographics, lifestyles); consumers' purchasing process (e.g., motives, perceptions); and competition. Thus, techniques such as factor analysis, cluster analysis, and discriminant analysis assist marketing managers in simultaneously assessing a set or sets of important variables.

■ **Distinguish between dependence and interdependence methods.**

Multivariate data analysis techniques can be classified into dependence and interdependence methods. A dependence method is one in which a variable or set of variables is identified as the dependent variable to be predicted or explained by other, independent variables. Dependence techniques include multiple regression analysis, and discriminant analysis. An interdependence method is one in which no single variable or group of variables is defined as being independent or dependent. The goal of interdependence methods is data reduction, or grouping things together. Cluster analysis, factor analysis, and multidimensional scaling are the most commonly used interdependence methods.

■ **Define and understand factor analysis and cluster analysis.**

Factor analysis and cluster analysis are both interdependence methods. Factor analysis is used to summarize the information contained in a large number of variables into a smaller number of factors. Cluster analysis classifies observations into a small number of mutually exclusive and exhaustive groups. In cluster analysis, these groups should have as much similarity within each group and as much difference between groups as possible.

■ **Define and use discriminant analysis.**

Multiple discriminant analysis is a dependence method. The purpose of techniques such as discriminant analysis is to predict a variable from a set of independent variables. Discriminant analysis uses independent variables to classify observations into mutually exclusive categories. Discriminant analysis can also be used to determine whether statistically significant differences exist between the average discriminant score profiles of two or more groups.

Key Terms and Concepts

Cluster analysis   599

Classification (or prediction) matrix   608

Dependence method   590

Discriminant analysis   606

Discriminant function   606

Discriminant function coefficients   608

Discriminant score   608

Factor analysis   591

Factor loading   592

Interdependence method   590

Multivariate analysis   588

Review Questions

1. Why are multivariate statistical analysis methods so important to managers today? How do multivariate methods differ from univariate methods?

2. What is the difference between dependence and interdependence multivariate methods?

3. What is the goal of factor analysis? Give an example of a marketing situation that would call for factor analysis.

4. How does cluster analysis differ from factor analysis? Give an example of how cluster analysis is used in marketing research.

5. Why would a marketing researcher use cluster analysis?

6. What is the purpose of discriminant analysis?

7. How might discriminant analysis be used to solve a marketing problem or identify a marketing opportunity?

8. Why would a marketing researcher want to use both discriminant analysis and cluster analysis on the same project to analyze the data?

Discussion Questions

1. Cluster analysis is a commonly used multivariate analysis technique in segmentation studies. Its primary objective is to classify objects into relatively homogeneous groups based on a set of variables. Once those groups are identified by a cluster analysis, what is the next logical analysis step a marketer might want to take? Will the results of a cluster analysis also reveal the characteristics of the members in each group? Why or why not?

2. Discriminant analysis is a frequently used multivariate technique when the objective is to identify important variables in identifying group membership of some type. What is the role of the discriminant function coefficients in identifying these important variables? In the chapter on regression, multicollinearity among the independent variables in a regression equation was highlighted as a potential problem for interpretation of the results. Do you think multicollinearity would also pose a problem for interpreting discriminant analysis results? Why or why not?

4. **EXPERIENCE THE INTERNET.** Access the Internet and select a particular search engine. Use various keywords and identify five major market research providers listed on the Web. Compare and contrast their Web sites and suggest the strength and weaknesses of each. Which would you choose to conduct a marketing research project for you? Why? Prepare a report for class so you can share your findings with other students.

5. **SPSS EXERCISE.** Using the Santa Fe Grill data set and the questionnaire found in Chapter 14, conduct the following tasks:
   a. Submit the data for questions 22, 23, 24 to an SPSS cluster analysis. Create a new variable called "Customer Commitment." Develop a three-group cluster solution identifying three levels of customer commitment.
   b. Using these new clusters as the dependent variable and questions 12 to 21 (restaurant perceptions variables) as the independent variables, perform a three-group discriminant analysis.

6. **SPSS EXERCISE.** Using the Santa Fe Grill data set and questionnaire, perform a factor analysis on the lifestyle variables. Are the results of the factor analysis acceptable, and if so why?

7. **SPSS EXERCISE.** Using the Santa Fe Grill data set and the questionnaire found in Chapter 14, conduct the following tasks:

   a. Conduct a factor analysis using the restaurant perceptions variables $(X_{12}-X_{21})$. After you find the best factor solution, label the factors based on which variables load on each factor.

   b. Calculate factor scores for the factor solution you developed. Use the factors scores as independent variables in a multiple regression with variable X_{22}—Satisfaction as the dependent variable. Interpret your findings and develop conclusions.

   c. Now run another regression using the same independent and dependent variables as in b. above, but now add variables X_{31} and X_{32} as independent dummy variables. What did you learn?

chapter 18

Preparing the Marketing Research Report and Presentation

Learning Objectives

After reading this chapter, you will be able to

1. Understand the primary objectives of a research report.

2. Explain how a marketing research report is organized.

3. List problems that can be encountered when preparing the report.

4. Understand the importance of presentations in marketing research.

5. Identify different software options available for developing presentations.

6. Understand the advantages and disadvantages of different software options available for developing presentations.

"Many times what you say may not be as important as how you say it."

—ANONYMOUS

Back Yard Burgers Focus Group Summary: Presenting Focus Group Results

To: All Executive Officers, Department Heads, Franchisees
Topic: Results and Dialogue from Focus Groups

Executive Summary

At Back Yard Burgers (BYB) we have just scratched the surface of the information needed to improve the climate in Little Rock, Arkansas. Many interesting comments were obtained in the focus group sessions. On the basis of this project it appears quite obvious that immediate attention must be given to operations and marketing in the Little Rock market. Overall, we lack consistency. More important, we need to enhance our commitment to solving the issues that need correction. These issues center on customer service, facility curb appeal, and general customer awareness. From this perspective, the following recommendations are set forth.

All stores in Little Rock need to be cleaned up. Exterior repairs, landscaping improvements, and enhancement of reader boards need to be systematically addressed. In-store employees need to improve their physical appearance and dress. This is particularly important for all customer-contact personnel. Cleanliness is a major issue with the Little Rock consumer. This is complicated by the fact that double drive-thru formats are evaluated on cleanliness based on their exterior appearance.

Regarding internal operations, we have three problems that need immediate attention: bland, mundane attitudes at point of sale; employee confusion in kitchen areas; and too many wrong customer orders. The surest way to alienate a Little Rock customer is to get his or her order wrong. Another big turnoff is charging the customer for additional condiments. In my opinion, there is no excuse for this, since by saving five cents we run the risk of losing long-term loyalty and revenue. Many of these problems can be eliminated with the quality service program. We need to implement this program in all Little Rock locations.

From a marketing perspective, we have great burgers, but beyond that customers don't know what we offer—they lack awareness of our menu variety. Given the fact that healthier food is desired by our patrons, we need to increase our emphasis on our chicken product line specifically and our full menu variety in general. Little Rock customers want to be treated with respect. They appreciate community involvement on the part of local businesses. They like to know who owns and operates those businesses. Given this attitude, BYB needs to implement a two-pronged approach to communication strategy. First, we need to project an overall image of how good we are regarding food and service. With a credible spokesperson, we need to tell the people of Little Rock that BYB is a great place to visit. Second, we need a tactical communication focused on our extensive menu variety, with an emphasis on our chicken line.

Coupons may not be an effective price incentive for Little Rock. Free samples, in-store point-of-sale price discounts, and employee/manager interaction at community events may prove more effective than coupons in generating first-time purchases. With the

high level of expectations for service quality among Little Rock customers, it is important that marketing be accountable for customer satisfaction. Therefore, marketing needs direct input into the quality service program and mystery shopper function. These programs are critical in developing lasting customer relationships and enhancement of our overall image. Given the substantial ramifications that can result from these programs, and the emphasis needed on curb appeal and customer contact personnel, marketing needs to accept responsibility for these programs.

Attached are the findings from the focus groups held in Little Rock. The report is in a question-and-answer format. We strongly urge all parties to read this report. It will provide insights into what customers believe to be occurring in this industry as well as in BYB operations. Also attached is a fax from one of the focus group participants regarding her most recent visit to BYB. Let's see if we can't prevent this from happening in the future.

Value of Preparing the Marketing Research Report

The opening example is an excerpt from an executive summary of a marketing research report for a set of focus groups. The excerpt includes recommendations that should be implemented on the basis of information obtained from focus groups. While this is not a complete executive summary, it illustrates some issues surrounding the purpose of the marketing research report.

No matter how perfectly the research project is designed and implemented, if the results cannot be effectively communicated to the client, the research project is not a success. An effective marketing research report is one way to ensure that the time, effort, and money that went into the research project will be completely realized. The purpose of this chapter is to introduce the style and format of the marketing research report. We identify how the marketing research report is designed, and explain the specific objectives of each section of the report. We then discuss industry best practices regarding effective presentation of the research report, focusing on the use of computer technology to build credibility. A complete marketing research report from a focus group interview is included in the Marketing Research in Action at the end of this chapter.

The Written Marketing Research Report

A professional marketing research report has four primary objectives: (1) to effectively communicate the findings of the marketing research project, (2) to provide interpretations of those findings in the form of sound and logical recommendations, (3) to establish the credibility of the research project, and (4) to serve as a future reference document for strategic or tactical decisions.

The first objective of the research report is to effectively communicate the findings of the marketing research project. Since a major purpose of the research project was to obtain information to answer questions about a specific business problem, the report must explain both how the information was obtained and what relevance it has to the research questions. A detailed description of the following factors should be communicated to the client:

1. The research objectives.

2. The research questions the study was to answer.

3. Procedural information about the collection of secondary data (if necessary).

4. A description of the research methods used.

5. Findings displayed in tables, graphs, or charts.

6. Interpretation and summation of the findings.

7. Conclusions based on data analysis.

8. Recommendations and suggestions for implementation of findings.

Too often researchers are so concerned about communicating results they forget to provide a clear, logical interpretation of those results. Researchers must recognize that clients are seldom knowledgeable about sampling methods and statistics. Thus, researchers must present technical or complex information in a manner that is understandable to all parties. Most researchers are comfortable with statistics, computer outputs, questionnaires, and other project-related material. In presenting such information to the client, researchers should keep the original research objectives in mind. The task is to focus on the objectives and communicate how each part of the project is related to the completion of that objective.

For example, Exhibit 18.1 illustrates a research objective that identifies significant predictors of heavy versus moderate users of family-style restaurants. While much numerical data was necessary to fulfill this objective, the use of appropriate terminology provides an understandable interpretation of the data. Exhibit 18.1 reveals that compared with moderate users, heavy users are less concerned about nutrition, particularly salt and fat, have a high child orientation, are innovators in terms of buying new and different things, are less concerned about food prices, have a lower preference for combo meals, and consider food quality and service relatively more important.

Credibility The quality of a report that is related to its accuracy, believability, and professional organization.

The research report must establish **credibility** for the research methods, findings, and conclusions. This can be accomplished only if the report is accurate, believable, and professionally organized. These three dimensions cannot be treated separately, for they collectively operate to build credibility in the research document. For the report to be accurate, all of the input must be accurate. No degree of carelessness in handling data, reporting of statistics, or incorrect interpretation can be tolerated. Errors in mathematical calculations, grammatical errors, and incorrect terminology are just a few types of inaccuracy that can serve to diminish the credibility of the entire report.

Believability The quality of a report that is based on clear and logical thinking, precise expression, and accurate presentation.

Clear and logical thinking, precise expression, and accurate presentation create **believability.** When the underlying logic is fuzzy or the presentation imprecise, readers may have difficulty understanding what they read. If readers do not understand what they read, they may not believe what they read. For example, a client may believe that half of all respondents find the company's store locations very convenient. If the actual results deviate from this expectation, the client may question the research results. In such cases,

EXHIBIT 18.1 Simple Interpretation of Data

Significant Predictors of User Class: Family Dining Segments

Predictor	Moderate Users	Frequent Users
Opinions		
Nutritious meals	High	Low
Information	Seekers	Leaders
Eating	Skip lunch	Routine
Children	Less child oriented	High child orientation
Eating	Sometimes avoid fat and salt	Little concern about fat and salt
Novelty	Sometimes buy new and different things	Often buy new and different things
Leadership	Follower	Leader
Restaurant Attitudes		
Food prices	Important	Less important
Food quality	Less important	Important
Combo meals	Prefer	Lower preference
Advertising impact	Moderate	High Importance
Service	Moderate	High Importance

the researcher needs to explain the findings clearly. Improper question wording, sampling bias, or nonresponse error can all create a discrepancy between the client's expectations and the findings.

Finally, the credibility of the research report is affected by the quality and organization of the document itself. The report must be clearly developed and professionally organized. Also, to the extent possible the document must reflect the preferences and technical sophistication of the reader.

The following is helpful in preparing the report: Make an outline of all major points, with supporting details in their proper position and sequence. Always keep the reader informed of where the topical development of the report is going. Use short, concise sentences and paragraphs. Always say exactly what you intend to say—don't leave the reader "grasping" for more information. Always select wording that is consistent with the background and knowledge of the reader. Rewrite the report several times. This will force you to remove clutter and critically evaluate the document for errors.

The fourth objective of the research report is to be a reference. Once it is completed, the research report will have a life of its own as a reference. Most marketing research studies cover a variety of different objectives and seek to answer several research questions. This is accomplished with large volumes of information in both statistical and narrative formats. To retain all of this information is virtually impossible for the client. Consequently, the research report becomes a reference document that is cited over an extended period.

Many marketing research reports become a part of a larger project conducted in various stages over time. It is not uncommon for one marketing research report to serve as a baseline for additional studies. Also, many reports are used for comparison purposes. They are used to measure promotional changes, image building tactics, or even strengths and weaknesses of the firm.

Format of the Marketing Research Report

Every marketing research report is unique in some way—due to client needs, research purpose, study objectives, and so on—yet all reports contain some common elements. Although the terminology may differ among industry practices, the basic format discussed in this section will help researchers plan and prepare reports for various clients. The parts common to all marketing research reports are the following:

1. Title page

2. Table of contents

3. Executive summary
   a. Research objectives
   b. Concise statement of method
   c. Summary of findings
   d. Conclusion and recommendations

4. Introduction

5. Research methods and procedures

6. Data analysis and findings

7. Conclusions and recommendations

8. Limitations

9. Appendixes

Title Page

The title page indicates the subject of the report and the name of the recipient, along with his or her position and organization. Any numbers or phrases to designate a particular department or division also should be included. Most important, the title page must contain the name, position, employing organization, address, and telephone number of the person or persons submitting the report, as well as the date the report is submitted.

Table of Contents

The table of contents lists the topics of the report in sequential order. Usually, the contents page will highlight each topical area, the subdivisions within each area, and corresponding page numbers. It is also common to include tables and figures and the pages where they can be found.

Executive summary
The part of a marketing research report that presents the major points; it must be complete enough to provide a true representation of the document but in summary form.

Executive Summary

The **executive summary** is the most important part of the report. Many consider it the soul of the report, insofar as many executives read only the report summary. The executive summary presents the major points of the report. It must be complete enough to provide a true representation of the entire document but in summary form.

The executive summary has several purposes: (1) to convey how and why the research was undertaken, (2) to summarize the findings, and (3) to suggest future actions.

In other words, the executive summary must contain the research objectives, a concise statement of method, a summary of the findings, and specific conclusions and recommendations.

Research objectives should be as precise as possible, and not longer than approximately one page. The research purpose along with the questions or hypotheses that guided the project should also be stated in this section. Next, a brief description of the sampling method, the research design, and any procedural aspects are addressed in one or two paragraphs. Following this is a statement of findings. The findings presented in the summary must agree with those found in the findings section of the full report. Include only key findings that relate to the research objectives. Finally, the summary contains a brief statement of conclusions and recommendations. Conclusions are given as opinions based on the findings. They are statements of what the research generated and what meaning can be attached to the findings. Recommendations, in contrast, are for appropriate future actions. Recommendations focus on specific marketing tactics or strategies the client can use to gain a competitive advantage. Conclusions and recommendations typically are stated in one to two paragraphs.

Introduction

The introduction contains background information necessary for a complete understanding of the report. Definition of terms, relevant background information, and the study's scope and emphasis are communicated in the introduction.

This section should also list specific research objectives and questions the study was designed to answer. Hypotheses, length and duration of the study, and any research-related problems are also contained in the introduction. Upon reading the introduction, the client should know exactly what the report is about, why the research was conducted, and what relationships exist between the current study and past or future research endeavors.

Research Methods and Procedures

The objective of the methods-and-procedures section is to communicate how the research was conducted. Issues addressed in this section include the following:

1. The research design used: exploratory, descriptive, and/or causal.

2. Types of secondary data included in the study.

3. If primary data were collected, what procedure was used (observation, questionnaire) and what administration procedures were employed (personal, mail, telephone, Internet).

4. Sample and sampling processes used. The following issues must be addressed:
    a. How was the sample population defined and profiled?
    b. Sampling units used (businesses, households, individuals, etc.).
    c. The sampling list used in the study.
    d. How was the sample size determined?
    e. Was a probability or nonprobability sampling plan employed?

Many times when generating the methods-and-procedures section, the writer gets bogged down in presenting too much detail. If on completion of this section, the reader can say what was done, how it was done, and why it was done, the objective of the writer has been fulfilled. The Marketing Research in Action at the end of the chapter exemplifies many of these principles.

Data Analysis and Findings

Because each project is so specific with regard to data analysis, little can be said in reference to the analysis techniques. Nonetheless, if the researcher is reporting the output of a Chi square, for example, best practices suggest covering the concept of statistical significance of the test, the general rationale for performing the test, and the assumptions associated with the procedure.

For more sophisticated analysis techniques, such as multiple regression or ANOVA, it is always good practice to provide a brief description of the technique along with why it is being used and what outcomes can occur.

The actual results of the study—the findings—will constitute the majority of this section of the report. Findings should always include a detailed presentation with supporting tables, figures, and graphs. All results must be logically arranged so as to correspond to each research objective or research question indicated earlier in the report. Best practices suggest that tables, figures, and graphs be used when results are presented. Illustrations should provide a simple summation of the data in a clear, concise, and nontechnical manner. For example, Exhibit 18.2 contains a table illustrating the results for the research question, "How frequently do you patronize the Santa Fe Grill?" This table illustrates the data output in a simple and concise manner, enabling the reader to easily view how frequently respondents patronize the Santa Fe Grill.

More sophisticated or technical exhibits should be reserved for the appendixes of the report. Unlike Exhibit 18.2, the information contained in Exhibit 18.3 is complex and more difficult to explain. While this information is directly related to the research objectives concerning factors influencing the image of the Santa Fe Grill, it needs detailed explanation to simplify the intent for the reader. Information such as this is better suited for the appendix section of the report.

Conclusions and Recommendations

Conclusions and recommendations are derived specifically from the findings. Conclusions can be considered broad generalizations that focus on answering questions related to the research objectives. They are condensed pieces of information derived from the findings

---

eXHIBIT 18.2 Findings Illustrating Simple Readable Results

How frequently do you patronize the Santa Fe Grill?

	Frequency	Percent	Cumulative Percent
Occasionally (less than once a month)	111	27.8	27.8
Frequently (1–3 times a month)	178	44.5	72.3
Very Frequently (4 or more times a month)	111	27.8	100.0
Total	400	100.0	

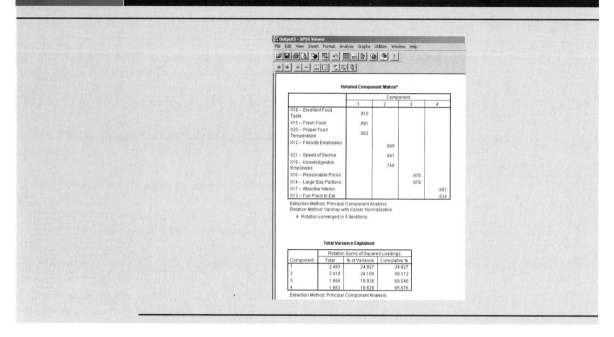

---

eXHIBIT | **18.3** **Findings Illustrating Complex Technical Results**

---

that communicate the results of the study to the reader. As illustrated in Exhibit 18.4, conclusions are descriptive statements generalizing the results, not necessarily the numbers generated by statistical analysis. Each conclusion is made in direct reference to the research objectives.

Recommendations are generated by critical thinking. The task is one where the researcher must critically evaluate each conclusion and develop specific areas of applications for

---

eXHIBIT | **18.4** **Illustration of Conclusions in a Marketing Research Report**

Conclusions

- Four primary factors are related to satisfaction with and patronage of the Santa Fe Grill—food quality, service, value, and atmosphere.
- Food quality is the most important factor influencing satisfaction with and patronage of the Santa Fe Grill.
- Service at the Santa Fe Grill is the second most important factor influencing satisfaction with and patronage of the restaurant.
- The Santa Fe Grill has favorable perceptions of its food quality and service.
- Perceptions of value and atmosphere are relatively less favorable.
- Perceptions of the Santa Fe Grill on all four factors—food, service, value, and atmosphere—are significantly less favorable for the less frequent patrons.
- More frequent patrons of the Santa Fe Grill have lifestyles that characterize them as Innovators and Influencers.

exhibit 18.5 Illustration of Recommendations in a Marketing Research Report

Recommendations

- Advertising messages should emphasize food quality and service, since these are the most important factors influencing satisfaction.
- If advertisements include people, they should be characterized as innovative in their lifestyles.
- Focus group research needs to be conducted to learn why perceptions of value and atmosphere are less favorable than perceptions of food quality and service.
- The focus group research also needs to examine why perceptions of less frequent patrons of the Santa Fe Grill are significantly less favorable than those of more frequent patrons.
- The current study collected data from customers of the Santa Fe Grill. In the future, data should be collected from noncustomers.

strategic or tactical actions. Recommendations must focus on how the client can solve the problem at hand through the creation of a competitive advantage.

Exhibit 18.5 outlines the recommendations that correspond to the conclusions displayed in Exhibit 18.4. You will notice that each recommendation, unlike the conclusions, is in the form of a clear action statement.

Limitations

Limitations Extraneous events that place certain restrictions on the report and are normally mentioned when results are being compared.

Researchers always strive to develop and implement a flawless study for the client. But extraneous events often place **limitations** on the project. Researchers must note the limitations of a project, and inform the client of such events. Common limitations associated with marketing research include sampling bias, financial constraints, time pressures, and measurement error.

Every study has limitations and it is the responsibility of the researcher to make the client aware of them. Researchers should not be embarrassed by limitations but rather admit openly that they exist. Treatment of limitations in the research report usually involves a discussion of results and accuracy. For example, researchers should tell clients about the generalizability of the results beyond the sample used in the study. Weaknesses of specific scales should be addressed, along with potential sources of nonsampling error. If limitations are not stated and later discovered by the client, mistrust and skepticism toward the entire report may result. Limitations rarely diminish the credibility of the report but rather serve to improve the perceptions clients hold toward the quality of the project.

Appendixes

Appendix A section following the main body of the report; used to house complex, detailed, or technical information.

An **appendix,** many times referred to as a "technical appendix," contains complex, detailed, or technical information not necessary for the formal report. Common items contained in appendixes include questionnaires, interviewer forms, statistical calculations, detailed sampling maps, and tables such as the one in Exhibit 18.6. Researchers know the appendix is rarely read in the same context as the report itself. In fact, most appendixes are treated as points of reference in the report. That is, information in the appendix is cited in the report to guide the reader to further technical or statistical detail.

---

e X H I B I T 18.6 **Example of Detailed Results Table Suitable for Appendix Section**

Output31 - SPSS Viewer
File Edit View Insert Format Analyze Graphs Utilities Window Help

Descriptives

		N	Mean	Std. Deviation	Std. Error	95% Confidence Interval for Mean		Minimum	Maximum
						Lower Bound	Upper Bound		
X22 -- Satisfaction	Occasionally	111	3.81	.694	.066	3.68	3.94	3	6
	Frequently	111	4.54	.829	.079	4.38	4.70	3	6
	Very Frequently	178	5.23	.735	.055	5.12	5.34	4	6
	Total	400	4.64	.955	.048	4.55	4.74	3	6
X23 -- Likely to Return	Occasionally	111	3.61	.822	.078	3.46	3.77	2	5
	Frequently	111	3.98	.820	.078	3.83	4.14	3	6
	Very Frequently	178	5.04	.833	.062	4.92	5.16	4	6
	Total	400	4.35	1.039	.052	4.25	4.45	2	6
X24 -- Likely to Recommend	Occasionally	111	2.88	.735	.070	2.74	3.02	2	5
	Frequently	111	3.14	.962	.091	2.96	3.33	2	5
	Very Frequently	178	4.01	.681	.051	3.91	4.11	3	5
	Total	400	3.46	.930	.047	3.37	3.55	2	5

ANOVA

		Sum of Squares	df	Mean Square	F	Sig.
X22 -- Satisfaction	Between Groups	139.439	2	69.720	123.482	.000
	Within Groups	224.151	397	.565		
	Total	363.590	399			
X23 -- Likely to Return	Between Groups	159.969	2	79.984	117.159	.000
	Within Groups	271.031	397	.683		
	Total	431.000	399			
X24 -- Likely to Recommend	Between Groups	102.129	2	51.064	83.375	.000
	Within Groups	243.149	397	.612		
	Total	345.278	399			

Common Problems in Preparing the Marketing Research Report

Often we get so involved with the writing of a research report that we fail to keep in mind key issues that later may present themselves as problems. Such simple things as language may even go overlooked in some cases. Industry best practices suggest five problem areas that may arise in writing a marketing research report.

1. *Lack of data interpretation.* In some instances, we get so involved in constructing results tables that we fail to provide proper interpretation of the data in the tables. The researcher always provides unbiased interpretation of any findings.

2. *Unnecessary use of multivariate statistics.* To impress clients, many researchers unnecessarily use sophisticated multivariate statistical techniques. In many research reports, the most sophisticated statistical technique required will be a Chi-square test. Avoid using statistical methods unless they are essential to derive meaning from the data.

A Closer Look at Research

What Is Marketing Research?

Apart from focus groups, marketing research consists mainly of sampling consumers, asking questions, adding up the answers, and supplying the results to clients. And the main change resulting from the convergence of computers, software, and telephones is the speed of getting answers. The slowest change has been in the presentation of results, and it is there that change is most needed. Speed of data collection has leapt ahead. But often the results are printed out on paper in too much detail and clients are bombarded with information.

In the Field

Progress in results presentation is essential. Nowadays most clients have PCs on their desks. The voice of the consumer should be made available to them in an interactive format that allows for immediate action.

This is far from conventional table analysis. It means quickly identifying what matters in the data, comparing it with past data for changes, and giving the client what is needed. In this way data can be used to make swift decisions and match the almost daily changes in the marketplace. To provide useful research, suppliers must know their clients' business. They can no longer be providers of tables only, but must provide data specifically tailored to the needs of their clients.

The future will see more specialization by research companies. There will be research companies collecting data and research companies using the data to inform clients. And most of the new developments will be in the area of presenting data in a form that clients can access easily, quickly, and use interactively. That's a long way from the old-style presentation of data in large bound volumes of tables.

3. *Emphasis on packaging instead of quality.* Many researchers go out of their way to make reports look classy or flamboyant using sophisticated computer-generated graphics. While graphic representation of the results is essential in the report, never lose sight of the primary purpose—to provide valid and credible information to the client.

4. *Lack of relevance.* Reporting data, statistics, and information that are not consistent with the study's objectives can be a major problem when writing the report. Always develop the report with the research objectives clearly in focus. Avoid adding unnecessary information just to make the report bigger. Always remain in the realm of practicality. Suggest ideas that are relevant, doable, and consistent with the results of the study. A further discussion of relevance appears in the Closer Look at Research box.

5. *Placing too much emphasis on a few statistics.* Never base all conclusions or recommendations on one or a few statistically significant questions or results. Always attempt to find supporting evidence for any recommendation or conclusion.

Always remember, the final research document is the end product of the researcher. Individual credibility can be enhanced or damaged by the report, and credibility is what helps a researcher gain repeat business and referrals from clients. The quality, dedication, and honesty one places into the report have the potential to generate future business, career promotions, and salary raises.

The Critical Nature of Presentations

Presentation of marketing research results can be as important as, if not more important than, the results of the research itself. This is true for several reasons. First, any research, no matter how well done or how important, cannot be properly acted upon if the results are not effectively communicated to those who will use the information in making decisions. Managers need accurate information if they are going to make good decisions, and if they do not understand the marketing research findings, they may well make poor decisions that lead to difficulty not only for the organization but also for individuals in the organization affected by those decisions. Second, the report or presentation is often the only part of the marketing research project that will be seen by those commissioning the report. Senior managers often do not have the time to review all aspects of a research project, so they rely on the researcher to carry out the research properly and then present the findings clearly and concisely. Third, the content and presentation form of the research are closely intertwined. Poorly organized presentations presented in an unclear, lengthy, difficult-to-access format often lead audiences to discount the content. Presentations that use high-technology applications and methods are often perceived as having more merit than presentations that use older, low-tech methods. Thus, the method of presentation can influence the perception of the value or merit of the information presented.

Presenting Marketing Research Results

Traditional presentation methods include chalkboards, whiteboards (dry-erase boards), and overhead projectors. These tried-and-true methods used to be acceptable. Today, however, they do not effectively communicate nearly as well. The desire to create cleaner, more professional-looking presentations of marketing research results has led to the development of a wide variety of computer-based presentation applications, from computer-generated overhead transparencies to full-blown multimedia presentations, complete with text, graphics, sound, and video or animation.

General Guidelines for Preparing the Visual Presentation

The visual presentation is many times referred to as a separate but equal component of the marketing research report. Equal because the visual presentation must reflect the exact content of the written marketing research report. Separate because based on the type of presentation and style preference of the presenter, it may not adhere to the same basic outline of the written research report. Regardless of the presentation style used, the visual presentation has one primary goal: to provide a visual summary of the marketing research report, designed in a manner that will complement and enhance oral communication of the written marketing research report.

In many cases, Microsoft PowerPoint is the preferred method of preparing the visual marketing research presentation. Given the versatility of PowerPoint, the visual presentation can be as simple as multiple slides reflecting summary statements of the written report, or as complex as a total multimedia presentation including the use of sound, animation, color graphics, and streaming video. Regardless of the complexity in the presentation, industry practices suggest the following guidelines:

1. Begin with a slide showing the title of the presentation and the individual(s) doing the presentation. In addition, the client and the marketing research firm should also be identified.

2. A sequence of slides should be developed indicating the objectives of the research and the specific research questions to be addressed, followed by the research methodology employed and a description of the sample surveyed.

3. Unlike the written research report, many times a visual presentation includes ancillary material such as environmental trends, market activities, customer behaviors, and other forms of secondary data.

4. Additional slides should be developed that highlight the research findings or particular results of the study which the researcher deems important for communication purposes.

5. Finally, the presentation should conclude with recommendations, conclusions, and research implications as they pertain to the study at hand.

A PowerPoint presentation illustrating many of the above suggestions can be reviewed at www.mhhe.com/hair06.

Using Computer Software to Develop Presentations

There are many computer presentation software packages. We focus on two major formats useful in presenting market research findings: computer screen projection and Web pages. Projecting the computer screen has several advantages. Researchers often find it easy to develop the presentation on a computer and import information from the research project computer files as needed. The computer helps the researcher stay organized during presentations, with little chance of lost or out-of-order transparencies. It also facilitates the use of sound, color, and other graphics. Finally, it enables presenters to reduce costs, since they no longer need to pay for costly color transparencies, and its electronic format means it can easily be e-mailed to clients ahead of time for review.

PowerPoint A software package used to develop slides for electronic presentation of research results.

One of the most widely used presentation software packages is Microsoft's **PowerPoint.** PowerPoint can develop transparencies, 35-mm slides, and on-screen electronic presentations. It can also be used to develop notes, audience handouts, and outlines, all from the same information. Thus, the presenter has to type or import information only once to develop the research presentation. Presentation software such as PowerPoint can be used to develop eye-catching, organized presentations that convey research findings clearly, concisely, and smoothly.

Hypertext markup language (HTML) Computer language used to create Web pages for communicating results on the Internet.

Another emerging format for presentations is the use of **hypertext markup language (HTML)** to create Web pages. This is the format for communication over the Internet. By using the Internet, researchers are able to communicate market information to their audiences around the world, without the restrictions of time or geography. No longer do all members of the audience need to be in the same location at a given time to receive information during a presentation. Marketing research results can be posted on Web pages and viewed at leisure. Furthermore, not only the presentation itself but also the supporting materials—including text, sound, graphics, and animation or movie files—are available for viewers to download and inspect, and articles on similar topics can be linked together for easy reference. Also, technology has made it possible to conduct real-time video conferencing where participants in different geographical locations take part in meetings, seeing and hearing each other through their computers over the Internet.

In developing Internet-based presentations, researchers have several options. They can put their information on a server for the world to view, and let those interested in the information know where and how to access it so they can receive the information independently, at their convenience. Or, if the researcher wants to present the information at a given time and location, he or she can place the information either on a server or on his or her own computer, and then personally lead the presentation of information to the audience, adding input and guiding the presentation along. In this section, we focus on the creation and development of Internet-based presentations that will be placed on a server for geographically dispersed audiences to view independently. But keep in mind that the presenter can just as easily use this format in actual presentations of research outcomes to a local audience. The flexibility and power of Internet-based presentations makes them an attractive format for use where time or distance is a problem in disseminating information.

Claris Home Page Software used to create Web pages that can integrate text and graphics with other types of computer files.

One easy-to-use software package is **Claris Home Page** (www.learningspace.org/tech/clrs_hmpg/chintro.html), which is used to create Web pages and can integrate text, graphics, and other types of computer files. While there are several software packages available for Web page development, they are similar enough in operation that an understanding of Claris Home Page should provide a sound foundation for using any of the other packages.

Advantages and Disadvantages of Computer Formats

Computer screen projection and Web page presentation formats each have their own advantages and disadvantages. Both formats enable presenters to easily import text outlines into the presentation software. Both formats also enable the integration of text and graphics to create eye-catching presentations and the use of coloring, background shading, and textures to highlight certain topics or major points. However, both formats also require at least the use of computers and their basic power requirements—it would be difficult to give a computer-based presentation to a group of farmers in a Kansas wheat field without a nearby source of electricity. Both formats also require the presenter, or both the presenter and the audience, to have some basic level of computer competence.

The use of software such as Microsoft PowerPoint in computer screen projection enables presenters to control their presentation in terms of timing, highlighting key points, and making transitions between topics. A disadvantage, however, is that it requires the audience to be physically present at a given location at a given time. Also, the amount of information presented is usually limited to the main points, with supporting documentation usually distributed in printed form, requiring added printing expense. Finally, animations and other high-tech graphics are not as easily integrated into this presentation format.

Internet-based presentations of marketing research have the primary advantage of not requiring the audience to be physically present at any given time or location. Members of the audience can access the information at any time, from many different locations. (One example of this is a student at the University of Memphis who accessed his marketing class's Web page and downloaded the reading materials while traveling from Nashville to Memphis, using a laptop computer and his wireless phone.) Further, additional information with supporting documentation, graphics, animation, or sounds can be readily available through the computer if requested. Also, information from other Web sites can be linked so the audience can easily and quickly access a wealth of relevant information. Finally, the Web itself can be used to conduct further investigations. Computer searches can be conducted to find out what other information is available, or possibly where it may be found.

Using the Internet has its drawbacks, however. The main drawback is that the presenter loses some control over the presentation, so the information must be presented in a more self-explanatory fashion. This requires presenters to spend more time in developing their presentations, with greater organization and an eye toward heading off possible misunderstandings. Another consideration is that the speed at which files are transmitted over the Internet can be a problem, particularly if large graphics files must be transmitted. Finally, creating Internet-based presentations requires presenters to have the relevant computer skills, since, for example, graphics files must often be converted and saved in particular file formats for use in Web pages.

mɑRKETIПG RESEɑRCH IП ɑCTIOП

Writing the Marketing Research Report for a Focus Group Interview

Jackson Community Business Environment

This illustration uses a focus group report that demonstrates many of the concepts addressed in this chapter.

Introduction

This focus group report is prepared for the area known as the Jackson community, located in the north central section of Memphis, Tennessee. The focus of this report is to communicate findings that were revealed in a focus group interview. Elements of discussion centered on the trends and market dynamics of the business environment within the Jackson community.

Research Purpose

Issues pertaining to the business climate of the Jackson community will be explored. The purpose of this study is twofold. First, to explore the business trends, market dynamics, and growth potential of the Jackson community for the purpose of providing insights into future business development in the area. Second, to obtain data on market characteristics to be used in a subsequent survey to determine residents' buying power and spending habits within the community. In order to address these issues, the following research objectives were developed.

Research Objectives

To obtain accurate data pertaining to future business development in the Jackson area, the following research objectives were agreed upon:

1. To determine the current level of saturation and possible oversaturation of business activities in the Jackson community.

2. To assess opportunities for new and emerging businesses regarding trends and potential of the Jackson market.

3. To discover potential barriers to entry and growth in such areas as capital, markets, banking, and suppliers.

4. To explore related business issues such as supplier/vendor relations, receivables, financial variables, leasing, and location, along with selling strategies.

5. To assess positive city-delivered services to the Jackson community.

6. To explore business and neighborhood relations.

7. To discuss what can be done to improve the Jackson community business environment.

8. To learn how businesses in the Jackson community market themselves.

9. To address the future of the economy and business climate regarding customer segments, spending behavior, and consumer decision making.

Sample Characteristics

On the basis of a random sample of the university business community, eight business owners/managers were used in the focus group procedure:

Mr. Harry Grayden	Johnson Supply
Mr. Warren Bowling	Plastic Fabrication
Ms. Emma Roberson	Temporary Employment
Ms. Anna Hogan	Sheet Metal Services, Inc.
Mr. Tom Brockway	Target Medical, Inc.
Mr. Sam Jorce	Retail Glass Co.
Mr. Andy Hammond	Retail Auto Parts
Mr. Hilliard Johnson	Carpet Cleaning

Research Findings

To best illustrate the findings of this focus group interview, results will be categorized in narrative form as they pertain to each research objective, following a general overview of the Jackson community.

General Overview of the Jackson Community

Major positive aspects. Jackson is a centralized location with easy access to all areas of the city and surrounding communities. It also is a good area to conduct manufacturing or wholesaling businesses. Stable, yet dependent on the economy—first area to lose jobs when the economy softens. Major competitive advantage is the central location.

Major negative aspects. Major problems in the area are sales of illegal drugs centering around two motels and the Paris adult bookstore. Also, crime is high—all participants in the study were victims of break-ins during the past two years. In addition, the uncertainty of the Sam Cooper Expressway extension has created a lot of anxiety among businesses.

1. Saturation and Oversaturation of Business Activities   Not unlike other areas of the city, Jackson is oversaturated in low-entry-barrier businesses. These include:

Pawn shops

Used-car lots

Credit agencies

Title companies

Small, home-based businesses

Medium-sized distribution businesses

A major concern of the participants was the increased number of small mom-and-pop businesses. The Jackson area has low-cost rental space that makes it attractive for many small, novice businesses to operate with a severe level of undercapitalization. The Broad/Tillman area is an example of undercapitalized businesses that often fail in the first year, leading to distressed commercial property.

2. Opportunity Assessment and Market Trends   Growth in the Jackson area is uncertain, given the extension of the Sam Cooper Expressway. High level of business turnover leads to both distressed commercial and residential property.

Several participants labeled Jackson as a good "incubation" area for small businesses, given its central location and low rent for commercial property.

Business trends and market potential. The Jackson area has an excellent opportunity for growth due to the high level of business turnover and low cost of rental property. Certain businesses can take advantage of a low barrier to entry but need to understand how to operate a business successfully without intensifying the level of saturation. Businesses that were identified by the participants include:

Hardware stores

Grocery stores

Movie theaters

Entertainment businesses

Large manufacturing plants

Warehousing and logistical businesses

Fast-food restaurants

Discount stores

All participants were in agreement that the Jackson area is a great magnet area due to the high level of employment that brings working people into the area.

3. Potential Barriers to Entry and Growth   The area is good for business growth if certain conditions exist. A neglected area that needs to be cleaned up is distressed property resulting from evicted tenants. There appears to be no code enforcement in the area. Drugs are keeping many businesses out.

4. Related Business Issues

- **Supplier/vendor relations.** No problems with suppliers because of the high volume of warehousing, distribution, and manufacturing in the community.

- **Controlling receivables.** Heavy inflow of dollars into the community from all parts of the metropolitan statistical area. Most accounts are large, high volume. Receivables are usually paid within 30 days; typical business cycles.

- **Financial variables.** Most financial institutions have moved out of the area due to crime. The level of financial support is still good in the community, but more so for service businesses and not as supportive for retail.

- **Leasing and location.** Low rent, convenient access, and central location are the major positives of the area. Yet many facilities are in the process of relocating because large spaces are not available in the area. Office space is high-priced relative to other areas, retail space is average, and warehousing and distribution space is very cheap in the community.

- **Selling strategies.** The community is excellent for business-to-business activity; not so good, given current conditions, for retail trade. Appeal to drive-up business, not a conducive area for pedestrian traffic. No real community support for retail business.

5. Positive Aspects of City Services   Businesses in the community are very disgruntled with city officials. Aside from electric and water they feel the community is ignored by the city—especially a lack of concern from the department of public works. Lack of city services detracts from the community, making it unappealing for consumers to shop in the area. The city has done nothing to promote the area in general, and nothing to promote business growth. The infrastructure of the community is deteriorating; high level of break-ins in the community.

6. Business and Neighborhood Relationships   Community commitment is low among both residential and business entities. The community has no sense of identity. Low community support for retail businesses. Heavy migration to East Memphis for shopping/specialty goods due to a lack of discount stores in the area and unpleasant shopping centers. The lack of adequate retailers is forcing people to other communities, specifically, east.

Curb appeal of many businesses is low. Unsightly areas need to be cleaned up, with emphasis on distressed property, both commercial and residential.

7. How to Improve the Business Environment in the Jackson Community

- Clean up distressed property; enforce city codes on property.

- Resolve the problems with the rail tracks.

- Provide some certainty as to the Sam Cooper Expressway extension.

- Add more foliage; make the streets look more attractive.

- Start enforcing housing codes for both residential and commercial property.

8. How Do Businesses Market Themselves?

- Focus on the business-to-business market, not on retail.

- Have good labor supply; provide security for the employees.

- Provide a safe, appealing, and convenient environment for customers and employees.

- Train employees.

- Take advantage of any form of low-cost advertising and promotions.

- Provide quality service; don't promise what you can't deliver.

9. Future Direction of the Economy and Business Community in the Jackson Area

- It is a static area—will probably go unchanged for the immediate future. Possibly a slow decline in the area due to larger businesses relocating to other parts of the city.

- Perception of the area needs to change if businesses are to remain there.

- Major opportunity for the community is to position it as a warehousing/distribution park.

- Not a good area for retail—too many distressed neighborhoods, too many home-based businesses.

- Sam Cooper Expressway extension will determine the future of the community; need better leadership by the city to correct crime problems.

- Area is ideally suited for small manufacturing businesses or transportation businesses. Not really conducive for retail—bad pedestrian traffic area.

- Provide the area with a focus of what it should be—industrial, residential, etc. Develop much of the vacant land with businesses that reinforce that focus.

Hands-On Exercise

1. What conclusions can be drawn from this focus group report?

2. Can strategy decisions be made for the Jackson Community using this focus group report, or will more research be necessary? If more research is necessary, what kind?

Summary of Learning Objectives

■ **Understand the primary objectives of a research report.**

The key objective of a marketing research report is to provide the client with a clear, concise interpretation of the research project. The research report is a culmination of the entire study and therefore must communicate the systematic manner in which the study was designed and implemented. Secondary objectives of the report are to provide accurate, credible, easy-to-understand information to the client. The end result of the report is its ability to act as a reference document to guide future research and serve as an information source.

■ **Explain how a marketing research report is organized.**

The research report generally includes the following: a title page, a table of contents, and an executive summary, which includes a statement of the research objectives, a detailed statement of the research method and procedures, a brief statement of findings, and conclusions and recommendations. Following the executive summary are the introduction of the report, a description of the methodology employed, and a discussion of data analysis techniques and findings. The final elements are conclusions and recommendations, and a description of limitations. An appendix may include technical explanations or documentation.

■ **List problems that can be encountered when preparing the report.**

Problem areas that may arise in the preparation of the research report are (1) lack of data interpretation, (2) unnecessary use of multivariate statistics, (3) emphasis on packaging rather than quality, (4) lack of relevance, and (5) placing too much emphasis on a few statistical outcomes.

■ **Understand the importance of presentations in marketing research.**

Presentations are important because research results must be effectively communicated to those seeking to use the information in decision making. The report or presentation may be the only part of the research project that will be seen by those commissioning the report. The content of the research and the presentation form of the research are closely intertwined.

■ **Identify different software options available for developing presentations.**

Computers can be used to create overhead transparencies, on-screen presentations based on slides or Web pages, and actual Web pages. The two major formats for presenting information are (1) computer screen projection, in which computer slides are projected to a live audience, and (2) Internet-based presentation to a live audience or to a general Internet audience.

■ **Understand the advantages and disadvantages of different software options available for developing presentations.**

Computer screen projection requires the audience to be physically present at a given time and location but allows the presenter to control the presentation, receive immediate feedback from the audience, and answer any questions. Internet presentations enable audiences to review the information anytime from anywhere they have computer access.

Key Terms and Concepts

Appendix 633

Believability 627

Claris Home Page 638

Credibility 627

Executive summary 629

Hypertext markup language (HTML) 637

Limitations 633

PowerPoint 637

Review Questions

1. What are the primary objectives of the marketing research report? Briefly discuss each objective and why they are so important.

2. In the context of the marketing research report, what is the primary goal of the executive summary?

3. What is the primary purpose of the research methods-and-procedures section of a marketing research report?

4. Why are conclusions and recommendations included in a marketing research report?

5. What are some common problems in preparing the marketing research report?

6. What are some general guidelines for preparing a visual presentation?

7. What is the value of computer software in developing marketing research presentations?

8. Why is Microsoft PowerPoint such a valuable tool for preparing marketing research presentations?

Discussion Questions

1. **EXPERIENCE THE INTERNET.** Go to the Web site www.intelliquest.com/resources, click on presentations, and select a presentation of your choice. Identify the presentation you selected, and provide a critical review of the effectiveness of that presentation.

2. **EXPERIENCE THE INTERNET.** Go to the Web site www.microsoft.com/Education/ Tutorials.aspx. Complete the Tutorials dialog box by typing in higher education in the Grade Level box, technology in the Learning Area box, and PowerPoint in the Product box. After selecting and completing the tutorial, provide written comments on the benefits you received by taking this tutorial.

3. On the basis of what you have learned about marketing research presentations, select the Santa Fe Grill data or one of the other databases provided with this text (see Deli Depot, MRIA, Chapter 14; Remingtons, MRIA, Chapter 15; Qualkote, MRIA, Chapter 16; or DVD Survey, MRIA, Chapter 17), analyze the data using the appropriate statistical techniques, prepare a PowerPoint presentation of your findings, and present it to your research class.

4. How can the Internet be used to facilitate communication of marketing research results?

5. **SPSS EXERCISE.** Using the Santa Fe Grill data set and the questionnaire found in Chapter 14, conduct the following tasks:
   a. Conduct a factor analysis using the restaurant perceptions variables (X_{12}–X_{21}). After you find the best factor solution, label the factors based on which variables load on each factor.
   b. Develop a PowerPoint presentation that visually displays the results.

6. **SPSS EXERCISE.** Using the Santa Fe Grill data set and the questionnaire found in Chapter 14, conduct the following tasks:

   a. Run a regression using the restaurant perceptions variables (X_{12}–X_{21}) as independent variables and variable X_{22}—Satisfaction as the dependent variable. Develop the best multiple regression solution (i.e., the one that has only the significant independent variables in the regression model) for this set of data.

   b. Prepare a PowerPoint presentation that visually displays the results.

glossary

ability to participate   The availability of both the interviewer and the respondent to get together in a question-and-answer interchange.

acquiescence error   A specific type of response bias that can occur when the respondent perceives what answer would be the most desirable to the sponsor.

active data   Data acquired by a business when customers interact with the business's Web site.

administrative error   Bias that can stem from data processing mistakes, interviewer distortion of the respondents' answers, or systemic inaccuracies created by using a faulty sampling design.

affect global approach   The theoretical approach of viewing the structure of a person's attitude as nothing more than the overall (global) expression of his or her favorable or unfavorable feeling toward a given object or behavior.

affective component   That part of an attitude which represents the person's feelings toward the given object, idea, or set of information.

alpha factor   The desired or acceptable amount of difference between the expected and the actual population parameter values; also referred to as the *tolerance level of error (α)*.

alternative hypothesis   A statement that is the opposite of the null hypothesis, where the difference in reality is not simply due to random error.

ambiguity   Contamination of internal validity measures due to unclear determination of cause–effect relationships between investigated constructs.

analysis of variance (ANOVA)   A statistical technique that determines whether two or more means are statistically different from each other.

anonymity   The assurance that the prospective respondent's name or any identifiable designation will not be associated with his or her responses.

appendix   A section at the end of the final research report used to house complex, detailed, or technical information.

appropriateness of descriptors   The extent to which the scale point elements match the data being sought.

archives   Secondary sources of recorded past behaviors and trends.

area sampling   A form of cluster sampling where clusters are formed by geographic designations such as cities, subdivisions, and blocks. Any geographic unit with boundaries can be used, with one-step or two-step approaches.

assignment   The scaling property that allows the researcher to employ any type of descriptor to identify each object (or response) within a set; this property is also known as *description* or *category*.

assignment property   The employment of unique descriptors to identify each object in a set.

attitude   A learned predisposition to react in some consistent positive or negative way to a given object, idea, or set of information.

attitude-toward-behavior model   A multiplicative-additive model approach that attempts to capture a person's attitude toward a behavior rather than to the object itself; where the attitude is a separate, indirectly derived composite measure of a person's combined thoughts and feelings for or against carrying out a specific action or behavior.

attitude-toward-object model   A multiplicative-additive model approach that attempts to capture a person's attitude about a specific object; where the attitude is a separate indirectly derived composite measure of a person's combined thoughts and feelings for or against a given object.

attribute-importance estimate   The importance of an attribute of an object as estimated by conjoint analysis. It is calculated by subtracting the minimum part-worth estimate from the maximum part-worth estimate.

auspices error   A type of response bias that occurs when the response is dictated by the image or opinion of the sponsor rather than the actual question.

automatic replenishment system (ARS)   A continuous, automated inventory control system designed to analyze inventory levels, merchandise order lead times, and forecasted sales.

availability of information   The degree to which the information has already been collected and assembled in some type of recognizable format.

bad questions   Any question or directive that obscures, prevents, or distorts the fundamental communications between respondent and researcher.

balancing positive/negative scale descriptors The researcher's decision to maintain objectivity in a scale that is designed to capture both positive and negative state-of-mind raw data from respondents; the same number of relative magnitudes of positive and negative scale descriptors are used to make up the set of scale points.

bar code A pattern of varied-width electronic-sensitive bars and spaces that represents a unique code of numbers and letters.

behavior intention scale A special type of rating scale designed to capture the likelihood that people will demonstrate some type of predictable behavior toward purchasing an object or service.

believability The quality achieved by building a final report that is based on clear, logical thinking, precise expression, and accurate presentation.

benefit and lifestyle studies Studies conducted to examine similarities and differences in needs; used to identify two or more segments within a market for the purpose of identifying customers for the product category of interest to a particular company.

beta coefficient An estimated regression coefficient that has been recalculated to have a mean of 0 and a standard deviation of 1. This statistic enables the independent variables with different units of measurement to be directly compared on their association with the dependent variable.

bias A particular tendency or inclination that skews results, thereby preventing accurate consideration of a research question.

bivariate regression analysis A statistical technique that analyzes the linear relationship between two variables by estimating coefficients for an equation for a straight line. One variable is designated as a dependent variable, and the other

as an independent (or predictor) variable.

Boolean operators Key words that form a logic string to sort through huge numbers of sites on the World Wide Web.

brand awareness The percentage of respondents having heard of a designated brand; brand awareness can be either unaided or aided.

business ethics The moral principles and standards that guide behavior in the world of business.

business intelligence A procedure for collecting daily operational information pertinent to the company and the markets it serves.

buying power index (BPI) A statistical indicator that provides weighted-average population, retail sales, and effective buying income data on different geographic areas of the United States.

call record sheet A recording document that gathers basic summary information about an interviewer's performance efficiency (e.g., number of contact attempts, number of completed interviews, length of time of interview).

cardinal numbers Any set of consecutive whole integers.

causal research Research that focuses on collecting data structures and information that will allow the decision maker or researcher to model cause–effect relationships between two or more variables under investigation.

census A study that includes data about or from every member of a target population. Sampling is often used because it is impossible or unreasonable to conduct a census.

central limit theorem (CLT) The theoretical backbone of sampling theory. It states that the sampling distribution of the sample mean

($\bar{x}$) or the sample proportion ($\bar{p}$) value derived from a simple random sample drawn from the target population will be approximately normally distributed provided that the associated sample size is sufficiently large (e.g., when n is greater than or equal to 30). In turn, the sample mean value ($\bar{x}$) of that random sample with an estimated sampling error (S_g) (estimated standard error) fluctuates around the true population mean value (μ) with a standard error of σ/n and has a sampling distribution that is approximately a standardized normal distribution, regardless of the shape of the probability frequency distribution curve of the overall target population.

cheating The deliberate falsification of respondents' answers on a survey instrument.

Chi-square (X^2) statistic The standardized measurement of the observed difference squared between two frequency distributions that allows for the investigation of statistical significance in analyzing frequency distribution data structures.

Claris Home Page A specific software program that can be used to create Web pages that can integrate both text and graphics with other types of computer files.

classification (or prediction) matrix The classification matrix in discriminant analysis that contains the number of correctly classified and misclassified cases.

cluster analysis A multivariate interdependence technique whose primary objective is to classify objects into relatively homogeneous groups based on the set of variables considered.

clusters The mutually exclusive and collectively exhaustive subpopulation groupings that are then randomly sampled.

cluster sampling A method of probability sampling where the sampling units are selected in groups (or clusters) rather than individually. Once the cluster has been identified, the elements to be sampled are drawn by simple random sampling or all of the units may be included in the sample.

code of ethics   A set of guidelines that states the standards and operating procedures for ethical decisions and practices by researchers.

coding   The activities of grouping and assigning values to various responses from a survey instrument.

coefficient alpha   See Cronbach's alpha.

coefficient of determination (r^2)   A statistical value (or number) that measures the proportion of variation in one variable accounted for by another variable; the r^2 measure can be thought of as a percentage and varies from .00 to 1.00.

cognitive component   That part of an attitude which represents the person's beliefs, perceptions, preferences, experiences, and knowledge about a given object, idea, or set of information.

commercial/syndicated data   Data that have been compiled and displayed according to some standardized procedure.

company ethics program   The framework through which a firm establishes internal codes of ethical behavior to serve as guidelines for doing business.

comparative scale   Scale used when the scaling objective is to have a respondent express an attitude, feeling, or behavior about an object (or person, or phenomenon) or its attributes on the basis of some other object (or person, or phenomenon) or its attributes.

competitive intelligence analysis   Specific procedures for collecting daily operational information pertaining to the competitive companies and markets they serve.

completely automated telephone survey (CATS)   A survey administered by a computer with no human interviewer. The computer dials a telephone number and the respondent listens to the electronic voice, responding by pushing keys on the Touch-Tone telephone pad.

completeness   The depth and breadth of the data.

completion deadline date   Part of the information included in a cover letter that directly communicates to a prospective respondent the date by which his or her completed questionnaire must be returned to the researcher.

complexity of the information   One of the two fundamental dimensions used to determine the level of information being supplied by the information research process; it relates to the degree to which the information is easily understood and applied to the problem or opportunity under investigation.

computer-administered survey   A survey design that incorporates the use of a computer to ask questions and record responses.

computer-assisted personal interviewing   An interview in which the interviewer reads respondents the questions from a computer screen and directly keys in the response.

computer-assisted self-interviewing   An interview in which respondents are directed to a computer where they read questions from the computer screen and directly enter their responses.

computer-assisted telephone interview (CATI)   The computer controls and expedites the interviewing process.

computer-assisted telephone survey   A survey that uses a fully automated system in which the respondent listens to an electronic voice and responds by pushing keys on a Touch-Tone telephone keypad.

computer disks by mail   A survey procedure in which computer disks are mailed to respondents; the respondents complete the survey on their own computer and return the disk to the researcher via the mail.

computer-generated fax survey   A survey procedure in which a computer is used to send a survey to potential respondents via fax; the respondent completes the survey and returns it via fax or mail.

computerized secondary data sources   Data sources designed by specific companies that integrate both internal and external data with online information sources.

conative component   That part of an attitude which refers to the person's behavioral response or specific action/reaction toward the given object, idea, or set of information; it tends to be the observable outcome driven by the interaction of a person's cognitive and affective components toward the object or behavior.

concept and product testing   Information for decisions on product improvements and new product introductions.

confidence interval   A statistical range of values within which the true value of the target population parameter of interest is expected to fall based on a specified confidence level.

confidence levels   Theoretical levels of assurance of the probability that a particular confidence interval will accurately include or measure the true population parameter value. In information research, the three most widely used levels are 90 percent, 95 percent, and 99 percent.

confidentiality to client   The agreement between a researcher and the client that all activities performed in the process of conducting marketing research will remain private and the property of the client, unless otherwise specified by both parties.

confidentiality to respondent The expressed assurance to the prospective respondent that his or her name, while known to the researcher, will not be divulged to a third party, especially the sponsoring client.

confirmation/invitation letter A specific follow-up document sent to prospective focus group participants to encourage and reinforce their willingness and commitment to participate in the group session.

conformance to standards The researcher's ability to be accurate, timely, mistake free, and void of unanticipated delays.

conjoint analysis A multivariate technique that estimates the utility of the levels of various attributes or features of an object, as well as the relative importance of the attributes themselves.

connectors Logic phrases and symbols that allow search terms to be linked together in a Boolean logic format.

connect time The length of time, frequently measured in minutes and seconds, that a user is logged on to an electronic service or database. The amount of connect time is generally used to bill the user for services.

consent forms Formal signed statements of agreement by the participants approving the taping or recording of the information provided in group discussions and releasing that data to the moderator, researcher, or sponsoring client.

constant sums rating scale A scale format that requires the respondents to allocate a given number of points, usually 100, among several attributes or

features based on their importance to the individual; this format requires a person to value each separate feature relative to all the other listed features.

construct development An integrative process of activities undertaken by researchers to enhance understanding of what specific data should be collected for solving defined research problems.

construct development error A type of nonsampling (systematic) error that is created when the researcher is not careful in fully identifying the concepts and constructs to be included in the study.

constructs Hypothetical variables composed of a set of component responses or behaviors that are thought to be related.

construct validity The degree to which researchers measure what they intended to measure, and to which the proper identification of the independent and dependent variables were included in the investigation.

consumer panels Large samples of households that provide certain types of data for an extended period of time.

content analysis The technique used to study written or taped materials by breaking the data into meaningful aggregate units or categories using a predetermined set of rules.

content validity That property of a test which indicates that the entire domain of the subject or construct of interest was properly sampled. That is, the identified factors are truly components of the construct of interest.

control group That portion of the sample which is not subjected to the treatment.

controlled test markets Test markets performed by an outside research firm that guarantees

distribution of the test product through prespecified outlets in selected cities.

control variables Extraneous variables that the researcher is able to account for according to their systematic variation (or impact) on the functional relationship between the independent and dependent variables included in the experiment.

convenience sampling A method of nonprobability sampling where the samples are drawn on the basis of the convenience of the researcher or interviewer; also referred to as *accidental sampling*. Convenience sampling is often used in the early stages of research because it allows a large number of respondents to be interviewed in a short period of time.

convergent validity The degree to which different measures of the same construct are highly correlated.

cost analysis An analysis of alternative logistic system designs that a firm can use for achieving its performance objective at the lowest total cost.

covariation The amount of change in one variable that is consistently related to the change in another variable of interest.

cover letter A separate letter that either accompanies a self-administered questionnaire or is mailed prior to an initial interviewer contact call and whose main purpose is to secure a respondent's willingness to participate in the research project; sometimes referred to as a *letter of introduction*.

cover letter guidelines A specific set of factors that should be included in a cover letter for the purpose of increasing a prospective respondent's willingness to participate in the study.

credibility The quality that comes about by developing a final report that is accurate, believable, and professionally organized.

critical questions   Questions used by a moderator to direct the group to the critical issues underlying the topics of interest.

critical tolerance level of error   The observed difference between a sample statistic value and the corresponding true or hypothesized population parameter.

critical z value   The book z value and the amount of acceptable variability between the observed sample data results and the prescribed hypothesized true population values measured in standardized degrees of standard errors for given confidence levels.

Cronbach's alpha   A widely used measurement of the internal consistency of a multi-item scale in which the average of all possible split-half coefficients is taken.

cross-tabulation   The process of simultaneously treating (or counting) two or more variables in the study. This process categorizes the number of respondents who have responded to two or more questions consecutively.

curbstoning   Cheating or falsification of data during the collection process that occurs when interviewers fill in all or part of a survey themselves.

curvilinear relationship   An association between two variables whereby the strength and/or direction of their relationship changes over the range of both variables.

customer-centric approach   Use of granular data to anticipate and fulfill customers' desires.

customer interaction   The relationship between the enterprise and the customer.

customer knowledge   The collection of customer interaction information used to create customer profiles that can be used to tailor interactions,

segment customers, and build strong customer relationships.

customer knowledge data   Information volunteered by customers that might be outside the marketing function of an organization.

customer relationship management (CRM)   Management of customer relationships based on the integration of customer information throughout the business enterprise in order to achieve maximum customer satisfaction and retention.

customer satisfaction studies   Studies designed to assess both the strengths and weaknesses customers perceive in a firm's marketing mix.

customer-volunteered information   Data provided by the customer without solicitation.

cycle time   The time that elapses between taking a product or service from initial consumer contact to final delivery.

cycle time research   A research method that centers on reducing the time between the initial contact and final delivery (or installation) of products.

data   Facts relating to any issue or subject.

data analysis error   A "family" of nonsampling errors that are created when the researcher subjects the raw data to inappropriate analysis procedures.

database   A collection of secondary information indicating what customers are purchasing, how often they purchase, and how much they purchase.

database technology   The means by which data are transformed into information.

data coding errors   The incorrect assignment of computer codes to the raw responses.

data editing errors   Inaccuracies due to careless verifying procedures of raw data to computer data files.

data enhancement   The process of weaving data into current internal data structures for the purpose of gaining a more valuable categorization of customers relative to their true value to the company.

data entry   The direct inputting of the coded data into some specified software package that will ultimately allow the research analyst to manipulate and transform the raw data into data structures.

data entry errors   The incorrect assignment of computer codes to their predesignated location on the computer data file.

data field   A basic characteristic about a customer that is filled in on a database.

data interaction matrix   A procedure used to itemize the type and amount of data required by each functional area of the company regardless of the cost of data collection.

data mining   The process of finding hidden patterns and relationships among variables/characteristics contained in data stored in the data warehouse.

data processing error   A specific type of nonsampling error that can occur when researchers are not accurate or complete in transferring raw data from respondents to computer files.

data silo   Collection of data by one area of a business that is not shared with other areas.

data structures   The output analysis results of combining a group of reported raw data using some type of quantitative or qualitative analysis procedure.

data validation   A specific control process that the researcher undertakes to ensure that his or her representatives collected the data as required. The process is normally one of recontacting about 20 percent of the selected respondent group to determine that they did participate in the study.

data warehouse   A central repository for all significant pieces of information that an organization collects.

debriefing analysis   The technique of comparing notes, thoughts, and feelings about a focus group discussion between the moderator, researcher, and sponsoring client immediately following the group interview.

decision opportunity   The presence of a situation in which market performance can be significantly improved by undertaking new activities.

decision problem   A situation in which management has established a specific objective to accomplish and there are several courses of action that could be taken, each with its own risks and potential benefits.

defined target population   A specified group of people or objects for which questions can be asked or observations made to develop the required data structures and information; also referred to as the *working population*. A precise definition of the target population is essential when undertaking a research project.

degree of manipulation   The extent to which data structures and results have been interpreted and applied to a specific situation.

deliberate falsification   When the respondent and/or interviewer intentionally gives wrong answers or deliberately cheats on a survey.

demand analysis   The estimating of the level of customer demand for a given product as well as the underlying reasons for that demand.

demand characteristics   Contamination to construct validity measures created by test subjects trying to guess the true purpose behind the experiment and therefore give socially acceptable responses or behaviors.

demographic characteristics   Physical and factual attributes of people, organizations, or objects.

deontologists   Individuals who emphasize good intentions and the rights of the people involved in an action; they are much less concerned with the results from any ethical decision.

dependence techniques   Appropriate multivariate procedures when one or more of the variables can be identified as dependent variables and the remaining as independent variables.

dependent variable   A singular observable attribute that is the measured outcome derived from manipulating the independent variable(s).

depth   The overall number of key data fields or variables that will make up the data records.

description   The process of discovering patterns, associations, and relationships among key customer characteristics.

descriptive questionnaire design   A questionnaire design that allows the researcher to collect raw data that can be turned into facts about a person or object. The questions and scales primarily involve the collecting of state-of-being and state-of-behavior data.

descriptive research   Research that uses a set of scientific methods and procedures to collect data structures that are used to identify, determine, and describe the existing characteristics of a target population or market structure.

diffusion of treatment   Contamination to construct validity measures due to test subjects discussing the treatment and measurement activities with individuals yet to receive the treatment.

direct cognitive structural analysis   A data analysis procedure in which respondents are simply asked to determine the extent to which an attribute is part of the construct's structural makeup and its importance to construct.

direct (positive) directional hypothesis   A statement about the perceived relationship between two questions, dimensions, or subgroups of attributes that suggests that as one factor moves in one direction, the other factor moves in the same direction.

directed data   Comprehensive data about customers collected through the use of computers.

direct mail survey   A questionnaire distributed to and returned from respondents via the postal service.

directness of observation   The degree to which the researcher or trained observer actually observes the behavior/event as it occurs; also termed *direct observation*.

direct observation   The process of observing actual behaviors or events and recording them as they occur.

direct self-administered questionnaire   A survey instrument designed to have the respondent serve as both an interviewer and a respondent during the question-and-answer encounter.

discretion of primary descriptors   The carefulness that a researcher must use in selecting the actual words used to distinguish the relative magnitudes associated with each of the primary descriptors in a scale design.

discriminant analysis   A multivariate technique for analyzing marketing research data when the dependent variable is categorical and the independent variables are interval.

discriminant function   The linear combination of independent variables developed by discriminant analysis which will best discriminate between the categories of the dependent variable.

discriminant function coefficient The multipliers of variables in the discriminant function when the variables are in the original units of measurement.

discriminant score In discriminant analysis, this represents the score of each respondent on the discriminant function.

discriminant validity The degree to which measures of different constructs are uncorrelated.

discriminatory power The scale's ability to significantly differentiate between the categorical scale responses (or points).

disguised observation An observation technique in which the test subjects are completely unaware that they are being observed and recorded.

disguised sponsorship When the true identity of the person or company for which the research is being conducted is not divulged to the prospective respondent.

disproportionate stratified sampling A form of stratified sampling in which the size of the sample drawn from each stratum is independent of the stratum's proportion of the total population.

distance property The scaling property that when activated allows the researcher and respondent to identify, understand, and accurately express in a unit measurement scheme the exact (or absolute) difference between each of the descriptors, scale points, or raw responses.

diversity of respondents The degree to which the respondents in the study share some similarities.

domain of observables The set of observable manifestations of a variable that is not itself directly observable. A domain represents an identifiable set of components that indirectly make up the construct of interest.

drop-off survey A questionnaire that is left with the respondent to be completed at a later time. The questionnaire may be picked up by the researcher or returned via some other mode.

dummy variables Artificial variables introduced into a regression equation to represent the categories of a nominally scaled variable (such as sex or marital status). There will be one dummy variable for each of the nominal categories of the independent variable, and the values will typically be 0 and 1, depending on whether the variable value is present or absent for a particular respondent (e.g., male or female).

editing The process in which the interviews or survey instruments are checked for mistakes that may have occurred by either the interviewer or the respondent during data collection activities.

effective buying income (EBI) The measure of personal income less federal, state, and local taxes.

electronic database A high-speed, computer-assisted information source or library.

electronic data interchange (EDI) A specific system designed to speed the flow of information as well as products from producer to distributor to retailer.

electronic test markets Test procedures that integrate the use of selected panels of consumers who use a special identification card in recording their product purchasing data.

element The name given to the object about which information is sought. Elements must be unique, countable, and, when added together, make up the whole of the target population.

e-mail survey A survey in which electronic mail is used to deliver a questionnaire to respondents and receive their responses.

empirical testing The actual collection of data in the real world using research instruments and then subjecting that data to rigorous analysis to either support or refute a hypothesis.

ending questions Questions used by a focus group moderator to bring closure to a particular topic discussion; encourages summary-type comments.

enterprise The total business unit, including all facets of the business as well as suppliers and retailers.

environmental forecasting The projection of environmental occurrences that can affect the long-term strategy of a firm.

environmental information Secondary information pertaining to a firm's suppliers and/or distributors.

equivalent form A method of assessing the reliability associated with a scale measurement; the researcher creates two basically similar yet different scale measurements for the given construct and administers both forms to either the same sample of respondents or two samples of respondents from the same target population.

error The difference between the true score on a research instrument and the actual observed score.

estimated sample standard deviation A quantitative index of the dispersion of the distribution of drawn sampling units' actual data around the sample's arithmetic average measure of central tendency; this sample statistical value specifies the degree of variation in the raw data responses in a way that allows the researcher to translate the variations into normal curve interpretations.

estimated sample variance The square of the estimated sample standard deviation.

estimated standard error of the sample statistic A statistical measurement of the sampling error that can be expected to exist between the drawn sample's statistical values and the actual values of all the sampling units' distributions of those concerned statistics. These indexes are referred to as *general precision.*

estimates Sample data facts that are transformed through interpretation procedures to represent inferences about the larger target population.

ethical dilemmas Specific situations in which the researcher, decision maker, or respondent must choose between appropriate and inappropriate behavior.

ethics The field of study that tries to determine what behaviors are considered to be appropriate under certain circumstances by established codes of behavior set forth by society.

evaluation apprehension Contamination to construct validity measures caused by test subjects being fearful that their actions or responses will become known to others.

executive interview A person-administered interview of a business executive. Frequently, these interviews will take place in the executive's office.

executive summary The part of the final research report that illustrates the major points of the report in a manner complete enough to provide a true representation of the entire document.

expected completion rate (ECR) The percentage of prospective respondents who are expected to participate and complete the survey; also referred to as the *anticipated response rate.*

experience surveys An informal gathering of opinions and insights from people who are considered to be knowledgeable on the issues surrounding the defined research problem.

experimental design reliability The degree to which the research design and its procedures can be replicated and achieve similar conclusions about hypothesized relationships.

expert systems Advanced computer-based systems that function in the same manner as a human expert, advising the analyst on how to solve a problem.

explained variance In multivariate methods, it is the amount of variation in the dependent construct that can be accounted for by the combination of independent variables.

exploratory research Research designed to collect and interpret either secondary or primary data in an unstructured format using sometimes an informal set of procedures.

external secondary data Data collected by outside agencies such as the federal, state, or local government; trade associations; or periodicals.

external validity The extent to which the measured data results of a study based on a sample can be expected to hold in the entire defined target population. In addition, it is the extent that a causal relationship found in a study can be expected to be true for the entire defined target population.

extraneous variables All variables other than the independent variables that affect the responses of the test subjects. If left uncontrolled, these variables can have a confounding impact on the dependent variable measures that could weaken or invalidate the results of an experiment.

extremity error A type of response bias when the clarity of extreme scale points and ambiguity of midrange options encourage extreme responses.

eye tracking monitor A device that observes and records a person's unconscious eye movements.

facilitating agencies Businesses that perform a marketing research function as a supplement to a broader marketing research project.

factor analysis A class of statistical procedures primarily used for data reduction and summarization.

factor loadings Simple correlations between the variables and the factors.

factor scores Composite scores estimated for each respondent on the derived factors.

facts Pieces of information that are observable and verifiable through a number of external sources.

faulty recall The inability of a person to accurately remember the specifics about the behavior under investigation.

fax survey A questionnaire distributed to the sample via fax machines.

field experiments Causal research designs that manipulate the independent variables in order to measure the dependent variable in a natural test setting.

finite correction factor (fcf) An adjustment factor to the sample size that is made in those situations where the drawn sample is expected to equal 5 percent or more of the defined target population. The fcf is equal to the overall square root of $N - n/N - 1$.

flowerpot approach A specific, unique framework or blueprint for integrating different sets of questions and scale measurements into an instrument that is capable of collecting the raw data needed to achieve each of the established information objectives.

focus group facility A professional facility that offers a set of specially designed rooms for conducting focus group interviews; each room contains a large table and comfortable chairs for up to 13 people, with a relaxed atmosphere, built-in audio equipment, and normally a one-way mirror for disguised observing by the sponsoring client or researcher.

focus group incentives Specified investment programs to compensate focus group participants for their expenses associated with demonstrating a willingness to be a group member.

focus group moderator A special person who is well trained in interpersonal communications; listening, observation, and interpretive skills; and professional mannerisms and personality. His or her role in a session is to draw from the participants the best and most innovative ideas about an assigned topic or question.

focus group research A formalized qualitative data collection method for which data are collected from a small group of people who interactively and spontaneously discuss one particular topic or concept.

follow-up test A statistical test that flags the means that are statistically different from each other; follow-up tests are performed after an ANOVA determines there are differences between means.

forced-choice scale measurements Symmetrical scale measurement designs that do not have a logical "neutral" scale descriptor to divide the positive and negative domains of response descriptors.

formal rating procedures The use of structured survey instruments or questionnaires to gather information on environmental occurrences.

formative composite scale Scale used when each of the individual scale items measures some part of the whole construct, object, or phenomenon.

F-ratio The statistical ratio of between-group mean squared variance to within-group mean squared variance; the F value is used as an indicator of the statistical difference between group means in an ANOVA.

free-choice scale measurements Symmetrical scale measurement designs that are divided into positive and negative domains of scale-point descriptors by a logical center "neutral" response.

frequency distributions A summary of how many times each possible raw response to a scale question/setup was recorded by the total group of respondents.

F-test The test used to statistically evaluate the difference between the group means in ANOVA.

full-text Option of having the entire document, news story, article, or numerical information available for downloading.

fully automated self-interviewing A procedure in which respondents independently approach a central computer station or kiosk, read the questions, and respond—all without researcher intervention.

fully automated telephone interviewing A data collection procedure in which the computer calls respondents and asks questions; the respondent records his or her answers by using the keypad of a Touch-Tone telephone.

fully automatic devices High-tech devices that interact with respondents without the presence of a trained interviewer during the question/response encounter.

functional relationship An observable and measurable systematic change in one variable as another variable changes.

garbage in, garbage out A standard phrase used in marketing

research to represent situations where the process of collecting, analyzing, and interpreting data into information contains errors or biases, creating less than accurate information.

gatekeeper technology Any device used to help protect one's privacy against intrusive marketing practices such as telemarketing solicitors, unwanted direct marketers, illegal scam artists, and "sugging" (caller ID, voice messengers, answering machines).

generalizability The extent to which the data are an accurate portrait of the defined target population; the representativeness of information obtained from a small subgroup of members to that of the entire target population from which the subgroup was selected.

generalizability of data structures The degree to which sample data results and structures can be used to draw accurate inferences about the defined target population, that is, the extent to which the research can extrapolate results from a sample to the defined target population.

general precision The amount of general sampling error associated with the given sample of raw data that was generated through some type of data collection activity; no specific concern for any level of confidence.

granular data Highly detailed, highly personalized data specifically structured around an individual customer.

graphic rating scale descriptors A scale point format that presents respondents with some type of graphic continuum as the set of possible raw responses to a given question.

group dynamics The degree of spontaneous interaction among group members during a discussion of a topic.

hits The number of documents or other items that meet the search terms in an online search.

human observation Data collection by a researcher or trained observer who records text subjects' actions and behaviors.

hypertext markup language (HTML) The language used to create Web pages for communicating the research results as well as other information on the Internet.

hypothesis A yet-unproven proposition or possible solution to a decision problem that can be empirically tested using data that are collected through the research process; it is developed in order to explain phenomena or a relationship between two or more constructs or variables.

hypothesis guessing Contamination to construct validity measures due to test subjects' believing they know the desired functional relationship prior to the manipulation treatment.

iceberg principle The general notion indicating that the dangerous part of many marketing decision problems is neither visible nor well understood by marketing managers.

importance-performance analysis A research and data analysis procedure used to evaluate a firm's and its competitors' strengths and weaknesses, as well as future actions that seek to identify key attributes that drive purchase behavior within a given industry.

inadequate preoperationalization of variables Contamination to construct validity measures due to inadequate understanding of the complete makeup of the independent and dependent variables included in the experimental design.

inappropriate analysis bias A type of data analysis error that creates the wrong data structure results and can lead to misinterpretation errors.

incidence rate The percentage of the general population that is the subject of the marketing research.

independent samples Two or more groups of responses that are tested as though they may come from different populations.

independent variable An attribute of an object whose measurement values are directly manipulated by the researcher, also referred to as a *predictor* or *treatment variable*. This type of variable is assumed to be a causal factor in a functional relationship with a dependent variable.

in-depth interview A formalized, structured process of a subject's being asked a set of semistructured, probing questions by a well-trained interviewer usually in a face-to-face setting.

indirect observation A research technique in which researchers or trained observers rely on artifacts that, at best, represent specific reported behavioral outcomes from some earlier time.

information The set of facts derived from data structures when someone—either the researcher or decision maker—interprets and attaches narrative meaning to the data structures.

informational data Data collected through On-Line Analytical Processing (OLAP) software for analysis purposes as a decision-making tool for marketing programs.

information objectives The clearly stated reasons why raw data must be collected; they serve as the guidelines for determining the raw data requirements.

information requirements The identified factors, dimensions, and attributes within a stated information objective for which raw data must be collected.

information research process The 10 systematic task steps involved in the four phases of gathering, analyzing, interpreting, and transforming data structures and results into information for use by decision makers.

information research questions Specific statements that address the problem areas the research study will attempt to investigate.

in-home interview A person-administrated interview that takes place in the respondent's home.

instrumentation Contamination to internal validity measures from changes in measurement processes, observation techniques, and/or measuring instruments.

intelligibility The degree to which questions can be understood by the respondents making up the defined target population to whom the scale will be administered.

intention to purchase A person's planned future action to buy a product or service.

interdependence techniques Multivariate statistical procedures in which the whole set of interdependent relationships is examined.

internal consistency reliability The extent to which the items of a scale represent the same domain of content and are highly correlated both with each other and summated scale scores. It represents the degree to which the components are related to the same overall construct domain.

internal quality movement One of the underlying factors for which many organizations are restructuring away from old traditional functional control/ power systems of operating to new cross-functional structures where team building, decision teams, and sharing of information and responsibility are the important factors, not control and power.

internal secondary data Facts that have been collected by the individual company for accounting and marketing activity purposes.

internal validity The certainty with which a researcher can state that the observed effect was caused by a specific treatment; exists when the research design accurately identifies causal relationships.

Internet A network of computers and technology linking computers into an information superhighway.

Internet survey The method of using the Internet to ask survey questions and record responses of respondents.

interpersonal communication skills The interviewer's abilities to articulate the questions in a direct and clear manner so that the subject understands what she or he is responding to.

interpretive bias Error that occurs when the wrong inference about the real world or defined target population is made by the researcher or decision maker due to some type of extraneous factor.

interpretive skills The interviewer's capabilities of accurately understanding and recording the subject's responses to questions.

interval scales Any question/scale format that activates not only the assignment and order scaling properties but also the distance property; all scale responses have a recognized absolute difference between each of the other scale points (responses).

interviewer error A type of nonsampling error that is created in situations where the interviewer distorts information, in a systematic way, from respondents during or after the interviewer/respondent encounter.

interviewer instructions The vehicle for training the interviewer on how to select prospective respondents, screen them for eligibility, and conduct the actual interview.

interviewer/mechanical devices The combination of highly skilled people who are aided by high-technology devices during the questioning/responding encounters with respondents.

introductory questions Questions used by a focus group moderator to introduce the general topic of discussion and opportunities of reflecting their past experiences.

inverse (negative or indirect) directional hypothesis A statement about the perceived relationship between two questions, dimensions, or subgroupings of attributes that suggests that as one factor moves in one direction, the other factor moves in an opposite fashion.

judgment sampling A nonprobability sampling design that selects participants for a sample based on an experienced individual's belief that the participants will meet the requirements of the research study.

junk mail A categorical descriptor that prospective respondents attach to surveys that are administered through the direct mail delivery system or an unwanted telephone interview that is viewed as being nothing more than a telemarketing gimmick to sell them something they do not want or need.

knowledge level of respondent The degree to which the selected respondents feel they have experience (or knowledge) with the topics that are the focus of the survey's questioning.

lead country test markets Field test markets that are conducted in specific foreign countries.

leading question A question that tends to purposely elicit a particular answer.

level of significance The amount of risk regarding the accuracy of the test that the researcher is willing to accept.

library A large group of related information.

lifetime value models Procedures developed using historical data, as well as actual purchase behavior, not probability estimates, to predict consumer behavior.

Likert scale A special rating scale format that asks respondents to indicate the extent to which they agree or disagree with a series of mental belief or behavioral belief statements about a given object; it is a cognitive-based scale measurement.

limitations A section of the final research report in which all extraneous events that place certain restrictions on the report are fully communicated.

linear relationship An association between two variables whereby the strength and nature of the relationship remains the same over the range of both variables.

listening skills The interviewer's capabilities of understanding what the respondent is communicating.

logistic assessment Information in logistics that allows market researchers to conduct total cost analysis and service sensitivity analysis.

lottery approach   A unique incentive system that pools together either individual small cash incentives into a significantly larger dollar amount or a substantial nonmonetary gift and then holds a drawing to determine the winner or small set of winners. The drawing procedure is designed so that all respondents who complete and return their survey have an equal chance of receiving the larger reward.

mail panel survey   A representative sample of individual respondents who have agreed in advance to participate in a mail survey.

mall-intercept interview   An interview technique in which mall patrons are stopped and asked for feedback. The interview may take place in the mall's common areas or in the research firm's offices at the mall.

managerial function software system   A computer-based procedure that includes forecasting, brand management, and promotional budget capabilities.

marketing   The process of planning and executing pricing, promotion, product, and distribution of products, services, and ideas in order to create exchanges that satisfy both the firm and its customers.

marketing decision support system (MDSS)   A computer-based system intended for use by particular marketing personnel at any functional level for the purpose of solving information and/or semistructured problems. Within this system databases are developed and used to analyze the firm's performance as well as control its marketing activities.

marketing knowledge   A characteristic that complements a researcher's technical competency.

marketing research   The function that links an organization to its

market through the gathering of information. The information allows for the identification and definition of market-driven opportunities and problems. The information allows for the generation, refinement, and evaluation of marketing actions.

market intelligence   The use of real-time customer information (customer knowledge) to achieve a competitive advantage.

market performance symptoms   Conditions that signal the presence of a decision problem and/or opportunity.

maturation   Contamination to internal validity measures due to changes in the dependent variable based on the natural function of time and not attributed to any specific event.

mean   The arithmetic average of all the raw responses; all values of a distribution of responses are summed and divided by the number of valid responses.

measurement   Rules for assigning numbers to objects so that these numbers represent quantities of attributes.

measurement/design error   A "family" of nonsampling errors that result from inappropriate designs in the constructs, scale measurements, or survey measurements used to execute the asking and recording of people's responses to a study's questions.

measures of central tendency   The basic sample statistics that could be generated through analyzing the collected raw data; they are the mode, the median, and the mean.

measures of dispersion   The sample statistics that describe how all the raw data are actually dispersed around a given measure of central tendency; they are the frequency distribution, the range, and the estimated sample standard deviation.

mechanical devices   High-technology instruments that can artificially observe and record either current behavioral actions or physical phenomena as they occur.

mechanical observation   Some type of mechanical or electronic device is used to capture human behavior, events, or marketing phenomena.

median   The sample statistic that splits the raw data into a hierarchical pattern where half the raw data is above the median statistic value and half is below.

media panels   Selected households that are primarily used in measuring media viewing habits as opposed to product/brand consumption patterns.

method bias   The error source that results from selecting an inappropriate method to investigate the research question.

misinterpretation error   An inaccurate transformation of data structures and analysis results into usable bits of information for the decision maker.

mode   The most frequently mentioned (or occurring) raw response in the set of responses to a given question/setup.

model *F* statistic   A statistic which compares the amount of variation in the dependent measure "explained" or associated with the independent variables to the "unexplained" or error variance. A larger *F*-statistic value indicates that the regression model has more explained variance than error variance.

moderator's guide   A detailed document that outlines the topics, questions, and subquestions that serve as the basis for generating the spontaneous interactive dialogue among the focus group participants.

modified Likert scale   Any version of the agreement/disagreement-based scale measurement that is not the original five-point "strongly agree" to "strongly disagree" scale.

monetary compensation   An individual cash incentive used by the researcher to increase the likelihood of a prospective respondent's willingness to participate in the survey.

monomethod bias   A particular type of error source that is created when only a single method is used to collect data about the research question.

moral philosophy   A person's basic orientation toward problem solving. Within the ethical decision-making process, philosophical thinking will come from teleology, deontology, and/or relativity orientations.

mortality   Contamination to internal validity measures due to changing the composition of the test subjects in the experiment.

multicollinearity   A situation in which several independent variables are highly correlated with each other. This characteristic can result in difficulty in estimating separate or independent regression coefficients for the correlated variables.

multiple-item scale designs   Method used when the researcher has to measure several items (or attributes) simultaneously in order to measure the complete object or construct of interest.

multiple regression analysis   A statistical technique which analyzes the linear relationships between a dependent variable and multiple independent variables by estimating coefficients for the equation for a straight line.

multivariate analysis (techniques)   A group of statistical techniques used when there are two or more measurements on each element and the variables are analyzed simultaneously.

mystery shopper studies   Studies in which trained, professional shoppers visit stores, financial institutions, or companies and "shop" for various products and assess service quality factors or levels.

nominal scales   Question/scale structures that ask the respondent to provide only a descriptor as the raw response; the response does not contain any level of intensity.

nomological validity   The extent to which one particular construct theoretically networks with other established constructs which are related yet different.

nonapplicable response descriptor   The alternative response attached to even-point (or forced-choice) scale designs that allows respondents not to directly respond to a given scale dimension or attribute if they feel uncomfortable about expressing thoughts or feelings about a given object because they lack knowledge or experience.

noncomparative scale   Scale used when the scaling objective is to have a respondent express an attitude, emotion, action, or intention about one specific object (person, phenomenon) or its attributes.

nondirectional hypothesis   A statement regarding the existing relationship between two questions, dimensions, or sub-groupings of attributes as being significantly different but lacking an expression of direction.

nonequivalent control group   A quasi-experimental design that combines the static group comparison and one-group, pretest-posttest preexperimental designs.

nonmonetary compensation   Any type of individual incentive excluding direct cash (e.g., a free T-shirt) used by the researcher to encourage a prospective respondent's participation.

nonprobability sampling   Sampling designs in which the probability of selection of each sampling unit is not known. The selection of sampling units is based on the judgment or knowledge of the researcher and may or may not be representative of the target population.

nonresponse error   An error that occurs when the portion of the defined target population not represented or underrepresented in the response pool is systematically and significantly different from those that did respond.

nonsampling error   A type of bias that occurs in a research study regardless of whether a sample or census is used.

North American industry classification system (NAICS)   Codes numerical industrial listings designed to promote uniformity in data reporting procedures for the U.S. government.

not at home   A specific type of nonresponse bias that occurs when a reasonable attempt to initially reach a prospective respondent fails to produce an interviewer/respondent encounter.

null hypothesis   A statement of the perceived existing relationship between two questions, dimensions, or subgroupings of attributes as being not significantly different; it asserts the status quo condition, and any change from what has been thought to be true is due to random sampling error.

object   Any tangible item in a person's environment that can be clearly and easily identified through the senses.

objectivity   The degree to which a researcher uses scientific procedures to collect, analyze, and create nonbiased information.

observation The systematic process of witnessing and recording the behavioral patterns of objects, people, and occurrences without directly questioning or communicating with them.

observing mechanism How the behaviors or events will be observed; *human observation* is when the observer is either a person hired and trained by the researcher or the researcher himself; *mechanical observation* refers to the use of a technology-based device to do the observing rather than a human observer.

odd or even number of scale points When collecting either state-of-mind or state-of-intention data, the researcher must decide whether the positive and negative scale points need to be separated by a neutral scale descriptor; even-point scales (known as *forced-choice scales*) do not require a neutral response, but odd-point scales (known as *free-choice scales*) must offer a neutral scale response.

one-group, pretest-posttest A pre-experimental design where first a pretreatment measure of the dependent variable is taken (O_1), then the test subjects are exposed to the independent treatment (X), then a posttreatment measure of the dependent variable is taken (O_2).

one-shot study A single group of test subjects is exposed to the independent variable treatment (X), and then a single measurement on the dependent variable is taken (O_1).

one-way tabulation The categorization of single variables existing in the study.

online focus groups A formalized process whereby a small group of people form an online community for an interactive, spontaneous discussion on one particular topic or concept.

online services Providers of access to electronic databases and other services in real time.

opening questions Questions used by a focus group moderator to break the ice among focus group participants; identify common group member traits; and create a comfort zone for establishing group dynamics and interactive discussions.

operational data Data collected through online transaction processing (OLTP) and used for the daily operations of the business.

operationalization The process of precisely delineating how a construct is to be measured. The variables are specified in such a manner as to be potentially observable or manipulable.

opportunity assessment The collection of information on product-markets for the purpose of forecasting how they will change in the future. This type of assessment focuses on gathering information relevant to macroenvironments.

optical scanner An electronic device that optically reads bar codes; this scanner captures and translates unique bar code numbers into product information.

order property The scaling property that activates the existence of relative magnitudes between the descriptors used as scale points (or raw responses); it allows the researcher to establish either a higher-to-lower or lower-to-higher rank order among the raw responses.

ordinally interval scales Ordinal questions or scale formats that the researcher artificially redefines as being interval by activating an assumed distance scaling property into the design structure; this hybrid-type scale format incorporates both primary ordinal scale descriptors and a secondary set of cardinal

numbers used to redefine the original primary descriptors.

ordinal scales A question/scale format that activates both the assignment and order scaling properties; the respondent is asked to express relative magnitudes between the raw responses to a question.

ordinary least squares A statistical procedure that estimates regression equation coefficients which produce the lowest sum of squared differences between the actual and predicted values of the dependent variable.

origin property The scaling property that activates a unique starting (or beginning) point in a set of scale points that is designated as being a "true zero" or true state of nothing.

overall incidence rate (OIR) The percentage of the defined target population elements who actually qualify for inclusion into the survey.

overall reputation The primary dimension of perceived quality outcomes. Quality of the end product can be gauged in direct proportion to the level of expertise, trust, believability, and contribution the research brings to the client.

overregistration When a sampling frame contains all of the eligible sampling units of the defined target population plus additional ones.

paired-comparison rating scale A scale format in which preselected groups of product characteristics or features are paired against one another and the respondents are asked to select which feature in each pairing is more important to them.

part-worth estimates Estimates of the utility survey that respondents place on each individual level of a particular attribute or feature.

passive data Data supplied to a business when a consumer visits the company's Web site.

Pearson correlation coefficient A statistical measure of the strength and direction of a linear relationship between two metric variables.

perceptual map A graphic representation of respondents' beliefs about the relationship between objects with respect to two or more dimensions (usually attributes or features of the objects).

performance rating scale descriptors A scale that uses an evaluative scale point format that allows the respondents to express some type of postdecision evaluative judgment about an object.

person-administered survey A survey in which an individual interviewer asks questions and records responses.

phantom respondents A type of data falsification that occurs when the researcher takes an actual respondent's data and duplicates it to represent a second (nonexisting) set of responses.

physical audits (or traces) Tangible evidence (or artifacts) of some past event or recorded behavior.

plus-one dialing The method of generating telephone numbers to be called by choosing numbers randomly from a telephone directory and adding one digit.

population The identifiable total set of elements of interest being investigated by a researcher.

population mean value The actual calculated arithmetic average parameter value based on interval or ratio data of the defined target population elements (or sampling units).

population proportion value The actual calculated percentage parameter value of the characteristic of concern held by the target population elements (or sampling units).

population size The determined total number of elements that represent the target population.

population specification error An incorrect definition of the true target population to the research question.

population standard deviation A quantitative index of the dispersion of the distribution of population elements' actual data around the arithmetic average measure of central tendency.

population variance The square of the population standard deviation.

positioning The desired perception that a company wants to be associated with its target markets relative to its products or brand offerings.

posttest-only, control group A true experimental design where the test subjects are randomly assigned to either the experimental or control group; the experimental group is then exposed to the independent treatment after which both groups receive a posttreatment measure of the dependent variable.

PowerPoint A specific software package used to develop slides for electronic presentation of the research results.

precise precision The amount of measured sampling error associated with the sample's raw data at a specified level of confidence.

precision The degree of exactness of the raw data in relation to some other possible response of the target population.

predictions Population estimates that are carried into a future time frame; they are derived from either facts or sample data estimates.

predictive bias A specific type of data analysis error that occurs when the wrong statistical facts and estimates invalidate the researcher's ability to predict and test relationships between important factors.

predictive questionnaire design A design that allows the researcher to collect raw data that can be used in predicting changes in attitudes and behaviors as well as testing hypothesized relationships. The question/scales primarily involve the collecting of state-of-mind and state-of-intention data.

predictive validity The extent to which a scale can accurately predict some event external to the scale itself.

pre-experimental designs A family of designs (one-shot study, one-group pretest-posttest, static group comparison) that are crude experiments that are characterized by the absence of randomization of test subjects; they tend not to meet internal validity criteria due to a lack of equivalent group comparisons.

pretesting The conducting of a simulated administering of a designed survey (or questionnaire) to a small, representative group of respondents.

pretest-posttest, control group A true experimental design where the test subjects are randomly assigned to either the experimental or the control group and each group receives a pretreatment measure of the dependent variable. Then the independent treatment is exposed to the experimental group, after which both groups receive a posttreatment measure of the dependent variable.

primary data Data structures of variables that have been specifically collected and assembled for the current research problem or opportunity situation; they represent "firsthand" structures.

primary information Firsthand facts or estimates that are derived through a formalized research process for a specific current problem situation.

probability distribution of the population The relative frequencies of a population's parameter characteristic emulating a normal bell-shaped pattern.

probability sampling Sampling designs in which each sampling unit in the sampling frame (operational population) has a known, nonzero probability of being selected for the sample.

probing questions The outcome of an interviewer's taking the subject's initial response to a question and using that response as the framework for asking the next question.

problem definition A statement that seeks to determine precisely what problem management wishes to solve and the type of information necessary to solve it.

product analysis Methods that identify the relative importance of product selection criteria to buyers and rate brands against these criteria.

project costs The price requirements of doing marketing research.

projective techniques A family of qualitative data collection methods where subjects are asked to project themselves into specified buying situations and then asked questions about those situations.

proportionate stratified sampling A form of stratified sampling in which the sample size from each stratum is dependent on that stratum's size relative to the total population.

protocol interviewing A technique that takes respondents into a specified decision-making situation and asks them to verbally express the process and activities considered when making the decision.

psychogalvanometer A device that measures a subject's involuntary changes in the electronic resistance of his or her skin, referred to as galvanic skin response (GVR).

pupilometer A device that observes and records changes in the diameter of a subject's pupils. Changes are interpreted as the result of unobservable cognitive activity.

purchase intercept interview An interview similar to a mall intercept except that the respondent is stopped at the point of purchase and asked a set of predetermined questions.

qualitative research Selective types of research methods used in exploratory research designs where the main objective is to gain a variety of preliminary insights to discover and identify decision problems and opportunities.

quality of the information One of the two fundamental dimensions that is used to determine the level of information being provided by the research process; it refers to the degree to which the information can be depended on as being accurate and reliable.

quantitative research Data collection methods that emphasize using formalized, standard, structured questioning practices where the response options have been predetermined by the researcher and administered to significantly large numbers of respondents.

quasi-experimental designs Designs in which the researcher can control some variables in the study but cannot establish equal experimental and control groups based on randomization of the test subjects.

query Part of an MDSS that enables the user to retrieve information from the system without having to have special software requirements.

questionnaire A set of questions and scales designed to generate enough raw data for accomplishing the information requirements that underlie the research objectives.

questionnaire development process A specific yet integrative series of logical activities that are undertaken to design a systematic survey instrument for the purpose of collecting primary raw data from sets of people (respondents).

questionnaire format/layout The integrative combination of sets of question/scale measurements into a systematic structured instrument.

question/setup element The question and/or directive that is asked of the respondent for which the respondent is to supply a raw response; it is one of the three elements that make up any scale measurement.

quota sampling The selection of participants based on specific quotas regarding characteristics such as age, race, gender, income, or specific behaviors. Quotas are usually determined by specific research objectives.

quota sheets A simple tracking form that enhances the interviewer's ability to collect raw data from the right type of respondents; the form helps ensure that representation standards are met.

random-digit dialing A random selection of area code, exchange, and suffix numbers.

random error An error that occurs as the result of chance events affecting the observed score.

randomization The procedure whereby many subjects are assigned to different experimental treatment conditions, resulting in each group's averaging out any systematic effect on the investigated functional relationship between the independent and dependent variables.

random sampling error The statistically measured difference between the actual sampled results and the estimated true population results.

ranges   Statistics that represent the grouping of raw data responses into mutually exclusive subgroups with each having distinct identifiable lower and upper boundary designation values in a set of responses.

rank-order rating scale   A scale point format that allows respondents to compare their responses to each other by indicating their first preference, then their second preference, then their third preference, etc., until all the desired responses are placed in some type of rank order, either highest to lowest or lowest to highest.

rating cards   Cards used in personal interviews that represent a reproduction of the set of actual scale points and descriptions used to respond to a specific question/setup in the survey. These cards serve as a tool to help the interviewer and respondent speed up the data collection process.

ratio scales   Question/scale formats that simultaneously activate all four scaling properties; they are the most sophisticated scale in the sense that absolute differences can be identified not only between each scale point but also between individuals' raw responses. Ratio scales request that respondents give a specific singular numerical value as their response to the question.

raw data   The actual firsthand responses that are obtained about the investigated object by either asking questions or observing the subject's actions.

reachable rate (RR)   The percentage of active addresses on a mailing list or other defined population frame.

reader-sorter   An electronic mechanism located at the point-of-

purchase (POP) that resembles a miniature automated bank teller machine. This device enables consumers to pay for transactions with credit cards, ATM cards, or debit cards.

real-time transactional data   Data collected at the point of sale.

reflective composite scale   Scale used when a researcher measures an individual subcomponent (dimension) of a construct, object, or phenomenon.

refusal   A particular type of nonresponse bias that is caused when a prospective respondent declines the role of a respondent, or simply is unwilling to participate in the question/answer exchange.

regression coefficient   The statistical measure of the slope coefficient (b) of an independent variable (x) that tells how much the researcher can expect the dependent variable (y) to change, given a unit change in (x).

related samples   Two or more groups of responses that originated from the sample population.

relational database system   A database in table format of rows and columns, with tables (not data fields) being linked together depending on the output requirements.

relationship marketing   A management philosophy that focuses on treating each customer as uniquely different with the overall goal of building a long-term, interactive relationship and loyalty with each customer.

relationships   The degree (relative magnitude) and direction of a consistent and systematic linkage (dependence) between two or more variables; this type of information can be derived from either facts or sample data estimates; in special cases, the researcher can determine the existence of cause–effect associations between two or more variables.

relativists   Individuals who let present practice set the standard for ethical behavior.

reliability   The extent to which the measurements taken with a particular instrument are repeatable.

reliability of data   Data structures that are consistent across observations or interviews.

reliability of the scale   The extent to which the designed scale can reproduce the same measurement results in repeated trials.

reliability of service   The researcher's ability to be consistent and responsive to the needs of the client.

reputation of the firm   The culmination of a research firm's ability to meet standards, reliability of service, marketing knowledge, and technical competency for purposes of providing quality outcomes.

research instrument   A microscope, radiation meter, ruler, questionnaire, scale, or other device designed for a specific measurement purpose.

research objectives   Statements that the research project will attempt to achieve. They provide the guidelines for establishing a research agenda of activities necessary to implement the research process.

research proposal   A specific document that serves as a written contract between the decision maker and researcher.

respondent characteristics   The attributes that make up the respondents being included in the survey; three important characteristics are diversity, incidence, and participation.

respondent error   The type of nonsampling errors that can occur when selected prospective respondents cannot be initially reached to participate in the survey process, do not cooperate, or demonstrate an unwillingness to participate in the survey.

respondent participation The overall degree to which the selected people have the ability and the willingness to participate as well as the knowledge of the topics being researched.

response error The tendency to answer a question in a particular and unique systematic way. Respondents may consciously or unconsciously distort their answers and true thoughts.

response rate The percentage of usable responses out of the total number of responses.

retailing research Research investigations that focus on topics such as trade area analysis, store image/perception, in-store traffic patterns, and location analysis.

role-playing interviews A technique in which participants are asked to take on the identity of a third person and are placed into a specific predetermined situation. They are then asked to verbalize how they would act in the situation.

sales forecasting A research method that uses variables that affect customer demand to provide estimates of financial outcomes for different price strategies.

sample A randomly selected group of people or objects from the overall membership pool of a target population.

sample design error A family of nonsampling errors that occur when sampling plans are not appropriately developed and/or the sampling process is improperly executed by the researcher.

sample mean value The actual calculated arithmetic average value based on interval or ratio data of the drawn sampling units.

sample percentage value The actual calculated percentage value of the characteristic of concern held by the drawn sampling units.

sample selection error A specific type of sample design bias that

occurs when an inappropriate sample is drawn from the defined target population because of incomplete or faulty sampling procedures or because the correct procedures have not been carried out.

sample size The determined total number of sampling units needed to be representative of the defined target population; that is, the number of elements (people or objects) that have to be included in a drawn sample to ensure appropriate representation of the defined target population.

sampling The process of selecting a relatively small number of elements from a larger defined group of elements so that the information gathered from the smaller group allows one to make judgments about that larger group of elements.

sampling distribution The frequency distribution of a specific sample statistic value that would be found by taking repeated random samples of the same size.

sampling error Any type of bias in a survey study that is attributable to mistakes made in either the selection process of prospective sampling units or determining the size of a sample required to ensure its representativeness of the larger defined target population.

sampling frame A list of all eligible sampling units for a given study.

sampling frame error An error that occurs when a sample is drawn from an incomplete list of potential or prospective respondents.

sampling gap The representation difference between the population elements and sampling units in the sample frame.

sampling plan The blueprint or framework used to ensure that the raw data collected are, in

fact, representative of a larger defined target population structure.

sampling units Those elements that are available for selection during the sampling process.

satisfaction of experience A person's evaluative judgment about his or her postpurchase consumption experience of a specified object.

scale dimensions and attributes element The components of the object, construct, or concept that is being measured; it identifies what should be measured and is one of the three elements of a scale measurement.

scale measurement The process of assigning a set of descriptors to represent the range of possible responses that an individual gives in answering a question about a particular object, construct, or factor under investigation.

scale points The set of assigned descriptors that designate the degrees of intensity to the responses concerning the investigated characteristics of an object, construct, or factor; it is one of the three elements that make up scale measurements.

scale reliability The extent to which a scale can produce the same measurement results in repeated trials.

scatter diagram A graphic plot of the relative position of two variables using a horizontal and a vertical axis to represent the values of the respective variables.

scientific method The systematic and objective process used to develop reliable and valid firsthand information by using the information research process.

scoring models Procedures that attempt to rank customer segments by their potential profitability to the company.

screening forms A set of preliminary questions that are used to determine the eligibility of a prospective respondent for inclusion in the survey.

screening question/scales Specific questions or scales that are used to qualify prospective respondents for a survey or eliminate unqualified respondents from answering question/scales in a study.

search A computer-assisted scan of the electronic databases.

search engine An electronic procedure that allows the researcher to enter keywords as search criteria for locating and gathering secondary information off the Internet.

search words The terms that the computer looks for in electronic databases.

secondary data Historical data structures of variables that have been previously collected and assembled for some research problem or opportunity situation other than the current situation.

secondary information Information (facts or estimates) that has already been collected, assembled, and interpreted at least once for some other specific situation.

selection bias Contamination of internal validity measures created by inappropriate selection and/or assignment processes of test subjects to experimental treatment groups.

selective perception bias A type of error that occurs in situations where the researcher or decision maker uses only a selected portion of the survey results to paint a tainted picture of reality.

self-administered survey A survey in which respondents read the survey questions and record their responses without the assistance of an interviewer.

semantic differential scale A special type of symmetrical rating scale that uses sets of bipolar adjectives and/or adverbs to describe some type of positive and negative poles of an assumed continuum; it is used to capture respondents' cognitive and affective components of specified factors and create perceptual image profiles relating to a given object or behavior.

semistructured question A question that directs the respondent toward a specified topic area, but the responses to the question are unbounded; the interviewer is not looking for any preconceived right answer.

separate sample, pretest-posttest A quasi-experimental design where two different groups of test subjects are drawn for which neither group is directly exposed to the independent treatment variable. One group receives the pretest measure of the dependent variable; then after the insignificant independent treatment occurs, the second group of test subjects receives a posttest measure of the dependent variable.

sequential database system A sorting procedure that displays data in a very simple pattern, usually where the data are organized by a simple path, linkage, or network.

service quality studies Studies designed to measure the degree to which an organization conforms to the quality level expected by customers; they concentrate on attributes determined to be most important to customers.

service sensitivity analysis A procedure that helps an organization in designing a basic customer service program by evaluating cost-to-service trade-offs.

silo Data in one functional area of a business not shared with other areas of the business.

similarity judgments A direct approach to gathering perceptual data for multidimensional scaling; where the respondents use a Likert scale to rate all possible pairs of brands in terms of their similarity.

simple random sampling (SRS) A method of probability sampling in which every sampling unit has an equal, nonzero chance of being selected. Results generated by using simple random sampling can be projected to the target population with a prespecified margin of error.

simulated test markets Quasi-test market experiments where the test subjects are preselected, then interviewed and observed on their purchases and attitudes toward the test products; also referred to as *laboratory tests* or *test market simulations.*

single-item scale descriptors A scale used when the data requirements focus on collecting data about only one attribute of the object or construct being investigated.

situation analysis An informal process of analyzing the past, present, and future situations facing an organization in order to identify decision problems and opportunities.

situational characteristics Factors of reality such as budgets, time, and data quality that affect the researcher's ability to collect accurate primary data in a timely fashion.

skip interval A selection tool used to identify the position of the sampling units to be drawn into a systematic random sample design. The interval is determined by dividing the number of potential sampling units in the defined target population by the number of units desired in the sample.

skip questions/scales Questions designed to set the conditions which a respondent must meet in order to be able to respond to additional questions on a survey; also referred to as *conditional* or *branching questions.*

snowball sampling A nonprobability sampling method that involves the practice of identifying a set of initial prospective respondents who can, in turn, help in identifying additional people to be included in the study.

social desirability A type of response bias that occurs when the respondent assumes what answer is socially acceptable or respectable.

Solomon Four Group A true experimental design that combines the pretest-posttest, control group and posttest only, control group designs and provides both "direct" and "reactive" effects of testing.

Spearman rank order correlation coefficient A statistical measure of the linear association between two variables where both have been measured using ordinal (rank-order) scale instruments.

split-half test A technique used to evaluate the internal consistency reliability of scale measurements that have multiple attribute components.

standard deviation The measure of the average dispersion of the values in a set of responses about their mean.

standard error of the population parameter A statistical measure used in probability sampling that gives an indication of how far the sample result lies from the actual population measure we are trying to estimate.

standard industrial classification (SIC) codes The numerical scheme of industrial listings designed to promote uniformity in data reporting procedures for the U.S. government.

staple scales Considered a modified version of the semantic differential scale; they symmetrically center the scale point domain within a set of plus (+) and minus (–) descriptors.

state-of-behavior data Raw responses that represent an individual's or organization's current observable actions or reactions or recorded past actions/reactions.

state-of-being data Raw responses that are pertinent to the physical and/or demographic or socioeconomic characteristics of individuals, objects, or organizations.

state-of-intention data Raw responses that represent an individual's or organization's expressed plans of future actions/reactions.

state-of-mind data Raw responses that represent the mental attributes or emotional feelings of individuals which are not directly observable or available through some type of external source.

static group comparisons A preexperimental design of two groups of test subjects; one is the experimental group (EG) and is exposed to the independent treatment; the second group is the control group (CG) and is not given the treatment; the dependent variable is measured in both groups after the treatment.

statistical conclusion validity The ability of the researcher to make reasonable statements about covariation between constructs of interest and the strength of that covariation.

statistical regression Contamination to internal validity measures created when experimental groups are selected on the basis of their extreme responses or scores.

statistical software system A computer-based system that has capabilities of analyzing large volumes of data and computing basic types of statistical procedures, such as means, standard deviations, frequency distributions, and percentages.

store audits Formal examinations and verifications of how much of a particular product or brand has been sold at the retail level.

strata The subgroupings that are derived through stratified random sampling procedures.

stratified random sampling (STRS) A method of probability sampling in which the population is divided into different subgroups (called strata) and samples are selected from each stratum.

structured questions Questions that require the respondent to make a choice among a limited number of prelisted responses or scale points; they require less thought and effort on the part of the respondent; also referred to as closed-ended questions.

structuredness of observation The degree to which the behaviors or events are specifically known to the researcher prior to doing the observations.

subjective information Information that is based on the decision maker's or researcher's past experiences, assumptions, feelings, or interpretations without any systematic assembly of facts or estimates.

subject's awareness The degree to which subjects consciously know their behavior is being observed; *disguised observation* is when the subject is completely unaware that he or she is being observed, and *undisguised observation* is when the person is aware that he or she is being observed.

supervisor instructions A form that serves as a blueprint for training people on how to execute the interviewing process in a standardized fashion; it outlines the process by which to conduct a study that uses personal and telephone interviewers.

survey instrument design error A "family" of design or format errors that produce a questionnaire that does not accurately collect the appropriate raw data; these nonsampling errors severely limit the generalizability, reliability, and validity of the collected data.

survey instrument error A type of error that occurs when the survey instrument induces some type of systematic bias in the response.

survey research methods Research design procedures for collecting large amounts of raw data using interviews or questionnaires.

symptoms Conditions that signal the presence of a decision problem or opportunity; they tend to be observable and measurable results of problems or opportunities.

syndicated (or commercial) data Data and information that have been compiled according to some standardized procedure which provides customized data for companies such as market share, ad effectiveness, and sales tracking.

systematic error The type of error that results from poor instrument design and/or instrument construction causing scores or readings on an instrument to be biased in a consistent manner; creates some form of systematic variation in the raw data that is not a natural occurrence or fluctuation on the part of the surveyed respondents.

systematic random-digit dialing The technique of randomly dialing telephone numbers, but only numbers that meet specific criteria.

systematic random sampling (SYMRS) A method of probability sampling that is similar to simple random sampling but requires that the defined target population be naturally ordered in some way.

table of random numbers A table of numbers that have been randomly generated.

tabulation The simple procedure of counting the number of observations, or data items, that are classified into certain categories.

target market analysis Information for identifying those people (or companies) that an organization wishes to serve.

target population A specified group of people or objects for which questions can be asked or observations made to develop required data structures and information.

task characteristics The requirements placed on the respondents in their process of providing answers to questions asked.

task difficulty How hard the respondent needs to work to respond, and the level of preparation required to create an environment for the respondent.

technical competency The degree to which the researcher possesses the necessary functional requirements to conduct the research project.

teleologists Individuals who follow a philosophy that considers activities to be ethical if they produce desired results.

telephone-administered survey A survey in which individuals working out of their homes or from a central location use the telephone medium to ask participants questions and record the responses.

telephone interview A question-and-answer exchange that is conducted via telephone technology.

test marketing A controlled field experiment conducted for gaining information on specified market performance indicators or factors.

test-retest A procedure used to assess the reliability of a scale measurement; it involves repeating the administration of the scale measurement to either the sample set of sampled respondents at two different times or

two different samples of respondents from the same defined target population under as nearly the same conditions as possible.

test-retest reliability The method of accumulating evidence of reliability by using multiple administrations of an instrument to the same sample. If those administrations are consistent, then evidence of test-retest reliability exists.

theory A large body of interconnected propositions about how some portion of a certain phenomenon operates.

topic sensitivity The degree to which a specific question or investigated issue leads the respondent to give a socially acceptable response.

topographically integrated geographic encoding and referencing (TIGER) system The U.S. government's new system that provides the researcher with the ability to prepare detailed maps of a variety of areas within the United States.

touchpoint Specific customer information gathered and shared by all individuals in an enterprise.

traditional test markets Test markets that use experimental design procedures to test a product and/or a product's marketing mix variables through existing distribution channels; also referred to as *standard test markets.*

trained interviewers Highly trained people, with excellent communication and listening skills, who ask research participants specific questions and accurately record their responses.

trained observers Highly skilled people who use their various sensory devices to observe and record either a person's current behaviors or physical phenomena as they take place.

transactional data Secondary information derived from transactions by consumers at the retail level.

transition questions Questions used by a moderator to direct a focus group's discussion toward the main topic of interest.

trilogy approach The theoretical approach of viewing a person's attitude toward an object as consisting of three distinct components: cognitive, affective, and conative.

true experimental designs Designs that ensure equivalence between the experimental and control groups of subjects by random assignment of subjects to the groups ("pretest-posttest, with control group," "posttest-only, with control group," Solomon Four Group).

t-test (also referred to as *t* statistic) A hypothesis test procedure that uses the *t*-distribution: *t*-tests are used when the sample size of subjects is small (generally less than 30) and the standard deviation is unknown.

Type I error The error made by rejecting the null hypothesis when it is true; represents the probability of alpha error.

Type II error The error of failing to reject the null hypothesis when the alternative hypothesis is true; represents the probability of beta error.

underregistration When eligible sampling units are left out of the sampling frame.

undisguised sponsorship When the true identity of the person or company for which the research is being conducted is directly revealed to the prospective respondent.

unexplained variance In multivariate methods, it is the amount of variation in the dependent construct that cannot be accounted for by the combination of independent variables.

unstructured questions Question/scale formats that require respondents to reply in their own words; this format requires more thinking and effort on the part of respondents in order to express their answers; also called *open-ended questions*.

validity The degree to which a research instrument serves the purpose for which it was constructed; it also relates to the extent to which the conclusions drawn from an experiment are true.

validity of data The degree to which data structures actually do represent what was to be measured.

variability A measure of how data are dispersed; the greater the dissimilarity or "spread" in data, the larger the variability.

variable Any observable, measurable element (or attribute) of an event.

variance The average squared deviations about a mean of a distribution of values.

virtual test markets Completely computerized systems that allow the test subjects to observe and interact with the product as though they were actually in the test store's environment.

voice pitch analyzer A computerized system that measures emotional responses by changes in the subject's voice.

Web-based TV test markets Use of broadband interactive TV (iTV) and advances in interactive multimedia communication technologies to conduct field experiments. Preselected respondents are shown various stimuli and asked questions online through their iTV.

Web home page The guide to a Web site; generally the home page is the first Web page accessed at the Web site.

Web page A source of secondary information that is likely to be linked to other complementary pages; includes text, graphics, and even audio.

Web site An electronic location on the World Wide Web.

width The total number of records contained in the database.

willingness to participate The respondent's inclination or disposition to share his or her thoughts and feelings.

World Wide Web (WWW) A graphical interface system that allows for text linkage between different locations on the Internet.

wrong mailing address A type of nonresponse bias that can occur when the prospective respondent's mailing address is outdated or no longer active.

wrong telephone number A type of nonresponse bias that can occur when the prospective respondent's telephone number either is no longer in service or is incorrect on the sample list.

z-test (also referred to as *z* statistic) A hypothesis test procedure that uses the *z* distribution; *z*-tests are used when the sample size is larger than 30 subjects and the standard deviation is unknown.

endnotes

Chapter 1

1. Annual Report, Dillard's Department Stores, Little Rock, Arkansas, 1997.

2. American Marketing Association, *Official Definition of Marketing Research,* www.marketingpower.com, 2004.

3. Michael R. Solomon, *Consumer Behavior,* 6th ed. (Upper Saddle River, NJ: Pearson/Prentice Hall, 2004), pp. 242–45.

4. *Research Topics in Cycle Time Research* (Memphis, TN: Center for Cycle Time Research, University of Memphis, 2003).

5. C. Lamb, J. Hair, and C. McDaniel, *Marketing,* 7th ed. (Cincinnati: Southwestern, 2004), pp. 592–93.

6. Kevin Lane Keller, *Strategic Brand Management,* 2nd ed. (Upper Saddle River, NJ: Prentice Hall, 2003).

7. "Value Added Research," *Marketing Research,* Fall 1997.

8. Ibid.

9. "Survey of Top Marketing Research Firms," *Advertising Age,* June 27, 1997.

10. "Fostering Professionalism," *Marketing Research,* Spring 1997.

11. AMA Code of Ethics, www.marketingpower.com, accessed June 2004.

Chapter 2

1. R. K. Wade, "The When/What Research Decision Guide," *Marketing Research: A Magazine and Application* 5, no. 3 (Summer 1993), pp. 24–27; and W. D. Perreault, "The Shifting Paradigm in Marketing Research," *Journal of the Academy of Marketing Science* 20, no. 4 (Fall 1992), p. 369.

2. Coca-Cola Company, Form 10-K (Washington, DC: Securities and Exchange Commission, September 16, 1996); and Mitchell J. Shields, "Coke's Research Fizzles, Fails to Factor in Customer Loyalty," *Adweek,* July 15, 1985, p. 8.

3. This example is adapted from a project conducted by one of the text's authors for the Ford Foundation's Amphitheater Design Team in Vail, Colorado.

Chapter 3

1. Stacey Bell, "Launching Profits with Customer Loyalty," *Customer Relationship Management,* April 2000, p. 58.

2. "The Dollar Sign: Secondary Data," *Database,* May 1997.

3. "Secondary Research," *Marketing Research Magazine,* Fall 1997.

4. William Pride and O. C. Ferrell, *Marketing,* 10th ed. (Boston: Houghton Mifflin, 2003).

5. *Sales & Marketing Management Magazine, Survey of Buying Power,* 2003; and Kansas Department of Revenue, 2003.

6. *Sales & Marketing Management Magazine, Survey of Buying Power,* 2003, www.salesandmarketing.com, accessed June 2004.

7. *Source Book of Demographics and Buying Power for Every Zip Code in the U.S.A.,* 2003.

8. *The Wall Street Journal Index,* www.wallstreetjournal.com, accessed June 2004.

9. NPD Group, www.npdgroup.com, accessed June 2004.

10. AC Nielsen Media Research, www.nielsenmedia.com, accessed June 2004.

11. Arbitron, www.arbitron.com, accessed June 2004.

12. Ibid.

Chapter 4

1. Stacy Bell, "Launching Profits with Customer Loyalty," *Customer Relationship Management,* April 2000, p. 58.

2. Meridith Levinson, "Getting to Know Them," *CIO Magazine,* February 15, 2004, www.cio.com, accessed June 2004.

3. David Roberts, "Turning Lemons to Lemonade," *Customer Relationship Management,* July 2000, p. 64.

4. Louis Fickel, "Know Your Customer," *CIO Magazine,* April 15, 1999.

5. "The Business Intelligence and Data Warehousing Glossary," www.sdgcomputing.com, June 2004.

6. C. Lamb, J. Hair, and C. McDaniel, *Marketing,* 7th ed. (Cincinnati: Southwestern, 2004), pp. 685–86.

7. Ibid., p. 687.

8. Bill Inmon, "Building the Data Warehouse," *The Data Warehousing Information Center,* June 21, 2001.

9. Peter Nolan, "Getting Started and Finishing Well," *Intelligent Enterprise Magazine,* May 7, 2001.

10. This is a Case-in-Point Report based on client files of Acxiom (www.acxiom.com) and other sources, including www.gemini.com, www.trustmark.com, www.netbank.com, and www.fingerhut.com.

Chapter 5

1. www.sears.com, www.searsmedia.com, and www.landsend.com, accessed June 2004; and A. Johnson, "Viewing Data in Real Time," *CIO Magazine,* December 1, 1999.

2. www.mdssworld.com and www.mdss.net, accessed June 2004.

3. L. Lodish, "On Measuring Advertising Effects," *Journal of Advertising Research,* September–October 1997.

4. www.gis.com, accessed June 2004; and adapted from Devlin Fung, "Managing by the Map," *Business Perspectives* 8, no. 2 (The University of Memphis: Spring 1995).

Chapter 6

1. Richard A. Krueger, *Focus Groups: A Practical Guide for Applied Research,* 2nd ed. (Thousand Oaks, CA: Sage, 1994), p. 233; T. L. Greenbaum, "It's Possible to Reduce Cost of Focus Groups," *Marketing News,* August 29, 1988, p. 43; also see T. C. Kinnear and J. A. Taylor, *Marketing Research: An Applied Approach,* 5th ed. (New York: McGraw-Hill, 1996), p. 312.

2. David J. Ortinau and Ronald P. Brensinger, "An Empirical Investigation of Perceived Quality's Intangible Dimensionality through Direct Cognitive Structural (DCS) Analysis," in Robert L. King, ed. *Marketing Perspectives for the 1990s,* (Richmond, VA: Society for Marketing Advances, 1993), pp. 214–19.

3. Adapted from suggestions offered in Richard A. Krueger, *Focus Groups: A Practical Guide for Applied Research,* 2nd ed. (Thousand Oaks, CA: Sage, 1994), pp. 79–82; also see Joe L. Welch, "Research Marketing Problems and Opportunities with Focus Groups," *Industrial Marketing Management* 14 (1985), p. 248.

4. Peter Cooper, "Comparison between the UK and US: The Qualitative Dimension," *Journal of the Marketing Research Society* 31 (4) (1991), pp. 509–20.

5. Dennis W. Rook, "Out-of-Focus Groups," *Marketing Research,* Summer 2003, pp. 10–15; also Cooper, "Comparison between UK and US."

6. Krueger, *Focus Groups;* also Lewis Winters, "What's New in Focus Group Research," *Marketing Research,* December 1999, pp. 69–70.

7. Naomi R. Henderson, "The Many Faces of Qualitative Research," *Marketing Research,* Summer 2002, pp. 13–17; "Focus Group Moderators Should Be Well Versed in Interpretative Skills," *Marketing News,* February 18, 1991, p. 23; also Thomas L. Greenbaum, "Do You Have the Right Moderator for Your Focus Groups? Here Are Ten Questions to Ask Yourself," *Bank Marketing* 23 (1) (1991), p. 43.

8. Alvin A. Achenbaum, "When Good Research Goes Bad," *Marketing Research,* Winter 2001, pp. 13–15; also B. G. Yovovick, "Focusing On Consumers' Needs and Motivations," *Business Marketing,* March 1991, pp. 41–43.

9. Krueger, 1994, 149–51.

10. Krueger, 1994, 165–66.

11. Thomas L. Greenbaum, "Understanding Focus Group Research Aboard," *Marketing News* 30, 12 (June 2, 1996), pp. H16, H36.

12. M. Zinchiak, "Online Focus Groups FAQs," *Quirk's Marketing Research Review,* July/August 2001, pp. 38–46; also "FocusVision Products and Services," Focusvision Worldwide, August 18, 2001, at http://focusvision.com/products/index.htm; also "A Feedback on the Phone," *Business Marketing,* March 1991, p. 46.

13. S. Jarvis and D. Szynal, "Show and Tell," *Marketing News,* November 19, 2001, pp. 1, 13; K. Lonnie, "Combine Phone and Web for Focus Groups," *Marketing News,* November 19, 2001, pp. 15–16; also Rebecca Piirto Heather, "Future Focus Groups," *American Demographics,* January 1, 1994, p. 6; and Tibbert Speer, "A Nickelodeon Puts Kids Online," *American Demographics,* January 1, 1994, p. 16.

14. G. Beistell and D. Nitterhouse, "Asking All the Right Questions," *Marketing Research,* Fall 2001, pp. 14–20; B. Wansink, "New Techniques to Generate Key Marketing Insights," *Marketing Research,* Summer 2000, pp. 28–36; David Ensing, "Web-based Reporting Makes for Easy Info," *Marketing News,* August 14, 2000, p. 15; and Berni Stevens, "Save Money with Online Analysis," *Marketing News,* November 6, 2000, pp. 27–28.

15. Marie Flores Letelier, Charles Sinosa, and Bobby J. Calder, "Taking an Expanded View of Consumers' Needs: Qualitative Research for Aiding Innovation," *Marketing Research,* Winter 2000, pp. 4–11; also see Gordon A. Wyner, "Anticipating Customer Priorities," *Marketing Research,* Spring 1999, pp. 36–38.

Chapter 7

1. Michael R. Czinkota and Ilkka A. Ronkainen, "Conducting Primary Market Research: Market Research for Your Export Operations, Part 2," *International Trade Forum,* January 1995, p. 18.

2. Robert M. Groves, Robert B. Cialdini, and Mick P. Couper, "Understanding the Decision to Participate in a Survey," *Public Opinion Quarterly* 56 (1992), pp. 475–95; Henry Assael and John Keon, "Nonsampling vs. Sampling Errors in Survey Research," *Journal of Marketing* 46 (Spring 1982), pp. 114–23; and Gary Lilien, Rex Brown, and Kate Searls, "Cut Errors, Improve Estimates to Bridge Biz-to-Biz Info Gap," *Marketing News* 25 (1) (January 7, 1991), pp. 20–22.

3. Terry L. Childers and Steven J. Skinner, "Toward a Conceptualization of Mail Survey Response Behavior," *Psychology and Marketing* 13 (2) (March 1996), pp. 185–225.

4. Kathy E. Green, "Sociodemographic Factors and Mail Survey Response Rates," *Psychology and Marketing* 13 (2) (March 1996), pp. 171–84.

5. M. G. Dalecki, T. W. Ilvento, and D. E. Moore, "The Effect of Multi-Wave Mailings on the External Validity of Mail Surveys," *Journal of Community Development Society* 19 (1988), pp. 51–70.

6. A. Ossip, "Likely Improvements in Data Collection Methods—What Do They Mean for Day-to-Day Research Management?" *Journal of Advertising Research,* October–November 1986, pp. RC9–RC12.

7. Arthur Saltzman, "Improving Response Rates in Disk-by-Mail Surveys," *Marketing Research: A Magazine of Management and Applications* 5 (Summer 1993), pp. 32–39.

8. Debby Hartke, "What Farmers Think of Market Research," *Agri Marketing* 34 (3) (March 1996), pp. 54–58.

9. Richard P. Bagozzi, "Measurement in Marketing Research: Basic Principles of Questionnaire Design," in *Principles of Marketing Research,* Richard P. Bagozzi, ed. (Cambridge, MA: Blackwell, 1994), pp. 1–49.

10. J. Yu and H. Cooper, "Quantitative Review of Research Design Effects on Response Rules to Questionnaires," *Journal of Marketing Research* 20 (February 1983), pp. 36–44.

11. R. Tourangeau and K. A. Rasinski, "Cognitive Process Underlying Content Effects in Attitude Measurement," *Psychological Bulletin* 103 (1988), pp. 299–314.

12. Patricia E. Moberg, "Biases in Unlisted Phone Numbers," *Journal of Advertising Research,* August–September 1982, p. 55.

13. Alan J. Bush and Joseph F. Hair, Jr., "An Assessment of the Mall Intercept as a Data Collect Method," *Journal of Marketing Research* 22 (May 1985), pp. 158–67.

14. J. Colombotos, "Personal vs. Telephone Interviews Effect Responses," *Public Health Reports,* September 1969, pp. 773–820; also see F. Kelly Shuptrine, "Survey Research: Respondent Attitudes Response and Bias," in R. L. King, ed., *Marketing Perspectives for the 1990s,* Southern Marketing Association Proceedings, November 1992, pp. 197–200.

15. William A. Lucus and William C. Adams, "An Assessment of Telephone Survey Methods," *Rand Report R-2135-NSF,* October 1997; also see T. F. Rogers, "Interviewing by Telephone and In-Person Quality of Response and Field Performance," *Public Opinion Quarterly,* Spring 1976, pp. 51–65.

16. Donald E. Stem, Jr., and Charles W. Lamb, Jr., "The Marble-Drop Technique: A Procedure for Gathering Sensitive Information," *Decision Sciences,* October 1981, pp. 702–8.

17. Todd D. Remington, "Telemarketing and Declining Survey Response Rates," *Journal of Advertising Research* 33 (1) (1993), pp. RC-6 and RC-7; also see T. Remington, "Rising Refusal Rates: The Impact of Telemarketing," *QUIRKS Marketing Research Review,* May 1992, pp. 8–15.

18. Diana K. Bowers, "Sugging Banned, At Last," *Marketing Research* 7 (4) (Fall 1995), p. 40.

19. Leif Gjestland, "Net? Not Yet: CATI Is Still Superior to Internet Interviewing but Enhancements Are on the Way," *Marketing Research: A Magazine of Management & Applications* 8 (1) (1996), pp. 26+; also see Peter J. DePaulo and Rick Weitzer, "Interactive Phone Technology Delivers Survey Data Quickly," *Marketing News* 28 (1) (January 4, 1994), p. 15.

20. Ju Long, Andrew B. Whinston, and Kerem Tomak, "Calling all Customers," *Marketing Research: A Magazine of Management & Applications,* Fall 2002, pp. 28–33.

21. Ibid.

22. Scott Dacko, "Data Collection Should Not Be Manual Labor," *Marketing News* 29 (18) (August 28, 1995), p. 31.

23. John P. Dickson and Douglas L. MacLachlan, "Fax Surveys?" *Marketing Research: A Magazine of Management & Applications* 4 (3) (September 1992), pp. 26–30; also see Aileen Crowley, "E-mail Surveys Elicit Fast Response, Cut Costs," *PC Week,* January 30, 1995.

24. John P. Dickson and Douglas L. MacLachlan, "Fax Surveys: Return Patterns and Comparison with Mail Survey," *Journal of Marketing Research* 33 (February 1996), pp. 108–13.

25. Paul R. Murphy and James M. Daley, "Mail Surveys: To Fax or Not to Fax," *Proceedings of the Association of Marketing Theory and Practice Annual Meetings* (Chicago, IL: American Marketing Association, 1995), pp. 152–57.

26. Ibid, Bowers, 1995, 40.

27. Dana James, "Old, New Make Up Today's Surveys," *Marketing News,* June 5, 2000, p. 4; also Dana James, "The Future of Online Research," *Marketing News,* January 3, 2000, p. 11.

28. Lisa Bertagnoli, "Middle East Muddle," *Marketing News,* July 16, 2001, pp. 1 and 9; also see "World's Online Population," *Nua Internet Surveys 2000,* as reported in *Marketing News,* July 3, 2000, p. 15.

29. Steve Jarvis, "U.S., EU Still Don't Agree on Data Handling," *Marketing News,* August 13, 2001, pp. 5–6; also see Maxine Lans Retsky, "Staying in Line with New Contest Legislation," *Marketing News,* July 31, 2000, p. 9.

30. Chad Rubel, "Researcher Praises On-Line Methodology," *Marketing News* 30 (12) (June 3, 1996), p. H18.

31. Scott Dacko, "Data Collection Should Not Be Manual Labor," *Marketing News* 29 (18) (August 28, 1995), p. 31; Michael Kraus, "Research and the Web: Eyeballs or Smiles," *Marketing News,* December 7, 1998, p. 18.

32. Patricia E. Moberg, "Biases in Unlisted Phone Numbers," *Journal of Advertising Research,* August–September 1982, p. 55.

33. Ibid, Hartke, 1996, 54–58.

Chapter 8

1. Betsy Peterson, "Trends Turn Around," *Marketing Research* 7 (3) (Summer 1995).

2. The opening example for Chapter 8 was specifically created by the authors for the third edition of *Marketing Research.*

3. William Rathje and Cullen Murphy, "Garbage Demographics," *American Demographics,* May 1992, pp. 50–53; Eugene J. Webb, Donald T. Campbell, Richard D. Schwartz, and Lee Sechrest, *Unobtrusive Measures: Nonreaction Research in the Social Sciences* (Chicago: Rand-McNally, 1971), pp. 113–14; and Joseph A. Cote, James McCullough, and Michael Reilly, "Effects of Unexpected Situations on Behavior-Intention Differences: A Garbology Analysis," *Journal of Consumer Research,* September 1985, pp. 188–94.

4. B. Becker, "Guidelines to Direct Observation," *Marketing News,* September 27, 1999, pp. 20, 29, 31, and 33.

5. See Bernie Whalen, "Marketing Detective Reveals Competitive-Intelligence Secrets," *Marketing News,* September 16, 1983, p. 1; also Witold Rybeznski, "We Are What We Throw Away," *New York Times Book Review,* July 5, 1992, pp. 5–6.

6. Webb et al., *Unobtrusive Measures,* chapter 2.

7. P. Kephart, "The Spy on Aisle 3," *American Demographics Marketing Tools,* October 1996, pp. 15–17.

8. James M. Sinkula, "Status of Company Usage of Scanner-Based Research," *Journal of the Academy of Marketing Science,* Spring 1986, pp. 63–71; and "Some Factors Affecting the Adoption of Scanner-Based Research in Organizations," *Journal of Advertising Research,* April/May 1991, pp. 50–55.

9. S. J. Hellebursch, "Don't Read Research by the Numbers," *Marketing News,* September 11, 2000, pp. 19, 25, and 34.

10. Thomas D. Cook and Donald T. Campbell, *Quasi-Experimentation: Design and Analysis Issues for Field Settings* (Boston, MA: Houghton Mifflin, 1979), pp. 39–41, 51, 59, 64, 70–73.

11. Edward G. Carmines and Richard A. Zeller, *Reliability and Validity Assessment* (Newbury Park, CA: Sage, 1979), pp. 9–48; also see Donald T. Campbell and Julian C. Stanley, *Experimental Designs for Research* (Skokie, IL: Rand-McNally, 1966).

12. B. J. Calder, L. W. Phillips, and A. M. Tybour, "The Concept of External Validity," *Journal of Consumer Research,* December 1992, pp. 240–44.

13. Gilbert A. Churchill, Jr., "A Paradigm for the Development of Better Measures of Marketing Constructs," *Journal of Marketing Research* 16 (February 1979), pp. 64–73.

14. William D. Crano and Marilyn B. Brewer, *Principles and Methods of Social Research* (Boston, MA: Allyn and Bacon, 1986), pp. 23–38.

15. Churchill, "A Paradigm."

16. Carmines and Zeller, pp. 9–48; Campbell and Stanley, *Experimental Designs;* and Fred N. Kerlinger and

Howard B. Lee, *Foundations of Behavior Research,* 4th ed. (Cincinnati: Wadsworth-Thomas Learning, 2000), pp. 324–26, 461–63.

17. Martin Fishbein, "Attitude and the Prediction of Behavior," in *Readings in Attitude Theory and Behavior,* M. Fishbein, ed. (New York: John Wiley and Sons, 1967), pp. 477–92.

18. S. Banks, *Experimentation in Marketing* (New York: McGraw-Hill, 1965), pp. 168–79.

19. Kerlinger and Lee, *Foundations of Behavior Research,* 4th ed.

20. Ibid.

21. Ibid.

22. Cook and Campbell, *Quasi-Experimentation,* pp. 39–41, 51, 59, 64, 70–73.

23. L. Brennan, "Test Marketing," *Sales and Marketing Management Magazine,* March 1988, pp. 140, 150–52.

24. Peterson, "Trends Turn Around."

25. Mark Gleason, "P&G Tests Smoothie," *Advertising Age* 66 (October 30, 1995).

26. Andrew Bernstein, "Spalding and Four Major Chains Launch Women's Theme Shops," *Sporting Goods Business* 28 (November 1985).

27. Robert Burgess, "Coors Chiller Fiasco Costs Brewer Dearly," *Denver Business Journal* 44 (32) (April 23, 1993), p. 1A.

28. Melvin Prince, "Choosing Simulated Test Marketing Systems," *Marketing Research* 4 (September 1992), pp. 14–16.

29. Ibid.

30. Raymond Burke, "Virtual Shopping: Breakthrough in Marketing Research," *Harvard Business Review,* March/April 1996.

31. Ibid.

32. Steve Jarvis, "iTV Finally Comes Home," *Marketing News,* (August 27, 2001), pp. 1, 19, and 20.

33. Burke, "Virtual Shopping."

34. Ibid.

35. Ibid. Burke. p. 120.

Chapter 9

1. www.surveysampling.com. Actual prices of lists will vary according to the number and complexity of characteristics needed to define the target population.

2. www.clickz.com/stats, accessed June 2004.

3. Source: www.dannon.com, accessed June 2004; and Paula Kephart, "The Leader of the Pack: How Dannon Yogurt Put Research to Work—And Came Out a Winner," *Marketing Tools,* September 1995, pp. 16, 18, 19.

Chapter 10

1. Daratech on-line: Digital Simulation and Prototyping, daratech.com, May 20, 2004.

2. Will Lester, "Pollsters Struggle To Balance Opportunities, Problems of the Internet, May 20, 2000, texnews.com

Chapter 11

1. William D. Crano and Marilyn B. Brewer *Principles and Methods of Social Research* (Boston, MA: Allyn and Bacon, 1986), pp. 23–38; Edward G. Carmines and Richard A. Zeller *Reliability and Validity Assessment* (Newbury Park, CA: Sage, 1979), pp. 9–48; and Paul E. Spector, *Summated Rating Scale Construction: An Introduction* (Newbury Park, CA: Sage, 1992), pp. 12–17, 46–65.

2. Gilbert A. Churchill, Jr. "A Paradigm for the Development of Better Measures of Marketing Constructs," *Journal of Marketing Research* 16 (February 1979), pp. 64–73.

3. Jum C. Nunnally, *Psychometric Theory,* 2nd ed. (New York: McGraw-Hill, 1978), p. 102.

4. David J. Ortinau and Ronald P. Brensinger, "An Empirical Investigation of Perceived Quality's Intangible Dimensionality through Direct Cognitive Structural (DCS) Analysis," in Robert L. King, ed., *Marketing: Perspectives for the 1990s* (New Orleans, LA: Southern Marketing Association, 1992), pp. 214–19.

5. These studies were conducted by one of the authors. Part of the results were reported in Ortinau and Brensinger, "An Empirical Investigation," pp. 214–19.

6. Ronald P. Brensinger, "An Empirical Investigation of Consumer Perceptions of Combined Product and Service Quality: The Automobile," unpublished doctoral dissertation (Tampa, FL: The University of South Florida, 1993), pp. 54–60.

7. Nunnally, *Psychometric Theory,* p. 3.

8. Stanley S. Stevens, "Mathematics, Measurement and Psychophysics," in S. S. Stevens, ed., *Handbook of Experimental Psychology* (New York: John Wiley and Sons, 1951).

9. Fred N. Kerlinger and Howard B. Lee, *Foundations of Behavioral Research,* 4th ed. (Cincinnati: Wadsworth-Thomas Learning, 2000), p. 403; also see Stanley S. Stevens, "On the Theory of Scales of Measurement," *Science* 103 (June 7, 1946), pp. 677–80.

10. Melvin R. Crask and Richard J. Fox, "An Exploration of the Interval Properties of Three Commonly Used Marketing Research Studies: A Magnitude Estimation Approach," *Journal of the Marketing Research Society* 29 (3) (1987), pp. 317–39.

11. Wendell R. Garner and C. D. Creelman, "Problems and Methods of Psychological Scaling," in Helson Bevan and William Bevan, eds., *Contemporary Approaches to Psychology* (New York: Van Nostrand, 1967), p. 4.

12. Stevens, "On the Theory of Scales of Measurement."

13. Kerlinger and Lee, *Foundations of Behavioral Research,* p. 405.

14. Ibid., p. 411.

15. William D. Perreault, Jr., and Forrest W. Young, "Alternating Least Squares Optimal Scaling: Analysis of Nonmetric Data in Marketing Research," *Journal of Marketing Research* 17 (February 1980), pp.1–13; also see Neil R. Barnard and Andrew S. C. Ehrenberg, "Robust Measures of Consumer Brand Beliefs," *Journal of Marketing Research* 27 (November 1990), pp. 477–84.

16. Crask and Fox, "An Exploration," p. 326.

17. Mark Taylor, "Ordinal and Interval Scaling," *Journal of the Marketing Research Society* 25 (4) (November

1977), pp. 297–303; Gerald Albaum, Robert Best, and Del I. Hawkins, "Measurement Properties of Semantic Scales Data," *Journal of the Marketing Research Society* 25 (1) (January 1977), pp. 21–28; and Norbert Schwarz et al., "Rating Scales: Numeric Values May Change the Meanings of Scale Labels," *Public Opinion Quarterly* 55 (Winter 1991), pp. 570–82.

18. John Gaito, "Measurement Scales and Statistics: Resurgence of an Old Misconception," *Psychological Bulletin* 87 (1980), pp. 564–67.

19. Garner and Creelman, "Problems and Methods of Psychological Scaling," p. 7; also see E. T. Goetz, P. A. Alexander, and M. J. Ash, *Educational Psychology* (New York: Macmillian, 1992), pp. 670–74.

20. Nunnally, *Psychometric Theory,* pp. 3–30, 86–90, 102, 225–40.

21. Albert R. Wildt and Michael B. Mazis, "Determinants of Scale Response: Labels versus Position," *Journal of Marketing Research* 15 (May 1978), pp. 261–67; also see Jacob Jacoby and Michael S. Matell, "Three Point Likert Scales Are Good Enough," *Journal of Marketing Research* 8 (November 1971), pp. 495–506.

22. "Measuring the Importance of Attributes," *Research on Research* 28 (Chicago, IL: Market Facts, Inc., undated).

23. Gilbert A. Churchill and J. Paul Peter, "Research Design Effects on the Reliability of Rating Scales: A Meta-Analysis," *Journal of Marketing Research* 21 (February 1984), pp. 360–75.

24. M. N. Segal, "Alternate Form Conjoint Reliability," *Journal of Advertising Research* 4 (1984), pp. 31–38.

25. L. J. Cronbach, "Coefficient Alpha and Internal Structure of Tests," *Psychometrika* 16 (1951), pp. 297–334.

26. H. Schuman and S. Pesser, *Questions and Answers in Attitude Survey* (New York: Academic Press, 1981), pp. 179–201.

27. Ibid., p. 192.

28. G. J. Spagna, "Questionnaire: Which Approach Do You Use?" *Journal of Advertising Research* (February–March 1984), pp. 67–70; also see E. A. Holdaway, "Different Response Categories and Questionnaire Response Patterns," *Journal of Experimental Education* (Winter 1971), p. 59.

29. K. C. Schneider, "Uninformed Response Rate in Survey Research," *Journal of Business Research* (April 1985), pp. 153–62; also see Del I. Hawkins and K. A. Coney, "Uninformed Response Error in Survey Research," *Journal of Marketing Research* 18 (August 1981), pp. 370–74.

30. Macro Consulting, Inc., 1998, www.macroinc.com/articles/imageq.htm, accessed June 2004.

Chapter 12

1. Thomas S. Robertson and Harold H. Kassarjian, *Handbook of Consumer Behavior* (Englewood Cliffs, NJ: Prentice Hall, 1991).

2. Martin Fishbein, *Readings in Attitude Theory and Behavior* (New York: John Wiley and Sons, 1967).

3. T. Robert, W. Wu, and Susan M. Petroshius, "The Halo Effect in Store Image Management," *Journal of Academy of Marketing Science* 15 (1987), pp. 44–51.

4. Rajendar K. Garg, "The Influence of Positive and Negative Wording and Issues Involvement on Response to Likert Scales in Marketing Research," *Journal of the Marketing Research Society* 38, no. 3 (July 1996), pp. 235–46.

5. Roobina Ohanian, "Construction and Validation of a Scale to Measure Celebrity Endorsers' Perceived Expertise, Trustworthiness, and Attractiveness," *Journal of Advertising* 19, no. 3 (1990), pp. 39–52.

6. Tony Siciliano, "Purchase Intent: Facts from Fiction," *Marketing Research* 21 (Spring 1993), p. 56.

7. Michael R. Solomon, *Consumer Behavior,* 6th ed. (Upper Saddle River, NJ: Pearson/Prentice Hall, 2004), pp. 242–45.

8. www.burke.com; and Amanda Prus and D. Randall Brandt, "Understanding Your Customers—What You Can Learn from a Customer Loyalty Index," *Marketing Tools,* July/August 1995, pp. 10–14.

9. Martin Fishbein, "Attitude and the Prediction of Behavior," in M. Fishbein, ed., *Readings in Attitude Theory and Behavior* (New York: John Wiley and Sons, 1967); also see Martin Fishbein, "An Investigation of the Relationships between Beliefs about an Object and the Attitude toward That Object," *Human Relations* 16 (1983), pp. 233–40.

10. Icek Ajzen and Martin Fishbein, *Understanding and Predicting Social Behavior* (Englewood Cliffs, NJ: Prentice Hall, 1980), pp. 53–89; and Icek Ajzen and Martin Fishbein, "Attitude-Behavior Relations: A Theoretical Analysis and Review of Empirical Research," *Psychological Bulletin* 84 (September 1977), pp. 888–948.

11. Y. Tsai, "On the Relationship between Cognitive and Affective Processes," *Journal of Consumer Research* 12, no. 3 (December 1985), pp. 358–62; also see P. A. Dabholkar, "Incorporating Choice into an Attitudinal Framework," *Journal of Consumer Research* 21, no.1 (June 1994), pp. 100–18.

12. Sharon E. Beatty and Lynn R. Kahle, "Alternative Hierarchies of the Attitude-Behavior Relationship," *Journal of the Academy of Marketing Science*, Summer 1988, pp.1–10; A. Sahni, "Incorporating Perceptions of Financial Control in Purchase Prediction," in Chris T. Allen and Debbie R. John, eds., *Advances in Consumer Research* XXI (Provo, UT: Association for Consumer Research, 1994), pp. 442–48; also see J. A. Cote, J. McCullough, and M. Reilly, "Effects of Unexpected Situations on Behavior-Intention Differences," *Journal of Consumer Research* 12, no. 3 (September 1985), pp.185–93.

13. These factors were adopted from the discussion in Del I. Hawkins, Roger J. Best, and Kenneth A. Coney, *Consumer Behavior: Building Marketing Strategy,* 7th ed. (New York: McGraw-Hill/Irwin, 1998), pp. 401–3.

Chapter 13

1. These characteristics are known as the cornerstones for conducting scientific inquiries into many different types of marketing phenomena. An excellent overview can be obtained by reading Stanley Payne's classic book *The Art of Asking Questions* (Princeton, NJ: Princeton University Press, 1951).

2. Ibid., pp. 8–9.

3. Maria Elena Sanchez, "Effects of Questionnaire Design on the Quality of Survey Data," *Public Opinion Quarterly* 56 (1992), pp. 208–17.

4. Pamela L. Alreck and Robert B. Settle, *The Survey Research Handbook*, 2nd ed. (New York: McGraw-Hill/Irwin, 1995), pp.120–22.

5. Robert A. Peterson, *Constructing Effective Questionnaires* (Thousand Oaks, CA: Sage, 2000), pp.1–2.

6. Ibid., p. 53.

7. Sanchez, "Effects of Questionnaire Design on the Quality of Survey Data," p. 209; also see James H. Barns and Michael J. Dotson, "The Effects of Mixed Grammar Chains on Response to Survey Questions," *Journal of Marketing Research* 26, no. 4 (November 1989), pp. 468–72.

8. Alreck and Settle, *The Survey Research Handbook*, pp. 97–100.

9. Susan Carroll, "Questionnaire's Design Affects Response Rate," *Marketing News* 28 (January 3, 1994), pp. 14, 23.

10. The "Flowerpot" design approach is a symbolic model developed in 1974 by David J. Ortinau while teaching at Illinois State University, Normal, Illinois.

11. M. Patten, *Questionnaire Research* (Los Angeles, CA: Pyrczak, 2001), pp. 8–12.

12. A. Diamantopoula, B. Schlegelmilch, and N. Wilcox, "The Pretesting in Questionnaire Design: The Impact of Respondent Characteristics on Error Detection," *Journal of Marketing Research Society* 35 (April 1994), pp. 295–314.

13. Carroll, "Questionnaire's Design Affects Response Rate," p. 23; also see D. Dillman, M. Sinclair, and J. Clark, "Effects of Questionnaire Length, Respondent Friendly Design, and a Difficult Question on Response Rates for Occupant-Addressed Census Mail Surveys," *Public Opinion Quarterly* 57 (1993), pp. 289–304.

14. Dillman et al., "Effects of Questionnaire Length," p. 294.

15. Patten, *Questionnaire Research*, p. 78.

16. R. Hubbard and E. Little, "Cash Prizes and Mail Response Rates: A Threshold Analysis," *Journal of the Academy of Marketing Science* (Fall 1988), pp. 42–44.

Chapter 14

1. Barry Deville, "The Data Assembly Challenge," *Marketing Research Magazine,* Fall/Winter 1995, p. 4.

2. Ibid., p. 15.

Chapter 15

1. Thomas T. Semon, "A Bad Picture Is Worth Very Few Words," *Marketing Research,* May 24, 1993, p. 11; and Edward R. Tufte, *The Visual Display of Quantitative Information* (Cheshire, CT: Graphics Press, 1983).

2. Thomas S. Gruca, "Reporting Poll Results: Focusing on Point Spreads Instead of Percentages Can Be Misleading," *Marketing Research,* Winter 1996, p. 29.

3. For a more detailed discussion of Analysis of Variance (ANOVA), see Gudmund R. Iversen and Helmut Norpoth, *Analysis of Variance* (Newbury Park, CA: Sage, 1987); and John A. Ingram and Joseph G. Monks, *Statistics for Business and Economics* (San Diego, CA: Harcourt Brace Janovich, 1989).

4. For a more detailed conceptual discussion of multiple analysis of variance (MANOVA), see Joseph F. Hair, Jr., et al., *Multivariate Data Analysis,* 6th ed. (Upper Saddle River, NJ: Prentice Hall, 2005).

5. "Hotel Chains Capitalize on International Travel Market," *Hotels and Restaurants International,* June 1989, pp. 81s–86s; and "Target Marketing Points to Worldwide Success," *Hotels and Restaurants International,* June 1989, p. 87s.

Chapter 16

1. For a detailed conceptual discussion of transformations, see Joseph F. Hair, Jr., Rolph E. Anderson, Ronald L. Tatham, and William C. Black, *Multivariate Data Analysis,* 5th ed. (Upper Saddle River, N.J.: Prentice Hall, 1998).

Chapter 17

1. For a conceptual discussion of these techniques, see Joseph F. Hair, Jr., Rolph E. Anderson, Ronald L. Tatham, and William C. Black, *Multivariate Data Analysis,* 5th ed. (Upper Saddle River, N.J.: Prentice Hall, 1998).

name index

679

subject index